Case Problems and Readings:
A SUPPLEMENT FOR
INVESTMENTS
AND PORTFOLIO MANAGEMENT

Case Problems and Readings:
A SUPPLEMENT FOR INVESTMENTS AND PORTFOLIO MANAGEMENT

Keith V. Smith
Purdue University

McGraw-Hill Publishing Company
New York   St. Louis   San Francisco   Auckland   Bogotá   Caracas
Hamburg   Lisbon   London   Madrid   Mexico   Milan   Montreal
New Delhi   Oklahoma City   Paris   San Juan   São Paulo   Singapore
Sydney   Tokyo   Toronto

Case Problems and Readings:
A Supplement for Investments and Portfolio Management

234567890 MAL MAL 893210

ISBN 0-07-058552-0

The editors were Suzanne BeDell and Joseph F. Murphy; the production supervisor
was Louise A. Karam.
The cover was designed by Caliber Design Planning, Inc.
Malloy was printer and binder.

Library of Congress Cataloging-in-Publication Data

Smith, Keith V.
    Case problems and readings: a supplement for investments and
portfolio management / Keith V. Smith.
        p.   cm. — (McGraw-Hill series in finance)
    ISBN 0-07-058552-0
    1. Investment analysis—Case studies.   2. Portfolio management—
Case studies.   I. Title.   II. Series.
HG4529.S55   1990
332.6—dc20   89-12738

About the Author

Keith V. Smith is professor of management at the Krannert Graduate School of Management, Purdue University.

Dr. Smith received a B.S. in engineering physics and an M.B.A., both from the Ohio State University. While working as an operations research analyst for the Space and Information Systems Division of North American Aviation, he did further graduate work in economics at the University of Southern California. He then taught economics at Purdue University where he completed a Ph.D. in finance.

Dr. Smith joined the faculty of the UCLA Graduate School of Management in 1966 as an assistant professor of business economics and finance. He also served as associate dean of the doctoral program. He returned to Purdue in 1979 as dean of the Krannert School. In 1983, he resumed a full-time faculty position.

Dr. Smith is the author of *Portfolio Management* (Holt, Rinehart and Winston, 1971), coauthor of *Essentials of Investing* (Richard D. Irwin, 1974) and *Guide to Working Capital Management* (McGraw-Hill, 1979), and coeditor of *Readings on Short-Term Financial Management* (West, 1988). He also has published numerous articles in professional journals on topics such as portfolio revision, option writing, performance evaluation, transportation system effectiveness, dividend policy, conglomerate mergers, trust department profitability, and real estate.

In addition to serving as a corporate director, Dr. Smith has been a consultant to numerous companies and financial institutions, with assignments in finance, investments, and strategic planning. He has experience as well in litigation consulting. He is a faculty associate of Management Analysis Center (MAC) and the Technical Assistance Program at Purdue University.

To Joel Mogy
with gratitude for
early racquetball, professional sharing and advice,
and lasting friendship

Contents

PART THREE
STOCK INVESTMENTS

PART FOUR
OTHER INVESTMENTS

PART FIVE
ASSET ALLOCATION

Case Problems:

Readings:

PART SIX
INSTITUTIONAL INVESTING

Case Problems:

Readings:

Preface

Most academic programs in management have a strong component in the field of finance. The usual curricular development in finance includes courses in three areas: corporate finance, financial institutions, and investments. To supplement advancements in the theory and practice of finance, case studies are used extensively in corporate finance, regularly in financial institutions, but only sporadically in investments. Selected readings from the academic literature also are used to supplement textbook coverage in each of the three areas of finance, although somewhat on an ad hoc basis.

The intent of this book is to present for the student or reader a new set of case problems, together with a selected choice of readings from the investments literature, that collectively will serve as a useful supplement to recent textbooks on investments. Hopefully, the book will be helpful in bringing theoretical advancements in investments closer to real-world practices of investments and portfolio management.

Twenty-six case problems are included. Each is relatively short. In each case problem, students are given a clear picture of the relevant issues for discussion and questions to be answered. Some of the case problems deal with investments and portfolio management by an individual or family. Other case problems deal with professional investments management. Certain of the case problems direct students to discuss readings that also are included in this book.

The case problems were written to supplement the teaching of investments management at Purdue University. They have been used extensively with graduate level courses in regular masters programs, as well as in executive masters programs. Many of the case problems also have been used at the undergraduate level. Our experience has been that students at all academic levels enjoy discussing brief cases to supplement textbook assignments. In other words, case problems serve as a bridge to the real-world practice of investments and portfolio management, as well as a useful vehicle for integrating modern portfolio theory and investment valuation with that practice.

Twenty readings are also included. Their authors are academics and/or practitioners whose works tend to reflect leading-edge research in investments and related fields. Many of the readings were published during the past five years, and thus the collection reflects latest developments in investments and portfolio management. There is a level of mathematical treatment in certain of the articles, but the readings overall stress application and practicality. Again, we believe that a study of these readings is helpful to students and readers in bridging the gap between theory and practice.

The twenty-six case problems and twenty readings are organized into six parts within the book. Part One deals with topics that are prerequisite to investment analysis and portfolio management. Bond investments are the subject of Part Two, stock investments are treated in Part Three, while other investments are considered in Part Four. Asset allocation, an increasingly important topic in investments, is the focus of Part five. Part Six deals with topics of investments and portfolio management from the viewpoint of professional investment managers and other institutional investors.

As reflected in the title of this book, our objective is to present a series of case problems and readings that would be useful in a supplemental context. Some instructors may wish to use many of the case problems and a few of the readings. Other instructors may prefer to use more of the readings and fewer of the case problems. In sum, we are hopeful that some combination of the case problems and selected readings will be helpful in a systematic study of investments and portfolio management at the appropriate level of study.

A number of talented persons have been helpful in the development of this collection of case problems and readings over a number of years. In particular, the contributions of Charles D'Ambrosio, Suzanne BeDell, David Eiteman, Jeanne Fitzgerald, Irving Frankman, Mark Hinesley, Philip Klinger, Joel Mogy, Joseph Murphy, Tyron Moser, David Rosenthal, Jamie Smith, and Robert Sorenson are acknowledged. I also appreciate the constructive comments and suggestions of my colleagues and many fine students at the Krannert School of Management. Naturally, errors and omissions are the sole responsibility of the author/editor.

Keith V. Smith

Case Problems and Readings:
A SUPPLEMENT FOR
INVESTMENTS
AND PORTFOLIO MANAGEMENT

PORTFOLIO ATTRIBUTES FOR DONALD ADAMS

Mr. Donald Adams is age 50 and has accumulated through savings and/or inheritance the portfolio shown below. He has always managed his own financial affairs, but has decided that he would like an outside evaluation of his portfolio. He provides the following information: (1) 40% tax bracket; (2) wife 48, three children 20, 17, and 14; (3) his objectives are to provide a retirement fund which can be used to supplement his pension and to provide protection against future inflation.

INVESTMENT PORTFOLIO

Bonds:

15 U.S. Treasury 9-5/8s of 1990	$15,100
Municipals (various maturities and yields)	102,500

Stocks:

700 ATT (current yield = 4.6%; P/E = 13)	18,200
500 General Motors (yield = 6.4%; P/E = 7)	39,000
1,500 Ingersoll Rand (yield = 2.6%; P/E = 18)	60,750
Total	$235,550

Based on this brief scenario, be prepared to discuss the following questions:

(1) What further information would you request in order to provide advice to Mr. Adams and his family?

(2) What investment attributes do you believe to be important to the Adams family?

(3) What is your overall assessment of Mr. Adam's portfolio relative to his expressed objectives?

FINANCIAL PLANNING FOR CLARICE JONES

Mr. Jeremiah Jones, a professional engineer, has just died of a heart attack at age 49. He did not qualify for social security. He left an estate after all taxes of approximately $210,000, which currently is invested in the following securities portfolio:

Bonds:

30 Texaco 9s of 1999	$28,800

Stocks:

1,500 Eastman Kodak	63,000
1,000 NCR	57,000
1,700 Sears	61,200
Total	$210,000

The market price of these securities approximates cost.

In addition to the $210,000 estate, Mrs. Clarice Jones was left with a comfortable home, subject to a $30,000 mortgage, with monthly payments of $450 remaining for ten years. She has a fully-paid new automobile, and all her home furnishings and personal possessions are in good order. She also has a savings account of about $2,000.

Mrs. Jones is 45 and enjoys good health. She has four daughters, ages 13, 15, 17, and 18. The girls are expected to attend college, with the oldest daughter beginning in six months at a nearby state university. Mrs. Jones has a college education but has never worked outside of the home. By attending college one more semester, she could obtain a teaching certificate -- and thus could expect to teach in the public schools at a salary of about $12,000 for nine months.

Living costs of the Jones' family were approximately $30,000 while Mr. Jones was still alive. They live in a midwestern city of 60,000 population. College expenses (i.e. tuition, room and board, etc.) are estimated to be $5,500 per daughter per year. Mrs. Jones has worked out a rough budget of current monthly

3

expenses on a pared-down basis. She estimates it will be $1,200 per month (of which $200 is deductible) in addition to mortgage and college costs. She expects to pay federal and state taxes at a rate of 25%. Assume 4% inflation over the next decade, and also a 9% expected rate of return on her investment portfolio.

Clarice Jones strongly desires to leave the estate intact for her children and possible grandchildren. You are a long-time friend of the Jones family, and Clarice comes to you for advice in investment and investment planning.

Specifically, here are some questions:

(1)   Based on the information provided, what would you project will happen to the estate during the next decade or so when the Jones girls are in college?

(2)   How sensitive is your answer (to the first question) to investment return, interest rates, inflation, educational costs, etc.?

(3)   What advice would you give to Clarice Jones about her investment portfolio?

(4)   What other topics and/or advice would you mention to Mrs. Jones?

DETERMINING EXPLICIT INVESTMENT GOALS

Carter and Hazel Surber are very concerned about their financial future. They come to you with several specific questions on whether or not they will have the financial resources to accomplish certain of their family goals, or whether they can expect to achieve the investment results to make those goals a reality.

Carter (41) and Hazel (43) live in a northern suburb of Indianapolis, Indiana with their two children -- Eleanor (17) who is just beginning her senior year in high school, and David (15) who will be a sophomore at the same school. Recent financial statements for the Surber family are as follows:

```
-----------------------------------------------------
                    Income:
    Carter's salary                      $37,300
    Hazel's salary                        32,400
    Investment income                      4,500
        Total                           $72,400
                   Expenses:
    Mortgage payment                      $9,800
    Taxes                                 16,700
    Food                                   6,200
    Home maintenance and utilities         7,300
    Consumer purchases and other          17,800
    Savings                               16,400
        Total                           $74,200

                    Assets:
    Home                                $121,800
    Retirement accounts                  163,400
    Savings accounts                      10,600
    Investment portfolio                  63,000
    Art and antiques                       6,700
    Automobiles (3)                       16,800
    Personal possessions                  26,900
        Total                          $409,200
                  Liabilities:
    Mortgage                             $77,400
    Credit card balances                   2,700
        Total                           $80,100

                 Family equity:
    Carter and Hazel Surber             $329,100
-----------------------------------------------------
```

Despite a sizable family equity, the Surbers' finances have been relatively tight in recent years. The situation improved significantly a year ago, however, when both kids were in high school and Hazel resumed her professional career. During the past year, in fact, the Surbers were able to add $16,400 to their savings, retirement programs, and investment portfolio.

Carter and Hazel both plan to work twenty more years until they are 61 and 63, respectively. Because of their joint income, the Surbers feel that they are in a relatively secure position financially. At the same time, they wonder if they will indeed have enough financial resources to pay for two college educations, some additional travel which they enjoy greatly, a comfortable standard-of-living after retirement, and possibly leave a significant estate for Eleanor and David.

That, of course, is why they came to you for some help in better planning their financial and investment future. After sharing their financial statements and broad hopes for the future, you suggest to the Surbers that they prepare a list of specific questions that need to be answered. A week later, they come up with the following list:

(1)   Eleanor plans to begin her study of mechanical engineering at Purdue University just a year from now. Fees, living costs, books, and spending money are estimated to average about $6,200 per year, and will be needed at the beginning of each academic year. How much should the Surbers set aside now in certificates of deposit that pay 6.5% per year (after tax) in order to provide for Eleanor's years at college?

(2)   In contrast, David expects to earn a full scholarship for his liberal arts (i.e. pre-law) studies at Notre Dame. Because of that, he is interested in saving money toward the purchase of a sports car at the beginning of his third year at Notre Dame. David works hard and believes he can save $200 per month during the next five years. If the sports car of his dreams is expected to cost about $18,500, what after-tax rate-of-return must David earn on his savings in order to afford the sports car?

(3)   Suppose that after putting aside adequate funds for Eleanor's college (and perhaps a bit to help David with his sports car), and the likely cost of a month long trip around the world in about nine years to celebrate Carter's fiftieth birthday, the Surber's find themselves with investment funds amounting to about $45,000. If those funds, together with an additional

savings of $12,000 each year, are invested in an equity
mutual fund that has an expected annual return of 9%
(after-tax), how much will that part of their total
portfolio be worth at the time of their retirement?

(4)   Assume that at retirement, the Surbers' retirement
      accounts have grown to $525,000 and is available to
      them along with the amount calculated for question (3).
      If they expect to earn 10% (after-tax) on their total
      wealth after retirement, and if they project annual
      expenses of $48,000, what will be the size of the
      estate which they will leave -- and assuming that they
      both live for 25 years after retirement?

(5)   How realistic are the rates-of-return and other
      assumptions which are reflected in these questions?

(6)   How sensitive are your answers to those assumptions?

Seven years ago, Pete Peterson and nine friends organized the Walnut Falls Investment Club (WFIC). The ten members are all in their late thirties, and all are employed professionally. Each member invested $1,500 at the beginning, and each has since contributed $250 at the end of each calendar quarter. The initial funds were invested in a portfolio of five common stocks. No cash withdrawals have been made, with all dividends and realized capital gains reinvested in the portfolio which now consists of twenty-one common stocks in varying amounts. Every year, each member pays his appropriate federal and state taxes on income and/or realized gains in the WFIC portfolio.

The objective of WFIC is capital preservation and growth over time. Income has never been given much consideration. The group makes decisions collectively based on information provided by their broker, ideas generated at their meetings, and especially as a result of research reports and special presentations made at the meetings of WFIC. Portfolio turnover has been relatively low as the group collectively seems to favor a very conservative and somewhat passive approach to investing. The treasurer of WFIC, Wally Cameron, reported a market value of $122,551.68 on the occasion of their seventh anniversary party.

WFIC meets bimonthly at members' homes on a rotating basis. A typical agenda is as follows:

(a)	Treasurer's report	10 minutes
(b)	New idea brainstorming	20 minutes
(c)	Investment research report	30 minutes
(d)	Special presentation	30 minutes
(e)	Beer and snacks (i.e. social)	??

Attendance at such meetings has been very steady over the years, and the ten members have developed a very close friendship. They decided at the outset to not allow new memberships until a charter member leaves -- and, thus far, that has not occurred.

The special presentation is made, again on a rotating basis, by either a member or his chosen guest. Pete Peterson has that assignment for the next meeting, and he has decided to handle it himself. He plans to discuss and compare two articles which he recently came across. The first was published in a 1979 issue of FINANCIAL ANALYSTS JOURNAL (see Reading #1), while the second appeared in a 1985 issue of BUSINESS WEEK (see Reading #4). In preparing his discussion, Pete is aware that the two articles are different in terms of their intended audiences, and also their general conclusions.

Pete Peterson also is aware that if he proceeds to introduce and discuss those two articles, his fellow members of the Walnut Falls Investment Club are likely to respond with serious questions about the articles and their implications for the group's collective investments. Specifically, he anticipates a series of questions such as the following:

(1) What is the compound before-tax annual return that WFIC has experienced since its beginning seven years ago? And what is the average after-tax annual return that Pete and his friends have experienced over that period?

(2) What are the major conclusions of the 1979 paper that was published in the FINANCIAL ANALYSTS JOURNAL? What are some questions that are not answered in that paper?

(3) What are the major conclusions of the article that was published in the 1985 issue of BUSINESS WEEK? Do those conclusions support or disagree with that from the first paper?

(4) Should either of the two articles cause any of the members to reconsider the long-term purposes and/or prospects of the Walnut Falls Investment Club?

Can Active Management Add Value?

Keith P. Ambachtsheer and James L. Farrell, Jr.

▶ To survive the onslaught of passive management, active management must produce returns large enough to offset its higher risks and fees. The authors identify the basic building blocks of a viable active management approach, shed light on the kinds of results that can be expected when these building blocks are integrated into an active management process and suggest some reasons why active management, although viable in theory, has often failed to outperform passive management in practice.

The five basic building blocks of active management are (1) judgments on the degree to which securities are under- or overvalued, (2) assessments of the correlation between these judgments and subsequent security returns, (3) conversion of the judgments into expected returns that are both unbiased and scaled to reflect the judgments' predictive power, (4) portfolio building rules that generate changes consistent with diversification requirements, transaction costs and legal and other considerations and (5) a mechanism for translating portfolio changes into actual buy and sell orders.

Tests suggest that existing research approaches are capable of generating judgments with low but significant predictive power, and that a combination of approaches will often yield results superior to those of any one approach. Superior results are forthcoming, however, only when the active manager devotes adequate attention to building blocks (2) through (5). ▶

T HE passive management of security portfolios has been elevated over the last few years from an oddity with subversive overtones to a viable and even attractive option for buyers and sellers of portfolio management services. The attraction lies partly in the fact that the product characteristics of passively managed portfolios can readily be described by sellers and understood by buyers. More importantly, the promise of diversification combined with reduced management and brokerage fees has proved hard to resist, especially for those responsible for the administration of large pools of pension assets.

The success of passive management has provided a healthy perspective from which to reexamine active management. The viability of active management hinges on whether it can produce over the long term incremental returns large enough to more than offset its greater risks and higher fees. The passive and active approaches are contrasted graphically in Figure I.

This article has three purposes—(1) to identify the basic building blocks of a viable active management approach, (2) to shed light on the kinds of results that can be expected when the building blocks are integrated into an active management "manufacturing process" and (3) to suggest a number of reasons why active management, while viable in theory, has often failed to succeed in practice.

Basic Building Blocks

It takes neither mysticism nor high-powered mathematics to list the basic components of successful active management. There are five—

1. *Judgments on the degree to which securities are under- or overvalued*: These can be judgments about individual securities (leading to "security selection"), groups of securities (leading to "group rotation") or classes of securities (leading to "market timing").
2. *Predictive ability*: There must be some positive correlation between the judgments and their subsequent actual outcomes. Without predictive ability, there is no basis for active management.
3. *Scaling*: To be useful, the judgments must be converted into return increments (decrements) that are unbiased and scaled to reflect the level of predictive ability embodied in them.
4. *Portfolio building rules*: Converting even properly scaled valuation judgments into portfolio rebalancing decisions is a complex task—especially when diver-

Keith Ambachtsheer is Director of Research for the investment management consulting firm Canavest House Inc., Toronto. James Farrell is a Vice President of Citibank, N.A., in New York.

The authors thank College Retirement Equities Fund, Citibank, N.A. and Canavest House for their financial support of this study.

sification requirements, transaction costs and other possible constraints must be considered. Portfolio building rules, which can be carried out by people, computers or some combination of the two, can greatly simplify the task.

5. *Buy and sell orders:* It is not enough to know what ought to be done. Successful active management requires that what ought to be done in theory actually be carried out in practice.

Figure I:
The Two Basic Portfolio Management Styles

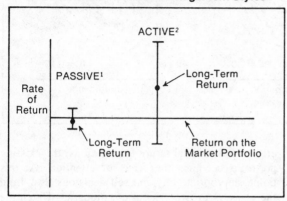

1. Passive Management leads to a long-term return slightly below that on the market portfolio because of management and brokerage charges. There is some period-to-period return variability, since it is typically not feasible to match the market portfolio exactly. This variability is represented by the bar.

2. Successful Active Management leads to a long-term positive increment of return (net of all fees) at the cost of greater period-to-period return variability.

Valuation Judgments

At least one aspect of past capital markets will surely apply in the future: Security prices will continue to fluctuate. Whether there exists some method of successfully predicting their fluctuations continues to be a subject of debate. Most of the currently used methods of predicting securities values fall into three broad categories.

The long-term fundamental approach (LTF) focuses on present value analysis. When applied to common stocks, LTF entails making long-term projections of dividends, earnings or cash flow and then relating the resulting payments stream back to current market values through a discount rate. This approach has become extremely popular over the last few years, and a significant number of investment management organizations currently use it in one form or another.[1]

The short-term fundamental approach (STF) has myriad specific applications in current use. Most revolve around analyzing earnings, earnings momentum and price-earnings multiples against a

background of historical relations. For many years Value Line has used an STF method to derive one-year price appreciation expectations on a large list of common stocks.

The technical approach focuses on deriving the demand and supply for securities through such devices as charting price and volume relations over time. Adherents claim that success with this approach demands subjective evaluation of patterns, making it a highly individualistic exercise not easily reduced to simple formulas or rules.

Other methods that do not fit into these three categories include those that focus on certain corporate balance sheet items or analysis of insider trading reports.

Predictive Ability

Successful active management obviously requires valuation judgments (acquired by whatever method) that have some predictive content. There is no one correct method of measuring the predictive content of such judgments. Canavest House has developed a method called "Information Coefficient Analysis" (or IC analysis), which is similar in spirit to the approach described by Treynor and Black.[2]

IC analysis is based on the thesis that, if a set of valuation judgments has predictive content, there should be some positive correlation between the judgments and subsequent stock price behavior. Figure II shows three possible cases: Case A suggests perfect predictive ability leading to an Information Coefficient (IC) of 1.0; Case B shows the logical consequence of no predictive ability at all—an IC of zero; Case C shows some predictive ability leading, in the example, to an IC of 0.15. In all cases the IC simply denotes the correlation between sets of codings denoting return expectations and sets of codings denoting subsequent return experience.

Results based on IC analyses of long-term and short-term fundamental valuation approaches (LTF and STF) suggest that carefully constructed valuation methods of both types appear capable of generating judgments having low but significant predictive content, with ICs typically in the 0.05 to 0.25 range.[3] These results are consistent with other scattered reports on the predictive content of appropriately designed and executed valuation methods.[4]

In the case of active management, the simple homily, "Two heads are better than one," takes the form, "Two valuation methods are better than one, as long as they approach the valuation problem through different perspectives."[5] It seems reasonable to assume that STF and LTF methods do provide different perspectives on the valuation of a given list of stocks. Insider trading data might provide a third perspective.

1. Footnotes appear at end of article.

11

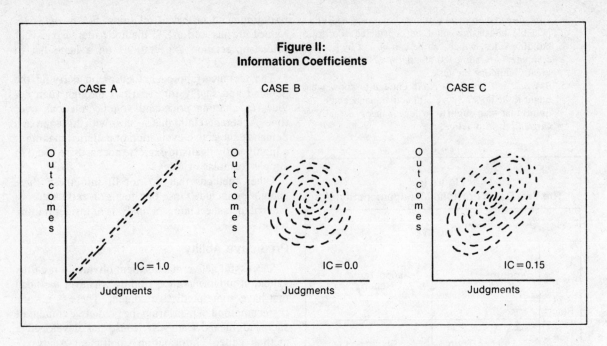

Figure II:
Information Coefficients

CASE A — Outcomes vs. Judgments — IC = 1.0

CASE B — Outcomes vs. Judgments — IC = 0.0

CASE C — Outcomes vs. Judgments — IC = 0.15

In statistical terms, composite forecasting means moving from simple ICs (denoting the correlation between valuation judgments based on a single method and actual results) to multiple ICs (denoting the correlation between valuation judgments based on multiple methods and actual results). Multiple ICs are higher than simple ICs as long as the valuation methods (i.e., the "explanatory variables") are not perfect substitutes for one another (i.e., perfectly correlated). In other words, predictive power can potentially be enhanced by using more than one valuation method. The appendix provides a more rigorous statement of the concept.

Scaling

Valuation judgments with positive predictive content are a means, not an end, the raw material from which incremental portfolio returns can be produced. Effective integration of valuation judgments and portfolio rebalancing decisions is highly dependent on the proper expression of the judgments.

The final output of the valuation process is, ideally, a set of expected residual returns (or alphas, in portfolio theory language) that have been adjusted to reflect their assumed level of predictive content. Traditionally, valuation judgments have not been expressed in terms of adjusted alphas, but as a wide variety of coding schemes such as "buy," "hold" or "sell." But procedures can be devised to convert any coding or rating scheme into an estimate of IC-adjusted alphas.[6]

Portfolio Building Rules

With the valuation judgments converted into prop-

erly scaled residual return expectations, the existing portfolio becomes the focus of attention. At this point, appropriate buy and sell decisions flow from the answers to two critical questions: (1) Given the portfolio's current structure, how much residual return (alpha) can be expected at the cost of how much incremental, non-market related, risk? and (2) What can be done to improve the incremental reward-risk characteristics of the existing portfolio?

The computer can answer the first question, but the second is a different matter. On one hand, rebalancing portfolios "manually" can lead to improper decisions, since proper rebalancing judgments require simultaneous consideration of residual returns, transaction costs and risk factors on a potentially very large list of securities. On the other hand, even highly sophisticated optimization programs cannot possibly deal with those subjective, qualitative aspects that are and will always continue to be part of the portfolio management function. The appropriate balance between man and machine can be struck by deriving a set of portfolio building rules that define the range of reward-risk characteristics desired while permitting portfolio managers discretion in terms of the specific securities and weights to be used.

An Application

We employed building rules along the lines proposed above to find out what a properly integrated active management process based on integrating the "basic building blocks" detailed above can produce. Our study began in September of 1973 with a "typical" institutional stock portfolio. We converted valuation judgments actually available at that time into IC-

TABLE A: Six-Month ICs

	9/73 3/74	3/74 9/74	9/74 3/75	3/75 9/75	9/75 3/76	3/76 9/76	Mean	Std. Dev.
LTF	0.12	0.16	0.01	0.13	0.08	0.31	0.135	0.100
STF	0.17	0.04	−0.09	0.16	0.11	0.01	0.067	0.100
Combined	0.17	0.18	0.00	0.16	0.10	0.30	0.152	0.099

adjusted expected residual returns and used these expectations, along with transaction cost assumptions and a set of formal portfolio building rules, to rebalance the portfolio. We repeated the rebalancing procedure in March 1974, September 1974, March 1975, September 1975 and March 1976.

We began with two sets of valuation judgments— LTF judgments acquired from Wells Fargo and STF judgments from Value Line—and a selection universe of 200 of the largest capitalization stocks common to both services.[7] We then used IC analysis to measure the predictive ability of each set over each six-month period. The IC statistics, shown in Table A, indicate that both LTF and STF methods delivered predictive power in a reasonably consistent fashion.[8]

Tests of independence between the two sets of valuation judgments for all six forecast dates suggested virtually no correlation. To test the "two heads are better than one" concept, we combined the LTF and STF judgments, using a two to one weighting scheme that reflected their relative predictive powers over the entire observation period, to create a third set of judgments. The IC statistics on the combined judgments set, also shown in Table A, are on average higher than those of either the LTF or STF set alone.

The Value Line STF judgments came in the form of a one-to-five rating scheme. For consistency, we scaled the Wells Fargo LTF "differences" (that is, the difference between each security's projected long-term return and its risk-adjusted required return) to a one-to-five rating scheme and used the two rating schemes to create ratings for the combined judgments. The three rating sets were converted to IC-adjusted alphas using IC assumptions of 0.15 for LTF, 0.075 for STF and 0.17 for the two combined (the latter being mathematically derived from the first two).[9]

Ideally, the LTF and STF IC assumptions should have been based on information generated outside the test period. This was not possible at the time the study was performed. Recent IC analyses suggest that the orders of magnitude assumed continue to be realistic, although LTF-based ICs have deteriorated somewhat while STF-based ICs have improved.[10]

While properly scaled residual return expectations can be used in all three areas of active management—market timing, group rotation and security selection—our study focused exclusively on the security selection component. We accomplished this by maintaining (1) portfolio market risk (beta) levels close to 1.0, (2) market (Standard & Poor's 500) weighting between the growth, cyclical, stable and oil sectors of the portfolio,[11] and (c) as a further risk control measure, a a 60-stock portfolio at all times, with no one stock exceeding three per cent of the total value of the portfolio.

Within these risk-related guidelines, our objective was simply to maximize expected portfolio alphas by taking advantage of any switch opportunities that offered a return greater than the three per cent round-trip transaction cost. With this objective in mind, we derived a set of portfolio building rules for a computer program that rebalanced the initial September 1973 portfolio and the resulting portfolios every six months thereafter.[12]

Study Results

Table B shows the three-year annualized rates of return (including income and after transaction costs but before management fees) for the following portfolios:

1. *The Combined Fund*—the "managed" fund based on the combined STF and LTF valuation inputs;
2. *The LTF Fund*—the "managed" fund based only on inputs from the long-term fundamental valuation method;
3. *The STF Fund*—the "managed" fund based only on inputs from the short-term fundamental valuation method;
4. *The S&P 500 Fund*—the unmanaged portfolio of 500 stocks as created by Standard & Poor's Corporation;
5. *The Universe (EW) Fund*—the unmanaged portfolio of 200 stocks used as the selection universe for the study, equally weighted;
6. *The Starting Fund*—a hypothetical portfolio of 60 stocks selected from our 200-stock universe and designed to meet the risk-related portfolio building rules created for the three "managed" funds but to have an alpha (given the September 1973 valuation judgments) of zero, in order to give performance equal to that of the universe;
7. *The Universe (CW) Fund*—the unmanaged portfolio of 200 stocks used as the selection universe for the study, capitalization weighted;
8. *The Becker Funds*—managed funds representing the 20th, 50th and 80th percentile breaks in the universe of the Becker Pension Fund Evaluation Service.[13]

Table B shows that the LTF and STF Funds each earned sufficient excess return to more than justify the

13

incremental management fee typically charged for active management. The Combined Fund produced an alpha that exceeded the better of the two single managed funds by one per cent. At the same time, the performances of the Universe Funds and the Starting Fund suggest that the performances of the three managed funds were not aided by the 200 stocks chosen as the selection universe. All three unmanaged funds marginally underperformed the S&P 500 Fund.

A detailed examination of performances within each of the six six-month sub-periods revealed that the Combined and LTF Funds outperformed the S&P 500 in each period. The STF Fund had a superior performance in five of the periods, versus one out of six periods for the 50th percentile Becker Fund. Figure III shows the cumulative wealth indexes for all funds over the three-year period.[14]

Table C shows the results of an *ex post* evaluation of the risk characteristics of the three managed and three unmanaged funds, performed by regressing the 36 observations of monthly returns against the returns of the S&P 500. The *ex post* betas of the managed portfolios (in the 1.00 to 1.07 range) suggest that market risk was reasonably well controlled over the three-year evaluation period. At the same time, the risk-related building rules produced superior levels of diversification, as evidenced by the R-squared and standard error statistics of the managed funds. Comparable statistics for the average pension fund over the test period were roughly 0.90 and 7.0 per cent, respectively.[15] The managed funds' results may be at least partially related to the conscious decision not to engage in either market timing or group rotation activity.

The somewhat higher specific, or non-market, risk of the LTF and Combined Funds (indicated by their standard errors) could reflect a tendency toward

TABLE B: Performance Results of Test Portfolios
(September 30, 1973 to September 30, 1976)

	ROR*
The Combined Fund	10.0%
The LTF Fund	9.0%
The STF Fund	5.5%
The S&P 500 Fund	3.3%
The Universe (EW) Fund	2.9%
The Starting Fund	2.5%
The Universe (CW) Fund	1.9%
The 20th Percentile Becker Fund	0.8%
The 50th Percentile Becker Fund	−2.9%
The 80th Percentile Becker Fund	−5.6%

* Annualized, including income, after transaction costs of 1.5 per cent each way, before management fees.

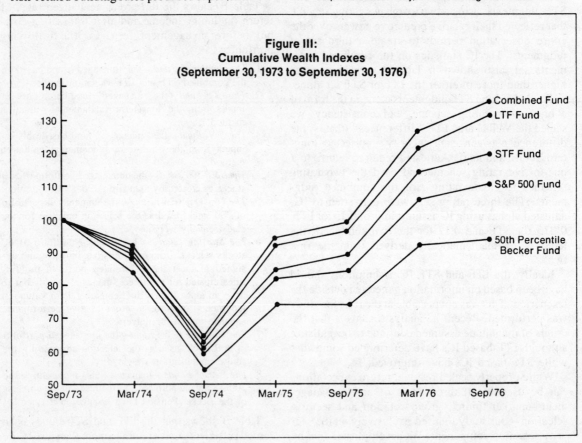

Figure III:
Cumulative Wealth Indexes
(September 30, 1973 to September 30, 1976)

14

	Regression Results**			
	% Annualized Alpha	Beta	R²	Annualized Std. Error
Combined Fund	6.7	1.03	0.93	6.0
LTF Fund*	5.7	1.00	0.93	5.8
STF Fund*	2.2	1.07	0.97	3.9
Starting Fund*	−0.6	1.03	0.95	5.3
S&P 500 Fund	0.0	1.00	1.00	0.0
Universe Fund (EW)	−0.4	1.07	0.98	3.5
Universe Fund (CW)	−1.3	1.02	0.99	2.1

* Adjusted monthly for dividends and transaction costs. (Transaction costs equal 1.5 per cent each way.)

** The monthly percentage change in the total return index for the portfolio minus the risk-free rate regressed against the monthly percentage change in the total return index for the S&P 500 minus the risk-free rate, using 36 observations.

higher yield exposure over the period. The dividend yields on the LTF and Combined Funds averaged 120 and 90 basis points, respectively, over the S&P 500 Fund's yield. By contrast, the STF Fund's dividend yield approximated the S&P 500's.

The bias in favor of high yield stocks on the part of the LTF and Combined Funds was rewarded over the evaluation period since high yield stocks generally outperformed low yield stocks. The alpha contribution of the high yield bias in the LTF and Combined Funds should not be exaggerated, however. Separate IC tests on the high and low yield subcomponents of the selection universe showed that the LTF valuation judgments discriminated successfully between under- and overvalued securities within *both* subcomponents. Recall also that all the funds were constrained to carry market (S&P 500) weights in the growth, cyclical, stable and oil sectors. Perhaps one per cent of the realized alpha on the LTF Fund and one-half per cent on the Combined Fund can be attributed to the high yield bias in these two funds over the test period.[16]

Portfolio Turnover Experience

Table D shows period-by-period and cumulative turnover rates for the three managed funds. Initial turnover was high for all three funds, reflecting the rebalancing of the original portfolio in September 1973. "Reweighting" held securities required about a seven per cent turnover on each subsequent rebalancing date. The remaining turnover reflects switches out of held securities into new ones.

The turnover numbers reemphasize the need for realistic IC assumptions and transaction cost estimates.[17] Too conservative assumptions depress turnover below the level warranted and lead to foregone return opportunities. Too optimistic assumptions cause excessive turnover, which can transform potential gains into losses.

TABLE D: Portfolio Turnover Rates

Date	LTF	STF	Combined
9/73	62%	27%	64%
3/74	30	22	31
9/74	34	23	36
3/75	32	32	33
9/75	24	23	25
3/76	25	23	25
Cumulative	207%	150%	214%

Can Active Management Add Value?

The results of our study reveal that successful active management is not dependent on the use of any one specific valuation approach. Indeed, some combination of approaches can yield results superior to those of any one approach. Nor does successful active management require valuation judgments with high levels of predictive content. The Information Coefficients reported in this article imply that only one to two per cent of the variance of residual returns on the 200-stock universe was "explained" by the STF and LTF judgments employed.

The alphas realized by the active management approaches used in our study arose purely from security selectivity within the growth, cyclical, stable and oil sectors of the sample stock universe. Market timing and group rotation strategies played no part in the superior results achieved by active management.

Successful active management is obviously not dependent on the use of sophisticated optimization models, as the relatively simple portfolio building rules used in the study demonstrate. Successful active management *is* dependent on (a) the availability of valuation judgments with some predictive content, (b) reasonable assumptions about the degree of predictive content embodied in each valuation judgment employed, (c) the conversion of valuation judgments into unbiased, properly scaled residual return expectations, (d) the existence of portfolio building rules that deal adequately with transaction costs and risk control and (e) the availability of computer aids to look after the very real data processing needs that the proper integration of the first four factors implies.

Some Caveats

Our STF, LTF and Combined Funds produced positive annual residual returns of 2.2, 5.7 and 6.7 per cent, respectively, with residual risk exposure equal to or less than that of actual equity components of pension funds. These results were achieved using valuation judgments with only modest predictive content (mean ICs of 0.067, 0.135 and 0.152 for STF, LTF and Combined Funds, respectively, over the test period).

Should these realized alphas be taken as targets for investment management organizations that assume they can make valuation judgments with Information Coefficients in the 0.067 to 0.152 range? First, consider that the reported results suffer from *ex post* bias, in the sense that we knew beforehand what order-of-magnitude ICs to assume for the STF and LTF methods over the September 1973 to September 1976 period. This luxury does not exist for the investment manager looking ahead. All he can practically do is to make informed IC judgments based on sound *a priori* reasoning and available *ex post* IC data. The availability of such data over an extended period of time clearly constitutes highly useful information on which to base *ex ante* judgments.

Furthermore, our study results were based on instantaneous implementation, in the sense that the valuation judgments for each six-month interval were assumed to have been received, turned into buy or sell decisions and executed all on the same day. This is hardly possible in reality (although a three-day turnaround time has been shown to be practical in one organization that uses the integrated building block approach outlined here).

The above arguments suggest that an organization using valuation methods with ICs in the 0.15 range should not necessarily promise clients a six per cent alpha; two to three per cent might be more realistic.[18] The real question at issue, however, is why actively managed funds are not achieving even this realistically modest level of return. The Becker results reported in Table B suggest that, during the 1973-76 period at least, over 80 per cent of actual funds realized *negative* alphas. This experience is likely to continue as long as investment management organizations fail to define the "product characteristics" of their active management services and to establish an integrated "manufacturing process" capable of converting low-grade valuation judgments into positive portfolio alpha realizations.[19]

Much of the active-passive debate over the last few years has focused on technical issues such as market efficiency. This article suggests that process design and organizational design considerations are at least equally important. Unless these issues are given the attention they deserve, active management will continue to lose ground to passive management in the years ahead. ∎

Footnotes

1. The long-term fundamental approach has been popularized through the efforts of the Wells Fargo Research Group. See, for example, William Fouse, "Risk and Liquidity Revisited," *Financial Analysts Journal*, January/February 1977.
2. Jack Treynor and Fischer Black, "How to Use Security Analysis to Improve Portfolio Selection," *Journal of Business*, January 1973. See also Robert Ferguson, "How to Beat the Index Funds," *Financial Analysts Journal*, May/June 1975 and Stuart Hodges and Richard Brealey, "Dynamic Portfolio Selection," *Financial Analysts Journal*, March/April 1973 for further exposition of these ideas.
3. Keith Ambachtsheer, "Where Are the Customers' Alphas?" *Journal of Portfolio Management*, Fall 1977 and "Profit Potential in an Almost Efficient Market," *Journal of Portfolio Management*, Fall 1974.
4. See, for example, Fischer Black, "Yes, Virginia, There is Hope: Tests of the Value Line System," *Financial Analysts Journal*, September/October 1973; Charles Dubois, "Insider Trading Information and Superior Portfolio Performance" (Institute for Quantitative Research in Finance, Spring Seminar, 1978); and Benjamin Korschot, "Measuring Research Analysts' Performance," *Financial Analysts Journal*, July/August 1978.
5. Robert T. Falconer and Charles M. Sivesind ("Dealing with Conflicting Forecasts: The Eclectic Advantage," *Business Economics*, September 1977) discuss this approach with respect to improving economic forecasts.
6. For a description of one such procedure, see Ambachtsheer, "Where Are the Customers' Alphas?"
7. Both Wells Fargo's Security Market Line Service and Value Line's One Year Price Appreciation Rankings were in existence prior to the test period and during the test period and continue to be available today. Both services have made some revisions to their methodologies over time.
8. We tested for the significance of the ICs from each model within each of the six sub-periods of the test. For a universe of 200 stocks (sample size), a correlation coefficient of 0.10 is significant at the 0.05 level. The LTF and combined approaches showed "t" statistics in excess of two (0.05 significance level) in five of the six periods of the test, while the STF model proved to be significant at the 0.05 level in three of the six periods.
9. The conversion process used is described in Ambachtsheer, "Where Are the Customers' Alphas?"
10. This deterioration was found to relate to industry group valuation and not to security valuation within industry groups.

11. James Farrell has shown that stocks within each of these four groups tend to move together even after the overall market effect has been removed. See "Analyzing Covariation of Returns to Determine Homogeneous Stock Groupings," *Journal of Business,* April 1974 and "Homogeneous Stock Groupings: Implications for Portfolio Management," *Financial Analysts Journal,* May/June 1975.

12. This computer program is part of the Equity Management and Control System of Canavest House.

13. We wish to thank Gil Beebower of A.G. Becker for providing this information.

14. Detailed period-by-period performance results are shown in the table below.

15. Gil Beebower, A.G. Becker.

16. The IC within the higher yielding class of securities was 0.13 vs. 0.06 within the lower yielding class of securities. These results compare with an IC of 0.14 across the entire selection universe. These numbers suggest that some of the overall predictive power resulted from the LTF approach correctly identifying high yield stocks as undervalued relative to low yield stocks. However, the weighted average of the two "within" class ICs was 0.11, suggesting significant predictive power even after the "across" class IC effect had been removed.

17. See Wayne Wagner and Larry Cuneo, "Reducing the Cost of Stock Trading," *Financial Analysts Journal,* November/December 1975.

18. Ambachtsheer, "Where Are the Customers' Alphas?" and "Profit Potential."

19. This statement does not imply that the "zero sum" nature of the active management game can be repealed. Instead, it suggests that steps can be taken to be a "winner" rather than a "loser" if the decision is made to play the game.

Detailed Performance Results

	9/73 to 9/76 Annualized ROR	3/76 to 9/76	9/75 to 3/76	3/75 to 9/75	9/74 to 3/75	3/74 to 9/74	9/73 to 3/74
Combined Fund	10.0	7.8	28.0	5.5	44.4	−28.9	− 9.0
LTF Fund	9.0	8.9	25.9	4.9	42.7	−28.3	−10.1
STF Fund	5.5	5.6	28.5	6.1	34.8	−31.4	− 9.8
S&P 500 Fund	3.3	4.4	25.0	2.7	34.5	−30.8	−11.7
Starting Fund (Zero Alpha)	2.5	6.3	20.3	3.0	35.4	−31.5	− 9.8
20th Percentile Becker Fund	0.8	5.3	26.2	3.1	44.2	−32.2	−14.1
50th Percentile Becker Fund	−2.9	2.5	22.3	−0.3	39.2	−35.2	−17.2
80th Percentile Becker Fund	−5.6	0.8	18.9	−3.4	35.2	−38.4	−20.5

APPENDIX

Combining Forecasts

This appendix illustrates the generalized procedure for combining forecasts from two different methods. In this regard, it might be easier to demonstrate the process by working with forecast errors, or the unexplained portion of realized return, rather than with the explained portion of returns, or correlation coefficient, on which the text focuses. Error reduction is the converse of maximizing correlation.

To begin with, we can designate the two forecasting methods as F_1 and F_2, and denote the variance of errors associated with each as VAR F_1 and VAR F_2 and the correlation between the errors of the two methods as P_{12}. Note that the method with the smaller error would be the one with the higher IC. In addition, the objective in combining forecasts would be to minimize forecast errors (which as noted would be equivalent to maximizing correlation). We can let k represent the weight of the first method and $(1-k)$ the weight of the second, thereby ensuring that the combined forecast is unbiased. The variance of errors in the combined forecast, VAR C, can then be written:

$$VAR(C) = k^2 \, VAR \, F_1 + (1-k)^2 \, VAR \, F_2 + 2P_{12} \, k(VAR \, F_1)^{1/2} (1-k)(VAR \, F_2)^{1/2} \, . \quad (1)$$

Note that the extent of error reduction depends on the correlation between methods (P_{12}). We can best illustrate this by analyzing two extreme cases mentioned in the body of the study—zero correlation and perfect correlation between methods.

First, assume that the forecasting methods have the same predictive power, or that VAR F_1 equals VAR F_2. Assume also that both forecasts carry the same weight in the combining formula, or that k equals one-half. Substituting in Equation (1) produces Equation (2):

$$VAR(C) = \tfrac{1}{2} \, VAR \, F + 2P_{12}(\tfrac{1}{4}) \, VAR \, F \, , \quad (2)$$

where VAR F is a general representation of the error from both methods.

Note that when the methods are independent, the variance of the combined forecast is one-half that of each individual forecast. This is because the zero correlation $(P_{12} = 0)$ eliminates the covariance term in the expression. On the other hand, when the correlation is perfect $(P_{12} = +1)$, the variance of the combined forecast is the same as that of each individual forecast. This is because the covariance term becomes equivalent to the error of an individual forecast.

Weighting forecasting methods in proportion to their forecasting power is optimal. We can specifically illustrate this by first differentiating Equation (1) with respect to k, then equating to zero. This provides Equation (3), where the combined error is minimal (combined IC is greatest):

$$k = \frac{VAR\ F_2 - P_{12}(VAR\ F_1)^{1/2}(VAR\ F_2)^{1/2}}{VAR\ F_1 + VAR\ F_2 - 2\ P_{12}(VAR\ F_1)^{1/2}(VAR\ F_2)^{1/2}} \ . \tag{3}$$

In the case where P_{12} equals zero, this reduces to:

$$k = \frac{VAR\ F_2}{VAR\ F_1 + VAR\ F_2} \ . \tag{4}$$

In the case where each method has equal forecasting power, the errors will be equal, and the numerator will be one-half the denominator. This indicates that equally powerful methods should be weighted equally to obtain the optimal reduction in forecasting error. In the case in the text, the LTF dividend discount method appeared to have about twice the forecasting power (IC) of the STF relative value/earnings momentum method, implying that the forecasting error of the LTF method was one-half that of the STF method, or that VAR STF equaled 2 VAR LTF. Using the preceding formula would indicate that the STF method should receive a weighting, k, of one-third and the LTF method a weighting of (1-k) or two-thirds. This was precisely the weighting used in our study.

Active Portfolio Management

How To Beat The Index Funds

Robert Ferguson

The Treynor-Black Model (TBM) is an idealized view of the investment world whose premises include some fairly unrealistic assumptions. Nevertheless, it offers the professional investor a new framework for viewing the investment process that can lead to a better understanding of the roles of various investment professionals (such as security analysts and portfolio managers) and more effective decision making.

TBM is based on the premise that investors like return and dislike risk. This view is probably consistent with the feelings of most investors although they may not agree on the definition of risk and the criterion they use to determine the attractiveness of a particular return-risk tradeoff.

The definition of risk used in TBM is a measure of the variability of return called the standard deviation of return (to save space it will be denoted by the symbol σ in what follows). Many investors may prefer other measures of risk, such as downside potential or the sensitivity of a portfolio (or security) to fluctuations of the market (beta, denoted by β). Most useful measures of risk are highly correlated with σ, and investors who prefer them can think of σ as a proxy that will rank portfolios in about the same way as their own measure of risk.

The definition of portfolio attractiveness used in TBM is based on a measure (denoted by P) in-

Robert Ferguson is Director of Computer Applications at Baker, Weeks & Co., Inc. and has had prior experience as a practicing security analyst and portfolio manager. An earlier version of this paper was presented at a seminar sponsored by the Institute of Quantitative Research in Finance.

troduced by Professor William F. Sharpe. The numerator (the top part) of this fractional measure is the amount by which the expected return of the portfolio (denoted by $\bar{R}_p$) exceeds the riskless rate of interest (R_F). The denominator (the bottom part) is the risk of the portfolio (σ_p). Symbolically, it is written as

$$P = \frac{\bar{R}_p - R_F}{\sigma_p}$$

The numerator is referred to as the portfolio's expected excess return ($\bar{r}_p$) and represents the anticipated reward for taking the risk σ_p.[1] Thus, Sharpe's measure,

$$P = \frac{\bar{r}_p}{\sigma_p} \quad , \tag{1}$$

is large when the anticipated reward per unit of associated risk is great. Choosing among portfolios on the basis of this measure is akin to buying meat at the store that sells the most pounds per dollar.

To avoid cumbersome notation, it is convenient to associate performance with the square of Sharpe's measure. This quantity (P^2), which ranks portfolios in exactly the same order as Sharpe's measure itself, is called the Sharpe Ratio.

$$P^2 = \frac{(\bar{R}_p - R_F)^2}{\sigma_p^2} = \frac{\bar{r}_p^2}{\sigma_p^2} \quad . \tag{2}$$

In the TBM view of the world, part of each security's excess return (denoted by r_i for security i)

---

1. Footnotes appear at end of article.

arises in association with changes in the market. This view is consistent with experience and with beta theory. It simply reflects the existence of economic and other factors that have an across the board impact on companies. That portion of a security's anticipated excess return ($\bar{r}_i$) related to the market's ($\bar{r}_M$) is called its market premium ($\bar{r}_{iM}$), and is assumed proportional to the market's anticipated excess return. The degree of sensitivity—essentially a beta concept—is denoted by β_i for security i. Symbolically the relationship is

$$\bar{r}_{iM} = \beta_i\, \bar{r}_M \quad . \tag{3}$$

The remaining portion of the i'th security's excess return is called its appraisal return (r_{iA}).[2] It is assumed to be associated with factors that only have an impact on the particular security in question. This assumption, while not entirely realistic, is a reasonable approximation in many instances.[3] It guarantees that each security's appraisal return is unrelated to its market return (r_{iM}). It also ensures that the appraisal return of one security is not related to that of another. The expected appraisal return for security i is denoted by $\bar{r}_{iA}$ and is called the appraisal premium.

For each security, then, expected excess return is the sum of two independent quantities, market premium and appraisal premium.

$$\bar{r}_i = \bar{r}_{iM} + \bar{r}_{iA} = \beta_i\, \bar{r}_M + \bar{r}_{iA} \quad . \tag{4}$$

The portion of a security's risk (σ_i) associated with its market return is called market risk (σ_{iM}), that associated with its appraisal return, appraisal risk (σ_{iA}). The independence assumption has the important consequence that the square of each security's risk (σ_i^2) is the sum of that associated with its market return (σ_{iM}^2) and that associated with its appraisal return (σ_{iA}^2).

$$\sigma_i^2 = \sigma_{iM}^2 + \sigma_{iA}^2 \quad . \tag{5}$$

The square of the standard deviation (i.e., risk) is called the variance (σ^2). Variance and risk rank portfolios (and securities) in the same order. Equation 5 states that a security's variance is the sum of its market variance and appraisal variance. But Equation 3 implies that

$$\sigma_{iM}^2 = \beta_i^2\, \sigma_M^2 \quad , \tag{6}$$

where σ_M^2 denotes the variance of the market, so that another way of writing the relationship is

$$\sigma_i^2 = \beta_i^2\, \sigma_M^2 + \sigma_{iA}^2 \quad . \tag{7}$$

In TBM, security characteristics are important only to the extent that they affect a portfolio's Sharpe Ratio. The question that must be answered at this juncture is how the Sharpe Ratio of a portfolio is related to the appraisal premium and appraisal risk and the market premium and market risk of its underlying securities.

Suppose the proportion of a portfolio devoted to security i is denoted by h_i. The portfolio's expected excess return is a weighted average of the expected excess returns of its underlying securities, with the weights being the allocation proportions.

$$\bar{r}_p = h_1\, \bar{r}_1 + h_2\, \bar{r}_2 + - - - + h_N\, \bar{r}_N \quad .$$

In this equation, there is one term for each security, representing its contribution to the portfolio's excess return. The number of securities in the portfolio is unspecified and is denoted by the letter N. A shorthand version of this equation is

$$\bar{r}_p = \sum h_i\, \bar{r}_i \quad , \tag{8}$$

where Σ is read as the sum over all values of i from 1 to N of terms of the form $h_i r_i$. Equations 4 and 8 imply that

$$\bar{r}_p = \beta_p\, \bar{r}_M + \left(\sum h_i\, \bar{r}_{iA} \right) \quad , \tag{9}$$

where β_p represents the beta of the portfolio. Just as in the case of a single security, the expected excess return of a portfolio (any portfolio) can be broken down into two independent portions: market premium ($\bar{r}_{PM}$) and appraisal premium ($\bar{r}_{PA}$), where we have

$$\bar{r}_{PM} = \beta_p\, \bar{r}_M \tag{10}$$

and

$$\bar{r}_{PA} = \sum h_i\, \bar{r}_{iA} \quad , \tag{11}$$

so that $\bar{r}_p$ can be expressed

$$\bar{r}_p = \text{market premium} + \text{appraisal premium}.$$

As intuition suggests, β_p is a weighted average of the betas of the underlying securities:

$$\beta_p = \sum h_i \beta_i \quad . \tag{12}$$

Given the perfect analogy between a security's return and a portfolio's return, and the similarity of Equations 7 to 4, it may not be too surprising that a portfolio's variance (σ_p^2) appears much like that of a security. The relationship is

portant function of the security analyst. Because none of the other quantities in Equation 17 is affected by security analysis, it follows that:

11. The role of the security analyst is to provide appraisal premiums and appraisal risks for the securities he follows.

Now consider a portfolio made up of securities with appraisal premiums. Such a portfolio is called an *active portfolio*.[4] Clearly, an active portfolio itself has an appraisal premium ($\bar{r}_{AA}$). As a consequence, it also has appraisal risk (σ_{AA}) and an appraisal ratio (γ^2). In general, it will have market premium ($\beta_A \bar{r}_M$) and market risk ($\beta_A \sigma_M$), too.

What will be the characteristics of a portfolio invested partly in an active portfolio and partly in the market? Referring to this portfolio as an active portfolio-market portfolio blend (AMB), the TBM shows that:

12. The market ratio (λ^2) of an AMB is equal to that of the market.
13. The appraisal ratio (γ^2) of an AMB is equal to that of the active portfolio.
14. The appraisal premium of an AMB ($\bar{r}_{PA}$) increases from 0.0 to the appraisal premium of the active portfolio ($\bar{r}_{AA}$) as the proportion of the AMB allocated to the active portfolio increases from 0.0 to 1.0.
15. The market premium of an AMB ($\bar{r}_{PM}$) changes from $\bar{r}_M$ to the market premium of the active portfolio ($\beta_A \bar{r}_M$) as the proportion of the AMB allocated to the active portfolio increases from 0.0 to 1.0.
16. The ratio of appraisal premium to market premium of an AMB ($\bar{r}_{PA}/\bar{r}_{PM}$) increases from 0.0 to that of the active portfolio ($\bar{r}_{AA}/\beta_A \bar{r}_M$) as the proportion of the AMB allocated to the active portfolio increases from 0.0 to 1.0.

But together with Equation 17, this implies that:

17. The entire impact on the performance of an AMB of a change in its allocation proportions arises from the associated change in its ratio of appraisal premium to market premium.

Is there a particular value for the ratio of appraisal premium to market premium in an AMB that makes the Sharpe Ratio a maximum? The answer is yes.

18. The performance of an AMB is at its highest when the ratio of appraisal premium to market premium is equal to the ratio of the active portfolio's appraisal ratio to its market ratio.

$$\frac{\bar{r}_{PA}}{\bar{r}_{PM}} = \frac{\gamma^2}{\lambda^2} \quad . \tag{20}$$

19. At this ratio of appraisal premium to market premium, the ratio of appraisal variance to market variance has the same value.

$$\frac{\bar{r}_{PA}}{\bar{r}_{PM}} = \frac{\gamma^2}{\lambda^2} = \frac{\sigma_{PA}^2}{\sigma_{PM}^2} \quad . \tag{21}$$

20. At this ratio of appraisal premium to market premium, the proportion of the AMB allocated to the active portfolio (h_A) is

$$h_A = \left| \frac{1}{\left(\dfrac{\bar{r}_{AA}}{\bar{r}_{AM}}\right)\beta_A \left(\dfrac{\lambda^2}{\gamma^2}\right) + (1 - \beta_A)} \right| . \tag{22}$$

21. At this ratio of appraisal premium to market premium, the Sharpe Ratio of the AMB is the sum of the market ratio and the active portfolio's appraisal ratio.

$$P^2 = \lambda^2 + \gamma^2 \quad . \tag{23}$$

Equation 23 says that the maximum Sharpe Ratio a portfolio manager can achieve by blending a particular active portfolio with the market is ($\lambda^2 + \gamma^2$). Thus the greater is the appraisal ratio of the active portfolio, the greater will be the performance of the associated best AMB. This, in turn, ensures that if the portfolio manager begins with an active portfolio whose appraisal ratio is as large as possible, the resulting optimum AMB will have the highest possible Sharpe Ratio. The following relatively simple two step procedure can be used to construct the best portfolio (in this sense) obtainable from a given set of analyst's recommendations:

  I. Using each security's appraisal premium and appraisal risk (as provided by the security analyst), construct an active portfolio whose appraisal ratio is as large as possible.
 II. Construct an AMB by allocating the proportion h_A (as given by Equation 22) of the AMB to the active portfolio and the remaining proportion to the market. This AMB has the highest possible performance.

It remains to determine how to maximize an active portfolio's appraisal ratio, given the appraisal premiums and appraisal risks of its underlying securities. According to the TBM:

22. The appraisal ratio of an active portfolio is maximized when the proportion allocated to each security (h_{Ai}) is proportional to the ratio

21

$$\sigma_p^2 = \beta_p^2 \sigma_M^2 + \left(\sum h_i^2 \, \sigma_{iA}^2 \right) \quad . \tag{13}$$

Thus a portfolio's variance also can be broken down into two related parts—market variance (σ_{PM}^2) and appraisal variance (σ_{PA}^2), where

$$\sigma_{PM}^2 = \beta_p^2 \sigma_M^2 \tag{14}$$

and

$$\sigma_{PA}^2 = \sum h_i^2 \, \sigma_{iA}^2 \quad , \tag{15}$$

so that

$$\sigma_p^2 = \text{market variance} + \text{appraisal variance.}$$

Equations 9 and 13 can be used to express a portfolio's Sharpe Ratio (P^2) in terms of the expected excess return and risk of the market; the betas, appraisal premiums and appraisal risks of its underlying securities; and the proportion of the portfolio allocated to each security. The result is the complicated looking expression

$$P^2 = \frac{\bar{r}_p^2}{\sigma_p^2} = \frac{[\,\beta_p \, \bar{r}_M + (\sum h_i \, \bar{r}_{iA})\,]^2}{[\,\beta_p^2 \, \sigma_M^2 + (\sum h_i^2 \sigma_{iA}^2)\,]} \quad . \tag{16}$$

A portfolio's Sharpe Ratio (P^2) is a reward/risk ratio based on total reward and total risk. In view of this, it seems plausible that it should depend in some way on two other reward/risk ratios:

A. The square of the ratio of market premium to market risk, called the market ratio (λ^2); and

B. The square of the ratio of appraisal premium to appraisal risk, called the appraisal ratio (γ^2).

This is in fact the case. The relationship is

$$P^2 = \frac{\left[1 + \left(\dfrac{\bar{r}_{PA}}{\bar{r}_{PM}} \right) \right]^2}{\left[\dfrac{1}{\lambda^2} + \left(\dfrac{\bar{r}_{PA}}{\bar{r}_{PM}} \right) \dfrac{1}{\gamma^2} \right]} \quad , \tag{17}$$

where the definitions of λ and γ are

$$\lambda \equiv \frac{\text{market premium}}{\text{market risk}} = \frac{\beta_p \, \bar{r}_M}{\beta_p \, \sigma_M} = \frac{\bar{r}_M}{\sigma_M} \tag{18}$$

and

$$\gamma \equiv \frac{\text{appraisal premium}}{\text{appraisal risk}} = \frac{\bar{r}_{PA}}{\sigma_{PA}} \quad . \tag{19}$$

Before discussing the implications of Equation 17, it is worth pointing out some properties of market premiums and appraisal premiums, and market ratios and appraisal ratios. To begin with:

1. The market ratio is the same for all portfolios (Equation 18).
2. The appraisal premium and appraisal risk of the market are zero (by definition).
3. The appraisal ratio of the market is undefined (because by definition its appraisal premium and appraisal risk are zero).

Together with Equations 16 and 17, these facts imply that:

4. The Sharpe Ratio of the market is the same as its market ratio.
5. The market ratio of all portfolios is equal to the market's Sharpe Ratio.
6. The Sharpe Ratio of all portfolios without appraisal premiums and appraisal risk is equal to the market's Sharpe Ratio.
7. The Sharpe Ratio of a portfolio that does not have an appraisal premium, but does have appraisal risk, is below that of the market.
8. The Sharpe Ratio of a portfolio that does not have an appraisal premium (such as the market) can be increased by adding a security that has an appraisal premium.
9. The Sharpe Ratio of a portfolio with no appraisal premium can be increased by blending it with a portfolio with an appraisal premium.

Points 8 and 9 assume that a security or portfolio with a positive appraisal premium is bought long and one with a negative appraisal premium is sold short, thereby achieving a positive appraisal premium in the final portfolio.

It should now be clear that the role of security analysis is somehow connected with appraisal premiums. If the security analyst can provide appraisal premiums for securities, the portfolio manager will be able to obtain performance superior to the market's. Conversely, if a portfolio's performance is superior to the market's it must be due to the presence of an appraisal premium. Evidently, one important role of the security analyst is to provide appraisal premiums for the securities he follows. But it seems intuitively clear that a reduction of appraisal risk should also improve performance. In fact, Equation 17 implies that:

10. The performance of a portfolio can be increased by decreasing its appraisal risk without changing its appraisal premium, market premium, or market risk.

Thus the reduction of appraisal risk is another im-of its appraisal premium to its appraisal variance:

$$h_{Ai} \; \alpha \; \frac{\bar{r}_{iA}}{\sigma_{iA}^2} \; ,$$

$$h_{Ai} = \frac{\bar{r}_{iA} \, / \, \sigma_{iA}^2}{\sum (\bar{r}_{iA} \, / \, \sigma_{iA}^2)} \qquad . \qquad (24)$$

23. With these allocation proportions, the appraisal ratio of the active portfolio will be the sum of the appraisal ratios of its underlying securities (γ_i^2):

$$\gamma^2 = \sum \left(\frac{\bar{r}_{iA}}{\sigma_{iA}} \right)^2 = \sum \gamma_i^2 \qquad . \qquad (25)$$

24. With the allocation proportions in the active portfolio given by Equation 24 and the allocation in the associated AMB given by Equation 22, the Sharpe Ratio of the AMB is the sum of the market ratio and the appraisal ratios of its underlying securities.

$$p^2 = \lambda^2 + \sum \gamma_i^2 \qquad . \qquad (26)$$

With all this in mind, we can draw the following conclusions:

25. The proper measure of the contribution of security analysis is the sum of the appraisal ratios of the securities followed.[5]
26. The proper measure of the contribution of a market forecast is the market ratio.[6]
27. The proper measure of the contribution of portfolio construction is the portfolio's Sharpe Ratio, less the contribution associated with security analysis and the market forecast.[7]

Point 27 follows because a Sharpe Ratio equal to ($\lambda^2 + \sum \gamma_i^2$) can be achieved if a portfolio is allocated properly. Any shortfall can be viewed as a negative contribution.

28. The contribution of a market forecast is equivalent to that of a forecast of the appraisal premium and appraisal risk for a single security.

Point 28 is true because the appearance of the market ratio (λ^2) in Equation 26 takes the same form as the appraisal ratio for a single security (γ_i^2). As a corollary:

29. If market forecasting is no more or less difficult than security analysis, then the effort put into market analysis should be about equal to that put into following a single security.[8]

It is difficult to reconcile the relative unimportance of the market implied by this result with everyday experience. To appreciate what is involved, consider the position of a portfolio manager who has available appraisal premiums and appraisal risks for a large number of securities. In constructing an active portfolio he appreciates that the more securities he includes, the lower will be the portfolio's appraisal risk (due to diversification). In the case of overpriced securities with negative appraisal premiums he can maintain a positive contribution to the portfolio's appraisal premium and still reduce its appraisal risk by holding a short position (see Equation 24). Now suppose the securities followed were originally selected at random. Then about half will be overpriced and held short. In this case, the beta of the active portfolio will be about zero. For all practical purposes, the active portfolio will have neither market premium nor market risk. Then in relation to the active portfolio, the market will appear to the portfolio manager as just another security having an independent return. He can further reduce his risk and increase his Sharpe Ratio by adding it to his active portfolio. Thus in constructing his AMB he will take a small long position in the market in the same way he would have allocated a small portion of his active portfolio to still another security (with a positive appraisal premium).

But what if all the securities followed are undervalued (positive appraisal premiums)? In this case, only long positions are called for and there will be no cancellation of beta. Typically, the beta of the active portfolio will not be much different from 1.0 and the active portfolio will contain about the same market premium and market risk as the market itself. Owing to the effects of diversification, its appraisal risk is likely to be small, and its appraisal ratio is likely to be large compared to the market ratio. Because of the predominance of market risk, its Sharpe Ratio may be about halfway between the market ratio and its appraisal ratio. Seeing this, the portfolio manager will wonder how he can move the portfolio's Sharpe Ratio closer to its appraisal ratio: A little reflection will convince him that shorting the market will permit him to offset all the active portfolio's market premium and market risk, leaving only appraisal premium and appraisal risk. Thus the Sharpe Ratio of the resulting portfolio will be equal to the active portfolio's appraisal ratio. But this portfolio has the same characteristics as the active portfolio in the previous example, and the same reasoning applies. The portfolio manager's final choice of allocation to the market in his AMB will be short in the amount necessary to reduce the AMB's total market position (including that inherent in the active portfolio) to an amount equivalent to that he would hold if it were just another security.

In both these examples, short selling permitted the portfolio manager to de-emphasize the market and increase the AMB's Sharpe Ratio to the maximum indicated by Equation 26. Unfortunately, short selling always will be necessary to achieve these results in practice. When short selling is permitted, the market portfolio can be used as a hedge against the active portfolio's exposure to market risk. The TBM shows that the portfolio balancing problem is then the same as if an extra security had been created which was the sole source of market premium and market risk. This equivalent situation is characterized by one security that has only market premium and market risk, and in the amounts contained in the market portfolio, and a set of securities equal in number to those in the active portfolio, each containing only the appraisal premium and appraisal risk of one of the active portfolio's securities. Viewed in this light, the purpose of blending the active and market portfolios is to obtain the proper (small) exposure to the "market security." The effect of disallowing short selling can be to prevent proper allocation to this "security." Without short selling, only allocations greater than a certain level can be achieved. The minimum level obtainable is the smaller of the allocations inherent in either the active portfolio or the market. If the optimum allocation is still smaller, the result is reduced performance. This and other complications are discussed in the final section of this article.

Point 22 and Equation 24 show that a security will be represented in the active portfolio in proportion to its appraisal premium. Thus:

30. All followed securities will have an appraisal premium; only the sign and magnitude will vary.
31. All followed securities will be in the active portfolio.

These two points suggest that:

32. A recommendation based on total return is meaningless.
33. A recommendation is meaningless.

What about the relationship between a portfolio's performance and the number of securities followed? Recognizing that each followed security's appraisal ratio (γ_i^2) is always positive, and recalling that this quantity is the security's contribution to performance (Points 24 and 25), it is clear that:

34. Portfolio performance is an increasing function of the number of securities followed.

Considering the fact that a security must be analyzed before it can be classified as over or underpriced, it probably is fair to view the selection of a security for analysis as a random draw from those available. This suggests that the individual analyst or research department need not be seriously concerned about diminishing returns. In this case:

35. The portfolio's Sharpe Ratio (P^2) is proportional to the number of securities followed.

An important implication of the last point is that:

36. If an increased requirement for liquidity is met by following and investing in fewer larger companies, performance will deteriorate;
37. If an increased requirement for liquidity is met by following and investing in more companies, performance will improve.

Measuring Talent

Up to now, the discussion has centered on portfolio and security characteristics as they appear at a particular point in time, based on a one period forecast. But talent can be differentiated from luck only by examining results averaged over many periods. Investors and management cannot afford to evaluate future performance and the reasons for it merely on the basis of a one period forecast. They must consider such things as the expected contribution of a security analyst over time, how to estimate it, and how to organize to make the most of it. A slight rephrasing of Point 25 provides a beginning.

38. The research contribution of any entity (C_E) (such as a security analyst, research department, portfolio manager or investment firm) at a point in time is the sum of the appraisal ratios of the securities it follows.

$$C_E = \sum \gamma_i^2 \quad .$$

39. The expected research contribution of any entity ($\overline{C}_E$) is the sum of the expected appraisal ratios ($\overline{\gamma_i^2}$) of the securities it follows.

$$\overline{C}_E = \sum \overline{\gamma_i^2} \quad . \qquad (27)$$

In particular:

40. The expected contribution of a security analyst ($\overline{C}_A$) is the sum of the expected appraisal ratios of the securities he follows.

$$\overline{C_A} = \sum \overline{\gamma_i^2} \quad . \qquad (28)$$

Point 40 provides a means of comparing the contributions of two or more analysts who follow different numbers of companies in different industries. If, for example, analyst A follows 20 companies and achieves an average appraisal ratio (γ_i^2) of 1.0 on each, his contribution is 20.0. Another analyst, B, may have an average appraisal ratio of 2.0. But if B achieves this higher level by restricting his attention to eight companies, his total contribution will only be 16.0, less than A's. A third analyst, C, may follow 40 companies but, not having time to study them closely enough, may only achieve an average γ_i^2 of 0.3, a contribution of only 12.0. This example illustrates a tradeoff that probably is familar to most readers.

If a security analyst follows only one security, he will have time to learn virtually everything about it that is relevant. In TBM terms, his expected appraisal ratio will be about as high as is possible. Suppose he is assigned a second company. He will probably still have sufficient time to analyze both very thoroughly. Perhaps the expected appraisal ratio for each security will be almost as great as it was for the single security, previously. If so, his expected contribution will have almost doubled. But this can not go on indefinitely. Eventually, the assignment of another security to follow will reduce his expected contribution because he will have insufficient time per company to accomplish meaningful analysis. Thus it is reasonable to think of the relationship between an analyst's expected contribution and the number of securities he follows as being first increasing and then decreasing. Such a curve is shown in Figure I. Ignoring costs:

41. The security analyst should follow that number of companies that maximizes his contribution as measured by the sum of the expected appraisal ratios of the securities he follows.

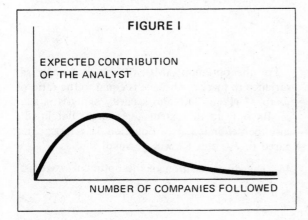

FIGURE I

EXPECTED CONTRIBUTION OF THE ANALYST

NUMBER OF COMPANIES FOLLOWED

Taking total research cost into account:

42. The research director should increase the number of analysts until the marginal revenue from their expected contribution falls to their marginal cost.

The optimum number of securities to follow will, in general, vary from analyst to analyst and from one industry to another. A plot of the marginal increase in expected contribution implied by Figure I is shown in Figure II.

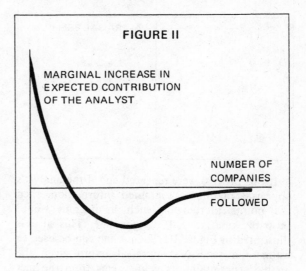

FIGURE II

MARGINAL INCREASE IN EXPECTED CONTRIBUTION OF THE ANALYST

NUMBER OF COMPANIES FOLLOWED

A little reflection now should persuade the reader that:

43. A limited research budget should be allocated among the available analysts such that the marginal increase in each analyst's expected contribution is the same.

Otherwise the expected contribution of the research department can be increased by shifting resources from analysts with smaller marginal impacts to those with larger marginal impacts.

All that is required now is an estimate of the expected contribution of a research entity. But this depends only on having an estimate for the expected appraisal ratio for each security it follows.

One way of thinking about this problem is to visualize it in the form of a scatter diagram. Imagine that an analyst makes a forecast of appraisal return (the appraisal premium) for a particular period. At the conclusion of the period, the actual appraisal return (z) will be known. These two numbers can be plotted on a chart whose horizontal axis represents the appraisal premium and whose vertical axis represents actual appraisal return. The format is illustrated in Figure III.

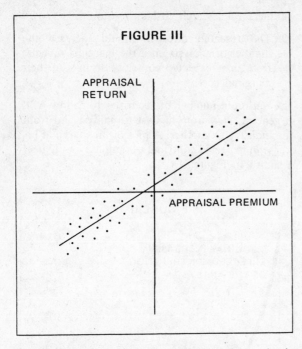

FIGURE III

APPRAISAL RETURN

APPRAISAL PREMIUM

If this process were repeated and if the analyst's appraisal premiums contained information, then the points plotted on such a diagram would probably tend to fall along a line. This also is illustrated in Figure III. Such a line can be used to estimate a security's appraisal return given the analyst's premium. Its value stems from the fact that it summarizes, and corrects for, any tendency on the part of the analyst to be too excitable, not excitable enough, optimistic or pessimistic. To use it for estimating, it is only necessary to locate the appraisal premium on the horizontal axis, move directly upward or downward to the estimating line, and then directly leftward or rightward to the vertical axis. The appraisal return corresponding to the resulting point on the vertical axis is the "appraisal premium" ($\mu_{z|\bar{r}_A}$) to be used in constructing the active portfolio. The appraisal risk ($\sigma_{z|\bar{r}_A}$) is indicated by the thickness of the scatter of points along a vertical line through the appraisal premium on the horizontal axis. The entire concept is that of a two-variable regression with the analyst's appraisal premium playing the role of the independent variable and the realized appraisal return playing that of the dependent variable. If the analyst's forecasting behavior is consistent, then the TBM shows that:

44. The expected appraisal ratio ($\overline{\gamma_i^2}$) for a security followed continuously is

$$\overline{\gamma_i^2} = \frac{P_i^2}{1 - P_i^2} \qquad (29)$$

where P_i is the correlation between the analyst's appraisal premium and the subsequent appraisal return for the i'th security.

This result must be modified if only securities with positive appraisal premiums are followed or if the regression model is applied to many securities over one period. In these cases, the average actual appraisal return (μ_z) and the standard deviation of actual appraisal return (σ_z) are important also. In general:

45. The expected appraisal ratio ($\overline{\gamma_i^2}$) for a security is:

$$\overline{\gamma_i^2} = \frac{\mu_{zi}^2 / \sigma_{zi}^2}{1 - P_i^2} + \frac{P_i^2}{1 - P_i^2} \qquad (30)$$

When a security is followed continuously, its long-term average appraisal return (μ_z) is zero. This is the reason for the simpler form of Equation 29.

The two-variable regression approach outlined above obviates the need for an estimate of appraisal risk from the analyst.

Diversification

Diversification is defined as the square of the correlation coefficient (R^2) between a portfolio's return and the market's return. Co-movement between a portfolio and the market arises from the market premium ($\bar{r}_{PM}$) present in the portfolio. If a portfolio has no appraisal risk, its movements will exactly parallel those of the market and its diversification will be 1.0, the maximum possible. If a portfolio has no market risk, its movements will be unrelated to those of the market and its diversification will be 0.0, the minimum possible. For a portfolio that has both market risk and appraisal risk, diversification will be between 0.0 and 1.0. The exact relationship is given by:

$$R^2 = \frac{1}{1 + \frac{\sigma_{PA}^2}{\sigma_{PM}^2}} \qquad (31)$$

For the optimum AMB, the ratio of appraisal variance to market variance is equal to the ratio of γ^2 to λ^2 (Point 19), and security analysis is successful only to the extent γ^2 is large. But in this case the denominator of Equation 31 is large compared to 1.0 and R^2 will be small.

46. The diversification of the optimum AMB is:

$$R^2 = \frac{1}{1 + \frac{\gamma^2}{\lambda^2}} \quad . \quad (32)$$

47. Success at security analysis implies lack of diversification.
48. Performance (the Sharpe Ratio) is inversely related to diversification.

A good portfolio is characterized by a large appraisal ratio. This implies low diversification, which means that the portfolio's fluctuations will be largely unrelated to those of the market. Thus the probability that the portfolio will perform below expectation at the same time that the market performs above expectation will approach 0.25. In fact, if the market's risk is sizable in relation to the portfolio's appraisal premium (which is likely to be the case), the probability of the portfolio declining (or at least doing considerably worse than the market) in a rising market also is substantial. Thus:

49. A good portfolio is likely to do poorly relative to the market, in many periods.
50. Many investors may not recognize, or be happy with, a good portfolio.

Limitations on Short Selling

One of the assumptions behind TBM is that short selling is possible. If short selling is not allowed, negative appraisal premiums in individual securities cannot be converted to positive appraisal premiums in the portfolio by shorting overvalued securities. About half the time an analyst selects and first analyzes a security its appraisal premium will be negative, and his effort will have been wasted. If, on the other hand, he follows a fixed list of securities, then at any point in time about half will have a negative appraisal premium and the effective number of securities being followed will be half the total. The elimination of short selling increases the cost of obtaining useful appraisal premiums. The magnitude of the appraisal premiums and appraisal ratios for the securities actually used would not be expected to change.

If, in effect, fewer securities are being followed, the active portfolio will contain fewer securities (roughly half), and its appraisal ratio will be smaller (Point 23). If only long positions are taken, the active portfolio almost certainly will contain substantial market risk, which is not diversifiable. Its beta can be expected to be about 1.0. At the same time its appraisal risk, which is diversifiable, will probably be much smaller, suggesting that its appraisal ratio may be large in relation to its market ratio.

According to Point 19 the proper balance in an AMB is struck when its ratio of appraisal variance to market variance is equal to γ^2 / λ^2, which could be large in this case. For the active portfolio, the ratio of appraisal variance to market variance is probably small. For the market portfolio, it is zero. For an AMB with a long position in the market, it is somewhere between the two. There can be too much market risk in each portfolio to achieve the proper large ratio of appraisal variance to market variance without shorting the market against the active portfolio. Thus, when short selling is not allowed, the proper AMB allocation may not be achievable. In this case, it may pay to trade off some of the active portfolio's appraisal premium if a relatively large reduction in beta can be achieved. The final portfolio, which no longer can be achieved through a simple two step procedure, will look much like the active portfolio, in that it will have many small commitments and will contain substantial market risk. Its Sharpe Ratio will almost certainly be well above λ^2 but less than ($\lambda^2 + \gamma^2$). Also, owing to the presence of substantial market risk in relation to appraisal risk, its diversification will be relatively high, as shown by Equation 31 (σ^2_{PA} is small in relation to σ^2_{PM} so R^2 is almost 1/1 or 1). This means that the market will have a substantial impact on the portfolio's behavior, and Point 29 no longer will be true. Point 49 will continue to be true, but the discrepancy will be much smaller than before.

When short selling is prohibited, the active portfolio's Sharpe Ratio—and, indeed, its expected return—will probably be attractive, but its risk (primarily market risk) may be too high for many investors. These investors may find it desirable to invest only part of their funds in the active portfolio and lend out the rest. However, this practical approximation to the optimal portfolio does not guarantee the highest level of return in relation to risk, and may not even come close.

Borrowing and the Sharpe Ratio

As noted above, using the Sharpe Ratio as a measure of portfolio attractiveness is equivalent to rating stores on the basis of pounds sold per dollar charged. This is fine if the store will sell the quantity desired. But it does not do the consumer much good to buy quality meat at $0.10 per pound if he can only get delivery on one ounce. What then should be made of a portfolio with an expected excess return of 1.0 per cent and a risk of 0.001 per cent? Although the portfolio's Sharpe Ratio is a heady 1.000.0, one might as well buy treasuries and skip the bother.

This portfolio will be unattractive to most investors unless they can borrow money. As an example, suppose the interest rate is 10.0 per cent and an investor puts $4.00 of borrowed money for each $1.00 of his equity into the portfolio. His expected gross return will be five times (10.0 + 1.0) = 55.0 per cent. Interest cost will be four times 10.0 = 40.0 per cent. His expected net return will be 55.0 − 40.0 = 15.0 per cent, 5.0 percentage points above the riskless rate, and his risk will be five times 0.001 = 0.005 per cent. The Sharpe Ratio will be 5.0/0.005 = 1000, the same as before.

Evidently:

51. Levering a portfolio (in either direction) does not change its Sharpe Ratio.

It only changes the amount of risk and return, and in proportion. Thus the use of the Sharpe Ratio implies that borrowing and lending are possible at the riskless rate. If borrowing is not possible then, even if they have a lower Sharpe Ratio, portfolios with both higher risks and returns than the optimum Sharpe portfolio will be preferred by some investors.

Transaction Costs

The TBM assumes that trading is free. One approach to visualizing the impact of transactions costs is to state returns after all costs of achieving them. Applying this rule is far from simple. For example:

A. The return from a security depends on whether it is a new commitment or is already in the portfolio;

B. The negative contribution to return associated with transactions costs cannot be converted to a positive contribution by selling short.

This suggests, in contrast with the pure TBM, where every security is held in some amount, that a security will not be added to an active portfolio unless the magnitude of its appraisal premium exceeds round-trip transaction costs. The full impact of transactions costs, however, is almost certainly more complex. ∎

Footnotes

1. By definition, the riskless interest rate, R_F, can be obtained without taking any risk. The holder of a portfolio is enduring risk in the hope of obtaining a greater return. He anticipates a greater return of $\overline{R}_p$. Thus he is enduring the risk σ_p in the anticipation of increasing his return by $(\overline{R}_p - R_F)$.

2. Called the unique return or independent return by some other authors.

3. The assumption that these factors have no impact on the market is realistic. But what about a Kodak and a Polaroid? It would seem that, owing to common non-market factors, the appraisal returns of these two securities would be related. To a degree, this problem can be overcome by imagining a single composite Kodak-Polaroid security that hedges away the interrelationships to the extent possible. The market share issue could be treated in this manner, for instance.

4. Appraisal premiums are assigned to securities as a result of security analysis. Thus, an "active portfolio" is made up of securities thought to be out of line with the current market consensus. As corrections occur and other securities move out of line, the composition of the active portfolio will be changed by the investor. The resulting activity is the motivation for naming it the active portfolio.

5. This presumes the traditional multiple role for the security analyst; including the determination of company output (perhaps based on a macroeconomic forecast), the conversion of output to profit or cash flow, and the valuation of that cash flow. In fact, no one person need be responsible for more than one of these activities and an organization's potential cannot be realized if this is not recognized.

6. Presumably, a market forecast requires an underlying macroeconomic forecast.

7. This always will be zero or negative. Zero is the highest contribution possible, and corresponds to the proportions in Equation 24 in the active portfolio and the proportions in Equation 22 in the associated AMB.

8. Which includes macroeconomic forecasting.

References

Sharpe, William F., "Mutual Fund Performance," *Journal of Business*, January 1966.

Treynor, Jack L. and Black, Fisher, "How to Use Security Analysis to Improve Portfolio Selection," *Journal of Business*, January 1973.

World wealth: Market values and returns

Roger G. Ibbotson, Laurence B. Siegel, and Kathryn S. Love

On two occasions in this Journal,[1] we have presented annual aggregate values and total returns for major asset classes in the U.S. and in foreign markets, and we have formed U.S., foreign, and world "market wealth portfolios." The portfolios are composed of five major categories of assets: equities (stocks), bonds, cash equivalents, real estate, and monetary metals (gold and silver). With a quarter century now elapsed since the appearance of accurate foreign equity data, we are newly motivated to examine the aggregate values of and total returns on the components of world wealth.

Why should we want to study the wealth of the world? First, a compendium of aggregate values and returns on investable assets serves the investor's and the researcher's need for data. Second, the concept of a market wealth portfolio is consistent with the principle of diversification that is the cornerstone of modern portfolio theory. Third, we feel compelled by the sheer size of foreign markets, as well as by their increasing importance to the U.S. investor, to regard the world rather than our own country as the appropriate field of view. Finally, we are motivated by curiosity — the need to know the past and current dimensions of the world market in which we invest

1. Footnote appears at the end of the article.

and to compare historical returns on a broad range of assets.

This article updates the World Market Wealth Portfolio study presented in Ibbotson and Siegel (1983). In addition, we incorporate some updates of the detailed data on U.S. markets first set forth in Ibbotson and Fall (1979).

CONSTRUCTION OF THE U.S., FOREIGN, AND WORLD PORTFOLIOS

This section describes the composition of the various portfolios and the techniques that we used to construct them. An appendix providing the basic sources of our data is available from the authors on request.

We have collected aggregate values over 1959-1984 and year-by-year returns over 1960-1984 for world equities, bonds, cash, and monetary metals plus real estate in the United States (the returns on foreign real estate being difficult to measure). The analysis covers the capital markets of the United States, Europe, Japan, Hong Kong, Singapore, Canada, Mexico, Australia, and South Africa.

Each category of assets includes several components. The three principal U.S. equity markets — the New York and American stock exchanges and the NASDAQ over-the-counter market — are measured

ROBER G. IBBOTSON is Professor in Practice of Finance at the Yale School of Management in New Haven (CT 06520). LAURENCE B. SIEGEL is Managing Partner and KATHRYN S. LOVE is Research Associate, Ibbotson Associates, Inc. in Chicago (IL 60603). The authors greatly appreciate the financial support for this study provided by the First National Bank of Chicago. They are indebted to Gary P. Brinson, Jeffrey J. Diermeier, and L. Randolph Hood, Jr. of the First National Bank of Chicago for their helpful comments, criticism, and advice. Mary Jo Kringas's assistance in collecting and updating the data was invaluable. They appreciate the help of Kate M. Green, Patrick McKee, and Donna Mills.

separately; we then aggregate them by market-value weighting to form a U.S. equity total. Foreign stocks are a value-weighted aggregate of returns in nineteen countries, with sub-portfolios representing Europe, Asia, and other non-U.S. markets. United States bonds include corporate issues (intermediate and long-term bonds plus preferred stocks) and government issues (Treasury notes, Treasury bonds, and agency issues). Foreign bonds include both domestic corporate and government bonds traded within a country's national capital markets and crossborder bonds traded outside the confines of any one country's markets. Cash includes U.S. issues (Treasury bills, commercial paper, and bankers' acceptances) and those of ten foreign countries. United States real estate is composed of business, residential, and farm components. Foreign real estate is excluded from the study except for a single estimate of market value as of the end of 1984. Monetary metals include the world supply of gold and the non-communist world supply of silver.

The aggregate market values of the categories serve as weights for the purpose of constructing value-weighted portfolios, including the World Market Wealth Portfolio and subsidiary portfolios. We have measured returns and have formed cumulative wealth indexes. We present these results in year-by-year form and as summary statistics. We include cross-correlations and regression results to measure the relationships among the series and between the series and inflation. Finally, we provide information on the sources of the market value and return data for each series.

THE WORLD MARKET WEALTH PORTFOLIO AND MODERN PORTFOLIO THEORY

As we said earlier, modern portfolio theory provides a theoretical reason for studying a market-value weighted World Market Wealth Portfolio. According to modern portfolio theory, the market portfolio — not just common stocks, and not just in the United States — is considered to be perfectly diversified with a capital asset pricing model (CAPM) beta of 1.0. A literal interpretation of the CAPM on a world basis would suggest that the ideal portfolio should represent each asset class in proportion to its prevalence in the world market — the ultimate index fund.

No individual or institutional investor, of course, would actually want to hold a world index fund. Each investor has his or her own risk preferences, tax considerations, information costs, and time horizons. The most obvious example is that only a high-tax investor would want to hold municipal bonds (which, incidentally, we have excluded from this study because of the effect of their tax-exempt

status on returns). Other clienteles would cluster in other ways. Suffice it to say that we wish to construct the World Market Portfolio not for its eventual purchase but for the insights it might reveal about the behavior of our capital markets.

WHAT SHOULD BE INCLUDED IN A MARKET WEALTH PORTFOLIO

Given that we want to construct a World Market Portfolio and subsidiary portfolios, what should we include in it? As stated earlier, we have included equities, bonds, cash, metals, and U.S. real estate. The astute reader will have already noted that the sum of these securities does not represent the "market." We have excluded huge categories of assets from the portfolio, while at the same time we have included categories that are not wealth at all.

As in our earlier work, the most important omission is human capital, which is probably the largest single component of world wealth. We have also excluded the value of foreign real estate (except as a rough illustrative estimate in Figure 1). We have excluded the value and returns from proprietorships and partnerships as well as many small corporations. We have excluded (except in Figure 1) personal holdings such as automobiles, cash balances, and various consumer capital goods. We have not only omitted a large proportion of wealth, but we also have little idea as to how large the omitted proportion is.

Our inclusions may misrepresent the market even more than our omissions. We have included U.S. and foreign government debt that is almost certainly not backed dollar-for-dollar by government-owned assets such as parks and bridges. More likely, it is backed by claims on a future tax base. Other inclusions in our portfolio also misrepresent wealth. For example, some corporations own parts of other corporations, causing double counting.

Therefore, while this study does not really measure the wealth of the world, it nevertheless presents market values and returns for asset classes that make up a large part of that wealth. We measure the values and returns of the capital market securities that are most marketable and most readily identifiable. These are the securities that make up the opportunity set faced by most investors.

FINDINGS: MARKET VALUES AND RETURNS

We now present the results, which appear in detail in the tables at the end of the article.

Figure 1 shows the approximate asset class composition of a broadly defined World Wealth Portfolio as of the end of 1984. We estimate that this broadly defined portfolio had a value of $27,681.5 billion. Foreign real estate is the largest component

FIGURE 1

FIGURE 2

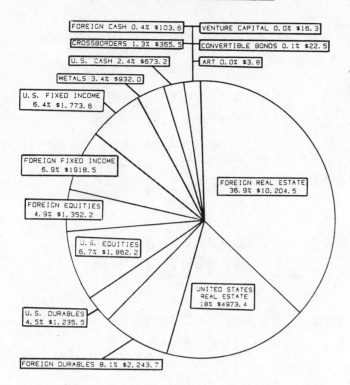

TOTAL WORLD WEALTH
1984 = $27,681.5 BILLION

FOREIGN CASH 0.4% $103.6
CROSSBORDERS 1.3% $365.5
U.S. CASH 2.4% $673.2
METALS 3.4% $932.0
U.S. FIXED INCOME 6.4% $1,773.6
FOREIGN FIXED INCOME 6.9% $1918.5
FOREIGN EQUITIES 4.9% $1,352.2
U.S. EQUITIES 6.7% $1,862.2
U.S. DURABLES 4.5% $1,235.5
FOREIGN DURABLES 8.1% $2,243.7
VENTURE CAPITAL 0.0% $16.3
CONVERTIBLE BONDS 0.1% $22.5
ART 0.0% $3.8
FOREIGN REAL ESTATE 36.9% $10,204.5
UNITED STATES REAL ESTATE 18% $4973.4

WORLD INVESTABLE WEALTH
1984 = $13,954.1 BILLION

U.S. CASH 4.8% $673.2
FOREIGN CASH 0.7% $103.6
METALS 6.7% $932.0
CROSSBORDERS 2.6% $365.5
UNITED STATES DOMESTIC BONDS 773.6
FOREIGN DOMESTIC BONDS 13.7% $1,919.5
OTHER EQUITIES 1.4% $193.0
EUROPE EQUITIES 3.5% $489.4
ASIA EQUITIES 4.8% $669.8
UNITED STATES EQUITIES 13.3% $1,862.2
UNITED STATES RESIDENTIAL REAL ESTATE 26.0% $3,631.1
U.S. FARM REAL ESTATE 4.9% $669.8
U.S. BUSINESS REAL ESTATE 4.7% $652.5

of the market, about $10 trillion, or 37% of the total.

Assets residing in foreign countries clearly make up a larger share of wealth than United States assets. Note that only nineteen of the most important foreign industrial countries were used to make these estimates; other countries also hold a substantial share of the world wealth. We see also that automobiles and other consumer durables, excluded in the main body of the study, comprise a substantial portion of world wealth.

In Figure 2, we show the distribution as of the end of 1984 of the asset classes included in the World Market Portfolio for which we measure returns. Here we exclude assets that are typically outside the U.S. institutional investor's opportunity set, namely durables, foreign real estate, art, venture capital, and convertible bonds. Of the remaining asset classes, U.S. real estate is the largest. By our measure, the investable World Market Portfolio at the end of 1984 was $13,022.1 billion excluding monetary metals, and $13,954.1 billion including these metals.

Figure 3 focuses on the United States. Residential real estate represents almost 40% of investable wealth, but note that most residential real estate, as well as farmland, is held by private (not institutional) investors. The large size of the New York Stock Exchange points out the important role of equities in the U.S. economy; this figure also reflects the importance of government debt (primarily Treasury notes

FIGURE 3

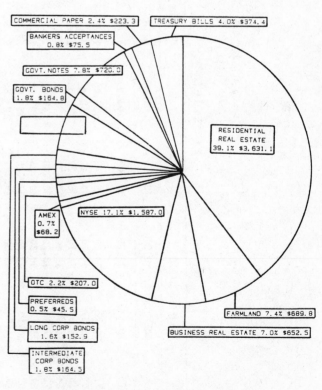

U.S. INVESTABLE WEALTH
1984 = $9,282.3 BILLION

COMMERCIAL PAPER 2.4% $223.3
BANKERS ACCEPTANCES 0.8% $75.5
GOVT. NOTES 7.8% $720.0
GOVT. BONDS 1.8% $164.8
AMEX 0.7% $68.2
OTC 2.2% $207.0
PREFERREDS 0.5% $45.5
LONG CORP BONDS 1.6% $152.9
INTERMEDIATE CORP BONDS 1.8% $164.5
TREASURY BILLS 4.0% $374.4
RESIDENTIAL REAL ESTATE 39.1% $3,631.1
NYSE 17.1% $1,587.0
FARMLAND 7.4% $689.8
BUSINESS REAL ESTATE 7.0% $652.5

and bills, and agency bonds) relative to corporate debt in the United States.

Table 1 shows aggregate market values of the various series and the total market on a year-by-year

31

TABLE 1

AGGREGATE VALUE OF CAPITAL
MARKET SECURITIES (BILLIONS OF DOLLARS)

EQUITIES / BONDS

YEAR END	UNITED STATES				FOREIGN				EQUITIES TOTAL	UNITED STATES - GOVT			
	NYSE	AMEX	OTC	TOTAL	EUROPE	ASIA	OTHER	TOTAL		NOTES	BONDS	AGENCIES	TOTAL
1959	309.25	20.13	23.70	353.08	103.00	14.6	23.40	141.03	494.11	43.29	74.96	7.3	125.55
1960	307.71	20.97	23.30	351.98	135.08	17.7	27.38	180.16	532.14	52.15	76.19	8.1	136.45
1961	388.05	26.37	30.70	445.12	168.40	20.5	32.62	221.52	666.64	71.77	70.79	8.8	151.36
1962	337.15	25.02	26.10	388.27	146.56	17.1	31.37	195.03	583.30	54.16	75.82	10.4	140.38
1963	401.64	26.68	31.40	459.72	153.86	23.1	34.23	211.19	670.91	58.46	82.33	12.0	152.79
1964	462.92	29.46	38.70	531.08	149.88	20.3	41.68	211.86	742.94	52.56	91.73	12.6	156.89
1965	523.84	31.12	50.30	605.26	145.08	18.5	40.85	204.43	809.69	49.78	97.75	14.7	162.22
1966	469.07	28.10	42.70	539.88	150.81	23.1	38.90	212.81	752.69	48.31	93.54	20.2	162.04
1967	585.17	44.94	65.80	695.91	174.89	27.5	42.76	245.15	941.06	51.47	92.76	20.3	164.52
1968	662.42	58.10	79.30	799.82	198.97	31.9	51.55	282.42	1082.24	78.51	72.24	24.1	174.85
1969	598.70	43.62	73.30	715.62	196.74	43.8	55.85	296.39	1012.01	77.61	57.45	33.8	168.86
1970	605.26	35.93	63.20	704.40	194.45	50.6	64.17	309.22	1013.62	100.81	50.90	43.6	195.31
1971	705.06	44.37	85.60	835.03	208.52	63.2	63.76	335.48	1170.51	110.67	46.90	49.5	207.07
1972	836.13	53.96	100.30	990.39	269.94	109.2	80.32	459.46	1449.85	122.55	40.68	57.9	221.13
1973	681.10	36.30	69.20	786.60	322.93	171.9	80.25	575.08	1361.68	123.52	29.72	77.9	231.14
1974	479.43	21.47	44.90	545.80	227.24	126.0	62.53	415.77	961.57	121.27	27.68	97.9	246.85
1975	648.76	28.60	58.20	735.56	242.06	143.7	66.53	452.29	1187.85	162.41	32.32	107.3	302.03
1976	812.04	33.59	65.20	910.83	233.49	176.9	82.66	493.05	1403.88	207.93	38.07	122.8	368.81
1977	761.57	33.12	72.70	867.39	247.29	195.9	78.66	521.85	1389.24	232.51	42.81	145.0	420.31
1978	790.27	33.80	78.80	902.86	300.54	267.1	92.53	660.17	1563.03	252.54	54.97	181.7	489.21
1979	918.13	54.01	91.70	1063.84	403.51	310.9	152.72	867.13	1930.97	267.93	64.80	230.3	563.03
1980	1194.54	72.32	122.40	1389.26	455.80	418.5	206.30	1080.60	2469.86	299.38	68.36	273.9	641.64
1981	1112.84	63.85	124.80	1301.49	411.40	479.8	184.10	1075.30	2376.79	356.91	76.90	319.4	753.21
1982	1294.66	62.57	153.10	1510.34	407.50	455.3	180.60	1043.40	2553.74	492.30	104.54	383.9	980.74
1983	1584.16	80.80	229.30	1894.26	488.30	573.9	217.90	1280.10	3174.36	574.80	124.00	451.7	1150.50
1984	1586.98	68.23	206.95	1862.16	489.40	669.8	193.00	1352.20	3214.36	720.00	164.80	525.9	1410.70

TABLE 1 (continued)

BONDS - CONT.

REAL ESTATE

YEAR END	UNITED STATES - CONT.				FOREIGN				BONDS TOTAL	UNITED STATES			
	CORPORATE			TOTAL	DOMESTIC		CROSS BORDERS	TOTAL		BUSINESS	RESIDENTIAL	FARM	TOTAL
	MED TERM	LONG TERM	TOTAL		CORP	GOVT							
1959	16.00	47.50	70.20	195.75	121.67	190.16	17.81	329.64	525.39	58.8	458.52	137.20	654.52
1960	16.20	52.30	75.20	211.65	139.99	235.56	18.64	394.19	605.84	61.9	476.88	138.53	677.28
1961	17.30	53.90	78.50	229.86	139.55	251.01	19.79	410.35	640.21	66.6	494.04	144.50	705.14
1962	20.80	55.00	83.50	223.88	136.85	257.59	21.37	415.81	639.69	71.4	514.68	150.20	736.28
1963	25.70	53.80	87.40	240.19	141.49	239.52	22.66	403.67	643.86	76.8	527.16	158.60	762.56
1964	28.50	52.90	89.70	246.59	139.23	234.10	24.00	397.33	643.92	82.5	562.44	167.50	812.44
1965	28.00	53.40	90.70	252.92	135.09	227.40	24.45	386.94	639.86	90.6	589.80	179.20	859.60
1966	28.30	50.80	88.80	250.84	133.06	225.19	24.56	382.81	633.65	100.6	635.28	189.10	924.98
1967	31.80	49.00	95.70	260.22	130.30	232.05	25.48	387.83	648.05	109.8	667.68	199.70	977.18
1968	31.10	55.30	110.90	285.75	128.19	229.97	27.08	385.24	670.99	120.6	745.32	209.20	1075.12
1969	30.00	53.90	106.50	275.36	121.64	214.35	27.06	363.05	638.41	139.9	813.00	215.80	1168.70
1970	38.70	64.60	127.20	322.51	125.41	233.21	30.34	388.96	711.47	156.1	870.72	223.20	1250.02
1971	41.50	86.50	155.50	362.57	163.20	297.70	34.19	495.09	857.66	170.4	960.24	239.60	1370.24
1972	45.80	98.80	171.80	392.93	187.98	321.67	39.65	549.30	942.23	187.8	1082.64	267.30	1537.74
1973	51.30	94.43	168.73	399.87	219.33	358.32	44.43	622.08	1021.95	216.8	1262.28	327.70	1806.78
1974	54.10	90.04	161.94	408.79	240.09	403.68	49.08	692.85	1101.64	267.9	1422.12	359.80	2049.82
1975	67.00	114.21	203.21	505.24	275.77	448.94	68.75	793.46	1298.70	269.8	1534.68	418.20	2222.68
1976	73.60	142.04	243.44	612.25	325.28	574.36	95.08	994.72	1606.97	280.8	1727.88	496.40	2505.08
1977	80.70	143.20	249.40	669.71	419.29	771.50	123.92	1314.71	1984.42	318.1	1959.48	554.60	2832.18
1978	78.31	137.14	239.45	728.66	538.19	1006.25	150.78	1695.22	2423.88	370.8	2340.60	655.10	3366.50
1979	79.59	129.00	233.19	796.22	553.44	1117.03	171.02	1841.49	2637.71	433.7	2607.12	763.28	3804.10
1980	90.12	121.51	239.04	880.68	615.82	1305.38	189.59	2110.79	2991.47	496.1	2862.96	843.66	4202.72
1981	98.90	112.21	234.84	988.05	618.76	1280.32	210.05	2109.13	3097.18	559.0	3116.28	843.30	4518.58
1982	137.92	147.61	319.31	1300.05	631.06	1341.60	257.63	2230.29	3530.34	594.0	3154.92	804.76	4553.68
1983	143.43	146.00	336.40	1486.90	653.56	1473.25	297.34	2424.15	3864.08	603.0	3318.96	794.03	4715.99
1984	164.46	152.92	362.86	1773.56	630.35	1288.17	365.47	2283.99	4057.55	652.5	3631.08	689.81	4973.39

TABLE 1 (continued)

MARKET WEALTH PORTFOLIOS

YEAR END	CASH					METALS			MARKET WEALTH PORTFOLIOS			
	UNITED STATES			FOREIGN	CASH TOTAL	WORLD		METALS TOTAL	U. S.	FOREIGN	WORLD EXCL. METALS	WORLD INCL. METALS
	TREASURY BILLS	COMMERCIAL PAPER	TOTAL	TOTAL		GOLD	SILVER					
1959	33.22	3.2	37.62	13.65	51.27	66.96	1.10	68.06	1240.98	484.32	1725.30	1793.36
1960	32.24	4.5	38.74	13.94	52.68	68.28	1.10	69.38	1279.64	588.29	1867.93	1937.31
1961	37.14	4.7	44.54	15.16	59.70	69.89	1.24	71.13	1424.66	647.03	2071.69	2142.82
1962	44.97	6.0	53.67	15.52	69.19	71.16	1.45	72.61	1402.09	626.36	2028.45	2101.06
1963	49.89	6.8	59.59	16.18	75.77	72.70	1.55	74.25	1522.06	631.04	2153.10	2227.35
1964	51.81	8.4	63.61	16.86	80.47	74.27	1.55	75.82	1653.71	626.05	2279.76	2355.58
1965	49.52	9.3	62.22	17.67	79.89	75.88	1.66	77.54	1780.00	609.04	2389.04	2466.58
1966	56.87	13.6	74.07	18.70	92.77	77.49	1.66	79.15	1789.77	614.32	2404.09	2483.24
1967	59.00	17.1	80.40	18.03	98.43	79.10	2.65	81.75	2013.71	651.01	2664.72	2746.47
1968	64.60	21.2	90.20	17.73	107.93	90.63	2.52	93.15	2250.89	685.39	2936.28	3029.43
1969	65.52	32.6	103.62	19.94	123.56	97.61	2.33	99.94	2263.29	679.38	2942.67	3042.61
1970	79.40	33.1	119.60	23.08	142.68	87.32	2.45	89.77	2396.52	721.26	3117.78	3207.55
1971	88.97	32.1	128.97	21.17	150.14	100.76	2.09	102.85	2696.81	851.74	3548.55	3651.40
1972	97.92	34.7	139.52	26.31	165.83	145.91	2.99	148.90	3060.58	1035.07	4095.65	4244.55
1973	100.53	41.1	150.53	32.16	182.69	247.83	4.73	252.56	3143.79	1229.32	4373.11	4625.67
1974	112.47	49.1	180.07	38.94	219.01	411.07	6.61	417.68	3184.48	1147.56	4332.04	4749.72
1975	150.37	47.7	216.77	47.09	263.87	421.84	6.09	427.93	3680.25	1292.84	4973.09	5401.02
1976	158.87	52.0	233.37	47.69	281.06	332.17	6.48	338.65	4261.53	1535.46	5796.99	6135.64
1977	156.28	63.9	245.88	59.40	305.28	399.08	7.02	406.10	4615.16	1895.96	6511.12	6917.22
1978	155.06	82.2	270.96	80.32	351.28	528.53	8.84	537.37	5268.98	2435.71	7704.69	8242.06
1979	148.80	110.9	305.00	71.90	376.90	851.47	32.47	883.94	5969.16	2780.52	8749.68	9633.62
1980	216.10	121.6	392.40	102.17	494.57	1654.73	27.13	1681.86	6865.06	3293.56	10158.62	11840.48
1981	245.00	161.1	475.30	112.15	587.45	1141.96	15.05	1157.01	7283.42	3296.58	10580.00	11737.01
1982	311.80	156.2	547.50	105.43	652.93	1320.83	20.30	1341.13	7911.57	3379.12	11290.69	12631.82
1983	343.80	175.2	597.30	104.24	701.54	1119.98	17.48	1137.46	8694.45	3808.49	12502.94	13640.40
1984	374.40	223.3	673.20	103.58	776.78	919.27	12.72	931.99	9282.31	3739.77	13022.08	13954.07

basis. Figure 4 graphically portrays the changing proportions for major categories. There is considerable change in the proportions within the period studied — most dramatically, the sharp 1973-74 decline in the equity proportion and the 1970s metals boom. The asset proportions at the end of 1984, however, are remarkably similar to those at the end of 1959; moreover, they have the same rank order in both years — real estate is largest, then bonds, equities, metals, and cash. While this consistency may be an artifact of the way the asset class aggregate values are measured, we may also speculate that it represents a fundamental characteristic of the way that society cuts shares of capital — a sort of optimal capital structure for the world economy.

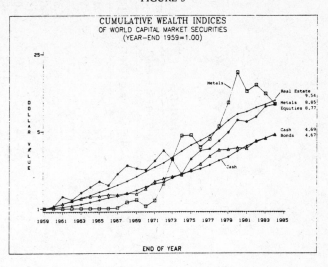

FIGURE 5

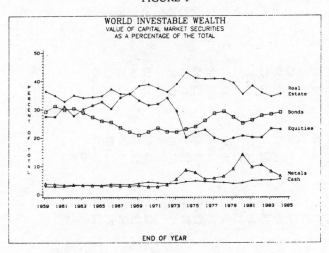

FIGURE 4

Table 2 presents the year-by-year total returns for the various components of the market portfolio, each component being grouped into one of the five major categories. The table includes returns for the U.S., Foreign, and World Market Wealth Portfolios. We also present returns for the world market both with and without monetary metals, since these metals have a large weight and unusual returns; thus, they alter the return on the world portfolio considerably. The returns are then linked (compounded) into cumulative wealth indexes, which are presented in Table 3. Each wealth index is initiated at 1.000 at year-end 1959 and includes reinvestment of all income as well as retention of all capital gains.

Figure 5 presents a graphic summary of the results in Table 3. U.S. real estate had the highest return over the period. Metals, the riskiest category, and equities, having substantial risk, had slightly lower but still generally good performance. Foreign equities outperformed U.S. equities, largely because

of the remarkable returns on equities in Japan and other Asian countries. We have almost certainly underestimated the risk of real estate here, due to the lesser marketability of real estate and the various smoothing effects inherent in our measures of annual returns.[2] Cash had returns that tracked the United States inflation rate. U.S. bonds were the worst performer, underperforming cash and, unlike cash, exhibiting appreciable risk. Foreign bonds had generally better results than U.S. bonds.

In Figure 6, we focus on returns in the U.S. market. Real estate and equities were the high-performing sectors of the market over the period studied.

FIGURE 6

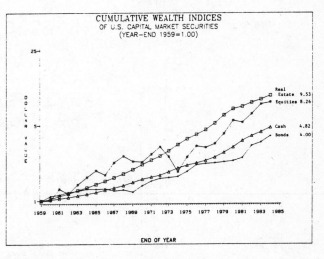

Cash equivalents and bonds were the low-performing sectors, with bonds underperforming cash as a consequence of generally rising interest rates over the period.

The results presented in Tables 2 and 3 are summarized statistically in Table 4. Looking at specific

TABLE 2

YEAR-BY-YEAR TOTAL RETURNS ON
CAPITAL MARKET SECURITIES (PERCENT)

YEAR END	EQUITIES									BONDS			
	UNITED STATES				FOREIGN				EQUITIES TOTAL	UNITED STATES - GOVT			
	NYSE	AMEX	OTC	TOTAL	EUROPE	ASIA	OTHER	TOTAL		NOTES	BONDS	AGENCIES	TOTAL
1960	0.60	4.16	1.93	0.90	13.65	38.50	-0.69	13.84	4.59	10.14	13.78	11.04	12.37
1961	27.17	25.76	35.35	27.63	15.11	-13.03	26.49	14.08	23.04	2.07	0.97	2.84	1.50
1962	-9.40	-5.11	-12.44	-9.35	-2.35	4.68	-3.42	-1.86	-6.86	5.07	6.89	5.79	5.96
1963	21.41	10.93	23.94	20.90	7.08	8.78	19.19	9.18	16.98	2.14	1.21	2.01	1.63
1964	16.36	13.20	26.02	16.84	-2.13	10.93	16.12	2.25	12.25	4.00	3.51	5.08	3.82
1965	13.99	15.50	32.90	15.45	3.74	21.39	-1.27	4.45	12.31	1.43	0.71	3.65	1.19
1966	-8.87	-7.70	-12.29	-9.10	-5.92	9.04	-3.92	-4.17	-7.85	5.02	3.65	3.74	4.08
1967	26.88	51.40	57.37	30.57	18.98	-4.85	22.42	17.02	26.74	1.79	-9.19	1.62	-4.57
1968	12.82	25.94	22.70	14.60	35.05	26.43	27.46	32.76	19.33	4.51	-0.26	4.02	1.76
1969	-9.82	-27.04	-5.80	-10.67	1.51	34.15	8.26	6.43	-6.21	-0.97	-5.08	-0.82	-2.65
1970	1.31	-18.14	-12.23	-1.26	-9.04	-4.09	-4.38	-7.43	-3.07	15.13	12.10	17.62	14.60
1971	15.81	17.86	37.19	17.83	27.33	48.41	10.91	27.37	20.74	8.20	13.23	8.75	9.63
1972	17.77	5.18	20.35	17.36	16.45	134.89	27.80	40.92	24.11	4.23	5.68	5.27	4.81
1973	-16.92	-30.09	-28.47	-18.81	-7.78	-24.62	-21.10	-14.11	-17.32	2.47	-1.11	3.47	2.07
1974	-26.80	-37.61	-32.71	-27.82	-23.34	-19.75	-35.98	-24.03	-26.22	6.50	4.35	12.69	8.31
1975	37.72	38.77	33.76	37.44	44.78	23.84	38.51	37.49	37.46	8.38	9.19	6.72	7.81
1976	26.26	28.25	29.20	26.57	-7.56	26.17	11.75	6.00	18.74	11.92	16.75	12.58	12.67
1977	-4.81	9.80	10.53	-3.18	21.26	13.39	4.61	15.65	3.43	2.29	-0.67	2.34	2.00
1978	7.39	16.95	15.81	8.46	25.51	51.13	19.79	34.27	18.15	3.22	-1.16	1.11	2.05
1979	21.82	58.47	31.91	24.07	15.38	-5.57	57.81	12.85	19.33	4.64	-1.22	5.54	4.32
1980	32.70	30.61	37.38	32.99	14.53	34.09	34.88	25.13	29.46	4.55	-3.95	3.55	3.16
1981	-4.22	-6.10	-0.01	-3.95	-8.93	12.90	-17.66	-2.14	-3.16	9.70	1.85	7.65	7.99
1982	20.72	4.93	21.87	19.98	5.74	-5.67	-1.29	-0.55	10.69	23.79	40.35	28.12	27.32
1983	23.00	28.27	22.17	23.09	22.84	24.06	32.85	25.11	23.92	7.52	0.68	7.78	6.89
1984	6.88	-5.45	-9.31	4.39	1.67	15.24	-13.76	5.13	4.69	13.29	15.43	13.88	13.75

TABLE 2 (continued)

BONDS – CONT.   REAL ESTATE

YEAR END	UNITED STATES – CONT.				FOREIGN					REAL ESTATE – UNITED STATES			
	CORPORATE MED TERM	CORPORATE LONG TERM	CORPORATE TOTAL	TOTAL	DOMESTIC CORP	DOMESTIC GOVT	DOMESTIC TOTAL	CROSS BORDERS	BONDS TOTAL	BUSINESS	RESIDENTIAL	FARM	TOTAL
1960	6.83	8.01	7.79	10.73	5.83	-0.25	2.26	4.66	5.41	2.49	4.99	4.07	4.57
1961	4.69	4.54	4.96	2.73	6.00	6.49	6.30	6.14	5.05	2.69	5.28	9.10	5.82
1962	1.59	6.73	5.91	5.94	4.44	7.93	6.74	7.99	6.46	3.29	4.79	8.98	5.51
1963	2.99	3.79	3.59	2.36	10.48	4.07	6.28	6.03	4.91	4.29	6.78	9.79	7.15
1964	3.72	5.19	4.75	4.16	5.52	1.71	3.28	5.90	3.61	2.99	5.83	7.58	5.91
1965	1.21	-5.19	-2.81	-0.27	4.82	1.94	2.95	1.87	1.72	4.09	6.24	12.64	7.34
1966	-2.75	-4.25	-4.26	1.09	6.14	4.15	4.61	0.48	3.22	4.89	5.76	12.23	7.02
1967	-1.21	-4.79	-3.91	-4.34	3.86	0.23	1.71	3.71	-0.68	6.39	6.83	10.30	7.49
1968	3.50	1.41	2.69	2.10	5.74	3.74	4.58	6.28	3.58	10.69	8.25	8.71	8.62
1969	-3.36	-8.78	-7.50	-4.53	2.78	-0.48	0.63	-0.08	-1.57	6.09	11.02	7.24	9.73
1970	14.15	15.25	14.00	14.37	9.02	9.33	8.91	5.03	11.26	9.99	12.16	7.77	11.09
1971	12.93	11.83	11.71	10.45	23.40	21.25	21.51	15.70	16.50	15.49	8.16	11.70	9.71
1972	8.15	7.35	7.12	5.80	9.88	2.78	5.73	11.53	5.76	9.49	6.73	18.94	9.21
1973	3.19	1.09	1.22	1.70	7.84	5.66	6.56	7.78	4.53	7.39	6.97	35.27	11.94
1974	1.06	-7.61	-5.70	2.40	4.94	3.15	4.01	6.34	3.38	8.09	13.50	19.80	13.99
1975	14.16	17.56	16.60	11.29	11.37	8.10	9.63	13.72	10.25	6.60	13.23	18.52	13.29
1976	14.63	21.03	19.03	15.23	16.74	9.16	12.53	17.64	13.58	8.55	7.51	19.54	9.90
1977	4.60	2.67	4.09	2.83	30.61	27.15	27.00	13.77	17.80	8.67	11.47	11.20	11.10
1978	1.65	-0.10	0.39	1.43	20.15	21.37	19.97	10.65	13.71	14.68	14.18	18.18	15.02
1979	3.35	-4.08	-2.12	2.20	-3.11	1.70	0.28	2.85	0.86	14.69	19.01	20.87	18.90
1980	5.34	-2.60	-0.31	2.15	7.13	2.71	4.00	2.24	3.44	12.92	14.75	12.63	14.12
1981	8.98	-0.15	3.42	6.75	-1.55	-6.69	-4.64	-0.54	-1.29	13.46	4.96	2.19	5.41
1982	30.02	44.52	38.33	29.93	7.79	10.84	11.21	23.49	17.18	10.38	11.82	-3.05	8.87
1983	10.66	8.32	9.20	7.46	4.54	4.19	4.69	7.62	5.71	16.00	7.35	-0.26	7.13
1984	14.87	17.66	15.63	14.18	10.16	0.63	4.43	10.65	8.14	9.99	5.62	-6.65	8.48

TABLE 2 (continued)

YEAR END	CASH — UNITED STATES TREASURY BILLS	CASH — UNITED STATES COMMERCIAL PAPER	CASH — UNITED STATES TOTAL	CASH FOREIGN TOTAL	CASH TOTAL	METALS WORLD GOLD	METALS WORLD SILVER	METALS TOTAL	MARKET WEALTH PORTFOLIOS U.S.	MARKET WEALTH PORTFOLIOS FOREIGN	MARKET WEALTH PORTFOLIOS WORLD EXCL. METALS	MARKET WEALTH PORTFOLIOS WORLD INCL. METALS
1960	2.66	3.85	2.79	0.84	2.27	0.00	0.00	0.00	4.44	5.59	4.77	4.58
1961	2.13	2.97	2.26	-0.33	1.57	0.00	13.19	0.21	11.20	8.53	10.36	10.00
1962	2.73	3.26	2.81	1.81	2.55	0.00	16.50	0.29	0.85	3.68	1.73	1.69
1963	3.12	3.55	3.18	3.62	3.28	0.00	7.50	0.15	10.04	7.12	9.14	8.83
1964	3.54	3.97	3.60	5.40	3.98	0.00	0.00	0.00	8.84	2.99	7.13	6.89
1965	3.93	4.38	4.00	6.78	4.59	0.00	0.00	0.00	8.68	3.56	7.28	7.04
1966	4.76	5.55	4.91	5.92	5.13	0.00	0.00	0.00	0.62	1.70	0.90	0.87
1967	4.21	5.10	4.40	-3.27	2.85	0.00	59.97	1.26	12.67	6.87	11.19	10.87
1968	5.21	5.90	5.39	6.80	5.64	12.29	-4.85	11.73	9.72	15.25	11.07	11.09
1969	6.58	7.83	6.92	8.72	7.22	5.60	-7.65	5.24	0.56	3.23	1.18	1.31
1970	6.53	7.72	6.95	12.90	7.91	-12.29	-9.94	-12.24	7.39	1.90	6.12	5.52
1971	4.39	5.11	4.62	14.03	6.14	13.19	-14.72	12.43	11.94	23.78	14.68	14.62
1972	3.84	4.69	4.09	0.80	3.63	42.23	42.45	42.23	11.03	19.46	13.05	13.88
1973	6.93	8.20	7.30	15.80	8.65	66.90	58.59	66.73	0.46	-2.38	-0.25	2.10
1974	8.00	10.05	8.67	14.52	9.70	63.29	39.81	62.85	1.80	-8.83	-1.19	2.31
1975	5.80	6.26	5.98	-2.14	4.53	1.13	-6.83	1.00	16.76	19.33	17.44	16.00
1976	5.08	5.24	5.12	9.46	5.90	-22.41	6.36	-22.00	13.68	10.13	12.76	10.01
1977	5.12	5.54	5.26	21.04	7.94	18.36	8.28	18.17	6.54	23.17	10.95	11.35
1978	7.18	7.94	7.47	18.88	9.69	30.55	25.90	30.47	11.41	23.87	15.04	15.95
1979	10.38	10.97	10.64	-2.32	7.68	58.83	367.45	63.91	17.05	3.60	12.80	16.13
1980	11.24	12.66	11.99	15.39	12.63	91.71	-24.78	87.43	15.78	10.88	14.22	20.94
1981	14.71	15.32	14.98	-1.16	11.65	-32.15	-49.66	-32.43	4.23	-3.71	1.66	-3.18
1982	10.54	11.89	11.19	-0.09	9.04	13.94	32.12	14.18	13.86	6.99	11.72	11.96
1983	8.80	8.88	8.85	3.10	7.88	-16.50	-17.89	-16.52	10.35	10.94	10.53	7.66
1984	9.85	10.10	10.12	-0.64	8.41	-19.19	-28.94	-19.34	8.67	4.53	7.41	5.17

TABLE 3

CUMULATIVE WEALTH INDICES OF CAPITAL
MARKET SECURITIES (YEAR-END 1959 = 1.00)

YEAR END	EQUITIES									BONDS			
	UNITED STATES				FOREIGN				EQUITIES TOTAL	UNITED STATES - GOVT			
	NYSE	AMEX	OTC	TOTAL	EUROPE	ASIA	OTHER	TOTAL		NOTES	BONDS	AGENCIES	TOTAL
1959	1.000	1.000	1.000	1.000	1.000	1.000	1.000	1.000	1.000	1.000	1.000	1.000	1.000
1960	1.006	1.042	1.019	1.009	1.136	1.385	0.993	1.138	1.046	1.101	1.138	1.110	1.124
1961	1.279	1.310	1.380	1.288	1.308	1.205	1.213	1.299	1.287	1.124	1.149	1.142	1.141
1962	1.159	1.243	1.208	1.167	1.277	1.261	1.213	1.274	1.199	1.181	1.228	1.208	1.209
1963	1.407	1.379	1.497	1.411	1.368	1.372	1.446	1.391	1.402	1.206	1.243	1.232	1.228
1964	1.637	1.561	1.887	1.649	1.339	1.522	1.679	1.423	1.574	1.255	1.286	1.295	1.275
1965	1.867	1.803	2.508	1.904	1.389	1.847	1.658	1.486	1.768	1.273	1.296	1.342	1.290
1966	1.701	1.664	2.199	1.730	1.307	2.014	1.593	1.424	1.629	1.337	1.343	1.392	1.343
1967	2.158	2.519	3.461	2.259	1.555	1.916	1.950	1.667	2.064	1.360	1.219	1.415	1.282
1968	2.435	3.173	4.247	2.589	2.100	2.423	2.485	2.213	2.463	1.422	1.216	1.472	1.304
1969	2.196	2.315	4.000	2.313	2.131	3.250	2.691	2.355	2.310	1.408	1.155	1.460	1.270
1970	2.225	1.895	3.511	2.284	1.939	3.117	2.573	2.180	2.239	1.621	1.294	1.717	1.455
1971	2.576	2.233	4.817	2.691	2.468	4.626	2.853	2.776	2.704	1.754	1.465	1.867	1.595
1972	3.034	2.349	5.797	3.158	2.874	10.867	3.646	3.912	3.356	1.828	1.549	1.966	1.672
1973	2.520	1.642	4.147	2.564	2.651	8.191	2.877	3.360	2.775	1.873	1.531	2.034	1.706
1974	1.845	1.025	2.791	1.851	2.032	6.573	1.842	2.553	2.047	1.995	1.598	2.292	1.848
1975	2.541	1.422	3.733	2.544	2.942	8.141	2.551	3.510	2.814	2.162	1.745	2.446	1.993
1976	3.208	1.823	4.822	3.220	2.720	10.271	2.851	3.721	3.342	2.420	2.037	2.754	2.245
1977	3.054	2.002	5.330	3.118	3.298	11.646	2.982	4.303	3.456	2.476	2.024	2.818	2.290
1978	3.280	2.341	6.173	3.381	4.139	17.601	3.572	5.777	4.084	2.555	2.000	2.849	2.337
1979	3.995	3.711	8.143	4.195	4.776	16.621	5.637	6.520	4.873	2.674	1.976	3.007	2.438
1980	5.301	4.847	11.187	5.579	5.470	22.286	7.604	8.158	6.309	2.795	1.898	3.114	2.515
1981	5.078	4.551	11.185	5.359	4.981	25.161	6.261	7.983	6.110	3.067	1.933	3.352	2.716
1982	6.130	4.775	13.632	6.430	5.267	23.735	6.181	7.939	6.763	3.796	2.713	4.295	3.458
1983	7.540	6.125	16.654	7.915	6.470	29.445	8.211	9.932	8.380	4.082	2.731	4.629	3.696
1984	8.058	5.791	15.103	8.262	6.578	33.932	7.081	10.441	8.773	4.624	3.153	5.271	4.204

TABLE 3 (continued)

BONDS - CONT.

YEAR END	UNITED STATES - CONT.				FOREIGN				BONDS TOTAL
	CORPORATE			TOTAL	DOMESTIC		CROSS BORDERS	TOTAL	
	MED TERM	LONG TERM	TOTAL		CORP	GOVT			
1959	1.000	1.000	1.000	1.000	1.000	1.000	1.000	1.000	1.000
1960	1.068	1.080	1.078	1.107	1.058	0.997	1.047	1.023	1.054
1961	1.118	1.129	1.131	1.137	1.122	1.062	1.111	1.087	1.107
1962	1.136	1.205	1.198	1.205	1.172	1.146	1.200	1.160	1.179
1963	1.170	1.251	1.241	1.234	1.294	1.193	1.272	1.233	1.237
1964	1.214	1.316	1.300	1.285	1.366	1.214	1.347	1.274	1.281
1965	1.228	1.247	1.264	1.281	1.432	1.237	1.372	1.311	1.303
1966	1.195	1.194	1.210	1.295	1.520	1.288	1.379	1.372	1.345
1967	1.180	1.137	1.163	1.239	1.578	1.291	1.430	1.395	1.336
1968	1.221	1.153	1.194	1.265	1.669	1.340	1.520	1.459	1.384
1969	1.180	1.052	1.104	1.208	1.715	1.333	1.519	1.468	1.362
1970	1.347	1.212	1.259	1.381	1.870	1.457	1.595	1.599	1.516
1971	1.522	1.356	1.406	1.526	2.308	1.767	1.846	1.943	1.766
1972	1.646	1.455	1.506	1.614	2.536	1.816	2.058	2.054	1.868
1973	1.698	1.471	1.525	1.642	2.734	1.919	2.218	2.189	1.952
1974	1.716	1.359	1.438	1.681	2.870	1.980	2.359	2.277	2.018
1975	1.959	1.598	1.677	1.871	3.196	2.140	2.683	2.496	2.225
1976	2.246	1.934	1.996	2.156	3.731	2.336	3.156	2.809	2.527
1977	2.349	1.986	2.077	2.217	4.873	2.971	3.590	3.567	2.977
1978	2.388	1.984	2.085	2.249	5.854	3.605	3.973	4.280	3.385
1979	2.468	1.903	2.041	2.298	5.672	3.667	4.086	4.292	3.414
1980	2.600	1.853	2.035	2.348	6.077	3.766	4.178	4.463	3.531
1981	2.833	1.851	2.105	2.506	5.983	3.514	4.155	4.256	3.486
1982	3.684	2.675	2.911	3.256	6.449	3.895	5.131	4.733	4.085
1983	4.076	2.897	3.179	3.499	6.742	4.059	5.522	4.955	4.318
1984	4.682	3.409	3.676	3.995	7.427	4.084	6.110	5.174	4.669

REAL ESTATE

YEAR END	UNITED STATES			
	BUSINESS	RESIDENTIAL	FARM	TOTAL
1959	1.000	1.000	1.000	1.000
1960	1.025	1.050	1.041	1.046
1961	1.052	1.105	1.135	1.107
1962	1.087	1.158	1.237	1.168
1963	1.134	1.237	1.359	1.251
1964	1.168	1.309	1.461	1.325
1965	1.215	1.391	1.646	1.422
1966	1.275	1.471	1.848	1.522
1967	1.356	1.571	2.038	1.636
1968	1.501	1.701	2.215	1.777
1969	1.593	1.888	2.376	1.950
1970	1.752	2.118	2.560	2.166
1971	2.023	2.291	2.860	2.377
1972	2.215	2.445	3.402	2.595
1973	2.379	2.615	4.601	2.905
1974	2.571	2.968	5.512	3.312
1975	2.741	3.361	6.533	3.752
1976	2.975	3.613	7.810	4.124
1977	3.233	4.028	8.684	4.581
1978	3.708	4.599	10.263	5.269
1979	4.253	5.473	12.405	6.265
1980	4.802	6.280	13.972	7.150
1981	5.449	6.592	14.278	7.536
1982	6.014	7.371	13.843	8.204
1983	6.976	7.913	13.807	8.790
1984	7.673	8.358	13.717	9.535

TABLE 3 (continued)

YEAR END	CASH					METALS			MARKET WEALTH PORTFOLIOS			
	UNITED STATES			FOREIGN	CASH TOTAL	WORLD		METALS TOTAL	U. S.	FOREIGN	WORLD EXCL. METALS	WORLD INCL. METALS
	TREASURY BILLS	COMMERCIAL PAPER	TOTAL	TOTAL		GOLD	SILVER					
1959	1.000	1.000	1.000	1.000	1.000	1.000	1.000	1.000	1.000	1.000	1.000	1.000
1960	1.027	1.038	1.028	1.008	1.023	1.000	1.000	1.000	1.044	1.056	1.048	1.046
1961	1.048	1.069	1.051	1.005	1.039	1.000	1.132	1.002	1.161	1.146	1.156	1.150
1962	1.077	1.104	1.081	1.023	1.065	1.000	1.319	1.005	1.171	1.188	1.176	1.170
1963	1.111	1.143	1.115	1.060	1.100	1.000	1.418	1.006	1.289	1.273	1.284	1.273
1964	1.150	1.189	1.155	1.118	1.144	1.000	1.418	1.006	1.403	1.311	1.375	1.361
1965	1.195	1.241	1.201	1.193	1.197	1.000	1.418	1.006	1.525	1.357	1.475	1.457
1966	1.252	1.310	1.260	1.264	1.258	1.000	1.418	1.006	1.534	1.380	1.489	1.469
1967	1.305	1.377	1.316	1.316	1.294	1.000	2.268	1.019	1.729	1.475	1.655	1.629
1968	1.373	1.458	1.387	1.306	1.367	1.123	2.158	1.139	1.896	1.700	1.838	1.810
1969	1.463	1.572	1.483	1.419	1.466	1.186	1.993	1.198	1.907	1.755	1.860	1.833
1970	1.559	1.693	1.586	1.603	1.581	1.040	1.795	1.052	2.048	1.788	1.974	1.934
1971	1.627	1.780	1.659	1.827	1.679	1.177	1.530	1.183	2.293	2.214	2.264	2.217
1972	1.690	1.863	1.727	1.842	1.739	1.674	2.180	1.682	2.545	2.645	2.559	2.525
1973	1.807	2.016	1.853	2.133	1.890	2.795	3.457	2.804	2.557	2.582	2.553	2.578
1974	1.951	2.219	2.013	2.443	2.073	4.563	4.834	4.567	2.603	2.354	2.522	2.637
1975	2.064	2.358	2.134	2.391	2.167	4.615	4.504	4.613	3.040	2.809	2.962	3.059
1976	2.169	2.481	2.243	2.617	2.295	3.581	4.790	3.598	3.456	3.093	3.340	3.365
1977	2.280	2.618	2.361	3.167	2.477	4.238	5.187	4.252	3.682	3.810	3.706	3.747
1978	2.444	2.826	2.538	3.766	2.717	5.533	6.530	5.547	4.102	4.720	4.263	4.344
1979	2.698	3.136	2.808	3.678	2.926	8.788	30.524	9.092	4.801	4.889	4.809	5.045
1980	3.001	3.534	3.144	4.244	3.296	16.847	22.960	17.041	5.559	5.422	5.492	6.102
1981	3.442	4.075	3.615	4.195	3.680	11.430	11.558	11.514	5.794	5.220	5.584	5.907
1982	3.805	4.559	4.020	4.192	4.012	13.024	15.271	13.146	6.597	5.585	6.238	6.614
1983	4.140	4.964	4.376	4.321	4.328	10.875	12.539	10.975	7.280	6.196	6.895	7.120
1984	4.548	5.466	4.819	4.294	4.692	8.788	8.910	8.852	7.912	6.477	7.405	7.488

TABLE 4

WORLD CAPITAL MARKET TOTAL ANNUAL RETURNS 1960-1984

	Compound Return	Arithmetic Mean	Standard Deviation
Equities			
United States			
NYSE	8.71%	9.99%	16.30%
Amex	7.28	9.95	23.49
OTC	11.47	13.88	22.42
United States Total	8.81	10.20	16.89
Foreign			
Europe	7.83	8.94	15.58
Asia	15.14	18.42	30.74
Other	8.14	10.21	20.88
Foreign Total	9.84	11.02	16.07
Equities Total	9.08	10.21	15.28
Bonds			
United States			
Corporate			
Intermediate-term	6.37	6.80	7.15
Long-term	5.03	5.58	11.26
Corporate Total*	5.35	5.75	9.63
Government			
Treasury Notes	6.32	6.44	5.27
Treasury Bonds	4.70	5.11	9.70
U.S. Agencies	6.88	7.04	6.15
Government Total	5.91	6.10	6.43
United States Total	5.70	5.93	7.16
Foreign			
Corporate Domestic	8.35	8.58	7.26
Government Domestic	5.79	6.04	7.41
Crossborder	7.51	7.66	5.76
Foreign Total	6.80	7.01	6.88
Bonds Total	6.36	6.50	5.56

	Compound Return	Arithmetic Mean	Standard Deviation
Cash Equivalents			
United States			
U.S. Treasury Bills	6.25%	6.29%	3.10%
Commercial Paper	7.03	7.08	3.20
U.S. Cash Total	6.49	6.54	3.22
Foreign	6.00	6.23	7.10
Cash Total	6.38	6.42	2.92
Real Estate**			
Business	8.49	8.57	4.16
Residential	8.86	8.93	3.77
Farms	11.86	12.13	7.88
Real Estate Total	9.44	9.49	3.45
Metals			
Gold	9.08	12.62	29.87
Silver	9.14	20.51	75.34
Metals Total	9.11	12.63	29.69
U.S. Market Wealth Portfolio	8.63	8.74	5.06
Foreign Market Wealth Portfolio	7.76	8.09	8.48
World Market Wealth Portfolio			
Excluding metals	8.34	8.47	5.24
Including metals	8.39	8.54	5.80
U.S. Inflation Rate	5.24	5.30	3.60

* Including preferred stock.
** United States only.

asset classes, we can see that the biggest winners over the period were Asian equities (with a 15.14% compound annual rate of return), U.S. farm real estate (11.86%), and U.S. over-the-counter equities (11.47%). Metals, which were among the highest returning assets over the 1960-1980 period studied in Ibbotson and Siegel (1983), fell sharply over 1981-1984, so that their returns over the whole period studied here, while above average, were not extraordinary. The least desirable investment was U.S. Treasury bonds. Despite the explosive 1982 bond rally, they earned a compound annual rate of return of only 4.70%. These bonds, along with long-term U.S. corporate bonds, were the only asset classes to return less then the U.S. inflation rate, and were also riskier than any class of cash or real estate (as measured) and the much better performing foreign bond portfolio.

The U.S. market wealth portfolio had positive returns in every year from 1960 to 1984. The year of highest return was 1979 (17.05%) and the lowest was 1973 (0.46%). The foreign market wealth portfolio was much riskier and, over this period, had a lower overall return. The year of highest return was 1978 (23.87%) and the lowest was 1974 (−8.83%).

The World Market Wealth Portfolio, excluding metals, had year-by-year returns ranging from 17.48% in 1975 to −1.35% in 1974. The World Market Wealth Portfolio, including metals, had returns ranging from 21.51% in 1980 to −3.32% in 1981 and had a slightly higher overall return. Thus, reflecting the counter-cyclical nature of monetary metal returns, the inclusion of metals produced a portfolio with positive total returns in every year except one from 1960 through 1984.

The Relationships Among the Series

We can get a good idea of the interrelationships among the series by looking at the cross-correlation matrix presented in Table 5. The various equity, bond, cash, real estate, and metal series exhibit high correlation *within* each category. Although world equities and world bonds have a correlation coefficient of only approximately 0.16, world cash and gold (sometimes considered a form of cash) are substantially correlated. Real estate is uncorrelated with equities and almost uncorrelated with bonds but highly correlated with cash and metals. These higher correlations probably reflect the impoundment of inflation rates into real estate returns and the tendency of hard, or tangible, assets to follow similar trends.

These results collectively suggest that two factors — economy or market risk and inflation risk — are important in determining security returns. We

proceed to investigate these influences by regression analysis.

Table 6 gives results for each of the excess return series regressed on the excess return series of the broader category in which the series appears. Each major category's excess return is then regressed on the excess return of the world market, excluding metals. Finally, the excess return of the world market, excluding metals, and the excess returns on metals are regressed on the excess return of the complete world market.

Excess returns in all cases are defined as the security return minus riskless (U.S. Treasury bill) return. Thus, in a market model context, the beta is a measure of the economy risk of the asset, and the R-square is a measure of the percent of the variance that is explained by the world market. The alpha expresses superior or inferior performance of an asset after adjusting for its beta on the world market.

The results show that world equities were a relatively poor performer, exhibiting a beta of 2.32 and an alpha of −1.14 relative to the total world market. Real estate and metals had positive alphas relative to the world market, while fixed-income securities accompanied equities with a negative alpha. Real estate also had a low beta, regressed on both the U.S. and world portfolios. Cash had a low alpha and essentially a zero beta. On a beta-adjusted basis, the U.S. market wealth portfolio outperformed the foreign market wealth portfolio.

Inflation appears to be the remaining factor that may describe the series. Table 7 presents the results of each of the return series regressed against U.S. inflation rates. A beta of one indicates that nominal returns on the asset fully impound inflation; a zero beta indicates that inflation has no effect on the nominal asset return.

Almost all categories of equities and bonds had negative betas when regressed on inflation; that is, higher inflation rates seemed to hurt returns on these assets and lower inflation rates helped. The beta T-statistics for these assets did not, however, support a statistically significant relationship. Cash and real estate had betas below but near one when regressed on inflation, with high T-statistics indicating that these assets are inflation hedges, although imperfectly so. Metals are extremely responsive to inflation, with a small rise in inflation producing a large rise in metals prices and vice versa.

[1] Ibbotson and Fall (1979); Ibbotson and Siegel (1983).

[2] See Ibbotson and Siegel [1984] for a full discussion of the difficulties in measuring the riskiness of real estate returns.

TABLE 5

WORLD CAPITAL MARKET SECURITY RETURNS
CORRELATION MATRIX

	NYSE	AMEX	OTC	U.S. TOTAL EQUITIES	EUROPE EQUITIES	ASIA EQUITIES	OTHER EQUITIES	FOREIGN TOTAL EQUITIES	WORLD EQUITIES	U.S. TREASURY NOTES	U.S. TREASURY BONDS	U.S. AGENCIES	U.S. TOTAL GOVT BONDS
NYSE	1.000												
AMEX	0.851	1.000											
OTC	0.900	0.897	1.000										
U.S. EQUITIES	0.997	0.883	0.929	1.000									
EUROPE EQUITIES	0.618	0.689	0.651	0.640	1.000								
ASIA EQUITIES	0.237	0.123	0.244	0.237	0.391	1.000							
OTHER EQUITIES	0.792	0.848	0.766	0.807	0.731	0.320	1.000						
FOREIGN EQUITIES	0.656	0.657	0.666	0.672	0.908	0.695	0.765	1.000					
WORLD TOTAL EQUITIES	0.955	0.879	0.914	0.964	0.787	0.409	0.853	0.841	1.000				
U.S. TREASURY NOTES	0.105	-0.102	-0.117	0.068	-0.159	-0.108	-0.252	-0.192	-0.037	1.000			
U.S. TREASURY BONDS	0.091	-0.153	-0.094	0.056	-0.130	-0.005	-0.266	-0.165	-0.041	0.904	1.000		
U.S. AGENCIES	0.007	-0.201	-0.187	-0.030	-0.280	-0.178	-0.342	-0.327	-0.156	0.962	0.904	1.000	
U.S. TOTAL GOVT BONDS	0.033	-0.183	-0.189	-0.006	-0.201	-0.067	-0.296	-0.226	-0.105	0.972	0.950	0.964	1.000
U.S. INTERMEDIATE TERM CORP BONDS	0.361	0.078	0.132	0.322	0.099	0.045	-0.028	0.072	0.242	0.900	0.865	0.848	0.887
U.S. LONG TERM CORP BONDS	0.341	0.058	0.110	0.302	0.095	0.022	-0.033	0.052	0.219	0.858	0.912	0.808	0.859
U.S. TOTAL CORP BONDS	0.361	0.083	0.132	0.323	0.117	0.033	-0.019	0.075	0.243	0.865	0.902	0.809	0.863
U.S. TOTAL BONDS	0.206	-0.047	-0.031	0.166	-0.045	-0.007	-0.160	-0.074	0.075	0.954	0.956	0.915	0.967
FOREIGN DOMESTIC CORP BONDS	0.044	0.025	0.107	0.050	0.315	0.269	-0.028	0.314	0.156	0.035	0.172	-0.008	0.085
FOREIGN DOMESTIC GOVT BONDS	0.010	0.078	0.097	0.024	0.345	0.084	0.058	0.255	0.115	0.061	0.190	0.044	0.117
FOREIGN CROSSBORDER BONDS	0.270	0.116	0.172	0.255	0.253	0.154	0.017	0.215	0.249	0.560	0.716	0.552	0.607
FOREIGN TOTAL BONDS	0.042	0.067	0.112	0.052	0.343	0.153	-0.028	0.281	0.144	0.097	0.239	0.072	0.153
WORLD TOTAL BONDS	0.136	0.035	0.069	0.124	0.248	0.122	-0.041	0.194	0.155	0.511	0.619	0.473	0.561
U.S. BUSINESS REAL ESTATE	0.159	0.227	0.138	0.164	0.268	0.218	0.243	0.332	0.233	0.262	0.036	0.179	0.206
U.S. RESIDENTIAL REAL ESTATE	0.123	0.213	0.090	0.125	0.207	-0.080	0.356	0.141	0.133	0.068	-0.039	0.095	0.066
U.S. FARM REAL ESTATE	-0.164	-0.093	-0.223	-0.171	-0.097	-0.003	-0.063	-0.065	-0.139	-0.315	-0.256	-0.273	-0.267
U.S. REAL ESTATE TOTAL	0.054	0.166	0.006	0.054	0.156	-0.033	0.288	0.129	0.083	-0.051	-0.138	-0.024	-0.040
U.S. TREASURY BILLS	-0.055	-0.063	-0.160	-0.070	-0.169	-0.157	-0.101	-0.153	-0.114	0.395	0.111	0.328	0.325
U.S. COMMERCIAL PAPER	-0.112	-0.130	-0.210	-0.127	-0.211	-0.176	-0.150	-0.199	-0.174	0.394	0.115	0.348	0.330
U.S. TOTAL CASH	-0.064	-0.080	-0.170	-0.079	-0.178	-0.159	-0.112	-0.162	-0.125	0.400	0.119	0.340	0.332
FOREIGN TOTAL CASH	-0.393	-0.355	-0.289	-0.386	-0.127	0.009	-0.270	-0.107	-0.311	-0.203	-0.183	-0.154	-0.143
WORLD TOTAL CASH	-0.225	-0.240	-0.284	-0.238	-0.212	-0.115	-0.225	-0.180	-0.242	0.270	0.032	0.237	0.236
GOLD	-0.094	-0.024	-0.067	-0.088	0.032	0.046	0.140	0.044	-0.058	-0.277	-0.252	-0.178	-0.206
SILVER	0.093	0.374	0.142	0.116	0.052	-0.181	0.410	-0.020	0.070	-0.131	-0.140	-0.064	-0.109
WORLD TOTAL METALS	-0.093	-0.011	-0.064	-0.086	0.032	0.036	0.152	0.039	-0.058	-0.279	-0.253	-0.177	-0.207
U.S. MARKET WEALTH PORTFOLIO	0.915	0.837	0.831	0.917	0.605	0.209	0.754	0.626	0.886	0.214	0.162	0.139	0.152
FOREIGN MARKET WEALTH PORTFOLIO	0.493	0.498	0.544	0.510	0.823	0.602	0.556	0.865	0.678	-0.086	0.021	-0.201	-0.083
WORLD MARKET WEALTH PORT (W/O METALS)	0.853	0.799	0.814	0.861	0.782	0.406	0.765	0.815	0.914	0.109	0.119	0.007	0.066
WORLD MARKET WEALTH PORT (W/ METALS)	0.747	0.723	0.727	0.757	0.706	0.351	0.753	0.732	0.805	-0.010	0.016	-0.059	-0.023

TABLE 5 (continued)

	U.S. INTERMED. CORP BONDS	U.S. LONG CORP BONDS	U.S. TOTAL CORP BONDS	U.S. TOTAL BONDS	FOREIGN CORP BONDS	FOREIGN GOVT BONDS	CROSS-BORDER BONDS	FOREIGN TOTAL BONDS	WORLD TOTAL BONDS	BUS. REAL ESTATE	RESI-DENTIAL STRUCTURES	FARM REAL ESTATE	TOTAL U.S. REAL ESTATE
U.S. INTERMEDIATE TERM CORP BONDS	1.000												
U.S. LONG TERM CORP BONDS	0.941	1.000											
U.S. TOTAL CORP BONDS	0.960	0.996	1.000										
U.S. TOTAL BONDS	0.956	0.956	0.962	1.000									
FOREIGN DOMESTIC CORP BONDS	0.211	0.263	0.264	0.180	1.000								
FOREIGN DOMESTIC GOVT BONDS	0.203	0.269	0.266	0.192	0.890	1.000							
FOREIGN CROSSBORDER BONDS	0.741	0.814	0.807	0.721	0.628	0.628	1.000						
FOREIGN TOTAL BONDS	0.260	0.326	0.323	0.242	0.950	0.985	0.689	1.000					
WORLD TOTAL BONDS	0.635	0.693	0.692	0.646	0.829	0.860	0.866	0.895	1.000				
U.S. BUSINESS REAL ESTATE	0.335	0.107	0.152	0.192	0.165	0.249	0.203	0.228	0.256	1.000			
U.S. RESIDENTIAL REAL ESTATE	0.085	-0.039	-0.030	0.017	0.091	0.293	0.108	0.225	0.191	0.493	1.000		
U.S. FARM REAL ESTATE	-0.252	-0.255	-0.273	-0.274	0.176	0.103	0.049	0.125	-0.013	0.016	0.214	1.000	
U.S. REAL ESTATE TOTAL	-0.004	-0.129	-0.123	-0.082	0.164	0.303	0.123	0.256	0.172	0.518	0.916	0.570	1.000
U.S. TREASURY BILLS	0.336	0.094	0.135	0.244	-0.269	-0.224	-0.060	-0.240	-0.091	0.685	0.428	-0.053	0.389
U.S. COMMERCIAL PAPER	0.313	0.070	0.108	0.230	-0.289	-0.232	-0.078	-0.254	-0.108	0.655	0.462	-0.040	0.415
U.S. TOTAL CASH	0.339	0.096	0.136	0.247	-0.265	-0.217	-0.054	-0.234	-0.085	0.681	0.447	-0.046	0.405
FOREIGN TOTAL CASH	-0.191	-0.225	-0.225	-0.192	0.616	0.617	0.101	0.608	0.393	0.231	0.317	0.306	0.529
WORLD TOTAL CASH	0.222	-0.005	0.029	0.141	0.048	0.080	0.007	0.065	0.106	0.705	0.528	0.096	
GOLD	-0.235	-0.316	-0.323	-0.280	0.001	0.107	-0.046	0.062	-0.079	0.219	0.586	0.517	0.684
SILVER	-0.150	-0.177	-0.187	-0.153	-0.286	-0.054	-0.076	-0.136	-0.177	0.188	0.532	0.351	0.580
WORLD TOTAL METALS	-0.239	-0.318	-0.326	-0.282	-0.011	0.104	-0.047	0.056	-0.085	0.220	0.596	0.526	0.696
U.S. MARKET WEALTH PORTFOLIO	0.446	0.367	0.393	0.284	0.153	0.171	0.395	0.191	0.288	0.394	0.422	-0.019	0.371
FOREIGN MARKET WEALTH PORTFOLIO	0.192	0.221	0.236	0.080	0.723	0.687	0.517	0.718	0.603	0.329	0.174	-0.008	0.177
WORLD MARKET WEALTH PORT (W/O METALS)	0.390	0.354	0.377	0.231	0.431	0.428	0.504	0.455	0.471	0.407	0.365	-0.014	0.332
WORLD MARKET WEALTH PORT (W/ METALS)	0.238	0.193	0.207	0.093	0.380	0.426	0.404	0.429	0.389	0.390	0.552	0.133	0.531

	U.S. TREASURY BILLS	U.S. COMMERCIAL PAPER	U.S. TOTAL CASH	FOREIGN TOTAL CASH	WORLD TOTAL CASH	GOLD	SILVER	WORLD TOTAL METALS	U.S. MARKET WEALTH PORTFOLIO	FOREIGN MARKET WEALTH PORTFOLIO	WORLD MARKET EXCL. METALS	WORLD MARKET INCL. METALS
U.S. TREASURY BILLS	1.000											
U.S. COMMERCIAL PAPER	0.990	1.000										
U.S. TOTAL CASH	0.999	0.995	1.000									
FOREIGN TOTAL CASH	-0.008	0.033	0.010	1.000								
WORLD TOTAL CASH	0.881	0.895	0.891	0.460	1.000							
GOLD	0.179	0.256	0.210	0.419	0.366	1.000						
SILVER	0.125	0.127	0.123	-0.203	-0.014	0.438	1.000					
WORLD TOTAL METALS	0.177	0.253	0.207	0.401	0.355	0.999	0.477	1.000				
U.S. MARKET WEALTH PORTFOLIO	0.133	0.088	0.130	-0.233	0.013	0.104	0.291	0.111	1.000			
FOREIGN MARKET WEALTH PORTFOLIO	-0.254	-0.298	-0.258	0.218	-0.122	0.025	-0.110	0.018	0.533	1.000		
WORLD MARKET WEALTH PORT (W/O METALS)	-0.033	-0.083	-0.037	-0.059	-0.053	0.075	0.142	0.077	0.925	0.812	1.000	
WORLD MARKET WEALTH PORT (W/ METALS)	-0.014	-0.027	-0.004	0.105	0.046	0.427	0.283	0.427	0.873	0.727	0.924	1.000

TABLE 6

REGRESSION RESULTS FOR MAJOR ASSET
CLASS RETURNS IN EXCESS OF U.S. TREASURY BILL RATES

Dependent Variable	Independent Variable	Alpha (%)	Alpha T Statistic	Beta	Beta T Statistic	Adjusted R2	Standard Deviation of Residuals	1st Order Autocorr. of Residuals
U.S. Equities-NYSE	U.S. Equities	-0.06	-0.22	0.96	63.54	0.994	1.32	0.04
AMEX	U.S. Equities	-1.10	-0.47	1.22	9.18	0.776	11.54	0.13
OTC	U.S. Equities	2.73	1.56	1.24	12.70	0.870	8.51	-0.05
U.S. Total Equities	World Equities	-0.22	-0.23	1.05	17.80	0.929	4.72	-0.05
Europe Equities	Foreign Equities	-1.57	-1.10	0.89	10.96	0.832	6.85	-0.48
Asia Equities	Foreign Equities	5.85	1.22	1.32	4.85	0.484	23.00	-0.15
Other Equities	Foreign Equities	-0.76	-0.26	0.99	5.95	0.589	14.02	-0.06
Foreign Equities	World Equities	1.19	0.64	0.90	7.90	0.719	9.10	-0.00
	World Wealth excl. metals	-1.14	-0.74	2.32	9.98	0.804	7.19	0.26
U.S. Corporate Bonds	U.S. Total Bonds	-0.05	-0.10	1.33	18.35	0.933	2.56	-0.28
U.S. Government Bonds	U.S. Total Bonds	0.12	0.36	0.84	18.61	0.935	1.60	-0.28
U.S. Total Bonds	World Total Bonds	-0.52	-0.47	0.72	4.37	0.430	5.46	0.20
Foreign Corporate Bonds	Foreign Total Bonds	1.56	3.31	1.02	17.70	0.929	2.35	-0.08
Foreign Government Bonds	Foreign Total Bonds	-1.00	-3.66	1.04	31.37	0.976	1.36	0.08
Crossborder Bonds	Foreign Total Bonds	0.91	1.04	0.64	6.07	0.599	4.33	0.12
Foreign Total Bonds	World Total Bonds	0.47	0.77	1.16	12.42	0.865	3.08	0.10
World Total Bonds	World Wealth excl. metals	-1.24	-1.08	0.67	3.82	0.362	5.39	0.17
U.S. Cash	World Cash	0.25	6.22	0.02	0.66	-0.024	0.20	0.26
Foreign Cash	World Cash	-0.73	-2.94	5.20	31.13	0.976	1.23	-0.26
World Cash	World Wealth excl. metals	0.05	0.16	0.04	0.72	-0.021	1.52	0.03
U.S. Business Real Estate	U.S. Real Estate	1.30	1.65	0.31	1.89	0.097	2.95	0.20
U.S. Residential Real Estate	U.S. Real Estate	-0.36	-0.87	0.94	10.94	0.832	1.55	0.11
U.S. Farm Real Estate	U.S. Real Estate	0.44	0.26	1.68	4.84	0.483	6.33	0.18
U.S. Real Estate	World Wealth excl. metals	2.52	3.71	0.31	3.03	0.254	3.20	0.57
U.S. Equities	U.S. Market Wealth	-3.17	-2.10	2.88	11.62	0.848	6.91	0.35
U.S. Bonds	U.S. Market Wealth	-1.34	-0.88	0.40	1.59	0.060	7.00	0.12
U.S. Cash	U.S. Market Wealth	0.28	6.58	-0.01	-1.49	0.048	0.19	0.00
U.S. Real Estate	U.S. Market Wealth	2.42	3.35	0.32	2.67	0.203	3.31	0.62
U.S. Market Wealth	World Wealth excl. metals	0.60	1.51	0.85	14.20	0.893	1.86	-0.06
Foreign Equities	Foreign Market Wealth	2.05	1.14	1.50	8.27	0.737	8.80	0.06
Foreign Total Bonds	Foreign Market Wealth	-0.48	-0.46	0.67	6.24	0.612	5.21	0.09
Foreign Cash	Foreign Market Wealth	-0.62	-0.41	0.31	2.04	0.116	7.45	0.05
Foreign Market Wealth	World Wealth excl. metals	-1.22	-1.19	1.38	8.87	0.764	4.83	-0.08
World Wealth excl. metals	World Wealth incl. metals	0.19	0.43	0.88	13.49	0.883	2.16	0.14
Gold	Metals	-0.04	-0.14	1.00	103.02	0.998	1.43	-0.42
Silver	Metals	6.61	0.47	1.20	2.55	0.186	69.07	-0.37
Metals	World Wealth incl. metals	2.89	0.48	1.53	1.77	0.082	28.66	0.39

TABLE 7

CAPITAL MARKET RETURNS REGRESSED ON U.S. INFLATION

Dependent Variable	Independent Variable	Alpha (%)	Alpha T Statistic	Beta	Beta T Statistic	Adjusted R²	Standard Deviation of Residuals	1st Order Autocorr of Residuals
U.S. Equities:	U.S. Inflation							
NYSE	"	14.22	2.39	-0.80	-0.86	-0.011	16.73	-0.11
AMEX	"	10.94	1.26	-0.18	-0.14	-0.043	24.48	0.13
OTC	"	20.43	2.51	-1.24	-0.97	-0.002	22.91	-0.07
U.S. Total Equities	"	14.50	2.35	-0.81	-0.84	-0.012	17.34	-0.09
Europe Equities	"	10.76	1.87	-0.34	-0.38	-0.037	16.19	-0.21
Asia Equities	"	24.75	2.19	-1.19	-0.68	-0.023	31.73	-0.07
Other Equities	"	9.06	1.17	0.22	0.18	-0.042	21.75	-0.04
Foreign Equities	"	12.95	2.18	-0.36	-0.39	-0.037	16.70	-0.08
World Equities	"	13.75	2.46	-0.67	-0.76	-0.018	15.73	-0.10
U.S. Corporate Bonds:								
U.S. Intermediate Term	"	7.45	2.82	-0.16	-0.39	-0.037	7.43	0.37
U.S. Long Term	"	10.42	2.61	-0.91	-1.46	0.046	11.23	0.18
U.S. Total Corporate Bonds	"	9.49	2.75	-0.70	-1.31	0.029	9.69	0.26
U.S. Government Bonds								
U.S. Treasury Notes	"	6.72	3.44	-0.05	-0.18	-0.042	5.49	0.15
U.S. Treasury Bonds	"	8.59	2.46	-0.66	-1.21	0.019	9.81	-0.01
U.S. Agencies	"	7.33	3.22	-0.09	-0.15	-0.042	6.40	0.05
U.S. Total Government Bonds	"	6.58	2.76	-0.09	-0.24	-0.041	6.70	0.14
U.S. Total Bonds	"	7.56	2.88	-0.31	-0.75	-0.018	7.38	0.22
Foreign Corporate Bonds	"	9.37	3.49	-0.15	-0.35	-0.038	7.55	0.35
Foreign Government Bonds	"	5.86	2.13	0.03	0.08	-0.043	7.72	0.27
Crossborder Bonds	"	8.84	4.18	-0.22	-0.68	-0.023	5.95	0.28
Foreign Total Bonds	"	7.30	2.86	-0.05	-0.14	-0.043	7.17	0.31
World Total Bonds	"	7.28	3.55	-0.15	-0.46	-0.034	5.77	0.28
U.S. Cash:								
U.S. Treasury Bills	"	3.11	3.77	0.60	4.66	0.464	2.32	0.74
U.S. Commercial Paper	"	3.63	4.48	0.65	5.14	0.514	2.28	0.74
U.S. Total Cash	"	3.18	3.78	0.63	4.83	0.482	2.36	0.75
Foreign Cash	"	2.37	0.97	0.73	1.91	0.099	6.88	-0.01
World Cash	"	3.05	4.52	0.63	6.02	0.595	1.90	0.39
U.S. Business Real Estate	"	5.08	4.01	0.66	3.33	0.296	3.56	0.44
U.S. Residential Real Estate	"	4.61	5.26	0.81	5.94	0.588	2.47	-0.08
U.S. Farm Real Estate	"	7.18	2.72	0.93	2.26	0.146	7.43	0.46
U.S. Real Estate	"	5.23	7.53	0.80	7.42	0.693	1.95	0.13
Gold	"	-15.97	-1.90	5.39	4.11	0.398	23.65	0.03
Silver	"	-25.73	-1.01	8.72	2.20	0.138	71.39	-0.19
Metals	"	-15.96	-1.92	5.39	4.15	0.404	23.40	0.06
U.S. Market Wealth	"	7.88	4.23	0.16	0.56	-0.030	5.24	-0.09
Foreign Market Wealth	"	9.59	3.07	-0.28	-0.58	-0.028	8.77	0.14
World Wealth excl. metals	"	8.32	4.28	0.03	0.09	-0.043	5.47	-0.00
World Wealth incl. metals	"	6.71	3.19	0.35	1.06	0.005	5.90	-0.17

SOURCES

1. *Capital International Perspective*. Geneva, Switzerland: Capital International, S.A., 1959-1984.

2. *CRSP Monthly Stock Returns File*. Machine-readable tape published by Center for Research in Security Prices (CRSP) [sponsored by Merrill, Lynch, Pierce, Fenner & Smith], Graduate School of Business, University of Chicago, annual; 1985 and earlier.

3. *Federal Reserve Bulletin*. Washington, D.C.: Board of Governors of the Federal Reserve System, January 1960-1984.

4. *Financial Statistics: Part I*. Paris: Organization for Economic Co-operation and Development, 1970-1984.

5. *Flow of Funds Accounts*. Washington, D.C.: Board of Governors of the Federal Reserve System, selected issues.

6. *Government Finance Statistics Yearbook*. Washington, D.C.: International Monetary Fund, 1959-1984.

7. Ibbotson, Roger G., Richard C. Carr, and Anthony W. Robinson. "International Equity and Bond Returns." *Financial Analysts Journal*, July/August 1982.

8. Ibbotson, Roger G., and Carol L. Fall. "The U.S. market wealth portfolio." *The Journal of Portfolio Management*, Fall 1979.

9. Ibbotson, Roger G. and Laurence B. Siegel. "Real Estate Returns: A Comparison With Other Investments." *American Real Estate & Urban Economics Association Journal*, Fall 1984.

10. ———. "The world market wealth portfolio." *The Journal of Portfolio Management*, Winter 1983.

11. *Interest Rates 1960-1974*. Paris: Organization for Economic Co-operation and Development, 1975.

12. *The Lehman Brothers Kuhn Loeb Bond Index*. New York: Shearson Lehman American Express (formerly Lehman Brothers Kuhn Loeb), 1984.

13. *Moody's Public Utility Manual*. New York: Moody's Investors Service, annual; 1985 and earlier.

14. *NASDAQ-OTC Market Factbook*. Washington, D.C.: National Association of Securities Dealers, selected issues.

15. *Outlook and Situation Summary: Agricultural Land Values*, U.S. Department of Agriculture, Economic Research Service, June 7, 1985.

16. *Stocks, Bonds, Bills, and Inflation: 1985 Yearbook*, Ibbotson Associates, Chicago, 1984. (Earlier editions published as Roger G. Ibbotson and Rex A. Sinquefield, *Stocks, Bonds, Bills, and Inflation: The Past and the Future*, 1982; also 1979, 1977 [titles vary]; Financial Analysts Research Foundation, Charlottesville, Va.)

17. *The Wall Street Journal*. Dow Jones and Company, New York: selected issues.

BUSINESS WEEK (February 4, 1985)

WHY MONEY MANAGERS DON'T DO BETTER

FOR ALL THEIR 'EXPERTISE,' THEY CAN'T EVEN BEAT THE S&P 500 INDEX

For two years, Joseph J. McCann watched impatiently as two professional money-management firms failed at what they are paid handsomely to do: "add value" to the $23 million profit-sharing trust McCann chairs for his employer, Ryan Homes Inc. In 1983, when the Standard & Poor's 500-stock index -- the yardstick by which stock market managers are measured -- moved up 22.4%, McCann's hired pros could muster only an anemic 8% total return. And like most of their brethren, the managers were in the red for at least part of 1984.

McCann, a Ryan Homes vice-president, has pretty much lost track of their performance -- because he replaced them last spring. "The money managers put you at such tremendous risk," he says. "And still they couldn't even beat a simple money market fund."

<u>Down</u> <u>to a</u> <u>Trickle</u>. Such experiences have put the institutional money-management industry -- which controls perhaps $1.5 trillion in assets and collects some $6 billion in fees -- in a crisis. And it isn't just that money mangers chalked up disastrous records in 1983 and 1984: Longer-term numbers suggest that managers on the whole are failing to achieve superior returns on their clients' money. This heightens the pressure on the money-management business at a time when new contributions are slowing to a trickle. Frustrated plan sponsors are taking their money from active managers and placing it in relatively low-cost "passive" investments such as index funds.

Why? Just look at the record (chart). Only 26% of the equity portfolios beat the S&P 500 last year, according to SEI Funds Evaluation Services. What's more, even in the longer time periods measured, most managers still failed to overcome the S&P 500.

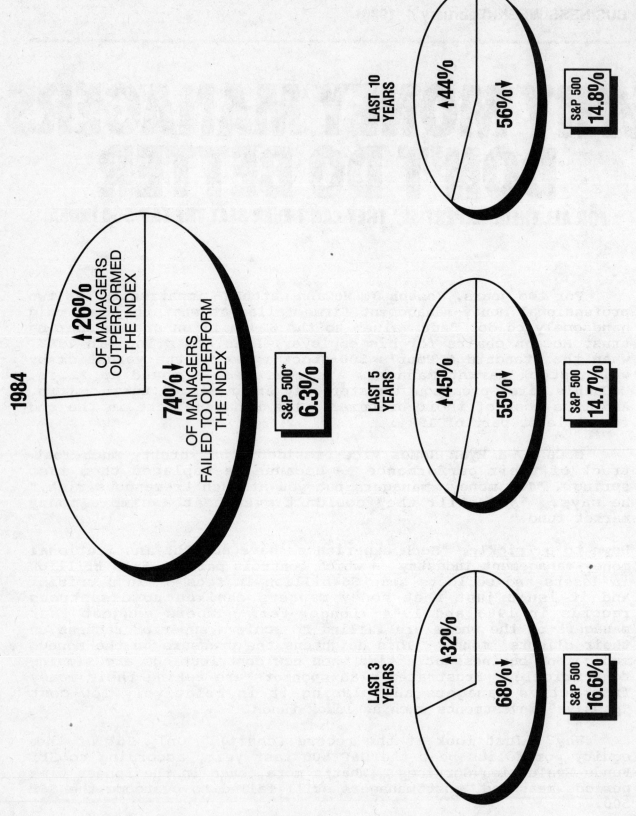

1984

↑26% OF MANAGERS OUTPERFORMED THE INDEX

74%↓ OF MANAGERS FAILED TO OUTPERFORM THE INDEX

S&P 500* 6.3%

LAST 3 YEARS

↑32%

68%↓

S&P 500 16.6%

LAST 5 YEARS

↑45%

55%↓

S&P 500 14.7%

LAST 10 YEARS

↑44%

56%↓

S&P 500 14.8%

DATA: SEI FUNDS EVALUATION SERVICES

* Compound annualized return of stocks in Standard & Poor's 500 index.

Fixed-income managers fared no better. According to SEI, only 29% topped the Shearson Lehman Government/Corporate Bond Index's 15% return in 1984. For 1982-84, only 41% of the managers beat the index's 17.6% compounded annualized return. And over 10 years, only 40% could summon enough smarts to outdo the index's 9.6% return.

Moreover, the SEI universe, though the largest data collection in the industry, probably overstates the returns. "No data base includes the managers whose results were so bad they didn't survive long enough to build a record," says Dennis Tito, president of Wilshire Associates, a pension-fund consulting firm. Unlike managers of publicly marketed mutual funds, money managers are under no legal obligation to post results. The only portfolios in the data bases are directed there by clients, or by money managers who want to measure themselves against competitors.

Loading the Dice. The conundrum of megabuck investing is this: The money management game employs the best talent on Wall Street, the most subtle strategies, the most finely honed tools. Why can't highly paid professional managers perform consistently better than any odd-lot trader? And what will become of the industry, which dominates today's securities markets, as clients lose patience and faith?

The answer to the first question may help determine the second. The structure of the institutional securities market may make it impossible to beat the averages -- at least for very long. And if the averages are unbeatable, what's the point of spending -- and risking -- a lot of money on professional help? If enough pension-fund sponsors begin to ask that question, there go the money managers.

Bad money management has grievous consequences. If a pension fund underperforms the S&P 500 by two percentage points a year, that compounds to 10.4% over five years and 34.6% in 20.

The problem of structure, which loads the dice against the money manager and his client, is an intricate one. In the first place, the indexes against which money management is measured are "transactional" -- they measure the performance of stocks and bonds in the marketplace without deducting the various costs of doing business. The performance of money managers, on the other hand, is reported after transaction costs. And transaction costs turn out to be "a lead anchor on performance," says Michael C. Jensen, a professor of finance and economics at the University of Rochester and now a visiting professor of finance at Harvard University's business school.

In a recent study for Harvard University, pension consultant James Meketa estimated basic money-management costs at 1% to 2%

of assets each year. That may not sound excessive, but consider this: If a $10 million account grosses 12%, or $1.2 million (a respectable return), a 2% overhead on assets is $200,000 -- or nearly 17% of the year's earnings. Where does the money go? Brokerage commissions and related transaction costs eat up 1/2% to 3/4% -- and are reflected in the results reported to the various industry data bases. But not included in such results are money managers' fees, which skim an average of 1/2% off the top. Nor do the results reflect fees paid to consultants, actuaries, or banks that act as custodians for the funds.

If the plan sponsor chooses some hotshot stock-pickers -- people expert in some fashionable specialty, such as high-tech stocks -- to manage the assets, costs can run up in the Tiffany range. Management fees can be double the average -- say, 1%. And hotshots with heavy reputations tend to incur higher transaction costs. They trade a lot more aggressively than the average manager, who trades about 70% of the portfolio's assets each year, according to Meketa's estimate. The more trading, the more commissions. Also, aggressive managers are attracted to less liquid, smaller company stocks where the opportunities for profit seem greater but the trading costs are higher. In short, the more aggressive the money manager, the more he must earn just to clear the hurdle of overhead.

In addition, size is the enemy of performance in the money-management business. "If you're very good and the value of your holdings increases substantially, it's harder and harder to repeat those kinds of gains," says Marshall E. Blume, a professor of finance at the University of Pennsylvania's Wharton School.

Business school professors have been arguing for years that no one can beat the averages over the long run. Now, however, a small but growing number of pension-plan sponsors are finally paying attention to theories of the "efficient market," which hold that quick distribution of information and competition between sophisticated investors keep stock prices where they should be. While some managers can outperform the market from time to time (like the lucky soul who pulls the arm on the slot machine when the jackpot comes up), the law of large numbers makes it impossible to win ad infinitum without taking significantly greater risks with pension money -- risks so large that they violate the "prudent man" rules that govern management of pension-fund assets.

Flip of a Coin. Efficient-market theories notwithstanding, academics can't ignore the riches reaped by some investors. As a result, theorists now allow for occasional "pockets of inefficiency" that investors may profitably exploit if they are smarter, quicker and better informed than competitors. "Hot stock-pickers come and go all the time. But no one has yet come up with any sure way of determining beforehand who that is going to be," says Jensen. "Hiring an active manager is a triumph of hope over experience," adds Dennis E. Logue, a Dartmouth College professor of finance and consultant to the U.S. on a study of pension-plan performance. "We all have an innate belief that good hard work will result in rewards, but no one should get their hopes up."

Wilshire's Tito tells of a finance instructor who asks each student to flip a coin. All those who turn up heads flip again; those with tails drop out. After 10 or so rounds, one student is left. "He'll be our money manager," says the instructor, "because he always wins."

Money managers naturally deplore such talk, since their jobs, their businesses, and their beach houses depend on beating the markets. They don't want to hear about coin-flipping -- but in fact they are not far from it. Pressured by clients to boost sagging performance at any cost, the pros have lost any vision they once might have had for long-term investing. "John Templeton, Warren Buffett, and Henry Singleton have been among the most successful investors of our time because they could recognize value and buy it dirt cheap, accumulate it, and hold it until it pays off," notes Ralph L. Knisley, a vice-president and manager of the Consulting Services Dept. at Irving Trust Co. "I doubt if they could have done it if they had to report quarterly returns to today's pension-plan sponsors." All three men are investors of legendary success who started their careers after World War II. None made his mark as a pension-plan money manager.

In fact, it's getting harder to make any record at all, largely because of the way clients manage their stables of money managers. For one thing, says Roy A. Schotland, a Georgetown University professor who has studied institutional investors, plan sponsors sometimes make it almost impossible for managers to do their jobs: "They jump through hoops to find the best money managers, and then they tell them what they can do and can't do -- like buy companies that do business in South Africa or demand a stock have a certain yield." Such constraints make it difficult to match, let alone beat, the S&P 500.

Even when plan sponsors are less inclined to interfere in day-to-day management of assets, there are rigidities in the system. To sell themselves to the pension committee, management firms typically roll out slide shows, flip charts, investment officers, and portfolio managers. In the end, the manager who gets the account is the one who best articulates his investment philosophy. Having bought a concept along with the money manager who devised it, plan sponsors not unreasonably expect that manager to stay with that concept.

Then, of course, when the concept no longer works -- and no investment strategy succeeds forever -- they pull their money out. Fayez Sarofim, a Houston money manager noted for his savvy with oil stocks, made a bundle in 1980 and attracted an even bigger stack of client money in 1981 -- just in time for the crash in oil prices. By the end of 1983, he had lost about $1 billion of nearly $9 billion in managed accounts, in part because clients pulled their money out. But because Sarofim stayed with oil, those who stuck with him or hired him when he was out of favor would have benefited handsomely in 1984, when he cashed in on the oil-company mergers and turned in a 12% gain.

'Greater Fool'. The consequence of plan sponsors' approaches to management is that they are forever chasing last year's fad and last year's manager, often to the detriment of the assets they are responsible for. Still, firings sometimes are unavoidable, says Stillman B. Brown, an executive vice-president at United Technologies Corp. who oversees the company's $4 billion pension fund, which is entrusted to 37 money-management companies. If any key portfolio managers leave or if a money firm changes ownership, Brown scales back the account or withdraws it entirely. "No matter what the performance was before the change, change does have an impact on investment performance," he says. Consequently, Brown fires three to five managers a year.

In their performance panic, money managers have been perfectly willing to dump stock abruptly. That may make sense to an individual manager, but when money managers do it collectively, the stampede can drive down the share prices of giants such as ITT, Digital Equipment, and Texas Instruments 30% in a few hours of fever-pitch selling. While the nimblest investors can make a lot of money on the ups and downs, how nimble can you be when you hold a million shares of a single stock? As a result, most money managers tend to do best when they spot a long trend and stick with it -- something they find harder and harder to do.

Violent swings in the market have had another peculiar consequence for the pros. They need the participation of individual investors, and they are no longer getting it. Individuals accounted for 85% of the trading activity on the New York Stock Exchange in 1965. Today they account for about 11%. As a result, there are fewer odd-lotters to fill a market role essential to the professionals. Who will play the "greater fool" on whom to unload doggy, overpriced stocks? "The institutional investors," the late stock market guru Benjamin Graham is reputed to have said, "are merely taking in each other's dirty laundry."

Small World. The melancholy thing about money managers is that they are still the nation's financial elite, controlling about two-thirds of the shares -- and accounting for nearly 90% of the trades -- on the Big Board. The pros are also responsible for virtually all the activity in the taxable bond market.

Considering its power, the universe of money managers is surprisingly small: More than 9,000 investment advisers, including newsletter writers, are registered with the Securities & Exchange Commission. New applications pour in at the rate of 200 per month. Yet only about 1,400 manage portfolios of more than $100 million in equities. Owners of successful management firms can earn millions of dollars each year.

Over the last decade, the tenfold increase in corporate and labor union pension funds fueled the money-management business far beyond anyone's expectations and allowed even the mediocre to survive. David L. Babson & Co., stuck in the bottom half of the performance rankings for most of the last 10 years, still manages almost $1 billion in institutional equity funds.

But new contributions to plans have slowed significantly, and many cash-starved corporations have discovered that they can tap their pension funds for a quick windfall (BW--Jan.21). The result is that new business is harder to come by. That ratchets up the desperation level. "Money management is a growth industry going into the early stages of maturity," says Kenneth L. Dowd, the Chemical Bank senior vice-president in charge of seven money-management subsidiaries whose combined assets total $12 billion.

True, emerging growth industries eventually will add to the pension assets. But high-tech America, with its young work force and few retired workers won't generate any large numbers from its pension assets for years. And when such companies jump into the pension benefit game, as Apple Computer Inc. did just six months ago, it usually is in the form of a defined-contribution plan. The company makes a prescribed payment to the employee's account, but the employee, not the company, selects one of several investment alternatives and bears the investment risk. Under more conventional defined-benefit plans, the company bears the risk, since it promises to pay a prescribed pension -- no matter how the pension account performed over the years.

Quotron Systems Inc., which recently adopted a defined-contribution plan, offers employees a choice of a guaranteed investment contract, a money market fund, or, for the daredevils, an S&P 500 index fund. "We'll accept a more modest rate of return because we want the employee's pension money to be absolutely secure," says Richard L. Little, the company's chief financial officer. Experience shows that when individuals take the risks, they prefer predictable returns such as those from guaranteed investment contracts to the uncertainties of stock-picking or interest-rate guessing. Even with defined-benefit plans, many corporations weary of the gyrations of the financial markets and become defensive in their investment policies. "Plan sponsors' first obligation is to preserve the pension fund assets, not to `grow' them,' says Meketa.

Aping the 500. Even if a company maintains a defined-benefit pension plan, the trend is to hew to a more "passive" investment policy. For example, a sponsor can purchase a nice portfolio of investment-grade bonds with a maturity and a yield that will produce the right amount of pension payments at the right time for any group of employees. The only drawback: Once the bonds are bought and turned over to a trustee, there's no chance of their earning a greater return -- or, therefore, of being able to reduce the corporate cash contribution in the coming years.

Another popular strategy, especially among the pension funds that are already too big to be very flexible in the market, is to invest part of the assets in a portfolio that mirrors the S&P 500-stock index -- in other words, an index fund. As in other investment strategies, the management fees can come to as little as 10% of the cost of managing the same size portfolio aggressively. Ironically, passive investment is considered a rather clever innovation in pension circles. But a decade ago, similar policies were excoriated as ineffective products of a cautious and plodding pension industry. In fact, passage of the Employee Retirement Income Security Act (ERISA), which just celebrated its 10th anniversary, was in part motivated by a desire to stimulate more aggressive investment and thus boost employee benefits.

The landmark legislation made corporate directors and other pension-plan trustees liable as fiduciaries for their employees' retirement funds. Nervous plan sponsors, fearful of employee lawsuits if they bungled pension investments, embraced independent "expert" money managers and investment-manager consultants, thus setting the stage for the prosperity of the money-management industry.

Since plan sponsors had a penchant for diversification and small management boutiques, the money was generously spread among a variety of managers. At one point before the company's breakup, American Telephone & Telegraph Co.'s $55 billion in pension funds was under the care of more than 100 outside investment managers. A post-divestiture AT&T pension fund, with a projected $18 billion to $20 billion in assets, will retain about 50 money managers.

Obviously, AT&T is still committed in principle to actively managing its funds. Nevertheless, says David P. Feldman, corporate vice-president for investment management, the company intends to make a major commitment to passive strategies, too. "When you look at the costs involved and the ability of large numbers of money managers to beat the market over time," he explains, "it's difficult to make a case against indexing substantial portions of your portfolio." That is why AT&T plans to index half the equity portion of its pension funds.

'Heat-Seeking Missile'. Even General Electric Co.'s pension fund, run by a team of in-house managers, recently placed $1.5 billion of its $5 billion in an index fund designed to track the S&P 500. Wells Fargo Investment Advisers, Mellon Capital Management, and Bankers Trust, all index-fund specialists, together took in more than $8 billion in new investments last year.

Index funds, which grew to $60 billion in only 10 years, "are like a heat-seeking missile on the tails of active equity managers," says Seth Lynn, president of Great American Core Investors Inc. Lynn, a former Bankers Trust Co. index fund manager, is now attempting to compete with his former employer. In fact, with a microcomputer and a telephone, there's no reason why he can't -- and thus undercut the already low rates that index funds charge for managing money. Index funds, says Lynn, "are becoming a commodity item."

Perhaps more threatening to active money managers are the new "second generation" index funds, which can be "tilted" toward a pension fund's particular bias. AT&T, for example, uses a "super" S&P fund that includes the 350 stocks ranked just below the 500 in market capitalization -- because, says AT&T's Feldman, those companies have tended to grow faster than the 500. Wilshire Associates manages a $1.6 billion index fund that replicates the performance of the top 5,000 stocks in the market without actually owning pieces of each. This is done by constructing a model and buying "sample" blocks of stocks in certain fixed proportions dictated by the model.

Is Less More? Although some of the largest private and some public employee pension funds are turning to investing by index, there still are those who believe they can beat the market with the right managers. If retaining one of a dozen consulting firms to conduct money-manager searches is any indication of plan sponsors' dissatisfaction, sponsors are miserable. SEI Evaluation Services conducted about 100 such searches last year, a 50% increase over 1983, says Howard H. Pohl, SEI's manager of consulting services.

But those who ultimately employ the managers, like Ryan Homes' McCann, are still smarting from bad experiences. And McCann says he will be far less patient with his two new managers, Sanford C. Bernstein & Co. and Avatar Associates. "I'd be disappointed if they didn't get us a 15% return" in 1985, he admits -- perhaps an unrealistic goal. "And if a manager digs a deep hole the first year, I'd seriously question whether we should stay with them."

There's no end to the frustrations. A switch in managers can itself eat up 1% to 2% of the value of an account, because of the commisssions and fees involved in unwinding an account and selling out positions. Thus if a fired manager loses 20% of the assets, the replacement has to make up 22% just to get his client even.

As companies concerned with the health of their pension plans and the welfare of their employees are beginning to realize, a little less pressure to manage aggressively probably produces about the same result at significantly less cost, less risk, and less disruption of the securities markets. Indeed, the inescapable conclusion to be drawn from the current crisis in money management is that less may well be more. The harder institutional investors try to get ahead of the S&P 500, the less likely they are to equal it.

[By Jeffrey M. Laderman in New York, with bureau reports]

DWIGHT EBERSOLE ANALYZES CORPORATE BONDS

Recently widowed and retired at age 62, Dwight Ebersole looks forward to the next phase of his life. As part of trying to remain active in retirement, Ebersole has decided to manage his investments more closely, and by himself rather than using a professional money manager. A substantial portion of his investment funds are likely to be in high-grade corporate bonds, and for that he seeks your help in analyzing some basics of bond investing.

Born and raised in St. Louis and educated in engineering at the University of Illinois, Mr. Ebersole spent virtually his entire working career in systems engineering and project management for Harris Corporation in Melbourne, Florida. He met and married Karen Clark soon after his graduation. Educated as a pharmacist, Karen decided not to pursue a career, preferring instead to stay at home and raise two girls and one boy. The three children are now all married and there are five grandchildren. Karen was diagnosed for cancer five years ago, and after three years of difficult radiation treatment, her health deteriorated steadily thereafter. Mrs. Ebersole passed away five months ago, just a few weeks before Dwight took early retirement from Harris.

Though he lives alone in a condominium in West Palm Beach, Mr. Ebersole is rarely alone and certainly never bored. He plays golf and tennis every week. He and three former colleagues at Harris jointly own an ocean-going yacht from which they enjoy deep sea fishing. He is active in his church. He attends Rotary on a regular basis. He tends his large flower garden and putters in his basement shop. And he visits his children and grandchildren in North Carolina and Massachusetts at every excuse.

All of this is possible financially because Harris has an excellent retirement program, and the Ebersoles saved well for many years when Dwight was well paid in his job with the company. As he begins his years of retirement, Mr. Ebersole finds that his retirement checks easily cover his living expenses and provide for his hobbies and for some travel.

His investment portfolio amounts to about $140,000. Over the years, the Ebersoles invested in common stocks, balanced mutual bonds, and occasional tax shelters. Fortunately, he was out of the stock market before the October 1987 crash. And so at this point, Dwight has decided to focus almost entirely on high-grade corporate bonds. While he has been willing to take on greater risk in the past, now he feels that he does not want to be in the stock market in the future. Thus his decision to focus only on corporate bonds. Moreover, the proceeds on his bond portfolio will amply provide for further travel when he wants, and also will allow him eventually to leave a modest estate to his heirs.

Although bonds were held in certain of the Ebersoles' mutual funds, he has had almost no experience investing in bonds directly. After reading as much as he could find in the local public library, Mr. Ebersole asks to meet with you to try and learn more about bond investing -- as well as to seek your advice about how he should go about beginning to build a portfolio of corporate bonds. You agree to try and help.

Because he was reared in St. Louis, and because he has been a longtime fan of the marvelous Clydesdale horses, Mr. Ebersole would like to investigate the corporate bonds of Anheuser-Busch Companies. Dwight owned shares of the Anheuser-Busch common stock over the years, but he never gave any thought to the bonds of the same company. He brings to your first meeting two sources of information. Exhibit 1 is a page on Anheuser-Busch from the Fall 1988 edition of MOODY'S HANDBOOK OF COMMON STOCKS. Exhibit 2 includes available data on Anheuser-Busch corporate bonds from the October 1988 issue of MOODY'S BOND RECORD.

As always, Dwight Ebersole is well organized -- as he presents to you the following list of specific questions on Anheuser Busch (the ticker symbol is "BUD") and its outstanding bonds:

(1)   Do the fifteen corporate bonds of BUD account for all of the almost $1.4 billion long term debt in the firm's capitalization?

(2)   For the BUD outstanding bonds, how does original cost compare with current market value? If there is a significant difference, how would you explain it?

(3)   Explain the maturity schedule of the BUD corporate bonds that range from 1990 to 2018.

(4)   Explain the Aa3 ratings assigned to BUD corporate bonds by Moody's. Are the yields-to-maturity on BUD bonds consistent with that assigned rating? Has BUD ever received other ratings on their corporate bonds?

(5)   Twelve of the BUD corporate bonds are callable, while the other three are non-callable? Why? Does callability matter to Anheuser-Busch? Does callability matter to investors who own BUD bonds?

(6) One issue of the BUD bonds is the 8.50 sinking fund debentures of 2017. What is a debenture? What is a sinking fund debenture? Is the current 88 bid price for that particular issue consistent with the 9.75% yield-to-maturity that is reported?

(7) How suitable would any of the BUD corporate bonds be for Dwight Ebersole as he begins to plan for his retirement? Which maturities would you recommend? Are the interest rates a factor to be considered by Mr. Ebersole?

Exhibit 1

ANHEUSER-BUSCH COMPANIES, INC.

LISTED	SYM.	LTPS♦	STPS♦	IND. DIV.	REC. PRICE	RANGE (52-WKS.)	YLD.
NYSE	BUD	131.6	95.0	$0.72	30	40 - 26	2.4%

HIGH GRADE. THIS COMPANY IS THE BREWING INDUSTRY'S LARGEST PRODUCER; STRONG BRAND NAMES HAVE LEADING MARKET POSITIONS.

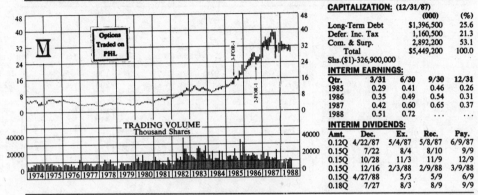

CAPITALIZATION: (12/31/87)

	(000)	(%)
Long-Term Debt	$1,396,500	25.6
Defer. Inc. Tax	1,160,500	21.3
Com. & Surp.	2,892,200	53.1
Total	$5,449,200	100.0

Shs.($1)-326,900,000

INTERIM EARNINGS:

Qtr.	3/31	6/30	9/30	12/31
1985	0.29	0.41	0.46	0.26
1986	0.35	0.49	0.54	0.31
1987	0.42	0.60	0.65	0.37
1988	0.51	0.72	...	...

INTERIM DIVIDENDS:

Amt.	Dec.	Ex.	Rec.	Pay.
0.12Q	4/22/87	5/4/87	5/8/87	6/9/87
0.15Q	7/22	8/4	8/10	9/9
0.15Q	10/28	11/3	11/9	12/9
0.15Q	12/16	2/3/88	2/9/88	3/9/88
0.15Q	4/27/88	5/3	5/9	6/9
0.18Q	7/27	8/3	8/9	9/9

BACKGROUND:

Anheuser-Busch Companies, Inc., is a holding company whose chief subsidiary is Anheuser-Busch, Inc., the world's largest brewer. In 1987, it accounted for about 40% of total brewing industry sales vs. 38% in 1986. Brands include MICHELOB, BUDWEISER, BUD LIGHT, BUSCH, NATURAL LIGHT, MICHELOB CLASSIC DARK, LA BRAND and KING COBRA. Beer volume sales in 1987 were 76.1 million barrels, compared with 72.3 million barrels in 1986. Other subsidiaries produce fresh baked goods and operate in the fields of container manufacturing and recycling, malt and rice production, wine, snack foods, baker's yeast, family entertainment cruise ships, major league baseball and transportation services. Dividends have been paid since 1932.

RECENT DEVELOPMENTS:

Net income for the quarter ended 6/30/88 rose 16% to a record $211.5 million compared with $181.8 million posted in 1987's similar period. Per share earnings gained 20% to $0.72, aided by fewer shares outstanding. Sales, excluding excise taxes, were up 7%. Earnings were fueled by continuing growth in beer operations. The brewing division sold 20.6 million barrels of beer, a 2.3% gain, reflecting high demand for BUDWEISER, BUSCH and light beer brands. Campbell Taggart and Busch Entertainment also recorded higher results.

PROSPECTS:

Anheuser-Busch has gained a 39.8% share of the U.S. beer market which should grow in the months ahead. Popularity of light beer augurs well for sales of BUD LIGHT, NATURAL LIGHT and MICHELOB LIGHT. Meanwhile, sales of BUDWEISER and BUSCH brands remain strong. International operations have benefited from a favorable export climate. BUDWEISER is sold in 47 countries and is brewed in Ireland and Denmark. A new brewery has been opened in Fort Collins to support increasing demand for the Company's products.

STATISTICS:

YEAR	GROSS REVS. ($mill.)	OPER. PROFIT MARGIN %	RET. ON EQUITY %	NET INCOME ($mill.)	WORK. CAP. ($mill.)	SENIOR CAPITAL ($mill.)	SHARES (000)	EARN. PER SH.$	DIV. PER SH.$	DIV. PAY. %	PRICE RANGE	P/E RATIO	AVG. YIELD %
	a	a											
78	2,259.6	9.8	14.7	111.0	236.4	427.3	270,828	0.41	0.14	33	4⅝ - 2⅞	9.2	3.6
79	2,775.9	8.9	15.8	196.4	100.7	507.9	271,572	h0.53	0.15	28	4½ - 3¼	7.3	3.9
80	3,295.4	9.5	16.6	171.8	38.9	743.8	271,104	0.64	0.17	26	5¼ - 4⅛	7.4	3.5
81	3,847.2	9.3	18.0	217.4	45.9	817.3	272,928	0.80	0.19	24	4⅞ - 4⅝	7.5	3.2
82	4,576.6	10.8	18.8	b274.0	45.8	969.0	289,752	b0.95	0.23	24	11¾ - 6⅜	9.6	2.5
83	6,034.2	11.7	19.7	347.8	175.1	1,247.4	290,370	1.09	0.27	25	12⅞ - 9¾	10.4	2.4
84	6,501.2	11.6	20.0	391.5	80.3	1,122.7	282,466	1.24	0.32	25	12⅜ - 8½	8.7	2.9
85	7,000.3	11.9	20.4	443.7	127.7	1,148.9	277,040	1.42	0.37	26	22⅞ - 11¾	12.2	2.1
c86	7,677.2	13.1	22.4	518.0	5.0	1,413.7	295,265	1.69	0.44	26	29¼ - 19¾	14.5	1.8
87	8,258.4	13.7	21.3	614.7	82.9	1,396.5	326,900	2.04	0.54	26	40½ - 25¾	16.1	1.6

♦Long-Term Price Score — Short-Term Price Score; see page 4a. STATISTICS ARE AS ORIGINALLY REPORTED. Adjusted for 3-for-1 stock split 6/85 and 2-for-1 split 9/86. a-Excludes excise taxes. b-Before gain from sale of property. c-Reflects change in accounting method for certain pension costs. h-Before accounting change.

INCORPORATED:
April 25, 1979 — Delaware

PRINCIPAL OFFICE:
One Busch Place
St. Louis, MO 63118
Tel: (314) 577-2000

ANNUAL MEETING:
Fourth Wed. in April

NUMBER OF STOCKHOLDERS:
64,343

TRANSFER AGENT(S):
Centerre Trust Co.
St. Louis, MO

REGISTRAR(S):
Mercantile Trust Co., N.A., St. Louis, MO
Centerre Trust Co., St. Louis, MO

INSTITUTIONAL HOLDINGS:
No. of Institutions: 587
Shares Held: 149,435,066

OFFICERS:
Chmn., C.E.O. & Pres.
A.A. Busch, III
V.P. & Secretary
J.L. Hayward
V.P. & Treasurer
G.C. Thayer
V.P. & Controller
O. Conrad

Exhibit 2

Issue	Interest Dates	Current Call Price	Moody's Rating	Current Price		Yield to Mat.	Price 1988 High	Price 1988 Low	Range 1946-87 High	Range 1946-87 Low	Amt. Outst. Mil.$	Sink. Fund Prov.	Legal Status	Fed. Tax	Issued	Price	Yld.
Anheuser-Busch Cos. nts. 14.00 1990[14]	F&A 4	N.C.	Aa3 r			-----	---	---	99⅞	99⅞	75.0	No	-------	N	1-22-87	99.88	14.05
do nts. 8.875 1994	M&S 1	[15] 100.00	Aa3 r	98¼	bid	9.26	102⅝	96⅝	99⅝	95½	100	No	-------	N	8-18-87	99.61	8.95
• do s.f.deb. 8.625 2016	J&D 1	§108.19▲	Aa3 r	90	bid	9.66	94⅛	85⅜	102	84¾	150	Yes	-------	N	Ref. fr. 12-1-96@	104.31	
do gtd.eurobonds 9.125 1992[16]	SEP 8	N.C.	Aa3	k 99¾	bid	9.20	101⅜	98⅜	---	---	100		-------	F	8-2-88	101.38	8.70
• do nts. 8.00 1996	A&O 1	[17] 100.00	Aa3 r	92½	bid	9.35	97¼	90⅛	102½	86⅛	100		-------	N	10-3-86	99.32	8.10
do s.f.deb. 10.00 2018	J&J 1	110.00▲	Aa3 r	100⅞	bid	9.90	100⅞	96¾	---	---	200	Yes	-------	N	6-23-88	100.00	10.00
do s.f.deb. 8.50 2017	M&S 1	§107.13▲	Aa3 r	88	bid	9.75	93⅜	84⅝	99	83⅜	150		-------	N	Ref. fr. 3-1-97@	103.75	
do euronts. 11.125 1993[18]	MAY30	[19] 101.00▲	Aa3	k103⅛	bid	10.26	105	102¾	113⅛	100	100		-------	F	4-22-85	100.00	11.13
do eurobonds 6.00 1994	APR 7	[20] 103.00▲	Aa3			-----	---	---	---	---	102	No	-------	F	4-7-86	100.00	6.00
do euroyen bonds 8.00 1995[21]	SEP20	N.C.	Aa3			-----	---	---	101	101	49.7	No	-------	F	9-10-85	101.00	7.85
•Anheuser-Busch Inc. s.f.deb. 5.45 1991	M&S 1	100.46▲	Aa3 r	92⅜	bid	9.00	97	89¾	103¼	63⅝	7.7	Yes	13	N	3-9-66	100.00	5.45
• do s.f.deb. 6.00 1992	J&J 1	100.75▲	Aa3 r	91⅞	sale	8.58	96½	89¾	100	58	7.7		13	N	7-19-67	100.00	6.00
• do s.f.deb. 7.95 1999	F&A 1	103.31▲	Aa3 r	94⅞	sale	8.71	96	90½	103¼	50¾	77.3		123	N	1-29-74	100.00	7.95
• do s.f.deb. 9.20 2005	A&O 1	104.42▲	Aa3 r	96	bid	9.69	100⅞	94⅜	112	57	134	Yes	123	N	4-10-75	100.00	9.20
• do s.f.deb. 8.55 2008	M&S 1	105.13▲	Aa3 r	90	bid	9.69	95	85	101	54	95.8	Yes	123	N	9-6-78	100.00	8.55

A CONVERTIBLE BOND FOR MILDRED HIGHTOWER

Mildred Hightower surprises you with a weekend telephone call. She is a longtime friend of your family, although you have not talked with her in several years. Upon learning that you are taking an investments course at Purdue University, she calls to ask for some advice.

Mildred is 53, divorced, and lives alone in a lovely home on the outskirts of Bloomington, Indiana. Her two children are grown and married, and she eagerly looks forward to grandchildren. Although she is well set financially, Mildred runs a stationery/gift shop out of her home on a part time basis. She is interested in investments -- and especially in some of the less traditional alternatives.

Recently, her stockbroker at E.G. Button recommended a new issue of convertible bonds by the Ralston Rubber Company. The bonds, rated Ba2 by Moody's, have a twenty year maturity and a 11% coupon. The bonds were just issued at $1,000 par value through an underwriting syndicate that includes E.G. Button. The convertible bonds have an 8-year deferred call provision. They are callable in the ninth year at $1,060 -- and at $5 less during each successive year.

Each bond is convertible into twenty shares of Ralston Rubber common stock that currently sells for $30 per share and pays an annual cash dividend of $2.50 per share. The research department at E.G. Button believes that earnings, dividends, and stock price of the common stock will grow 8% annually (indefinitely). They also indicate that Ba2 nonconvertible bonds currently sell to yield 12%.

Mrs. Hightower admits to not understanding the significance of all these bond features -- and hence her telephone call to you. Her stockbroker, who has been helpful in the past, seems unusually eager for her to buy some of the new issue.

After briefly discussing the recent Indiana-Purdue football game, she asks for your overall advice on whether she should purchase 10-15 of the convertible bonds. You agree to take a look at the convertible bond issue and discuss it with her in a few days. A number of questions occur to you as you begin your analysis for Mrs. Hightower:

(1)   What should be the approximate market price of 20-year, 11% coupon, straight bonds that are rated Ba2?

(2) Assuming no change in the yield structure, what should happen to the market price of such straight bonds between now and maturity in twenty years? Draw a graph of that expected bond price behavior.

(3) What is the expected price behavior of the Ralston Rubber Company common shares that are equivalent to one of the convertible bonds? Plot that behavior on the same graph. When would you expect the straight bond and common stock equivalents to sell at about the same price?

(4) How does the call feature of the convertible bond impact your analysis? Would you expect conversion at some future date?

(5) Based on your analysis for the above questions, what do you expect to happen to the market price of the Ralston Rubber Company convertible bond that Mrs. Hightower is considering?

(6) What is the yield-to-maturity on the convertible bond? Is that yield consistent with the yields on straight bonds and Ralston common stock, respectively?

(7) How would your analysis change if the operating results and future prospects for Ralston Rubber Company were to improve and its convertible bond rating was raised to Baa?

FLEMING RE-ASSESSES JUNK BONDS

On May 26, 1988, Dr. Martin Fleming returns home after a busy day of medical practice at the Spencer Family Clinic. After dinner with his wife and two teenage children, he settles down on his patio to review the day's mail and newspapers. When he finally gets to the WALL STREET JOURNAL, Fleming immediately notices and carefully reads a front-page article entitled "Junk Juggernaut: How Drexel Wields Its Power For High-Yield Bonds." The article is very disturbing to him and he decides to call his stockbroker, Jason Kell, the next morning.

Martin Fleming grew up in a medium-size community of southern Michigan. He was an excellent student and athlete in high school, thus earning himself a scholarship to the University of Michigan. Although Martin made the Wolverine baseball team his freshman year as a left-handed relief pitcher, a bad elbow curtailed his athletic career during his sophomore year. With all his energies thus devoted to academic studies, Fleming graduated with honors in pre-med, and was admitted to the School of Medicine at the same institution.

Five years later, Dr. Martin Fleming graduated from the University of Michigan with his medical degree, married Donna Ringel whom he met and dated steadily during the last two years of medical school, and accepted a position at a family practice clinic in Detroit, and relatively near their parents.

Dr. Fleming's general practice grew steadily from the very outset, and he looked forward to a busy but fulfilling career. After their daughter and son were about to begin grade school, MarTin and Donna began planning for both geographical and occupational change. Donna was eager to begin her career as a speech therapist, while Martin was interested in a smaller medical practice wherein he would have a greater say in policy- making and overall administration. The Flemings also were interested in a smaller community and school system for their two children.

Fortunately, those objectives were accomplished when the Flemings decided to move to a progressive community on the outskirts of St. Paul, Minnesota. Donna was chosen to fill a new position as speech consultant for the local school district, while Martin joined a small medical practice as one of the more senior partners. With the combined income of their two professional positions, the Flemings looked forward to very comfortable years in Minnesota.

After settling into their new home and surroundings, Martin and Donna began planning for their financial future. In addition to their home, possessions, and generous retirement programs, they rather quickly began to accumulate an investment portfolio, the proceeds of which they hope will provide educational expenses for their two kids, occasional international travel, and supplemental funding for their eventual retirement. In view of their considerable conservatism, it is perhaps not surprising that their initial investments were in a balanced mutual fund (no-load), and a few round lots of the common shares of three or four blue-chip common stocks.

Two years ago, after a couple of years in which their particular stocks did not fare very well, Martin Fleming began to wonder if he and Donna were on the best track in terms of their investment portfolio. After considerable reading and numerous requests for investment advice from friends and professionals, he was led to a new relationship with Jason Kell, an account executive at a leading securities firm in Detroit. Kell was quite friendly, knowledgeable, and seemed to understand quickly what the Flemings needed from their investment portfolio.

Although Mr. Kell was able to handle a variety of investment alternatives for his varied clients, his specialty turned out to be in "high yield" bonds of corporations that were experiencing some degree of financial difficulty. Martin eventually decided that Jason Kell was suggesting an investment opportunity that has become known as "junk bonds." Kell indicated his belief that families such as the Flemings could probably afford to take on an above-average level of risk -- and, if so, they could expect to receive an unusually large rate of return on their investment. Kell proceeded to describe in some detail the particular high-yield bonds which he felt were the best alternatives at the present time.

After considerable discussion with Jason Kell, the Flemings decided to switch about half of their investment funds to a series of four bonds proposed by the account executive. Their investment results for the eighteen months were extremely positive, to the point that Martin Fleming became a very strong advocate of investing in these "junk bonds that very few investors are willing to touch at all." Donna remained a bit skeptical about their riskier investment -- but, as Martin reminded her, who can argue with such positive results?

Three months ago, however, Martin noticed in his monthly statement that their total portfolio value was down by a few thousand dollars. He immediately called Jason Kell and was informed that one of their four bonds was experiencing considerable difficulty, and that its market value had dropped by a rather significant percentage. He tried to explain that the Flemings had done quite well with their revised portfolio strategy, and that the latest development should be viewed as somewhat normal for high-return, high-risk investments of that type. To provide further information on the results of investing in high-yield bonds, Mr. Kell mailed to Fleming a copy of a recent article by Professor Edward Altman of New York University (see Reading #5).

The Flemings were, of course, quite concerned about this recent development of their investment portfolio -- but they decided to just wait and see would happen in the future. And that was the mind-set of Martin Fleming as he re-read the WALL STREET JOURNAL article, after a long day in his professional practice. Later, Martin shared with Donna -- his growing concern about their investment portfolio. Per her inquiry, Martin reported to Donna that their portfolio currently had a total market value of $84,500 -- with $31,200 in common stocks and $53,300 in high-yield bonds.

As a result of their family conversation, Martin did call Jason Kell the next morning. Apparently Kell had had a very busy morning in answering the inquiries of a number of concerned families who had followed his recommendations in revising their investment portfolios toward a relatively large position in junk bonds.

If you were Kell, how would you respond to the following questions as part of the ensuing conversation:

(1) Just how do "junk bonds" fit into the spectrum of possible investments for a professional family such as Donna and Martin Fleming?

(2) Does the considerable predominance of the Drexel firm in this new market a positive or negative factor? What else should the Flemings know about what is going on?

(3) Is there some way to measure the true downside risk of the junk bonds? Do we have enough experience in May 1988 to really know what is going on in this development?

(4) Is the portfolio mix of the Fleming portfolio still appropriate for a family in their particular position?

(5) Given subsequent experience, what portion of the Flemings' total investment portfolio should be allocated to "junk bonds"?

69

BOND PORTFOLIO FOR BETSY MORTON

Mrs. Betsy Morton became a widow in late 1988 at the age of 70. After collecting modest life insurance held by her late husband, the settling of his estate, and the sale of an income property held for many years by the family, Mrs. Morton finds herself in a relatively secure financial position. Her modest home in a midwestern suburban area is paid in full, she owns a new model automobile, her personal possessions are in good order, and she has no debts. Unfortunately, Mrs. Morton has no social security or other retirement benefits from her husband. She does have a passbook savings account of approximately $25,000 that earns 5.5% annually. She views this as her emergency funds. Mrs. Morton also expects to receive about $350 per month from the second mortgage which arose from the sale of the income property.

Her other asset is $200,000, the cash proceeds from the sale of the income property. Mrs. Morton has come to you for advice on how to proceed with that investment. She informs you that she is interested in income from her investment, as well as in safeguarding the principal. The income will allow her to do some traveling and to give some gifts to her four grandchildren.

Remembering the depression, Mrs. Morton is quite reluctant to invest in the stock market or in any securities for that matter. However, after careful explanation, you convince her that investing in corporate and government bonds is a relatively safe way to invest her funds. Her only additional constraint is that there likely will be federal taxes of approximately $15,000 due in April of 1989 as a result of the sale of the income property. It also would be desirable for her monthly income to be reasonably constant during the year.

Your task, therefore, is to construct a $200,000 bond portfolio for Mrs. Morton that reflects her goals, constraints, and current financial status. You decide to limit selection to U.S. government securities and to higher quality corporate bonds. In preparing specific recommendations, you consider the following questions:

(1) In terms of diversification, how many different bond issues would you recommend for Mrs. Morton? How would you decide on an appropriate mix between corporate and government bonds?

(2) Given Mrs. Morton's great concern for safety, what bond ratings would you consider?

(3)   What range of bond maturities would you include in the
      recommended bond portfolio?

(4)   Since the interest on most bonds is paid semi-annually,
      how would you construct the bond portfolio so that Mrs.
      Morton can expect a relatively constant monthly income?
      Do you recommend high or low coupons?

(5)   How important will transaction costs be for the bond
      portfolio of Betsy Morton?

(6)   In view of these considerations, what specific
      portfolio of bonds do you recommend for Mr. Morton?

The Anatomy of the High-Yield Bond Market

Edward I. Altman

Between June 1986 and April 1987, the high-yield debt market grew from $93 billion to over $125 billion. High-yield debt is now approaching 20 per cent of the total corporate straight-debt market. "Fallen angels" comprise about 30 per cent of the high-yield total, but original issues continue to gain ground. In 1986, new-issue high-yield debt broke all previous records, accounting for 22 per cent of the total corporate straight debt issued that year; about 50 per cent of the new-issue dollars went for merger and acquisition-related activities.

The total amount of high-yield debt defaulting in 1986 also shattered the previous record. Over 55 per cent of the $3 billion total was related to the giant LTV bankruptcy. Although not a record, the default rate—3.39 per cent of total straight debt outstanding as of mid-1986—was high for a non-recession year and heavily concentrated in steel and energy issues. Even after accounting for defaults, however, the total rate of return on a diversified portfolio of high-yield issues was a respectable 16.1 per cent for the year.

An examination of the credit quality of the high-yield market reveals that, while overall quality declined, the quality of lower-rated debt and of new issues improved. The Zeta credit scoring model red-flagged all the 1986 defaults. This would have allowed investors to save between 29 and 40 per cent by selling prior to default.

BY ALMOST ANY STANDARD (excepting total annual rate of return), the high-yield bond market enjoyed a record year in 1986. The volume and dollar amount of new-issue high-yield debt rose substantially, both in absolute terms and relative to the total corporate straight-debt market. Competition for new underwritings and secondary market-making intensified. And the amount of high-yield debt defaulting shattered all previous records, thanks in large measure to the giant LTV bankruptcy in July.

Edward Altman is a Consultant to Morgan Stanley & Co., Incorporated and Professor of Finance at the Graduate School of Business Administration of New York University.

Portions of this article are reproduced, with permission, from E. Altman, 'The Anatomy of the High Yield Debt Market: 1986 Update," Morgan Stanley & Co., Incorporated, April 1987.

The large number of defaults in 1986 has added significantly to our database for calculating default rates and losses, for analyzing short-term price change after default and for evaluating the correspondence between credit quality and default. This article examines the anatomy of the current high-yield debt market—its size and rate of return, its default rates and losses and its overall quality.

Market Size and Rates of Return

The high-yield debt market climbed in relative importance from 14.1 per cent of total corporate publicly traded straight debt in June 1985 to 18.4 per cent one year later (Table I). The average outstanding issue size grew impressively (to $85 million), as did the average issuer amount. We estimate that the market totaled about $93 billion as of June 1986 and was over $125 billion as

Table I Public Straight Debt Outstanding, 1970–1986 (millions of dollars)

Year	Par Value Public Straight Debt Outstanding Over Year[a]	Low-Rated Debt[b]			
		Straight Public Debt	% of Public St. Debt	Amount Outstanding Per Issuer	Amount Outstanding Per Issue
1986	$505,150	$92,985	18.4%	$181	$85
1985	419,600	59,178	14.1	135	55
1984	358,100	41,700	11.6	125	49
1983	319,400	28,223	8.8	93	39
1982	285,600	18,536	6.5	69	33
1981	255,300	17,362	6.8	62	32
1980	265,100	15,125	5.7	59	31
1979	269,900	10,675	4.0	47	30
1978	252,200	9,401	3.7	49	30
1977	237,800	8,479	3.5	46	27
1976	219,200	8,015	3.7	41	27
1975	200,600	7,720	3.8	41	27
1974	167,000	11,101[d]	6.6	59	35
1973	154,800[c]	8,082	5.2	45	29
1972	145,700	7,106	4.9	45	29
1971	132,500	6,643	5.0	45	29
1970	116,200	6,996	6.0	48	32

a. Average of beginning and ending years' figures (1974–86).
b. Source: *Standard & Poor's Bond Guide* and *Moody's Bond Record*, July issues of each year. Defaulted railroads excluded. Also includes non-rated debt equivalent to rated debt for low-rated firms.
c. Estimates for 1973 and earlier based on linear regression of this column vs. the Federal Reserve's Corporate Bonds Outstanding figures (*Federal Reserve Bulletin*).
d. Includes $2.7 billion in Con Edison debt.

of April 1, 1987. These figures include both "fallen angels" and original-issue high-yield debt.

Fallen angels comprised 31.8 per cent of the market in June 1986 and, by preliminary estimates, amounted to about 30.0 per cent as of March 1, 1987 (Table II). The fallen angel proportion was swelled by about $4 billion of USX Corporation debt, which was dropped to non-investment-grade status in February 1987 by both Standard & Poor's and Moody's. This continues a trend of industrial fallen angel debt displacing electric utility issues within the high-yield population. The utilities' proportion continued to decrease.

Returns

In 1986, a diversified portfolio of high-yield debt returned 16.09 per cent (Table III).[1] The

1. Footnotes appear at end of article.

Table II Fallen Angel (FA) Proportion of the High-Yield Debt (HYD) Market

Fallen Angel Totals	December 1985		June 1986		March 1987	
Rated Issues						
Amount (millions)	$23,165		$29,564		$36,101	
No. of issues	350		321		339	
No. of issuers	72		92		100	
Utilities						
Amount (millions)	$ 8,758		$ 4,929		$ 5,054	
No. of issues	196		107		108	
No. of issuers	13		7		7	
Total FA Dollars	$23,165	= 31.1%	$29,564	= 31.8%	$36,101	= 30.0%
Total HYD Outstanding	$74,514		$92,985		$120,336	
Total FA Issues	350	= 29.9%	321	= 29.4%	339	= 24.0%
Total HYD Issues Outstanding	1,170		1,093		1,410	
Total FA Issuers	72	= 14.8%	92	= 17.9%	100	= 12.3%
Total HYD Issuers Outstanding	488		514		815	

Table III Annual Returns, Yields and Spreads on Long-Term (LT) Government Bonds and High-Yield (HY) Bonds

Year	Return (%)			Promised Yield (%)[a]		
	HY[b]	LT Govt[c]	Spread	HY	LT Govt	Spread
1987	N.A.	N.A.	N.A.	12.67	7.60	5.07
1986	16.09	24.08	−7.99	14.45	9.55	4.90
1985	22.51	31.54	−9.03	15.40	11.65	3.75
1984	8.50	14.82	−6.32	14.97	11.87	3.10
1983	21.80	2.23	19.57	15.74	10.70	5.04
1982	32.45	42.08	−9.63	17.84	13.86	3.98
1981	7.56	0.48	7.08	15.97	12.08	3.89
1980	−1.00	−2.96	1.96	13.46	10.23	3.23
1979	3.69	−0.86	4.55	12.07	9.13	2.94
1978	7.57	−1.11	8.68	10.92	8.11	2.81
Arithmetic Averages:						
1978–1983	12.01	6.64	5.37	14.33	10.68	3.65
1978–1986	13.24	12.25	0.99	14.54	10.80	3.74
Compound Averages:						
1978–1983	11.45	5.62	5.83			
1978–1986	12.80	11.21	1.59			

a. Promised yield as of beginning of year. It represents the internal rate of return based on the security's current price and scheduled payments of interest and principal.
b. Morgan Stanley composite generated from over 440 high-yield issues. Actual portfolio ranged in size from 153 in 1978 to 339 issues in 1983. This database goes through 3/31/84; Morgan Stanley estimates based on Standard & Poor's data for 1985–86.
c. Shearson Lehman Long-Term Government Index.

arithmetic and geometric average returns for the 1978–86 period were 13.24 and 12.80 per cent, respectively, resulting in return spreads (over long-term government bonds) of 0.99 and 1.59 per cent—positive, but small. High-yield composite return is calculated net of defaults; the higher coupon appears to compensate for the greater default risk.

Return spreads for each of the last three years were negative, as long-term governments performed exceptionally well in a consistently declining interest rate environment. As the average duration on high-yield debt is more than two years less than that of the Shearson-Lehman goverment index, we are not surprised by this differential. Over this same three-year period, however, yield spreads widened from 310 basis points at the start of 1984 to 507 basis points at the start of 1987. (Yield spreads have fallen considerably since the beginning of 1987.) This indicates that, while interest rates in general have declined, yields on high-yield debt have remained relatively high. There are several possible reasons, including the large volume of new issues requiring attractive promised yields and the continuing concern with the credit quality in the market.

Figure A illustrates the performances of fixed income mutual funds over various 10-year periods; Figure B shows their performances over the last three years, as well as in 1985 and 1986 alone.[2] These results, while always lower than composite indexes (because of fees, transaction costs and other expenses), reflect the same relative long and short-term performance numbers. For example, the compound rate of return on high-current-yield funds over the 10-year period 1977–86 was 166.6 per cent, compared with 156.8 per cent for government bond funds and 159.1 per cent for Single-A funds. The picture is very different, however, over the last three years (1984–86), with high-yield funds trailing all other fixed income portfolios.

A Record New-Issue Year

The past year set records for the amount of new high-yield debt issued, the number of issues, the average size of new issues and the proportion of total new corporate straight debt comprising high-yield issues. Net new high-yield issues totaled $34.177 billion (Table IV)— far more than 1984 and 1985 combined—bringing the total new high-yield debt issued since 1978 to just under $80 billion. The 1986 total does *not* include exchange offers and recapitalizations of $9.6 billion and private placements coming public of $3.4 billion.

High-yield debt comprised 22 per cent of the total corporate straight debt market, easily surpassing the prior year's high (15.8 per cent in 1983). Of the year's 234 issues (a 25 per cent increase over 1985), 11 were greater than $500

Figure A   Selected Groups of Long-Term Taxable Bond Funds:
Total Reinvested Return for 10-Year Periods

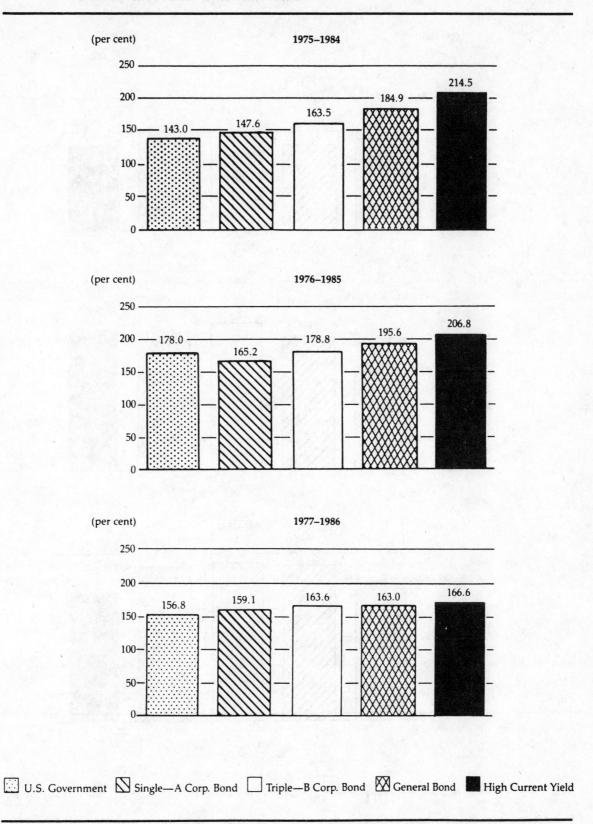

Source: Lipper Analytical Services, Inc., New York.

Figure B   Selected Groups of Long-Term Taxable Bond Funds:
Total Reinvested Return for One and Three-Year Periods, 1984 to 1985

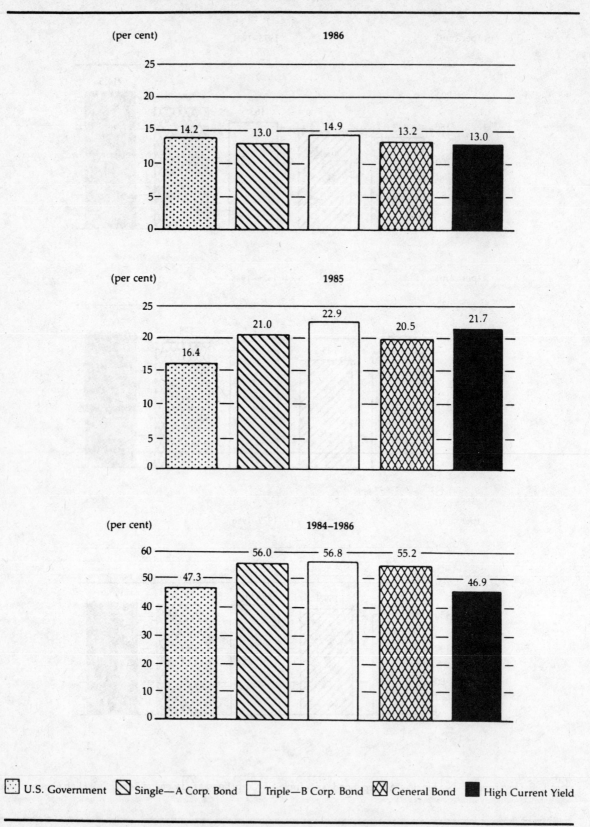

Source: Lipper Analytical Services, Inc., New York.

Table IV New Non-Convertible Domestic Debt Issues, 1978–1986[a] (millions of dollars)

Year	Total Par Value New Public Straight Debt Issues		Total Par Value New High-Yield Debt Issues		% New Issue Dollars	Variable Rate Debt	
	Amount	No.	Amount	No.	Pct.	Amount	No.
1986[b]	$155,672	1,041	$34,177	234	22.0%	$ 661	8
1985	101,098	1,212	14,670	188	14.5	2,543	12
1984	99,416	721	14,952	124	15.0	3,927	27
1983	46,903	511	7,417	86	15.8	—	—
1982	47,798	513	2,798	48	5.9	40	1
1981	41,651	357	1,648	32	4.0	104	2
1980	37,272	398	1,442	43	3.9	137	4
1979	25,678	277	1,307	45	5.0	—	—
1978	22,416	287	1,493	52	6.7	—	—
Total	$577,904	5,317	$79,904	852	12.0%	$7,412	54

Source: Morgan Stanley & Co., Incorporated and *Investors Dealers Digest*.
a. Not including exchange offers, secondary offerings, tax exempts, convertibles of government agencies.
b. In 1985, exchange offers and reorganization issues totaled $3.96 billion; retirements were $1.62 billion and secondary issues were at least $1.1 billion. In 1986, exchange offers and recapitalizations totaled $9.6 billion and retirements were over $8 billion. Private placements coming public totaled $3.4 billion.

million and 54 (23 per cent) were greater than $200 million (Table V), compared with 19 (10 per cent) greater than $200 million in 1985. The average issue size was $146 million. Table VI gives the breakdown by Standard & Poor's original-issue bond rating. About 57 per cent of the new issues in 1986, comprising 62 per cent of the new-issue dollars, were rated B.

We estimate that about 50 per cent of the new-issue dollars went for merger and acquisition-related deals, including LBO activity. The reason we are somewhat vague about the exact percentage is that the proceeds from a new issue may not be used entirely for the merger, and the exact purpose is not always clear. Still, 50 per cent is a relatively high proportion and the dollars involved are substantial. We can probably expect that amount to diminish in 1987 if takeovers meet legislative resistance and the stock market continues to rise (as it has in the early months of 1987), making LBOs and other acquisitions more costly.

Exchange debt in 1986 grew dramatically, reaching over $9.6 billion on 27 issues (Table VII); $5.8 billion of the total was used in LBO activity, $3.8 billion (19 issues) for other purposes. Most of these "other" purposes involved distressed company exchange issues. Some of these (including LTV, Crystal Oil, Petro Lewis and Damson Oil) were not successful. Still, the default rate would no doubt have been higher without these distressed exchange issues.

Underwriting Activity

Much has been made of late about the increased competitive nature of new-issue underwritings in the high-yield debt market and the apparent increased liquidity of issues in secondary markets, as well. Table VIII reinforces these observations. It appears that Drexel Burnham Lambert, while still the dominant firm, has seen its market share cut somewhat, from 69 per cent in 1984 to about 46 per cent in 1986. In terms of new-issue size, Drexel's average issue was larger ($191 million) than any other firm's. Merrill Lynch was second in total dollars and number of issues, with 11 per cent of the market and an average size of $151 million. Morgan Stanley's average size ($188 million) was just below Drexel's, and its overall amount put it in a third place tie with Salomon Brothers.

Default Rates and Losses

Defaults, defined as either debt issues dropping to a D rating or involved in a formal bankruptcy (whichever comes first) reached record levels in 1986. The $3.156 billion in defaults easily sur-

Table V Distribution of 1986 New Issues by Size of Issue

Size (Millions of Dollars)	No. of Issues	Percentage of Total
0.0–24.9	11	4.70
25.0–49.9	42	17.95
50.0–99.9	52	22.22
100.0–199.9	75	32.05
200.0–499.9	43	18.38
500.0 +	11	4.70
	234	100.00

Table VI Rating of Public High-Yield New Issues[a]

Year	S&P Rating	Total Amount Issued (thousands)	Number of Issues	Average Years to Maturity	Average Issue Amount (thousands)
1986[b]	BBB/Ba[c]	$ 765,000	7	10	$109,000
	BB	7,098,000	37	12	192,000
	B	21,260,000	133	11	160,000
	CCC	4,618,000	40	12	115,000
	No Rating	436,000	17	12	26,000
		34,177,000	234	11	146,000
1985	BBB/Ba	1,065,000	11	10	96,818
	BB	2,040,750	23	11	88,728
	B	6,038,033	77	11	78,416
	CCC	1,668,000	14	11	119,143
	No Rating	3,858,641	63	11	61,248
		14,670,424	188	11	78,034
1984	BBB/Ba	1,290,000	5	9	258,000
	BB	4,698,000	23	13	204,260
	B	6,484,500	68	11	95,360
	CCC	1,476,000	9	12	164,000
	No Rating	1,003,469	19	13	52,814
		14,951,969	124	12	120,580
1983	BBB/Ba	—	—	—	—
	BB	2,893,738	24	17	120,572
	B	3,713,451	46	14	80,727
	CCC	285,000	5	17	57,000
	No Rating	525,000	11	11	47,727
		7,417,189	86	15	86,246
1982	BBB/Ba	60,000	2	11	30,000
	BB	1,378,000	16	12	86,125
	B	1,122,292	24	14	46,762
	CCC	145,050	2	13	72,525
	No Rating	92,311	4	23	23,078
		2,797,653	48	14	58,284
1981	BBB/Ba	$ 290,000	4	11	$ 72,500
	BB	290,000	6	19	48,333
	B	893,667	15	18	59,578
	CCC	—	—	—	—
	No Rating	174,500	7	11	24,929
		1,648,167	32	16	51,505
1980	BBB/Ba	50,000	1	7	50,000
	BB	418,000	9	18	46,444
	B	878,625	28	19	31,379
	CCC	25,000	1	15	25,000
	No Rating	70,000	4	14	17,500
		1,441,625	43	18	33,526
1979	BBB/Ba	—	—		—
	BB	359,000	8	18	44,875
	B	852,600	33	18	25,836
	CCC	91,400	3	15	30,467
	No Rating	4,000	1	15	4,000
		1,307,000	45	18	29,044
1978	BBB/Ba	40,000	1	20	40,000
	BB	407,875	10	19	40,787
	B	1,029,025	39	19	26,385
	CCC	12,000	1	15	12,000
	No Rating	4,000	1	15	4,000
		1,429,900	52	19	28,710
Total 1978–1986		$79,903,927	852	13	$93,784

Source: Morgan Stanley & Co., Incorporated.

a. Does not include convertibles, secondary offerings, exchange or best efforts offerings.

b. Aggregate amounts for all public straight debt excluding exchange issues and private placements going public. Also does not include $8.4 billion of convertible debt.

c. BBB included if Moody's ranked below investment grade.

Table VII High-Yield Exchange Debt Issues, 1978–1986

Year	Number of Issues	Dollar Amount (millions)	Average Amount (millions)
1986*	27	$9,643	$357
1985	27	2,725	101
1984	10	702	70
1983	16	486	30
1982	5	529	106
1981	2	323	162
1980	5	645	129
1979	6	227	38
1978	12	662	55

* Includes recapitalization issues and $5.8 billion of LBO-related exchange debt. Non-LBO exchange debt in 1986 was $3.8 billion on 19 issues.

passed the next highest year—1985, with under $1 billion (Table IX). We include all defaulting debt in the totals, not just original-issue high-yield bonds. LTV-related defaulting debt totaled $1.766 billion, or 56 per cent of the total defaulting straight debt in 1986.[3]

The default rate in 1986 was 3.39 per cent of the amount of straight debt outstanding as of June 30, 1986. As Table X indicates, the 1986 rate was relatively high, although not a record; however, the amount easily broke the prior calendar-year high. Only in 1977 was the default rate higher than 1986, and the market was much smaller then, consisting of virtually 100 per cent fallen angels.

Analyzing the Default Rate

The 1986 default rate is somewhat difficult to analyze. On the one hand, the rate is quite high, especially for a non-recession year, reflecting an increased overall vulnerability to distress, and the rate would have been higher if exchange issues for distressed firms had not been successful in avoiding some defaults. On the other hand, despite the 3.39 per cent rate, and a somewhat lower loss rate, the total rate of return on a diversified portfolio of high-yield debt was a respectable 16.1 per cent. And if one excludes LTV, the default rate was only about 1.50 per cent—close to the average annual rate of 1.53 per cent for the 1974–85 period.

It appears that the combination of a bad recessionary period *and* two or three really large defaults would be necessary to cause default rates to rise to the 4 to 5 per cent range in the future. For 1987, a default rate of 4 per cent would mean about $5 billion in defaults—a number that "requires" many large defaults.

Table VIII New Issues by Leading Underwriters, 1982–1986 (millions of dollars)

Underwriter	1986				1985				1984				1983				1982			
	Amount	%	Number	%	Amount	%	Number	%	Amount	%	Number	%	Amount	%	Number	%	Amount	%	Number	%
Drexel Burnham Lambert	15,775	45.86	82	35.04	7,239	49.71	83	44.15	10,358	69.28	67	54.03	4,346	58.60	46	53.49	1,544	55.18	28	58.33
Merrill Lynch	3,782	10.95	25	10.68	666	4.57	9	4.79	530	3.54	4	3.23	427	5.76	5	5.81	699	24.99	7	14.58
Morgan Stanley	2,817	8.16	15	6.28	1,050	7.21	13	6.91	319	2.13	5	4.03	80	1.08	1	1.16	—	—	—	—
Salomon Brothers	2,814	8.15	16	6.41	1,464	10.06	13	6.91	865	5.79	9	7.26	423	5.70	4	4.65	—	—	—	—
Shearson Lehman	1,903	5.51	11	4.60	708	4.86	8	4.26	718	4.80	8	6.45	230	3.10	1	1.16	25	0.89	1	2.08
First Boston	1,650	4.78	11	4.60	640	4.39	9	4.79	390	2.61	5	4.03	325	4.38	3	3.49	—	—	—	—
Goldman Sachs	1,228	3.56	9	3.77	615	4.22	5	2.66	100	0.67	1	0.81	125	1.69	1	1.16	—	—	—	—
Bear Stearns	1,145	3.32	14	5.86	456	3.13	7	3.72	360	2.41	4	3.23	380	5.12	5	5.81	35	1.25	1	2.08
Kidder Peabody	880	2.55	7	2.93	—	—	—	—	—	—	—	—	—	—	—	—	—	—	—	—
PaineWebber	545	1.58	4	2.93	206	1.41	2	1.06	65	0.43	1	0.81	235	3.17	3	3.49	225	8.04	1	2.08
E.F. Hutton	370	1.07	5	2.09	280	1.92	2	1.06	145	0.97	3	2.42	190	2.56	2	2.33	83	2.95	2	4.17
Prudential-Bache	357	1.03	4	1.67	435	2.99	8	4.26	950	6.35	13	10.48	275	3.71	6	6.98	40	1.43	1	2.08
Donaldson, Lufkin & Jenrette Inc.	338	0.98	7	2.93	—	—	—	—	—	—	—	—	—	—	—	—	—	—	—	—
Others	864	2.50	24	9.62	804	5.52	29	15.43	152	1.02	4	3.23	381	5.14	9	10.47	147	5.27	7	14.58
Totals	34,117		234		14,562		188		14,952		124		7,417		86		2,798		48	

Table IX Public Corporate Debt Defaulting on Interest and/or Principal, 1970–1986[a] (millions of dollars)

Year of Default	Straight Debt	Convertible Debt	Total Debt in Default
1986	$3,155.16	$ 299.62	$ 3,455.38
1985	992.10	310.02	1,302.12
1984	344.16	279.95	624.11
1983	301.08[b]	111.55	412.63
1982	752.34[c]	243.29	995.63
1981	27.00	52.61	79.61
1980	224.11	31.60	255.71
1979	20.00	10.70	30.70
1978	118.90	73.30	192.20
1977	380.57	74.21	454.78
1976	29.51	83.99	113.50
1975	204.10	115.63	319.73
1974	122.82	165.87	288.69
1973	49.07	150.84	199.91
1972	193.25	79.34	272.59
1971	82.00	42.90	124.90
1970	796.71	135.81	932.52
Total	$7,793.48	$2,261.23	$10,054.71

a. Also includes those issues whose ratings dropped to D because of missed interest payments, but did not legally default.
b. Although Baldwin United's debt in 1983 was not rated investment grade just prior to default, we are told that it was not possible to trade these issues after it dropped below triple-B.
c. Includes $175 million in Johns Manville debt rated investment grade prior to default.

Of course, one must include LTV in default rate calculations, and it brings the average annual rate over the 1974–86 period to 1.67 per cent, with a slightly higher 1.73 per cent over the last four years (1983–86). The default rate on all corporate straight debt—investment and noninvestment grade—rose to about 0.20 of 1 per cent for the 1970–86 period and 0.19 of 1 per cent for the more recent 1978–86 period. This reflects the record (except for 1970) rate of 0.636 per cent in 1986 (Table XI).

Table XII gives the breakdown of defaults by industrial sector over the 1970–86 period. Defaults were heavily concentrated in steel and energy issues, reflecting the economic realities of the country.

Between 1985 and 1986, oil and gas-related defaults went from 18 to 29, with a 12.7 per cent increase in amounts.[4] The relative proportion of this sector's contribution to total defaults increased from 15 to over 20 per cent. General manufacturing, including steel, showed the greatest increase, from 9 per cent of the total (1970–85) to over 29.5 per cent, mainly fueled by LTV. Counting LTV as just one default, the number of general manufacturing defaults increased to 23 from 18. (If one includes each of

LTV's issuing subsidiaries, 1986 defaults numbered 33 and general manufacturing defaults would number 31 over the last 17 years.) Railroad proportions continue to fall, from 27 to 16 per cent. These statistics show vividly the marked impact of the two sick industries—energy and steel. The shakeout in these industries is probably not complete.

Table XIII breaks down defaults over the 1970–86 period by their rating distributions at various times prior to default.[5] Between 1985 and 1986, the proportion of fallen angel defaulting debt dropped from 28.0 per cent (based on 125 issues) to 23.6 per cent (based on 182 issues). This reflects the increasing proportion of original-issue high-yield defaults in a growing and maturing market.

At one year prior to default, the proportion of investment-grade debt naturally decreases. That proportion is now 6.5 per cent, down from 9.1 per cent over the 1970–85 period. At the six-month mark, the proportion is now 2.5 per cent, versus 2.8 per cent for 1970–85.

Default Losses

We adjusted the annual default rate to allow for the investor's important option of selling the debt just after default, thereby realizing at least a partial return of capital. Any calculation of

Table X Default Rates on Low-Rated, Straight Debt (millions of dollars)

Year	Par Value Outstanding with Utilities	Par Value Defaulted	Default Rate
1986	$92,985	$3,155.76	3.394%
1985	59,078	992.10	1.679
1984	41,700	344.16	0.825
1983	28,233	301.08	1.066
1982	18,536	577.34	3.115
1981	17,362	27.00	0.155
1980	15,126	224.11	1.482
1979	10,675	20.00	0.187
1978	9,401	118.90	1.265
1977	8,479	380.57	4.488
1976	8,015	29.51	0.368
1975	7,720	204.10	2.644
1974	11,101	122.82	1.106
1973	8,082	49.07	0.607
1972	7,106	193.25	2.719
1971	6,643	82.00	1.234
1970	6,996	796.71	11.388

Average Default Rate 1970 to 1986:	2.216%
Average Default Rate 1974 to 1986:	1.671%
Average Default Rate 1978 to 1986:	1.451%
Average Default Rate 1983 to 1986:	1.727%

Table XI Historical Default Rates, All Ratings (millions of dollars)

Year	Par Value of Straight and Convertible Public Debt Outstanding[a]	Par Value of All Public Defaults	Default Rate	Par Value of Public Straight Debt Outstanding[a]	Par Value of Straight Debt Defaulted	Default Rate
1986	$542,900 (est.)	$3,455.38	0.636%	$505,150 (est.)	$3,155.76	0.625%
1985	454,900	1,302.02	0.286	419,600	992.40	0.237
1984	387,750	624.11	0.161	358,100	344.16	0.096
1983	347,800	412.63	0.118	319,400	301.08	0.094
1982	317,600	995.63	0.313	285,600	725.34	0.263
1981	289,900	79.61	0.027	255,300	27.00	0.011
1980	281,900	255.71	0.091	265,100	224.11	0.084
1979	281,700	30.70	0.011	269,900	20.00	0.007
1978	258,600	192.20	0.074	252,200	118.90	0.047
1977	248,300	454.78	0.183	237,800	380.57	0.160
1976	229,100	113.50	0.049	219,200	29.51	0.013
1975	209,900	319.73	0.152	200,600	204.10	0.102
1974	183,500	288.69	0.157	175,200	122.82	0.070
1973	162,900[b]	199.91	0.123	158,800[b]	49.07	0.031
1972	154,400	272.59	0.176	150,900	193.25	0.128
1971	143,000	124.90	0.087	140,500	82.00	0.058
1970	125,500	932.52	0.743	124,400	796.71	0.640
Average Default Rate 1970 to 1986:			0.199%			0.157%
Average Default Rate 1974 to 1986:			0.173%			0.139%
Average Default Rate 1978 to 1986:			0.190%			0.163%

a. These numbers are averages of beginning and ending year outstanding amounts from 1981 to 1986. End-of-year totals for prior years. Total corporate, publicly held outstanding debt at the end of 1986 was $591.5 billion. Source: *Prospects for Financial Markets in 1987*, Salomon Brothers Inc.

b. Estimates for 1973 and earlier based on linear regression of this column vs. the Federal Reserve's *Corporate Bonds Outstanding* figures, *Federal Reserve Bulletin*.

default *loss* should also consider the forgone interest payment on one semiannual coupon installment.

In 1986, the average price at the end of the default month on 56 defaulting issues was 35.5 per cent of par, or a principal loss of 64.5 per cent (assuming purchase at par). The average coupon rate on the 56 issues was 10.4 per cent

Table XII Public Defaults by Industry Sector, 1970–1986 (millions of dollars)

	Number of Companies	Straight Debt	Percentage of Total Straight	Convertible Debt	Total in Default	Percentage of Total
Industrial						
Retailers	15	$ 556.74	7.14	$211.87	$ 768.61	7.70
General Mfg.	23	2,301.49	29.53	331.64	2,563.73	25.68
Elec./Computer & Comm.	22	200.79	2.58	413.58	614.37	6.15
Oil & Gas	29	1,581.09	20.29	449.65	2,030.74	20.34
Real Estate-Const., Supplies	13	103.93	1.33	126.55	230.48	2.31
Misc. Industrials	18	570.30	7.32	177.68	747.98	7.49
Total	120	$5,314.34	68.19	$1,710.97	$6,955.91	69.66
Transportation						
Railroads	9	$1,260.22	16.17	$ 31.10	$1,291.32	12.93
Airlines/Cargo	7	211.81	2.72	122.81	334.62	3.35
Sea Lines	4	243.00	3.12	123.10	366.10	3.67
Trucks/Motor Carriers	3	48.31	0.62	9.75	58.06	0.58
Total	23	$1,763.34	22.63	$286.76	$2,050.10	20.53
Finance						
Financial Services	11	$436.09	5.60	$164.04	$600.13	6.01
REITs	12	279.71	3.59	99.46	379.17	3.80
Total	23	$715.80	9.18	$263.50	$979.30	9.81
Total	166	$7,793.48	100.00	$2,261.23	$10,054.71	100.00

Table XIII Rating Distribution of Defaulting Issues at Various Points Prior to Default, 1970–1986

Original Rating	AAA	AA	A	BBB	BBB	B	CCC	CC	Total
Number	0	3	11	29	26	79	33	1	182
Percentage	0.00%	1.65%	6.04%	15.93%	14.29%	43.41%	18.13%	0.55%	100.00%
Rating One Year Prior	AAA	AA	A	BBB	BB	B	CCC	CC	Total
Number	0	0	2	11	29	81	67	9	199
Percentage	0.00%	0.00%	1.01%	5.53%	14.57%	40.70%	33.67%	4.52%	100.00%
Rating Six Months Prior	AAA	AA	A	BBB	BB	B	CCC	CC	Total
Number	0	0	2	3	11	77	95	15	203
Percentage	0.00%	0.00%	0.99%	1.48%	5.42%	37.93%	46.80%	7.39%	100.00%

(11.2 per cent median), resulting in an average net default loss of 2.24 per cent. The calculations are given in Table XIV.

The weighted average default loss over the 1974–86 period was 1.54 per cent, or 154 basis points. The 1986 experience accounts for 44 per cent of the weighting over the entire 13-year period. As 1986 had a relatively high default loss, the average loss increased from 0.99 per cent for the 1974–85 period to 1.54 per cent for the 1974–86 period.

Investors in and analysts of high-yield securities are, of course, interested in default losses over much shorter horizons than these comprehensive figures cover. One might be concerned, for example, with the portfolio's exposure as of the beginning of the calendar year as well as the issuing date. Another benchmark is the price change and loss on defaulting issues from just prior to default to just after default. The latter might be called the "default announcement effect."

We analyzed the price decline of 195 defaulting issues over the 1970–86 period and found that the average price decline from January 1st of the defaulting year to the end of the defaulting month was 40.11 per cent over an average number of 5.73 months, compared with an average price decline of approximately 61.12 per cent from the original issue date (assuming issuance at par).

This calculation included all defaulting issues—convertible debt and fallen angels as well as original-issue high-yield debt. Indeed, seven of the 49 convertible issues included were among the top 10 losers. These included price declines of 92.0 per cent (FSC Corp.), 88.4 per cent (Interstate Dept. Stores) and 87.3 per cent (Nucorp Energy). The largest straight debt declines were FSC Corp. (86.7 per cent), Omega-Alpha (84.3 per cent) and Crystal Oil (76.5 per cent). All these big losers, however, had relatively small amounts outstanding (under $60 million).

Table XIV Default Loss to Investors, 1986 (based on 56 defaulting issues)

Background Data

Average Default Rate 1986		= 3.394%
Average Loss of Principal Based on Average Price After Default		= 64.5% (35.5% of Par)
Average Coupon Payment		= 10.4%
Median Coupon Payment		= 11.2%

Default Loss Computation

Default Rate	3.394%
x Loss of Principal	0.645
Loss from Principal	2.189%
+ ½ Coupon Loss	0.052
Default Loss (1986)	2.241%

1974–86 Statistics

		Loss	No. Issues	Wgt.
Default Loss 1974–85	=	0.990%	70	0.56
Default Loss 1986	=	2.241	56	0.44
Weighted Avg. Default Loss 1974–86	=	1.540%	126	1.00

Table XV Average Zeta Scores by Rating Agency and Rating Category (senior debt bond rating)

	1986	1985	1984	1983	1982	1981	1980	1979	1978
Moody's									
AAA	9.54	10.75	11.55	10.90	10.54	9.87	9.80	9.34	9.16
AA	7.36	8.03	7.77	7.74	7.57	7.61	7.48	7.56	7.49
A	5.05	5.32	5.48	5.35	5.42	5.60	5.62	5.23	5.28
BAA	2.97	3.30	3.42	2.96	2.88	3.43	3.44	3.08	2.93
BA	1.47	0.66	0.75	0.81	1.29	1.00	0.87	0.89	1.06
B	−1.25	−1.50	−1.62	−2.18	−1.62	−0.69	−0.24	−1.80	−2.56
CAA	−6.32	−7.63	−6.95	−4.51	−4.97	−3.69	−6.08	−5.45	−5.50
NR	−0.22	0.35	1.33	1.09	1.36	—	—	—	—
S&P									
AAA	8.78	9.95	11.01	10.80	10.34	10.03	10.00	9.49	9.33
AA	6.82	7.55	7.48	7.58	7.29	7.58	7.48	7.32	7.30
A	5.19	5.34	5.47	5.20	5.39	5.65	5.62	5.30	5.29
BBB	2.87	3.26	3.51	2.83	2.71	3.61	3.75	3.51	3.31
BB	1.47	1.08	0.86	0.78	1.09	1.38	1.03	1.20	1.73
B	−0.59	−1.88	−2.08	−1.56	−1.43	−0.79	−0.52	−1.42	−1.60
CCC	−8.36	−5.24	−4.35	−4.08	−4.23	−2.59	−2.45	−4.29	−5.35
NR	2.83	4.20	4.52	0.82	0.64	—	—	—	—

Source: Zeta Services Corp's, "Bond Rating Analysis" section in the quarterly *Analysis Book*, Winter-Spring 1987 (Hoboken, N.J.).

The largest issues suffering big losses were Republic Steel's $193 million issue (75.9 per cent), followed by Crystal Oil's $175 million (66.4 per cent), Petro Lewis' $103 million (62.3 per cent) and Global Marine's $100 million (62.0 per cent). The largest single issue default in our sample was Lykes Corp.'s $206 million (7.55 per cent of 1994) with a loss of 54.6 per cent. The percentage loss of defaulting straight debt only was 36.6 per cent, compared with the 40.1 per cent on all debt. On average, convertible defaulting debt fell slightly more than straight debt.

Observing the immediate default announcement impact, we found that the one-month percentage drop in price on the same 195-bond sample was 25.88 per cent. This indicates that, while the market does react negatively to a firm's deterioration prior to default, there is still a significant price decline around the announcement date. The largest one-month price declines were 89.4 per cent for Interstate Department Stores' convertible issues and 77.3 per cent for Altec's straight debt issue.[6] Again, the amounts

Table XVI Zeta Scores for 1986 New High-Yield Bond Issuers

	Zeta Score Before Issue	Zeta Score After Issue	Total
Number of Firms	56	35	91
Median Zeta	0.25	0.22	0.24
Average Zeta	0.26	0.05	0.18
Standard Deviation	3.93	2.56	3.47

of these defaults were very small. In 18 of the 195 cases, prices actually rose between the month-end prior to default and the month-end after default; interestingly, the three big "winners" were also convertibles. In 10 cases, there was no price change.

Credit Quality and Default Prediction

The Zeta credit scoring model can be used to assess a number of risk aspects in the high-yield debt market.[7] We have coined the term "quality junk" to indicate a firm whose outstanding debt is rated non-investment grade but whose financial profile, objectively scored on the basis of Zeta's seven-variable model, matches that of investment-grade firms.

Table XV shows the latest Zeta score compilation by bond rating. It appears that the latest scores based on 1986 data show a deterioration in the average Zeta score for many of the bond rating categories, with the exception of the lower ratings. Admittedly, the samples are not large and do not capture even a majority of the outstanding issues in each category. Still, it is interesting to note that only in the BB (Ba) and B categories do we see an improvement over 1985.

This could be due to a number of factors. For instance, if these categories are now populated by more fallen angels whose financial Zeta profiles are still better than the lower-rated firms, then the average would be expected to increase. This factor probably explains less of the improvement, however, than the fact that

Table XVII   Zeta Score Distribution for 1986 New High-Yield Bond Issuers

Zeta Score	Number of Firms
< = −5.00	5
−4.99 to −4.00	4
−3.99 to −3.00	3
−2.99 to −2.00	11
−1.99 to −1.00	15
−0.99 to 0.00	3
0.01 to 1.00	18
1.01 to 2.00	11
2.01 to 3.00	3
3.01 to 4.00	4
4.01 to 5.00	8
> 5.00	6
Total	91

new-issue scores in the high-yield sector actually increased.

In 1986, the average Zeta score on new high-yield bond *issuers* was up to +0.18 from −0.86 in 1985. The median increased from −0.24 to +0.24. The 1986 numbers reflect the latest scores available, which in 35 cases were calculated *after* the new issue and in 56 cases *before* the issue (Table XVI). The total of 91 issuers is roughly half of all of the new issuers. Note that the averages are higher *before* the issue compared with after—as one would expect, given the increase in debt associated with new issuance.

The higher average Zeta in 1986 flies in the face of numerous accusations that the latest volume of new issues has caused a deterioration of credit quality as the markets dig deeper into the credit barrel for eligible issuers. If we observe the trend in new-issuer Zeta scores over the 1978–86 period, we see a slight improvement (see Figure C). In three recent years— 1982, 1984 and 1986—the average was above zero. The increase in 1986 is impressive and it certainly does *not* indicate a decline in credit quality.

Table XVII shows the distribution of new-issuer Zeta scores. The distribution is quite wide, with about 35 per cent above 1.0—a respectable score—and 20 per cent indicating investment-grade quality (equivalent to the Triple-B average or better).

Figure C   Zeta Scores: New vs. Existing Issuers by S&P Rating

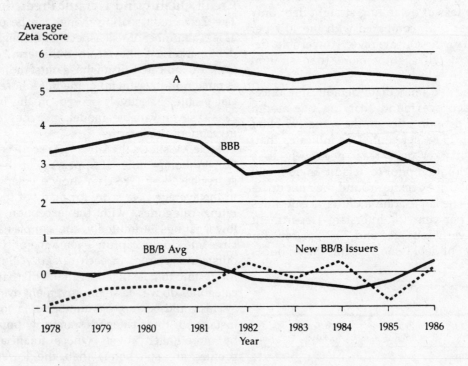

Source: Zeta Services, Inc.

Table XVIII Zeta Scores for 1986 High-Yield Bond Defaults

Company	Default Date	Latest Zeta Score	Zeta One Yr. Prior
Argo Petroleum	Jan 86	−11.33	−3.09
Crystal Oil	Apr 86	−3.44	−2.86
Damson Oil	June 86	−8.28	−2.61
Digicon Inc.	June 86	−8.84	−5.97
ICO Inc.	July 86	−4.07	−3.55
Ideal Basic Industries	July 86	−12.13	−12.28
Kenai Corporation	Mar 86	−12.53	−7.14
LTV Corp.	July 86	−6.54	−4.27
McLean Ind.	July 86	−3.36	−1.32
Petro-Lewis	Aug 86	−11.12	−3.70
Western Co. N.A.	Apr 86	−1.37	0.80
Zapata Corp.	Sep 86	−1.53	0.55
Average		−6.66	−3.34

rate in 1986, the market remains intact. Performance over the first two months of 1987 has been impressive, with total returns exceeding 6 per cent, compared with about 1.7 per cent on the Shearson-Lehman long-term government index.

Attempts to regulate investments in high-yield debt by state insurance departments and possible legislation on state and federal levels in the insurance field, as well as the takeover arena, suggest some future rocky periods. Furthermore, the new tax laws will perhaps reduce debt activity in the coming months, as firms sort out the net benefit of debt financing. In our opinion, however, the market is resilient enough to withstand these largely exogenous shocks. ∎

Zeta Scores and Defaults

We looked back on 1986 defaults and tracked Zeta scores over the prior two periods to see if Zeta's record of signaling virtually all recent defaults remained intact. As Table XVIII indicates, Zeta did indeed red-flag every default for which scores were available (13 defaulting companies), with an average score of −6.66.

The average score is very deep into the "distress zone" and indicates legitimate, serious concern prior to default. The average prior notice was about four months. Our price decline data (discussed earlier) indicate that an average of between 29 and 40 per cent could have been saved if these issues had been sold prior to default.

Note that the average Zeta score was still a dismal −3.34 a year prior to the latest score, although in three cases the score was positive. These three issues indicate a shorter early warning of the eventual default than prevailed for the other issues.

Conclusion

The high-yield debt market is now bigger, deeper, more liquid and more controversial than ever before. Despite the relatively high default

Footnotes

1. The 1986 results for other high-yield debt indexes were 19.27 per cent (Drexel), 17.45 per cent (Shearson), 16.06 per cent (Salomon) and 15.63 per cent (First Boston).
2. At the end of 1986, there were 55 open-end mutual funds investing in high-current-yield corporate debt, with total net assets of $25.9 billion—an increase of $2.8 billion over the last quarter of 1986. See *Lipper Fixed-Income Fund Performance Analysis* (New York: Lipper Analytical Services, Inc., 1986).
3. See our prior compilation of all defaulting firm names and amounts (1970–85) in E. Altman and S. Nammacher, *Investing in Junk Bonds: Inside the High Yield Debt Market* (New York: J. Wiley & Sons, 1986), pp. 112–119.
4. *Ibid.*, p. 24.
5. *Ibid.*, p. 131.
6. Interstate's bankruptcy gave rise to one of the most incredible success stories, involving the turnaround of Toys "R" Us. Investors can make significant returns on investing in defaulted debt and sometimes the equity as well.
7. See Altman and Nammacher, *Investing in Junk Bonds, op. cit.*, Chapters 6 and 7 or Altman, *Corporate Financial Distress* (New York: J. Wiley & Sons, 1983), Chapter 4.

Interest rate risk, immunization, and duration

A general model relating interest rate risk to holding period and to yield curve shifts.

Kevin J. Maloney and Jess B. Yawitz

Theoretical and empirical research on fixed-income securities, with special emphasis on maturity selection strategies, has been a major area of investigation during the last several years. In fact, one might argue that in no other area of financial research is the application of theory to practice more rapid nor the intersection of interests between academics and practitioners greater. While it is difficult to attribute this heightened interest in fixed-income research to a specific event, there is no doubt that the increased volatility of interest rates and the introduction of innovative financing features have been important factors.

The purpose of this paper is to develop a general model designed to specify how interest rate risk is related to the investor's holding period and to the particular stochastic process assumed to generate yield curve shifts. While each of these individual questions has been studied extensively, the literature has devoted relatively little attention to the development of a unifying model.[1] In positioning this

1. Footnotes appear at the end of the article.

paper in the existing literature, our purpose has been to consolidate and extend the recent research that has addressed the question of interest rate risk in fixed-income securities.

The remainder of our paper is organized as follows. After briefly summarizing the relevant literature, we turn to the source of interest rate risk and develop an intuitive model to explain the relationship between an investor's holding period and interest rate risk for both a single cash flow and for securities and portfolios containing several cash flows. We then develop a general model of immunization that highlights the specific risk contribution of individual cash flows.

Following the model, we then discuss the relationship between this general model and some recent work in the duration and immunization literature. In particular, we demonstrate that several of the specific duration models that have been developed to accommodate particular stochastic interest rate processes are simply special cases of this general model. Next, we develop a simple example to highlight the important aspects of the analysis in this

KEVIN J. MALONEY is Assistant Professor of Finance at the Amos Tuck School, Dartmouth College, at Hanover (NH 03755). JESS B. YAWITZ is Director of Financial Strategies at Goldman Sachs in New York (NY 10004). The authors would like to thank present and former colleagues at Dartmouth College and Washington University, St. Louis, an anonymous referee, and Frank Fabozzi for helpful comments on earlier drafts of this paper.

paper. Using both a graphical and a numerical example, we are able to augment the intuition underlying this unifying model. Finally, we conclude with a brief summary of results and suggestions for future research, particularly empirical testing.

LITERATURE REVIEW

From a historical perspective, it is useful to divide the literature on interest rate risk in fixed-income investments into two time periods, before and after publication of the Fisher and Weil study in 1971. While there was some limited empirical research prior to 1971, the primary contribution from this earlier era was the necessary analytical foundation for future work. The most important contributions of this period are found in Macaulay (1938), Hicks (1939), Samuelson (1945), and Redington (1952).

The Fisher and Weil study represents the first attempt to conduct a thorough testing of the usefulness of the duration concept in a maturity selection strategy designed to eliminate interest rate risk. This strategy, first called "immunization" in 1952 by Redington, has over the last 15 years been the dominant focus for researchers seeking to analyze the riskiness of fixed-income securities.

As Bierwag, Kaufman, and Toevs (1983) point out, much of this research has considered the implications of relaxing one or more of the assumptions made in the early literature on immunization. Specifically, the assumptions of (1) a parallel change in the yield curve, (2) an immediate one-time shift in yields, and (3) a single investor holding period have received considerable attention.

INTEREST RATE RISK AND THE INVESTOR'S HOLDING PERIOD

In this section, we develop our analytical model designed to demonstrate the importance of an investor's holding period in specifying the source of interest rate risk from a single cash flow and from a series of cash flows. We then discuss the importance of simple duration indexes and transformations of these indexes as summary measures of interest rate risk for multiple cash flow portfolios. This discussion is then extended to immunization strategies based upon these duration measures.

Interest Rate Risk

If we limit the menu of securities that can be purchased for a portfolio to default-free fixed-income instruments with known cash flows, the only risk to the nominal rate of return is from the effect of interest rate changes on the portfolio's value at the end of the holding period. We will refer to this relationship simply as *interest rate* risk. For the discussion that follows, we define the holding period to be the length of time until the portfolio must be liquidated into cash, perhaps for the purpose of funding a specific liability. Quite simply, interest rate risk is present whenever the investor must enter the market in the future either to purchase additional cash flows or to sell cash flows that have not yet matured.

We can categorize interest-rate risk into two distinct components. When cash is received prior to the end of the holding period, we say that it subjects the investors to *reinvestment risk*. On the other hand, a cash flow to be received after completion of the holding period subjects investors to *price risk*, since they must sell the claim to this cash flow at the end of the holding period. Clearly, movements in interest rates cause opposite changes in the end-of-period value of cash flows received prior to, and after the end of, the holding period.

(i) A Single Cash Flow

A brief discussion of interest rate risk for a single payment discount instrument will serve to set the stage for consideration of more complicated securities. The interest rate risk of a single cash flow can be shown to be completely specified by interest rate volatility, the cash flow's maturity, and the investor's holding period. Let $V_{O,t}$ be the present value of \$1 to be received t periods from today. That is:

$$V_{O,t} = (1 + R_t)^{-t}, \quad (1)$$

where R_t is the t-period term structure rate. The value of \$1 received at time t, evaluated M periods from now is:

$$V_{M,t} = (1 + R_M)^M (1 + R_t)^{-t}. \quad (2)$$

That is, $V_{M,t}$ represents the forward price at time M of \$1 to be delivered at time t.

Consider an investor with a claim to \$1 in period t and with a holding period of length M. This investor is concerned about the effect of interest rate changes on the value at the end of the holding period, $V_{M,t}$. The percentage change in the holding period value ($V_{M,t}$) of this cash flow can be shown to be a function of time to receipt of the cash flow (t), the time to the end of the holding period (M), and the percentage changes in the M and t period term structure rates.

In particular, for small changes in R_M and R_t, we obtain the following formula:

$$\dot{V}_{M,t} = \frac{\Delta V_{M,t}}{V_{M,t}} = M \frac{\Delta(1 + R_M)}{(1 + R_M)} - t \frac{\Delta(1 + R_t)}{(1 + R_t)}. \quad (3)$$

Equation (3) indicates that the variability in the holding period value of \$1 to be received in t periods is simply a weighted average of the variability in the M period and t period rates, where the weights are M and $-t$, respectively. Note that in the special case (usually assumed in the immunization literature) of an equal percentage change in all rates, the variability in the holding period value is strictly proportional to $M - t$.

We can rewrite Equation (3) to obtain a more convenient expression for $\dot{V}_{M,t}$. If we let R_1 be the one-period spot rate and η_i be the elasticity between $(1 + R_i)$ and $(1 + R_1)$, $\dot{V}_{M,t}$ can be written as follows:[2]

$$\dot{V}_{M,t} = [M \, \eta_M - t\eta_t] \frac{\Delta(1 + R_1)}{(1 + R_1)} . \qquad (4)$$

Equation (4) contains an important insight. It indicates that the impact of interest rate changes on the holding period value of a given cash flow can be immediately determined if we have knowledge of the relative volatility between the one-period term structure rate and longer maturity rates. Again, note that if all rates change by the same percentage ($\eta_M = \eta_t$), $V_{M,t}$ is proportional to $(M - t)$.[3] In general, however, we should not expect this to be the case. In particular, it is reasonable to argue that for $i > 1$, $\eta_i < 1$, and that η_i should fall as i increases.[4] Stated simply, short rates should be more volatile than long rates. Finally, the special case of $M = 0$ provides some useful insights into the duration and immunization literature. When $M = 0$, Equation (4) reduces to the following expression:

$$\dot{V}_{0,t} = - t \, \eta_t \frac{\Delta(1 + R_1)}{(1 + R_1)} . \qquad (5)$$

The concept of duration for a particular cash flow is a measure of the elasticity of its present value to a given change in interest rates.[5] While most discussions of duration and immunization assume all rates change by the same percentage amount, Equation (5) offers an alternative approach that does not require this assumption.

We define the *adjusted duration* of a given cash flow to be received in time t as *minus* the percentage change in the present value of that cash flow when the one-period spot rate increases by 1%. As we can see from Equation (5), the adjusted duration of this cash flow is simply $t \, \eta_t$. In the next section, we demonstrate that this term measures the contribution of each cash flow in a portfolio to the volatility of the portfolio as a whole.

(ii) A Multiple Cash Flow Portfolio

Now let us extend the preceding discussion to consider a series of default-free cash flows that orig-

inate either from one security with multiple payments or from a portfolio of securities. The holding period value of a multiple cash flow portfolio, T_M, can be expressed as follows:

$$T_M = \sum_{t=1}^{N} C_t \, V_{M,t}, \qquad (6)$$

where C_t is the cash flow from the portfolio at time t. Using the logic behind Equation (4), we can express the percentage change in T_M as follows:

$$\dot{T}_M = \frac{\sum_{t=1}^{N} C_t \, V_{M,t} \, \dot{V}_{m,t}}{\sum_{t=1}^{N} C_t \, V_{M,t}}$$

$$= \frac{\sum_{t=1}^{N} C_t \, V_{M,t} [M \, \eta_M - t \, \eta_t] \frac{\Delta(1 + R_1)}{(1 + R_1)}}{\sum_{t=1}^{N} C_t \, V_{M,t}} . \qquad (7)$$

Equation (7) indicates that the percentage change in the holding period value of a portfolio is equal to a weighted sum of the percentage changes in the holding period value of \$1 amounts received at each time period t. The weights are simply the proportion of the holding period value that is attributed to each cash flow.

We can simplify Equation (7) by noting that the holding period value weight of any cash flow,

$$\frac{C_t \, V_{M,t}}{\sum_{t=1}^{N} C_t \, V_{M,t}} ,$$

will always be equal to its present value weight

$$\frac{C_t \, V_{0,t}}{\sum_{t=1}^{N} C_t \, V_{0,t}} ,$$

which we will denote by W_t. Since these weights must sum to unity, Equation (7) simplifies to the following form:

$$\dot{T}_M = [M \, \eta_M - \sum W_t \eta_t] \frac{\Delta(1 + R_1)}{(1 + R_1)} . \qquad (8)$$

Equation (8) indicates that the percentage change in the holding period value of the portfolio that accompanies a one percent change in one plus the spot rate is simply the adjusted duration of a cash flow received at the end of the holding period, minus a value-weighted sum of the adjusted durations of each cash flow in the portfolio.

The following exercise provides an improved insight into this expression. If M is equal to zero, then Equation (8) indicates that the percentage change in a portfolio's present value that results from a given percentage change in the one-period rate is *minus* the value-weighted sum of the adjusted durations of its composite cash flows:

$$\dot{T}_O = - \left[\sum_{t=1}^{N} W_t t \eta_t \right] \frac{\Delta(1 + R_1)}{(1 + R_1)} . \qquad (9)$$

This then can be properly referred to as the portfolio's *adjusted duration,* which we denote D^*. This adjusted duration measure reflects the modification that is necessary when all term structure rates do not change by the same percentage.

Equation (9) shows that $\dot{T}_O$ is negative for increases in the one-period rate, revealing that every cash flow contributes price risk to the portfolio's current value. As the holding period increases from zero to some positive time period M, we see from Equation (8) that $\dot{T}_M$ increases (becomes less negative). This reflects the reduction in the price risk associated with each cash flow. When the holding period exceeds the maturity of the shortest cash flow, then that cash flow will contribute reinvestment risk to the portfolio, which also serves to increase $\dot{T}_M$.

This pattern continues as M is increased until at some holding period $\dot{T}_M$ will equal zero. For this holding period, the price risk in the portfolio is exactly offset by the reinvestment risk. Such a portfolio is *immunized* against changes in the one-period spot rate. The precise condition for immunization can be obtained by setting the bracketed term in Equation (8) equal to zero. Thus, a portfolio will be immunized when its adjusted duration, D^*, is equal to the adjusted duration of a single cash flow received at the end of the holding period:

$$D^* = M \eta_M. \qquad (10)$$

Intuitively, this condition states that a portfolio is immunized when its cash flow profile has identical interest rate risk (adjusted duration) as an M-period single-payment discount instrument.

RELATIONSHIP TO PREVIOUS LITERATURE

We now briefly redirect our analysis to consider several special cases of this general model. By imposing specific assumptions about the stochastic process that generates yield curve shifts, we are able to obtain some results that have previously appeared in the literature in addition to other interesting special cases. In particular, we demonstrate that the adjusted duration framework and its associated immunization criterion can be utilized to replicate the results in Bierwag (1977) and Khang (1979). We accomplish this task by specifying the vector of yield volatility elasticities to account for their proposed stochastic processes. We have chosen these examples to demonstrate the general nature of this model, although we could also

replicate other measures.

As discussed earlier, the original Macaulay-Hicks duration measure is useful in immunization strategies if the term structure is assumed to be flat and subject only to parallel shifts. In our general model, this corresponds to a special case in which $\eta_t = 1$ and R_t equals a constant for all t. Since the assumptions of a flat term structure subject only to parallel shifts is restrictive, researchers have sought to analyze other interest rate structures.

Bierwag (1977) demonstrated that, under the assumption of multiplicative shocks to the term structure, he could modify the original Macaulay-Hicks duration measure to design immunization strategies even when the term structure was not flat. This modification requires one to replace yields in the original Macaulay duration measure with the appropriate term structure rates. The multiplicative shock scenario analyzed by Bierwag is a case where all term structure rates $(1 + R_t)$ change by the same percentage. As indicated previously, this is also equivalent to the assumption that η_t is equal to unity for all t. Thus, the Bierwag duration measure for multiplicative shocks is a special case of the adjusted duration measure where $\eta_t = 1$ for all t. Furthermore, the immunization condition in Equation (10) reduces in this case to the traditional "holding period equal to duration" condition.

In this same article, Bierwag discussed the possibility of additive shock (parallel shifts) in non-flat yield curves. He correctly demonstrated that the duration measure used for immunization strategies in this case must be appropriately modified. By assuming that all term structure rates change by the *absolute* amount, Bierwag implicitly assumed that

$$\eta_t = \frac{(1 + R_1)}{(1 + R_t)} .$$

By substituting this measure for η_t into Equation (9), we obtain the same duration measure as Bierwag for the additive shock scenario. Note that D^* in this case differs from the traditional duration measure for multiplicative shocks when the term structure is not flat.

Citing the historic behavior of interest rates, Khang (1979) argued that a maturity-dependent stochastic process would provide a better description of interest rate movements than either the additive or multiplicative assumptions of Bierwag. He then postulated two alternatives, an "additive maturity-dependent process" and a "multiplicative maturity-dependent process," as substitutes for Bierwag's two stochastic processes. Khang's additive maturity-independent process implies that the elasticity measure η_t will equal

$$\frac{\ln{(1 + \alpha t)} (1 + R_1)}{t \ln(1 + \alpha) (1 + R_t)},$$

which results in the adjusted duration measure in Equation (11):

$$D^* = \sum W_t \frac{\ln{(1 + \alpha t)} (1 + R_1)}{\ln{(1 + \alpha)} (1 + R_t)}. \qquad (11)$$

Note that this is identical to the measure derived by Khang.

In a similar fashion, we can replicate the results from Khang's "multiplicative maturity-dependent process." Under that case,

$$\eta_t = \frac{\ln(1 + \alpha t)}{t \ln(1 + \alpha)},$$

and D^* is given by Equation (12):

$$D^* = \sum_{t=1}^{N} W_t \frac{\ln(1 + \alpha t)}{\ln(1 + \alpha)}. \qquad (12)$$

Another feasible stochastic process for interest rates is one in which the volatility of the one-period forward rates implicit in the term structure follow a simple decay process. If we denote the one-period forward rate spanning time periods i and i + 1 as $_if_{i+1}$, then a simple decay process for the elasticities between one-period forward rates and the spot rate could be written as follows:

$$\frac{d(1 + _if_{i+1})}{d(1 + R_1)} \frac{(1 + R_1)}{(1 + _if_{i+1})} = \alpha^i. \qquad (13)$$

Given this stochastic process for one-period forward rates, we can demonstrate that

$$\eta_t = \frac{1 - \alpha^t}{t(1 - \alpha)}. \qquad 7$$

The adjusted duration measure for this stochastic assumption is given by Equation (14):

$$D^* = \sum_{t=1}^{N} \frac{W_t(1 - \alpha^t)}{(1 - \alpha)}. \qquad (14)$$

We have demonstrated in this section that our general model of interest rate risk includes as special cases some results found in the previous literature. In the next section, we provide a numerical example to further the intuition behind this general model.

AN ILLUSTRATIVE EXAMPLE

Table 1 presents an example that illustrates the various concepts discussed in the development of our model. Our intention here is to provide a more intuitive understanding of the mathematical results in the previous two sections.

Consider a portfolio consisting of a ten-year level annuity paying $100 per year. We chose a level annuity to represent the cash flow stream because it allows us to illustrate the key concepts discussed above without the need to be concerned with the additional complexities associated with unequal cash flows.

Column (1) of Table 1 lists the years to receipt for each cash flow in the portfolio. Column (2) lists the dollar amounts of the cash flow associated with each time period.

The first transformation is to compute the present value of each cash flow. This is calculated assuming a flat term structure with all rates equal to 20%; we use a flat term structure for ease of exposition, and we use the 20% rate to dramatize the results. This information is listed in Column (3) of the table. The sum of the entries in this column provides the present

TABLE 1

The Annuity Example
M = 3, R = .2

(1) Year	(2) C	(3) $C(1 + R)^{-t}$	(4) $-tC(1 + R)^{-t}$	(5) η_t	(6) $-C\eta_t t(1 + R)^{-t}$	(7) $C(1 + R)^{M-t}$	(8) $(M - t)C(1 + R)^{M-t}$	(9) $(\eta_M M - \eta_t t)C(1 + R)^{M-t}$
1	100	83.33	−83.33	1	−83.33	144	288	246.24
2	100	69.44	−138.89	.950	−131.94	120	120	97.20
3	100	57.87	−173.61	.903	−156.83	100	0	0
4	100	48.23	−192.90	.860	−165.85	83.33	−83.33	−60.75
5	100	40.19	−200.94	.819	−164.57	69.44	−138.89	−96.19
6	100	33.49	−200.94	.781	−156.92	57.87	−173.61	−114.33
7	100	27.91	−195.36	.745	−145.60	48.23	−192.90	−120.90
8	100	23.26	−186.05	.712	−132.46	40.19	−200.94	−119.97
9	100	19.38	−174.43	.681	−118.72	33.49	−200.94	−114.39
10	100	16.15	−161.51	.651	−105.19	27.91	−195.36	−106.14
COLUMN SUMS	1000	419.25	−1707.96	——	−1361.41	724.46	−777.97	−389.24

SIMPLE DURATION = 4.07 Years

ADJUSTED DURATION = 3.25 Years

90

value of the annuity, $419.25. Column (4) multiplies the present value of each cash flow by minus the number of years until that payment is received. This represents the change in the present value of each cash flow that would occur if $(1 + R)$ increased by 1%.

The calculations to this point are sufficient to compute the Macaulay-Hicks duration measure for this annuity: Sum the series in Column (4), change the sign, and divide by the present value of the entire annuity. Given the parameters from the numerical example, this yields a duration of 4.07 years.

Now we demonstrate the effect of introducing a term structure that need not be subject to equal percentage shifts. The assumption underlying the Macaulay-Hicks duration measure is that the elasticity of every term structure rate with respect to the one-period rate is equal to one, but empirical evidence shows that this elasticity decreases monotonically with the maturity of the term structure rate.

The particular representation of this phenomenon employed in this example is the forward rate decay model introduced in the previous section. That is, we assume that the elasticity of the forward rate spanning periods i and i + 1 is α^i. This implies that the elasticity between the t-period and one-period term structure rates is

$$\frac{(1 - \alpha^t)}{t(1 - \alpha)},$$

as demonstrated in footnote 7.

For our example, we chose α equals .9. The vector of elasticities generated by this assumption is listed in Column (5). Multiplying the entries in Column (4) by this vector of elasticities yields Column (6). This transformation has the effect of "deflating" all of the terms in Column (4) except the first one. This then represents the impact on the present value of the annuity if one plus the one-period spot rate increases by 1% and all other term structure rates adjust according to the elasticities for rate.

Summing the terms in Column (6) and dividing by the present value of the annuity yields the adjusted duration of this cash flow stream. In this example, the adjusted duration equals 3.25 years. Note that the introduction into the analysis of declining yield volatility across the term structure reduces the risk profile of this annuity by .82 years, or approximately one-fifth. Figure 1 provides a graphical exposition of these numbers, where we graph the transformations of the cash flows in Columns (3), (4), and (6).

We can also use this example to illustrate the effect on interest rate risk from varying the assumed holding period. Returning to Table 1, we can compute

FIGURE 1

SELECTED ENTRIES FROM TABLE 1

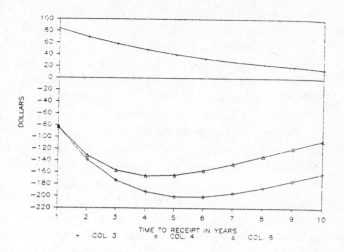

the value of each cash flow at the end of a three-year holding period, given the current term structure, by multiplying the present value of each cash flow (the entries in Column (3)) by $(1 + R)^3$. This series is presented in Column (7). With t < 3, the dollar value of the cash flow is compounded forward, while for t > 3 the cash flow is discounted backward. When t = 3, the entry in Column (2) equals the entry in Column (7). The sum of the entries in this column, $724.46, is the three-year holding period value of the annuity.

If we multiply each term in Column (7) by (3 − t), we obtain Column (8). The values obtained by multiplying the holding period value of each cash flow by the number of periods separating the end of the holding period and the maturity of the cash flow are sufficient to compute a measure of the effect of interest rate changes on holding period value. When $(1 + R)$ increases by one percent uniformly across the maturity structure, the sum of the entries in Column (8) equals the change in the holding period value of the annuity. From the entries in this column, we can see that cash flows received prior to period 3 when interest rates rise have the effect of increasing the end-of-period value due to increased reinvestment income, while flows received after period 3 reduce the holding period value of the portfolio due to reduced prices upon sale.

If we sum the entries in Column (8), change the sign, and divide by the holding period value of the annuity, we obtain the net risk position of this portfolio, measured in terms of the Macaulay-Hicks duration number. The value of 1.07 obtained from this calculation is thus the duration of the portfolio (4.07) minus the length of the holding period (3).

We can again incorporate the assumption that rate variability decreases monotonically with maturity as follows. In moving from Column (7) to Column (8), we multiplied each entry by (M − t). In computing the entries in Column (9), we multiply each entry in Column (7) by $(M\eta_M - t\eta_t)$. As indicated earlier, this is the appropriate measure of the risk associated with the timing of cash flows for the general case when discount factors change by different percentages. The sum of the entries in Column (9) represents the change in the end-of-period value of the portfolio when one plus the one-period spot rate increases by one percent and all other discount factors change according to their elasticity measures.

Finally, if we divide the sum of the entries in Column (9) by the holding period value of the annuity, we obtain the net risk position of the portfolio, incorporating relative interest rate volatility. This calculation yields a value of .54. This is equal to the adjusted duration of the portfolio (3.25) minus the product of the holding period (3) and the elasticity of the three-year term structure rate (.903). As indicated above, this is the appropriate comparison when yield volatility is incorporated into the analysis.

Figure 2 provides a graphical presentation of the transformations described above. Note that the lines representing Columns (8) and (9) cross the X-axis at three years: For an investor with a three-year holding period, a portfolio with a single cash flow at the end of three years would be an immunized portfolio. Cash flows received prior to (after) period 3 contribute reinvestment (price) risk to the portfolio.

This example has illustrated the theoretical concepts introduced in this paper with some actual numbers. The discussion shows that yield volatility

and the holding period are important determinants of the net risk contributed by a particular security or portfolio of securities.

CONCLUSIONS

The literature on interest rate risk, duration, and immunization has been expanding rapidly in recent years. In this paper we have developed a general model of interest rate risk that enhances the intuition underlying the concept of duration and summarizes recent advances in the literature. In particular, our adjusted duration index provides an important summary measure of interest rate risk that is sufficiently general to include many previous results in the literature as special cases.

This measure also focuses attention on important parameters that need to be investigated empirically. Specifically, additional tests must be conducted using actual bond data to measure the importance of the various assumptions required if the Macaulay-Hicks duration measure is employed. A subset of this research must test whether an alternative specification of interest rate volatility, perhaps the decay model presented here, has enduring explanatory power. We would expect that such a specification would dominate the equal percentage shift assumption, if only from the casual observation that short rates are more volatile than longer-term rates.

---

[1] The paper by Babbel (1983) is perhaps the best previous attempt to develop such a unifying model.

[2] While we have chosen the one-period spot rate as the base, the analysis is equally relevant with a different rate as the base rate.

[3] If all rates change by the same percentage amount, then for $i \neq j$, $\eta_i = \eta_j$. What is less clear is that each of these elasticities must equal one. This is obvious when we consider that these elasticities are defined using the one-period rate. Thus, η_1 must equal one, and equality of all elasticities means $\eta_i = 1$ for all i.

[4] We feel that a compelling theoretical argument can be presented to support the empirical finding that on average yield volatility decreases with maturity. Yields change when one-period forward rates change, and forward rates are primarily influenced by revaluations in expected future rates. A less than unitary elasticity of expectations between changes in the current one-period rate and changes in expected future one-period rates is most reasonable from the following perspective. Just as current market conditions determine the one-period rate of interest, the expected market conditions in each period in the future determine expected future one-period rates. Therefore, the effects of a change in current market conditions on expected future market conditions would decay with the number of periods into the future. To this extent, the change in one-period forward rates would decrease with the number of periods into the future. Since multi-period yields are a geometric mean of

FIGURE 2
SELECTED ENTRIES FROM TABLE 1

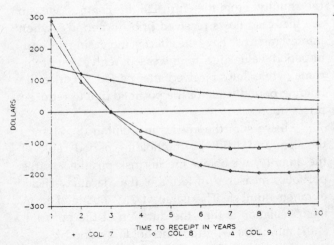

the current one-period rate and the one-period forward rates, yield volatility should decrease monotonically with maturity. Empirical work by Babbel (1983) and everyday experience confirm this hypothesis.

[5] See Bierwag, Kaufman, and Toevs (1983).

[6] The additive shock assumption of Bierwag is equivalent to assuming that $d(1 + R_t) = \lambda$ for all t. In that case,

$$\frac{d(1 + R_t)}{d(1 + R_1)} = 1 \text{ and } \eta_t = \frac{(1 + R_1)}{(1 + R_t)} .$$

[7] The relationship between the t-period yield R_1 and the vector of one-period forward rates is:

(F1) $(1 + R_t)^t = (1 + R_1)(1 + {}_1f_2)(1 + {}_2f_3) \ldots (1 + {}_{t-1}f_t).$

Differentiating both sides with respect to $(1 + R_1)$ and imposing Equation (14) from the text yield the following result:

(F2) $t(1 + R_t)^{t-1} \dfrac{\Delta(1 + R_t)}{\Delta(1 + R_i)} = \dfrac{(1 + R_t)^t}{(1 + R_1)} + \displaystyle\sum_{i=1}^{t-1} \dfrac{(1 + R_t)^t \alpha^i}{(1 + R_1)} .$

Rearranging terms and simplifying this equation yield the following expression for η_t:

(F3) $\eta_t = \dfrac{1}{t} \left[1 + \displaystyle\sum_{i=1}^{t-1} \alpha^i \right] = \dfrac{(1 - \alpha^t)}{t(1 - \alpha)} .$

BIBLIOGRAPHY

D. F. Babbel. "Duration and the Term Structure of Interest Rate Volatility." In G. O. Bierwag, G. Kaufman, and A. Toevs, *Innovations in Bond Portfolio Management: Duration Analysis and Immunization,* JAI Press, 1983.

G. O. Bierwag. "Immunization, Duration, and the Term Structure of Interest Rates." *Journal of Financial and Quantitative Analysis,* January 1977, pp. 725-42.

G. O. Bierwag, G. Kaufman, and A. Toevs. "Uses of Duration in Bond Portfolio Strategies: A Survey Review." *Financial Analysts Journal,* July/August 1983.

L. Fisher and R. Weil. "Coping with the Risk of Interest Rate Fluctuations: Returns to Bondholders from Naive and Optimal Strategies." *Journal of Business,* October 1971, pp. 408-31.

J. R. Hicks. *Value and Capital.* Oxford: Clarendon Press, 1939.

Chulsoon Khang. "Bond Immunization when Short-term Rates Fluctuate More Than Long-term Rates." *Journal of Financial and Quantitative Analysis,* 1979.

F. Macaulay. *Some Theoretical Problems Suggested by the Movement of Interest Rates, Bond Yields, and Stock Prices in the U.S. Since 1856.* New York: National Bureau of Economic Research, 1938.

F. Redington. "Review of the Principle of Life Office Valuations." *Journal of the Institute of Actuaries,* 18(1952), pp. 286-340.

P. Samuelson. "The Effect of Interest Rate Increases on the Banking System." *American Economic Review,* 55(1945), pp. 16-27.

The equity component of corporate bonds*

Consideration of this component is essential for optimal bond portfolio management strategies.

Mark Weinstein

A corporate bond is a hybrid security: a combination of risk-free government debt and equity in the firm that issued the bond. This view of corporate bonds has a number of important implications for active corporate bond portfolio management. This paper presents estimates that demonstrate the impact of the equity component on the total return of a corporate bond.

A corporate bond has some characteristics of a government bond. The income is relatively certain, and the value of the bond changes with changes in the yield curve. To the extent that the payments of coupons and principal depend on the value of the issuing firm, however, the bond also has characteristics of equity in that firm. When the firm's prospects improve, the probability of default goes down and the values of the bond and the common stock increase. If interest rates are declining when the firm's prospects are improving, then both effects (the change in the yield curve and the increased value of the equity) will contribute to an increase in the price of the bond. If, on the other hand, interest rates are rising when the firm's prospects are improving, the two effects work in opposite directions.

This view of corporate bond pricing leads to three conclusions:

1. The corporate bond portfolio manager who accurately anticipates movements in the overall equity market will outperform the manager who ignores this information.

2. Optimal duration strategies must take into account anticipated performance in the equity market.

3. Even if interest rates are stable, active corporate bond trading strategies can be based on changes in the value of the firm.

What determines the behavior of the equity part of a corporate bond? Like any other equity, the returns to the equity part of the bond are correlated with the returns on the market portfolio. The strength of this correlation depends upon: 1) the strength of the correlation between changes in the firm's market value and the overall market return and 2) the importance of the equity component of the bond relative to the debt component. In turn, the relative importance of the equity component depends upon characteristics of the bond, the issuer, and the market. In particular, the importance of the equity component of the corporate bond increases with:

- term to maturity,
- leverage, and
- the volatility of the percentage change in the value of the firm

and decreases with:

- increases in the coupon rate and
- increases in the level of the yield curve.[1]

EMPIRICAL RESULTS

An examination of the monthly holding period returns (coupon plus capital gain) on a sample of 90 corporate bonds over the 50-month period from June 1970 to July 1974[2] demonstrates the importance of the equity component of corporate bonds. During this

* Financial support for this research was provided by A. B. Laffer Associates. The author has benefited from comments by Charles Kadlec, Arthur Laffer, Thomas Nugent, and Marc Reinganum. The usual disclaimer applies.

1. Footnotes appear at the end of the article.

period, the variability of corporate bond prices showed a marked increase when compared to the previous 20 years. This variability lends itself to active portfolio management.

The estimated effects of the equity component of the bond are based on the coefficients of a regression presented in detail in the Appendix. While the estimates of the effects may vary with the time period analyzed, the conclusions, which are supported by economic theory, should not.

For this analysis, I constructed a market index composed of the CRSP value-weighted New York Stock Exchange index (70%) and an index of corporate bond returns (30%). The weights approximate the relative market values over this period. The addition of bond returns to the stock market portfolio provides a measure of the performance of the overall corporate sector, as opposed to the performance of the equity component of this sector alone. This approach captures the direct effects of changes in interest rates and other economic variables on the total value of the firm. In other work with this data base, I have used a number of different market indexes, but the conclusions reached have been unaffected by the choice of the market index.

The common problem of simultaneous equations bias arises in this approach. To the extent that one believes that the bond market *causes* movements in the stock market, a problem exists because then the independent variable in the regression (the stock market return) is caused by the dependent variable (the return on bonds). This problem is different from the problem that arises when we run simple market model regressions (there, as here, the dependent variable is a constituent of the independent variable). Unfortunately, a solution to the simultaneity problem is beyond the scope of this paper.

THE IMPORTANCE OF THE MARKET PORTFOLIO

A sensitivity analysis shows the importance of the return on the market portfolio to the total return of corporate bonds. In this analysis, predicted returns for the average corporate (AC) bond in the sample are calculated for hypothetical periods of below-average, average, and above-average market portfolio returns, respectively.

The discussion that follows presents the salient features of the interaction of market returns and the other factors that influence bond returns. Detailed results are available from this author on request.

When the return on the market portfolio is at its average value, 75 basis points per month, the AC bond earns 61 basis points per month. If the market return is 320 basis points per month (one standard deviation above average), the AC bond returns 211 basis points per month — an increase of 150 basis points. On the other hand, if the market return is −170 basis points per month (one standard deviation below average), the bond will lose 88 basis points per month — a decline of 149 basis points.

This relationship by itself indicates that the equity component of an average corporate bond is an important determinant of its total return. Moreover, other determinants of AC bond returns, including the level of interest rates and duration, can have markedly different effects on the total return of the bond depending on whether the market return is above or below its average.

INTEREST RATES AND AVERAGE CORPORATE BOND RETURNS

When the market return is at its average value, the expected return on an average corporate bond is inversely related to the level of interest rates. When the T-bill rate is at its low value (387 basis points per annum), the expected monthly AC bond return is 96 basis points, 70 basis points higher than when the T-bill rate is at its high value of 742 basis points.[3]

The relationship between the level of interest rates and the market return is more important. The lower the level of interest rates, the more pronounced the effect of movements in the market portfolio return; this result can be traced to the implicit change in leverage associated with different levels of interest rates. When interest rates are low, bond values are high, and, holding the value of the firm's assets fixed, effective leverage is high. Not surprisingly, the more highly levered the firm, the more sensitive is the total return of its debt to movements in the market portfolio. Thus, the total return of an AC bond under a low interest rate scenario increases by 427 basis points as the market return changes from −170 to 320 basis points. By contrast, under the high interest rate scenario, the total return of the average corporate bond increases by only 172 basis points.

TERM TO MATURITY AND CORPORATE BOND RETURNS

When the market return is at its average level, increases in term to maturity decrease expected average corporate bond returns. For example, the typical bond with a term to maturity of 7.33 years earns 69 basis points per month when the market return is at its average value. If this bond had 22.34 years to maturity, its predicted return would be only 53 basis points.

The strength and direction of the term-to-maturity effect depend upon the behavior of the market portfolio. When the market return is low, investors are better off in shorter-term bonds. The increase in maturity from 7.33 to 22.34 years results in a decline in predicted return of 81 basis points (-48 basis points to -129 basis points). In contrast, if the return on the market portfolio is high, the optimal strategy is to switch into longer-term bonds. The same increase in term to maturity now leads to an increase in predicted returns of 50 basis points per month. Thus, whether a manager should shift into long- or short-term corporate bonds depends upon the anticipated market return.

COUPON RATES AND BOND RETURNS

A reversal in bond returns is also experienced with coupon rates. When the market return is low, an increase in the coupon rate is associated with an increase in AC bond return. An increase in the coupon rate from 3½% to 6½% leads to an increase of 46 basis points per month to -65 basis points in expected return. The opposite result occurs when the return on the market is high. In this case, the AC bond return falls by 21 basis points per month (to 200 basis points from 221 basis points) as the coupon rate increases to 6½%.

The importance of the market portfolio's return also varies with the coupon rate. The lower the coupon rate, the more sensitive the AC bond return is to movements in the market.

DURATION EFFECT

The effects of term to maturity and coupon rate taken jointly imply that the anticipated performance of the market portfolio is an important input in devising a duration strategy. If the market is expected to perform well, an increase in duration will lead to high average corporate bond returns. If the market is expected to decline, the duration of the portfolio should be shortened. Further, changes in the market are more important for long-duration bonds than for bonds with short duration.

LEVERAGE AND CORPORATE BOND RETURNS

In contrast to the above results, the interaction between the leverage of the firm (book value of long-term debt to total assets) and the market is relatively unimportant. When the market is doing well, an increase in leverage from .19 to .49 increases expected AC bond return by only 23 basis points per month. When the market is doing poorly, the relation is reversed: An increase in leverage now produces a decrease in expected return of 20 basis points. Once again, anticipation of market movements should be considered when factoring in leverage to a corporate bond strategy.

CHANGES IN BOOK VALUE AND BOND RETURNS

The relationship between the volatility of percentage changes in the book value of the issuing firm and expected AC bond returns also depends on the performance of the market. When the market return is low, an increase in volatility from its low value of .01% to its high value of .55% reduces predicted AC bond return by 17 basis points.[4] When the market is doing well, the increase in firm volatility increases predicted bond return by 63 basis points per month. Furthermore, the more volatile the firm, the more sensitive are the returns of its bonds to movements in the market portfolio.

These results are not surprising, since leverage and firm risk are highly correlated with bond rating. When the market is expected to do well, low-rated bonds will outperform high-rated bonds and should be considered for the portfolio; when the market is doing badly, low-rated bonds should be avoided.

CONCLUSION

The results of this paper provide strong evidence that investors should view the traditional elements of bond analysis within the context of the behavior of the overall market, including equities. The strategy that is appropriate when the market return is high may be precisely the wrong one when the market return is low. Consideration of the equity component of corporate bonds can yield higher returns on corporate bond portfolios.

APPENDIX

The results presented in the text are based on a regression equation designed to explain cross-sectional and time-series variability in monthly returns (price appreciation plus coupon yield) for a sample of 90 bonds during the 50-month period from June 1970 to July 1974. The regression equation, a generalization of the standard "market model" regression, is derived in the following way.

Start with the standard market model regression:

$$(1) \qquad R_{it} = \alpha_i + \beta_i R_{mt} + \epsilon_{it},$$

where:

R_{it} is the return on bond i at time t,

R_{mt} is the return on the market portfolio at time t,

ϵ_{it} is the unobservable residual, and

α_i and β_i, the slope and intercept parameters are the well known alpha and beta.

In Equation (1), the return on the bond is a function of only a single variable, the return on the market, and the sensitivity of the bond to the market, β_i, is assumed constant over time (there is no t subscript attached to β_i).

The model is first extended by considering the possibility of additional explanatory variables as follows:

$$(2) \quad R_{it} = \alpha_i + \beta_i R_{mt} + \delta_1 \tau_{it} + \delta_2 C_i + \delta_3 r_t + \delta_4 L_{it} + \delta_5 \sigma_{it} + \epsilon_{it},$$

where, in addition to the variables in Equation (1):

τ_{it} is the term to maturity of bond i at time t,

C_i is the coupon rate on bond i,

r_t is the level of short-term interest rates at time t,

L_{it} is the leverage ratio for bond i at time t, and

σ_{it} is the volatility of the percentage change in the value of the issuer of bond i at time t.

Equation (2) differs from Equation (1). It cannot be estimated separately for each bond, because the coupon level (for nonfloating rate bonds) does not change. Thus, the only way to estimate the effect of varying coupon on bond return is to combine data from a number of bonds with different coupons. Although it might seem appropriate in this case to estimate the model from cross-sectional data, cross-sectional data are also insufficient. In particular, the variables R_{mt} and r_t are the same for all bonds at a given moment. Consequently, the only way to estimate all of the parameters in Equation (2) is to combine the data from a number of bonds into one pooled time-series cross-sectional regression.

The next step in the analysis is to drop the assumption that β_i is constant. Rather, following Galai-Masulis (1976), let β be described by:

$$(3) \quad \beta_{it} = \gamma_0 + \gamma_1 \tau_{it} + \gamma_2 C_i + \gamma_3 r_t + \gamma_4 L_{it} + \gamma_5 \sigma_{it}.$$

Equation (3) is not a regression equation. Rather, it is a theoretical model of the determinants of β.[5] The theory predicts that γ_1, γ_4, and γ_5 will be positive and that γ_2 and γ_3 will be negative. Thus, longer term-to-maturity bonds are riskier, in a systematic risk sense, than shorter term-to-maturity bonds. The same is true for bonds issued by riskier (measured by σ) firms, and/or by firms with higher leverage ratios.[6]

While this is of some interest, at this point it is only a theory. The empirical relevance of Equation (3) can be examined by substituting Equation (3) for β in Equation (2), giving:

$$(4) \quad R_{it} = \alpha_i + [\gamma_0 + \gamma_1 \tau_{it} + \gamma_2 C_i + \gamma_3 r_t + \gamma_4 L_{it} + \gamma_5 \sigma_{it}] R_{mt}$$
$$+ \delta_1 \tau_{it} + \delta_2 C_i + \delta_3 r_t + \delta_4 L_{it} + \delta_5 \sigma_{it} + \epsilon_{it}.$$

Dropping the i subscript on α (that is, assuming the intercept is the same for each bond) and expanding the product terms on the first line of (4), we obtain:

$$(5) \quad R_{it} = \alpha + \gamma_0 R_{mt} + \gamma_1 [\tau_{it} R_{mt}] + \gamma_2 [C_i R_{mt}] + \gamma_3 [r_t R_{mt}]$$
$$+ \gamma_4 [L_{it} R_{mt}] + \gamma_5 [\sigma_{it} R_{mt}] + \delta_1 \tau_{it} + \delta_2 C_i + \delta_3 r_t + \delta_4 L_{it}$$
$$+ \delta_5 \sigma_{it} + \epsilon_{it}.$$

In this model, each variable-R_m, τ, C, r_t, L, and σ-enters directly as a determinant of the return on the bond. Additionally, there are interaction terms that measure the effects of τ, C, r, L and σ on the β and hence the return of the bond.

This paper is concerned with the significance of the γ terms in Equation (5). If γ_0 is significant, then the portfolio manager must consider the behavior of the equity market when making predictions about the corporate bond market. If the coefficients of the interaction effects ($\gamma_1 - \gamma_5$) are significant, then not only must portfolio managers consider the behavior of the market portfolio, but they must also consider the way that differences in the market return affect the relation between bond return and the other variables (τ, C, r, L and σ).

Table 1 presents the results of estimating Equation (5) on the sample of bond returns. The measure of r is the realized return on the shortest term Treasury bill still outstanding at the end of the month. Leverage is measured by the ratio of Total Long Term Debt to Total Assets from the Compustat tapes. The measure of σ is the standard deviation of the percentage change in Total Assets over the five fiscal years prior to the month of observation. The market index used is a weighted average of a value weighted NYSE return and the return on a sample of corporate bonds. The weights were chosen to approximate market value weights over this period.[7]

The evidence presented in Table 1 shows the importance of the return on the market portfolio and the interaction terms in explaining bond returns. Of the six independent variables, the highest t-statistic is associated with R_m, the market return. That is not to say that the yield curve is unimportant. The coefficients of τ and C are significantly negative and positive, respectively. This indicates that short-duration bonds outperformed long-duration bonds over this period, as is well known. Leverage seems to play no direct role, but σ, a measure of the operating risk of the underlying issuer of the bond, does have a statistically significant effect.

The most interesting findings in Table 1, however, lie in the analysis of the interaction effects. For every variable, the t-statistic associated with the interaction effect exceeds that associated with the corresponding direct effect. Furthermore, the interaction effects are not simply proxying for the direct effects. The coefficients of $[\tau_{it} R_{mt}]$ and $[C_{it} R_{mt}]$ are both statistically significant and of opposite sign to the direct effects of τ and C.

Further, even though the direct effect of L_{it} is unimportant (the t-statistic is only 1.05) the interaction term is significant, with a t-statistic of 3.41. The domination by the interaction terms shows that the manager must consider the differential effects of τ, C, r, L, and σ at various levels of R_m and cannot simply consider R_m, by itself, as an additional explanatory variable.

The F-statistics report the significance of the direct effects taken as a group (F_2) and the interaction effects taken as a group (F_1). Although both are statistically significant, it seems obvious that the interaction effects make a stronger contribution to explaining bond returns than do the direct effects. This is also shown in the R^2 of this and other unreported regressions. In other work, regressions are estimated with only R_{mt} ($R^2 = .13$), R_{mt} and the direct effects ($R^2 = .15$), R_{mt} and the interaction terms ($R^2 = .23$).

It is clear that the interaction terms provide incremental explanatory power that is not provided by the direct terms.[8] The obvious conclusion to reach from this analysis is that the return on the market portfolio, because of both its direct effect (γ_0) and its role in mediating the effects of the other determinants of bond returns, is too important to be ignored by the portfolio manager.

TABLE 1

Estimates of Indirect and Direct Effects on Bond Returns

Dependent Variable	Const. × 10²	R_m	Indirect Effects (thru β)				
			τ × 10²	Coupon × 10¹	r	L	σ
R_d	.651	1.29	.148	−.480	−184.15	.313	.303
	(1.15)	(4.90)	(7.00)	(−3.52)	(−4.24)	(3.41)	(9.27)

Direct Effects							
τ × 10²	Coupon × 10¹	r	L	σ	R^2	F_1 (D.O.F.)	F_2 (D.O.F.)
−.002	.008	−1.10	−.002	.002	.23	102.18	14.30
(−3.54)	(2.30)	(−1.00)	(1.05)	(2.60)		(5,4488)	(5,4488)

F_1 tests hypothesis that all indirect coefficients are 0.

F_2 tests hypothesis that all direct coefficients are 0.

The "Interaction Effects" independent variables were first multiplied by R_m.

The numbers in parentheses are t-statistics.

D.O.F. is the degrees of freedom for the F-Statistic.

R_d = bond return for monthly holding period
R_m = market return for monthly holding period
τ = term to maturity (months)
coupon = coupon level (in percent)
r = realized return on short maturity Treasury bill
L = debt/value ratio
σ = std. deviation of returns on book value of total assets

---

[1] The derivation of these relations can be found in Merton (1974), Galai-Masulis (1976), and Weinstein (1983).

[2] Details of the analysis may be found in the Appendix to this paper, and in Weinstein (1983).

[3] At first this result seems counterintuitive; normally, high interest rates are associated with higher total returns. In part, this result occurred because interest rates were generally rising during the sample period. The result also reflects the impact of higher interest rates on the value of the corporate bond relative to the firm's assets, which have not necessarily dropped in value. A period-to-period comparison would show that when interest rates are high, the value of the bonds is low. By contrast, when interest rates are low, the value of the bonds is high. Thus, holding assets constant, the higher the interest rates, the lower the effective leverage of the firm (value of the debt to value of the total assets). Conversely, when interest rates are low, the value of the debt is high, and the effective leverage of the firm is high. As a result, when interest rates are high, corporate bonds are less risky than when interest rates are low and all else held constant, they would be expected to provide a lower rate of return.

[4] The high and low values for σ, the variability of percentage change in total assets, were calculated differently from the high and low values for the other variables. This variable has a low mean and its distribution is highly skewed to the right. The mean value of σ is .12472, and the sample standard deviation is .42969. Subtracting the sample standard deviation from the sample mean would have led to a negative test value, a nonsensical result. The value .01, which is one of the lower observed values of σ, was used instead.

[5] In fact, the theory does not predict that Equation (3) will be a linear equation. The linearity assumption should be viewed as a useful approximation.

[6] In this analysis, the systematic risk of the firm is assumed constant through time and across firms. Also, no difference is being made between junior and senior debt.

[7] In other work with these data, the results have been unaffected by the choice of weights. In fact, the inferences drawn are unaffected even if a stock market index is used. The choice of a weighted stock and bond market index is made because the theory alluded to earlier suggests that it is appropriate to view a bond as a portfolio of risk-free debt and equity in the unlevered firm. The combined index approximates the behavior of the corporate sector without regard for the effect of leverage. A stock market index, on the other hand, presents the performance of levered equity. Because this work stresses the non-yield curve determinants of bond returns, it seems reasonable to use the combined index. Details of the Generalized Least Squares estimation procedure can be found in Weinstein (1983).

[8] The R^2 reported may seem low compared with other market model regressions; however, the comparison is invalid. In this paper we are not reporting the results of separate regressions for each of the 90 bonds. Rather, we are reporting the results of estimating one equation with only 12 estimated parameters for all 90 bonds simultaneously. The regression attempts to explain not only the time-series variation in bond returns, but also the cross-sectional variation.

REFERENCES

Galai, D., and Masulis, R. "The Option Pricing Model and the Risk Factor of Stock." *Journal of Financial Economics*, Vol. 3 (1976).

Merton, R. "On the Pricing of Corporate Debt; The Risk Structure of Interest Rates." *Journal of Finance*, Vol. 29 (1974).

Weinstein, M. "Bond Systematic Risk and the Option Pricing Model." *Journal of Finance*, Vol. 38 (1983).

MARGARET EATON'S CHOICE OF AN INDUSTRY

Margaret Eaton, age 31, was born and raised in Colorado. She received a B.A. degree in history from the University of Denver in 1975. Lacking a clear career focus and not willing to do much interviewing, she worked the next five years as a secretary, and ultimately as an administrative assistant, at the University of Colorado in Boulder.

Her last boss at Boulder, Dr. Kalman Sperry, recognized Ms. Eaton's intelligence, integrity, and motivation -- to the point that Sperry convinced her to return to graduate school at Boulder in September 1980 to pursue an MBA degree. Still single, and with moderate savings, Margaret quickly and enthusiastically followed that advice. In June 1982, she emerged with her MBA degree, specializing in finance and investments, the fourth highest GPA in her class of 180 MBAs, with considerable poise and self confidence -- and with a much clearer career focus toward the investments/securities industry. Deftly handling fifteen interviews, eleven corporate visits, and seven impressive offers, Margaret decided on a well-paying position as a security analyst for Bank Two in Columbus, Ohio.

Six years later, Ms. Eaton is viewed as one of the top four or five security analysts at Bank Two. One reason for that is that Margaret has exhibited rapid learning and mastery of three rather diverse industries in those six years. She seems to be able to quickly understand an industry, to get to know the right people in each firm, and to conceptually integrate a myriad of institutional detail, research reports, et.al., toward a concise understanding of what really matters in an industry, and what the investment future is likely to be for that industry.

As a result of such credentials and promise, Bank Two very much wanted to retain Ms. Eaton. The Bank has given her several generous salary increases as well as additional perks within the organization. Nevertheless, Margaret decides to leave Columbus and return to the Denver area. In addition to not liking the Columbus social scene, Margaret simply wants to work for a smaller organization in which she can more fully exercise her entrepreneurial skills.

In July 1988, Margaret Eaton accepts a job as "senior analyst" with the investment advisory firm of Duncan, Evans, and Farquarth (DEF). DEF is a relatively small firm but with an excellent reputation among the elite of Denver. Ms. Eaton's credentials and reputation from Bank Two are so impressive that she is literally offered "almost any industry" within DEF as her initial assignment.

To clarify her initial industry assignment, she is asked to select an industry, plus two competing firms within that industry. Then using annual reports, 10-Ks, and other available information, Ms. Eaton is to perform careful but crisp analyses of the industry in general, and the selected firms in particular. These analyses should lead toward determining the short/long term prospects for the industry and the two firms, and ultimately to specific buy/hold/sell recommendations.

Margaret Eaton ponders this initial assignment, and, in particular, the following initial questions:

(1) What industry should she select? What information sources might be helpful to her in that decision?

(2) What two firms in that industry should she select? What information sources might be helpful to her?

(3) What analyses for the selected industry and two firms ought she do for this initial assignment?

(4) What are the key variables that are likely to be germane to her final recommendations for each firm?

(5) Assuming that her initial work results in her being assigned to the industry and firms of her choice, how should she proceed in her work on a longer-term basis?

COMMON STOCK ANALYSIS FOR THE SEMINAR

Jack Walker did rather well in his studies of mechanical engineering at Rice University in Texas. As a result, he obtained an excellent job as a project engineer for an oil services firm in Dallas upon his graduation. He liked the technical work in the Texas oil business and was rewarded with a series of initial salary increases far beyond his initial expectations.

Gradually, however, Jack began to feel that he really would like to get into management as soon as possible. He talked with key managers of his company, and they agreed to help him plan for additional coursework and experiences that would expedite his being prepared for project management.

Part of that planning involved in-house training sessions. Another part was the possibility of attending some management seminars in the Dallas area. Two of his older colleagues at work strongly recommended that he attend "Fundamentals of Accounting and Finance," a three-day seminar put on periodically by one of the leading professional management associations. They found that particular seminar to be well designed, very demanding, and very rewarding as a result. Walker discovers that the seminar will be given again in about five weeks -- and his firm agrees to pay the $850 registration, and to let him attend on company time.

One of the reasons why that particular seminar is so demanding is that attendees are expected to do reading and other work in advance. The reading includes selected chapters from one of the leading finance textbooks. The advance work also includes a special project -- namely, a careful financial analysis of a recent annual report. In this instance, each attendee is to do an analysis of the 1987 financial statements of the R.R. Donnelley Company.

According to the instructions which are sent out to each registrant, Jack Walker is to read the financial section of the 1987 Donnelley annual report (enclosed with the instructions), and to respond to the following:

(1) How would you summarize the nature and importance of the following topics as discussed in the footnotes to the 1987 financial statements:

(a) Inventory accounting
(b) Depreciation accounting
(c) Major corporate acquisitions
(d) The stock split

(e)   The change in pension fund accounting

(2)   Calculate financial ratios and other suitable measures for the following:

   (a)   size
   (b)   liquidity
   (c)   activity
   (d)   leverage
   (e)   profitability
   (f)   ownership

   Do you notice any significant changes from 1986 to 1987?

(3)   Calculate the "duPont" system of financial control for R.R. Donnelley for both 1986 and 1987. Any changes?

(4)   Calculate measures of sustainable growth for the firm for each of the two years.

(5)   Calculate Altman's "Z-score" for bankruptcy prediction for each of the two years.

(6)   Based on all of these ratios and measures, what would you conclude about the financial health and future prospects of the R.R. Donnelley Company?

(7)   Based on all of the above common stock analyses, calculate your best estimate of what R.R. Donnelley is worth today. How does your estimate of value compare to its current market value? Do you judge the Donnelley common stock to be overvalued or undervalued?

(8)   In terms of a potential addition to a well-diversified portfolio of common stocks, would you recommend the inclusion of R.R. Donnelley?

R. R. Donnelley & Sons Company is a major participant in the communications industry, providing a broad range of printing and related services to publishers of magazines and books, as well as merchandisers, the telephone industry, financial institutions and other firms requiring substantial amounts of printing and other communication services. The Company is the largest supplier of commercial printing services in the United States and a major supplier in the United Kingdom. In the United States, it produces catalogs and newspaper inserts, magazines, books, directories, computer documentation and financial printing. The principal services provided to customers are presswork and binding, along with all pre-press operations necessary to create a printing image, and planning for truck, rail and air distribution of the printed product. Through Metromail Corporation, a wholly owned subsidiary, the Company provides list and list enhancement services to direct mail merchandisers. The Company also provides design and related creative services, cartographic services and diskette replication services. Due to the range of services it provides, the Company is uniquely positioned to meet the information and communication needs of its customers.

The relative contribution of each of the Company's major product areas to its total sales for the five-year period ended December 31, 1987, is shown in the following table. In 1986 and 1987, the acquisition of Norwest Publishing Company accounted for much of the increase in Directories' relative contribution.

	1987	1986	1985	1984	1983
Catalogs	34%	37%	40%	40%	39%
Magazines	21	22	23	25	26
Books	18	17	18	17	16
Directories	20	19	15	14	14
Other	7	5	4	4	5

Consolidated Statement of Income

R. R. Donnelley & Sons Company and Subsidiaries

Year Ending December 31 Thousands of Dollars	1987	1986	1985
Net Sales	$2,482,865	$2,233,511	$2,038,408
Cost of Sales	1,970,788	1,776,514	1,606,483
Gross Profit	512,077	456,997	431,925
Selling & Administrative Expenses	233,044	206,238	195,789
Earnings from Operations	279,033	250,759	236,136
Gain on Sale of Cable Company	64,986	—	—
Interest on Marketable Securities	7,046	12,675	15,638
Other Income—net	5,411	3,128	4,113
Total Other Income—net	77,443	15,803	19,751
Earnings Before Income Taxes	356,476	266,562	255,887
Income Taxes	138,280	108,294	107,473
Net Income	$ 218,196	$ 158,268	$ 148,414
Net Income per Share of Common Stock*	$ 2.80	$ 2.03	$ 1.94

*Reflects 2-for-1 common stock split effective May 30, 1987

See accompanying Notes to Consolidated Financial Statements

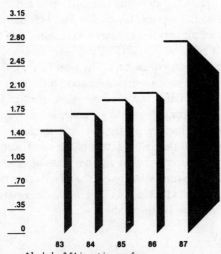

Earnings Per Share*
(in dollars)

* Includes $.51 in net income from
Cablevision sale in 1987

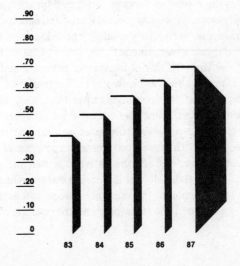

Dividends Per Share
(in dollars)

105

The Consolidated Statement of Income summarizes income and expense for the last three years. The accounting policies used by the Company are discussed in Notes to Consolidated Financial Statements. The following discussion covers major year-to-year changes in operating results for each of the last three years.

Comparison of 1987 with 1986

Net sales in 1987 increased 11% over 1986. Management estimates that substantially all of the sales increase is due to increased volume of services performed for customers and the sales contributed by Metromail since its acquisition. Price pressures continue to be experienced but the reductions are not as severe as in 1986. Gross profit increased 12% and the gross profit rate of 20.6% was greater than the 1986 rate of 20.5%. Higher volume, the inclusion of Metromail results and reduced pension expenses resulting from the adoption of SFAS No. 87 "Employers' Accounting for Pensions" (see Benefit Plans note on page 31) contributed to the increase in gross profit. Selling and administrative expenses increased 13% over 1986 resulting from the sales increase, the continuing expansion of the sales force, the opening of new sales offices and the inclusion, since August, of Metromail Corporation. Total other income—net increased $62 million primarily due to the gain on the sale of Rockford/Park Cablevision, Inc., a wholly owned subsidiary. The gain was partially offset by less interest income on marketable securities as a result of lower investment balances and yields. Earnings before income taxes increased 34% as a result of the items discussed above. The effective tax rate of 38.8% in 1987 was lower than the 1986 rate of 40.6% principally reflecting the net favorable effect of provisions in the Tax Reform Act of 1986. Net income increased 38% as a result of the items discussed above.

Comparison of 1986 with 1985

Net sales in 1986 increased 10% over 1985. Management estimates that substantially all of the sales increase represents an increase in the volume of services performed for customers. Significant pressures on price were experienced and demand was soft in several areas, particularly catalogs and magazines, due primarily to sluggish advertising activity. Gross profit increased 6%, a rate lower than the rate of increase in net sales, and the gross profit rate of 20.5% was below the 1985 rate of 21.2%. These lower comparative percentages reflect the price pressures noted above and certain higher period-to-period expenses, particularly start-up expenses and depreciation and amortization expenses associated with the capital investment program of 1986 and prior years. Selling and administrative expenses increased 5% over 1985. Essentially all of this increase was in selling expense, up as a function of the sales increase, as well as the continuing expansion of the sales force and the opening of new sales offices. Other income—net decreased 20%, representing less interest income on marketable securities as a result of lower investable balances and yields, along with higher amortization expense associated with the investment in safe-harbor leases. The higher amortization expense was more than offset by the favorable income tax provision effect discussed below. Earnings before income taxes increased 4% as a result of the items discussed above. The effective tax rate of 40.6% in 1986 was lower than 1985's 42% effective tax rate, reflecting the net favorable effect in 1986 of certain provisions in the Tax Reform Act of 1986. The adverse effect of the retroactive repeal of the investment tax credit was more than offset by the favorable effect of the Act on the Company's investments in safe-harbor leases. Net income increased 7% as a result of the items discussed above.

Comparison of 1985 with 1984

Net sales in 1985 increased 12% over 1984. Management estimates that substantially all of this increase represents increased volume of services performed for customers. The volume increase reflects generally high operating levels, combined with the utilization of increased capacity which resulted from the continued expansion of the Company. Gross profit increased at a higher rate of 15% primarily due to improved manufacturing performance, a decrease in the LIFO provision and reduced employee benefits plan expense. The lower benefits plan expenses result from the Company's contribution to its voluntary employees' beneficiary association (VEBA) to fund certain existing employee benefits. The VEBA was established in late 1984 to provide future benefits to employees in a more cost-effective manner. The lower year-to-year LIFO provision results from the Company's successful efforts to minimize the investment in inventories and because of less materials cost inflation. Further, the higher gross profit rate in the period (21.2% as compared to 20.8% in 1984) was achieved despite an increase in start-up costs related to expansion programs, including the start-up of a new division in October, 1985 in Danville, Kentucky. The 14% increase in selling and administrative expenses was mainly due to higher selling costs required to support the greater sales volume, the effect of continuing expansion of the sales force, the opening of new sales offices, start-up activities and expanding customer support services. Other income—net decreased by $6 million or 23%. This was primarily due to a smaller average investment in marketable securities during the year as a result of the VEBA contributions and the amortization of the investment in safe-harbor leases. Earnings before income taxes increased 11% as a result of the items discussed above. The effective tax rate of 42% in 1985 was equal to that in 1984. Net income increased 11% as a result of the items discussed above.

Consolidated Balance Sheet
R. R. Donnelley & Sons Company and Subsidiaries

December 31 Thousands of Dollars	1987	1986
Assets		
Cash and equivalents	$ 38,605	$ 25,420
U.S. government and other marketable securities, at cost approximating market	21,752	94,883
Receivables, less allowances for doubtful accounts of $12,535 in 1987 and $13,904 in 1986	462,618	394,170
Inventories, principally at LIFO cost	172,759	128,205
Progress billings	(58,791)	(51,321)
Prepaid expenses	35,421	72,402
Total Current Assets	672,364	663,759
Property, plant and equipment, at cost	1,868,477	1,675,394
Accumulated depreciation	(777,720)	(678,008)
Net Property, Plant and Equipment	1,090,757	997,386
Investment in acquired tax benefits	45,663	56,152
Franchise costs, net of accumulated amortization of $9,249 in 1986	—	15,666
Goodwill, net of accumulated amortization of $2,739 in 1987 and $44 in 1986	242,040	1,289
Other	35,563	6,999
Total Other Assets	323,266	80,106
Total Assets	$2,086,387	$1,741,251
Liabilities		
Accounts payable	$ 141,346	$ 126,805
Accrued compensation	46,996	32,204
Short-term debt	55,706	66,594
Deferred income taxes	55,550	60,437
Other accrued liabilities	84,094	81,090
Total Current Liabilities	383,692	367,130
Long-term debt	193,787	18,444
Deferred income taxes	280,675	288,818
Deferred investment credit	46,799	51,553
Other noncurrent liabilities	26,345	10,298
Total Noncurrent Liabilities	547,606	369,113
Shareholders' Equity		
Common stock at stated value ($1.25 par value)		
Authorized shares: 200,000,000; Issued: 79,304,400 in 1987 and 1986*	231,481	181,916
Earnings reinvested in the business, including $6,146 of cumulative translation adjustment in 1987 and ($2,838) in 1986	984,226	863,641
Reacquired common stock, at cost	(60,618)	(40,549)
Total Shareholders' Equity	1,155,089	1,005,008
Total Liabilities & Shareholders' Equity	$2,086,387	$1,741,251

*Reflects 2-for-1 common stock split effective May 30, 1987

See accompanying Notes to Consolidated Financial Statements

The Consolidated Balance Sheet presents the Company's financial position at the end of each of the last two years. The statement lists the Company's assets, liabilities and the equity of its shareholders. Major changes in the Company's financial position are summarized in the Consolidated Statement of Funds Flow which appears on page 26. The Funds Flow Statement summarizes the changes in our cash and marketable securities balance for each of the last three years and helps to show the relationship between operations (presented in the Consolidated Statement of Income) and liquidity and financial resources (presented in the Consolidated Balance Sheet).

The Company continues in a strong financial position. At December 31, 1987, cash and marketable securities totaled $60 million, down $60 million from the prior year end. Working capital at year end was $289 million, down $8 million from the prior year end. These reductions resulted from the Company's acquisition of Metromail in August of 1987. The acquisition was initially funded by Company funds of approximately $85 million and commercial paper debt of $200 million. At December 31, 1987, $192 million of the commercial paper remains outstanding and $173 million is classified as long-term debt as explained in

Notes to Consolidated Financial Statements. Working capital and cash flow continue to be adequate for the operation and growth of the business. Working capital—particularly cash, accounts receivable and inventories—is closely controlled and continually monitored. Emphasis continues on asset management, particularly the Company's investment in inventories and receivables.

Capital expenditures in 1987 were $210 million. As in past years, the major portion of these expenditures was financed primarily by internally generated funds. The Company estimates that capital spending during 1988 will exceed $200 million. Other cash expenditures in 1988 are expected to be in line with the growth in sales, earnings and cash flow. In 1987, net funds (cash and marketable securities) were reduced primarily due to the acquisition of Metromail. In 1988 net funds are expected to be provided from operations.

Total short- and long-term debt was 21.6% of total shareholders' equity at December 31, 1987, compared to 8.5% in 1986. The increase from 1986 represents funds required for the purchase of Metromail which are expected to be retired at a rate of approximately $50 million per year.

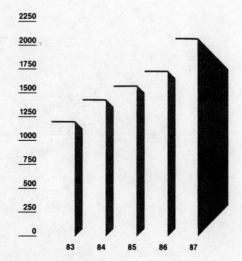

Total Assets
(millions of dollars)

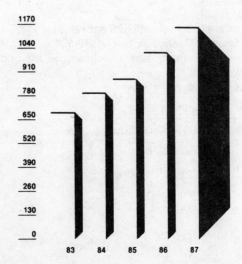

Total Shareholders' Equity
(millions of dollars)

Consolidated Statement of Funds Flow
R. R. Donnelley & Sons Company and Subsidiaries

Year Ending December 31 Thousands of Dollars	1987	1986	1985
Funds (Cash & Marketable Securities) at Beginning of Year	$120,303	$161,614	$180,607
Provided From Operations			
Net income	218,196	158,268	148,414
Depreciation and amortization	140,300	119,054	103,710
Deferred income taxes and investment credits	3,428	3,060	59,187
Net book value of cable company assets sold	23,458	—	—
Reduction of noncurrent VEBA asset	—	55,000	—
Other	11,929	—	1,382
Total	397,311	335,382	312,693
Used in Operations			
Purchase of property, plant and equipment	210,482	254,646	162,841
Net change in working capital (excluding cash & marketable securities)	51,989	62,281	83,425
Addition to noncurrent VEBA asset	—	—	55,000
Net assets of businesses acquired (including goodwill of $243 million, net of working capital of $22 million in 1987)	272,485	6,954	—
Other	—	600	—
Total	534,956	324,481	301,266
Net Funds Provided From (Used in) Operations	(137,645)	10,901	11,427
Provided From (Used For) Financing Activities			
Deferred tax benefits from investment in tax leases	(16,325)	5,345	21,097
Increase (decrease) in long-term debt	171,123	(2,394)	722
Disposition of reacquired common stock	10,799	12,967	10,486
Acquisition of common stock	(33,372)	(18,906)	(18,376)
Cash dividends paid	(54,526)	(49,224)	(44,349)
Total	77,699	(52,212)	(30,420)
Funds (Cash & Marketable Securities) at End of Year	$ 60,357	$120,303	$161,614
Increase (Decrease) in Working Capital			
Receivables	$ 68,448	$ 71,886	$ 39,993
Inventories—net	37,084	(612)	3,648
Prepaid expenses	(36,981)	(15,674)	8,029
Accounts payable	(14,541)	(7,741)	52,419
Accrued compensation	(14,792)	7,205	19,057
Short-term debt	10,888	8,574	(26,607)
Deferred income taxes	4,887	13,518	(11,341)
Other accrued liabilities	(3,004)	(14,875)	(1,773)
Net Change	51,989	62,281	83,425
Change in Cash & Marketable Securities	(59,946)	(41,562)	(18,993)
Increase (Decrease) in Working Capital	$ (7,957)	$ 20,719	$ 64,432

See accompanying Notes to Consolidated Financial Statements

Consolidated Statement of Shareholders' Equity

R. R. Donnelley & Sons Company and Subsidiaries

Year Ending December 31 Thousands of Dollars	1987	1986	1985
Common Stock			
Beginning of Year	$ 181,916	$ 180,916	$180,916
Pooling of interests—Norwest Publishing	—	1,000	—
Par value of common stock issued in 2-for-1 split effective May 30, 1987	49,565	—	—
End of Year, as restated	231,481	181,916	180,916
Reacquired Common Stock			
Beginning of Year	(40,549)	(31,933)	(23,632)
Cost of purchased shares	(33,372)	(18,906)	(18,376)
Cost of common shares issued under stock programs	13,303	10,290	10,075
End of Year	(60,618)	(40,549)	(31,933)
Earnings Reinvested in the Business			
Beginning of Year	863,641	746,920	641,199
Pooling of interests—Norwest Publishing	—	4,885	—
Beginning of Year, as restated	863,641	751,805	641,199
Net income	218,196	158,268	148,414
Cash dividends	(54,526)	(49,224)	(44,349)
Par value of common stock issued in 2-for-1 split effective May 30, 1987	(49,565)	—	—
Common shares issued under stock programs	(2,504)	2,677	411
Translation adjustment	8,984	115	1,245
End of Year	984,226	863,641	746,920
Shareholders' Equity	$1,155,089	$1,005,008	$895,903

See accompanying Notes to Consolidated Financial Statements

Funds Provided From Operations
(millions of dollars)

Additions To Property, Plant And Equipment
(millions of dollars)

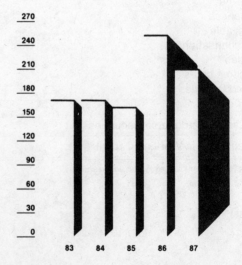

Summary of Significant Accounting Policies—*Basis of Consolidation* The consolidated financial statements include the accounts of the Company and its operating subsidiaries, all of which are wholly owned. Intercompany items and transactions are eliminated in consolidation. The 71% investment in Lakeside Bank is carried at underlying book value. Commencing in 1988, the Company will include the Lakeside Bank as a consolidated, majority-owned subsidiary (Statement of Financial Accounting Standards No. 94); the effects of such consolidation are not anticipated to be significant. Certain 1985 and 1986 amounts have been reclassified to conform with the 1987 presentation. The consolidated funds flow for the year ending December 31, 1986, has been prepared as if the Company and Norwest Publishing Company, acquired in October, 1986 and accounted for as a pooling of interests, had been consolidated at January 1, 1986.

Nature of Operations All operations of the Company are in the communications industry. The Company produces a wide variety of printing and related services for specific customers, virtually always under contract. Some contracts provide for progress payments from customers as certain phases of the work are completed. Revenue is recognized after production has been completed in accordance with the terms of the contracts. Some customers furnish paper for their work, while in other cases the Company purchases the paper. International operations represent less than 7% of consolidated results and assets.

Inventories Inventories include material, labor and factory overhead and are substantially all carried at LIFO cost. This method reflects the effect of inventory replacement costs on earnings—accordingly, charges to cost of sales reflect recent costs of material, labor and factory overhead.

Foreign Currency Translation Translation gains and losses of the Company's international financial statements are reflected in "Earnings Reinvested in the Business" in the accompanying consolidated financial statements.

Earnings per Share Earnings per share are computed on the basis of average shares outstanding during each year. No material dilution would result if effect were given to the exercise of outstanding stock options and stock units.

Benefit Plans The Company's Retirement Benefit Plan (the Plan) is a non-contributory defined benefit pension plan covering substantially all employees. Normal retirement age is 65, but provision is made for earlier retirement. Benefits are based on members' annual career earnings data. In 1987, the Company adopted the principles of Statement of Financial Accounting Standards No. 87, "Employers' Accounting for Pensions," which requires use of the projected unit credit actuarial cost method for financial reporting purposes. Prior to 1987, the Company used the attained age normal actuarial cost method for financial reporting purposes and continues to use that method for funding purposes. This latter method recognizes all benefits expected to accrue to Plan members during their working career and spreads the cost of those benefits on a level (as a percentage of salary) basis, thereby reflecting currently the increasing pension cost associated with earnings growth and aging of the work force. The projected unit credit actuarial cost method assigns an annual normal cost equal to the present value of the portion of total career benefits earned in each year. Therefore, as participants age, the normal cost as a percentage of payroll will increase due to the shorter discounting period.

In conjunction with this method and the adoption of SFAS No. 87, the Company will amortize excess gains and losses (using the corridor method), prior service costs and the transition credit (the excess of Plan assets plus balance sheet accruals over the projected benefit obligation, all as of January 1, 1987—the date of adoption of SFAS No. 87) over the remaining service life of its active employee population, currently 19 years. The Company's benefit plans are discussed further in a separate note.

Capitalization, Depreciation and Amortization Fixed assets are stated at cost. Depreciation is computed principally on the straight-line basis. Maintenance and repair costs are charged to expense as incurred. Major renewals are capitalized. When properties are retired or disposed, the costs and related depreciation reserves are eliminated and the resulting profit or loss is recognized in income. Goodwill is amortized principally over 40 years.

Income Taxes Deferred income taxes relate principally to accelerated depreciation methods, the investment in safe-harbor leases, the use of the installment sales method for certain receivables and the contributions to the voluntary employees' beneficiary association (VEBA). Investment tax credits are reflected in earnings over the depreciable lives of the associated assets; therefore, the portion of the credit attributable to future years has been deferred. Tax benefits purchased under the safe-harbor leasing provisions of the Economic Recovery Tax Act of 1981 and the transitional provisions of the Tax Equity and Fiscal Responsibility Act of 1982 are recorded as an investment in acquired tax benefits. The Company recognizes amortization of the investment, not directly recovered through tax credits, when the agreements provide net positive cash flows. The amortization expense is offset by a reduction to income tax expense for the tax benefit of deductions.

Acquisitions and Dispositions—In August, 1987, the Company acquired Metromail Corporation for approximately $285 million, including related expenses. Metromail is a leading provider of list, list enhancement and other services to the direct mail marketing industry. The Metromail acquisition was accounted for using the purchase method; accordingly, Metromail's assets and liabilities have been recorded at their estimated fair values at the date of acquisition. The excess of purchase price over the fair value of the net assets acquired ("goodwill" of $242 million) is being amortized on a straight-line basis over 40 years. Metromail's results of operations have been included in the consolidated results of operations since the date of acquisition. The following table presents the unaudited pro forma results of operations as if the acquisition had occurred on January 1, 1986. These pro forma results have been prepared for comparative purposes only and do not purport to be indicative of what would have occurred had the acquisition been made at the beginning of 1986 or of results which may occur in the future.

Thousands of Dollars Except Per Share Data (Unaudited)	1987	1986
Net sales	$2,545,216	$2,321,683
Earnings before income taxes	357,138	263,794
Net income	217,713	154,948
Net income per share of common stock	$2.80	$1.98

In September, 1987, the Company sold the assets of Rockford/Park Cablevision, Inc., a wholly owned subsidiary, for approximately $90 million in cash. The resulting pre-tax gain of approximately $65 million (which contributed $.51 per share to net income) is included separately in total other income—net. The results of operations of this subsidiary are included in the consolidated results of operations through the date of sale and were not material to the consolidated results of operations.

In August, 1986, the Company purchased CSA Press, Incorporated of Hudson, Massachusetts for cash. In March, 1985, the Company purchased the assets of Index Printers and Thompson Photo-Litho of Dunstable, England from Reed International (PLC) for cash. The results of operations of these acquisitions have been included in the consolidated results of operations since the dates of purchase and were not material to the consolidated results of operations.

In October, 1986, the Company acquired all of the outstanding common stock of Norwest Publishing Company (Norwest) of Portland, Oregon and Greeley, Colorado in exchange for 1,600,904 shares of common stock. This transaction was accounted for as a pooling of interests. Accordingly, the consolidated results of operations and consolidated funds flow for 1986 include the results of operations and funds flow of Norwest for the full year ending December 31, 1986. The 1985 consolidated financial statements have not been restated because the acquisition was not material to the consolidated financial statements.

Inventories—The components of the Company's inventories as of December 31, 1987 and 1986, were as follows:

Thousands of Dollars	1987	1986
Work in process	$165,697	$121,052
Operating supplies	7,062	7,153
Total	$172,759	$128,205

LIFO inventories at December 31, 1987 and 1986, were $145,131,000 and $109,141,000, respectively. Under the average cost method of accounting, inventories would have been $78,918,000 and $76,736,000 higher than those reported at December 31, 1987 and 1986, respectively.

Income Taxes—The components of income tax expense for the years ending December 31, 1987, 1986 and 1985, were as follows:

Thousands of Dollars	1987	1986	1985
Federal			
Current	$120,165	$ 93,317	$ 27,632
Deferred	863	6,123	66,085
State	22,005	12,262	8,700
Investment credit—net	(4,753)	(3,408)	5,056
Total	$138,280	$108,294	$107,473

The deferred taxes associated with the current portion of the Company's contributions to its voluntary employees' beneficiary association (VEBA) and the use of the installment sales method for certain receivables are included in current liabilities in the accompanying consolidated financial statements.

The difference between the statutory tax rate and the effective tax rate is primarily attributable to the state tax provision, amortization of investment tax credits ($7,555,000, $7,408,000 and $6,480,000 in 1987, 1986 and 1985, respectively) and the cumulative favorable impact of the Tax Reform Act of 1986 on the Company's investment in safe-harbor leases which was recognized as a reduction of deferred income tax expense in the fourth quarter of 1986.

In December, 1987, the Company entered into certain agreements with a corporation established pursuant to the Alaska Native Claim Settlement Act (ANC) for the purpose of purchasing certain tax benefits. The amount of benefits ultimately available will be determined in 1988 when the final effects of the agreements can be determined. The tax liabilities in the consolidated balance sheet include the estimated liabilities due the ANC corporation and the potential benefits.

In December, 1987, the Financial Accounting Standards Board issued Statement No. 96, "Accounting for Income Taxes." The Company is required to adopt the new accounting and disclosure rules no later than 1989. The Company has not decided when it will adopt the new standard or if it will restate prior periods. This new standard introduces complex concepts, methods and terminology; accordingly, the Company cannot yet estimate the impact the standard will have on the consolidated financial statements.

Commitments—Authorized expenditures on incomplete projects for the purchase of property, plant and equipment, as of December 31, 1987 totaled $190,007,000. Of this total, $54,148,000 has been paid and an additional $59,955,000 has been committed for payment upon completion of the contracts. The Company has a variety of commitments with suppliers for the purchase of paper and other materials for delivery in future years at prevailing market prices. The Company has operating lease commitments approximating $153,700,000 extending through various periods to 2008. The lease commitment is $21,400,000 for 1988, ranges from $10,500,000 to $17,400,000 in each of the years 1989-1992, and totals $78,900,000 for future periods.

Debt Financing and Interest Expense—At December 31, 1987, the Company had available credit facilities of $250 million to provide support for the issuance of commercial paper and other credit needs. The facilities are represented by lines of credit ($200 million) and a revolving credit agreement ($50 million) with various banks, expiring on various dates from January 1, 1989 to April 30, 1989. Borrowings under the facilities bear interest at various rates not exceeding the banks' prime rate. The Company pays a fee of 0.1% per annum on the total commitment.

At December 31, 1987, the Company had $228 million of commercial paper and short-term debt outstanding, of which $173 million is classified as long-term since the Company has the ability (see above) and intent to refinance such debt on a long-term basis. The weighted average interest rate on all commercial paper debt outstanding was 7.9%.

The following table summarizes interest expense:

Thousands of Dollars	1987	1986	1985
Interest incurred	$11,948	$8,767	$6,352
Amount capitalized as property, plant and equipment	(6,459)	(8,767)	(6,352)
Net Interest Expense	$ 5,489	$ 0	$ 0

Stock Split—On April 23, 1987, the Board of Directors declared a 2-for-1 common stock split. The stock split was completed on May 30, 1987, by the distribution of one share of common stock, par value $1.25 per share, for each share held by stockholders of record on May 8, 1987. Information relating to stock options, stock appreciation rights, reacquired common stock, the shareholder rights plan, net income and dividends per share included in the Consolidated Financial Statements and related footnotes reflect the stock split.

Common and Preferred Stock—The Company has 2,000,000 shares of $1.00 par value preferred stock authorized for issuance. The Board of Directors may divide the preferred stock into one

or more series and fix the redemption, dividend, voting, conversion, sinking fund, liquidation and other rights. The Company has no present plans to issue any preferred stock. 1,000,000 of the shares are reserved for issuance under the Shareholder Rights Plan discussed below.

As a result of the shares issued in 1986 in connection with the acquisition of Norwest, the number of common shares issued increased by 1,600,904, from 77,703,496 shares outstanding as previously reported in 1985, to 79,304,400. The following table summarizes the activity in reacquired common stock during the three years ending December 31, 1987:

	1987	1986	1985
Number of shares reacquired at beginning of year	1,380,526	1,343,060	1,196,052
Purchased during the year	939,063	580,980	653,732
Issued under stock programs	(503,524)	(543,514)	(506,724)
Number of shares reacquired at end of year	1,816,065	1,380,526	1,343,060

Shareholder Rights Plan—On July 24, 1986, the Company adopted a Shareholder Rights Plan (the Plan) designed to deter coercive or unfair takeover tactics, to prevent a person or group from gaining control of the Company without offering fair value to all shareholders and to deter other abusive takeover tactics which are not in the best interests of shareholders.

Under the terms of the Plan, each share of common stock is accompanied by one-half of a Right; each full Right entitles the shareholder to purchase from the Company, one one-hundredth of a newly issued share of Series A Junior Participating Preferred Stock at an exercise price of $225.

The Rights only become exercisable ten days after a public announcement that an Acquiring Person (as defined in the Plan) has acquired 20% or more of the outstanding common stock of the Company (the Stock Acquisition Date) or ten days after the commencement of a tender offer which would result in a person owning 30% or more of such shares. The Company can redeem the Rights for $.05 per Right at any time until twenty days following the Stock Acquisition Date (the 20-day period can be shortened or lengthened by the Company). The Rights will expire on August 8, 1996 unless earlier redeemed by the Company.

If, subsequent to the Rights becoming exercisable, the Company is acquired in a merger or other business combination at any time when there is a 20% or more holder, the Rights will then entitle a holder to buy shares of common stock of the acquiring company with a market value equal to twice the exercise price of each Right. Alternatively, if a 20% holder acquires the Company by means of a merger in which the Company and its stock survive, or if any person acquires 30% or more of the Company's common stock, each Right, not owned by a 20% or more shareholder, would become exercisable for common stock of the Company (or, in certain circumstances, other consideration) having a market value equal to twice the exercise price of the Right.

Benefit Plans—*Retirement Benefit Plan (the Plan)* Net pension costs (credits) included in operating results for the Plan were $(2,214,000) in 1987, $20,700,000 in 1986, and $21,555,000 in 1985. The net pension credit in 1987 was composed of:

Thousands of Dollars	
Service cost	$12,607
Interest cost on the projected benefit obligation	30,656
Actual return on Plan assets	(502)
Amortization of excess Plan net assets at adoption of SFAS No. 87 and deferrals ($48.6 million)	(58,450)
Supplemental early retirement costs	13,475
Total	$ (2,214)

The 1987 actuarial computations assumed a discount rate on projected benefit obligations of 9.5% (8.5% at January 1, 1987), an expected long-term rate of return on Plan assets of 9% and annual salary increases of 5%. The effect of the 1987 adoption of SFAS No. 87, "Employers' Accounting for Pensions," was to reduce 1987 pension costs, net of the cost of supplemental early retirements, by approximately $23 million.

Plan assets include government and corporate debt securities, marketable equity securities, commingled funds, real estate and a group annuity contract purchased from a life insurance company. The funded status and prepaid pension cost (included in Other Assets on the accompanying balance sheet) are as follows:

Thousands of Dollars	December 31, 1987	January 1, 1987
Fair value of Plan assets	$551,300	$554,269
Actuarial present value of benefit obligations:		
Vested	305,589	305,535
Non-vested	7,731	9,996
Total accumulated benefit obligations	313,320	315,531
Additional amounts related to projected salary increases	46,892	54,576
Projected benefit obligations for services rendered to date	360,212	370,107
Excess of Plan assets over projected benefit obligations	191,088	184,162
Unrecognized net losses	7,848	—
Unrecognized net excess Plan assets to be amortized over 19 years	(177,295)	(187,145)
Prepaid pension costs	$ 21,641	$ (2,983)

In the event of Plan termination, the Plan provides that no funds can revert to the Company, and any excess assets over Plan liabilities must be used to fund retirement benefits.

Other Post-retirement Benefits In addition to pension benefits, the Company provides certain health care and life insurance benefits for retired employees. Substantially all of the Company's domestic, full time employees become eligible for those benefits upon reaching age 55 while working for the Company and having 10 years' continuous service at retirement. The cost ($4,451,000 in 1987, $4,553,000 in 1986 and $3,383,000 in 1985) of retiree health care and life insurance benefits is recognized as expense when paid.

VEBA In 1984, a Voluntary Employees' Beneficiary Association was established to fund benefits to employees in a more cost-effective manner. Those contributions from the Company to the Trust which will be used to fund benefits as they become payable during the next twelve months are included in "Prepaid expenses" in the accompanying consolidated financial statements. That portion of 1985's contributions which funded post-1986 expenses was included in "Other" (noncurrent) Assets at December 31, 1985.

Employee Stock Ownership Plan (ESOP) Contributions to the Company's ESOP were discontinued in response to the change in tax law that eliminated the previously available tax credit. Under this plan, 865,206 shares are held in trust as of December 31, 1987, for formerly eligible employees. There are no charges to operations for this plan, except for certain administrative expenses.

Fixed Assets—The following table summarizes the components of Property, Plant and Equipment (at cost):

Thousands of Dollars	1987	1986
Land	$ 48,998	$ 28,549
Buildings	364,761	329,315
Machinery and equipment	1,454,718	1,317,530
Total	$1,868,477	$1,675,394

Stock and Incentive Programs for Management Employees—*Stock Units Awards* At December 31, 1987 and 1986, the Company had outstanding 480.916 and 551,594 stock units, respectively, which had been granted to officers and selected managers.

Certain of these units are payable upon or subsequent to termination of employment and others are payable upon vesting, normally five years after the date of grant. Payment of these awards will be made in shares of common stock equal to the number of units awarded or, at the Company's option, in cash equal to the market value at the date of distribution, or a combination thereof.

When an award of stock units is paid, the recipient will receive an additional amount in cash equal to dividends paid on an equivalent number of shares of common stock during the time between grant and payment of the award, plus interest. The value of the dividends and interest accounts was $2,230,000 and $2,113,000 at December 31, 1987 and 1986, respectively.

The value of the stock units was $15,690,000 ($32.63 per share) at December 31, 1987 and $16,962,000 ($30.75 per share) at December 31, 1986. Charges to expense for these stock units plans were $2,574,000 in 1987, $2,949,000 in 1986 and $3,003,000 in 1985.

Stock Options The Company granted stock options in 1977, 1981, and 1983 to 1987. Option prices were 100% of the market price of common stock on the date of grant, and the period of exercise ranges up to ten years from the date of grant.

Under the 1986 Stock Incentive Plan, a maximum of 2,321,900 shares were available for future grants of stock options and stock units as of December 31, 1987. No charges to income will be made with respect to the stock options. No options were granted under the 1981 Stock Incentive Plan after the termination date of March 25, 1986.

The Company has followed a policy of granting stock appreciation rights (rights) related to certain outstanding options during the options' final year of exercise and, in the case of awards of stock units, of paying part of such awards in cash. Reflecting its intention to grant rights (relating to options already granted) in the future, and to pay cash in lieu of shares for a portion of the shares covered by awards of stock units, the Company currently provides for the expected costs associated with the rights and cash payments based on the vesting portion of the related rights and stock units.

During 1987, the Company granted 72,380 stock appreciation rights with respect to shares of common stock then covered by stock options granted in 1977 (the "related options") at an option price of $5.75 per share. No stock appreciation rights were granted in 1986.

Stock Purchase Plan The Company has a stock purchase plan for selected managers and key staff employees. The number of shares required for the plan for the year 1987 will depend on the extent to which eligible participants subscribe during the subscription period (January 25, 1988 to February 19, 1988) and the price of the stock on February 22, 1988. The Company is required to contribute an amount equal to 70% of participants' contributions, of which 50% is applied to the purchase of stock and 20% is paid in cash. Amounts charged to expense for this plan were $3,229,000 in 1987, $2,919,000 in 1986 and $2,954,000 in 1985.

Incentive Compensation Plans The Company has incentive compensation plans covering selected officers and executives. Amounts charged to expense for supplementary compensation, which is determined from participants' base salaries and factors relating to profits, sales performance, and other items, were $2,352,000 in 1987, $2,180,000 in 1986 and $2,431,000 in 1985.

Other Information Under the stock programs, authorized unissued shares or treasury shares may be used. If authorized unissued shares are used, not more than 5,445,802 shares may be issued in the aggregate. The Company intends to reacquire shares of its common stock to meet the stock requirements of these programs in the future.

Information relating to the stock options and stock appreciation rights for the years ended December 31, 1987 and 1986, is shown below:

1987	Number of Shares	Per Share Option Price on Date of Grant		
Stock options granted	299,000			$32.38
Stock options canceled or expired	96,514	$5.75	to	$31.91
Stock options exercised	276,324	$5.75	to	$31.91
Stock appreciation rights exercised in lieu of related options	22,330			$5.75
At end of year				
Stock options outstanding	1,442,986	$9.25	to	$32.38
Stock options exercisable	223,314	$9.25	to	$31.91
1986				
Stock options granted	575,500			$31.31
Stock options canceled or expired	55,588	$21.50	to	$31.91
Stock options exercised	241,640	$5.22	to	$22.88
Stock appreciation rights exercised in lieu of related options	113,000			$5.22
At end of year				
Stock options outstanding	1,539,154	$5.75	to	$31.91
Stock options exercisable	392,314	$5.75	to	$31.91

Statement of Management Responsibility
R. R. Donnelley & Sons Company and Subsidiaries

Auditors' Report

The consolidated financial statements of R. R. Donnelley & Sons Company and Subsidiaries are the responsibility of management, and those statements have been prepared in accordance with generally accepted accounting principles. All available information and management's judgment of current conditions and circumstances have been reflected. Management accepts full responsibility for the accuracy, integrity and objectivity of the financial data included in this report.

To provide reasonable assurance that assets are safeguarded against loss from unauthorized use or disposition and that accounting records are reliable for preparing financial statements, management maintains systems of accounting and internal controls, including written policies and procedures, which are communicated to all levels of the Company. Management believes that the Company's accounting and internal control systems provide reasonable assurance that assets are safeguarded and financial information is reliable. Key employees are periodically given written communications concerning their responsibilities for integrity.

Maintenance of sound internal control by division of responsibilities is augmented by internal audit programs and an Audit Committee of the Board of Directors comprised solely of directors independent of management. The Audit Committee reviews the scope of the audits performed by the independent public accountants, Arthur Andersen & Co., and the Company's Internal Audit Department, together with their audit reports and any recommendations made by them. The Committee reviews in January each year, the results of the audit for the prior fiscal year with the independent public accountants before the earnings report for such fiscal year is released publicly. The independent accountants have free access to meet with the Audit Committee and the Board of Directors with or without management representatives present.

To the Shareholders of R. R. Donnelley & Sons Company:
We have examined the consolidated balance sheet of R. R. Donnelley & Sons Company (a Delaware corporation) and Subsidiaries as of December 31, 1987 and 1986, and the related consolidated statements of income, shareholders' equity and funds flow for each of the three years in the period ended December 31, 1987. Our examinations were made in accordance with generally accepted auditing standards and, accordingly, included such tests of the accounting records and such other auditing procedures as we considered necessary in the circumstances.

In our opinion, the financial statements referred to above present fairly the financial position of R. R. Donnelley & Sons Company and Subsidiaries as of December 31, 1987 and 1986, and the results of their operations and funds flow for each of the three years in the period ended December 31, 1987, in conformity with generally accepted accounting principles which, except for the change, with which we concur, in the method of accounting for pension expense, were applied on a consistent basis.

Arthur Andersen & Co.
Chicago, Illinois,
January 28, 1988

Financial Summary
R. R. Donnelley & Sons Company and Subsidiaries

Thousands of Dollars Except Per Share Data	1987	1986	1985
Operating Statistics			
Net Sales	$2,482,865	$2,233,511	$2,038,408
Cost of Sales	1,970,788	1,776,514	1,606,483
Selling and Administrative Expenses	233,044	206,238	195,789
Depreciation and Amortization	140,300	119,054	103,710
Earnings Before Income Taxes	356,476	266,562	255,887
Income Taxes	138.280	108,294	107,473
Net Income	218,196	158,268	148,414
Per Common Share*			
Net Income	2.80	2.03	1.94
Cash Dividends	.70	.64	.58
Shareholders' Equity	14.83	12.87	11.72
Financial Statistics			
Current Assets	672,364	663,759	639,005
Current Liabilities	383,692	367,130	342,023
Working Capital	288,672	296,629	296,982
Property, Plant and Equipment—Net	1,090,757	997,386	811,082
Total Assets	2,086,387	1,741,251	1,593,345
Capital Expenditures	210,482	254,646	162,841
Short-Term Debt	55,706	66.594	49,983
Long-Term Debt	193,787	18,444	15,002
Total Shareholders' Equity	1,155,089	1,005,008	895,903
Average Common Shares Outstanding*	77,872	78,086	76,464

*Based on average common shares outstanding during each year, which reflects 2-for-1 common stock split effective May 30, 1987.

Shareholders' Information Thousands of Dollars Except Per Share Data	First Quarter*	Second Quarter*	Third Quarter*	Fourth Quarter
Interim Financial Information				
1987				
Net sales	$510,568	$574,684	$624,551	$773,062
Gross profit	95,824	116,763	137,106	162,384
Net income	30,174	41,435	89,379	57,208
Net income per common share**	.39	.53	1.15	.73
Interim Financial Information				
1986				
Net sales	$492,217	$500,823	$560,808	$679,663
Gross profit	93,346	105,695	120,792	137,164
Net income	28,162	35,287	44,720	50,099
Net income per common share**	.36	.45	.57	.64

*1986 restated to include results of operations of Norwest Publishing Company, an acquisition completed October 31, 1986, and accounted for as a pooling of interests.
**Reflects 2-for-1 common stock split effective May 30, 1987.

1984	1983	1982	1981	1980	1979	1978	1977
$1,814,486	$1,545,750	$1,404,206	$1,243,859	$1,111,258	$957,807	$780,193	$661,844
1,437,401	1,216,160	1,124,155	1,004,215	895,996	770,213	621,915	521,341
172,016	144,735	130,026	107,510	94,752	80,725	66,337	58,096
90,250	71,892	71,445	53,078	43,084	35,300	33,040	27,756
230,850	200,768	162,475	146,516	129,561	115,937	101,055	90,507
96,957	86,332	71,300	67,500	60,600	52,600	46,100	41,300
133,893	114,436	91,175	79,016	68,961	63,337	54,955	49,207
1.75	1.50	1.20	1.05	.93	.86	.74	.66
.50	.41	.35½	.32	.28½	.25	.22	.18
10.44	9.25	8.23	7.44	6.70	6.04	5.43	4.85
606,328	440,851	305.933	277,244	267,030	261,820	268,938	254,523
373,778	280,153	184,841	199,590	197,272	162,107	123,925	106,084
232,550	160,698	121,092	77,654	69,758	99,713	145,013	148,439
745,954	669,094	572,064	548,052	495,213	400,661	292,759	246.930
1,445,793	1,204,117	971,831	865.797	771,749	670,083	569,526	504,836
175,370	172,779	124,040	106,656	137,547	143,654	79,395	47,292
23,376	29,337	14,544	16,968	32,728	5,243	4,361	1,260
14,280	14,026	13,934	11,637	11,589	12,949	4,535	—
798,483	705,341	624,986	560,021	499,046	446,895	400,773	361,229
76.472	76,280	75,980	75,250	74,466	74,032	73,788	74,510

	First Quarter	Second Quarter	Third Quarter	Fourth Quarter	Full Year
Stock Market Data*					
1987					
High	$39¼	$39¾	$45⅜	$43	$45⅜
Low	30¾	31¹¹⁄₁₆	36¼	25½	25½
1986					
High	$39¹³⁄₁₆	$40	$39⁷⁄₁₆	$33⁵⁄₁₆	$40
Low	30³⁄₁₆	34½	29⁷⁄₁₆	29½	29⁷⁄₁₆
Dividend Summary*					
1987	$.17½	$.17½	$.17½	$.17½	$.70
1986	.16	.16	.16	.16	.64
1985	.14½	.14½	.14½	.14½	.58
1984	.12½	.12½	.12½	.12½	.50
1983	.10	.10	.10½	.10½	.41

*Reflects 2-for-1 common stock split effective May 30, 1987.

SCREENING FOR SUITABLE STOCKS

Daniel Chamberlin, founder and senior partner of Daniel Chamberlin Investment Counsel, has just subscribed to a computerized database provided by Jorgenson Investment Services. The service includes a program disk and a monthly data disk. The database includes over fifty variables (see Exhibit 1 below) for each of 1,500 common stocks. Mr. Chamberlin hopes that this periodic information will be helpful to him in building an approved list of common stocks for his business. He asks Keith Rosenthal, a graduate student at Emory University who works part time for Chamberlin's firm, to help him make use of the new data.

Daniel Chamberlin Investment Counsel is a small but growing investment advisory firm in Atlanta, Georgia. In addition to Mr. Chamberlin, there are two younger partners, a staff of five (including an office manager, two research assistants, and two secretaries), and two part-time graduate students. The firm manages something over $200 million, including individual accounts, pension funds, and the portfolios of a few non-profit organizations. Although the fee income of the firm has grown steadily in recent years, Mr. Chamberlin is increasingly concerned about the level and volatility of the stock market -- and is one reason for the new database subscription.

The firm's expressed investment philosophy is to focus on high quality securities, to be well diversified at all times, to not consider options and futures, and to have low portfolio turnover over time. Each portfolio is tailored to client needs in terms of both asset allocation (equity, bonds, and cash) and yield versus appreciation for equity investments. Each portfolio is managed by one of the three partners, although Mr. Chamberlin keeps an eye on all of them. The three partners also serve as an investment committee to consider asset allocation policies and the composition of the firm's approved list.

Chamberlin and his colleagues normally limit their equity purchases to an approved list of approximately fifty common stocks. In the past, the approved list has been reviewed quarterly, and occasional changes have been made based on research information provided by the four or five securities firms that Chamberlin does business with on a regular basis.

Mr. Chamberlin instructs Keith Rosenthal to become familiar with the computerized data base, and to make recommendations on how it should be used over time. Apparently, the program disk allows the user to print selected data for any or all stocks in the universe, as well as to calculate averages for selected sectors of the universe. In addition, there is a capability to develop screens using one or more of the variables. In other words, the user could ask for a listing of all common stocks that are in the highest two quality categories and have a current dividend yield exceeding 8%. Daniel Chamberlin is particularly interested in what variables and parameters would lead to useful screens for monitoring and revising his firm's approved list.

Keith Rosenthal begins to work on his assignment for Mr. Chamberlin by becoming familiar with the monthly database. In so doing, he begins to anticipate several questions which he feels that he may be asked in the near future.

(1) What are the <u>three</u> most important variables (see Exhibit 1) that are provided monthly for each of the 1,500 common stocks?

(2) What are the <u>five</u> most important variables?

(3) What are the <u>ten</u> most important variables?

(4) If Rosenthal is given the database for each of the past twelve months, how should he utilize that data to build screens that select attractive common stocks from the universe?

(5) In preparing screens, it is possible to rank those common stocks that survive. What do you suggest about rankings?

(6) What additional data should be utilized in developing an approved list for the firm?

120

Exhibit 1
VARIABLE LISTING AND EXPLANATION
JORGENSON INVESTMENT SERVICES

The computerized database provided by Jorgenson Investment Services covers 1,500 common stocks. The data are updated monthly. The database is available on-line via a modem, or it is provided on a floppy disk no later than the sixth working day of the next month. The following variables are available for each common stock:

---

1. Company name
2. Ticker symbol
3. Month-end share price
4. Quality rating (1 highest to 9 lowest) -- based on financial strength and earnings stability over time
5. Current/normal earnings ratio
6. Growth rate -- estimated for earnings and dividends during the next five years
7. Current price/earnings ratio
8. Normal price/earnings ratio
9. Normal price/earnings ratio divided by estimated growth rate
10. Market price/book value ratio
11. Price/cash flow per share ratio
12. Share price/sales per share ratio
13. Total return (growth plus dividend yield)
14. Internal rate of return
15. Price/intrinsic value ratio
16. Price/intrinsic value ratio relative to the stock universe
17. Current 12-month earnings per share
18. Normal 12-month earnings per share
19. Cash flow per share
20. Earnings variability (past five years)
21. Dividend payout ratio
22. Current dividend per share
23. Current yield
24. Net profit margin on sales
25. Return on equity
26. Return on assets
27. Intrinsic value per share
28. Foreign-based company indicator
29. Listed options indicator
30. Exchange indicator
31. DJIA/S&P550/Value Line indicator
32. Buy/Hold/Sell indicator
33. Earnings per share growth rate (past five years)
34. Sales growth rate (past five years)
35. Dividends per share growth rate (past five years)
36. Average price/earnings ratio (past five years)

121

37. Average price/intrinsic value ratio (past five years)
38. Previous month-end share price
39. Percentage price gain (during last month)
40. Percentage price gain (last five years)
41. Annual total return (last five years)
42. Beta -- based on last five years
43. Common shares outstanding
44. Company annual sales
45. Common shares held by institutional investors
46. Market capitalization
47. Preferred equity/sales ratio
48. Common equity/sales ratio
49. Long term debt/assets ratio
50. Other liabilities/assets ratio
51. Total assets
52. Current ratio
53. Total debt/assets ratio
54. Long term debt/equity ratio

STOCK PORTFOLIO FOR THE BROPHYS

After graduation from a midwestern university, classmates David Brophy and Cathy Sorenson married and set forth on a well-conceived career plan. They proceeded to work for five years in their chosen professions as an electrical engineer and home economist, respectively. At the end of that period, they invested their savings in the purchase of a hardware store in the small town where they were high school sweethearts.

For the next twenty-five years, they both devoted long hours to the management of their business. David was in the store at all times and specialized in helping customers on the design and eventual construction of home improvements. Cathy handled all of the purchasing, accounting, and personnel matters. Because of their easy and helpful manner with customers, the business grew steadily, and the Brophys, not able to have children, were able to save a good deal of their earnings. Five years later, they opened a second hardware store in a neighboring town, and after three more years, they purchased a lumber yard in their town. Their devotion to customer service, positive treatment of their personnel, and overall concern for all details of their three businesses consistently led to profitability.

When at mid-year 1987, they reached age of fifty, the Brophys fulfilled their career goal of retiring. They proceeded to sell the three businesses, as well as other investment property that had been bought along the way. The results of their years of work included their home comfortably furnished and paid for, a vacation home also furnished and paid for, plus after-tax wealth of $450,000.

Though highly successful in the hardware and lumber businesses, the Brophys do not pretend to have much expertise in investing. However, they have seen first-hand the effect of inflation, and thus are determined to not invest in fixed-income securities. They come to you for advice on how to construct a portfolio of common stocks. They stipulate that their $450,000 be invested in a portfolio of common stocks that generates reasonable income, and overall a fair return for the risk undertaken. They also stipulate that their portfolio be tailored to their particular needs, and not just be put in either a common trust fund or a mutual fund. With the proceeds of their portfolio, the Brophys plan to do some traveling, to contribute to some of their favorite charities, and overall to enjoy their relatively early retirement.

A recent research report from Goldman Sachs is enclosed. You decide to limit your analysis and portfolio construction to the 302 common stocks covered in that report. Be specific in your recommendation. And be prepared to discuss the following questions:

Safety Volatility
Return
Income

(1) What criteria will you utilize in selecting common stocks the Brophys' portfolio?

10 or 20 or 40

(2) How will you determine the number of common stocks to be included?

a) Equally
b) ($ Return)

(3) What criteria will you utilize in allocating the Brophys' $450,000 to the common stocks so selected?

@ 2% = 9000

(4) Approximately how much will be spent in brokerage fees to purchase the Brophys' common stock portfolio?

Annual Income Quart

(5) In view of these considerations, what specific portfolio of common stocks do you recommend for the Brophys?

(6) What annual income can the Brophys expect from their portfolio?

Not given

(7) How would you suggest that David and Cathy go about revising their common stock portfolio over time?

124

Exhibit 1

Portfolio Strategy

June 1987

Risk, Return, and Equity Valuation

Monthly Update

Steven G. Einhorn

Patricia C. Shangkuan

Appendix I

Definition of Column Headings .

Column 1
Indicates the rank of the company by risk-adjusted excess annual return.

Column 2
Current price of the stock.

Column 3
Estimated trend growth rate in earnings per share for the next five years.

Column 4
The estimated justifiable price in 1991 based on normalized dividends (1987) earnings growth (1987-1991), and sustainable return on equity (1987-1991). Derivation of the theoretical price is detailed in Appendix A of our initial publication dated January 13, 1978.

Column 5
The estimated risk index of the security, computed over the most recent 40-quarter interval. The risk index is a weighted average of a fundamental beta (40% weighting), developed by our Portfolio Strategy Group, and an inflation risk index (60% weighting). A detailed explanation is available on request.

Column 6
The sensitivity of the security's internal rate of return to a one-percentage-point change in the estimated growth rate (column 3). For example, we are currently estimating a 7.0% trend rate of growth in earnings for the S&P 500 over the next five years. At its current price, the S&P 500 has an estimated 3.2% internal rate of return. If we assume a 9.0% growth rate, the internal rate of return is increased by 5.4 percentage points (2x2.7 = 5.4) to 8.6%. With the market's required return unchanged, risk-adjusted excess return is also increased by 5.4 percentage points. Column 6 permits the user to quickly compute security excess returns under different assumptions for trend growth in earnings.

Column 7   Indicates the internal annual rate of return for
                  each security. This rate equates the current stock
                  price to the sum of dividends over the next five
                  years and the security's theoretical (1991) price.

Column 8   Indicates the required rate of return for each
                  security, which is based on the company investment
                  risk measure and the required return assumed for
                  the market. The derivation of required rate of
                  return is given in Appendix B of our January 13,
                  1978 report.

Column 9   Risk-adjusted excess return is the difference
                  between a security's internal rate of return
                  (column 7) and its required rate of return (column
                  8).

Column 10   Current price divided by normalized earnings per
                  share. Normalized earnings are estimated by our
                  analysts.

Column 11   Theoretical (1991) price, given in column 4,
                  divided by normalized earnings in 1991. Normalized
                  earnings 1991 are obtained by compounding the 1987
                  earnings per share at the rate given in column 3.

APPENDIX I

RANKING OF

COMMON STOCK RISK ADJUSTED EXCESS RETURNS

COMPANY	(1) RANK BY RISK ADJ EXCESS ANNUAL RETURN	(2) PRICE (5/29/87)	(3) TREND GR RATE EPS (87-91)	(4) THEORETICAL PRICE (1991)	(5) GS&C RISK INDEX	(6) INTERNAL RATE OF RETURN CHANGE	(7) INDCTD ANNUAL RETURN (%)	(8) REQR'D ANNUAL RETURN (%)	(9) RISK ADJ EXCESS ANNUAL RETURN (%)	(10) NORMALIZED PE RATIO (1987)	(11) PE RATIO (1991)	
*S&P COMPOSITE AVERAGE	255	290.10	7.0	285	1.01	2.7	3.2	10.6	-7.4	14.7	11.0	1
*AAR CORP	51	30.38	18.0	74	1.22	2.2	22.6	11.1	11.5	17.9	22.4	2
*ASK COMPUTER SYSTEMS	151	13.00	17.0	23	1.58	2.4	13.3	12.0	1.3	18.6	17.9	3
*ABBOTT LABS	155	60.13	15.0	93	1.00	2.2	11.5	10.6	1.0	21.3	18.9	4
*ADAMS-RUSSELL CO	275	23.88	12.0	25	1.39	2.7	0.7	11.5	-10.8	18.4	12.1	5
*AETNA LIFE & CASUALTY	21	57.25	11.0	160	0.99	2.8	28.2	10.5	17.7	7.9	14.5	6
*AGNICO EAGLE	297	24.88	15.0	14	1.67	1.8	-10.4	12.2	-22.7	54.1	17.6	7
*AHMANSON(H.F.)& CO	16	21.00	11.0	71	2.26	3.0	33.1	13.7	19.4	6.2	13.8	8
*ALBERTSON'S INC	167	49.50	12.0	74	0.83	2.6	10.5	10.1	0.4	15.2	14.4	9
*ALCO STANDARD CORP	54	48.38	14.0	110	0.93	2.4	21.6	10.4	11.3	13.4	18.0	10
*ALLIED SIGNAL	29	40.50	12.0	109	1.08	2.7	26.6	10.8	15.9	9.0	15.5	11
*AMERADA HESS CORP	287	36.88	8.0	26	1.12	4.5	-4.0	10.9	-14.8	24.6	12.8	12
*AMDAHL CORP	229	36.88	16.0	52	1.86	2.2	8.1	12.7	-4.6	23.0	17.9	13
*AMERICAN CYANAMID CO	130	90.63	13.0	148	1.17	2.8	13.6	11.0	2.6	18.9	19.0	14
*AMERICAN GENERAL CORP	56	36.00	10.5	84	1.44	2.8	22.7	11.6	11.1	8.6	13.4	15
*AMERICAN GREETINGS CP	68	25.50	12.0	56	1.04	2.8	20.5	10.7	9.8	10.2	14.4	16
*AMERICAN HOME PRODS CP	194	82.63	8.0	102	0.96	4.5	8.9	10.4	-1.5	14.7	13.3	17
*AMERICAN INT'L GROUP	84	64.38	15.0	150	1.48	2.7	20.0	11.8	8.2	12.0	16.0	18
*AMERICAN MEDICAL	143	17.50	8.0	26	1.20	3.9	12.8	11.0	1.8	10.8	11.9	19
*AMERICAN STANDARD	75	42.38	10.0	84	0.88	2.6	19.4	10.2	9.1	11.0	14.9	20
*AMDCO CORP	278	83.38	6.0	62	0.82	2.3	-2.0	10.1	-12.1	19.4	11.5	21
*ANALOG DEVICES	295	21.63	15.0	14	1.09	2.1	-8.6	10.8	-19.3	41.6	15.5	22
*ANHEUSER BUSCH INC	156	33.50	14.0	52	1.06	2.3	11.4	10.7	0.7	18.4	16.9	23
*APPLE COMPUTER	288	79.00	15.0	70	1.76	2.2	-2.4	12.5	-14.8	30.5	15.5	24
*APOLLO COMPUTER	276	24.00	15.0	24	1.45	2.3	0.4	11.7	-11.3	26.7	15.5	25
*APPLIED MAGNETICS	296	36.00	12.0	21	1.39	2.4	-10.8	11.5	-22.3	32.7	12.1	26
*ASHLAND OIL. INC	251	62.63	4.0	60	0.97	2.9	4.2	10.5	-6.2	10.4	8.5	27
*ASHTON-TATE	235	24.25	15.0	33	1.42	2.4	6.5	11.6	-5.1	20.2	15.5	28
*ATLANTIC RICHFIELD CO	267	87.63	6.0	71	0.73	2.3	0.1	9.9	-9.8	19.5	12.5	29
*AUTOMATIC DATA PROCESS	201	46.38	16.0	65	1.09	2.1	8.6	10.8	-2.1	24.9	19.2	30
*AVERY INTL INC	95	24.00	15.0	47	1.00	2.4	17.1	10.5	6.6	16.0	18.0	31

* (ASTERISKED) COMPANIES REFLECT GOLDMAN SACHS ESTIMATES FOR TREND GROWTH IN EARNINGS PER SHARE
AND SUSTAINABLE RETURN ON EQUITY. WHERE WE DO NOT MAINTAIN COVERAGE, ESTIMATES FOR GROWTH IN EARNINGS
FOR NON-ASTERISKED COMPANIES. PER SHARE AND RETURN ON EQUITY ARE DERIVED FROM HISTORICAL (LAST 5 YEARS) COMPANY INFORMATION.

APPENDIX I

RANKING OF
COMMON STOCK RISK ADJUSTED EXCESS RETURNS

	COMPANY	(1) RANK BY RISK ADJ EXCESS ANNUAL RETURN	(2) PRICE (5/29/87)	(3) TREND GR RATE EPS (87-91)	(4) THEORETICAL PRICE (1991)	(5) GS&C RISK INDEX	(6) INTERNAL RATE OF RETURN CHANGE	(7) INDCTD ANNUAL RETURN (%)	(8) REQR'D ANNUAL RETURN (%)	(9) RISK ADJ EXCESS ANNUAL RETURN (%)	(10) NORMALIZED PE RATIO (1987)	(11) NORMALIZED PE RATIO (1991)
32	*AVON PRODUCTS INC	10	29.88	9.0	97	1.10	2.8	33.6	10.8	22.7	9.1	21.1
33	*BAIRNCO	218	38.88	10.0	48	1.04	2.6	6.7	10.6	-3.9	15.4	12.9
34	*BANC ONE CORP	81	24.63	10.0	49	1.00	2.8	19.1	10.5	8.5	9.7	13.3
35	*BANK OF BOSTON CORP	144	34.00	9.0	54	1.35	2.9	13.2	11.4	1.8	10.4	11.7
36	*BANK OF NEW ENGLAND	22	32.00	12.0	94	1.26	2.8	28.9	11.2	17.7	7.9	14.9
37	*BANK OF NEW YORK CORP	46	40.13	10.0	94	1.14	2.9	23.3	10.9	12.4	8.3	13.2
38	*BANKERS TRUST NY CORP	15	47.38	12.0	154	1.22	3.0	30.9	11.1	19.8	6.9	14.3
39	*BARD(C.R.) INC NJ	285	44.75	11.0	37	1.21	2.4	-2.6	11.1	-13.6	23.7	13.0
40	*BARNETT BANKS OF FLA	47	37.63	14.0	95	1.27	2.6	23.5	11.2	12.3	11.1	16.6
41	*BAXTOR TRAVENOL	233	22.88	12.0	27	1.02	2.2	5.9	10.6	-4.7	20.4	15.5
42	*BECTON DICKINSON & CO	137	54.50	14.0	90	1.11	2.3	12.8	10.8	2.0	17.1	16.7
43	*BELL INDUSTRIES	284	20.63	10.0	18	0.97	2.9	-2.7	10.5	-13.1	16.5	9.9
44	*BIG BEAR INC	294	21.50	8.0	15	1.08	3.3	-7.4	10.5	-18.1	15.3	7.8
45	*BOEING CO	40	45.25	16.0	114	0.90	2.4	23.6	10.3	13.3	14.1	19.6
46	*BOISE CASCADE CORP	210	68.88	9.0	89	1.55	2.5	8.8	11.9	-3.2	13.8	12.6
47	*BORG-WARNER	200	45.50	11.0	60	1.10	2.4	8.8	10.8	-2.0	17.1	14.9
48	*BRISTOL-MYERS CO	78	97.00	15.0	203	0.93	2.2	19.3	10.4	9.0	20.1	24.0
49	*BURLINGTON INDS INC	289	75.75	8.0	53	1.17	4.5	-4.2	11.0	-15.2	24.4	12.6
50	*CIGNA CORP	23	59.25	11.0	174	1.43	2.9	29.3	11.6	7.7	7.3	14.1
51	*CPC INTL INC	138	52.25	13.0	81	0.92	2.3	12.3	10.4	2.0	18.0	17.2
52	*CABOT CORP	227	37.00	8.0	43	1.05	2.8	6.1	10.7	-4.6	12.3	10.6
53	*CAMPBELL RED LAKE	300	27.75	8.0	8	1.09	4.5	-20.0	10.4	-30.8	64.5	14.4
54	*CAMPBELL SOUP CO	154	62.88	11.0	93	0.91	2.4	11.3	10.3	1.0	15.0	14.6
55	*CAPITAL HOLDING CO	141	29.75	8.0	46	1.09	3.0	12.6	10.8	1.8	9.1	10.4
56	*CHAMPION INTL CORP	196	34.63	10.0	48	1.22	2.7	9.3	11.1	-1.8	13.1	12.4
57	*CHASE MANHATTAN CORP	4	38.63	11.0	145	1.27	3.1	36.4	11.2	25.2	5.6	13.9
58	*CHEMICAL NEW YORK CORP	8	42.00	10.0	145	1.24	3.1	34.6	11.1	23.5	5.6	13.2
59	*CHEVRON CORP	286	58.38	6.0	40	1.00	2.2	-3.4	10.5	-14.0	22.5	12.3
60	*CHUBB CORP	13	58.00	12.5	198	1.44	3.0	31.9	11.6	20.3	6.8	14.5
61	*CHURCH'S FRIED CHICKEN	9	9.75	12.0	33	0.89	2.6	33.4	10.3	23.1	12.5	26.8
62	*CITICORP	30	56.13	10.0	149	1.03	3.1	26.5	10.6	15.9	7.0	12.7
63	*CITIZ & SOUTHERN CORP	70	26.38	10.0	57	1.47	2.8	21.3	11.7	9.6	9.2	13.5
64	*CLOROX CO	136	53.88	10.0	84	1.19	2.5	13.0	11.0	2.0	13.0	13.8
65	*COCA-COLA CO	174	42.88	10.0	61	1.05	2.3	10.7	10.7	0.0	18.6	18.0
66	*COLEMAN COMPANY	230	34.88	7.0	39	1.15	2.8	6.3	10.9	-4.6	12.7	10.9

* (ASTERISKED) COMPANIES REFLECT GOLDMAN SACHS ESTIMATES FOR TREND GROWTH IN EARNINGS PER SHARE
AND SUSTAINABLE RETURN ON EQUITY. WHERE WE DO NOT MAINTAIN COVERAGE, ESTIMATES FOR GROWTH IN EARNINGS
FOR NON-ASTERISKED COMPANIES, ESTIMATES FOR GROWTH IN EARNINGS
PER SHARE AND RETURN ON EQUITY ARE DERIVED FROM HISTORICAL (LAST 5 YEARS) COMPANY INFORMATION.

APPENDIX I

RANKING OF

COMMON STOCK RISK ADJUSTED EXCESS RETURNS

	COMPANY	(1) RANK BY RISK ADJ EXCESS ANNUAL RETURN	(2) PRICE (5/29/87)	(3) TREND GR RATE EPS (87-91)	(4) THEORETICAL PRICE (1991)	(5) GS&C RISK INDEX	(6) INTERNAL RATE OF RETURN CHANGE	(7) INDCTD ANNUAL RETURN (%)	(8) REQR'D ANNUAL RETURN (%)	(9) RISK ADJ EXCESS ANNUAL RETURN (%)	(10) NORMALIZED PE RATIO (1987)	(11) PE RATIO (1991)	
67	*COLGATE PALMOLIVE CO	87	44.63	12.0	88	0.98	2.4	18.4	10.5	7.9	16.2	20.3	67
68	*COMBINED INTL	57	24.63	9.0	53	1.09	2.8	21.8	10.8	11.0	8.4	12.7	68
69	*COMPUTER ASSOCIATES	216	28.00	20.0	38	0.99	2.0	6.7	10.5	-3.8	32.9	21.6	69
70	*COMPUTER SCIENCES CORP	236	53.13	16.0	74	1.78	2.4	7.2	12.5	-5.3	21.7	16.7	70
71	*COMPUTERVISION	199	17.75	15.0	27	1.31	2.5	9.4	11.3	-1.9	17.8	15.5	71
72	*CONAGRA INC	36	26.75	15.0	69	0.89	2.5	24.4	10.3	14.1	12.7	18.7	72
73	*CONTINENTAL CORP	14	43.75	9.0	127	0.93	2.8	30.3	10.4	19.9	9.0	18.6	73
74	*CONTINENTAL ILLINOIS	179	4.88	8.0	8	1.51	3.3	11.6	11.8	-0.2	8.3	9.4	74
75	*COOPER INDS INC	153	54.38	11.0	84	1.06	2.7	11.9	10.7	1.2	13.6	13.8	75
76	*CORESTATES FIN'L CORP	52	35.50	10.0	81	1.11	2.9	22.2	10.8	11.4	8.2	12.7	76
77	*DANA CORP	208	46.88	9.0	58	1.01	2.5	7.6	10.6	-3.0	15.6	13.6	77
78	*DAYTON HUDSON CORP	149	46.88	12.0	73	1.00	2.5	12.0	10.5	1.4	14.9	14.8	78
79	*DELUXE CHECK PRINTERS	82	31.50	15.0	65	1.07	2.2	19.1	10.7	8.4	19.1	22.6	79
80	*DIEBOLD INC	247	54.63	10.0	62	1.25	2.4	5.1	11.2	-6.1	17.6	13.5	80
81	*DIGITAL EQUIPMT. CORP	139	157.38	15.0	271	0.88	2.6	12.2	10.2	1.9	15.7	15.5	81
82	*DILLARD DEPT STORES	140	41.63	14.0	73	1.17	2.6	12.8	11.0	1.8	14.1	14.7	82
83	*WALT DISNEY CO	265	64.00	15.0	69	1.20	2.2	2.4	11.0	-8.6	27.8	17.2	83
84	*DOME MINES LTD	302	14.00	5.0	2	0.92	1.8	-31.2	10.4	-41.5	87.5	10.6	84
85	*DONNELLEY(R.R.) & SONS	192	66.50	11.0	93	1.15	2.6	9.5	10.9	-1.4	15.3	14.0	85
86	*DOVER CORP	271	64.63	10.0	62	1.14	2.4	1.0	10.9	-9.9	19.6	12.8	86
87	*DOW JONES 30 IND. AVG	268	2291.57	6.0	1970	0.98	2.6	0.7	10.5	-9.8	15.1	10.3	87
88	*DU PONT (EI)	213	112.75	9.0	137	1.13	2.5	7.2	10.9	-3.7	16.1	13.8	88
89	*DUN & BRADSTREET CORP	59	119.25	16.0	274	1.08	2.2	21.6	10.7	10.8	22.5	28.5	89
90	*DURR-FILLAUER	145	12.00	13.0	21	1.39	2.7	13.3	11.5	1.8	13.3	14.3	90
91	*E-SYSTEMS,INC	272	30.63	8.0	30	1.62	2.9	1.8	12.1	-10.3	13.5	9.9	91
92	*EATON CORP	211	90.00	10.0	118	1.21	2.7	7.8	11.1	-3.3	13.6	12.2	92
93	*ECHLIN INC	66	17.38	12.0	37	0.89	2.5	20.4	10.3	10.1	11.9	16.0	93
94	*ECHO BAY MINES	290	36.13	20.0	26	0.87	1.7	-6.1	10.2	-16.3	66.9	23.3	94
95	*EMERSON ELECTRIC CO	257	103.00	8.0	100	0.95	4.5	2.8	10.4	-7.6	17.3	12.4	95
96	*EXXON CORP	258	87.00	5.0	77	0.95	2.4	2.7	10.4	-7.7	15.5	11.3	96
97	*FARMERS GROUP	89	42.25	12.0	84	1.17	2.6	18.3	11.0	7.3	11.8	15.0	97
98	*FEDERAL MOGUL CORP	43	42.63	12.0	100	0.97	2.6	23.2	10.5	12.8	10.6	15.8	98
99	*FEDERAL NATL MTG ASSN	1	38.00	20.0	176	1.31	2.5	39.0	11.3	27.6	10.1	22.6	99
100	*FEDERAL SIGNAL CORP	55	22.75	12.0	51	1.03	2.4	21.8	10.6	11.2	13.5	19.3	100
101	*FEDERATED DEPT STORES	198	44.63	8.0	57	0.88	2.8	8.4	10.3	-1.9	11.8	11.0	101

* (ASTERISKED) COMPANIES REFLECT GOLDMAN SACHS ESTIMATES FOR TREND GROWTH IN EARNINGS PER SHARE
  AND SUSTAINABLE RETURN ON EQUITY.
  FOR NON-ASTERISKED COMPANIES, WHERE WE DO NOT MAINTAIN COVERAGE, ESTIMATES FOR GROWTH IN EARNINGS
  PER SHARE AND RETURN ON EQUITY ARE DERIVED FROM HISTORICAL (LAST 5 YEARS) COMPANY INFORMATION.

APPENDIX I

COMMON STOCK RISK ADJUSTED EXCESS RETURNS
RANKING OF

	COMPANY	(1) RANK BY RISK ADJ EXCESS ANNUAL RETURN	(2) PRICE (5/29/87)	(3) TREND GR RATE EPS (87-91)	(4) THEORETICAL PRICE (1991)	(5) GS&C RISK INDEX	(6) INTERNAL RATE OF RETURN CHANGE	(7) INDCTD ANNUAL RETURN (%)	(8) REQR'D ANNUAL RETURN (%)	(9) RISK ADJ EXCESS ANNUAL RETURN (%)	(10) NORMALIZED PE RATIO (1987)	(11) PE RATIO (1991)	
102	*FIELDCREST CANNON	222	36.38	8.0	45	1.22	3.0	6.8	11.1	-4.4	11.2	10.1	102
103	*FINANCIAL CORP OF AMER	114	6.38	6.0	13	1.78	4.5	17.1	12.5	4.6	3.4	5.7	103
104	*FIRESTONE TIRE & RUBBE	283	39.25	7.0	30	1.03	2.5	-2.4	10.6	-13.1	18.3	10.7	104
105	*FIRST BANK SYSTEM	67	29.88	10.0	66	1.22	2.9	21.1	11.1	10.0	8.4	12.5	105
106	*FIRST CHICAGO CORP	12	29.13	10.0	93	1.10	3.1	31.9	10.8	21.1	5.8	12.7	106
107	*FIRST INTRSTA BANCORP	5	53.63	12.0	196	1.12	2.9	35.4	10.8	24.5	6.5	15.2	107
108	*FIRST WACHOVIA CORP	58	40.13	12.0	92	1.19	2.7	22.0	11.0	10.9	10.2	15.0	108
109	*FLEET FINANCIAL GROUP	85	27.50	11.0	56	1.09	2.7	18.9	10.8	8.1	10.3	13.8	109
110	*FLOWERS IND	122	23.75	13.0	41	1.11	2.5	14.4	10.8	3.6	15.3	16.3	110
111	*FOOTE, CONE & BELDING	92	55.88	10.0	102	0.87	2.6	17.0	10.2	6.8	13.8	17.2	111
112	*FORD MOTOR CO	108	90.88	9.0	165	1.19	3.0	16.1	11.0	5.1	8.7	11.2	112
113	*FORT HOWARD PAPER CO	175	53.38	13.0	80	1.32	2.3	11.3	11.3	-0.1	18.2	16.7	113
114	*GAP INC	74	60.25	23.0	146	1.74	2.0	21.6	12.4	9.2	26.4	27.9	114
115	*GARAN INC	163	24.38	8.0	34	1.05	2.7	11.2	10.7	0.5	11.4	11.8	115
116	*GENERAL ELECTRIC CO	253	52.00	8.0	52	1.03	3.1	3.3	10.6	-7.3	16.0	11.9	116
117	*GENERAL MILLS CORP	125	54.00	13.0	88	0.87	2.2	13.4	10.2	3.2	19.0	19.0	117
118	*GENERAL RE CORP	131	50.75	13.0	88	1.56	2.5	14.5	11.9	2.6	15.0	16.0	118
119	*GENUINE PARTS CO	190	34.63	10.0	46	0.89	2.4	9.0	10.3	-1.2	18.9	17.2	119
120	*GEORGIA-PACIFIC CORP	133	42.25	12.0	68	1.13	2.4	13.1	10.9	-2.3	15.1	15.5	120
121	*GERBER PRODUCTS CO	240	48.75	9.0	54	0.99	2.4	5.0	10.5	-5.5	19.3	15.1	121
122	*GIANT FOOD	189	29.63	10.0	42	1.21	2.7	9.9	11.1	-1.2	13.5	12.9	122
123	*GIBRALTAR FIN CP CALIF	71	9.75	7.0	22	1.31	4.2	20.8	11.3	9.5	4.3	7.6	123
124	*GILLETTE CO	195	29.25	10.0	39	1.09	2.4	9.1	10.8	-1.7	16.3	14.7	124
125	*GOLDEN WEST FINANCIAL	86	37.13	10.0	92	2.20	3.6	21.5	13.5	7.9	6.0	10.2	125
126	*GOODYEAR TIRE & RUBR	299	66.75	9.0	24	1.13	2.1	-18.4	10.9	-29.3	45.4	11.4	126
127	*GRAINGER(W.W.) INC	292	50.50	7.0	32	1.08	2.7	-7.0	10.8	-17.8	18.8	9.2	127
128	*GREAT NORTHN NEKOOSA	205	38.00	11.0	48	0.93	2.4	7.7	10.4	-2.7	17.1	14.4	128
129	*GREAT WESTN FINL CORP	50	20.38	11.0	50	1.26	3.0	22.8	11.2	11.6	8.0	12.8	129
130	*GREYHOUND CORP	19	43.75	16.0	136	1.25	2.4	30.0	11.2	18.8	13.0	22.3	130
131	*GUILFORD MILLS INC	262	31.38	8.0	34	1.68	2.9	3.9	12.3	-8.3	12.6	10.0	131
132	*HANNAFORD BROS	197	45.50	14.0	65	1.26	2.3	9.3	11.2	-1.9	20.0	16.8	132
133	*HARLAND (JOHN) CORP	182	24.38	14.0	36	1.16	2.3	10.5	11.0	-0.4	19.8	17.4	133
134	*HARTMARX CORP	169	27.75	8.0	39	1.15	2.3	11.1	10.9	0.2	11.3	11.6	134
135	*HEINZ(H.J.) CO	128	43.50	13.0	71	0.91	2.3	13.1	10.3	2.8	16.4	16.4	135
136	*HERSHEY FOODS CORP	142	25.50	12.0	39	0.91	2.4	12.1	10.3	1.8	15.9	15.6	136

* (ASTERISKED) COMPANIES REFLECT GOLDMAN SACHS ESTIMATES FOR TREND GROWTH IN EARNINGS PER SHARE
  AND SUSTAINABLE RETURN ON EQUITY.
  FOR NON-ASTERISKED COMPANIES, WHERE WE DO NOT MAINTAIN COVERAGE, ESTIMATES FOR GROWTH IN EARNINGS
  PER SHARE AND RETURN ON EQUITY ARE DERIVED FROM HISTORICAL (LAST 5 YEARS) COMPANY INFORMATION.

APPENDIX I

COMMON STOCK RISK ADJUSTED EXCESS RETURNS

RANKING OF

	COMPANY	(1) RANK BY RISK ADJ EXCESS ANNUAL RETURN	(2) PRICE (5/29/87)	(3) TREND GR RATE EPS (87-91)	(4) THEORETICAL PRICE (1991)	(5) GS&C RISK INDEX	(6) INTERNAL RATE OF RETURN CHANGE	(7) INDCTD ANNUAL RETURN (%)	(8) REQR'D ANNUAL RETURN (%)	(9) RISK ADJ EXCESS ANNUAL RETURN (%)	(10) NORMALIZED PE RATIO (1987)	(11) NORMALIZED PE RATIO (1991)
137	*HEWLETT-PACKARD CO	254	65.13	15.0	74	1.07	2.3	3.4	10.7	-7.4	25.5	16.6
138	*HILTON HOTELS CORP	171	85.50	12.0	123	0.96	2.3	10.5	10.5	0.0	19.1	17.4
139	*HOSPITAL CP OF AMERICA	206	46.75	10.0	62	1.04	2.8	7.9	10.6	-2.7	12.9	11.7
140	*HUBBELL INC	264	35.88	8.0	35	1.14	2.6	2.5	10.9	-8.4	16.2	11.6
141	*HUFFY CORP	207	21.50	10.0	27	0.88	2.7	7.2	10.3	-3.0	14.3	12.4
142	*HUMANA INC	123	23.38	9.0	38	1.04	2.7	14.1	10.6	3.5	10.7	12.3
143	*INGERSOLL-RAND CO	118	75.50	9.0	127	1.15	2.8	14.8	10.9	3.9	10.1	12.0
144	*INTERCO INC	76	40.13	10.0	82	1.12	2.6	20.0	10.8	9.1	12.2	17.0
145	*INTL BUSINESS MACHINES	135	160.00	10.0	242	0.93	2.4	12.4	10.4	2.0	14.5	15.0
146	*INTERNATIONAL PAPER CO	160	45.38	10.0	66	0.98	2.4	11.2	10.5	0.7	16.5	16.3
147	*INTERPUBLIC GROUP	117	33.38	13.0	60	1.31	2.4	15.5	11.3	4.2	15.2	16.7
148	*IRVING BANK CORP	18	41.00	9.0	122	1.14	3.2	30.0	10.9	19.1	5.5	11.6
149	*JWT GROUP INC	214	35.25	11.0	44	1.22	2.3	7.3	11.1	-3.7	20.1	16.5
150	*JEFFERSON-PILOT CORP	129	29.88	7.0	45	0.88	3.0	13.0	10.3	2.7	8.8	10.1
151	*JOHNSON & JOHNSON	165	86.00	13.5	130	1.09	2.3	11.2	10.8	0.5	18.7	17.1
152	*K-MART CORP	146	59.88	10.0	92	0.99	2.6	12.1	10.5	1.5	12.2	12.8
153	*KELLOGG CO	184	60.50	13.0	86	0.89	2.3	9.7	10.3	-0.6	18.9	16.5
154	*KEYSTONE INTL	60	18.38	15.0	42	1.05	2.3	21.5	10.7	10.8	16.0	20.7
155	*KIDDE INC	110	34.38	9.0	58	1.07	2.6	15.6	10.7	4.8	12.6	15.2
156	*KIMBERLY-CLARK CORP	132	54.63	12.0	86	0.89	2.4	12.7	10.3	2.4	15.5	15.6
157	*KRAFT INC	176	58.00	11.0	82	0.99	2.4	10.3	10.5	-0.2	16.1	14.9
158	*KROGER COMPANY	53	31.63	11.0	68	0.74	2.6	21.2	9.9	11.3	13.0	18.5
159	*LILLY (ELI) & CO	193	88.00	12.0	120	1.11	2.3	9.4	10.8	-1.4	19.3	16.8
160	*LIMITED (THE) INC	105	40.13	25.0	85	1.63	1.9	17.3	12.1	5.2	33.4	28.9
161	LINCOLN NATIONAL CORP	44	49.00	10.0	112	0.94	2.8	23.0	10.4	12.6	8.8	13.6
162	*LITTON INDUSTRIES INC	237	91.50	12.0	115	1.24	2.6	5.8	11.1	-5.3	16.3	13.1
163	*LIZ CLAIBORNE	101	60.75	20.0	120	0.81	2.1	16.2	10.1	6.1	24.3	23.1
164	*LOCKHEED CORP	298	50.63	2.0	23	1.35	4.5	-12.5	11.4	-23.9	7.9	3.3
165	*LORAL CORP	183	40.13	12.0	62	1.52	2.5	11.3	11.8	-0.5	14.3	14.1
166	*LOTUS DEVELOPMNT CORP	277	34.38	15.0	34	1.37	2.3	-0.3	11.5	-11.8	27.5	15.5
167	*LUBY'S CAFETERIA	203	31.50	13.0	41	0.98	2.2	7.9	10.5	-2.6	23.2	18.4
168	*LUCKY STORES INC	126	27.00	8.0	40	0.92	4.5	13.3	10.4	3.0	12.5	13.5
169	*MCA INC	232	48.00	11.0	56	0.74	2.4	5.2	9.9	-4.7	17.3	13.4
170	*MANAGEMENT SCIENCE	49	14.00	16.0	39	1.71	2.7	24.3	12.3	12.0	10.8	16.7
171	*MANUFACTURERS HANOVER	25	41.00	6.0	102	1.17	3.4	27.9	11.0	17.0	4.8	9.5

* (ASTERISKED) COMPANIES REFLECT GOLDMAN SACHS ESTIMATES FOR TREND GROWTH IN EARNINGS PER SHARE
AND SUSTAINABLE RETURN ON EQUITY.
FOR NON-ASTERISKED COMPANIES, WHERE WE DO NOT MAINTAIN COVERAGE, ESTIMATES FOR GROWTH IN EARNINGS
PER SHARE AND RETURN ON EQUITY ARE DERIVED FROM HISTORICAL (LAST 5 YEARS) COMPANY INFORMATION.

COMMON STOCK RISK ADJUSTED EXCESS RETURNS

RANKING OF EXCESS RETURNS

	COMPANY	(1) RANK BY RISK ADJ EXCESS ANNUAL RETURN	(2) PRICE (5/29/87)	(3) TREND GR RATE EPS (87-91)	(4) THEORETICAL PRICE (1991)	(5) GS&C RISK INDEX	(6) INTERNAL RATE OF RETURN CHANGE	(7) INDCTD ANNUAL RETURN (%)	(8) REQR'D ANNUAL RETURN (%)	(9) RISK ADJ EXCESS ANNUAL RETURN (%)	(10) NORMALIZED PE RATIO (1987)	(11) PE RATIO (1991)
172	*MARRIOTT CORP	109	40.25	20.0	79	1.09	2.1	15.9	10.8	5.1	24.0	22.7
173	*MARTIN MARIETTA CORP	103	44.38	11.0	82	1.13	2.7	16.4	10.9	5.6	11.1	13.6
174	*MARYLAND NATL CORP	38	42.38	11.0	108	1.17	2.9	24.7	11.0	13.7	8.0	13.5
175	*MASCO CORP	120	35.38	17.0	63	1.05	2.2	14.4	10.7	3.7	21.1	20.1
176	*MAXWELL LAB	80	14.25	15.0	33	0.97	2.7	19.0	10.5	8.6	11.9	15.5
177	*MAY DEPT STORES	181	43.88	11.0	63	1.06	2.5	10.3	10.7	-0.4	15.1	14.2
178	*MCDONALDS CORP	187	78.75	14.0	116	0.98	2.4	9.6	10.5	-0.9	18.2	15.9
179	*MCDONNELL DOUGLAS CORP	291	68.50	3.0	42	1.20	3.9	-6.2	11.0	-17.2	9.3	5.1
180	*MEAD CORP	62	65.50	15.0	150	1.02	2.4	21.1	10.6	10.5	14.1	18.3
181	*MEDTRONIC	42	95.00	18.0	250	1.01	2.4	23.5	10.6	13.0	15.1	20.4
182	*MELLON BANK CORP	2	32.00	8.0	117	1.10	3.4	38.0	10.8	27.3	4.2	11.2
183	*MERCK & CO	178	158.38	16.0	235	1.11	2.0	10.6	10.8	-0.2	28.3	23.2
184	*MICHIGAN NATIONAL	7	37.25	15.0	137	1.17	2.7	34.7	11.0	23.7	8.9	18.7
185	*MINNESOTA MNG & MFG CO	134	127.88	10.0	199	1.03	2.5	12.9	10.6	2.3	16.3	17.3
186	*MOBIL CORP	238	46.63	6.0	47	1.00	2.4	5.2	10.6	-5.4	15.5	12.4
187	*MORGAN(J.P.) & CO INC	26	44.00	12.0	126	1.07	2.9	27.5	10.7	16.8	8.0	14.5
188	*MORTON THIOKOL INC	172	42.50	11.0	63	1.10	2.6	10.8	10.8	0.0	13.7	13.4
189	*MURRAY OHIO	266	24.50	8.0	23	1.19	2.5	1.7	11.0	-9.3	16.9	11.7
190	*NCNB CORP	35	23.50	11.0	61	1.34	2.8	25.7	11.4	14.3	8.1	13.9
191	*NEC CORP	301	66.38	15.0	21	1.69	1.7	-21.4	12.3	-33.7	94.8	16.8
192	*NATIONAL CITY CORP	48	31.88	11.0	75	1.10	2.8	22.9	10.8	12.1	9.0	13.9
193	*NATIONAL MEDICAL	158	26.13	10.0	38	1.04	2.6	11.3	10.6	0.7	13.2	13.2
194	*NORSTAR BANCORP	39	32.38	11.0	77	0.90	2.6	23.9	10.3	13.6	10.4	16.3
195	*NORWEST CORP	27	39.88	10.0	107	1.14	2.7	27.7	10.9	16.8	9.5	17.4
196	*OGILVY CORP	104	29.75	12.0	54	1.04	2.4	16.0	10.6	5.4	13.5	15.5
197	*ON-LINE SOFTWARE	242	17.00	17.0	22	1.49	2.2	6.1	11.8	-5.7	25.4	17.9
198	*OXFORD INDS	170	15.50	8.0	22	1.26	2.9	11.3	11.2	0.1	10.3	10.9
199	*PHH GROUP	223	38.13	9.0	45	1.16	2.6	6.6	10.9	-4.4	15.0	12.5
200	*PNC FINANCIAL CORP	41	45.38	12.0	111	1.14	2.6	24.0	10.9	13.1	9.9	15.4
201	*PANSOPHIC SYSTEMS	280	21.00	18.0	20	1.50	2.0	-0.6	11.8	-12.4	38.2	19.1
202	*PARKER HANNIFIN CORP	217	31.75	9.0	39	1.15	2.6	7.1	10.9	-3.8	14.1	12.2
203	*PENNEY(J.C.) CO	243	51.38	8.0	57	1.05	2.8	5.0	10.7	-5.7	12.9	10.6
204	*PENNWALT CORP	244	59.00	8.0	62	0.96	4.5	4.5	10.5	-6.0	16.2	12.5
205	*PEPSICO INC	185	35.00	12.0	49	0.88	2.4	9.5	10.3	-0.8	17.3	15.4
206	*PFIZER INC	152	65.13	11.0	98	1.08	2.4	12.0	10.7	1.2	15.0	14.9

* (ASTERISKED) COMPANIES REFLECT GOLDMAN SACHS ESTIMATES FOR TREND GROWTH IN EARNINGS PER SHARE
AND SUSTAINABLE RETURN ON EQUITY. WHERE WE DO NOT MAINTAIN COVERAGE, ESTIMATES FOR GROWTH IN EARNINGS
FOR NON-ASTERISKED COMPANIES ARE DERIVED FROM HISTORICAL (LAST 5 YEARS) COMPANY INFORMATION.
PER SHARE AND RETURN ON EQUITY ARE DERIVED FROM HISTORICAL (LAST 5 YEARS) COMPANY INFORMATION.

133

APPENDIX I

RANKING OF
COMMON STOCK RISK ADJUSTED EXCESS RETURNS

	(1) RANK BY RISK ADJ EXCESS ANNUAL RETURN	COMPANY	(2) PRICE (5/29/87)	(3) TREND GR RATE EPS (87-91)	(4) THEORETICAL PRICE (1991)	(5) GS&C RISK INDEX	(6) INTERNAL RATE OF RETURN CHANGE	(7) INDCTD ANNUAL RETURN (%)	(8) REOR'D ANNUAL RETURN (%)	(9) RISK ADJ EXCESS ANNUAL RETURN (%)	(10) NORMALIZED PE RATIO (1987)	(11) NORMALIZED PE RATIO (1991)
207	3	*PHILIP MORRIS COS	85.38	18.0	333	0.94	2.4	35.9	10.4	25.5	11.1	22.4
208	241	*PHILLIPS NV	23.38	6.0	25	1.08	2.9	5.1	10.8	-5.6	11.0	9.3
209	248	*PHILLIPS PETROLEUM CO	15.63	6.0	15	0.71	2.6	3.7	9.8	-6.1	14.2	10.9
210	261	*PHILLIPS-VAN HEUSEN	48.13	9.0	51	0.88	3.0	2.0	10.3	-8.2	13.3	9.9
211	121	PILLSBURY COMPANY	38.75	12.0	64	0.91	2.4	14.0	10.3	3.6	14.9	15.7
212	173	*POLICY MANAGMNT SYSTMS	25.50	18.0	39	0.50	2.2	9.3	9.3	0.0	24.3	19.1
213	6	*PRICE COMPANY	43.25	30.0	182	1.42	2.0	35.4	11.6	23.8	23.8	35.0
214	269	*PRIME COMPUTER	27.13	15.0	30	1.55	2.4	2.0	11.9	-9.9	24.7	15.5
215	166	*PROCTER & GAMBLE CO	91.50	9.0	130	0.97	2.5	10.9	10.5	0.4	17.4	17.6
216	188	*QUAKER OATS CO	49.50	12.0	69	1.02	2.4	9.5	10.6	-1.1	17.4	15.4
217	83	*RJR NABISCO	50.75	11.0	100	0.99	2.5	18.8	10.5	8.3	11.4	14.8
218	127	*RAINIER BANCORP	47.50	11.0	79	1.22	2.6	14.0	11.1	2.9	12.8	14.0
219	113	*RALSTON PURINA CO	80.63	14.0	143	0.99	2.3	15.2	10.5	4.6	16.8	17.7
220	119	*RAYTHEON CO	71.75	12.0	126	1.05	2.7	14.4	10.7	3.7	12.8	14.3
221	91	*REPUBLIC NY CORP	48.25	10.0	94	1.27	2.8	18.1	11.2	6.9	9.5	12.7
222	164	*REPUBLICBANK	23.75	5.0	29	0.98	2.5	11.0	10.5	0.5	11.3	11.5
223	150	*REYNOLDS & REYNOLDS	33.75	10.0	52	1.13	2.6	12.2	10.9	1.3	12.5	13.0
224	96	*RITE AID CORP	33.38	15.0	65	1.08	2.3	17.2	10.8	6.4	17.0	18.9
225	94	*ROCKWELL INTL CORP	26.00	11.0	51	1.18	2.8	17.7	11.0	6.7	10.1	13.2
226	250	*ROYAL DUTCH PETROL	125.38	6.0	122	0.92	2.5	4.1	10.4	-6.2	14.8	11.4
227	219	*RUBBERMAID INC	29.38	15.0	37	1.14	2.1	6.7	10.9	-4.2	26.2	18.9
228	11	*RUSS BERRIE & CO	36.88	20.0	126	0.50	2.4	31.0	9.3	21.7	14.5	23.8
229	252	*RUSSEL CORP	16.50	9.0	18	1.01	2.9	3.5	10.6	-7.0	13.2	10.3
230	77	*SAFECO CORP	56.50	10.0	120	1.27	2.9	20.2	11.2	9.0	8.6	12.5
231	79	*ST PAUL COMPANIES	44.00	10.0	93	1.38	2.9	20.3	11.5	8.8	8.8	12.7
232	282	*SALANT CORP	12.38	8.0	11	1.30	3.4	-1.6	11.3	-12.9	11.5	7.8
233	186	*SARA LEE CORP	41.75	12.0	58	0.94	2.3	9.5	10.4	-0.9	17.9	15.7
234	159	*SCHERING PLOUGH CORP	92.75	13.0	139	1.06	2.3	11.4	10.7	0.7	18.4	17.0
235	202	*SCOTT PAPER CO	67.38	10.0	88	1.10	2.6	8.2	10.8	-2.6	14.1	12.7
236	124	*SEAGATE TECHNOLOGY	44.75	15.0	89	1.80	2.6	15.8	12.5	3.2	13.6	15.5
237	106	*SEARS, ROEBUCK & CO	51.00	9.0	89	1.17	2.7	16.1	11.0	5.2	11.7	14.4
238	32	*SECURITY PAC CORP	38.00	10.0	100	1.11	3.1	26.3	10.8	15.4	7.1	12.7
239	115	*SHAKLEE CORP.	22.13	10.0	41	1.93	2.5	17.1	12.9	4.3	14.4	18.0
240	260	*SHELL TRANS & TRADNG	84.63	6.0	75	0.91	2.3	2.4	10.3	-8.0	17.6	12.4
241	93	*SHERWIN-WILLIAMS	34.75	15.0	73	1.71	2.3	19.1	12.3	6.8	15.9	19.0

* (ASTERISKED) COMPANIES REFLECT GOLDMAN SACHS ESTIMATES FOR TREND GROWTH IN EARNINGS PER SHARE AND SUSTAINABLE RETURN ON EQUITY.
FOR NON-ASTERISKED COMPANIES, WHERE WE DO NOT MAINTAIN COVERAGE, ESTIMATES FOR GROWTH IN EARNINGS PER SHARE AND RETURN ON EQUITY ARE DERIVED FROM HISTORICAL (LAST 5 YEARS) COMPANY INFORMATION.

APPENDIX I

RANKING OF
COMMON STOCK RISK ADJUSTED EXCESS RETURNS

	COMPANY	(1) RANK BY RISK ADJ EXCESS ANNUAL RETURN	(2) PRICE (5/29/87)	(3) TREND GR RATE EPS (87-91)	(4) THEORETICAL PRICE (1991)	(5) GS&C RISK INDEX	(6) INTERNAL RATE OF RETURN CHANGE	(7) INDCTD ANNUAL RETURN (%)	(8) REQR'D ANNUAL RETURN (%)	(9) RISK ADJ EXCESS ANNUAL RETURN (%)	(10) NORMALIZED PE RATIO (1987)	(11) PE RATIO (1991)	
242	*SHONEY'S INC	98	27.25	18.0	56	1.18	2.3	17.3	11.0	6.3	19.2	20.4	242
243	*SIGMA-ALDRICH	191	44.00	20.0	68	1.56	1.9	10.7	11.9	-1.3	31.4	23.6	243
244	*SINGER CO	228	43.50	10.0	59	1.68	3.0	7.7	12.3	-4.6	11.8	10.9	244
245	*SMITHKLINE BECKMAN CP	224	108.50	8.0	122	0.94	2.6	5.9	10.4	-4.5	14.1	11.7	245
246	*SOUTHEAST BANKING CORP	99	27.75	9.0	52	1.14	3.0	17.2	10.9	6.3	8.7	11.5	246
247	*SOUTHLAND CORP	147	54.50	11.0	87	1.11	2.7	12.3	10.8	1.5	12.8	13.4	247
248	*SOVRAN FINANCIAL CORP	17	31.75	12.0	97	1.12	2.8	30.1	10.9	19.3	8.0	15.4	248
249	*SPRINGS INDS	225	30.75	8.0	36	1.05	2.7	6.2	10.7	-4.5	12.8	10.9	249
250	*SQUARE D COMPANY	270	52.75	5.0	44	1.05	2.7	0.8	10.7	-9.9	13.4	9.3	250
251	*SQUIBB CORP	249	173.75	15.0	200	1.13	2.1	4.8	10.9	-6.1	29.1	19.1	251
252	*STANADYNE INC	88	45.50	12.0	92	1.17	2.7	18.6	11.0	7.7	11.6	15.0	252
253	*STERLING DRUG	107	51.38	12.0	91	1.08	2.4	15.9	10.8	5.1	15.8	17.8	253
254	*STEVENS J P & CO INC	246	43.88	8.0	48	1.19	2.7	5.0	11.0	-6.0	13.5	11.0	254
255	*STRATUS COMPUTER	102	38.00	25.0	79	1.16	1.9	16.7	10.9	5.7	33.0	28.1	255
256	*STUDENT LOAN MKTG ASSN	37	70.50	20.0	193	0.95	2.3	24.3	10.4	13.9	17.2	22.7	256
257	*SUN CO	281	65.38	7.0	49	0.86	2.3	-2.4	10.2	-12.6	21.8	12.4	257
258	*SUNDSTRAND CORP	97	55.75	11.0	105	0.99	2.7	16.9	10.5	6.4	11.1	13.8	258
259	*SUNTRUST BANKS INC	63	23.00	12.0	53	1.19	2.7	21.5	11.0	10.5	10.0	14.5	259
260	*SUPER VALU STORES INC	90	26.75	15.0	54	0.99	2.3	17.7	10.5	7.2	16.0	18.3	260
261	*SYNTEX CORP	45	75.75	17.0	190	1.30	2.2	23.8	11.3	12.5	19.9	26.7	261
262	*SYSTEMATICS INC	245	29.25	16.0	38	1.62	2.2	6.1	12.1	-6.0	24.4	17.5	262
263	*TRW INC	31	100.50	14.0	268	1.03	2.4	26.3	10.6	15.6	12.2	19.3	263
264	*TAMBRANDS INC	61	56.88	13.0	125	1.02	2.4	21.1	10.6	10.5	15.8	21.3	264
265	*TANDEM COMPUTERS	204	67.50	20.0	103	1.57	2.1	9.3	12.0	-2.7	29.3	21.6	265
266	*TEXACO INC	177	37.75	7.0	48	1.04	2.4	10.4	10.6	-0.2	13.7	13.3	266
267	*TEXAS INSTRUMENTS	273	175.63	12.0	170	1.10	2.4	0.4	10.8	-10.4	22.7	13.9	267
268	*TEXTRON INC	111	29.00	9.0	51	1.17	3.0	15.8	11.0	4.8	9.2	11.5	268
269	*TORCHMARK CORP	65	26.50	10.0	57	1.16	2.8	21.1	10.9	10.2	8.8	13.0	269
270	*TORO CO	168	25.63	10.0	39	1.14	2.8	11.2	10.9	0.3	11.6	12.0	270
271	*TOYS R US	24	35.00	25.0	110	0.70	2.1	27.2	9.8	17.4	21.9	28.1	271
272	*TRACOR INC	220	19.38	9.0	25	1.66	2.8	8.0	12.2	-4.2	12.1	11.2	272
273	*TRANSAMERICA CORP	72	33.50	8.0	63	1.03	4.5	19.9	10.6	9.3	9.4	13.1	273
274	*TRAVELERS CORP	33	43.38	9.5	106	0.99	2.9	25.3	10.5	14.8	8.0	13.6	274
275	*TULTEX CORP	256	18.75	8.0	21	1.72	2.9	4.8	12.4	-7.5	12.5	10.3	275
276	*UAL INC.	293	86.50	8.0	59	1.47	2.7	-6.2	11.7	-17.9	19.2	9.7	276

* (ASTERISKED) COMPANIES REFLECT GOLDMAN SACHS ESTIMATES FOR TREND GROWTH IN EARNINGS PER SHARE
AND SUSTAINABLE RETURN ON EQUITY. WHERE WE DO NOT MAINTAIN COVERAGE, ESTIMATES FOR GROWTH IN EARNINGS
FOR NON-ASTERISKED COMPANIES, ARE DERIVED FROM HISTORICAL (LAST 5 YEARS) COMPANY INFORMATION.
PER SHARE AND RETURN ON EQUITY ARE DERIVED FROM HISTORICAL (LAST 5 YEARS) COMPANY INFORMATION.

RANKING OF
COMMON STOCK RISK ADJUSTED EXCESS RETURNS

	COMPANY	(1) RANK BY RISK ADJ EXCESS ANNUAL RETURN	(2) PRICE (5/29/87)	(3) TREND GR RATE EPS (87-91)	(4) THEORETICAL PRICE (1991)	(5) GS&C RISK INDEX	(6) INTERNAL RATE OF RETURN CHANGE	(7) INDCTD ANNUAL RETURN (%)	(8) REQR'D ANNUAL RETURN (%)	(9) RISK ADJ EXCESS ANNUAL RETURN (%)	(10) NORMALIZED PE RATIO (1987)	(11) PE RATIO (1991)
277	*USF&G CORP	20	37.75	9.0	104	1.17	3.0	29.0	11.0	18.0	6.6	12.8
278	*UNIFI	209	15.50	12.0	24	1.80	3.0	9.4	12.5	-3.1	12.4	12.1
279	*UNION CAMP CO	148	59.50	10.0	89	0.97	2.5	11.9	10.5	1.5	13.5	13.8
280	*UNION PAC CORP	239	70.75	8.0	79	1.15	2.6	5.5	10.9	-5.5	14.1	11.5
281	*U S BANCORP	73	25.88	10.0	55	1.18	2.8	20.3	11.0	9.3	8.9	12.8
282	*U.S. TOBACCO CO	28	26.25	12.0	70	0.99	2.5	26.6	10.5	16.0	12.7	21.4
283	*UNITED TECHNOLOGIES CP	226	45.50	7.0	53	1.25	2.9	6.7	11.2	-4.5	11.2	10.0
284	*UNOCAL	274	37.63	7.0	31	0.79	2.6	-0.6	10.0	-10.7	17.9	11.2
285	*UPJOHN CO	259	45.25	14.0	48	1.15	2.0	3.2	10.9	-7.8	28.3	17.9
286	*USLIFE CORP	157	38.13	7.0	56	1.22	3.1	11.8	11.1	0.7	8.5	9.5
287	*VF CORP	231	36.88	9.0	45	1.31	2.7	6.7	11.3	-4.6	13.4	11.6
288	*VALLEY NATIONAL CORP	116	37.38	7.0	63	1.19	3.3	15.3	11.0	4.3	7.2	9.3
289	*VULCAN MATERIALS CO	112	134.13	12.0	234	0.92	2.5	15.0	10.4	4.7	13.9	15.4
290	*WAL-MART STORES	69	58.50	25.0	145	1.48	1.9	21.5	11.8	9.8	28.5	29.0
291	*WALGREEN CO	234	36.75	12.0	45	1.27	2.3	6.4	11.2	-4.9	19.3	15.1
292	*WARNER-LAMBERT CO	34	67.75	13.0	174	1.15	2.5	25.6	10.9	14.6	11.2	17.7
293	*WATKINS JOHNSON	212	32.00	10.0	44	1.39	2.9	8.2	11.5	-3.4	12.1	11.3
294	*WEIS MARKETS INC	279	29.75	9.0	25	1.05	2.6	-1.6	10.7	-12.3	18.6	11.2
295	*WELLS FARGO & CO	64	52.88	11.0	117	1.17	2.8	21.2	11.0	10.2	9.5	13.9
296	*WEST POINT-PEPPERELL	221	69.25	8.0	77	0.95	4.5	6.1	10.4	-4.3	15.4	12.6
297	*WESTINGHOUSE ELECTRIC	263	59.63	6.0	57	1.14	2.9	2.5	10.9	-8.4	12.2	9.2
298	*WESTVACO CORP	215	42.50	9.0	51	1.01	2.7	6.7	10.6	-3.8	13.9	11.9
299	*WEYERHAEUSER CO	162	49.00	10.0	72	1.11	2.4	11.4	10.8	0.6	17.1	17.1
300	*WHIRLPOOL CORP	161	37.00	9.0	53	1.11	2.7	11.4	10.8	0.6	12.3	12.6
301	*WITCO CORP	180	39.13	9.0	55	1.08	2.7	10.5	10.7	-0.3	12.0	12.0
302	*WOOLWORTH(F.W.) CO	100	47.50	12.0	92	1.33	2.5	17.6	11.4	6.2	12.5	15.3

AVERAGE WEIGHTED BY CAPITALIZATION = 1.08   11.5 10.7 0.8

* (ASTERISKED) COMPANIES REFLECT GOLDMAN SACHS ESTIMATES FOR TREND GROWTH IN EARNINGS PER SHARE
AND SUSTAINABLE RETURN ON EQUITY.
FOR NON-ASTERISKED COMPANIES, WHERE WE DO NOT MAINTAIN COVERAGE, ESTIMATES FOR GROWTH IN EARNINGS
PER SHARE AND RETURN ON EQUITY ARE DERIVED FROM HISTORICAL (LAST 5 YEARS) COMPANY INFORMATION.

THE RINGER FAMILY UTILIZES PORTFOLIO THEORY

The Ringer family lives in a lovely suburb of Dallas, Texas. Barry Ringer (age 42) is a successful sales engineer for a leading computer manufacturer. His wife, Helen (39), works part- time in the public library, while Scott (16) and Tammy (14) are both doing well in the local high school. Helen and Barry are both involved in a number of civic activities, and, overall, their family is very well respected in the community.

The Ringers have worked hard, saved consistently, and planned well for retirement. As a result, they currently own their home, a vacation cabin in southern Texas, a very good retirement plan (social security, IRAs, etc.), plus a special fund which will provide for their kids' college education.

In addition, Mr. Ringer has accumulated $148,000 in a "cash management" type account at a leading Dallas brokerage firm. Currently, the Ringers' $148,000 is invested as follows: 40% in a money market fund, 30% in Aaa and Aa corporate bonds, and 30% in a common stock mutual fund. Mr. Ringer has decided that he should leave about $50,000 in the money market fund, and put all the remaining funds (about $98,000) in a more actively managed portfolio of common stocks. In his best judgment, the expected return and standard deviation of those existing funds are 10% and 16%, respectively. In contrast, the Ringers seek 25% expected return, but with the thought of minimizing risk in so doing.

Fortunately, Barry Ringer has tried to do a bit of homework on what he ought to do. First, and as a part of his business training at the University of Texas, Ringer took two courses in investments management. One dealt with security analysis, while the subsequent course focused on portfolio management. As part of the latter, he was exposed to "modern portfolio theory," consisting of portfolio theory, capital asset pricing theory, and considerable empirical evidence on market efficiency.

Mr. Ringer was especially struck by the power of portfolio theory -- and how it can be utilized to help manage one's own portfolio of common stocks. His course notes are somewhat sketchy, however, and thus he has a number of specific questions. All of his questions are based on the following information on fourteen assets, i.e. distinct securities and portfolios, which resulted from his own research, plus numerous conversations with his account executive and other security analysts at his brokerage firm:

Security or Portfolio	Expected Return	Standard Deviation
A	26%	22%
B	20	19
C	25	18
D (Ringers')	10	16
E	13	12
F (riskless)	6	0
G	5	10
H	18	8
I	13	5
J	3	3
K	21	11
L	15	16
M (market)	8	14
N	9	9

Your first suggestion to Jerry Ringer is that he should carefully plot the fourteen assets on a graph, with expected return on the vertical axis and standard deviation on the horizontal axis. Based on that plot of return and risk, the following tasks and questions should be addressed:

(1) Sketch the "efficient frontier" from among the risky securities and portfolios.

(2) Identify the tangent portfolio along the efficient frontier.

(3) What is the risk level of a portfolio that best satisfies the Ringers' goal of expected return?

(4) Locate a new investment that would be equivalent to selling short asset G. Assume no dividends for that asset.

(5) Locate the new return-risk position of asset C if a 25% tax were to be levied on both dividend income and capital gains.

(6) Locate the new return-risk position of asset N if it were purchased on full margin. The initial margin requirement is 50%, and interest of 6% is paid on the amount borrowed.

$$R_p = -1(6\%) + 2(9\%) = 12\%$$

$$\sigma^2 = w_1^2 \sigma_1^2 + w_2^2 \sigma_2^2 + 2w_1 w_2 \sigma_{12}$$

$$\sigma^2 = w_2^2 \sigma_2^2$$

$$= (2)(9) = 18\%$$

(7)   Ignoring taxes and transaction costs, should the Ringers prefer to revise their holdings from D to B or from D to E, and why?

(8)   What is the maximum amount of transaction costs that the Ringers should be willing to pay to revise their existing portfolio to the tangent portfolio identified above? $R_H = 18$ $R_{\bar{R}} 10 = 8\%$

(9)   If the correlation between assets G and L is zero, what dollar allocations to G and L would minimize risk for that two-asset portfolio?

(10) If security L has a correlation of 0.8 with the market, what is the effective "beta" for security L?

(9) $\sigma_p^2 = w_1^2 \sigma_1^2 + w_2^2 \sigma_2^2 + 2 w_1 w_2 \sigma_{12}$

$$= w_1^2 \sigma_1^2 + (1-w_1)^2 \sigma_2^2$$

$$\sigma_p^2 = w_1^2 \sigma_1^2 + (1 - 2w_1 + w_1^2) \sigma_2^2$$

$$\frac{\partial \sigma_p^2}{\partial w_1} = 2 w_1 \sigma_1^2 + (-2 + 2w_1)\sigma_2^2 = 0$$

$$2 w_1 (\sigma_1^2 + \sigma_2^2) = 2 \sigma_2^2$$

$$w_1 = \frac{\sigma_2^2}{\sigma_1^2 + \sigma_2^2} = \frac{16^2}{10^2 + 16^2} = \frac{256}{356} = .72(\%)$$

(10) $\beta = \frac{Cov_{L,M}}{\sigma_m^2} = \frac{\rho_{L,M} \sigma_L \sigma_m}{\sigma_m^2} = \frac{0.8(16)}{(14)} = 0.91$

A Simplified Common Stock Valuation Model

Russell J. Fuller and Chi-Cheng Hsia

A simplified stock valuation model based on the general principle that the price of a common stock equals the present value of its future dividends, the H-model is more practical than the general dividend discount model, yet more realistic than the constant growth rate model. The H-model assumes that a firm's growth rate declines (or increases) in a linear fashion from an above-normal (or below-normal) rate to a normal, long-term rate. Given estimates of these two growth rates, the length of the period of above-normal growth, and the discount rate, an analyst may use the H-model to solve for current stock price.

Like the popular three-phase model, the H-model allows for changing dividend growth rates over time. The H-model thus yields results similar to those of the three-phase model. But the H-model is much easier to use, requiring only simple arithmetic. Furthermore, it allows for direct solution of the discount rate, or cost of equity, whereas more complicated models can give numerical solutions only through trial and error.

SECURITY ANALYSTS NEED common stock valuation models to estimate "correct" prices for shares of common stock and to determine the stock's expected return, given its current price. Ideally, practitioners—and academics—would like a model that (1) is conceptually sound, (2) requires relatively few estimates, (3) allows some flexibility in describing dividend growth rate patterns, and (4) allows straightforward calculation of either the price (given the discount rate) or the discount rate (given the price). None of the common valuation models currently in use satisfies more than three of these objectives. The H-model, described below, satisfies all four.

Current Models

The general dividend discount model states that current stock price equals the present value of all expected dividends. This is stated mathematically as:

$$P_0 = \sum_{t=1}^{\infty} \frac{D_t}{(1 + r)^t}, \qquad (1)$$

where

P_0 = the current stock price,

D_t = expected dividend in period t, and

r = the appropriate discount rate.

Although theoretically sound, the dividend discount model is not practical because it requires the estimates of an infinite, or at least a very long, dividend stream. In addition, it does not allow for direct solution of the discount rate.

The more practical constant growth dividend discount model greatly simplifies the problem of estimating future dividends. It assumes that dividends grow at a constant rate forever, so that the price of a share of common stock may be calculated as follows:

$$P_0 = \frac{D_0(1 + g)}{r - g}, \qquad (2)$$

where

D_0 = the dividend paid in the most recent 12 months and

Russell Fuller is Vice President of Conners Investor Services and Chi-Cheng Hsia is Professor of Finance at Washington State University.

Figure A Constant Growth Model

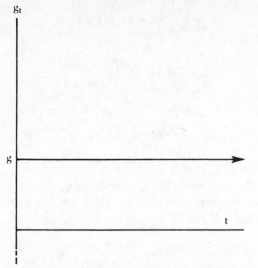

Figure B Three-Phase Model

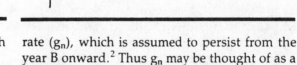

g = the constant, perpetual dividend growth rate.

Figure A illustrates the pattern of dividend growth rates over time (g_t) according to the constant growth model.

In addition to simplicity, one of the advantages of the constant growth model is that it allows for direct solution of the discount rate, given the current stock price and an estimate of g. One merely has to rearrange the terms of Equation (2) to get:

$$r = \frac{D_0(1 + g)}{P_0} + g. \qquad (3)$$

The problem with the constant growth model, however, is that dividend growth rates are *not* constant. The growth rates of many stocks fluctuate so much that the constant growth model cannot even provide a good first approximation.

Security analysts have developed alternative valuation models that tend to be more complicated than the constant growth model but not as complex as the general dividend discount model. The three-phase dividend discount model, for example, is based on a dividend growth rate pattern similar to that illustrated in Figure B.[1] In Phase 1, dividends are expected to grow at a constant rate (denoted g_a) for a period of A years. During Phase 2 (a transition phase lasting for B − A years), the dividend growth rate declines in a linear fashion to a constant growth

rate (g_n), which is assumed to persist from the year B onward.[2] Thus g_n may be thought of as a long-run, steady-state, or "normal" growth rate for the firm.

In practice, the three-phase model allows for calculation of all future dividends, given estimates of the growth rate during Phase 1 (g_a), the length of Phases 1 (A) and 2 (B), the long-run, normal growth rate during Phase 3 (g_n), and the appropriate discount rate (r). The present value (PV) of all future dividends may be written as:[3]

$$P_0 = PV \text{ (Phase 1)} + PV \text{ (Phase 2)}$$
$$+ PV \text{ (Phase 3)},$$

or

$$P_0 = D_0 \sum_{t=1}^{A} \left(\frac{1 + g_a}{1 + r} \right)^t$$
$$+ \sum_{t=A+1}^{B} \left(\frac{D_{t-1}(1 + g_t)}{(1 + r)^t} \right)$$
$$+ \frac{D_B(1 + g_n)}{(1 + r)^B(r - g_n)}, \qquad (4)$$

where D_B is the dividend in year B and growth declines during the transition phase in the following linear fashion:

$$g_t = g_a - (g_a - g_n) \frac{t - A}{B - A},$$

for

$$(A + 1) \le t \le B.$$

---

1. Footnotes appear at end of article

The three-phase model has several attributes that make it popular with practitioners. First, because it assumes constant growth in Phase 3, the analyst does not have to estimate a perpetual stream of dividends. Instead, only five estimates are needed to calculate the stock price. Second, the model is much more flexible than the constant growth model, because it allows for some change in dividend growth rates over time. Finally, although the necessary calculations are fairly complex, Equation (4) may be solved by developing algorithms for use on programmable calculators or computers.[4]

The three-phase model does have drawbacks, however. First, if Phases 1 and 2 cover more than two or three years, solving for the price becomes tedious. Second, Equation (4) does not allow one to solve analytically for r; rather, one has to "guess" at a discount rate, solve for P_0, compare this figure with the current market price, then guess again using a higher (lower) discount rate if the calculated P_0 was higher (lower) than the current price. This iterative process is continued until one arrives at a discount rate that results in a price that approximates current market price.

Deriving the H-Model

Consider the "two-step" dividend growth rate pattern illustrated in Figure C. Initially, dividends grow at a constant rate of g_a for A years. Thereafter, dividends grow at a constant rate of g_n. Given these assumptions, the present value of the future dividend stream can be calculated as:[5]

$$P_0 = PV \text{ (Step 1)} + PV \text{ (Step 2)},$$

or

$$P_0 = D_0 \sum_{t=1}^{A} \left(\frac{1 + g_a}{1 + r} \right)^t$$

$$+ D_A \sum_{t=A+1}^{\infty} \left[\frac{(1 + g_n)^{t-A}}{(1 + r)^t} \right], \quad (5)$$

where D_A is the dividend in year A.

If we solve for the geometric progressions and assume that r exceeds g_n, Equation (5) may be simplified to:

$$P_0 = \frac{D_0(1 + g_a)}{r - g_a}$$

$$\left[1 - \left(\frac{1 + g_a}{1 + r} \right)^{A-1} \left(\frac{g_a - g_n}{r - g_n} \right) \right] \quad (6)$$

Equation (6) could be used to estimate P_0, but it has two drawbacks as a common stock valuation model. First, it is very tedious to solve for r, the discount rate, directly from Equation (6). Second, the dividend growth rate pattern assumed—that is, a constant growth rate for A years followed by a sudden jump to a long-run, normal growth rate—is highly unlikely.

A more realistic, yet operational, model is given by Equation (7), which approximates Equation (6):[6]

$$P_0 = \frac{D_0}{r - g_n} [(1 + g_n) + A(g_a - g_n)]. \quad (7)$$

This general process may be extended beyond two steps. For example, a three-step growth rate pattern is illustrated in Figure D. In this case, dividends are expected initially to grow at a constant rate of g_a for A years; the growth rate then jumps to a level of g_b, which lasts for B − A years; at the end of B years, the growth jumps to a long-run, normal level of g_n. The present value of dividends for this three-step model can be approximated as:

$$P_0 = \frac{D_0}{r - g_n} [(1 + g_n) + A(g_a - g_n)$$

$$+ (B - A)(g_b - g_n)]. \quad (8)$$

This general procedure can be repeated for as many "steps" as one wishes to consider.[7] We

Figure C Two-Step Growth Rate

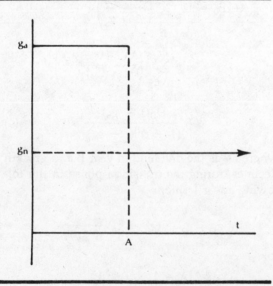

Figure D Three-Step Growth Rate

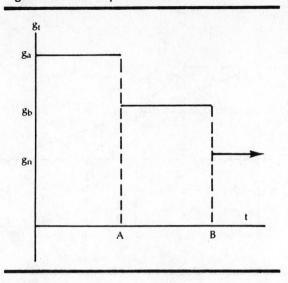

will stop at three steps here, however, for two reasons. First, increasing the number of steps increases the complexity of the model until it approaches the complexity of Equation (1), the general dividend discount model. As we add more steps, we begin to defeat our purpose, which is to develop a simple and operational model. Second, by making one additional assumption, we can modify Equation (8) so that it is very similar to the three-phase model in current use and, at the same time, further simplify Equation (8).

To do this, assume that g_b, the "middle step" growth rate, is exactly halfway between g_a and g_n, so that:

$$g_b = \frac{g_a + g_n}{2}.$$

Substituting this into Equation (8) yields:

$$P_0 = \frac{D_0}{r - g_n}\left[(1 + g_n) + \frac{A + B}{2}(g_a - g_n)\right].$$

Now substitute H for (A + B)/2, and we have the H-model:

$$P_0 = \frac{D_0}{r - g_n}[(+ g_n) + H(g_a - g_n)]. \quad (9)$$

We have eliminated g_b from the equation and have to estimate only the beginning growth rate (g_a) and the long-run growth rate (g_n). We have made H the "halfway" point for the period of above-normal growth.

Suppose, for illustration, that an analyst esti-

mates that XYZ Company, which has just paid a one dollar dividend, will experience a long-run normal growth rate of 8 per cent and that the appropriate discount rate is 14 per cent. The analyst expects, however, that the growth rate will be above normal for the next 10 years, starting out at 12 per cent and declining in a linear fashion until it reaches 8 per cent at the end of the 10 years. Because the total period of above-normal growth is 10 years, the halfway point (H) is five years. The analyst thus has the following estimates:

g_a = 12%
g_n = 8%,
r = 14%,
D_0 = \$1.00, and
H = 5 years.

Using Equation (9), he can estimate the price for the stock as follows:

$$P_0 = \frac{\$1.00}{0.14 - 0.08}[1.08 + 5(0.12 - 0.08)]$$

$$= \$21.33.$$

H-Model Features

The H-model has several pleasing features. There are no exponential terms; solving for P_0 involves only simple arithmetic. Also, to solve analytically for the discount rate, the terms in Equation (9) have only to be rearranged as follows:

$$r = \frac{D_0}{P_0}[(1 + g_n) + H(g_a - g_n)] + g_n. \quad (10)$$

If g_a equals g_n, Equation (10) reduces to Equation (3) of the constant growth model. In any case, solving for r by Equation (10) is straightforward.

The H-model implies a growth rate pattern over time that seems (to us at least) to be plausible for many firms.[8] Figure E illustrates the implicit pattern. The growth rate, beginning at g_a, declines in a steady fashion from g_a to g_n over a period of 2H years. The growth rate is halfway between g_a and g_n at year H and reaches g_n at the year 2H. (If g_a is estimated to be less than g_n, then the line would slope upwards toward g_n over time.) This growth rate pattern seems more likely than a two or three-step pattern (Figures C and D) with sudden jumps from g_a to g_b to g_n, and perhaps more likely than the linear segments of the three-phase model (Figure B).

143

Figure E H-Model Implicit Growth Rate

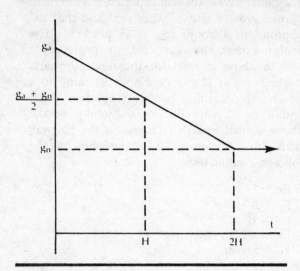

Figure F H-Model vs. Three-Phase Model

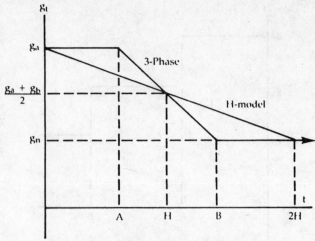

Analysts should also find the H-model intuitively appealing. Suppose investors believe that a firm's normal growth rate is equal to g_n, but believe that the firm currently has unusual investment opportunities and therefore will grow at an above-normal rate for the next 2H years. In this case, Equation (9) of the H-model indicates that the value of the stock is equal to the capitalized value of the dividends assuming normal growth (g_n) plus the additional value from the above-normal growth (g_a). This interpretation becomes clearer if we rewrite Equation (9) as follows:

$$P_0 = \frac{D_0(1 + g_n)}{r - g_n} + \frac{D_0H(g_a - g_n)}{r - g_n}. \quad (11)$$

The second term represents the incremental value due to the temporary above-normal growth. Consider, for example, the case of XYZ Company. Using Equation (11), we can see that its total price of $21.33 is composed of $18.000 from normal growth prospects and $3.33 from temporary, above-normal growth, or:

$$P_0 = \frac{\$1.00(1.08)}{0.14 - 0.08} + \frac{\$1.00(5)(0.12 - 0.08)}{0.14 - 0.08}$$

$$= 18.00 + 3.33 = \$21.33.$$

Finally, the H-model is directly comparable to the three-phase model. Both models require an estimate of the initial growth rate (g_a), the long-run, normal growth rate (g_n) and the discount rate (r). The three-phase model requires an estimate of Phase 1 (A years) and Phase 2 (B-A years), whereas the H-model requires only an estimate of H—the halfway point.

Figure F compares the growth rate pattern of the three-phase model with the implicit growth rate pattern of the H-model. The H-model's assumption that g_b equals $(g_a + g_n)/2$ puts H exactly halfway between the A and B of the three-phase model. Thus H can be thought of in either of two ways—(1) as one-half the time required for the firm's growth rate to decline from its initial level (g_a) to the firm's long-run normal growth rate (g_n) or (2) as the point halfway through the transition phase (Phase 2) of the three-phase model.

As Equation (4) suggests, the three-phase model is relatively complex and requires either a programmable calculator or a computer, or a lot of time and patience. The H-model can be solved using simple arithmetic. In addition, the H-model can be used to solve analytically for the discount rate, using Equation (10). By contrast, the three-phase model requires an iterative process to solve for r. If the H-model generates results that are similar to those of the three-phase model, then it might be considered as a replacement for the three-phase model.

H-Model Results

Table I presents for six hypothetical cases estimated prices generated by the H-model and the three-phase model. In Case 1, g_a, g_n and r estimates are 7, 4 and 9 per cent, respectively, for both models. For the three-phase model, A (the length of Phase 1) is estimated at five years

Table I H-Model vs. the Three-Phase Model

Case No.	Common Assumptions* g_a	Common Assumptions* g_n	Common Assumptions* r	Three-Phase A	Three-Phase B	Three-Phase P_0	H-Model H	H-Model P_0	Ratio of Estimated Prices
1	7%	4%	9%	5 yr.	7 yr.	$23.97	6 yr.	$24.40	0.98
2	12	4	9	5 yr.	7 yr.	30.17	6 yr.	30.40	0.98
3	12	4	9	5 yr.	15 yr.	37.66	10 yr.	36.80	1.02
4	−2	4	9	3 yr.	5 yr.	17.12	4 yr.	16.00	1.07
5	20	4	9	7 yr.	13 yr.	68.18	10 yr.	52.80	1.29
6	20	4	9	3 yr.	7 yr.	38.04	5 yr.	36.80	1.03

* D_0 equals $1.00 in each case.

and B (the end of Phase 2) is estimated at seven years. The transition period, B-A, thus lasts for two years. Given these assumptions, and the one dollar dividend assumption, the three-phase model generates a price of $23.97. The H-model, where H is set at six years (halfway through the transition phase of the three-phase model), generates a price of $24.40.

In Case 2, the beginning growth rate assumption is increased to 12 per cent, while other estimates remain the same. The results of the two models are again extremely close—$30.17 for the three-phase model, versus $30.40 for the H-model. In Case 3, the transition period for the three-phase model is lengthened to 10 years, so that H, the halfway point of the H-model, becomes 10 years. Again, the answers generated by the two models are similar—$37.66 versus $36.80.

Case 4 covers the possibility that the beginning growth rate is less than the long-run, normal growth rate. Although the answers generated by the two models in this case are not as close as in the first three cases, they are only $1.12 apart—$17.12 versus $16.00.

Case 5 illustrates the circumstances under which the two models will give answers that are not reasonably close. This will occur when (1) there is a large difference between the beginning growth rate and the long-run, normal growth rate; (2) the time period over which the annual growth rates approach g_n is relatively long; and (3) the difference between the discount rate and the initial growth rate is relatively large.[9] In Case 5, the three-phase model generates a price of $68.18, whereas the H-model generates a price of $52.80.

It seems unlikely that such a wide difference between the beginning growth rate and the long-run growth rate—20 per cent versus 4 per cent— would persist for very long. Over shorter periods, however, such a difference may not be uncommon. Case 6 shows that, under these conditions, the two models provide very similar prices—$38.04 versus $36.80.

Under most plausible circumstances, then, the two models provide price estimates that are remarkably similar. This is borne out by the last column of Table I, which presents the ratio of the prices generated by the two models. With the exception of Case 5, the ratios are close to 1.0, indicating that the prices are within a few percentage points of one another.[10]

Using the H-Model

To see exactly how the H-model might be used to identify under or overpriced stocks, consider the case of IBM. In February 1982, IBM was selling for $62 per share. At that time, Value Line was forecasting a dividend growth rate of 12 per cent for IBM for the next five years. Value Line does not publish estimates of long-run, normal growth rates or transition periods, but we will assume that IBM's long-run, normal dividend growth rate is 7 per cent, or slightly above the average growth rate for industrial stocks.[11] We'll further assume that its growth rate will decline from 12 to 7 per cent over a period of 22 years, so that the halfway point, H, is 11 years. We thus have:

$g_a = 12\%$,
$g_n = 7\%$, and
$H = 11$.

To determine the appropriate discount rate, or the "required return," we'll use the following Security Market Line:[12]

$$\text{required } r = 10\% + 6\%. \qquad (12)$$

Using Value Line's estimate of IBM's beta in 1982—0.95—gives us a required return of 15.7 per cent. Given these estimates and IBM's 1981 dividend of $3.44, the H-model gives us a price for IBM of $64.06. Comparing this model price with the market price of $62 suggests that IBM was slightly underpriced. Of course, different estimates of the dividend growth rates and the required return would yield different results. The H-model, like every other model, can be no better than the estimates used as inputs.

The H-model can also be used to determine the cost of equity, or expected return. This is the return investors expect, given the current stock price and their estimates of future dividend growth rates. For example, given the market price of $62 and the above estimates for IBM, the expected return for IBM would be 16.0 per cent, based on Equation (10) of the H-model:

$$\text{expected } r = \frac{\$3.44}{\$62} \left[(1.07) + 11(0.12 - 0.07) \right]$$
$$+ 0.07 = 0.160.$$

Calculating the cost of equity using the H-model is straightforward. By contrast, the same calculation using the three-phase model requires an iterative process and, for all practical purposes, a computer.

Finally, the H-model allows investors to calculate security alphas—i.e., the difference between the expected return and the required return. IBM's alpha would be calculated as follows:

$$\text{IBM alpha} = 16.0\% - 15.7\% = +0.3\%.$$

The positive alpha is consistent with the earlier conclusion that IBM was slightly underpriced.

We hope the H-model will prove to be a useful addition to the analyst's tool kit. Like any other tool, however, it is only of value when properly used. Without sound estimates of growth rates and required returns, the H-model can provide little useful information. With them, it offers a theoretically sound and practically efficient approach to stock valuation. ■

Footnotes

1. The three-phase model has been proposed in the literature by Nicholas Molodovsky, Catherine May and Sherman Chottiner, "Common Stock Valuation—Principles, Tables, and Applications," *Financial Analysts Journal*, March/April 1965; W. Scott Bauman, "Investment Returns and Present Values," *Financial Analysts Journal*, November/December 1969; and Russell J. Fuller, "Programming the Three-Phase Dividend Discount Model," *Journal of Portfolio Management*, Summer 1979.

2. The growth rate during Phase 1 (g_a) does not have to be greater than the constant, steady-state growth rate (g_n) assumed for Phase 3. If g_n exceeds g_a, then the growth rate increases in a linear fashion from g_a to g_n during Phase 2, the transition phase. However, g_n does have to be less than r; otherwise, the stock price would be infinite because dividends would be growing at a faster rate than the rate at which they are being discounted.

3. For the derivation of the three-phase model, see Fuller, "Programming the Three-Phase Dividend Discount Model," *op cit.*

4. *Ibid.*

5. This two-step model has been presented previ-

continued

ously in the literature in an attempt to provide a common stock valuation model that is more realistic than the constant growth model. See J. Fred Weston and Eugene F. Brigham, *Managerial Finance* (Hinsdale, Ill.: The Dryden Press, 1978), pp. 690–692.

6. The formal derivation of the H-model as well as the N-step model is available from the authors.

7. The generalized N-step model is:

$$P_0 = \frac{D_0}{r\text{-}g_n}[(1+g_n) + X_1(g_1-g_n) + X_2(g_2-g_n) + \ldots + X_n(g_n-g_n)],$$

where the "X"s represent the length of time for each step.

8. In the process of deriving the H-model, the time dimension was suppressed. (Note there is no subscript t in Equation (9)). Thus there is only an implicit growth rate pattern over time in the H-model. However, it can be shown that the implicit growth rate pattern begins at g_a and declines (or rises) in a linear fashion, reaching g_n at the point in time of 2H, as Figure E illustrates.

9. If a discount rate of 15 per cent is used in Case 5, the difference between g_a and r is 0.05 (0.20 − 0.15) instead of 0.11 (0.20 − 0.09). Under these circumstances, the three-phase model price would be $25.98, the H-model price would be $24.00, and the ratio of the two would be 1.08. Thus if the difference between g_a and r is relatively small, the results of the two models are similar, even if there is an unusually large difference between g_a and g_n and the transition period is relatively long.

10. If, as in Case 5, g_a is much greater than r and g_a approaches g_n over a long time period, then the three-phase model will always generate answers that are substantially larger than the H-model's. Under these circumstances, the analyst will have to decide which growth rate pattern most closely resembles the pattern he foresees for the firm's dividend stream.

11. Most studies of historical stock returns have found the average dividend growth rate to be in the 4 to 5 per cent range over the period from 1926 to the late '70s. We increased this to 7 per cent for IBM to adjust for a higher long-run state of inflation and slightly better long-run prospects for IBM than the typical stock.

12. Historically, the Security Market Line has averaged approximately a 4 per cent intercept (roughly the risk-free rate) and a 5 per cent risk premium, where risk is measured in terms of beta. Thus the typical stock has averaged approximately a 9 per cent return in the past. To adjust for current market conditions, we increased the risk-free rate to 10 per cent and the risk premium to 6 per cent.

The Anatomy of a Stock Market Winner

Marc R. Reinganum

An examination of 222 firms whose stocks at least doubled in price during one year of the 1970–83 period reveals several distinct features shared by the majority of companies. For example, investment advisers on average more than doubled their claims in these winners while stock prices were advancing. Also, the firms' pretax profit margins rose by about 2 per cent during the period of rapid price appreciation, while their growth rates based on five years of quarterly earnings data advanced from an average of 23 per cent to 38.2 per cent. Indeed, changes in earnings growth rates and profit margins probably fueled the price advances.

Of perhaps greater interest are the shared features that revealed themselves prior to the rapid price appreciation. The winners, for example, generally sold at a price less than their book value prior to their substantial price advances. Their quarterly earnings accelerated in the quarters preceding the price rise, and their relative-strength ranks, while already high, increased further.

Nine characteristics common to the 222 stock market winners were used to form the basis of a trading strategy that was applied to 2,057 NYSE and AMEX firms over the 1970–83 period. The trading strategy significantly outperformed the S&P 500 index. After one year, the average holding-period return of the selected firms equaled 30.6 per cent, versus 6.9 per cent for the S&P 500. By the end of two years, the sample firms' average holding-period return was 65.4 per cent, versus 14.7 per cent for the index. These return differentials amount to excess returns for the trading strategy of 23.7 and 50.7 per cent after one and two years, respectively. These results cannot be explained by the firms' historical betas or stock market capitalizations.

MOST ACADEMIC RESEARCH during the 1960s and early 1970s supported the hypothesis that capital markets are efficient, hence that investors cannot systematically outperform naive investment strategies such as buying and holding a market index. Technical and fundamental research based on publicly available information would improve investment performance only marginally at best, and probably not at all. Throwing darts to select stocks would be just about as effective.

Serious chinks in this simple view of investment performance began to appear by the late 1970s and early 1980s. Basu, drawing on earlier work by Nicholson, reported that portfolios comprised of stocks with low price/earnings ratios outperformed portfolios with high price/earnings ratios by about 7 per cent per year, even after adjusting returns for the beta risk of the Capital Asset Pricing Model.[1] Banz and

Marc Reinganum is Phillips Professor of Finance at the College of Business Administration of The University of Iowa.

The author thanks Nai-Fu Chen, Charles D'Ambrosio, Kim Dietrich, Wayne Ferson, Larry Harris, Al MacGregor, William O'Neil, Jack Treynor, Robert Vishny and Mark Weinstein for their helpful comments.

Partial funding and research support for this study were provided by the William O'Neil Company, the University of Chicago and the University of Southern California.

1. Footnotes appear at end of article.

Reinga[...] very small market [...] rmed large-capitaliza[...] 0 per cent on an ann[...] nt anomalies," char[...] s in the timing of st[...] ranging from a month [...] fect to a week-of-the-m[...] e-week effect and eve[...] he-day effect.[3] While ea[...] used on a different problem[...] at least one conclusion: Investors may be able to beat stock performance benchmarks using publicly available information. (Whether the potential superior performance reflects deficiencies in the benchmark or informational inefficiencies in the stock market is still being debated.)

This article analyzes characteristics of past stock market winners to see whether they may yield some insights into successful investment strategies. Earlier research has isolated a particular attribute (such as P/E or size) and then investigated its associated return behavior; we take the opposite tack. We single out stocks with exceptionally high returns to see whether these firms share any common attributes. If history does repeat itself, these common attributes may suggest an investment strategy.

The Data

Our research differs not only in its experimental design, but also in its data. We turned to the *Datagraph* books (published by William O'Neil + Co. and sold primarily to institutional investors), which report a host of fundamental and technical information about firms traded on listed exchanges and the OTC markets.[4] In a search for common attributes among stock market winners, these data offer a much wider choice of potential candidates than CRSP or Compustat data. We also garnered our list of "winners" from an O'Neil publication, *The Greatest Stock Market Winners: 1970–1983*, which contains 272 episodes of explosive price appreciation for companies that traded on the NYSE, AMEX and OTC markets.

The Set Of Winners

We considered the universe of winners comprising the firms contained in *The Greatest Stock Market Winners: 1970–1983*. Several companies were classified as "great" winners during two separate episodes over the 1970–83 period. To be considered a great winner, a company typi-cally had to at least double in value within a calendar year; there were a few exceptions to this guideline, and not all companies that doubled in value were selected.[5]

We merged the list of great winners with a file containing historical information on 2,279 NYSE and AMEX companies; these data were published in various issues of O'Neil's *Datagraph* over the 1970–83 period. Of 272 winning cases, 222 could be matched with the *Datagraph* information; the unmatched companies were OTC firms not covered in the historical files or firms whose CUSIP numbers could not be matched because of name changes. The complete list of 272 winners enjoyed average price appreciation of 361 per cent; the matched list of 222 winners increased in value by an average 349 per cent.

To compute the price appreciation of the winners, we assigned them hypothetical buy and sell dates. These dates were selected *ex post facto*, hence were not generated from actual stock market recommendations. The number of weeks between hypothetical purchase and sale varied from company to company. Panel A of Table I summarizes the price appreciations of the 222 winners between the buy and sell dates. While the average advance of 349 per cent was pulled up by the performance of a couple of stocks with astronomical price advances (4009 and 2554 per cent), more than half the firms increased in value by at least 237 per cent. One-quarter of these firms earned more than 370 per cent, and more than 95 per cent at least doubled in value.

Panel B of Table I displays the number of weeks that elapsed between buy and sell dates. Half the firms were held for less than 60 weeks. One-tenth of the firms were held for more than

Table I Price Appreciation and Length of Time Position Held

Panel A: Price Appreciation (per cent)					
		Percentiles			
Mean	349	5%	104	95%	945
Median	237	10%	119	90%	652
		25%	159	75%	370
Panel B: Elapsed Time Between Buy and Sell Dates (in weeks)					
		Percentiles			
Mean	77	5%	26	95%	178
Median	60	10%	34	90%	155
		25%	44	75%	96

(handwritten note in right margin:) per year?

three years. Only 5 per cent of the firms were held for less than 26 weeks.

Regardless of the precise method by which companies were chosen for inclusion in *The Greatest Stock Market Winners*, the performance of the sample firms is truly exceptional by any standard. Below, we compare the firms' financial conditions in the buy quarter with their conditions in the sell quarter and in the quarters immediately preceding the buy signal.

Characteristics of the Winners

We classified each variable contained in the *Datagraph* files into one of five categories.[6] The first category, "smart money," includes the behaviors of professionally managed funds and corporate insiders. The second category contains valuation measures such as price/book and price/earnings ratios. The third grouping includes technical indicators such as relative strength. The fourth class consists of accounting earnings and profitability measures. The final category contains some miscellaneous variables that did not seem to fit into the other four groups.

"Smart Money" Variables

The "smart money" variables reveal the stock holdings of professionally managed investment funds and corporate insiders. Even if they are not clairvoyants, money managers and corporate insiders are probably well-informed. We broke professionally managed funds down into four groups—investment advisers, banks, mutual funds and insurance companies. For each of these groups, O'Neil reports the number of institutions holding a particular issue as well as the aggregate holdings of these institutions as percentages of the outstanding common stock. We will focus on the holdings of investment advisers, which exhibit the most pronounced changes; the results for the other groups are qualitatively similar.[7]

Table II provides data on *investment adviser holdings* in the sell quarter, the buy quarter and the eight quarters preceding the buy date. Between the buy and sell dates, the number of investment advisers owning the 222 winners more than doubled, increasing from an average of 9.3 advisers per company to 20.9. The change in investment adviser ownership claims is just as dramatic; these more than doubled on average. The percentage of outstanding stock held by investment advisers rose from an average of 7.2 per cent in the buy quarter to 14.9 per cent in the sell quarter.

As a group, investment advisers concentrated their holdings in fewer companies than banks or mutual funds. Of the 222 winners, only 103 and 145 were in the portfolio of at least one invest-

Table II Investment Adviser Holdings in Sell, Buy and Eight Preceding Quarters

Panel A: Number of Investment Advisers Owning Shares										
		Percentile								
Quarter	Mean	1st	5th	10th	25th	50th	75th	90th	95th	99th
Sell	20.9	0	0	0	0	14	31.0	47.0	74.5	125
Buy	9.3	0	0	0	0	0	13.0	26.4	35.8	110
Buy-1	7.7	0	0	0	0	0	9.0	23.7	30.8	100
Buy-2	7.2	0	0	0	0	0	8.2	22.7	30.8	96
Buy-3	7.2	0	0	0	0	0	7.0	21.0	31.8	105
Buy-4	7.2	0	0	0	0	0	7.0	21.0	36.0	107
Buy-5	7.2	0	0	0	0	0	6.5	20.4	34.2	110
Buy-6	7.2	0	0	0	0	0	6.0	20.5	30.7	117
Buy-7	7.2	0	0	0	0	0	5.0	22.0	27.5	115
Buy-8	7.2	0	0	0	0	0	4.0	22.0	28.2	121

Panel B: Percentage of Outstanding Stock held by Investment Advisers										
		Percentile								
Quarter	Mean	1st	5th	10th	25th	50th	75th	90th	95th	99th
Sell	14.9	0	0	0	0	10.5	25.0	36.0	40.7	82.3
Buy	7.2	0	0	0	0	0.0	13.0	23.0	31.8	58.1
Buy-1	6.3	0	0	0	0	0.0	10.2	20.7	31.5	58.0
Buy-2	5.8	0	0	0	0	0.0	9.2	21.0	27.8	44.0
Buy-3	6.3	0	0	0	0	0.0	8.5	21.6	26.3	36.0
Buy-4	6.3	0	0	0	0	0.0	8.0	20.0	27.0	37.0
Buy-5	6.3	0	0	0	0	0.0	7.0	20.2	29.1	38.0
Buy-6	6.3	0	0	0	0	0.0	8.0	22.5	27.0	34.1
Buy-7	6.3	0	0	0	0	0.0	6.5	21.0	24.6	35.1
Buy-8	6.3	0	0	0	0	0.0	7.0	19.0	25.6	36.2

ment adviser in the buy and sell quarters, respectively. But although investment advisers avoided placing funds in a substantial fraction of the winners, they appear to have been very aggressive with their investments in the companies they did purchase.

Despite the investment advisers' aggressive positioning during the period of major price appreciation, their sponsorship data hold little promise of forecasting the big price change. Although there is a slight increase in sponsorship by investment advisers in the quarter or two preceding the buy date, the change is minuscule compared with that observed between the buy and sell dates. While these data do not indicate whether investment advisers jumped on the bandwagon or followed it, they suggest that these institutions cannot serve as the bellwether of stock price surges. The past behavior of investment advisers is not apt to be a good predictor of future stock price movements.

We can draw several general observations from the professionally managed funds as a whole. If hindsight were foresight, one would like to know of impending significant increases in the sponsorship of stock held by banks, mutual funds and investment advisers. Between the buy and sell dates, these groups of professionally managed funds increased their average ownership stakes in the 222 winners by 25, 60 and 107 per cent, respectively. At least at the conclusion of the rapid price advance, these funds were where the action was. Prior to the buy quarter, the ownership claims of these managed funds tended to rise only slightly; the big increase in sponsorship occurred as prices began to escalate sharply. Thus professional money managers may participate in, but do not prophesy, extraordinary price appreciation.

Corporate insiders form another group that may be privy to information about a company's prospects. Will tracking their transactions lead to profitable trading? Several prior studies have suggested that insider trading does predict future price changes.[8] Panel A of Table III gives summary statistics for the number of insiders purchasing our sample stocks. The data do not indicate any great changes in the pattern of insider trading.

For most companies, no corporate insiders bought stock either prior to the large price advance or after it; there was no flurry of insider buying prior to the big price run-up. Selling transactions seem equally uninformative. One might expect insider selling to subside prior to the major price advance. In fact, insider selling for these 222 companies actually increased

Table III   Corporate Insider Transactions in the Sell, Buy and Eight Preceding Quarters

		Panel A: Number of Insiders Buying Stock								
					Percentile					
Quarter	Mean	1st	5th	10th	25th	50th	75th	90th	95th	99th
Sell	0.44	0	0	0	0	0	1	2	2.84	3.77
Buy	0.37	0	0	0	0	0	1	1	2.00	3.77
Buy-1	0.31	0	0	0	0	0	0	1	2.00	3.00
Buy-2	0.35	0	0	0	0	0	0	1	2.00	4.00
Buy-3	0.21	0	0	0	0	0	0	1	1.00	2.86
Buy-4	0.32	0	0	0	0	0	1	1	2.00	3.00
Buy-5	0.30	0	0	0	0	0	0	1	2.00	3.02
Buy-6	0.21	0	0	0	0	0	0	1	1.00	2.15
Buy-7	0.29	0	0	0	0	0	0	1	2.00	4.00
Buy-8	0.29	0	0	0	0	0	0	1	1.00	3.12
		Panel B: Number of Insiders Selling Stock								
					Percentile					
Quarter	Mean	1st	5th	10th	25th	50th	75th	90th	95th	99th
Sell	1.80	0	0	0	0	1	3	5	6	10
Buy	1.38	0	0	0	0	1	2	4	5	8
Buy-1	0.84	0	0	0	0	0	1	3	4	9
Buy-2	0.72	0	0	0	0	0	1	3	4	6
Buy-3	0.80	0	0	0	0	0	1	2	4	7
Buy-4	0.68	0	0	0	0	0	1	2	3	5
Buy-5	0.75	0	0	0	0	0	1	2	4	9
Buy-6	0.67	0	0	0	0	0	1	2	4	6
Buy-7	0.78	0	0	0	0	0	1	3	4	7
Buy-8	0.69	0	0	0	0	0	1	3	3	7

Table IV Price/Book and Price/Earnings Ratios in the Sell, Buy and Eight Preceding Quarters

		Panel A: Price/Book Ratios								
						Percentile				
Quarter	Mean	1st	5th	10th	25th	50th	75th	90th	95th	99th
Sell	2.64	0.17	0.33	0.42	1.15	2.24	3.43	4.95	6.49	11.26
Buy	0.95	0.07	0.12	0.20	0.31	0.60	1.10	2.14	2.74	6.92
Buy-1	0.69	0.04	0.08	0.14	0.26	0.45	0.80	1.52	1.94	5.28
Buy-2	0.62	0.04	0.08	0.13	0.26	0.40	0.68	1.39	1.86	4.74
Buy-3	0.58	0.04	0.07	0.11	0.22	0.41	0.66	1.33	1.89	4.75
Buy-4	0.49	0.05	0.07	0.11	0.18	0.40	0.60	1.10	1.41	2.83
Buy-5	0.52	0.05	0.07	0.10	0.20	0.38	0.61	1.06	1.58	3.19
Buy-6	0.50	0.05	0.07	0.10	0.18	0.38	0.63	1.03	1.71	2.82
Buy-7	0.49	0.05	0.06	0.09	0.18	0.34	0.57	0.95	1.55	3.35
Buy-8	0.45	0.04	0.07	0.09	0.18	0.29	0.50	0.96	1.46	2.52

		Panel B: Price/Earnings Ratios								
						Percentile				
Quarter	Mean	1st	5th	10th	25th	50th	75th	90th	95th	99th
Sell	29.4	7.0	9.0	11.0	16.5	24.0	37.0	59.0	71.1	92.1
Buy	13.6	2.0	4.0	5.0	7.0	10.0	14.0	20.0	27.8	119.7
Buy-1	11.7	2.0	4.0	5.0	6.0	8.0	12.0	18.0	23.0	152.0
Buy-2	10.8	1.9	4.0	5.0	6.0	9.0	13.0	17.0	21.0	36.3
Buy-3	10.9	1.9	5.0	5.0	6.0	9.0	13.0	18.0	23.4	48.6
Buy-4	11.1	1.9	5.0	5.0	6.0	8.0	13.0	18.0	27.1	68.0
Buy-5	12.1	2.0	4.6	5.0	7.0	9.0	13.0	21.0	34.0	66.7
Buy-6	12.5	2.0	4.0	5.0	7.0	9.0	14.0	21.0	26.4	100.0
Buy-7	11.7	2.0	4.0	5.0	7.0	9.0	14.0	21.0	27.5	59.0
Buy-8	11.7	2.0	4.0	5.0	6.0	9.0	14.0	19.2	25.6	76.2

slightly before the advance, rising from an average of 0.84 insider sales per company to 1.38. Insider selling continued slightly higher after the large price advance, which is consistent with expectations. But insider buying was also somewhat greater, which runs contrary to expectations. In short, the buying and selling transactions of corporate insiders do not adumbrate the large price advances of the 222 winners.

While the "smart money" variables may reflect the actions of well-informed investors, the evidence suggests that well-informed investors do not predict major price advances. The transactions of corporate insiders do not suggest either a leading or contemporaneous relation with the large price changes. The actions of professional money managers do not reveal a leading relation with the large price changes, although significant shifts in institutional ownership seem to be contemporaneously correlated with large price movements.

Valuation Measures

We looked at five different valuation variables—(1) price/book ratio, (2) price/earnings ratio, (3) stock price level, (4) stock market capitalization and (5) beta. Prior research has discovered a relation between each of these variables and performance.

Price/book ratio compares the market value of equity to its book value. A ratio less than 1.0 indicates that the market value of a company is less than its book value and might suggest that the stock is "underpriced." Panel A of Table IV shows the sample's ratios.

Among the 222 winners, 164 were selling for less than book value in the buy quarter. The median price/book ratio for the 222 winners was 0.60. In the two quarters prior to the buy date, 183 and 184 of the 222 winners were selling at market prices less than their book values. While a price/book value less than one may not be a perfect indicator of a stock market winner, a price/book value less than one does seem to be a common characteristic of these 222 winners. This suggests that *an investment strategy should isolate firms that sell below book value.*

Panel B of Table IV gives the distribution of *price/earnings ratios* (P/E). In the buy quarter, the average P/E ratio equaled 13.6; the median P/E, which is less influenced by the extreme values, was 10. Although previous research has reported an association between high performance and low P/E, the P/E ratios for this set of 222 winners do not tend to be very small.[9] In fact, only one of every 10 of these firms had P/E ratios less than five in the buy quarter. This

Table V Share Prices and Market Capitalizations

Panel A: Share Prices on the Buy Date (dollars)

		Percentiles			
Mean	27.69	5%	10.71	95%	58.59
Median	24.07	10%	12.80	90%	49.70
		25%	17.32	75%	32.81

Panel B: Stock Market Capitalizations on Buy Date (millions of dollars)*

		Percentiles			
Mean	484.3	5%	19.3	95%	1,375.5
Median	120.1	10%	30.9	90%	802.9
		25%	53.9	75%	316.4

* Stock market captializations are defined as price per share times number of shares outstanding.

indicates that very low P/E ratios are *not* a necessary ingredient of a successful investment strategy.

Prior research has found that small firms outperform their larger cousins. Our 222 winners, however, are not characterized by either low *stock prices* or small *stock market capitalizations* (number of shares times price per share). Panel A of Table V shows that the median share price on the buy date was $24.07. Only nine companies sold for less than $10 a share. The median capitalization was $120.1 million—a figure that would fall in the upper half of an NYSE-AMEX capitalization ranking.[10] Only one of the 222 winners had a market capitalization less than $10 million, and only 12 had capitalizations less than $20 million. This evidence suggests that small size, whether measured by share price or stock market capitalization, is not a necessary component of a successful investment strategy.

To test whether the extraordinary rates of return earned by the 222 winners might be compensation for riskiness, we looked at the stocks' *betas* (Table VI). The average and median beta of these firms was 1.14.[11] Fewer than 5 per cent of the companies had betas greater than 2.0. While the firms as a group were slightly riskier than the market as a whole, the additional beta risk cannot account for the extraordinary returns of these winners.

The valuation evidence indicates that companies whose market values are less than their book values are potential winners. This is not startling or new. The more surprising discovery is that the 222 winners did *not* have low-priced stocks or low P/Es or small market capitalizations.[12] While low price, low P/E or small capitalization may be an integral part of some successful investment strategies, these charac-

teristics are not essential to every successful strategy.

Technical Indicators

Panel A of Table VII gives the *relative-strength ranks* of the 222 winners. The ranks range from 1 (lowest) to 99 (highest). The relative strength of a stock is the weighted average of quarterly price changes during the previous year, where the most recent quarter receives a weight of 40 per cent and the other three quarters each receive weights of 20 per cent. The sample's median rank in the buy quarter was 93; 212 of the 222 firms possessed relative-strength measures in excess of 70. Between the buy-1 and buy quarters, the median relative-strength rank jumped from 81 to 93. In fact, the relative-strength measures for 170 of the 222 winners increased between these two dates. These findings have two implications for investment strategy: First, one should *seek out firms with relative strength ranks of at least 70*; second, one should try to identify firms that exhibit *a positive change in their relative strength rank* from the prior quarter.

Table VI Stock Betas*

		Percentiles			
Mean	1.14	5%	0.41	95%	1.97
Median	1.14	10%	0.52	90%	1.78
		25%	0.79	75%	1.46

* Betas are calculated using weekly returns during the period two years prior to the buy date. The proxy for the market portfolio is a value-weighted index of all New York and American stock exchange companies.

The *datagraph ratings* of the 222 winners also tended to be high in the quarter of the buy date (Panel B of Table VII). The datagraph rating is based on a proprietary formula that assigns weights to "reported earnings [primary operating], capitalization, sponsorship, relative strength of stock, price-volume characteristics, group rank and other factors." The datagraph rating can range from 1 (lowest) to 99 (highest). The sample's median rating in the buy quarter was 80; the ratings for 188 firms exceeded 70. Thus the set of winners was characterized by a *datagraph rating in excess of 70* in the buy quarter. One might also consider incorporating positive changes in datagraph ratings into an investment strategy, although there is substantial overlap between these changes and changes in relative strength.

153

Table VII Relative-Strength Ranks and Datagraph Ratings in the Sell, Buy and Eight Preceding Quarters

Panel A: Relative-Strength Ranks (99 = highest, 1 = lowest)

						Percentile				
Quarter	Mean	1st	5th	10th	25th	50th	75th	90th	95th	99th
Sell	74.0	5.2	20.0	37.0	62.0	82.0	93.0	97.0	98.0	99.0
Buy	90.2	52.1	72.0	78.0	87.0	93.0	97.0	99.0	99.0	99.0
Buy−1	78.1	21.6	45.0	50.0	69.0	81.0	92.0	96.0	98.0	99.0
Buy−2	70.0	6.7	23.0	32.9	56.0	78.0	90.0	96.0	98.0	99.0
Buy−3	64.4	1.1	11.0	17.0	48.0	69.0	87.0	94.0	98.0	99.0
Buy−4	57.9	1.0	11.0	18.0	37.0	61.0	82.0	92.0	96.0	98.0
Buy−5	58.4	3.7	9.0	16.0	35.5	63.0	83.5	94.0	96.5	98.1
Buy−6	60.6	4.4	10.0	16.0	40.0	63.0	86.0	95.0	97.0	99.0
Buy−7	58.6	1.0	8.2	15.0	37.0	61.5	83.7	93.0	98.0	99.0
Buy−8	60.8	1.8	9.0	17.1	39.0	65.5	84.0	95.0	97.0	99.0

Panel B: Datagraph Ratings (99 = highest, 1 = lowest)

						Percentile				
Quarter	Mean	1st	5th	10th	25th	50th	75th	90th	95th	99th
Sell	72.2	40.3	50.1	55.0	64.0	73.0	81.5	88.0	91.0	96.7
Buy	78.3	1.2	60.0	64.0	73.0	80.0	87.0	93.0	96.0	99.0
Buy−1	67.4	1.4	45.0	51.0	58.0	70.0	77.0	85.0	89.0	97.0
Buy−2	63.9	23.4	37.0	43.0	54.0	66.0	75.0	84.0	86.0	94.8
Buy−3	61.8	20.1	29.0	37.0	50.0	63.0	76.0	83.0	90.5	96.9
Buy−4	57.7	10.6	29.8	35.0	46.0	59.0	70.0	77.0	83.0	94.1
Buy−5	59.9	21.8	34.0	38.0	49.0	59.0	71.0	83.2	88.6	97.1
Buy−6	60.9	10.6	29.0	37.0	49.0	63.0	74.0	85.0	92.2	97.0
Buy−7	58.4	16.8	26.2	34.0	46.0	58.5	71.0	84.5	89.0	96.3
Buy−8	56.9	1.0	24.1	33.0	43.2	58.0	70.7	81.0	85.0	94.5

Earnings and Profitability Measures

Panel A of Table VIII shows the *pretax profit margins* of the 222 winners. The average pretax margin in the buy quarter equaled 12.3 per cent. In the buy-1 quarter, this margin was slightly smaller, at 12.0 per cent. By the sell quarter, however, the pretax profit margin had increased to 14.5 per cent on average. Along with the great run-up in price, the firms experienced an increase in pretax margins. Indeed, the nearly 2 per cent increase in the pretax margins may have contributed to the price appreciation of these firms. Prior to the period of rapid price appreciation, pretax profit margins increased gradually. However, 216 of the 222 winners had positive pretax margins in the buy quarter and 215 had positive margins in the buy-1 quarter. This evidence clearly indicates that a *positive pretax profit margin* should be one of the selection screens in an investment strategy.

Panel B of Table VIII presents *changes in quarterly earnings* on a percentage basis. These were not seasonally adjusted in any way and represent changes in the raw accounting earnings. Quarterly earnings in the buy quarter rose nearly 45.9 per cent, on average, from the previous quarter. Quarterly earnings in the buy-1 quarter registered an average increase of 60.8 per cent. A notable feature of the data is the change between the buy-2 and buy-1 quarters. (Because of the lag in the release of accounting information, the accounting data from these quarters are the last that could be used as a leading indicator of the price advance.) The average change in quarterly earnings from 50.4 to 60.8 per cent between the buy-2 and buy-1 quarters represents a positive change in the change in quarterly earnings—i.e., an acceleration in quarterly earnings. Thus another investment rule suggested by the 222 winners is to seek out firms with a *positive change in the change in quarterly earnings—that is, earnings acceleration*.

The behavior of *changes in quarterly sales* (Panel C of Table VIII) closely parallels that of changes in quarterly earnings. Quarterly sales, like quarterly earnings, accelerated during the buy-2 and buy-1 quarters. The average rates of change were positive and increasing. Average sales during the buy-1 quarter rose by 11.8 per cent over the previous quarter; the buy-2 quarter witnessed an average increase of 6.7 per cent. In general, the information contained in the changes in quarterly sales duplicates the information incorporated in the changes in quarterly earnings.

Table IX reveals a picture of earnings over a

Table VIII Pretax Profit Margins and Changes in Quarterly Earnings and Sales in the Sell, Buy and Eight Preceding Quarters

Panel A: Pretax Profit Margins (per cent)

		Percentile								
Quarter	Mean	1st	5th	10th	25th	50th	75th	90th	95th	99th
Sell	14.5	−3.2	3.7	5.7	8.2	13.0	18.5	26.4	33.0	46.3
Buy	12.7	−3.5	2.9	4.0	7.0	11.2	16.2	23.5	28.2	39.6
Buy−1	12.3	−6.0	2.2	3.5	6.5	10.8	15.7	24.5	30.6	45.0
Buy−2	12.0	−6.0	2.0	3.4	6.1	10.5	15.3	23.9	32.1	45.4
Buy−3	11.1	−6.4	1.6	2.4	5.5	10.0	14.8	21.6	28.4	38.6
Buy−4	10.2	−6.9	1.4	2.2	4.9	9.3	13.5	20.8	26.7	37.9
Buy−5	9.7	−14.5	0.5	1.8	4.4	8.5	12.7	19.8	24.8	38.1
Buy−6	9.8	−6.0	0.6	1.9	4.3	8.3	12.5	20.1	28.4	40.6
Buy−7	9.0	−24.2	0.4	1.8	4.1	8.2	12.2	18.9	24.9	40.7
Buy−8	8.4	−24.4	−3.1	1.8	4.1	7.8	11.9	17.7	25.1	40.9

Panel B: Changes in Quarterly Earnings (percentages)

		Percentile								
Quarter	Mean	1st	5th	10th	25th	50th	75th	90th	95th	99th
Sell	16.9	−70	−44	−32	−10	8.05	29.4	66	113	262
Buy	45.9	−82	−41	−26	0	7.40	39.0	103	179	1747
Buy−1	60.8	−63	−42	−22	0	14.10	41.7	108	232	1731
Buy−2	50.4	−91	−60	−33	−4	3.00	35.7	100	241	1158
Buy−3	22.6	−90	−50	−40	−3	0.00	33.3	100	150	500
Buy−4	29.0	−97	−73	−45	−11	0.00	34.3	100	180	867
Buy−5	32.7	−92	−54	−37	−14	0.00	43.1	137	221	603
Buy−6	41.5	−276	−76	−50	−16	0.00	30.4	97	147	1925
Buy−7	19.2	−700	−81	−53	−7	1.90	42.3	100	194	484
Buy−8	35.8	−326	−59	−37	−10	4.00	40.0	131	257	828

Panel C: Changes in Quarterly Sales (percentages)

		Percentile								
Quarter	Mean	1st	5th	10th	25th	50th	75th	90th	95th	99th
Sell	8.4	−29	−21	−9	−1.5	7.10	14.8	29.7	40.4	96.8
Buy	9.5	−48	−22	−10	−1.4	7.30	16.0	32.9	40.4	93.9
Buy−1	11.8	−35	−14	−7	0.2	9.25	16.0	30.6	54.2	153.1
Buy−2	6.7	−30	−25	−17	−2.7	5.20	14.0	25.2	34.8	114.1
Buy−3	8.5	−47	−31	−15	−4.3	6.00	16.3	30.9	44.1	99.7
Buy−4	7.1	−74	−29	−13	−3.7	4.40	15.5	27.5	40.7	158.8
Buy−5	9.8	−29	−15	−9	−1.2	5.60	15.7	32.6	49.1	86.5
Buy−6	3.9	−36	−24	−18	−4.7	4.30	12.0	22.1	29.2	57.9
Buy−7	7.0	−52	−32	−17	−4.4	4.20	14.4	31.2	51.8	144.5
Buy−8	10.7	−41	−19	−7	0.0	9.30	18.9	34.6	45.2	95.3

longer period of time, as reflected by the *five-year quarterly earnings growth rates*. These rates were computed with five years of quarterly earnings data and then annualized. In the buy and buy-1 quarters, the sample's average growth rates equaled 23.0 and 21.6 per cent, respectively. By the sell quarter, the average earnings growth rate increased dramatically, to 38.2 per cent. This increase can be explained by the fact that the calculation of the growth rates

Table IX Five-Year Earnings Growth Rates in the Sell, Buy and Eight Preceding Quarters

		Percentile								
Quarter	Mean	1st	5th	10th	25th	50th	75th	90th	95th	99th
Sell	38.2	−14.0	3.3	10.6	18.0	30.0	48.5	83.8	98.1	156
Buy	23.0	−22.5	−10.5	−4.0	8.5	17.0	31.0	55.0	70.5	131
Buy−1	21.6	−24.5	−10.7	−5.0	7.0	16.0	29.5	54.0	70.2	128
Buy−2	21.4	−28.6	−13.0	−6.2	6.0	16.0	30.0	52.2	71.6	137
Buy−3	20.1	−29.2	−13.0	−7.0	4.0	16.0	29.0	54.0	69.0	152
Buy−4	21.5	−20.8	−10.1	−4.6	6.2	16.0	30.7	54.6	72.6	159
Buy−5	21.2	−18.6	−9.6	−4.0	5.0	17.0	31.5	55.6	73.2	114
Buy−6	22.9	−16.8	−7.0	−4.0	6.5	17.0	33.5	58.0	76.0	137
Buy−7	24.7	−14.7	−8.5	−3.0	9.0	19.0	36.7	63.1	78.1	178
Buy−8	24.2	−13.7	−8.6	−0.6	8.0	19.0	36.2	62.3	75.0	90

Table X Common Shares Outstanding in the Sell, Buy and Eight Preceding Quarters (in thousands)

Quarter	Mean	Percentile								
		1st	5th	10th	25th	50th	75th	90th	95th	99th
Sell	23360	1431	2034	2985	5895	10925	25652	47805	65924	328405
Buy	13885	712	1301	1583	2637	5740	11355	21113	34899	308358
Buy−1	13197	712	1257	1506	2577	5145	10832	19317	34827	281323
Buy−2	13098	712	1131	1493	2557	4955	10767	19317	34258	281323
Buy−3	13110	711	1110	1434	2540	4930	10845	18652	33114	294743
Buy−4	12834	710	1110	1420	2560	5050	11320	18820	32490	315620
Buy−5	12883	705	1110	1414	2522	5110	11275	19033	32518	323784
Buy−6	12915	680	1116	1420	2440	5090	11320	19388	30762	337393
Buy−7	12899	678	1115	1380	2385	5090	10955	19590	30975	342838
Buy−8	12871	677	1111	1359	2387	4875	10712	19302	31755	360903

discards the low rates from several years prior and replaces them with the high earnings growth rates these firms experienced during the large price advance. Over the buy-1 and previous quarters, the average five-year rates remained very stable. In the buy-1 quarter, however, more than 85 per cent of the firms exhibited positive five-year quarterly earnings growth rates. This suggests that one should select companies from the set of those that possess *positive five-year quarterly earnings growth rates*.

Miscellaneous Measures

Table X presents data on common shares outstanding. In the buy quarter, the sample had an average of about 13.8 million outstanding shares; the median number is much less, 5.7 million. In the sell quarter, the average and median number of outstanding shares nearly doubled. This probably indicates that many of the firms split their shares of stock during the period of rapid increase in price. Perhaps the only salient point about these data that might be relevant for an investment strategy is that nearly 90 per cent of the firms had fewer than 20 million shares of stock outstanding. One might limit one's selection to firms with *fewer than 20 million outstanding shares of stock*.

Table XI gives the *ratio of the price on the buy*

Table XI Ratio of Price on Buy Date to Maximum Price During Previous Two Years*

			Percentile		
Mean	0.899	5%	0.699	95%	1.000
Median	0.922	10%	0.785	90%	0.996
		25%	0.871	75%	0.969

* Computed by dividing the price of the stock on the buy date by its maximum price during the previous two-year period. All prices have been adjusted for stock splits.

date to the maximum price during the two previous years—one measure of whether these firms had "fallen out of favor" in the investment community. This variable measures the extent to which the extraordinary success of these 222 winners might have been captured by a "contrarian" investment strategy of selecting stocks that have suffered substantial price declines. The data indicate that it is unlikely these stock would have been selected by a contrarian rule. More than half the winners were selling on the buy date within 8 per cent of their previous two-year high. Only one company was selling at a price less than half its previous two-year high. More than 80 per cent of the firms were selling within 15 per cent of their previous two-year high. An investment strategy that *selects stocks that are selling within 15 per cent of their maximum price during the previous two years* would capture a characteristic common to the 222 stock market winners.

Trading Strategy Results

Given the number of variables examined, we could come up with myriad potential investment strategies. We will limit our investigation here to two.

The first strategy examined includes the nine technical and fundamental variables that either changed noticeably before the big price run-up or seemed to be pervasive among the winners; this strategy thus overlays nine investment screens on the data. The second strategy uses a subset of four of these nine investment screens. As we did not define these strategies after an exhaustive search of all possible strategies, we can make no claim that they represent the best possible strategies. They do, however, illustrate that lessons learned from an examination of the empirical regularities associated with the biggest winners may be applied profitably to a broader universe of companies.

The rules for each trading strategy were straightforward. After a buy signal was generated, we waited 63 trading days before assuming a position in the stock; this delay ensured that accounting information assumed known had actually been released. The stock purchased was held for two years; no sell signal, other than the lapse of two years, was investigated. We calculated the cumulative holding-period return through each of the eight quarters. We then compared the cumulative holding-period returns of each selected stock with the cumulative returns of the S&P 500 index over the identical time period; the difference was labeled an excess return. In cases where a buy signal for a particular company was generated at different times, we tracked the return for each buy signal separately.

The data employed to generate the buy signals were contained on an O'Neil data tape that gave the fundamental and technical variables for 2,279 NYSE and AMEX firms over the 1970–83 period. Any firm on our list of 222 winners was excluded from the trading strategy.[13] Thus 2,057 companies were considered. The return data for the individual securities and the S&P 500 index were gathered from the files provided by the University of Chicago's Center for Research in Security Prices (CRSP).

A Nine-Screen Strategy
Under the first trading strategy using nine investment screens, a firm receives a buy signal when all the following conditions are met:

(1) price-to-book ratio is less than 1.0;
(2) five-year growth rate based on quarterly earnings is positive;
(3) quarterly earnings are accelerating (i.e., there is a positive change in the percent-

age change in quarterly earnings);
(4) pretax profit margins are positive;
(5) fewer than 20 million common shares are outstanding;
(6) relative-strength rank is at least 70;
(7) relative-strength rank of the stock in the current quarter is greater than the rank in the previous quarter;
(8) O'Neil datagraph rating is at least 70; and
(9) stock is selling within 15 per cent of its maximum price during the previous two years.

These nine investment screens were not determined from an analysis of the universe of 2,057 firms contained on the large O'Neil tape. Rather, these are prespecified conditions based upon the investigation into the common characteristics of O'Neil's 222 greatest stock market winners.

The investment strategy results, shown in Table XII, are impressive. The strategy generated 453 buy signals for 319 different companies over the 1970–83 period. On average, the cumulative holding-period returns of the selected securities exceeded the equivalent return for the S&P 500 index in each of the eight quarters. After one quarter (buy+1), these stocks outperformed the S&P 500 by about 6 per cent. Over the two-year interval, the selected firms outperformed the S&P 500 index by more than 50 per cent. That is, the individual firms appreciated on average by more than 65 per cent, while the S&P 500 managed gains of only about 15 per cent. Furthermore, the excess returns were not concentrated in a few firms: More than 79 per cent of the firms outperformed the S&P 500 index over a two-year period. On an annual basis, the firms selected by the nine investment screens earned excess holding-period returns of about 23 per cent per year.

Table XII Distribution of Cumulative Excess Holding-Period Returns from Nine-Screen Strategy (per cent)*

		Percentile								
Quarter	Mean	1st	5th	10th	25th	50th	75th	90th	95th	99th
Buy+1	5.97	−24.7	−18.2	−12.2	−3.7	4.7	14.8	26.0	31.6	46.2
Buy+2	11.56	−30.0	−22.1	−13.8	−5.2	9.8	22.6	37.1	54.1	89.6
Buy+3	18.20	−34.6	−23.1	−17.4	−2.7	14.7	34.5	55.8	72.2	133.4
Buy+4	23.71	−36.0	−25.4	−17.7	−3.8	17.4	43.5	74.1	96.8	158.2
Buy+5	30.20	−40.4	−25.1	−16.5	−2.3	20.5	51.7	91.2	113.3	182.6
Buy+6	37.80	−56.5	−29.0	−18.2	0.1	27.6	62.6	114.5	144.3	219.9
Buy+7	44.09	−53.1	−33.6	−18.7	5.5	34.5	71.1	126.1	160.1	242.3
Buy+8	50.65	−56.2	−32.4	−20.2	5.1	39.4	83.4	132.0	170.1	303.8

* An excess return is defined as the difference between the holding-period return on the security and the holding-period return on the S&P 500 index over the same period of time.

Table XIII Betas, Stock Market Capitalizations, Share Prices and Shares Outstanding for Firms Selected by the Nine Investment Screens

Panel A: Betas*

		Percentiles			
Mean	1.03	5%	0.29	95%	1.95
Median	0.99	10%	0.45	90%	1.66
		25%	0.69	75%	1.34

Panel B: Stock Market Capitalizations (millions of dollars)

		Percentiles			
Mean	182.9	5%	11.0	95%	614.0
Median	102.3	10%	19.6	90%	441.9
		25%	40.8	75%	241.3

Panel C: Share Prices (dollars)

		Percentiles			
Mean	28.21	5%	7.88	95%	58.50
Median	26.25	10%	11.30	90%	45.70
		25%	18.25	75%	34.82

Panel D: Common Shares Outstanding (thousands)

		Percentiles			
Mean	5649	5%	921	95%	15052
Median	3958	10%	1246	90%	12797
		25%	2108	75%	7890

* Betas are calculated relative to the S&P 500 index using weekly returns during the period two years prior to the buy date.

The higher returns earned by the investment strategy need not be "abnormal"; they may merely reflect compensation for bearing additional risk. But risk (at least as measured by historical betas) does not explain the average 23 per cent per year excess return earned by the selected firms. The betas, computed with weekly returns for individual securities and the S&P 500 index, averaged only 1.03 in the two-year period preceding the buy date (Panel A of Table XIII). Half the firms possessed betas of *less* than 1.0. The betas of 80 per cent of the selected companies ranged between 0.45 and 1.66. (Similar values were obtained when a value-weighted NYSE-AMEX market index was used as the market proxy.)

Recent research has suggested that stock market capitalization may be a very good proxy for risk.[14] Reinganum reported that firms with a median capitalization of $4.6 million earned about 32 per cent per year on average over the 1963–82 period; the excess returns of these very small firms are of about the same magnitude as the excess returns associated with the investment strategy reported here.[15] However, the firms selected by this investment strategy are not particularly small (Panel B of Table XIII). Their median stock market capitalization of $102.3 million compares to the median capital-

ization of Reinganum's seventh decile, $119 million. Firms in this decile earned average returns of 15.6 per cent per year over the 1963–82 period. Firms selected by the nine investment screens in the 1970–83 period earned an average of 30.6 per cent in the first year after they were bought. Thus firms selected by the nine-screen investment strategy apparently outperformed a portfolio of firms with comparable stock market capitalization. Stated differently, the excess returns earned by this investment strategy cannot be attributed to the "small firm effect." This is not particularly surprising, as fewer than 5 per cent of the firms could be considered to be very small.

Panels C and D of Table XIII present the distributions of the two components of stock market capitalization—share prices and shares outstanding. The median share price was $26.25. One-quarter of the firms were priced over $34.82; only 8 per cent sold at less than $10.00 on the day they were purchased. The selected companies are clearly not in general low-priced stocks. The median number of shares outstanding was slightly less than four million; the dispersion in outstanding shares was fairly large, with 80 per cent of the companies falling in the range between 1.2 million shares and 12.8 million shares.

A Four-Screen Strategy

To assess the sensitivity of the strategy's results to all nine criteria, we generated an alternative strategy that employed only four of these criteria. To choose which four criteria to use, we applied each investment screen to the 222 winners and selected the four screens that produced the highest median returns. For example, of the 222 winners, those with price-to-book values less than 1.0 possessed a median return of 260 per cent, versus the median return for all 222 winners of 237 per cent. The four investment screens associated with the highest median returns were:

(1) price-to-book ratio less than 1.0 (260 per cent);
(2) accelerating quarterly earnings (253 per cent);
(3) a relative-strength rank of the stock in the current quarter greater than the rank in the previous quarter (253 per cent); and
(4) fewer than 20 million common shares outstanding (251 per cent).

Table XIV   Distribution of Cumulative Excess Holding-Period Returns from Four-Screen Strategy (per cent)*

Quarter	Mean	Percentile								
		1st	5th	10th	25th	50th	75th	90th	95th	99th
Buy+1	3.04	−37.5	−24.7	−18.4	−8.3	1.4	11.4	24.8	36.8	68.0
Buy+2	8.19	−45.3	−29.8	−21.7	−8.6	4.4	19.8	40.3	57.5	108.1
Buy+3	12.65	−53.3	−34.8	−25.3	−9.5	7.3	26.9	53.8	75.3	148.6
Buy+4	16.67	−60.1	−39.1	−27.9	−9.8	9.7	33.7	65.1	93.1	170.2
Buy+5	20.84	−65.8	−44.6	−31.5	−10.9	12.7	41.0	78.9	111.2	215.8
Buy+6	26.10	−70.0	−45.5	−31.6	−9.4	15.6	48.1	92.7	131.3	243.6
Buy+7	31.13	−71.1	−47.2	−34.1	−9.3	18.5	56.0	106.4	148.1	267.6
Buy+8	37.14	−74.0	−48.3	−33.1	−7.6	22.3	64.2	118.7	161.6	319.3

* Excess return is defined as the difference between the holding-period return on the security and the holding-period return on the S&P 500 index over the same period of time.

A buy signal was generated whenever the above four criteria were satisfied. (The 222 winners were excluded from the analysis.) As might be expected, more buy signals were generated with only four filters than with nine. The four-screen filter rule generated 10,543 buy signals, whereas the more restrictive nine-screen filter rule produced only 453. Clearly, the other five investment screens severely limit the selection of firms. But do these other five screens seem to matter?

Table XIV gives the performance results for the investment strategy with only four filters; these results should be compared with those in Table XII. The strategy with four screens still does well relative to the S&P 500 index. After one year, the selected firms experienced an average excess holding-period return of 16.67 per cent, versus 23.71 per cent for the nine-screen firms; they appreciated in value by 23.85 per cent, whereas the S&P 500 advanced by only 7.18 per cent. After two years, the excess holding-period returns increased to an average of 37.14 per cent, versus 50.65 per cent for the nine-screen firms.

The performance results with four screens are impressive; they fall short, however, of the excess holding-period returns earned when all nine investment screens are applied. At the margin, the other five investment rules seem to improve performance.

Obviously, these results should not be construed to mean that these four investment screens are the four best filters. They do suggest, however, that the nine investment rules are not entirely redundant. It seems unlikely that any one of the investment rules will yield better performance results than all nine jointly.

Finally, the absence of certain characteristics from the trading strategies merits mention. What is truly remarkable about the strategies is that they do not exploit characteristics that prior research has revealed to be associated with superior performance. The strategies are not tilted in favor of stocks with very small market capitalizations. Nor are firms with low share prices singled out, or those with low price/earnings ratios. The strategies are not "contrarian" in the sense that companies with substantial previous price declines are selected. Indeed, only firms that are selling near their maximum price for the two previous years are eligible for inclusion. Despite the absence of these characteristics, the trading strategies produce excess returns that are economically significant. This suggests that there may be more than one way to skin the performance cat! ∎

Footnotes

1. See S. Basu, "The Investment Performance of Common Stocks in Relation to Their Price-Earnings Ratios: A Test of the Efficient Market Hypothesis," *Journal of Finance* 32 (1977), pp. 663–682 and S. Francis Nicholson, "Price Earnings Ratios," *Financial Analysts Journal*, September/October 1960, pp. 43–45.

2. R.W. Banz, "The Relationship Between Return and Market Value of Common Stocks," *Journal of Financial Economics* 9 (1981), pp. 3–18 and M.R. Reinganum, "Misspecification of Capital Asset Pricing: Empirical Anomalies Based on Earnings Yields and Market Values," *Journal of Financial Economics* 9 (1981), pp. 19–46.

3. See D.B. Keim, "Size-Related Anomalies and Stock Return Seasonality—Further Empirical Evidence," *Journal of Financial Economics* 12 (1983), pp. 13–32; R.A. Ariel, "A Monthly Effect in Stock

Returns" (Working Paper No. 1629–84, Sloan School, M.I.T., 1984); K. R. French, "Stock Returns and the Weekend Effect," *Journal of Financial Economics* 8 (1980), pp. 55–69; M.R. Gibbons and P. Hess, "Day of the Week Effects and Asset Returns," *Journal of Business* 54 (1981), pp. 579–596; and L. Harris, "A Transaction Data Study of Weekly and Intradaily Patterns in Stock Returns," *Journal of Financial Economics* 16 (1986), pp. 99–117.

4. For this research, William O'Neil + Co. provided me with a specially formatted computer tape containing the information on NYSE and AMEX firms from the *Datagraph* books. This is the first time William O'Neil + Co. has made these proprietary data available for an academic study.

5. O'Neil personnel employed criteria other than just price appreciation to choose firms. However, such criteria are not explicitly stated. Based on the University of Chicago's CRSP tapes, there are 4,049 occurrences of a NYSE or AMEX firm doubling in value within a given calendar year during the 1970–83 period. For example, one additional criterion seemingly applied to stocks by O'Neil personnel is related to the price per share of a stock. In O'Neil's universe of 272 firms, fewer than 5 per cent sold at a price less than $10 a share. Of the list of 4,049 firms that doubled, if one eliminated those selling for less than $10, the number would dwindle to 1,311 companies. Given the customer base subscribing to this publication, such a price level screen is not all that surprising. Furthermore, it does not bias this analysis. At worst it might caution one against applying the findings from this research to stocks selling for less than $10.

6. These categories are strictly the author's and are not part of the O'Neil data.

7. Upon request, the author will provide similar data for the banks, mutual funds and insurance companies.

8. See J.F. Jaffe, "Special Information and Insider Trading," *Journal of Business* 47 (1974), pp. 410–428 and H. N. Seyhun, "Insiders' Profits, Costs of Trading, and Market Efficiency," *Journal of Financial Economics*, June 1986, pp. 189–212.

9. See Basu, "The Investment Performance of Common Stocks," *op. cit.* and Reinganum, "Misspecification of Capital Asset Pricing," *op. cit.*

10. See M. R. Reinganum, "The Anomalous Stock Market Behavior of Small Firms in January: Empirical Tests for Tax-Los Selling Effects," *Journal of Financial Economics*, June 1983, pp. 89–104.

11. Betas were calculated using ordinary–least-squares regressions and weekly returns during the two-year period prior to the buy date. The proxy for the market portfolio is a value-weighted index of all NYSE and AMEX companies.

12. One cannot rule out the possibility that O'Neil personnel implicitly (it is not stated in the publication) applied some of these criteria to define a great winner. For example, given their institutional customers, it might make commercial sense for them to exclude most companies selling at a price less than $10 or whose market capitalizations are smaller than $20 million.

13. To the extent that the samples of 222 winners and other firms are correlated, some subtle biases may remain. Application of the trading strategies in other time periods should eliminate any remaining biases.

14. See K.C. Chan and N-F. Chen, "Estimation Error of Stock Betas and The Role of Firm Size as an Instrumental Variable for Risk" (CRSP Working Paper No. 179, University of Chicago, 1986).

15. See Reinganum, "Anomalous Stock Market Behavior," *op. cit.*

How Many Stocks Make a Diversified Portfolio?

Meir Statman*

Abstract

We show that a well-diversified portfolio of randomly chosen stocks must include at least 30 stocks for a borrowing investor and 40 stocks for a lending investor. This contradicts the widely accepted notion that the benefits of diversification are virtually exhausted when a portfolio contains approximately 10 stocks. We also contrast our result with the levels of diversification found in studies of individuals' portfolios.

I. Introduction

How many stocks make a diversified portfolio? Evans and Archer [9] concluded that approximately ten stocks will do. They stated that their results "Raise doubts concerning the economic justification of increasing portfolio sizes beyond 10 or so securities" (p. 767). Evans and Archer's conclusion has been widely adopted and cited in many current textbooks, but is it correct? No. The primary purpose of this paper is to show that no less than 30 stocks are needed for a well-diversified portfolio. A secondary purpose is to compare this finding to the levels of diversification observed in studies of individual investors' portfolios.

II. Portfolios and Risk

The risk of a stock portfolio depends on the proportions of the individual stocks, their variances, and their covariances. A change in any of these variables will change the risk of the portfolio. Still, it is generally true that when stocks are randomly selected and combined in equal proportions into a portfolio, the risk of a portfolio declines as the number of different stocks in it increases. Evans and Archer observed that the risk reduction effect diminishes rapidly as the number of stocks increases. They concluded that the economic benefits of diversification are virtually exhausted when a portfolio contains ten or so stocks.

Evans and Archer's conclusion has been cited in many textbooks. For example, Francis ([10], p. 749) wrote:

---

* Leavey School of Business Administration, Santa Clara University, Santa Clara, CA 95053. The author thanks Melanie Austin, Ivan Brick, Wayne Lee, and especially an anonymous *JFQA* referee for helpful comments, but retains full responsibility for all errors. He acknowledges the support of a Batterymarch Fellowship.

[P]ortfolio managers should not become overzealous and spread their assets over too many assets. If 10 or 15 different assets are selected for the portfolio, the maximum benefits from naive diversification most likely have been attained. Further spreading of the portfolio's assets is *superfluous diversification* and should be avoided. [Emphasis in the original.]

Stevenson and Jennings ([22], pp. 532–533) wrote:

The results of the Evans and Archer study indicate that a portfolio of approximately eight to sixteen randomly-selected stocks will closely resemble the market portfolio in terms of fluctuations in the rate of return. Other studies have shown similar results and an unusual consistency using different time periods, different groups of stocks, and different research techniques. Consequently, while the CAP model requires the purchase of the market portfolio, essentially the same result can be achieved from a practical standpoint with a much smaller portfolio.

Gup ([11], pp. 363–364) wrote:

Proper diversification does not require investing in a large number of different industries or securities . . . [T]he diversifiable risk is reduced as the number of stocks increases from one to about eight or nine . . . [W]hen the number of securities is increased to about nine, almost all of the diversifiable risk is eliminated.

Reilly ([18], p. 101) wrote:

In terms of overdiversification, several studies have shown that it is possible to derive most of the benefits of diversification with a portfolio consisting of from 12 to 18 stocks. To be adequately diversified does *not* require 200 stocks in a portfolio [Emphasis in the original.]

Early studies, including that by Evans and Archer, reached their conclusions by simulating the relationship between risk and the number of stocks. Elton and Gruber [7] investigated the relationship between risk and the number of stocks in a portfolio further and provided an analytical solution for the relationship between the two.[1] Elton and Gruber's results, presented in Table 1, imply that 51 percent of a portfolio standard deviation is eliminated as diversification increases from 1 to 10 securities. Adding 10 more securities eliminates an additional 5 percent of the standard deviation. Increasing the number of securities to 30 eliminates only an additional 2 percent of the standard deviation.

III. The Costs and Benefits of Diversification

The principle that marginal costs should be compared to marginal benefits in determining the optimal levels of production or consumption is fundamental to economic theory. The fact that "almost all" of the portfolio's unsystematic risk is eliminated when it contains 10 or 100 stocks is meaningless when presented by itself.

Diversification should be increased as long as the marginal benefits exceed the marginal costs. The benefits of diversification are in risk reduction. The costs are transaction costs. The usual argument for limited diversification is that marginal costs increase faster than marginal benefits as diversification increases. For

---

[1] Bird and Tippett [1] have shown that studies using the simulation methodology are deficient. In particular, simulation studies tend to exaggerate the rate of decline in portfolio risk as the number of stocks in the portfolio increases.

TABLE 1
Expected Standard Deviations of Annual Portfolio Returns

Number of Stocks in Portfolio	Expected Standard Deviation of Annual Portfolio Returns	Ratio of Portfolio Standard Deviation to Standard Deviation of a Single Stock
1	49.236	1.00
2	37.358	0.76
4	29.687	0.60
6	26.643	0.54
8	24.983	0.51
10	23.932	0.49
12	23.204	0.47
14	22.670	0.46
16	22.261	0.45
18	21.939	0.45
20	21.677	0.44
25	21.196	0.43
30	20.870	0.42
35	20.634	0.42
40	20.456	0.42
45	20.316	0.41
50	20.203	0.41
75	19.860	0.40
100	19.686	0.40
200	19.423	0.39
300	19.336	0.39
400	19.292	0.39
450	19.277	0.39
500	19.265	0.39
600	19.247	0.39
700	19.233	0.39
800	19.224	0.39
900	19.217	0.39
1000	19.211	0.39
Infinity	19.158	0.39

Source: Elton and Gruber [8], p. 35. Portfolios are equally weighted. Elton and Gruber reported variances of weekly returns. We have converted these to standard deviations of annual returns.

example, Mayshar [17] developed a model that shows that it is optimal to limit diversification in the presence of transaction costs.

Comparison of benefits and costs requires a common measure. We use returns as our measure. The risk reduction benefits of diversification, in units of expected return, can be determined through a simple comparison of any two portfolios. The analysis is similar to that by Blume and Friend ([5], pp. 52–58).

We use a 500-stock portfolio as our benchmark portfolio and compare other, less diversified portfolios to it. We use a 500-stock portfolio as an example of an attainable, fairly diversified portfolio, but we claim neither that a 500-stock portfolio is a proxy for the market portfolio, nor that we cannot obtain better diversified portfolios.

The 500-stock portfolio can be levered, through borrowing or lending, to form portfolios $P(n)$ with combinations of expected returns and standard deviations according to the equation

$$(1) \qquad E\left[R_{P(n)}\right] = \left(R_F + \alpha\right) + \left\{\frac{E\left[R_{P(500)}\right] - \left(R_F + \alpha\right)}{\sigma_{P(500)}}\right\}\sigma_{P(n)} ,$$

where $E[R_{P(n)}]$ = the expected return of portfolio $P(n)$,

$\qquad R_F$ = the risk-free rate,

$\qquad \alpha$ = the excess of the borrowing rate over the lending or risk-free rate for a borrowing investor, and zero for a lending investor,

$\qquad E[R_{P(500)}]$ = the expected return of the 500-stock portfolio,

$\qquad \sigma_{P(n)}$ = the standard deviation of portfolio $P(n)$, and

$\qquad \sigma_{P(500)}$ = the standard deviation of the 500-stock portfolio.

Equation (1) defines what we will call the 500-stock line and all portfolios $P(n)$ lie on it (see Figure 1). The 500-stock line is composed of two segments. The first, from R_F to $P(500)$, represents the portfolio combinations for a lending investor. The lending rate is R_F, the risk-free rate. The second, from $P(500)$ through $P(10)$, represents the portfolio combination for a borrowing investor. The borrowing rate is $R_F + \alpha$, where α is the excess of the borrowing rate over the lending rate.

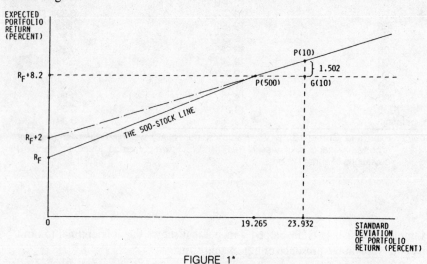

FIGURE 1*

* An expected return 1.502 percent higher than that of a 500-stock portfolio, P(500), is necessary to offset the higher risk, due to limited diversification, of the 10-stock portfolio G(10). A portfolio P(10) can be constructed by leveraging P(500) where the expected return of P(10) is 1.502 percent higher than that of G(10), while the two have identical risks. Data on standard deviations of portfolio returns are from Table 1. An estimate of 2 percent was used for α, the excess of the borrowing rate over the lending rate. An estimate of 8.2 percent was used for the risk premium.

Markowitz [16] developed a formula for the expected variance of a portfolio on n securities. That formula has been used by Elton and Gruber. We assume, as in Elton and Gruber, that an investor draws randomly from all stocks to form portfolios that differ in the number of stocks but have identical expected returns. We use the findings of Ibbotson Associates [12] about the risk premium on a particular 500-stock portfolio, the Standard and Poor's (S&P) 500 Index. Note that the S&P 500 Index is one attainable 500-stock portfolio. While Elton and Gruber use equally weighted portfolios, the S&P 500 Index is value weighted. We assume, for now, that the cost of maintaining an equally weighted 500-stock portfolio is identical to the cost of maintaining a value weighted 500-stock portfolio.

We use an Ibbotson Associates ([12], p. 42) estimate of the risk premium on the 500-stock portfolio, $E[R_{P(500)}] - R_F$. The arithmetic mean of the risk premium over the period 1926–1984 is 8.2 percent per year. We use 2.0 percent per year as an estimate of α, the excess of the borrowing rate over the risk-free or lending rate. The estimate is based on a comparison between the Treasury Bill rate, a proxy for the lending rate, and the Call Money rate. The Call Money rate is the rate charged on loans to brokers on stock exchange collateral (i.e, margin loans), and it provides a starting point for the estimate of the borrowing rate. The Call Money rate is less than 2 percent higher than the Treasury Bill rate (see Table 2). However, brokers typically charge their borrowing customers somewhat more than the Call Money rate. An estimate of 2 percent for α seems reasonable.

TABLE 2

Difference between the Call Money Rate and the Treasury Bill Rate

Date	(1) Call Money Rate (percent)	(2) Treasury Bill Rate (percent)	(1)−(2) Difference
Jan. 15, 1985	9.25	7.74	1.50
Feb. 15, 1985	9.38	8.20	1.18
March 15, 1985	9.75	8.48	1.27
April 15, 1985	9.50	8.14	1.36
May 15, 1985	9.00	7.69	1.31
June 14, 1985	8.63	7.21	1.42
July 15, 1985	8.63	6.92	1.71
Aug. 15, 1985	9.25	7.14	2.11
Sept. 15, 1985	8.75	7.22	1.53
Oct. 17, 1985	8.88	7.20	1.68
Nov. 15, 1985	9.13	7.21	1.92
Dec. 16, 1985	9.00	7.05	1.95
			1.58

Source: Data are from the Money Rate tables of the *Wall Street Journal* on the specified dates. We used data from the *Wall Street Journal* for the 15th of each month during 1985, or a date close to the 15th if data for the 15th were not available. The Call Money rate is the mean of the range of rates provided. The Treasury Bill rate is the rate for the most recent auction of 13-week bills.

To calculate the risk reduction benefits of diversification, compare, for example, a portfolio of ten randomly selected stocks, $G(10)$, to a portfolio $P(10)$, that lies on the 500-stock line and has a standard deviation identical to that of portfolio $G(10)$. We know from Elton and Gruber (Table 1) that portfolio $G(10)$

has an expected standard deviation, $\sigma_{G(10)}$ of 23.932 percent, and that the expected standard deviation of the 500-stock portfolio, $\sigma_{P(500)}$, is 19.265 percent. The standard deviation, $\sigma_{G(10)}$, exceeds $\sigma_{P(500)}$ as portfolio $G(10)$ contains more diversifiable risk than portfolio $P(500)$.

If stocks are chosen randomly, every stock and every portfolio has an expected return of $R_F + 8.2$ percent, composed of the risk-free rate and an 8.2-percent risk premium. Thus, the expected returns of both the 10-stock portfolio, $G(10)$, and the 500-stock portfolio, $P(500)$, are equal to $R_F + 8.2$ percent.

How much would a portfolio $P(10)$, that levers the 500-stock portfolio, $P(500)$, be expected to yield if $P(500)$ were levered so that the standard deviation of the returns on portfolio $P(10)$ is 23.932 percent? Using Equation (1) we find that

$$E\left[R_{P(10)}\right] = \left(R_F + 2\right) + \left\{ \frac{\left(R_F + 8.2\right) - \left(R_F + 2\right)}{19.265} \right\} 23.932 = R_F + 9.702 \ .$$

An investor obtains the $R_F + 9.702$-percent expected return on portfolio $P(10)$ by borrowing 0.242 of his or her wealth and investing 1.242 of his or her wealth in the 500-stock portfolio (see Figure 1).

The return differential between the levered 500-stock portfolio, $P(10)$, and the 10-stock portfolio, $G(10)$, is $E[R_{P(10)}] - E[R_{G(10)}] = [R_F + 9.702] - [R_F + 8.2] = 1.502$.

The 1.502-percent differential in the expected return between the levered 500-stock portfolio $P(10)$ and the 10-stock portfolio $G(10)$ can be interpreted as the benefit that an investor derives from increasing the number of stocks in the portfolio from 10 to 500. In general, the benefit from increasing the number of stocks in a portfolio from n to 500 is

$$(2) \quad E\left[R_{P(n)}\right] - E\left[R_{G(n)}\right] = \left\{ \frac{\sigma_{P(n)}}{\sigma_{P(500)}} - 1 \right\} \left\{ E\left[R_{G(n)}\right] - \left(R_F + \alpha\right) \right\} \ .$$

For the 10-stock portfolio, discussed earlier, we have

$$E\left[R_{P(10)}\right] - E\left[R_{G(10)}\right] = \left\{ \frac{23.932}{19.265} - 1 \right\} \left\{ \left(R_F + 8.2\right) - \left(R_F + 2\right) \right\} = 1.502 \ .$$

Benefits, in terms of expected returns, of increasing the number of stocks in various portfolios to 500 are presented in Table 3.

We turn now from the measurement of the benefits of diversification to the measurement of its costs. Assume, for now, that no costs are incurred in buying, selling, and holding of portfolios $G(n)$ composed of less than 500 stocks. A leveraged 500-stock portfolio, $P(n)$, is preferable to a portfolio $G(n)$ if the costs of $P(n)$ are lower than the benefits that come with increased diversification.

A 500-stock portfolio is available to all investors in the form of the Vanguard Index Trust, a no-load index fund that mimics the S&P 500 Index. The fund provides a return that is lower than that of the S&P 500 Index because investors pay transaction costs and administrative expenses. The mean annual re-

TABLE 3

Difference between Expected Annual Return of a Portfolio of *n* Stocks, *G(n)*, and Expected
Annual Return of a Portfolio *P(n)* That Levers a 500-Stock Portfolio Such That Standard
Deviations of Returns of Portfolios *G(n)* and *P(n)* Are Equal[a]

Number of Stocks in Portfolio (*n*)	Return Differences for Borrowing and Lending Investors	
	Borrowing Investor	Lending Investor
10	1.502	1.986
20	0.776	1.027
30	0.517	0.683
40	0.383	0.507
50	0.302	0.399
100	0.135	0.179

[a] The figures in this table were calculated using Equation 2 with data from Table 1. The risk premium is estimated as 8.2 percent, the arithmetic mean risk premium. Risk premium data are from Ibbotson Associates [12], p. 42. The value of α, the excess of the borrowing rate over the lending rate, was estimated as 2 percent.

turn differential for the years 1979–1984 is 0.49 percent (see Table 4). Of course, 0.49 is less than 1.502, so the Vanguard portfolio dominates a ten-stock portfolio even when the cost of buying, selling, and holding these ten securities is zero.

TABLE 4

Comparison of Returns to Investors in the Standard and Poor's (S&P)
500 Index and Vanguard Index Trust, 1979–1984

Year	(1) Rate of Return on S&P 500 Index (percent)	(2) Rate of Return on Vanguard Index Trust (percent)	Difference (1) − (2)
1979	18.44	18.04	0.40
1980	32.42	31.92	0.50
1981	−4.91	−5.21	0.30
1982	21.41	20.98	0.43
1983	22.51	21.29	1.22
1984	6.27	6.21	0.06
		Mean	0.49

Source: Vanguard Index Trust returns data are from Wiesenberger Financial Services [23]. S&P 500 Index returns data are from Ibbotson Associates [12].

Note that the Vanguard Index Trust serves only as an example of an attainable well-diversified and unmanaged mutual fund. Similar funds with various combinations of securities would be offered, if investors demand them.

A comparison of the 0.49-percent figure to the figures in Table 3 makes clear that the Vanguard Index Trust dominates a 30-stock portfolio, *G(30)*, for a borrowing investor, and a 40-stock portfolio, *G(40)*, for a lending investor, even if we assume that no costs exist for buying, selling, and holding stocks in portfolios *G(30)* and *G(40)* while the Vanguard Index Trust costs are paid.

The figures quoted above were obtained under a set of particular assumptions, and they may increase or decrease as the assumptions change. We will consider here some prominent cases.

First is the issue of transaction costs. So far we have assumed that investors pay the costs of the Vanguard Index Trust, but they pay nothing for buying and selling and holding stocks of less diversified portfolios, $G(n)$. This assumption leads to an underestimation of the advantage of the Vanguard Index Trust over portfolios $G(n)$. For example, consider the case where costs associated with portfolios $G(n)$ amount to 0.1 percent per year of the value of the portfolio. The effect of these costs on the relative positions of portfolios $G(n)$ and the Vanguard Index Trust is equal to the effect of reducing the Vanguard Index Trust annual costs by 0.1 percent, from 0.49 to 0.39. Such a change makes the Vanguard Index Trust superior to a portfolio of 35 stocks, rather than 30 stocks, for the case of a borrowing investor, and 50 stocks, rather than 40 stocks, for the case of a lending investor.

The estimation of annual costs associated with portfolios $G(n)$ is difficult because they depend on the interval between stock trades; costs are higher for those who trade frequently. However, the earlier example probably underestimates the advantages of the Vanguard Index Trust. The cost of a round trip stock trade is probably not lower than 1 percent, and the mean holding period of a stock is probably not much higher than one year. (See [20], p. 306.)

Second, the reliability of the standard deviation estimate for returns of portfolios consisting of few stocks is low relative to that of portfolios of many stocks. Elton and Gruber ([7], Table 8) reported that the standard deviation of the estimate of the standard deviation of the portfolio return is 1.8 percent for a portfolio of 10 stocks, and 0.3 percent for a portfolio of 50 stocks, but it drops to virtually zero for a portfolio of 500 stocks. We do not know how to measure the loss that is due to the inherent unreliability of the estimate of the standard deviation of portfolio returns in portfolios of few stocks. However, it is another disadvantage of low levels of diversification.

The case for the Vanguard Index Trust may have been overstated because of two reasons. First, investors may be able to choose superior stocks and use the returns on these stocks to compensate for the additional risk due to lack of diversification. Indeed, there is some evidence that investors are able to choose stocks that offer return advantages sufficient to eliminate some of the negative effects of transaction costs. For example, Schlarbaum, Lewellen, and Lease ([20], Table 14) found that individual investors had mean returns, after transaction costs, that were identical to the mean returns of mutual funds. However, Schlarbaum et al. adjusted only for the systematic risk of stocks in both individuals' portfolios and mutual funds. The lack of diversification in individuals' portfolios relative to that of mutual funds implies that individuals may do worse than mutual funds when proper consideration is given to both systematic and unsystematic risk.

Second, stocks in the Vanguard Index Trust are value weighted while the analysis here is based on equally weighted portfolios. It is possible that the cost of the Vanguard Index Trust underestimates the costs of an equally weighted 500-stock portfolio, since transaction costs per dollar investment are generally higher for small company stocks than for large company stocks.

IV. Do Individuals Follow Markowitz's Prescription on Diversification?

The framework in which individuals construct portfolios by choosing combinations of expected return and risk, measured as the standard deviation of the return, is a crucial building block for much work in finance. Markowitz developed the prescriptive (normative) framework.

An important prediction of the CAPM, a descriptive (positive) model based on Markowitz's idea, is that every investor would hold a portfolio of all securities available in the market (given efficient markets, perfectly divisible securities, and no transaction costs).

Evidence, however, suggests that the typical investor's stock portfolio contains only a small fraction of the available securities. Blume, Crockett, and Friend [3] found that in 1971, 34.1 percent of investors in their sample held only one dividend-paying stock, 50 percent held no more than 2 stocks, and only 10.7 percent held more than 10 stocks. A 1967 Federal Reserve Board Survey of Financial Characteristics of Consumers showed that the average number of stocks in the portfolio was 3.41 (see [4]). A survey of investors who held accounts with a major brokerage company revealed that the average number of stocks in a portfolio ranged from 9.4 to 12.1, depending on the demographic group [15].

Of course, the number of securities in the portfolio is not the sole determinant of the degree of diversification. Studies by Jacob [13] and others have shown that an investor can reduce unsystematic risk significantly with few securities if he or she chooses securities judiciously. However, there is no evidence that investors follow the suggested rules on optimal diversification with few securities. Blume and Friend ([5], p. 49) reported that the actual degree of diversification in 70 percent of the investors in their study *was lower* than suggested by the number of securities in the portfolios. Blume and Friend concluded that

> The empirical results show, however, that many investors, particularly those of limited means, do not hold well-diversified portfolios. The analysis of the returns realized by them confirms that these investors have exposed themselves to far greater risks than necessary (p. 58).

Observing individuals' stock portfolios provides only limited information about the level of diversification in their overall portfolios. While we know that there are only few stocks in the typical portfolio, it is possible that diversification is accomplished through bonds, real estate, and other assets. However, recent evidence by King and Leape [14] strongly suggests that limited diversification is observed even where assets other than stocks are included. Their study was based on a detailed survey of 6,010 U.S. households conducted in 1978. The survey oversampled high-income families and therefore provides a rich source of information on the composition of portfolios. One conclusion of King and Leape was that

> the differences in portfolio composition across households cannot be fully explained within the framework of the conventional portfolio choice model. The households in our sample, though wealthy, own a surprisingly small number of assets and liabilities, and this lack of diversification was found to be important when estimating asset demand equations. Given that the mean net worth of the sample was almost a quarter of a million dollars in 1978, it is hard to imagine that transactions costs, as traditionally defined, played a decisive role in producing incomplete portfolios (pp. 33–34).

It seems that a descriptive theory of portfolio construction, based on Markowitz, does not hold. People forego available opportunities for diversification, and transaction costs are not likely to provide a complete explanation for it.

V. Conclusion

We have shown that a well-diversified stock portfolio must include, at the very least, 30 stocks for a borrowing investor, and 40 stocks for a lending investor. This conclusion contradicts earlier results, quoted in many current textbooks, that the benefits of diversification for stock portfolios are exhausted when the number of stocks reaches 10 or 15. Moreover, observation of individuals' portfolios suggests that people do not hold portfolios that are well diversified.

Why do people forego the benefits of diversification? Maybe investors are simply ignorant about the benefits of diversification. If ignorance is the problem, education may be the solution. However, existing evidence does not warrant a claim that investors should indeed be educated to increase diversification.

Alternative approaches to portfolio construction exist. One is the framework in which investors are concerned about the skewness of the return distribution as well as with the mean and variance. (See, for example, [6].) The other is the "safety first" framework (see [19]). However, we are not sanguine about the ability of either of these two theories to provide an adequate description of the way portfolios are built because neither is consistent with the following two common observations.

First, people do not seem to treat their assets as parts in an integrated portfolio. For example, some people borrow at 15-percent interest to finance a car rather than "borrow" from the college education fund they have set for their young chidren that pays only 10 percent interest. As Black [2] wrote, people "keep their money in separate pockets." Second, people display risk seeking and risk aversion that varies with the various "pockets." Many people seek risk by buying lottery tickets, while they are extremely risk averse with assets in retirement accounts. (For a discussion of these issues in the context of portfolio construction, see [21].)

We have to know much more about investors' goals and preferences to develop a framework that describes how they form portfolios. Meanwhile, we should not rush to conclude that investors should be educated to hold fully diversified portfolios.

References

[1] Bird, R., and M. Tippett. "Naive Diversification and Portfolio Risk: A Note." *Management Science*, 32 (Feb. 1986), 244–251.

[2] Black, F. "The Future for Financial Services." Working Paper, M.I.T. (Oct. 1982).

[3] Blume, M. E.; J. Crockett: and I. Friend. "Stock Ownership in the United States: Characteristics and Trends." *Survey of Current Business*, 54 (Nov. 1974), 16–40.

[4] Blume, M. E., and I. Friend. "The Asset Structure of Individual Portfolios and Some Implications for Utility Functions." *Journal of Finance*, 30 (May 1975), 585–603.

[5] —————————. *The Changing Role of the Individual Investor: A Twentieth Century Fund Report*. New York: John Wiley & Sons (1978).

[6] Conine, T. E., and M. J. Tamarkin. "On Diversification Given Asymmetry in Returns." *Journal of Finance*, 36 (Dec. 1981), 1143–1155.

[7] Elton, E. J., and M. J. Gruber. "Risk Reduction and Portfolio Size: An Analytical Solution." *Journal of Business*, 50 (Oct. 1977), 415–437.

[8] —————————. *Modern Portfolio Theory and Investment Analysis*, 2nd ed. New York: John Wiley & Sons (1984).

[9] Evans, J. L., and S. H. Archer. "Diversification and the Reduction of Dispersion: An Empirical Analysis." *Journal of Finance*, 23 (Dec. 1968), 761–767.

[10] Francis, J. C. *Investments: Analysis and Management*, 4th ed. New York: McGraw-Hill (1986).

[11] Gup, B. E. *The Basics of Investing*, 2nd ed. New York: John Wiley & Sons (1983).

[12] Ibbotson Associates. *Stocks, Bonds, Bills, and Inflation: 1985 Yearbook*. Chicago: Ibbotson Associates, Inc. (1985).

[13] Jacob, N. L. "A Limited-Diversification Portfolio Selection Model for the Small Investor." *Journal of Finance*, 29 (June 1974), 837–857.

[14] King, M. A., and J. I. Leape. "Wealth and Portfolio Composition: Theory and Evidence." #1468, NBER Working Paper Series, Cambridge, MA: National Bureau of Economic Research (Sept. 1984).

[15] Lease, R. C.; W. Lewellen; and G. Schlarbaum. "Market Segmentation: Evidence on the Individual Investor." *Financial Analysts Journal*, 32 (Sept. 1976), 53–60.

[16] Markowitz, H. *Portfolio Selection: Efficient Diversification of Investments*. New York: John Wiley & Sons (1959).

[17] Mayshar, J. "Transaction Cost in a Model of Capital Market Equilibrium." *Journal of Political Economy*, 87 (Aug. 1979), 673–700.

[18] Reilly, F. K. *Investment Analysis and Portfolio Management*, 2nd ed. San Francisco: Dryden Press (1985).

[19] Roy, A. D. "Safety-first and the Holding of Assets." *Econometrica*, 20 (July 1952), 431–449.

[20] Schlarbaum, G. G.; W. G. Lewellen; and R. C. Lease. "Realized Returns on Common Stock Investments: The Experience of Individual Investors." *Journal of Business*, 51 (April 1978), 299–325.

[21] Shefrin, H. M., and M. Statman. "A Mental Accounting-Based Portfolio Theory." Working Paper, Santa Clara Univ. (Nov. 1985).

[22] Stevenson, R. A., and E. H. Jennings. *Fundamentals of Investments*, 3rd ed. San Francisco: West Publ. Co. (1984).

[23] *Wiesenberger Investment Companies Service: Investment Companies 1985*. New York: Wiesenberger Financial Services. (1985).

AN EMPIRICAL ANALYSIS OF BEN GRAHAM'S NET CURRENT ASSET VALUE RULE

*Joseph D. Vu**

This paper presents evidence that the net current asset value rule developed by Ben Graham in 1930 is still profitable in the 1970s and early 1980s. The abnormal gain is not due to future mergers because both the merged and nonmerged subsamples have positive and statistically significant returns in the post-event period.

INTRODUCTION

The net current asset value (NCAV) rule is a simple trading technique: buy all the stocks that sell for less than the net current asset value per share. The NCAV is defined as current assets minus all liabilities including long-term debt and preferred stock. Buying stocks below NCAV, the investor pays nothing at all for the fixed assets. Ben Graham developed the NCAV rule in 1930, claiming that stocks selected by this technique substantially outperform the market.

Graham [11, p. 85] more recently tests the NCAV rule by buying one share of each of the 85 companies that meet the selection criterion on December 31, 1957, and holding them for two years. The gain for the NCAV portfolio is 75 percent, against 50 percent for the Standard and Poor's 425 industrials. What is more remarkable is that none of the issues shows significant losses, seven are about even, and 78 show substantial gain. Graham also claims that the investment strategy based on the NCAV rule is uniformly good for about 30 years prior to 1957.

Oppenheimer [15] and Oppenheimer and Schlarbaum [16] test Graham's stock selection criteria for "defensive" investors and conclude that these criteria result in above-average

*University of Illinois at Chicago, Chicago, IL 60680. The author is grateful for partial funding for this research from the University of Illinois at Chicago, and thanks Mary Lunberg for her research assistance. Special thanks are given to Beni Lauterbach and Michael Long for many helpful comments.

return even after adjusting for market risk. In 1984, Oppenheimer and Schlarbaum [17] test the NCAV rule directly. They find that this stock selection criterion is still profitable in the 1970s. The NCAV stock portfolios outperform relevant market benchmarks on both raw return and risk-adjusted return basis. This study has some limitations. First, portfolios are formed on an arbitrarily chosen simulated date of purchase—the last business day of December. The method may include stocks that no longer satisfy the NCAV rule in December because the stock price used is the November closing price. In addition, this method ignores stocks that meet the NCAV selection criterion in earlier months but rise above the NCAV in December. Second, the beta (systematic risk) estimate of NCAV stocks might be incorrect because many stocks remain below NCAV for a period of more than a year, causing the portfolio selected in the following period to be highly correlated with the portfolio of the previous period. The estimated beta in such a situation would be based on the same period in which excess returns have already been reported.

This paper analyzes the performance of stocks that meet the NCAV, using a different method than that of Oppenheimer and Schlarbaum [17]. The selection method and data are described in the second section. The third section presents the results. The data suggest that the NCAV stock selection criterion is still profitable in the 1977–1984 period. The final section gives the conclusions and summary.

DATA AND METHOD

Data of all stocks selling below NCAV are collected from the *Value Line Investment Survey* from April 1977 to December 1984. This list of stocks begins on April 8, 1977, and is updated every week. This stock selection method is better than that of Oppenheimer and Schlarbaum because it includes *all* stocks selling below NCAV at any time. Since *Value Line* is published weekly, new stocks meeting the NCAV can enter the portfolio continuously at the end of each month, not on an arbitrary date such as December 31. Each stock can enter the portfolio only once during a two-year period, and each stock carries the same weight in the portfolio. For stocks that are acquired or liquidated, the final stock price is used in calculating monthly returns. These returns are available on the Center for Research in Security Prices (CRSP) monthly return tapes at the University of Chicago. Restricting the sample to common stock issues included in the CRSP files means that only firms listed on the New York Stock Exchange or the American Stock Exchange are studied. From April 1977 through December 1984, the sample size is 107 stocks. In a bearish market such as 1977, 50 out of the 107 satisfy the selection criteria. However, in periods of a rising market, few stocks satisfy the NCAV. For example, no stock meets the NCAV in 1983 and only two satisfy the NCAV in 1984. The NCAV stocks on average belong to small firms with above average systematic risk. The mean market value of equity is $51.3 million, and the mean beta is 1.38.

The method used to compute the risk-adjusted stock returns is similar to that of Fama et al. [9] and to that endorsed by Brown and Warner [5]. The month in which the stock is first identified by *Value Line* as being traded below NCAV is designated as month 0. Because Graham [10, 11] suggests that stocks selling below NCAV be held for about two years, monthly excess returns on a portfolio of NCAV stocks are computed for 24 months prior to the event (month 0) and 24 months after.

RESULTS

Table 1 shows the performance of 107 NCAV stocks. Column (1) shows the months relative to the date that stocks selling below NCAV are identified in the *Value Line*. The average common stock raw (unadjusted) returns and cumulative raw returns are reported in columns (2) and (3), respectively.

Although the month 0 raw return of -0.9 percent is not significantly different from zero ($t = -1.12$), month -1 return of -5 percent is significant at the 0.01 level ($t = -5.42$). Five out of seven months before the event date have negative raw returns. These results indicate that stocks that satisfy the NCAV selection criterion tend to fall in the previous few months. For the pre-event period (month -24 to month -1), the average cumulative raw return is 21 percent with a t-value of 1.76. The null hypothesis that the cumulative raw return equals zero is not rejected at the 0.05 level of significance. The post-event cumulative raw return of 61.7 percent is significant at the 0.01 level ($t = 5.93$).

Similar to the result of raw returns, the excess return of -0.4 percent in month 0 is not significantly different from zero ($t = -0.66$), but month -1 excess return of -3.2 percent is significant at the 0.01 level ($t = -3.87$). Because the average

TABLE 1

PERFORMANCE MEASURES OF 107 STOCKS SELLING BELOW
NET CURRENT ASSET VALUE

Month (1)	Raw Return (2)	Cumulative Raw Return (3)	Excess Return (4)	Percentage of Positive Excess Return (5)	Cumulative Excess Return (6)
– 24	.032**	.032	– .001	45.3	– .001
– 23	.021*	.053	– .014	36.8	– .015
– 22	.018	.071	.001	42.5	– .014
– 21	.018	.089	.023	58.5	.009
– 20	.023*	.112	.003	40.6	.012
– 19	.009	.121	.007	49.1	.019
– 18	.013	.134	– .028**	36.8	– .009
– 17	.025**	.159	.007	45.3	– .002
– 16	.006	.165	– .017	36.8	– .019
– 15	.075**	.240	.017*	50.0	– .002
– 14	.029	.269	.029**	56.2	.027
– 13	.010	.279	– .005	47.7	.022
– 12	– .009	.270	– .012	42.1	.010
– 11	– .023	.247	– .023	37.4	– .013
– 10	.022**	.269	– .004	41.6	– .017
– 9	.001	.270	– .006	43.9	– .023
– 8	.006	.276	– .007	40.6	– .030
– 7	– .002	.274	– .015	44.9	– .045
– 6	– .025**	.249	– .011	38.5	– .056
– 5	– .005	.244	– .005	43.0	– .061
– 4	.025**	.269	– .007	41.1	– .068
– 3	.009	.278	.009	57.9	– .059
– 2	– .018	.260	– .014	43.9	– .073
– 1	– .050**	.210	– .032**	33.6	– .105
0	– .009	.201	– .004	46.7	– .109
1	.012	.213	– .002	46.2	– .111
2	.060**	.273	.020*	49.0	– .091
3	.014	.287	.010	52.4	– .081
4	.019*	.306	.020*	57.4	– .061
5	.039**	.345	.024*	55.0	– .037
6	.019*	.364	.013	52.5	– .024
7	.051**	.415	.009	53.5	– .015
8	.006	.421	– .019	40.8	– .034
9	.010	.431	.013	54.1	– .021
10	.046**	.477	.036**	64.3	.015
11	.049**	.526	.018	43.3	.033
12	.060**	.586	.012	49.5	.045
13	.044**	.630	.016	51.0	.061
14	.020*	.650	.014	49.0	.075
15	.028	.678	.001	44.7	.076
16	.015	.693	.006	45.3	.082
17	– .002	.691	– .001	43.2	.081
18	– .020	.671	.003	44.2	.084
19	.011	.682	– .014	40.0	.070
20	.033**	.715	.011	50.5	.081

TABLE 1 CONTINUED

PERFORMANCE MEASURES OF 107 STOCKS SELLING BELOW NET CURRENT ASSET VALUE

Month (1)	Raw Return (2)	Cumulative Raw Return (3)	Excess Return (4)	Percentage of Positive Excess Return (5)	Cumulative Excess Return (6)
21	.033**	.748	.013	47.9	.094
22	.008	.756	.015	52.1	.109
23	.026	.782	− .002	41.9	.107
24	.035**	.817	.025*	55.4	.132

*Significant at the 5 percent level.

**Significant at the 1 percent level.

beta (systematic risk) of NCAV firms is 1.38, after adjusting for risk the returns in the pre-event period are mostly negative. In 11 out of 12 months before the event, the excess returns are negative. However, the average drop in cumulative excess return in the entire pre-event period (month − 24 to month − 1) is − 10.5 percent, which is not statistically significant at the 0.05 level ($t = -1.45$). The post-event cumulative excess return of 24.1 percent is significant at the 0.01 level ($t = 3.90$).

The results are similar to those reported by Oppenheimer and Schlarbaum: the NCAV stock selection criterion is still profitable in the 1970s and early 1980s. These authors could not explain the magnitude of the abnormal gain in their sample, after adjusting for the firm size, the January effect, and the holding period. One possible explanation for the observed high post-event return is that the NCAV criterion is sensitive in picking stocks that are potential merger candidates. In our sample of 107 NCAV stocks, 18 of them (17 percent) later merged. To investigate the merger explanation further, the overall sample is broken into merged and nonmerged subsamples. The performance measures of 18 merged stocks are shown in Table 2.

The month 0 raw return of − 1.9 percent is not significantly different from zero ($t = -1.01$), but the month − 1 raw return of − 6.7 percent is significant at the 0.01 level ($t = -2.67$). This result indicates that the NCAV criterion tends to select stocks that recently decline in value. For the pre-event

TABLE 2

PERFORMANCE MEASURES OF 18 MERGED STOCKS SELLING BELOW NET CURRENT ASSET VALUE

Month (1)	Raw Return (2)	Cumulative Raw Return (3)	Excess Return (4)	Percentage of Positive Excess Return (5)	Cumulative Excess Return (6)
−24	.004	.004	−.037	44.4	−.037
−23	.040	.044	.012	44.4	−.025
−22	.015	.059	.009	33.3	−.016
−21	.013	.072	.016	50.0	−.000
−20	.025	.097	.000	27.8	.000
−19	.013	.110	.020	38.9	.020
−18	−.027	.083	−.059*	38.9	−.039
−17	.069**	.152	.044	61.1	.005
−16	.020	.172	.003	33.3	.008
−15	.082**	.254	.013	38.9	.021
−14	.061**	.315	.071**	66.7	.092
−13	.037	.352	−.002	50.0	.090
−12	−.048	.304	−.046	33.3	.044
−11	.010	.314	.019	61.1	.063
−10	.068**	.382	.027	58.8	.090
−9	−.018	.364	−.028	38.9	.062
−8	−.004	.360	−.020	38.9	.042
−7	.024	.384	−.000	44.4	.042
−6	−.044*	.340	−.014	37.5	.028
−5	.009	.349	−.009	33.3	.019
−4	.029	.378	−.004	44.4	.015
−3	.001	.379	−.004	44.4	.011
−2	−.035	.344	−.019	38.9	−.008
−1	−.067**	.277	−.042	22.2	−.050
0	−.019	.258	−.027	33.3	−.077
1	.011	.269	−.007	44.4	−.084
2	.051**	.320	.020	50.0	−.064
3	.013	.333	.003	55.6	−.061
4	.036	.369	.037	55.6	−.024
5	.053	.422	.047	50.0	.023
6	.011	.433	.008	55.6	.031
7	.071**	.504	.017	66.7	.048
8	−.013	.491	−.022	32.3	.026
9	.009	.500	.023	58.8	.049
10	.029	.529	.019	52.9	.068
11	.032	.561	−.008	41.2	.060
12	.023	.584	−.015	41.2	.045
13	.028	.612	.009	41.2	.054
14	.056**	.668	.057**	64.7	.111
15	.009	.677	−.002	46.7	.109
16	.022	.699	.011	56.3	.120
17	−.003	.696	.020	62.5	.140
18	−.001	.695	.009	50.0	.149
19	−.000	.695	−.026	31.3	.123
20	.030	.725	.011	56.3	.134

Table 2 Continued

PERFORMANCE MEASURES OF 18 MERGED STOCKS SELLING BELOW NET CURRENT ASSET VALUE

Month (1)	Raw Return (2)	Cumulative Raw Return (3)	Excess Return (4)	Percentage of Positive Excess Return (5)	Cumulative Excess Return (6)
21	.099**	.824	.079**	75.0	.213
22	.011	.835	.033	62.5	.246
23	.092**	.927	.055*	53.3	.301
24	.061	.988	.052*	64.3	.353

*Significant at the 5 percent level.

**Significant at the 1 percent level.

period, the average cumulative raw return rises 27.3 percent, with a t-value of 1.45. The null hypothesis that the cumulative raw return equals zero is not rejected at the 0.05 level of significance. The post-event cumulative raw return of 73.0 percent is significant at the 0.01 level ($t = 4.77$).

Column (4) of Table 2 shows that the excess return of − 2.7 percent in month 0 is not significantly different from zero ($t = -1.13$). The small decline of − 1.3 percent in cumulative excess returns in the pre-event period is not significant ($t = -0.09$). However, the increase of 43 percent in cumulative excess return in the post-event period is significant at the 0.01 level ($t = 3.13$). The magnitude of the increase in two measures of cumulative return for the merged stocks is larger than that of the overall sample. This result is consistent with the findings of Mandelker [14], Langetieg [13], Dodd [8], Asquith and Kim [3], Asquith [2], and Dennis and McConnell [7] that the common stocks of acquired firms earn positive and statistically significant abnormal returns.

Table 3 shows the performance measures of the 89 non-merged stocks in the original sample. Column (2) of Table 3 shows that the month 0 raw return of − 0.7 percent is not significantly different from zero ($t = -0.77$). However, the month − 1 raw return of − 4.7 percent is significant with a t-value of − 4.75. Column (3) shows that the increase in cumulative raw return of 15.4 percent in the pre-event period is not significant

TABLE 3

PERFORMANCE MEASURES OF 89 NONMERGED STOCKS SELLING BELOW NET CURRENT ASSET VALUE

Month (1)	Raw Return (2)	Cumulative Raw Return (3)	Excess Return (4)	Percentage of Positive Excess Return (5)	Cumulative Excess Return (6)
-24	.039**	.039	.007	45.1	.007
-23	.016	.055	-.021	45.1	-.014
-22	.019	.074	.000	39.6	-.014
-21	.018	.092	.023	52.2	.009
-20	.022*	.114	.004	46.7	.013
-19	.012	.126	.008	51.1	.021
-18	.018	.114	-.024	45.6	-.003
-17	.016	.160	.001	50.0	-.002
-16	.002	.162	-.023	50.6	-.025
-15	.073**	.235	.016	47.2	-.009
-14	.021	.256	.019	47.7	.010
-13	.005	.261	-.007	51.1	.003
-12	.004	.265	.000	47.8	.003
-11	-.034**	.231	-.036**	45.6	-.033
-10	.014	.245	-.010	47.2	-.043
-9	.004	.249	-.001	46.1	-.044
-8	.007	.256	-.005	44.3	-.049
-7	-.007	.249	-.018	42.7	-.067
-6	-.021*	.228	-.010	43.2	-.077
-5	-.008	.220	-.004	39.3	-.081
-4	.025*	.245	-.008	42.7	-.089
-3	.009	.254	.012	46.1	-.077
-2	-.014	.240	-.013	44.9	-.090
-1	-.047**	.193	-.030**	36.0	-.120
0	-.007	.186	-.000	49.4	-.120
1	.012	.198	-.001	46.6	-.121
2	.062**	.260	.020*	48.8	-.101
3	.016	.276	.014	52.3	-.087
4	.016	.292	.015	57.1	-.072
5	.039**	.331	.018	56.0	-.054
6	.020*	.351	.012	51.8	-.042
7	.045**	.396	.006	50.6	-.036
8	.010	.406	-.014	43.4	-.050
9	.008	.414	.002	51.8	-.048
10	.050**	.464	.042**	66.3	-.006
11	.052**	.516	.021	43.9	.015
12	065**	.581	.014	50.0	.029
13	.046**	.627	.017	53.1	.046
14	.014	.641	.009	46.9	.055
15	.030	.671	.001	43.8	.056
16	.013	.684	.006	43.8	.062
17	-.002	.682	-.004	39.2	.056
18	-.024	.658	.002	43.0	.058
19	.014	.672	-.011	41.8	.047
20	.034**	.706	.011	49.4	.058

TABLE 3 CONTINUED

PERFORMANCE MEASURES OF 89 NONMERGED STOCKS SELLING BELOW NET CURRENT ASSET VALUE

Month (1)	Raw Return (2)	Cumulative Raw Return (3)	Excess Return (4)	Percentage of Positive Excess Return (5)	Cumulative Excess Return (6)
21	.019	.725	− .001	42.3	.057
22	.008	.733	.011	50.0	.068
23	.014	.747	− .013	39.7	.055
24	.029**	.776	.019	53.8	.074

*Significant at the 5 percent level.

**Significant at the 1 percent level.

(t = 1.32). The post-event cumulative raw return of 59 percent is significant at the 0.01 level (t = 5.45).

Similar to the result of raw returns, the excess return of 0 percent in month 0 is not significantly different from zero (t = − 0.22), but the month − 1 excess return of − 3 percent is significant at the 0.01 level (t = − 3.43). Moreover, for one year prior to the event, 10 months have negative excess return. This return is similar to previous findings that the NCAV criterion tends to pick stocks that recently fall in value. Column (6) of Table 3 shows that for the entire pre-event period, the decline of − 12.7 percent in cumulative excess return is not significant with a t-value of − 1.69. The post-event period increase of 19.4 percent in cumulative excess return is significant at the 0.01 level (t = 3.12). This result indicates that even if adjustment is made for merged stocks, the NCAV criterion is still profitable.

CONCLUSION

This paper presents evidence that the net current asset value criterion developed by Ben Graham in 1930 is still profitable in the 1970s and early 1980s. A possible explanation for this anomaly is that the financial market does not seem to pay much attention to this selection criterion. (Arbel and Strebel [1] find that firms that are relatively neglected by security analysts exhibit superior performance compared with those that are intensively researched.) At the time of the first publication of the

NCAV stocks in the *Value Line Investment Survey* (month 0 and month + 1), both the raw and excess returns are not significantly different from zero for all three samples. Moreover, most of these NCAV stocks are not recommended by *Value Line,* which has a good reputation in stock selection (see Black [4], Holloway [12], Copeland and Mayers [6], and Stickel [18]). *Value Line* ranks 1700 common stocks into 5 groups based on their projected relative price performance over the next 12 months. Rank 1 stocks are expected to have the best relative price performance over the next 12 months, while rank 5 stocks are expected to perform the worst. From a sample of 107 NCAV stocks, none has rank 1, 6 stocks have rank 2, 38 stocks have rank 3 (average price performance), 42 stocks have rank 4, and 21 stocks have rank 5. Although 63 NCAV stocks (59 percent of the sample) have below average or the worst relative price performance, the NCAV portfolio substantially outperforms the market benchmark in both raw and excess returns during the two years subsequent to the first publication in *Value Line.* The abnormal gain is not due to future mergers because both the merged and nonmerged subsamples have positive and statistically significant returns in the post-event period. Future research is needed to determine if the NCAV rule continues its past trend and to determine if certain adjustments for firm size can change the profitability of this trading rule.

REFERENCES

[1] Arbel, A., and P. Strebel. "Pay Attention to Neglected Firms! Even When They're Large." *Journal of Portfolio Management* 9(Winter 1983):37-42.

[2] Asquith, P. "Merger Bids, Uncertainty, and Stockholder Returns." *Journal of Financial Economics* 11(April 1983):51-83.

[3] Asquith, P., and E. H. Kim. "The Impact of Merger Bids on the Participating Firms' Security Holders." *Journal of Finance* 37(December 1982):1209-1228.

[4] Black, F. "Yes, Virginia, There Is Hope: Tests of the Value Line Ranking System." Working paper, Graduate School of Business, University of Chicago, May 1971.

[5] Brown, L., and J. Warner. "Measuring Security Price Performance." *Journal of Financial Economics* 8(September 1980):205-258.

[6] Copeland, T., and D. Mayers. "The Value Line Enigma (1965-1978): A Case Study of Performance Evaluation Issues." *Journal of Financial Economics* 10(November 1982): 289-321.

[7] Dennis, D., and J. McConnell. "Corporate Mergers and Security Returns." *Journal of Financial Economics* 16(June 1986):143–187.

[8] Dodd, P. "Merger Proposals, Management Discretion and Stockholder Wealth." *Journal of Financial Economics* 8(June 1980):105–138.

[9] Fama, E., L. Fisher, M. Jensen, and R. Roll. "The Adjustment of Stock Prices to New Information." *International Economic Review* 10(February 1969):1–21.

[10] Graham, B. *The Intelligent Investor.* New York: Harper & Row, 1949.

[11] ———. *The Intelligent Investor.* 4th rev. ed. New York: Harper & Row, 1973.

[12] Holloway, C. "A Note on Testing an Aggressive Investment Strategy Using Value Line Ranks." *Journal of Finance* 36(June 1981):711–719.

[13] Langetieg, T. "An Application of a Three-Factor Performance Index to Measure Stockholder Gains from Merger." *Journal of Financial Economics* 6(December 1978):365–383.

[14] Mandelker, G. "Risk and Return: The Case of Merging Firms." *Journal of Financial Economics* 1(December 1974):303–335.

[15] Oppenheimer, H. "Common Stock Selection: An Analysis of Benjamin Graham's 'Intelligent Investor' Approach." Ann Arbor, Michigan: UMI Research Press, 1981.

[16] Oppenheimer, H., and G. Schlarbaum. "Investing with Ben Graham: An Ex Ante Test of the Efficient Market Hypothesis." *Journal of Financial and Quantitative Analysis* 3(September 1981):341–360.

[17] ———. "Ben Graham's Net Current Asset Values: Risks, Returns, and Market Efficiency." Working paper, Texas Christian University, Fort Worth, December 1984.

[18] Stickel, S. "The Effect of Value Line Investment Survey Rank Changes on Common Stock Prices." *Journal of Financial Economics* 14(March 1985):121–143.

EVALUATION OF A GROWTH MUTUAL FUND

A distant relative of yours, Mr. Hubert Hummel, contacts you upon learning that you are doing graduate work in investments. Mr. Hummel is seeking advice on how to evaluate a particular mutual fund, the Babson Growth Fund (BGF). BGF is one member of a group of six mutual funds managed by David Babson & Co., a respected investment advisory firm in Cambridge, Massachusetts. To get you started on such a mission, Mr. Hummel sends you a copy of the latest BGF annual report (see Exhibit 1 below).

Hubert Hummel, a lawyer, aged 50, is widowed with no children, and is in excellent health. His annual income exceeds his annual living expenses and taxes by about $7,000 per year. Mr. Hummel plans to practice law for another ten years and then retire at age 60. His law firm provides excellent working conditions but no retirement benefits, and so he must generate retirement benefits by himself.

To date, Mr. Hummel has accumulated about $250,000 in common stocks and corporate bonds. His securities account, at a local brokerage firm, has not performed well in recent years, and Mr. Hummel has decided to switch his funds into a common stock mutual fund. A colleague at his law firm recommended the Babson Growth Fund. After reading the latest annual report for BGF, Hummel is not sure what to do, and hence his inquiry for you. He indicates at the outset that he is willing to pay for your help.

Assuming that you are interested in helping him, here are some questions that need to be considered:

(1) If his invest funds generate an after-tax return of 7%, what wealth should Hummel expect to have at retirement?

(2) Given the brief scenario, does BGF seem to be a reasonable investment alternative for Mr. Hummel?

(3) How do you appraise the BGF portfolio holdings at mid-year 1988?

(4) How would you assess the risk of BGF?

(5) How do you evaluate the achieved performance of BGF during the last decade? During the last five years?

What performance comparisons will you use in doing such an evaluation?

No time value of money
No market comparisons
No inter fund comparisons

(6) In turn, how would you assess the performance methodology used in the BGF annual report?

(7) Review other information sources for mutual funds such as Wiesenberger Investment Companies Service, FORBES (annual issue in September), MONEY magazine (periodically), and United Business Service Co. Do those sources support your performance analysis of the Babson Growth Fund?

Exhibit 1

The BABSON Funds

Babson Growth Fund

Annual Report June 30, 1988

David L. Babson
Growth Fund Inc.

A no-load mutual fund invested in a diversified list of common stocks selected for their long-term possibilities of both capital and income growth.

It was founded particularly for those investors who believe in the Fund's fundamental investment policy, and who wish to receive, through ownership of the Fund's shares, continuous portfolio supervision by the staff of David L. Babson & Co. Inc.

To The Shareholders:

David L. Babson Growth Fund completed a very successful 28th fiscal year on June 30, 1988. Distributions to shareholders in the past year have been substantial. The timing of several of these payments was dictated by changes in the tax law.

Date	Distribution of	
	Income	Capital Gains
July 1, 1987	$0.16	$0.69
December 18, 1987	0.1475	0.7525
December 31, 1987	–	0.06
June 30, 1988	0.145	1.53

The Fund's net asset value on June 30, 1988 was $11.66, reflecting the fiscal year-end distributions. In the June quarter of 1988 (the last fiscal quarter for the Fund) the total return (including income and principal) was 5.2%, bringing the return for the first six months of calendar 1988 to 15.1%. This compares favorably with the 12.7% figure for the Standard & Poor's 500 and 13.6% for the average growth mutual fund as measured by Lipper Analytical Services, Inc. For the 1988 fiscal year, which included the October, 1987 market collapse, the Fund declined 6.2%, while the average growth fund declined 6.3%.

Over the past five years Babson Growth Fund has done well. Its total return of 79.1% has been substantially above the 53.5% increase of the average of 249 Growth Funds and the 57.9% average gain of 709 General Equity Funds measured by Lipper. The following graph depicts this record, with dividends and capital gains reinvested, compared to the Lipper Growth Funds Average.

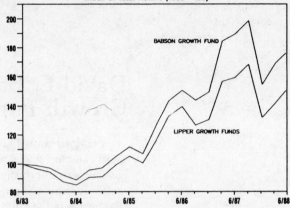

BABSON GROWTH FUND VS. LIPPER GROWTH AVERAGE
Index Of Total Return (1983 = 100)

This strong performance places Babson Growth Fund in the top quartile of all Growth Funds with a five-year record in the Lipper universe.

Changes in the portfolio during the past twelve months were not dramatic. Worthy of note, however, were reductions in chemical, paper, photography, and retail stocks where relative valuations were high. Proceeds were used to take advantage of new investment opportunities which included increases in the transportation and service areas of the economy.

We continue to find attractive new investments in more modest-sized companies. Nearly one-third of the companies in the Fund have a market value of less than $1 billion.

The Economic and Portfolio Review on pages 4-5 of this report contains some interesting comments by David L. Babson & Co. on the current economic and investment situation, and its relationship to the investment position of the Fund.

We appreciate your interest and participation in Babson Growth Fund. If you have questions or suggestions about this or any of the other Babson Funds, please let us know.

Sincerely,

Larry D. Armel

Larry D. Armel
President

Economic and Portfolio Review

In the face of a roller coaster stock market during the past 12 months, in which investor psychology swung rapidly from great enthusiasm to deep pessimism and part way back, business activity and corporate profits have grown at a steady, strong pace. Despite the fears of many economists, the real world of business has been virtually unaffected by last Fall's dramatic shift in the attitude of investors and in the market value of their portfolios.

Consumer spending is determined primarily by the pattern of consumer income. So far in 1988 disposable income has been boosted by a reduction in the personal tax burden as the final phase of the Tax Reform Act of 1986 has been implemented, and by continued rapid increases in employment. (In just the past 12 months two million additional people have found jobs in the U.S.)

As shown in the chart below, after a brief dip following the October, 1987 stock market break, consumption spending has advanced quite consistently. The rate of increase has been slightly lower than the growth in income, which is providing a long-awaited boost in the savings rate. This is a positive development because individuals have accumulated a record amount of debt during the 1980s and if that trend continued unabated, it would be dangerous.

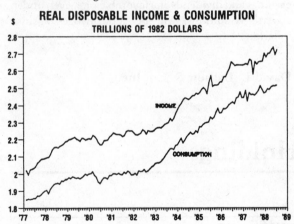

REAL DISPOSABLE INCOME & CONSUMPTION
TRILLIONS OF 1982 DOLLARS

The greatest area of strength in the American economy in the past year has been manufacturing. Thanks to the decline in the dollar relative to many of the world's currencies and to the strenuous efforts of American companies to improve their efficiency and the quality of their products, U.S. goods producers are now much more competitive in world markets. This turnabout has stimulated a sizable increase in exports and thus in our industrial production.

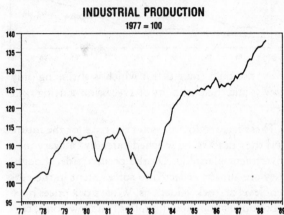

INDUSTRIAL PRODUCTION
1977 = 100

As a result of these favorable business trends, corporate sales, cash flow and profits are rising more rapidly than they have for a number of years. Earnings for the Standard & Poor's 500 companies are now estimated to increase 20-25% in 1988 and the recent pace of dividend increases has been close to 10%, more than double the rate of inflation.

Despite all this good news, investors this summer are quite cautious, even skeptical. This attitude is demonstrated in high cash positions and historically low stock percentages in corporate pension funds and most individuals' portfolios, and in a very moderate level of price/earnings ratios.

The primary concerns appear to be: the overburden of debt and a massive amount of bad loans which have not yet been absorbed, the persistently high federal budget deficit which may well cause tax increases in

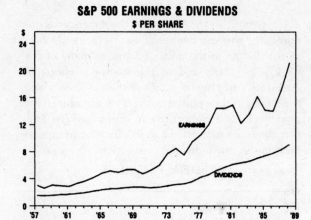

S&P 500 EARNINGS & DIVIDENDS
$ PER SHARE

1989, the high trade deficit which is shrinking only slowly, and the possibility of a recession starting next year.

These factors do pose potential risks for the future and they need to be weighed carefully in everyone's investment planning. On the positive side, though, they are already reflected to some extent in the current level of stock valuations. While stock prices have rebounded about 20% from last Fall's low point, corporate profits have risen much more, so the average price/earnings ratio on the Standard & Poor's 500 is now down to 12. That is the lowest level in three years and significantly under the average multiple of 14 which has prevailed over the past three decades.

In today's somewhat calmer but still uncertain environment, Babson Growth Fund's portfolio is concentrated in companies which have demonstrated superior earnings and dividend growth over the past decade and are expected to maintain their favorable trends in the next few years—and whose shares are reasonably valued.

The average company in the Fund achieved annual earnings growth of 9% from 1977 through 1987, compared with 5% for the 500 companies in the Standard & Poor's index. Over the same period, dividend growth for the Fund's portfolio holdings averaged 11% per year versus 7% for the S&P.

Despite their distinctly superior growth trends, the Fund's stocks had an average price/earnings ratio of 11 on June 30, 1988, compared with the multiple of 13 on the S&P 500 (based on trailing 12 months' earnings).

We believe this combination of good growth and reasonable valuation has been a major factor in the Fund's superior investment record in the past few years.

While inflation has dropped to a rather moderate level since the early 1980s, an acceleration of price increases is a distinct possibility for the future. One of the purposes of equity investing is to protect capital (and the income it generates) against the erosion of inflation. In selecting stocks for the Babson Growth Fund portfolio, we generally try to pick companies which have better-than-average ability to cope with inflationary pressures. Those that can increase their earnings and dividends at a favorable rate, even under adverse conditions, will be good hedges against inflation.

David L. Babson & Co. Inc.

The Fund's Ten Largest Holdings

1988 Rank	1987 Rank	Company	Owned by the Fund Since	Market Value	Percent of Portfolio	S&P Rating
1	1	IBM	1960	$10,190,000	4.29%	A+
2	2	Digital Equipment	1978	6,892,500	2.90%	B+
3	9	Johnson & Johnson	1974	5,556,250	2.34%	A
4	7	Royal Dutch Petroleum Co.	1983	5,506,250	2.32%	A
5	12	Delta Air Lines, Inc.	1984	5,500,000	2.32%	B
6	15	Georgia-Pacific Corp.	1984	4,606,250	1.94%	B
7	17	SmithKline Beckman Corp.	1985	4,462,500	1.88%	A+
8	6	Philip Morris Cos., Inc.	1984	4,187,500	1.76%	A+
9	—	Community Psychiatric Ctrs.	1987	3,894,375	1.64%	A
10	—	Leggett & Platt, Inc.	1987	3,828,125	1.61%	A

Historical Record

Progress of the Fund Since it was Founded in 1960

FISCAL YEAR ENDED JUNE 30	TOTAL NET ASSETS	NET ASSET VALUE PER SHARE	*ORDINARY INCOME DIVIDENDS PER SHARE	*LONG-TERM CAPITAL GAINS DISTRIBUTIONS PER SHARE	*SHORT-TERM CAPITAL GAINS DISTRIBUTIONS PER SHARE	NET ASSET VALUE PER SHARE WITH CAPITAL GAINS DISTRIBUTIONS REINVESTED	NET ASSET VALUE PER SHARE WITH DIVIDENDS and CAPITAL GAINS DISTRIBUTIONS REINVESTED
1960 *(Inception April 30)*	$ 128,066	$ 4.87	$ —0—	$ —0—	$ —0—	$ 4.87	$ 4.87
1961	1,236,869	5.62	0.050	—0—	—0—	5.62	5.67
1962	1,823,440	4.31	0.030	0.08	0.020	4.37	4.45
1963	2,914,824	5.31	0.100	—0—	—0—	5.39	5.59
1964	4,112,818	6.21	0.100	—0—	—0—	6.30	6.64
1965	5,176,041	6.36	0.100	0.07	—0—	6.52	6.97
1966	7,606,119	6.71	0.110	0.12	—0—	6.99	7.59
1967	10,574,446	7.43	0.130	—0—	—0—	7.74	8.55
1968	15,774,577	8.35	0.130	0.04	—0—	8.74	9.82
1969	22,679,878	8.72	0.120	0.13	0.020	9.27	10.56
1970	28,729,379	7.16	0.170	0.02	—0—	7.63	8.87
1971	54,672,327	9.60	0.190	—0—	—0—	10.23	12.15
1972	77,860,344	10.90	0.180	—0—	—0—	11.62	14.05
1973	106,017,401	10.66	0.160	0.09	—0—	11.46	14.05
1974	143,011,492	9.34	0.200	—0—	—0—	10.04	12.54
1975	207,734,395	10.22	0.220	—0—	—0—	10.99	14.09
1976	224,727,885	10.00	0.250	—0—	—0—	10.75	14.16
1977	217,273,868	9.27	0.240	—0—	—0—	9.97	13.46
1978	217,114,139	9.40	0.280	—0—	—0—	10.11	14.06
1979	218,528,345	10.20	0.320	—0—	—0—	10.97	15.76
1980	234,348,577	11.25	0.390	—0—	—0—	12.08	18.01
1981	281,980,936	12.74	0.410	—0—	—0—	13.68	21.04
1982	205,749,921	9.67	0.440	0.79	—0—	11.24	17.97
1983	249,201,722	14.40	0.380	0.19	0.040	16.96	27.97
1984	208,290,661	10.85	0.380	1.615	—0—	14.68	24.91
1985	215,374,722	13.40	0.4025	1.6285	0.2225	18.14	31.36
1986	253,780,848	13.62	0.3525	1.3725	—0—	22.89	42.37
1987	288,727,782	16.25	0.305	1.29	0.005	28.45	53.43
1988	237,465,629	11.66	0.2925	2.3425	—0—	26.09	50.10

*Includes dividends and distributions applicable to the fiscal year which may have been paid soon after the fiscal year-end.

Financial Statements

Statement of Net Assets
June 30, 1988

S&P RATING*	NUMBER OF SHARES	COMPANY	COST	MARKET VALUE
COMMON STOCKS — 97.49%				
BASIC MATERIALS — 6.26%				
A –	50,000	Air Products & Chemicals, Inc.	$ 234,887	$ 2,531,250
A	100,000	Avery International	1,004,198	2,450,000
A	80,000	EcoLab, Inc.	2,167,084	1,800,000
B +	35,000	Hercules, Inc.	1,610,770	1,658,125
A –	100,000	James River Corp. of Virginia	2,200,000	2,575,000
B +	50,000	Lubrizol Corp.	1,896,100	1,837,500
A –	50,000	Scott Paper Co.	1,797,680	2,012,500
			10,910,719	14,864,375
CAPITAL GOODS — 12.09%				
B +	33,300	Carlisle Cos., Inc.	1,033,266	1,132,200
B –	50,000	Deere & Co.	1,974,650	2,300,000
B +	100,000	Emhart Corp.	1,829,000	2,225,000
B	110,000	Georgia-Pacific Corp.	2,266,330	4,606,250
A	40,000	Grainger, (W.W.), Inc.	715,800	2,435,000
B +	75,000	Ingersoll-Rand Co.	1,449,900	3,140,625
A –	30,000	Martin Marietta Corp.	1,254,900	1,342,500
A	40,000	McDonnell Douglas	2,087,047	2,565,000
B	100,000	Potlatch Corp.	2,620,933	3,087,500
B	60,000	Rohr Industries, Inc.	1,911,060	1,935,000
B	30,000	Sundstrand Corp.	1,607,400	1,698,750
A –	40,000	Thomas & Betts Corp.	794,870	2,240,000
			19,545,156	28,707,825
CONSUMER CYCLICAL — 15.14%				
B –	100,000	Armtek Corp.	2,018,400	3,125,000
B	40,000	Eaton Corp.	1,643,325	3,325,000
A –	200,000	Echlin, Inc.	3,564,759	3,425,000
B +	100,000	Fleetwood Enterprises	2,430,471	2,487,500
NR	20,000	Honda Motor Co. ADR	1,111,600	2,540,000
B +	100,000	K mart	2,277,538	3,512,500
A	125,000	Leggett & Platt, Inc.	3,860,270	3,828,125
B +	100,000	Lowe's Cos., Inc.	3,213,588	2,150,000
A +	50,000	McDonald's Corp.	729,055	2,306,250
A +	30,000	Melville Corp.	2,060,061	2,058,750
A –	30,000	Penney, (J.C.), Inc.	1,209,840	1,458,750
B +	50,000	Tandy Corp.	2,088,578	2,400,000
B +	50,000	West Point-Pepperell, Inc.	1,560,300	1,900,000
A	50,000	Whirlpool Corp.	1,327,750	1,437,500
			29,095,535	35,954,375
CONSUMER STAPLES — 14.58%				
NR	125,000	Alco Health Services Corp.	2,234,240	3,625,000
A +	100,000	Anheuser-Busch Cos., Inc.	613,835	3,187,500
A	155,000	Community Psychiatric Centers	3,380,428	3,894,375
A	40,000	Fleming Cos., Inc.	1,638,680	1,375,000
A	70,000	Johnson & Johnson	2,129,519	5,556,250
A	150,000	National Medical Enterprises, Inc.	3,685,575	3,393,750
A +	50,000	Philip Morris Cos., Inc.	1,389,106	4,187,500
A –	50,000	Pioneer Hi-Bred International, Inc.	2,025,000	1,900,000
A +	100,000	SmithKline Beckman Corp.	3,159,903	4,462,500
B +	100,000	Universal Foods Corp.	2,703,000	3,037,500
			22,959,286	34,619,375

S&P RATING*	NUMBER OF SHARES	COMPANY	COST	MARKET VALUE
ENERGY—11.17%				
C	40,000	Amerada Hess Corp.	$ 1,113,850	$ 1,035,000
B	75,000	Coastal Corp.	2,104,725	2,165,625
B	70,000	Dresser Industries	1,353,089	2,038,750
A	80,000	Exxon Corp.	584,235	3,630,000
B	40,000	Halliburton Co.	565,834	1,175,000
B	50,000	Kerr-McGee Corp.	1,682,462	1,750,000
B—	60,000	Louisiana Land & Exploration Co.	2,132,160	1,852,500
B	80,000	Mobil Corp.	2,352,240	3,490,000
A	50,000	Royal Dutch Petroleum Co.	2,202,875	5,506,250
A—	75,000	Schlumberger, Ltd.	1,050,898	2,512,500
A—	50,000	Sonat, Inc.	1,684,263	1,368,750
			16,826,631	26,524,375
FINANCIAL—9.56%				
A+	50,000	Banc One Corp.	1,225,134	1,375,000
A—	75,000	Comdisco, Inc.	1,485,741	1,828,125
A—	75,000	Corroon & Black Corp.	2,483,202	2,362,500
NR	70,000	Fireman's Fund Corp.	1,802,500	2,301,250
A—	70,000	First Fidelity Bancorp.	2,532,915	2,835,000
B+	40,000	Household International, Inc.	1,765,740	2,350,000
B+	80,000	Norwest Corp.	2,056,400	3,800,000
B	80,000	Salomon, Inc.	2,040,375	1,990,000
B+	50,000	St. Paul Cos., Inc.	2,262,500	2,162,500
B	50,000	Transamerica Corp.	1,661,791	1,693,750
			19,316,298	22,698,125
TECHNOLOGY—12.42%				
B—	200,000	Cullinet Software, Inc.	1,942,675	1,725,000
A	50,000	Diebold, Inc.	2,685,229	2,037,500
B+	60,000	Digital Equipment	1,560,775	6,892,500
A+	80,000	International Business Machines Corp.	3,929,576	10,190,000
NR	100,000	MCI Communications	975,000	1,400,000
B	200,000	Scientific-Atlanta, Inc.	3,060,209	2,775,000
NR	150,000	Seagate Technology	1,561,885	2,700,000
A	40,000	Wallace Computer Services, Inc.	1,709,383	1,775,000
			17,424,732	29,495,000
TRANSPORTATION & SERVICES—8.91%				
A—	50,000	Burlington Northern, Inc.	2,396,425	3,506,250
B	150,000	Canadian Pacific, ORD	2,210,750	2,887,500
A—	100,000	Carolina Freight Corp.	2,356,560	2,350,000
B	100,000	Delta Air Lines, Inc.	4,530,910	5,500,000
B+	80,000	Foote, Cone & Belding Communications, Inc.	2,325,804	2,120,000
NR	100,000	KLM Royal Dutch Airlines	1,831,850	1,850,000
B	125,000	Overseas Shipholding Group, Inc.	3,089,960	2,937,500
			18,742,259	21,151,250

Financial Statements (Continued)

Statement of Net Assets (Continued)
June 30, 1988

S&P RATING*	NUMBER OF SHARES	COMPANY	COST	MARKET VALUE
COMMON STOCKS—97.49% *(Continued)*				
UTILITIES—7.36%				
A	100,000	Arkla, Inc.	$ 1,783,324	$ 1,887,500
A+	50,000	Central & South West Corp.	1,529,000	1,587,500
B+	100,000	Louisville Gas & Electric Co.	2,900,367	3,425,000
A−	120,000	Pacific Telesis Group	1,959,330	3,600,000
A−	90,000	Southwestern Bell Corp.	1,733,600	3,588,750
A−	60,000	U.S. West, Inc.	2,281,383	3,397,500
			12,187,004	17,486,250
TOTAL COMMON STOCKS—97.49%			**$167,007,620**	**$231,500,950**
Face Amount				
SHORT-TERM CORPORATE NOTES—2.95%				
$1,000,000		General Electric Capital Corp., 7.35%, due July 18, 1988	$ 1,000,000	$ 1,000,000
1,000,000		General Electric Capital Corp., 7.35%, due July 22, 1988	1,000,000	1,000,000
1,000,000		General Electric Capital Corp., 7.35%, due July 25, 1988	1,000,000	1,000,000
1,000,000		General Motors Acceptance Corp., 7.40%, due July 29, 1988	1,000,000	1,000,000
1,000,000		General Motors Acceptance Corp., 7.40%, due August 5, 1988	1,000,000	1,000,000
1,000,000		General Motors Acceptance Corp., 7.40%, due August 12, 1988	1,000,000	1,000,000
1,000,000		General Motors Acceptance Corp., 7.40%, due August 19, 1988	1,000,000	1,000,000
TOTAL SHORT-TERM CORPORATE NOTES—2.95%			**$ 7,000,000**	**$ 7,000,000**
TOTAL INVESTMENTS—100.44%			**$174,007,620**	**$238,500,950**
Other assets less liabilities—(0.44%) (Note 4)				(1,035,321)
TOTAL NET ASSETS—100.00%				
(equivalent to $11.66 per share; 100,000,000 shares of $1.00 par value common stock authorized; 20,365,656 shares outstanding) (Note 5)				**$237,465,629**

*Standard & Poor's ratings are derived from statistical measurements of past earnings and dividend stability and growth.
The accompanying notes to financial statements are an integral part of this statement.

Statement of Operations
For the year ended June 30, 1988

INVESTMENT INCOME:

Income:		
Dividends	$ 6,796,251	
Interest	674,656	
	7,470,907	
Expenses:		
Management fees (Note 3)	1,978,276	
State registration fees	20,221	
	1,998,497	
Net investment income	5,472,410	

REALIZED AND UNREALIZED GAIN (LOSS) ON INVESTMENTS (Note 1):

Realized gain from investment transactions:	
Proceeds from sales	656,813,241
Cost of securities sold	614,744,595
Net realized gain	42,068,646
Unrealized appreciation on investments:	
Beginning of year	130,239,964
End of year	64,493,330
Decrease in net unrealized appreciation on investments	(65,746,634)
Net loss on investments	(23,677,988)
Decrease in net assets resulting from operations	**($18,205,578)**

The accompanying notes to financial statements are an integral part of this statement.

Financial Statements (Continued)

Statements of Changes in Net Assets
For the two years ended June 30, 1988

	1988	1987
NET ASSETS AT BEGINNING OF YEAR	$288,727,782	$253,780,848
FROM INVESTMENT ACTIVITIES:		
Net investment income	5,472,410	5,522,425
Dividends to shareholders (Note 6)	(7,972,360)	(2,714,170)
Undistributed net investment income included in price of shares sold and redeemed (Note 1)	(130,614)	(29,541)
Increase (decrease) in undistributed net investment income	(2,630,564)	2,778,714
Net realized gain from investment transactions (Note 1)	42,068,646	23,005,782
Less distributions to shareholders (Note 6)	(54,267,254)	(10,522,303)
Increase (decrease) in net unrealized appreciation on investments (Note 1)	(65,746,634)	32,408,840
Net increase (decrease) in net assets from investment activities	(80,575,806)	47,671,033
FROM CAPITAL SHARE TRANSACTIONS:		
Proceeds from 1,919,926 and 1,736,925 shares sold	25,447,614	24,960,302
Net asset value of 4,769,655 and 950,340 shares issued for reinvestment of dividends and distributions	59,077,354	12,625,999
Cost of 4,094,491 and 3,548,801 shares redeemed	(55,211,315)	(50,310,400)
Net increase (decrease) in net assets from capital share transactions	29,313,653	(12,724,099)
Total net increase (decrease) in net assets for the year	(51,262,153)	34,946,934
NET ASSETS AT END OF YEAR	$237,465,629	$288,727,782

The accompanying notes to financial statements are an integral part of these statements.

Notes to Financial Statements

1. Significant Accounting Policies:

The Fund is registered under the Investment Company Act of 1940, as amended, as a diversified open-end management company. A summary of significant accounting policies that the Fund uses in the preparation of its financial statements follows. The policies are in conformity with generally accepted accounting principles.

Investments—Common stocks traded on a national securities exchange are valued at the last reported sales price on the last business day of the year or, if no sale was reported on that date, at the average of the last reported bid and asked prices. Common stocks traded over-the-counter are valued at the average of the last reported bid and asked prices. Investment transactions are recorded on the date securities are purchased or sold. Dividend income and distributions to shareholders are recorded on the ex-dividend dates. Realized gains and losses from investment transactions and unrealized appreciation and depreciation of investments are reported on the identified cost basis.

Federal Income Taxes—The Fund has complied with the Internal Revenue Code requirements applicable to regulated investment companies and will distribute all income to its shareholders. Therefore, no Federal income tax provision is required.

Equalization—The Fund follows the accounting practice known as equalization in which the price of capital shares sold and repurchased between dividend dates includes a proportionate share of the undistributed net investment income for the period. As a result, undistributed net investment income per share is not affected by sales or repurchases of capital shares.

2. Purchases and Sales of Securities:

The aggregate amount of security transactions during the years ended June 30, 1988 and 1987, was as follows:

	1988	1987
Purchases:		
Common stocks	$ 62,357,556	$ 34,517,945
Corporate notes	95,989,061	83,550,000
Repurchase agreements	472,480,000	257,549,000
	$630,826,617	$375,616,945
Sales:		
Common stocks	$ 46,425,534	$ 35,140,285
Corporate notes	93,989,061	82,550,000
Repurchase agreements	474,330,000	255,699,000
	$614,744,595	$373,389,285
Realized gain from investment transactions if the average cost basis had been used would approximate	$ 40,451,708	$ 22,245,564
Cost for Federal income tax purposes of investments owned was	$173,902,947	$157,754,310

Notes to Financial Statements (Continued)

3. Management Fees:

Management fees, which include all normal expenses of the Fund other than taxes, fees and other charges of governmental agencies for qualifying the Fund's shares for sale, special legal fees, interest and brokerage commissions, are paid to Jones & Babson, Inc., an affiliated company. These fees are based on average daily net assets of the Fund at the annual rate of .85 of one percent on net assets up to $250,000,000, and .70 of one percent on net assets exceeding that amount. Certain officers and directors of the Fund are also officers and/or directors of Jones & Babson, Inc.

4. Other Assets and Liabilities:

Other assets consist of cash ($148,012), dividends receivable ($407,850) and interest receivable ($40,887). Liabilities consist of dividends payable to shareholders ($1,632,070).

5. Net Asset Value:

The June 30, 1988 net asset value consists of capital stock ($20,365,657), paid-in capital ($152,856,891), accumulated undistributed loss ($117,513), accumulated undistributed realized loss on investments ($132,736) and accumulated unrealized appreciation on investments ($64,493,330).

6. Shareholder Distributions:

Dividend and capital gain distributions of $7,972,360 and $54,267,254 ($.45 and $3.03 per share), respectively, were declared to shareholders during the fiscal year ended June 30, 1988.

Supplementary Information

The following table sets forth information as to capital and income changes for a share outstanding throughout the five fiscal years ended June 30, 1988:

	1988	1987	1986	1985	1984
Net asset value, beginning	$16.25	$13.62	$13.40	$10.85	$14.40
Income	.40	.41	.44	.48	.45
Expenses	(.11)	(.11)	(.10)	(.09)	(.10)
Net investment income	.29	.30	.34	.39	.35
Dividends from net investment income	(.45)	(.15)	(.55)	(.21)	(.38)
Net realized and unrealized gain (loss) on investments	(1.40)	3.08	3.64	2.38	(1.90)
Distribution from realized capital gains	(3.03)	(.60)	(3.21)	(.01)	(1.62)
Net asset value, ending	$11.66	$16.25	$13.62	$13.40	$10.85
Ratio of expenses to average net assets	.81%	.74%	.75%	.76%	.76%
Ratio of net investment income to average net assets	2.21%	2.12%	2.65%	3.23%	2.64%
Portfolio turnover rate	26%	14%	20%	35%	52%
Number of shares outstanding at end of period (000 omitted)	20,366	17,771	18,632	16,078	19,193

Independent Auditor's Report

To the Shareholders and Board of Directors of David L. Babson Growth Fund, Inc.:

We have audited the accompanying statement of net assets of David L. Babson Growth Fund, Inc. as of June 30, 1988, the related statement of operations for the year then ended, the statements of changes in net assets for each of the two years in the period then ended, and the selected per share data and ratios for each of the five years in the period then ended. These financial statements are the responsibility of the Fund's management. Our responsibility is to express an opinion on these financial statements and per share data and ratios based on our audits.

We conducted our audits in accordance with generally accepted auditing standards. Those 'standards require that we plan and perform the audit to obtain reasonable assurance about whether the financial statements and per share data and ratios are free of material misstatement. An audit includes examining, on a test basis, evidence supporting the amounts and disclosures in the financial statements. Our procedures included confirmation of securities owned as of June 30, 1988, by correspondence with the custodian. An audit also includes assessing the accounting principles used and significant estimates made by management, as well as evaluating the overall financial statement presentation. We believe that our audits provide a reasonable basis for our opinion.

In our opinion, the financial statements and selected per share data and ratios referred to above present fairly, in all material respects, the financial position of David L. Babson Growth Fund, Inc. as of June 30, 1988, the results of its operations for the year then ended, the changes in its net assets for each of the two years in the period then ended, and the selected per share data and ratios for each of the five years in the period then ended, in conformity with generally accepted accounting principles.

ARTHUR ANDERSEN & CO.

Kansas City, Missouri,
August 5, 1988.

The Babson Funds

EQUITIES

DAVID L. BABSON GROWTH FUND – invests in a diversified list of common stocks selected for their long-term possibilities of both capital and income growth.

SHADOW STOCK FUND – designed to achieve long-term growth of capital by investing in common stocks of small, established, profitable companies presently neglected by analysts and institutional investors.

BABSON ENTERPRISE FUND – invests in common stocks of a carefully selected group of smaller, faster-growing companies for their long-term growth of capital possibilities. The Enterprise Fund can provide an important element of vitality in the overall program of an investor seeking long-term capital appreciation who can afford to take greater risk to achieve greater return.

BABSON VALUE FUND – seeks long-term growth of capital and income by investing in a diversified portfolio of common stocks which are considered to be undervalued in relation to earnings, dividends and/or assets.

BABSON-STEWART IVORY INTERNATIONAL FUND – for investors seeking international diversification and favorable total return, this Fund includes equities of various developed investment markets in the free world, principally Western Europe and certain areas of the Pacific Basin.

FIXED INCOME

D. L. BABSON BOND TRUST – emphasizes current income return and relative stability of principal by investing in corporate bonds, U.S. Government issues and other fixed-income securities of high quality. The Fund offers two portfolios: Portfolio S normally with average maturities of less than 5 years, and Portfolio L of more than 5 years (currently about 11 years).

D. L. BABSON MONEY MARKET FUND – provides investors the opportunity to manage their money over the short term by investing in high-quality, domestic, short-term debt instruments for the purpose of maximizing income to the extent consistent with safety of principal and maintenance of liquidity. It offers two portfolios, Prime and Federal.

D. L. BABSON TAX-FREE INCOME FUND – invests principally in quality municipal securities, the income from which is judged exempt from federal income tax. The Fund offers a choice among three separate portfolios of investment-grade securities, differing only in average length of maturity – Longer Term (Portfolio L), Shorter Term (Portfolio S) and Money Market (Portfolio MM).

Emerson "Ozzie" Parker is a longtime friend and high school classmate of your father. They both graduated from Swanton (Ohio) High School in the mid-fifties. While your father pursued an engineering/business college education and career, Emerson Parker always wanted to be a lawyer. To do that, he earned a B.S. in economics/political science from Toledo University, and, three years later, he received his law degree from the University of Michigan.

After graduation from law school, Ozzie returned to Swanton to join the legal firm in which his father was co-founder and co-senior partner of that prestigious firm. Two decades later, Ozzie is the senior and only partner, and thus leader of now a larger law firm that has seven proven lawyers, plus an experienced legal staff. As a result, Ozzie's firm has a most successful practice in Swanton, as well as much of northwestern Ohio, including several key corporations in Toledo.

In addition to his successful legal career, Ozzie has -- from all indications -- an equally successful family life. He is happily married, and all three of his children have good educations and good marriages. In sum, Ozzie is thankful for his family, and he believes that basic values prevail at home, as well as in his professional practice.

The major uncertainty in Ozzie's life for the past few years has been the status and prospects for his investment portfolio. Ozzie began systematic savings soon after he graduated from Michigan. By now, near the end of September 1987, the Parker family portfolio consists of the following common stocks:

# Shares	Issue	Cost Basis	Market Value
500	AMP	$15,800	$22,500
800	Baxter Travenol	12,400	18,400
400	Chubb	16,600	23,600
500	Coca Cola	14,300	19,500
800	R.R. Donnelley	19,200	24,000
500	Eastman Kodak	14,400	24,000
600	General Mills	26,200	27,000
400	General Motors	23,100	23,600
250	IBM	13,600	29,500
600	Ingersoll Rand	16,800	19,800
400	3M	17,600	25,200
600	McDonalds	14,900	27,000

600	Mobil	11,700	21,600
700	J.P. Morgan	16,100	23,800
300	Philip Morris	21,400	27,000
800	Schlumberger	15,800	25,600
650	Upjohn	14,400	20,800
700	Walgreen	16,500	21,000
600	Waste Management	13,700	21,000
400	Xerox	17,800	22,400
	Totals	$332,300	$467,300

As seen from this portfolio update, Ozzie has put together a rather well-diversified portfolio. It consists of twenty common stocks, each from a different industry, and with current market valuations rather evenly distributed. There is a capital gain for each of the 20 issues -- with an aggregate gain of $135,000, or 40.6%, at present. Emerson Parker is proud of this result, and he very much wants to protect his "paper" profit.

Ozzie's portfolio decisions in building this portfolio have been based on extensive consideration of personal advice, plus extensive hours of reading of investment reports provided by his two account executives from the two leading brokerage firms in Toledo. Parker is pleased with his progress to date, but he is continually concerned about the future of his equity investments.

Two events have complicated Parker's current attitude toward his investment portfolio. In June 1987, at his high school's twentieth anniversary, classmate Donald Galliers, by now a commissioned officer in the United States Navy, shared with Ozzie his belief that the stock market is near its likely high for many years. Knowing a bit about the status of Parker's portfolio, Commander Galliers suggests that Ozzie ought to place with his account executives a series of stop loss orders on all of his common stock holdings -- so as to minimize the chances of significant loss if the current bull market were to turn around suddenly. Galliers argued strongly to Parker, albeit after an evening of festive fellowship, that "stops" are the most effective way of avoiding downside risk.

Emerson Parker pondered these thoughts and suggestions, without action, for two months. Then, in late-September 1987, a member of Ozzie's golfing foursome gave him a copy of a First Boston equity research report (see Exhibit 1 below) on put options that he recently received from his account executive. It apparently suggests that protective puts are another way of dealing with downside risk when the stock market is presumed to be near a relative/absolute high. Unfortunately, that research report contains complex diagrams and is more difficult to read.

As a result of these two events and inputs, Emerson Parker is now thoroughly confused about what to do. He calls your father, who immediately defers to you -- by now a second-year graduate student at a southern state university -- and who your father remembers is just about to start a graduate course in investments. Your father mails to you a copy of the First Boston research report, as well as the current listing of Emerson Parker's common stock portfolio. Unfortunately, your task is complicated because many market commentators feel that the stock market has finally reached a level of "over-valuation," while other commentators feel that the stock market has quite a bit further to go.

In particular, your father asks you to review these materials -- and, as a favor to him, to call Mr. Parker at an early date. Specifically, he asks you to consider the following questions:

(1) How would you assess the level of the stock market in late-September 1987?

(2) How would you assess Parker's portfolio at the same time?

(3) What do you think of Galliers' recommendation for stop-loss orders as a means of reducing downside risk?

(4) How do you evaluate First Boston's recommendation for protective put options?

(5) Based on the above, what do you recommend to Ozzie Parker with regard to an investment strategy for minimizing risk?

----

(6) How would you answer these questions today, in view of what has happened since September 1987?

Exhibit 1

Equity Research

First Boston

Industry: **Stock Index Markets**
September 16, 1987
ST2482

Stephen Figlewski

Topics in Stock Index Futures and Options

Buying Puts: A Defensive Strategy for an Uncertain Market

This publication is the first in a series of research reports that will cover basic strategies and other aspects of the stock index futures and options markets. In it we describe stock index put options and discuss how to use a "protective put" strategy to manage risk exposure effectively in an equity portfolio.

Buying Puts: A Defensive Strategy for an Uncertain Market

The stock market has shown extraordinary strength during 1987. New all-time highs are being set, only to be broken immediately as the market charges further ahead. From January through August, the Standard & Poor's 500 index rose from 242.17 to 329.80, an increase of 36.2%. In nine months investors have already earned profits that would look very good for a whole year's performance.

This raises a dilemma. No one believes the market can continue at this pace forever. Whether the bull market will carry stocks another 1, 5, or 20 percent higher, no one can tell. But we may be confident that eventually stock prices will decline from whatever peak they achieve.

The traditional way a portfolio manager protects his investments in an uncertain market is to sell equities and shift funds into bonds or cash. But timing this move correctly is not easy. Those who got out of stocks into cash too early have now missed out on a substantial runup. And shifting from stocks to bonds during the first half of 1987 turned out to be a disaster, as the bond market collapsed while stock prices kept soaring.

Stock index puts offer a solution to the timing dilemma. Adding put options to an equity portfolio is like buying insurance against the market going down. For a fixed cost, the investor limits the amount his portfolio can lose no matter how far the market may drop, while he does not give up the potential for further profits if the market continues higher. This report will describe what stock index puts are and how they can be used to protect an equity portfolio and will briefly discuss some of the choices that must be made in designing a good put buying strategy.

Stock Index Put Options

A put option is the right to sell a specified amount of some underlying asset at a fixed "exercise" or "strike" price on or before an expiration date. The puts we will be concerned with are those based upon one of several stock indexes. Table 1 shows the five most important market indexes on which put contracts are currently traded.

Let us take, as an example, the August 1987 OEX 300 puts. On July 15, 1987, the Standard & Poor's 100 index closed at 305.65 and these puts closed at $3^5/8$. The underlying asset for this contract was 100 "shares" of the index, that is, an amount of the S&P 100 stock portfolio having a current value of $30,565. Like stock index futures, all index options are settled in cash; there is no delivery of actual shares. Thus, the option contract gives the buyer the right to a cash payment from the writer of $100 times the exercise price minus the closing value of the index on the day the put option is exercised.

$$\text{Put payoff} = \$100 \times \left(\begin{array}{cc} \text{exercise} \\ \text{price} \end{array} - \begin{array}{cc} \text{closing index} \\ \text{value} \end{array} \right)$$

OEX options are "American" so the put could be exercised on any day the buyer chose, up until its expiration on the third Friday of the expiration month, in this case August 21. If the buyer did not choose to exercise his put because the index remained higher than the strike price, the option would expire worthless. For this right to choose, the buyer paid the seller $362.50 at the outset.

Table 1
Stock Index Option Contracts

Stock Index	Ticker Symbol	Contract Value	Open Interest	Trading Volume	Description
Standard & Poor's 100	OEX	$31,000	745,000	187,000	Index of 100 large stocks with options
Major Market Index	XMI	$51,000	74,000	24,000	Index of 20 large stocks designed to mimic the DJIA
Standard & Poor's 500	SPX	$31,000	233,000	7,000	Option on S&P 500. Unique feature is options are European: no early exercise
Institutional Index	XII	$32,000	99,000	5,000	Index of stocks with major institutional interest
NYSE Composite	NYA	$18,000	20,000	4,000	Market value weighted index of all NYSE stocks

Note: All exchange-traded stock index options are for $100 times the underlying stock index. Open interest and trading volume are for puts only. All figures are as of September 9, 1987, rounded to the nearest 1,000.

Figure 1 shows the net profit per "share" on the option contract as a function of the level of the index at expiration date. At any index value above 300, the put expires worthless and the initial price is lost. Below 300, the put is in the money. If the index falls below the strike price minus the initial option premium $(300 - 3.63) = 296.37$, the option will be far enough in the money to be worth more than its initial cost. The put purchase then begins to show a profit that increases point for point as the index drops lower.

Clearly, buying this option alone on July 15 would be a bearish strategy, and quite risky. It is out of the money at the outset, and as we have just seen, the S&P 100 index would have to drop by more than nine points for the trade to show a profit at expiration. But that is not an appropriate way to think about what buying this put would do *in the context of an investor's overall portfolio strategy,* any more

than thinking that buying fire insurance on one's home is nothing more than making a bet that the house will burn down.

Consider what buying this put would do to the overall profit for an investor who was already holding the stocks in the S&P 100 index portfolio. (We will discuss the more general case where the stock portfolio is different from the index later.) By July 15, he has seen the value of his portfolio rise by more than 32% since the beginning of the year. Now he is thinking about selling the stocks to realize these profits, but he is not sure if the rally is entirely over. So instead of selling, he buys the August 300 put.

Figure 2 shows the profits that would be earned on the put alone, the stocks alone, and the combined position. The profit profile for the stock portfolio simply shows that its value moves point for point with the S&P 100 index.

Figure 1
Net Profit at Expiration on
OEX August 300 Put Purchased at 3⅝

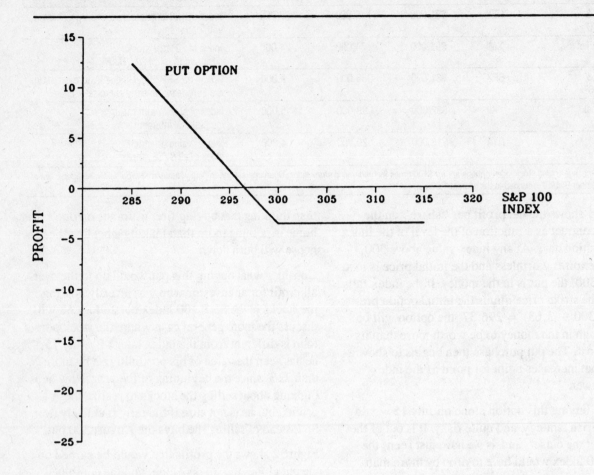

Figure 2
Net Profit at Expiration on Portfolio Plus Protective Put
Long S&P 100 Portfolio at 305.65
Long August 300 Put at 3⅝

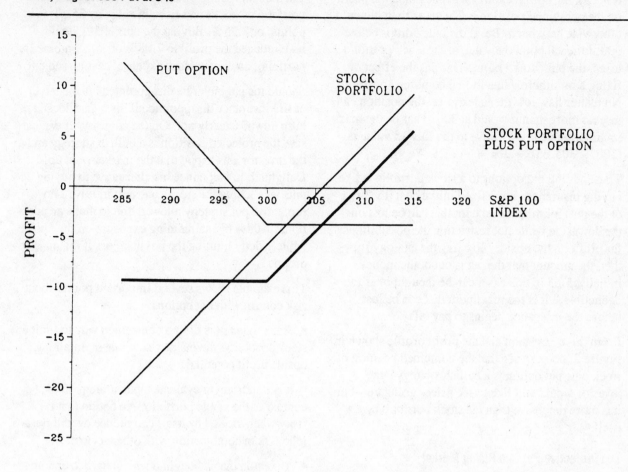

Adding the put option to this portfolio has the effect of splitting the overall profit profile into two regions. If the index ends up above 300 on expiration day, the option expires worthless and the profit on the combined position is $3\frac{5}{8}$ lower than it would otherwise have been. But if the index drops below 300, for each point the value of the stock portfolio loses, the put gains a point. This has the effect of fixing a minimum value for the combined position. No matter how low the index goes, the position can lose no more than it would at 300. That is, the maximum possible loss relative to the July 15 value is $(300 - 305.65) - 3\frac{5}{8} = -9.28$.

Thus, adding put options to a stock portfolio is like buying insurance. For a fixed initial cost (the price of the put) it limits the amount that can be lost on the downside while not restricting the possibilities for profit on the upside. To carry the analogy further, the amount that the put is out of the money initially, 5.65 in this case, can be thought of as the "deductible." It is the maximum that can be lost before the insurance begins to pay off.

From this discussion and the profit profile shown in Figure 2, one can see that the combined position of stock plus put option is a bullish strategy—the investor would still like to see prices going up—but it is more defensive than the stock portfolio by itself.

The Protective Put in a Rising Market

How did this particular strategy work in practice? The first part of Table 2 shows the result. On July 15, the stock portfolio was worth 305.65 and the put option cost $3\frac{5}{8}$, for a total investment of 309.28 in the protected portfolio. On expiration day, August 21, the S&P 100 index closed at 331.16 and the August 300 puts expired worthless. The portfolio of stocks had risen in value by 25.51 points, or 8.35%. Buying the puts at $3\frac{5}{8}$ would have reduced the profit to 7.08% on the combined portfolio, an unnecessary expense, as it turned out.

Should the put buyer be disappointed? Is the buyer of fire insurance disappointed if his house doesn't burn down? Clearly not. On the contrary, as we just saw, the protected position is a bullish strategy and the investor was happy that the market went up. Delighted, in fact, since his alternative to buying puts was selling the stocks outright in July! The protective put strategy allowed him to make an additional 7.08% by maintaining exposure on the upside while strictly limiting the possible loss if the market dropped.

This example shows several important points about risk control with put options:

■ Stock index puts offer a convenient way to limit a stock portfolio's downside risk while maintaining upside profit potential.

■ It is important to evaluate a put strategy in the context of the whole portfolio. An option that is risky when viewed by itself can reduce overall portfolio risk in combination with other securities.

■ An option that is bought does not have to end up in the money for the strategy to be successful.

Table 2
The Protective Put Strategy

	Value of Position			Realized Return	
	July 15	**August 21**	**September 9**	**Points**	**Percent**
Case 1: Buying Puts in a Rising Market					
S&P 100 Portfolio	305.65	331.16	—	25.51	8.35%
August 300 OEX Put	3.63	0.00	—	(3.63)	(100.00)%
Protected Portfolio	309.28	331.16	—	21.89	7.08%
Case 2: Buying Puts in a Falling Market					
S&P 100 Portfolio	—	331.16	310.06	(21.10)	(6.37)%
September 325 OEX Put	—	3.88	15.13	11.25	290.32%
Protected Portfolio	—	335.04	325.19	(9.85)	(2.94)%
Case 3: Longer-Term Protection with Index Puts					
S&P 100 Portfolio	305.65	331.16	310.06	4.41	1.44%
August 300 OEX Put	3.63	0.00	—	(3.63)	(100.00)%
September 325 OEX Put	—	3.88	15.13	11.25	290.32%
Protected Portfolio	309.28	327.29	325.19	12.03	3.89%

The Protective Put in a Falling Market

Now let us look at how the put strategy performs when the market drops. With the OEX index at 331.16 on August 21, suppose the investor buys the September 325 puts for 3⅞. The second part of Table 2 shows what happened to this position from August 21 to September 9. In this period, the stock market sold off sharply. The S&P 100 index portfolio dropped more than 6% to 310.06 and the September 325 puts went up in price to 15⅛. This cushioned the loss on the stocks, so that the protected portfolio ended up losing only 2.94%.

Comparing these results to those in the first part of Table 2 illustrates two features of the protective put strategy that we have already mentioned:

- The strategy is bullish. The protected portfolio is profitable if the price of the underlying asset rises and it loses money when the underlying asset falls.

- It is less risky than the stock portfolio alone. It makes less profit in up markets but has smaller losses in down markets.

Protection with Stock Index Puts Over the Longer Run

Both of the examples we have discussed involved put options with short maturities. While index options are traded with expiration dates as far as nine months in the future, the market for long-duration options is less liquid than for those closer to expiration. An investor who wants to be protected for a long period will normally have to roll over the position as the puts expire.

To see a couple of the issues that are raised by the need to roll over the hedge, let us think about how a protective put strategy spanning the whole period from July 15 through September 9 would have worked. This is shown in the third part of Table 2.

The first stage of the strategy is the same as shown in the first part of the table. The stocks are worth 305.65 at the beginning and the August 300 put is purchased for 3⅝. By August 21, the stocks have risen and the put expires worthless.

At this point, the investor is faced with the decision of how best to proceed. That will depend on what his current evaluation of the market is. For example, after the strength shown by stocks in early August he might decide that a protective put was no longer needed. On the other hand, he might feel that the rally has finally run its course and it is now time to sell out the stock portfolio.

Or he might have begun the strategy with the intention of fixing a minimum level of 300 for the portfolio over the long run and not wish to change at this point. On August 21 he could have rolled the hedge forward into the September 300 contract at a price of only 5/16 or $31.25 per contract, since it was so far out of the money at that point. This is substantially less than it cost to buy the August 300's in July. But while this option was very cheap, it also did not provide much protection for the current value of the portfolio: the index now had to drop more than 30 points before the put would begin to offset the losses. An important thing to see in this example is that the cost of a longer-term protective strategy is not just the price of a short-term option multiplied by the number of times it will be rolled over. In this case it was much less.

A more typical response to a rapid market advance such as was experienced in August would be to lock in some of the latest gains by rolling over the put position to one with a higher strike price, like the September 325s. This is the strategy shown in Table 2. The portfolio was worth 331.16 on August 21. Deducting the cost of the September 325 put left 327.29. When the stock market dropped sharply over the next few weeks, the position could have been liquidated on September 9 at a value of 325.19. This represented a gain over the full period of 3.89% on the protected portfolio as opposed to only 1.44% for the stocks alone.

Notice that by the time the index hit 310.06, the September 325 puts were trading almost at their intrinsic value, that is, the amount that would be realized if they were exercised immediately $(325 - 310.06) = 14.94$. This is normal for deep-in-the-money puts. To continue the protection beyond this point, the options could have been rolled into the October 325 contract at $16\frac{1}{8}$. Thus, it was possible to buy an additional month of insurance for just one point. Once again, the cost of longer-term protection is not found by multiplication.

What is the cost of a protective put strategy if, as we have argued, it is not just given by the prices of the puts that are purchased? This is actually a fairly complex issue and a complete treatment of it will have to be deferred to a later report. However, the way to think about it is the following. An option contract is a "wasting" asset—if there is no change in the market, it loses value daily as expiration approaches. This erosion of value over time can be estimated from an option valuation model and is known as the rate of time decay, or "theta." The actual cost to holding an options position is a function of its rate of time decay. This will depend on the option's strike price, market volatility, the interest rate and all of the other factors that determine option value.

This section has shown that:

- A longer-term protective put strategy will frequently involve a sequence of shorter-term hedges.

- With a sequential hedge, it is not necessary for the market to go down over the whole period for the protected portfolio to outperform the unprotected portfolio. The puts let you profit from short-run rallies while protecting you from short-run sell-offs.

- The cost of a longer-term protective put strategy is not the price of a single option contract multiplied by the number of times it will be rolled over. Rather, it is a function of the rate of time decay on the options that are purchased.

Setting Up a Protective Put Strategy

The first part of this report illustrated how a protective put strategy would work. In setting up a put buying plan to protect a particular portfolio, there are a number of choices to be made with regard to the particular index and contract month to use, the number of contracts to trade and the strike price to pick. These are choices for which there is no single answer. The correct strategy will depend on a number of factors, including the investor's planning horizon, market expectations, risk tolerance, and so on. In this section we will discuss the trade-offs involved in these choices.

Which Index to Trade

Table 1 shows a variety of stock indexes for which traded options exist. Other contracts are also traded and new offerings are being created by the exchanges regularly. There are two basic aspects to the choice of index: tracking error and liquidity. With the exception of the Standard & Poor's 500, little institutional money is invested in stock portfolios that exactly duplicate one of the optionable stock indexes. This means that there will typically be some degree of tracking error (or "basis risk") in the payoff profile for a protective put.

Tracking error means that the value of the stock portfolio that is being protected will not move exactly in tandem with the stock index that the put option is tied to. Total return will be a function of both how the stock market moves (as measured by the option's index) and how the stock portfolio does relative to the index. To the extent that the stocks held outperform the index, the total return on the position is enhanced.

For most diversified institutional portfolios, the tracking error in a protective put is fairly small. For example, over the last year the correlation between daily changes in the S&P 100 and the S&P 500 indexes was over 0.95. But to minimize uncertainty caused by tracking error risk, one should trade puts based on the index that is most correlated with one's stock portfolio.

However, the other element of the choice of contract is liquidity. The more liquid the contract, the smaller will be the market impact of a trade. The open interest and volume figures in Table 1 give an indication of the liquidity of the different contracts. If an institutional investor needs to protect a very large stock position, it might pay to use a contract with greater liquidity even if it is not the most highly correlated with his portfolio.

Which Expiration Month to Pick

This issue is somewhat similar to the last one. If the investor has a specific time horizon over which he wants to be protected, the most predictable results will be achieved by using an option with the same maturity, other things being equal. The total cost of the strategy is known at the outset and there is no risk from changes in market volatility.

This is one important difference between protecting a stock portfolio with stock index puts versus following a "portfolio insurance" scheme. Portfolio insurance involves a dynamic trading strategy that duplicates, in principle, the payoff on a stock portfolio with a protective put by systematically varying the fraction of the portfolio held in stocks and in cash. While portfolio insurance does allow the investor to fix the minimum value for the insured portfolio, the cost of the strategy depends on how much trading is required and on how volatile the market is over the insurance period. Since these can't be known ahead of time, how a portfolio insurance scheme actually performs will be significantly affected by random factors other than the final prices of the stocks in the portfolio.

But while index puts with maturities matching the target horizon reduce uncertainty, as we mentioned before, the markets for distant maturities can be substantially less liquid than for near maturities. In many cases this will make the strategy of rolling over shorter-term puts easier to set up. While such a sequence of options will involve more transactions, this may be offset by narrower bid/ask spreads and greater depth in the market. Also, by holding shorter-term puts, one has the flexibility to choose whether, when, and how to roll the position forward. A portfolio manager may be able to reduce costs and improve performance by adjusting the position in response to market developments and by rolling at times when the spread is relatively favorable.

Which Strike Price to Pick

One of the most common questions raised about a protective put strategy is which strike price one should use. As we saw above, this choice involves a trade-off between the cost of the options and the degree of protectiveness. Better insurance costs more. An inexpensive out-of-the-money put provides only "disaster insurance" against a large drop in the market but costs little if the market rises and it expires worthless. An in-the-money put locks in a high minimum value for the position, but at the cost of a much larger reduction in profits if the market goes up.

To illustrate the trade-off between protection on the downside and profit reduction on the upside for puts with different strike prices, Table 3 shows the possibilities that were available in the market on August 21. For six strike prices it shows the minimum value that is locked in on the position, the increase in the index that would be required for the position to break even, and the rate of return earned on the whole position for changes in the index between down 10% and up 10%. The position ends up at its minimum value if the S&P 100 index at expiration on September 18 is less than the option's strike price. Table 3 shows how market exposure is reduced as higher strike price puts are used, at the cost of higher break-even prices.

How Many Contracts to Trade
The overall payoff profile for a put-protected portfolio will depend entirely on the number of contracts traded. This article has focused on a strategy of protecting a stock portfolio by buying stock index puts on an equal amount of stock. To compute the number of contracts needed for a given stock portfolio, divide the dollar value of the portfolio by the dollar value of the amount of stock underlying one contract, 100 times the current index.

$$\text{Number of contracts to buy} = \frac{\text{Value of stock portfolio}}{100 \times \text{option index}}$$

For example, suppose that on July 15, the investor's portfolio contained $10 million worth of S&P 100 stocks. The protective put strategy described in Table 2 would call for him to buy $10,000,000/100 \times 305.65 = 327$ August 300 put contracts.

Conclusion

The introduction of exchange-traded options and futures contracts based on stock indexes has enormously expanded the range of risk management strategies available to equity portfolio managers. In this article, we have focused on one important defensive strategy, the protective put. In analyzing a few specific cases we were able to see many of the basic properties of stock index options. In future reports we will examine other strategies involving stock index calls and futures contracts. These new instruments present almost limitless opportunities that prudent portfolio managers should be aware of for enhancing investment performance.

Table 3
Comparison of Protective Puts with Different Strike Prices
August 21 S&P 100 Index: 331.16

Strike Price	Option Cost	Minimum Value for Portfolio	Upside Break-Even	Percent Return on Protected Portfolio if S&P 100 Is				
				Down 10%	Down 5%	Unchanged	Up 5%	Up 10%
310	15/16	309.06	332.10	(6.67)	(5.28)	(0.28)	4.72	9.72
315	19/16	313.44	322.72	(5.35)	(5.35)	(0.47)	4.53	9.53
320	29/16	317.44	333.72	(4.14)	(4.14)	(0.77)	4.23	9.23
325	37/8	321.13	335.04	(3.03)	(3.03)	(1.17)	3.83	8.83
330	57/8	324.13	337.04	(2.12)	(2.12)	(1.77)	3.23	8.23
335	83/8	326.63	339.54	(1.37)	(1.37)	(1.37)	2.47	7.47

Note: Closing prices for September Standard & Poor's 100 puts August 21.
   Payoffs are based on the level of the S&P 100 Index at option expiration, September 18.

OPTION STRATEGIES FOR PROFESSOR CULBERT

Jason Culbert is an eccentric professor of behavioral science at the University of California, Santa Barbara. Perhaps best known for "hot tub" graduate seminars at his beachside home, Professor Culbert is also an amateur investor with great intensity and willingness to take on considerable risk. His "risky" funds are currently about $35,000. His expressed objective is to make as much money as soon as possible. And he will simply "start over" if he loses his $35,000. Clearly, he is willing to take on considerable risk in the process.

Over the years, Professor Culbert has read widely in the investments literature -- especially the books advertised and reviewed in the WALL STREET JOURNAL, BARRON'S, and other popular magazines. As a result, he has tried all sorts of wild and risky investment strategies. Overall, his investment performance would best be described as "dismal." He dismisses that performance as consistent with his ability to take on great risk. Quite simply, Professor Culbert is not interested in any type of conservative investment strategy.

Recently, Culbert read a "leading book" on how to make money using put and call options. In typical fashion, he is all excited about yet another strategy that will make him a lot of money to support his expensive lifestyle. You are a distant cousin, and he asks to meet with you to discuss his newest investment interest -- and, in particular, to consider possible option strategies.

As your meeting begins on 9 November 1988, you explain to your distant cousin that while options generally are viewed as quite risky, there are certain strategies involving options that actually lead to reduced risk. Culbert seems puzzled by that observation, and so you decide that it would be well to review with your cousin some of the basics of option investing. Rather than working with several different examples, you decide that it may be helpful to focus on strategies involving options of a single firm. When asked to identify a favorite common stock for use in your analysis, Professor Culbert selects Sears Roebuck -- where he has shopped for many years.

Perusal of the WALL STREET JOURNAL for that day reveals the following option quotations for Sears on the Chicago Board Option Exchange:

OPTION & NY CLOSE	STRIKE PRICE	CALLS-LAST			PUTS-LAST		
		NOV	DEC	JAN	NOV	DEC	JAN
Sears	35	8	7 5/8	8	r	3/16	3/8
42	40	2 7/16	3 3/8	4 1/8	3/8	1 1/4	1 7/8
42	45	5/8	1 9/16	2 5/16	3 1/2	4 5/8	4 1/2
42	50	3/16	3/4	1 5/16	7 3/4	r	r
42	55	s	5/16	3/4	s	r	r

Note: r -- option not traded   s -- no option offered

In reviewing with Culbert how to interpret these option quotations for Sears, you further explain that possible outcomes of various option strategies depend critically on what is expected to happen to the underlying common stock. Professor Culbert has followed Sears common stock for some time now, and after some prodding on your part, he comes up with the following probability distribution for Sears Roebuck common stock price between now and the third week of January 1989, when the January calls and puts expire:

Sears' Stock Price	Probability
$38	10%
40	10
42	20
44	25
46	20
48	10
50	5

Although Sears currently pays an annual cash dividend of $2.00 per share, there will be no dividend payment between now and the expiration of January options. In addition, you decide for simplicity to ignore transaction costs in your analysis.

Based on that probability distribution and the available premia for Sears' call and put options, you and Culbert begin working on the following questions:

(1) What is the expected return (i.e. return) and standard deviation of return (i.e. risk) from holding Sears' common stock for the next ten weeks?

(2) What is the return and risk for a strategy of buying a January 40 call?

(3) What is the return and risk for a strategy of selling (i.e. "writing") a January 45 put?

(4) What is the return and risk for a strategy of buying a straddle, consisting of a January 40 call and a January 40 put?

(5) What is the return and risk for a strategy of engaging in a spread, consisting of buying a January 40 call and writing a January 45 call?

(6) If Professor Culbert currently owns 100 shares of Sears common stock, what is the return and risk of writing a covered call, i.e holding the common stock and writing a January 40 call?

(7) If Professor Culbert currently owns 100 shares of Sears common stock, what is the return and risk of holding the common stock and buying a January 45 put?

(8) Based on your calculations, what do you conclude about the return and risk of option strategies for Culbert?

(9) In view of his apparent investment goals, what would you recommend for Professor Jason Culbert?

BLACKMAN EVALUATES HIS APARTMENT PROJECT

Joshua Blackman is determined to complete an analysis of one of his rental apartment complexes before he and his wife Janet leave on a two-week vacation in Europe. The urgency of the analysis is prompted by Blackman's accountant, David Patrick, who feels that it may be beneficial tax wise if Joshua sells one or two of his apartment projects before the end of the year.

At first glance, the nine-unit "Sepulveda" complex would seem to be a logical choice -- since the annual cash flows which it generates are relatively small, and there apparently are a couple of interested buyers for the rental property. Mr. Blackman is not sure, however, and he wants to review the numbers carefully before considering a sale. You and Joshua have been good friends for many years, and because of your interest in finance and computers, he shares with you a spreadsheet analysis of his Sepulveda investment.

Joshua Blackman was born and raised in Pennsylvania and has a masters degree in civil engineering from a prestigious eastern school. He and Janet were married soon after graduation and started a family almost immediately. The Blackmans and their two children moved to Los Angeles three years later when Joshua accepted an engineering position with a large aerospace firm. After accumulating a few thousand dollars in the company's credit union, the Blackmans decided to invest in a four-unit rental income property. Their first investment went very well, and they were able to purchase two additional rental properties during the next five years.

During that period, the Blackmans intensified their interest and capability in real estate. Janet earned her real estate license and, adroitly balancing home and career, steadily built a successful business in real estate sales. Meanwhile, Joshua earned a contractor's license, and began planning for the design and construction of their first new apartment complex. During the construction phase of that project, Joshua became so upset with sloppy work by a concrete subcontractor that he decided that he really could not keep on top of his real estate business on a part-time basis. Accordingly, he resigned from the aerospace firm and set up a small office in the San Fernancdo Valley for himself and for Janet's real estate sales business.

The Blackmans never regretted that key career decision. For over the next fifteen years, Janet's perceptive understanding of real estate values and trends, coupled with Joshua's attention to considerable detail and understanding of all phases of design and construction, proved to be a most synergetic combination. Project after project proved to be successful. So much so that by late

217

1989, they owned 323 rental units -- mainly in Los Angeles, but also apartment complexes in Seattle and Nashville where, conveniently from a tax standpoint, they could visit their grown children and marvelous grandchildren. In sum, Mr. and Mrs. Blackman have attained a very comfortable lifestyle as a result of their investments and hard work in real estate.

Three years ago, Joshua purchased a personal computer for use in his real estate business. He did not use it for several months, but finally David Patrick convinced Joshua to acquire a software package that would allow him to keep track of rent payments, expenses, and occupancy statistics for his several apartment complexes. A year later, Joshua purchased a leading spreadsheet software and now is trying to develop his own computerized capability to analyze new investment opportunities, as well as to re-assess his existing apartment complexes.

Late last week, Joshua shared with you his spreadsheet analysis of the Sepulveda rental property (see Exhibit 1 below). He indicates that the Sepulveda property, which is not quite three years old, consists of nine units, including four one--bedrooms, one town house, and four two-bedrooms. Rents range from $648 to $810 and total $6,534 per month. Blackman's vacancy experience has been quite low for newer apartments, and so he uses 2% vacancy in his analysis. Property taxes, insurance, and other operating expenses total $14,210 for the year.

Based on a multiple of nine times annual gross rent, the market value of the Sepulveda project is estimated to be $705,672. Because Mr. Blackman effectively did the construction, the project has a $369,424 cost basis (original cost minus depreciation to date) that is well below that estimate. So much so that Joshua recently took out a first mortgage of $425,000 that exceeds his investment to date. The 30-year, 12% mortgage has annual payments of $52,616, of which $51,212 is interest during the next year. Annual depreciation, based on a 15-year accelerated schedule, amounts to $18,056 for the next year.

Based on these estimates and financial obligations, Joshua's analysis shows for the next year a net operating income of $62,630, a taxable loss of $6,638, and an after-tax cash flow of $11,872. The Blackmans' equity in the property is shown to be $280,672. If they were to sell the apartment complex, pay off the mortgage, and pay the resulting capital gains tax, they would end up with a cash residual of $161,118. Joshua reasons that they thus are earning 7.4% (11,872/161,118) on their effective investment. Including the approximate equity build-up of $1,404 per year, that rate increases to 8.2%.

Those rates-of-return are not all that high, and that is why David Patrick feels that perhaps the Sepulveda property would be a candidate to be sold. Still, Blackman is not certain that his analysis is either complete or comprehensive enough to justify selling that apartment complex at this time.

It is thus in a mood of uncertainty that Joshua sits down to talk with you about the analysis that he has done so far. A series of questions come up during your ensuing discussion:

(1) Is there anything that has not been included that might serve to increase the estimated rate-of-return on the Seulveda project?

(2) How sensitive are the results of the analysis to Joshua's assumption of a 2% vacancy rate? What if it were 5%? Or even 10%?

(3) Although Blackman has not increased rents at the Sepulveda property since it was opened in1986, he feels that an increase of 5-6% would not unduly upset existing tenants. What would be the impact of such a rental increase?

(4) What if operating expenses were to increase by 10%?

(5) You point out **to Joshua that his 28% tax rate is** just the federal rate. What if the California tax rate of 11% is included?

(6) What rate-of-return should Joshua use to decide whether or not to sell the Sepulveda property?

Exhibit 1
ANALYSIS OF A RENTAL PROPERTY
JOSHUA M. BLACKMAN

Annual gross rent		78,408
- Vacancy (2%)		1,568
Estimated annual rent		76,840
Property taxes	5,480	
Insurance	1,530	
Maintenance	1,200	
Utilities	2,400	
Advertising	600	
Trash removal	600	
Manager's fee	2,400	
- Total operating expenses		14,210
Net operating income		62,630
- Mortgage payments		52,616
Before-tax cash flow		10,014
Net operating income		62,630
- Loan interest		51,212
- Depreciation		18,056
Taxable income (loss)		(6,638)
Tax due (savings)		(1,859)
After-tax cash flow		11,873
+ Equity build-up		1,404
Cash flow plus equity build-up		13,277
Market price (multiple = 9)		705,672
- First mortgage		425,000
Equity		280,672
Market price		705,672
- Sales costs (5%)		35,284
- Cost basis		369,424
Taxable gain		300,964
- Tax on gain (28%)		84,270
Net cash proceeds		161,118

Annual return on net cash	7.4%
Annual return including equity build-up	8.2%

The use of options in performance structuring

Molding returns to meet investment objectives.

Richard Bookstaber

During the first ten years of listed option trading, options were viewed as tactical, if not outright speculative, instruments. Investors purchased calls to gain leverage, bought puts to lock in gains or speculate on declines, and used covered writes to enhance yields on sluggish issues. The implications of options positions for the return characteristics of the overall portfolio were rarely a consideration; the concern in option trading was trade-by-trade profitability, not cumulative portfolio effects. As option markets have matured, however, and as new instruments such as index and interest rate options and futures have been introduced to address the major sources of financial risk, the emphasis has shifted toward using options strategically in portfolio management.

The purpose of this paper is to address the role of options in portfolio management; to explain the concepts behind option-related techniques for structuring portfolio returns and controlling financial risks, and to lay out both the opportunities and difficulties these techniques present.

The topic of options we will address is more general than it might at first seem. Broadly speaking, options are instruments with a payoff that is contingent on the value of another, underlying security. Listed options are traded on a number of exchanges, but options can also be traded over the counter and, most important, can be created synthetically through the proper set of transactions in other securities. Listed options, while the most visible option contracts, are only a small part of the picture.

When dealing with option strategies, the topic of portfolio management also covers a broad area. We can think of portfolio management as the management of overall investment or financial risk. Besides the management of equity and bond investment portfolios, portfolio management includes balancing asset and liability risk in banks and in savings and loans, creating payment streams to match obligations in insurance companies and pension funds, and constructing securities to satisfy the financing patterns required by corporations.

Portfolio management is typically approached as a two-dimensional tradeoff between the mean and variance of returns. The mix of risky assets and cash is the only tool that managers have at their disposal in adjusting the portfolio. The mix dictates the mean-variance tradeoff the portfolio will face.

Figures 1-A and 1-B illustrate this tradeoff. These figures depict portfolio returns with the familiar bell-shaped curve of the normal distribution. In this setting, a two-dimensional mean-variance tradeoff is a natural way of looking at returns, since the mean and variance completely describe the normal distribution. A more conservative manager will move funds from risky assets into cash, ending up with a return distribution such as Figure 1-B, with less vari-

RICHARD BOOKSTABER is Research Manager at Morgan Stanley & Co. Inc. in New York (NY 10020).

FIGURE 1-A

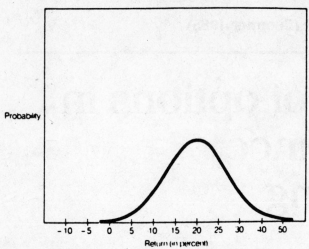

Return distribution of a stock portfolio. Mean return is 20 percent, with a standard deviation of 30 percent.

FIGURE 1-B

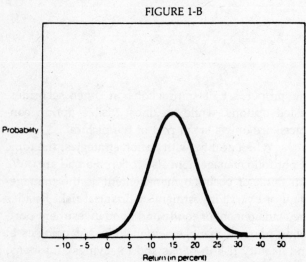

Return distribution of a stock portfolio. Mean return is 15 percent, with a standard deviation of 20 percent. Compared to the return portfolio of Figure 1-A, the investor has both lower expected return and lower risk. The returns continue to be normally distributed, however.

ance and a lower expected return. A more aggressive manager will go in the opposite direction, levering to achieve a higher expected return at the cost of higher variance. In either case, the manager can measure the alterations in the structure of returns simply in terms of mean and variance.

Comfortable and intuitive though it is, this two-dimensional tradeoff will not always result in a return distribution that meets portfolio objectives. A manager might prefer to control some other aspect of returns. For example, a manager may wish to achieve some guaranteed minimum return while retaining a portion of the upward return potential.[1] This objective would imply a non-symmetric return distribution such as that shown in Figure 1-C. This distribution

1. Footnotes appear at the end of the article.

FIGURE 1-C

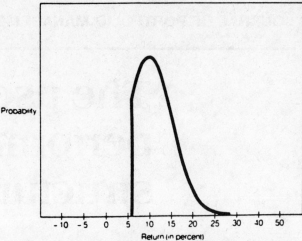

The return distribution that might be preferred by the portfolio manager. The probability of a large loss is eliminated.

truncates the downside risk while the right-hand tail still maintains some of the upside potential. Forming this return distribution requires more than mean-variance tradeoffs — it cannot be constructed using the conventional procedures of portfolio management.

The ability to form distributions of this type may have a value far beyond simply meeting subjective preferences. For example, the very pattern of liabilities may lead to a need for non-symmetric, non-normal returns. The obligation of a pension fund to meet a minimum actuarial payoff would lead to a return distribution like that shown in Figure 1-C. Other complex payoffs, such as those generated by the carefully tailored annuity products of the life insurance industry or the variable rate liabilities of many corporations and thrift institutions, will lead to return objectives that cannot be met by simple mean-variance adjustments.

Options are the building blocks for constructing the payoffs to meet these complex return objectives. We can use options to create the portfolio insurance depicted in Figure 1-C, or to mold returns to conform with virtually any other feasible distribution. This capacity for options to expand the set of contingencies has been established theoretically.[2] Here we will deal with the practical issues of how managers can implement these strategies.

THE INSURANCE FEATURE OF OPTION CONTRACTS

Let us begin by looking at an option as an insurance contract. The premium for the insurance is part of the option price. The variety of payoffs from option strategies comes from taking selective positions in the insurance — buying some insurance protection over one range of security prices, selling some insurance over another.

We can see the essential insurance feature of an option contract by constructing an option through an insurance-motivated transaction. Suppose an investor buys a security worth $1200 by investing $200 directly and borrowing the remaining $1000. The security is retained as collateral by the lender, to be released to the investor in one year upon repayment of the $1000 loan. Further, suppose the investor wishes to have protection should the security decline in value before the loan comes due and therefore arranges for the loan on a no-recourse basis. Then, if the investor fails to make the $1000 payment in one year, the lender will receive ownership of the security and will have no further recourse to the investor. This no-recourse feature amounts to giving the investor an insurance contract on the investment, with a deductible equal to the $200 initial investment.

At the end of the year, what will be the best strategy for the investor to pursue? Obviously, the investor will pay back the loan if the security value at the end of the year is at least as great as the $1000 necessary to gain clear ownership. The investor's profit in doing so will be the security value, S^*, less the loan payment, or $S^* - 1000$. If the security is worth less than the loan payment, the investor will be better off simply to walk away from the loan and let the lender take ownership, since the $1000 payment to claim the security will net the investor a loss. The payoff pattern from this insured loan is identical to that of a call option on the security with an exercise price of $1000. The call option gives the right to buy the security for $1000 and has a payoff that is the security price minus the exercise price, $S^* - \$1000$, or zero, whichever is greater.

Using this no-recourse loan as a vehicle for analyzing a call option, we see the price of the call option can be broken up into three parts. First, there is the initial payment of $200. This payment, the difference between the security price and the $1000 exercise price, is called the *intrinsic value* of the option. Second, there is an interest carrying cost from holding the security in escrow. The investor pays the exercise price at the end of the year, but the lender has the $1000 tied up in the security over the loan period. Given an interest rate of r, this interest cost will be $(r/(1 + r)) 1000$. The third part of the option price is the insurance cost of the downside protection. Since the lender is absorbing the loss, there will be an insurance premium, P, implicit in the price of the call option.

Combining these three terms, and denoting the exercise price by E, we can express the call option as

$$C = (S - E) + E(r/(1 + r)) + P.$$

This expression shows the option price consists of intrinsic value, prepaid interest, and insurance against loss.

To gain more insight into the nature of the insurance premium, P, consider the contract the lender would need in order to overcome the risk from the loan's no-recourse feature. If the security is worth more than the exercise price at the end of the year, the lender will receive the $1000 payment and no other compensation will be necessary. If the value is less than the exercise price, the lender will have paid $1000 for a security that is now worth less than that; the lender will have lost $1000 − S*. The compensating contract, then, must give a payout equal to the difference between the exercise price and security price when the security price is less than the exercise price; it must give no payout when the security price is equal to or greater than the exercise price. This is exactly the payout given by a *put option*. A put option gives the right to sell the underlying security at the exercise price; its payout is the maximum of zero and $(E - S)$, the exercise price minus the security price.

Put and Call Options Redefined

The insurance premium for the no-recourse loan, P, is thus equal to a put option with one year to maturity and an exercise price of $1000. In this context, then, we can define a call option and a put option as follows:

Call option: A contract giving the holder the underlying security at maturity while insuring against any loss during the term of the contract beyond a deductible equal to the intrinsic value of the option.

Put option: An insurance contract that pays off to cover fully any security price decline below the face value of the contract, which is the put option's exercise price.

Some of the characteristics of option pricing are evident from viewing options in this insurance context. First, just as insurance premiums increase with an increase in riskiness, so option prices increase with an increase in the price volatility of the security. Second, call prices are an increasing function of interest rates, since higher interest rates increase the interest carrying cost. Third, just as insurance premiums decline as the amount of the deductible increases, so the insurance cost, P, drops as the intrinsic value of the call option increases. Fourth, the longer the term of the coverage, i.e., the longer the time to expiration of the option, the more the option will cost.[3]

Different patterns of returns are possible by properly selecting the option coverage. Indeed, given options at all exercise prices and all times to expiration, we could construct the entire range of attainable return structures.

To see this more concretely, consider a strategy of buying one option with an exercise price of $100, writing two options each with an exercise price of $101, and buying one option with an exercise price of $102. This position, called a butterfly spread, will lead to a payoff of $1 if the underlying security is at $100 at the time of option expiration, and a payoff of zero otherwise. Such a binary payoff can be used as the basic building block from any payoff schedule.[4]

TABLE 1

Security price	Value of option with exercise price of $49	Value of option with exercise price of $50	Value of option with exercise price of $51	Total strategy value
–	–	–	–	–
–	–	–	–	–
–	–	–	–	–
46	0	0	0	0
47	0	0	0	0
48	0	0	0	0
49	0	0	0	0
50	1	0	0	1
51	2	−2	0	0
52	3	−4	1	0
53	4	−6	2	0
–	–	–	–	–
–	–	–	–	–
–	–	–	–	–

Obviously, only a small part of this set of options are actually traded on the listed exchanges. These institutional limitations would seem to be a serious constraint for turning the great theoretical potential of performance structuring into a real opportunity. As we will see in the next section, however, we are not restricted to listed options. We can construct synthetic options of any exercise price and any time to expiration through the use of dynamic trading strategies.

THE CREATION OF OPTION POSITIONS USING DYNAMIC TRADING TECHNIQUES

The key difficulty in employing option methods is that the appropriate option contracts often do not exist in the market place. While a growing number of markets and securities are covered by option instruments, these may not match the terms of the option contract required for the portfolio strategy. For example, the maturity of the traded options may not match the manager's time horizon, or the security underlying the option contract may not match the asset mix of the portfolio. Fortunately, the principles of option theory can be applied to create the option contract synthetically even when the required option does not exist in the market. This is done by a dynamic reallocation of funds across sets of assets, or by a dynamic readjustment of positions in listed options and futures contracts.

To develop the dynamic strategy, we will concentrate on the creation of insurance provided by the protective put option. We can apply the same principles in forming other option positions and creating other return structures.

Dynamic Strategies as Multi-Point Stop-Loss Strategies

The simplest and most widely known technique for achieving downside protection is the stop-loss order. An investor can assure a $100 floor on a security price by stopping out of the security at a price equal to the present value of $100, $100(1/(1 + r))^T$, and putting the funds in the risk-free asset for the remaining time period, T. Once stopped out, the funds will accrue interest at the rate r and will be worth $100 at the end of the time period.

For example, if there is a year left in the holding period for the strategy and if r is 10%, then the security would be stopped out at $91. Putting the $91 in the risk-free asset at 10% would give the desired $100 return by the end of the year.

Figure 2 illustrates this stop-loss order. The figure overlays the security price with the percentage of

FIGURE 2

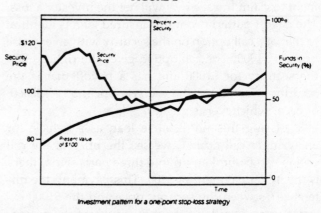

Investment pattern for a one-point stop-loss strategy

the portfolio invested in the security. Note that the level of the stop approaches the floor as the end of the holding period approaches, because the funds have less and less time to accrue interest. Once the security price drops below the stop, all funds are taken out of the security.

This insurance method is effective, but is also costly. It fails to take into account the possibility that the security may rebound from the decline, eliminating any possibility of sharing in later increases in the security price.

We can remedy this deficiency to a limited degree by allowing the stop to be reversible. Rather than pursuing this one-point stop-loss strategy, suppose we employ a two-point strategy where the investment is stopped out of the security when the price drops below the stop, and the security is bought when the price moves back through the stop-loss point. This will allow the required downside protection while no longer shutting the investor completely out of possible appreciation. This strategy is illustrated in Figure 3.

FIGURE 3

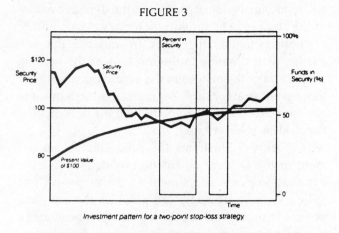

Investment pattern for a two-point stop-loss strategy.

This two-point strategy, while superior to the simple stop-loss strategy, still imposes its own costs. In addition to imposing greater transaction costs, every reversal leads to a loss equal to the distance between the selling and buying point. Setting the points close together will not eliminate these costs. The closer these two points, the smaller the cost per reversal but the more frequently such reversals will occur. This cost will be greatest if the security vibrates around the breakeven point and will be smallest if the breakeven point is never hit.

Both the nonreversible one-point stop-loss strategy and the two-point stop-loss strategy will thus lead to a reduction in the expected return. This risk-return tradeoff is as expected, since the strategies provide a reduction of downside risk. The two-point stop-loss strategy will have the higher return, since it gives the opportunity to gain from price appreciation.

Given the results of the two-point strategy, we should logically consider the effects of extending the flexibility further. If we are confident the security in question will remain risky over the holding period — that is, if we believe the security will continue to be volatile — then there is no need to sell off completely when the security reaches the breakeven point of $100(1/(1 + r))^T$. Instead, we might move in or out of the security gradually as the security moves away from the breakeven point. This will lessen the chance of being whipsawed by repeated reversals.

Given the time left in the holding period, security volatility will make periodic moves around the breakeven point likely. Such moves will be more likely the longer the time left, the greater the volatility, and the closer the security price is to the breakeven point. Accordingly, the proportion of the security we stop out should take all of these factors into account. Furthermore, the breakeven point for the stop will change over time and with interest rates.

Thus, the rule we use for moving in and out of the security should be a function of the security price, the insured price, the holding period of the strategy, the interest rate, and the volatility of the security. Since these stop-loss strategies all mimic the sort of non-linearities common to options, it is not surprising these are the same factors we discussed above as determining the price of an option.

Obviously, an unlimited number of stop-loss adjustments are available to us with these factors in mind. Figure 4 shows the return to one particular strategy. With this alternative, we hold 50% of the funds in the security and 50% in the risk-free asset when we hit the breakeven point; we move completely in or out of the security only when the price has moved a significant distance away from the breakeven point. We let this strategy stop out completely at a point with twice the time factor as the breakeven point, $100(1/(1 + r))^{2T}$, stop out one half at the breakeven point, $100(1/(1 + r))^2$, and fully invest at $100 (1 + r)^T$. This three-point stop-loss strategy continues to give the required protection. Furthermore, by making finer adjustments and by retaining a partial holding over more of the range of the security price, the strategy will provide the protection for the least cost of the three strategies considered so far.

FIGURE 4

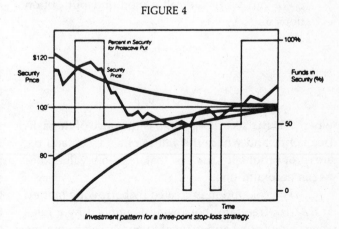

Investment pattern for a three-point stop-loss strategy.

A Put Option as the Least-Cost Insurance Strategy

A cost is imposed by the insurance protection because the dynamic adjustments gradually pull funds out of the security as it declines and only gradually put funds back into the security as it appreciates.

Hence, the insured position cannot fully participate in the appreciation.

Our objective is to find the lowest-cost insurance contract. The best adjustment strategy will be the strategy that provides the downside protection while allowing the greatest sharing of security appreciation on the upside. We already know that the put option represents the ideal insurance contract for protecting against downside risk. If we could find a dynamic stopless strategy that replicated the behavior of a put option with a time to expiration equal to the investor's time horizon, and an exercise price of $100, we would have protection that precisely meets the insurance objectives, and, given efficient markets, that gives the protection at the lowest price.

All three stop-loss strategies considered above approximate a put option. They all give downside protection similar to that of a put option. And, like a put option, the two-point and three-point stop-loss strategies share in some of the upward potential of the security as well. On the other hand, they are not perfect replicas of a put option; they move in jumps as the security price changes, rather than in the smooth, continuous fashion of a put option. Nevertheless, they do suggest that an extension of the dynamic stop-loss strategy will move us closer to the pure put option protection desired.

Option pricing theory has shown this is in fact the case; we can create an option position by pursuing a strategy that dynamically adjusts the proportion of the underlying security and the risk-free asset.[5] Since an option can be replicated by such a strategy, this further implies the option price must always equal the cost of this replicating portfolio.

We can write the call option and put option equations as :

$$C = a_c - b_c B$$

and

$$P = -a_p S + b_p B,$$

where S is the security price, B is the price of the risk-free bond, and where the values of a_c, a_p, b_c, and b_p, are proportionality factors that take on values between zero and one.[6]

The call option is created by borrowing money at the risk-free rate (borrowing is implied by a negative value for b_c) and using it to purchase an amount a_c of the security. The borrowing leads to the leverage that is characteristic of a call option. The put is created by shorting the security (shorting is implied by a negative value for a_p) and putting an amount equal to b_p into the risk-free asset. When the put option position is combined with a long position in the security to form an insured position, the net effect of combining the initial long position in the security with the short position required to replicate the put option is a positive, but less than full, investment in the security.[7]

As was suggested by the three-point stop-loss strategy, the proportion of stocks and bonds in the option replication varies both over time and as the security price changes. The replicating portfolio must be continuously adjusted; hence, the dynamic nature of the strategy. The proportion terms a_c, a_p, b_c and b_p are not constants; rather, they are variables that will change with the time to the maturity of the holding period and with changes in the security price. As the three-point strategy further suggests, these terms will also be a function of the volatility of the security and the riskless interest rate.

Figure 5 illustrates the proportion of investment in the security when the investor follows the dynamic stop-loss adjustment of the protective put option strategy. This strategy provides the complete downside protection at the lowest cost. The strategy is overlaid on the three-point strategy described in Figure 4.

FIGURE 5

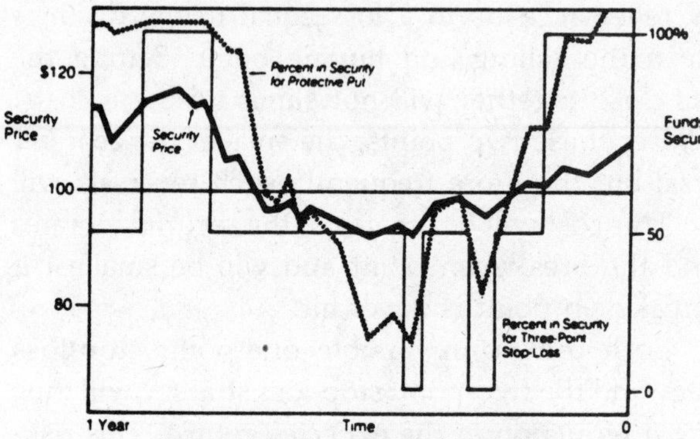

Investment pattern for a protective put option strategy, compared with the three-point stop-loss of Figure 8.

The naive one-point stop-loss strategy has been proposed in a number of insurance settings. For example, the original construction of the contingent immunization strategy for bond portfolios involves stopping out of an interest-sensitive bond position once a critical portfolio price or interest rate level is passed.[8] It should be clear from this discussion that such strategies, while providing the desired protection, are a more costly means of securing that protection than a strategy that more closely approximates the return structure of a put option.

VARIATIONS ON THE DYNAMIC STRATEGY: USING LISTED FUTURES AND OPTION CONTRACTS

As with any strategy, the dynamic strategy presents practical difficulties. These include:

226

1. The need for continuous adjustment.

   Theoretically, the option position requires continuous portfolio adjustments. The appropriate mix of the security and riskless asset changes over time and with changes in the security price. Discrete adjustments, by failing to account for the continuous nature of the movement of the security price and of time, will lead to a margin of error in the payoff of the option, as well as in its cost.

2. The accurate estimation of security price volatility.

   The appropriate portfolio mix will also depend on the volatility of the security. A highly volatile security will be more costly to insure, since the adjustments will catch less of each price swing. If the volatility of the security is forecast incorrectly, the result may lead to a higher cost or to less than complete protection.

3. The specification of the stochastic process driving security prices.

   The functional form of the proportionality terms in the option model depends on the nature of security price movements. The direction of the price movements has no bearing on the option model, but the way price movements tend to evolve does matter. For example, a security price that is typified by large periodic jumps will lead to a model specification, and hence to a different dynamic strategy, than a security whose price never experiences discrete jumps. Accuracy in the specification of the stochastic process is as important as accuracy in the estimation of the security price volatility emerging from that process.[9]

Just how critical these factors are to the successful implementation of the dynamic option strategies is an empirical question that cannot be answered here. Some of these problems are mitigated by using listed futures and option contracts in forming the dynamic strategy. We will discuss these variations on the dynamic strategy next.

Using Futures in Dynamic Strategies

The essential feature of the dynamic strategy is that the position in the security varies as the time to maturity and the security price vary. Obviously, one way to vary the size of the position is by transacting directly in the security itself. When there are futures on the security, we can also vary the position by leaving the actual security holdings unchanged and transacting in the futures contract instead.

For example, a put option on a well-diversified stock portfolio can be replicated by using a short position in an index future. As the portfolio value declines, requiring a smaller position in the portfolio, the short position will be increased. The short position will react in a direction opposite the portfolio position, leaving a net return to market movements that is essentially the same as if a portion of the portfolio itself had been sold off and transferred to the risk-free asset. The futures act as a damper on the effective portfolio position. The futures position is an alternative for the construction of dynamic strategies for any position that is highly correlated with the movement of traded futures, be they stocks, stock portfolios, bonds, foreign exchange, metals, or commodities.

Futures have a number of attractive features. First, because they combine a position in the asset with borrowing, they can lead to less costly transactions than the investor would incur with transfers between the security and cash. Second, execution is often better in the futures than in the cash market. This is particularly true when a single futures contract can be substituted for a portfolio-wide transaction, as in the case of stock or bond portfolios. Third, since futures are levered instruments, less cash is necessary to carry out the dynamic strategy.

The third point is especially important when the dynamic strategy is pursued separately from the portfolio holdings. For example, consider a pension sponsor with a number of outside managers, each managing a fraction of the fund. If the sponsor decides to pursue a dynamic strategy, the sponsor could conceivably have each manager restructure its management methods to incorporate the dynamic strategy.

There are obvious practical and administrative difficulties in doing this. And even if it were done successfully, the end result of having options on each of the individual portfolios would be an inefficient means of attaining the desired option on the overall pension fund investment.[10] On the other hand, the alternative of having the sponsor retain enough of the fund to make the market/cash adjustments itself would greatly reduce the amount retained under the outside managers, and would therefore change the character of the fund.

We can overcome these difficulties by using futures as the vehicle for making the dynamic adjustments. The pension fund sponsor, pursuing a dynamic strategy with futures, would need only retain enough cash to meet margin requirements. The sponsor could monitor its overall fund value, and, assuming its holdings are closely correlated with the overall market, use index futures to create a position that would be equivalent to selling off the necessary proportion of its holdings. The sponsor could do this without making any alteration in the managers' roles, without significant changes in the amount under management, even without the knowledge of the managers. With protection against poor performance, any superior management performance will still lead to relative performance gains under the dynamic strategy.

Strictly speaking, the replication of a put or call option requires a proper balancing of positions in the riskless asset as well as risky security. The position in the riskless asset serves to make the position self-financing, i.e., the position neither requires further funding nor gives out payments from the time it is initiated until the expiration of the option contract. The self-financing feature is critical to the theoretical development of option pricing. Options are, after all, self-financing instruments: Once an option is purchased, no cash flow takes place until its exercise or expiration. Shifting between the risky security and the riskless asset maintains an economy in the development of the theoretical pricing argument since no other assets or transactions need to be tracked.

Nevertheless, when our attention moves from option pricing to hedging, and from theoretical development to practical implementation, the stringent requirements of maintaining a self-financing portfolio no longer apply. In practice, our concern is only with maintaining a position that gives a security payoff equal to that of an option. Failure to hold the proper proportion of funds in the riskless asset will not affect this essential return structure. It will affect only the ex post cost of the protection.

For example, if the manager chooses to place funds made available from the strategy into another risky asset rather than into the riskless asset, the overall cost of the dynamic strategy may now be thought to depend on the performance of that risky asset. But clearly that facet of the strategy can easily be separated from the insurance service the strategy is delivering.[11]

It is important to recognize this role of the riskless asset when using futures contracts in constructing dynamic hedges, because the most efficient use of futures may not maintain the theoretically correct position in the risk-free asset. Because they are levered, futures implicitly contain a short position in the risk-free asset, but this position will not necessarily equal that required for the strategy to be self-financing.

The most efficient use of futures may lead to periodic payments or cash requirements. When properly treated, these cause no difficulties for the construction or evaluation of the strategy. On the contrary, they may lead to important advantages over transactions in the security itself.

Using Options to Create Options

A second variation on dynamic strategies is the use of listed options. As with futures, listed options may exist on indexes and securities that are closely correlated with the security of interest. Obviously, if there is a listed option that is fairly priced and that exactly meets the time and contract specifications for hedging, then it will be preferred to constructing the option synthetically. Frequently, however, there is a listed option that only partially fits the hedging requirements. For example, the listed option may be on a slightly different underlying asset, perhaps on a Treasury bond futures contract when the underlying asset is a corporate bond portfolio, or on a stock index that does not exactly match the construction of the underlying stock portfolio, or the listed option may have too short a time to maturity or be at the wrong exercise price.

The first of these problems will not be unique to the use of the listed options. It will exist for futures and may also exist when a dynamic strategy is pursued directly through the underlying asset. Dynamic adjustments of stock or bond portfolios must be done piecemeal. The subset of securities to be adjusted will not exactly match the overall portfolio. As a result, it is possible the discrete adjustment of the dynamic strategy may induce more basis risk than the use of listed options that, although not perfectly correlated with the underlying asset, overcome the problems related to discrete adjustments.

The second problem of listed options — a time to expiration that is shorter than the time horizon demanded for the option protection — is probably considered the greatest barrier to using listed options. Listed options often cannot be found more than three months out, while the time horizon for dynamic strategies is typically one year or more. On the other hand, these short-term listed options can themselves be employed in a dynamic strategy for creating synthetic longer-term options. This strategy is similar to rolling over short-term futures contracts to create longer-term protection.

For example, suppose an investor were interested in a $100 floor for a security price for one year, and put options existed with three months to maturity. The investor might buy a three-month put with an exercise price of $100, and upon expiration of that put buy another three-month put with the same exercise price. The position would be liquidated at the end of six months, a new three-month option purchased, and the procedure would be repeated again at the end of nine months.

If the option expired out of the money, there would be no proceeds from the strategy, and more funds would be necessary to roll over the strategy. If the security dropped below the floor, the put option would return the difference between the floor price and the security price, covering the loss and providing the intrinsic value for buying the next contract.[12]

The actual cost of this technique depends on the path the security price takes. To see this, consider a security currently priced at $100 together with a call option purchased on the security with an exercise price of $100. Suppose a six-month option cost $10 while a three-month option cost $6. If the security is again at $100 when the three-month option expires, a second $6 option will have to be purchased, and the total cost of the rolling over strategy will be $12, or $2 more than the cost of the six-month option. If, on the other hand, the stock drops to $80 in three months, the price of the call option for the next three months will be far less, since the option is now $20 out of the money. The next option may cost only $1, leading the rolling over strategy to be less costly. The same will be true if the security rises substantially, to, say, $120. The first of the three-month options will then pay off $20 at expiration, and the second option, being in the money, will have a small premium above their intrinsic value, selling for, say, $21. The total cost of the rolling over strategy will then be $7, compared to the $10 cost for the straight six-month option.

This path dependence adds uncertainty to the cost of the strategy, and this may dampen its desirability. It also presents an opportunity to improve return potential by the selection of the options used each time the position is rolled over. For example, the investor can choose the time to roll over to maximize gain from mispricing between options, and can choose different exercise prices to alter the strategy if past performance warrants it.[13]

The use of listed options does have a number of particularly attractive features not shared by the other dynamic methods. First, the transaction costs and the timing of the transaction are known in advance. Second, like futures, the options are already levered, requiring less of a cash commitment than the straight security/bond strategy. And third, the option contract is protected against unforeseen jumps in the security price or changes in the security price volatility.

In a perfect market setting, the standard dynamic return structuring techniques using reallocations between the security and the riskless asset will replicate the desired option contract exactly. In practice, however, transaction costs, basis risk, capital constraints, and fundamental uncertainty about the return process and return volatility of the security make the proper choice of return structuring techniques more difficult.

We can, however, overcome some of the difficulties by making dynamic adjustments with the futures rather than the cash instrument, or by constructing the return structuring by rolling over listed options. Furthermore, having a number of alternative routes to achieving the desired return structuring permits the exploitation of mispricing in the various instruments. For example, if listed options are considered to be underpriced, they may be preferred to the dynamic strategy on that basis alone. These methods are not always a practical alternative, however. Since listed options and futures may not exist on the underlying security itself, the problems of basis risk may be accentuated. These aspects of return-structuring techniques should be the subject of further empirical testing and comparison.

APPLICATIONS OF PERFORMANCE STRUCTURING

The flexibility of dynamic strategies allows the return distribution to be molded in a wide variety of ways. We can also apply such strategies beyond the creation of the portfolio insurance we have dealt with here to more complex and specialized applications ranging from hedging single-premium deferred annuities in the life insurance industry to asset-liability management for thrift institutions. In this section, I will present three examples intended to be more or less generic and to cover a range of possible strategies.

Cutting Losses: Protective Portfolio with Options

Protective puts are the best known and most widely used option-type strategy. There are a number of variations on portfolio insurance designed to adapt the basic concept of the protective put to particular markets and risks. For example, protective puts can be extended beyond the bond and equity markets to insure floor prices for commodities or foreign exchange, can be set to assure returns equal to a pension plan's actuarial interest rate assumptions, or can be modified to express the floor return as a fixed differential off the Treasury bill rate or other interest rates.[14]

Table 2 presents the results of creating the simple dynamic put option on an equity portfolio. The objective here is to achieve a floor return of 0% from the portfolio, while maximizing the share of any increase in the equity position. The strategy used here is repeated each year with an end-of-year horizon each year. That is, a new protective put with one year to expiration is constructed each January. Hence, we can look at the performance as a series of independent trials.

The table shows the annual results of this strategy for the years 1973-83. The first column of the table gives the returns to equity (the S&P 500 Composite). The next two columns relate to the performance of the synthetic option strategy. The first of these columns gives the annual return to the strategy, the second gives the capture of the strategy.

The capture is the return to the synthetic option

TABLE 2

PROTECTIVE PUT STRATEGY SIMULATION
COMPARISON OF ANNUAL RETURNS

Year	Equity	Dynamic Strategy With Floor Exercise Price	Capture	Dynamic Strategy With Variable Exercise Price	Capture
1973	−14.9%	−0.52%	Floor	−0.99%	Floor
1974	−25.2	−0.71	Floor	−0.99	Floor
1975	34.1	20.68	61%	31.20	91%
1976	23.0	14.99	65	22.42	98
1977	−7.2	−0.38	Floor	−1.02	Floor
1978	6.5	4.55	70	0.35	5
1979	18.5	16.62	90	18.48	100
1980	33.4	26.89	81	30.00	90
1981	−5.6	−0.38	Floor	−1.13	Floor
1982	20.8	11.30	54	1.96	9
1983	22.2	18.94	85	22.17	100

Cumulative Returns for 11 Years Compounded:

7.80%	9.76%	10.40%

- 52-week periods were used instead of exact calendar years.
- EQUITY: S&P 500 Stock Index adjusted for dividends
- Capture is the dynamic strategy return as a percent of the return to the equity portfolio when the equity portfolio return exceeds the 0% floor.
- Includes transactions costs of $25 per contract round trip.
- Assets are reallocated once every week.

strategy as a percent of the equity portfolio. Since replicating an option position involves a gradual shift into equity as the equity increases in value, only part of the equity performance will be shared by the option position. The incomplete capture is a direct implication of option price behavior; option prices move less than one-to-one with changes in the price of the underlying asset. The incomplete capture of potential gains can be thought of as a cost of pursuing the option strategy. This serves to emphasize that option-related strategies have tradeoffs consistent with market efficiency. Changes in return structure are met with commensurate costs. The cost for the repeated one-year protective put positions used in this example is greater than a single longer-term put option would be. The capture can be increased by taking a longer investment horizon in the performance structure.

It is evident from Table 2 that the portfolio performed as expected in providing the 0% floor return. In the four years that the equity market saw negative returns, the return to the structured portfolio was 0%. In the years of positive return, the structured portfolio shared to varying degrees in that return. In most cases, the protective put returned over 75% of the return to the equity portfolio. The capture was higher in years of higher equity return and was also higher the longer the equity sustained a high rate of return. This is an attractive and natural feature of option prices. The proportion of funds in equity is the average of proportions held over the annual period. In the simulation, these proportions were readjusted weekly.[15]

How much would it be worth to be able to receive a perfect stock-bond market timing service, a service that could always pick when holding stocks would do better than holding bonds? It is possible to create and price such a service through the simple option strategy of buying an index call option and placing the remainder of the portfolio in bonds.

To see this, select the call option to have an exercise price that equals the return possible through a bond investment. Then, if the option pays off, it will give a return equal to the stock market return less the bond price, while if the option expires worthless, the overall portfolio return will still equal the bond return. The net effect of this strategy will be to give a return equal to the equity or the bond, whichever is greater. This is the return that would be generated by following the advice of a perfect market timer. The cost of this strategy is the cost of the call option on the market.[16]

As this perfect market-timing example illustrates, options can perform a strategic as well as defensive role in portfolio management. The proper dynamic allocation between equities and bonds will replicate a call option on the market and provide a return equal to the greater of the two. Added onto an actively managed stock portfolio, such an allocation strategy can accentuate gains by increasing market participation during upswings while moving out of the market during downturns.[17] Table 3 shows the annual results of pursuing this strategy over the 1973-1983 period.

The gradual adjustments that constitute the dynamic technique lead the structured market-timing strategy to capture only a portion of the return of the better performing asset. As we discussed in the last example, this is a result of the core feature of option returns of reacting less than one-to-one with price changes in the underlying security.

In two instances, however, the option return actually is lower than either the bond or equity return. In 1976 the structured return was 16.6%, compared to 18.4% for bonds and 23% for equity; in 1981 it was −10.6%, compared to −1% for bonds and −5.6% for equity. This failure in the strategy is the result of employing only weekly adjustments in the historical simulation. While generally adjustments in the proportions of security holdings need to be made only infrequently, adjustments in the times of dramatic price movements may need to be made more than once a week to replicate the option position. These two years were marked by such price movements, and the inability of the simulation to make immediate allocation changes led to the inferior performance. This serves to emphasize the need for good monitor-

TABLE 3

MARKET TIMING STRATEGY SIMULATION
COMPARISON OF ANNUAL TOTAL RETURNS

Year	Bond	Equity	Dynamic Strategy	Capture
1973	0.83%	−14.86%	−5.96%	57%
1974	2.77	−25.25	−6.23	68
1975	6.96	34.15	26.34	71
1976	18.39	22.07	17.78	Floor
1977	−0.64	−7.20	−4.44	42
1978	−1.19	6.48	1.64	37
1979	−1.58	18.48	14.21	79
1980	−2.95	33.38	21.68	68
1981	−0.98	−5.58	−7.74	Floor
1982	44.99	20.79	34.93	58
1983	1.03	22.17	16.32	75

Cumulative Returns for 11 Years Compounded:

5.41%   7.80%   8.94%

- 52-week periods were used instead of exact calendar years.
- For purposes of this study, the asset classes are defined as follows:
  BOND: 20-year Treasury Bonds
  EQUITY: S&P 500 Stock Index adjusted for dividends
- Capture is the absolute difference of the dynamic strategy return and the lower of the bond or equity return, divided by the absolute difference of the bond and equity return.
- Includes transactions costs of $25 per contract round trip.
- Assets are reallocated once every week.

ing and execution facilities in following dynamic strategies.

This market-timing strategy can be adapted to other portfolio management settings. For example, it can be used to accentuate the performance of a number of managers by creating an option that will lead to a return equal to the largest of the managers' returns. The same method could be used to focus in on the best of a number of investment themes. A manager who, for example, is interested in both energy-intensive industries and recreation-related industries could create options on each area to increase the leverage of the better performing area.

Combined Strategies: Extensions to Multiple Risky Assets

Having presented examples both for cutting losses through portfolio insurance and for accentuating gains through call option positions, the next logical step is to combine the two.[18] The resulting strategy will give the greater of the bond or equity return with a floor return equal to the short-term rate.

Table 4 presents the result of combining the two previous strategies in this way. Over the eleven-year period from 1973 to 1983, all three assets in the strategy came into use at some point. From 1973 to 1980, returns shifted between the floor of 0% and some capture of the equity rate. The capture was almost 100% in 1976 and 1979, and roughly two-thirds in 1975 and 1979. In 1982 the bond market had twice the return of equity and over three times the return

of cash, and the dynamic strategy shifted toward bonds. The stock-bond option in this strategy, which represents the market-timing aspect of the strategy, was sensitive enough to capture 81% of this return.

This strategy is easily extended to other risk-

TABLE 4

MULTIPLE RISKY ASSET STRATEGY SIMULATION
COMPARISON OF ANNUAL TOTAL RETURNS

Year	Asset Class		Dynamic Strategy	
	Bond	Equity	Floor Exercise Price	Capture
1973	0.83%	−14.86%	0.44%	53%
1974	2.77	−25.25	0.11	4
1975	6.96	34.15	16.39	48
1976	18.39	22.97	11.67	51
1977	−0.64	−7.20	0.01	Floor
1978	−1.19	6.48	3.84	59
1979	−1.58	18.48	13.20	71
1980	−2.95	33.38	16.59	50
1981	−0.98	−5.58	−0.04	Floor
1982	44.99	20.79	24.38	54
1983	1.03	22.17	13.74	62

Cumulative Returns for 11 Years Compounded:

5.41%   7.80%   8.81%

- 52-week periods were used instead of exact calendar years.
- For purposes of this study, the asset classes are defined as follows:
  BOND: 20-year Treasury Bonds
  EQUITY: S&P 500 Stock Index adjusted for dividends
- Capture is the dynamic strategy return as a percent of the return to the equity portfolio when the equity portfolio return exceeds the 0% floor.
- Includes transactions costs of $25 per contract round trip.
- Assets are reallocated once every week.

return considerations, and to more than two risky assets. One way to look at the combined strategy is as a call option on the best performing of the risky assets with a residual position in cash. The call option gives the leverage on the upside while giving out protection on the downside. Furthermore, the call option can be selected before the fact to act like a call option only on the asset that turns out to be the best performer. If one of the areas does well, the options will pay off for that area; if they all do poorly and the option expires out of the money, the cash position will still guarantee a floor return.

THE IMPLICATIONS OF PERFORMANCE STRUCTURING FOR PORTFOLIO EVALUATION

Care must be taken in evaluating portfolios with return distributions altered by option strategies. Methods of performance evaluation that depend on mean and variance measures of returns — as all of the common methods do — cannot be applied to portfolios resulting from dynamic strategies for the simple reason that those portfolios depend on more than mean and variance.[19] These strategies mold the return distributions, bringing the higher moments, such as skewness and kurtosis, into play.

For example, the protective put leads to a truncation of the left tail of the portfolio return distribution and a leftward shift of the distribution. The truncation reflects the protection from downside loss, and the shift reflects the cost of the insurance. Figure 6 shows the distribution of the underlying portfolio, with the familiar normal distribution and the distribution that

FIGURE 6

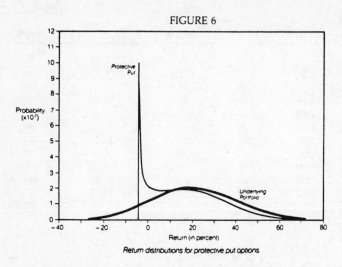

Return distributions for protective put options.

results when a put option is purchased on that portfolio.

In contrast to this strategy, consider the distributional effect of writing a covered-call option on the same underlying portfolio. The covered call has the opposite effect of the put option. It truncates the right tail of the distribution while shifting the distribution to the right. The truncation is the result of selling off the upward potential to the call buyer, and the shift reflects the premium received from that sale. Figure 7 compares the distribution of covered-call writing with that of the underlying portfolio.

Even a cursory reference to Figures 6 and 7 demonstrates that distributions resulting from option strategies cannot be understood by looking at the

FIGURE 7

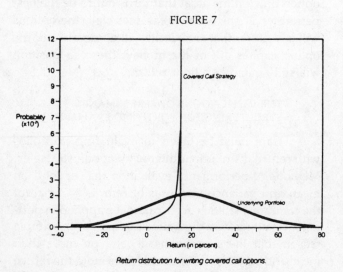

Return distribution for writing covered call options.

mean and variance alone. Indeed, in this particular case, an analysis based solely on expected return and variance of return will make call writing appear superior to put buying. The two strategies have much the same effect on expected return. The expected return drops from 18% for the underlying stock portfolio to 13.6% for the portfolio fully covered by a call option, and to 14.5% for the portfolio fully covered by the protective put. But the standard deviation of returns drops from 20% for the underlying portfolio to only 16.7% for the put strategy, while it is cut to 5.8% for the covered call strategy. The put strategy has a standard deviation that is nearly three times higher than for call writing. If standard deviation or variance is used as a proxy for risk, writing a covered call will be preferred to buying a protective put.[20]

Variance is not a suitable proxy for risk, however, since the option strategies reduce risk *asymmetrically*. The call truncates the right-hand side of the distribution and thereby reduces the desirable upside variance. The put, on the other hand, reduces the variance on the undesirable left-hand portion of the return distribution. It is natural, then, for a reduction in variance to be compensated differently for the two strategies.

This example illustrates the shortcomings of evaluation methods that rely on summary statistics such as mean and variance in dealing with option-related strategies. By trading off between the mean and the higher moments of the distribution, many unusual mean-variance relationships are possible.

For example, it is possible to construct a covered call strategy with both a higher expected return *and* a lower variance than the underlying portfolio. Or, by using far-out-of-the-money call options, it is possible to construct a portfolio insurance strategy that yields the same return floor as a protective put but with a higher expected return. (This strategy will give a high probability of achieving only the floor return and a small chance of receiving a very high return.) Such a strategy may not, in fact, lead to a desirable return structure. Strictly on a mean-variance basis, however, it certainly appears superior to the conventional insurance strategy of using a protective put.[21]

These two examples show the potential for misleading statements and inaccurate evaluations of alternative strategies. The incomplete state of performance evaluation may foster conflict between portfolio and management objectives. The strategies that lead to good measures of management success may not be those which best address the portfolio objectives. Given techniques that extend performance structuring beyond the two-dimensional plane of mean and variance, it is natural to expect that evaluation methods for these techniques must also break out of the mean-variance framework. We need a new set of performance techniques for the quantitative evaluation of portfolios engaged in these strategies.

Misinterpretations are also likely in the qualitative review of the performance of dynamically structured portfolios. For example, the portfolio insurance strategy requires selling off the security as the price declines and gradually buying it back as the price rises. Viewed outside the context of dynamic management, such a pattern of trading does not lead to favorable conclusions as to the manager's trading skills. Furthermore, most managers are evaluated by rankings based on realized return performance rather than on meeting distributional objectives. In these rankings, a manager's successful pursuit of a strategy for meeting a specified return objective may be overshadowed if a drop in realized return was a necessary cost of meeting that objective.[22] As with the misinterpretations inherent in applying the quantitative evaluation methods, the possibility of the manager pursuing a dynamic strategy may convey a mistaken impression that could keep these strategies from being correctly selected or effectively implemented.

CONCLUSION

The opportunities that option strategies present for molding the return distributions to meet investment objectives apply to a wide number of portfolio management and risk control problems. In their most general form, option strategies allow the manager to expand the set of insurable contingencies far beyond those available with static hedging methods. The use of dynamic hedging strategies to create the desired option-type payoffs allows returns to be structured even further than is possible with listed options; risks can be defined according to the specific asset/liability mix and risk preferences of management. The tools of option theory provide the technology for expanding the dimensions of risk management to meet the specialized demands of business.

We can summarize the technology of option theory as a payoff processor which reshapes return distributions.

The set of return distributions for the assets enter the processor, where the dynamic hedging technology remolds them to specification. The payoffs exit the processor with distributions of the desired shape.

Naturally, the benefits of dynamic return structuring are not gained without a cost. The protection of portfolio insurance is not free. Its cost, explicit in the price of a put option, is implicit in the dynamic strategy for replicating a put option, since, as we have seen, such a strategy leads only to partial participation in price increases. To state without qualification that a protective put strategy, or any other dynamic strategy, is superior to holding the uninsured portfolio

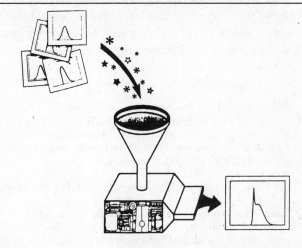

FIGURE 8
The Payoff Processor
Molding Returns to Meet Risk Management Objectives

ignores the risk-return tradeoffs that form the basis of asset pricing. While it is no doubt true that ex post the insured strategy will do better over some particular time period, ex ante the insurance will impose a cost. The same point applies to other strategies as well.[23]

The major issue we have addressed in this paper is how to minimize the cost of performance structuring, that is, how to find the dynamic strategy that best fulfills a given objective while still preserving the other features of the portfolio distribution. The least-cost dynamic strategy for meeting the objective of portfolio insurance will be the strategy which best replicates a put option. This conclusion flows over into a wide range of other portfolio objectives. In general, the least-cost means of return structuring can be represented through the appropriate set of put and call options on the underlying asset. This leads the goal of minimizing costs one step further, to finding the dynamic strategy which best replicates the required set of put and call options.

We have dealt with this and with the related issue of finding the most effective strategy, the strategy that gives the greatest chance of meeting the investment objectives under all possible market scenarios. We have addressed only indirectly a second vital issue of performance structuring: finding the strategy that meets the needs and objectives of the investor. Poorly written insurance policies can be formed just as easily with dynamic strategies as with more conventional insurance techniques. A strategy must not only meet its objectives, and do so at the least cost; the objectives themselves must also be intelligently conceived.

Like creating policies in insurance or contracts in law, creating the proper performance structure in finance is possible only when the nature of the risks and the objectives of the client are known. This requires more than an understanding of the tools of performance structuring. It requires a knowledge of the business being analyzed. The investment needs of the pension fund differ in scope and complexity from those of the insurance company, which in turn differ from those of the thrift institution. This is an area that is part art and part science, where judgment and experience are of key importance.

[1] The desirability of this type of insured portfolio is discussed in Leland, and in Brennan and Solanki. Skewness preference, i.e. a preference for a return distribution characterized by a degree of skewness as well as mean and variance, is discussed by Kraus and Litzenberger.

[2] See Ross, Breeden and Litzenberger, and Arditti and John.

[3] These characteristics, and a readable presentation of the nature of option pricing, can be found in Bookstaber. A more rigorous and detailed treatment can be found in Rubinstein and Cox.

[4] The creation of these binary payoffs, called primitive securities, through the use of option positions is covered in Breeden and Litzenberger (1978).

[5] The procedure for replicating an option through a dynamically adjusted position in the underlying security and risk-free asset is implied in the original work on option pricing by Black and Scholes (1973) and by Merton (1973). This procedure is discussed in simpler terms in Rubinstein and Leland, and in Chapter 4 of Bookstaber. The operaional considerations of these techniques are discussed in Platt and Latainer (1983a, 1983b).

[6] The exact functional form these factors take on depends on the assumptions of the model being used, particularly the distributional assumptions. If stock prices are assumed to be described by a lognormal distribution, the well-known Black-Scholes model will be appropriate. The binomial model of Cox, Ross, and Rubinstein will be an approximation for this same distribution. Merton has developed a model for a jump-diffusion process, a process that allows for discrete jumps in the security price. Cox has a model that allows the volatility of the security price to vary as a function of the security price. These models differ from the Black-Scholes model in terms of the functional form for a and b.

[7] The portfolio for replicating a put option is directly related to the replicating portfolio for a call option. This relationship can be expressed by the put-call parity formula presented in the first section of this paper:

$$C = (S - E) + E(r/(1 + r)) + P,$$

or

$$C = S - E(1/(1 + r)) + P.$$

As this formula shows, a call option can be created by holding the security, S, borrowing $E(1/(1 + r))$, and thus repaying E at expiration, and holding a put option. This creates a protective put on a portfolio that is similar to holding a call option on the portfolio. In fact, the only difference between the two is that a call option is levered through borrowing while the protective put position is not.

[8] For example, see Leibowitz and Weinberger.

[9] In particular, if there are sudden jumps in the underlying security while the Black-Scholes model is being used, the position will be subject to unexpected losses. The strategy will be unsuccessful in replicating an option position.

[10] This happens because an option on a portfolio of securities will not behave in the same way as a portfolio of options on each of the individual securities. The portfolio of options will be more expensive than the option on the portfolio. This is discussed in Merton (1973).

[11] The role of the riskless asset in creating a synthetic option is similar to its role in creating a synthetic forward contract for foreign exchange. The textbook method for creating a synthetic forward contract involves borrowing in one currency and converting it in the spot market into a second currency where the funds are then loaned out at the risk-free rate until the maturity of the contract. The result of these transactions is an obligation to deliver the first currency (to pay off the loan) and to receive the second currency. In practice, the funds need not actually be borrowed nor do they need to be loaned out as a riskless asset in the second currency. For example, the firm's own funds could be converted and the converted funds could be used for working capital needs. The end result of creating a forward contract will still be met, although the contract would be entangled with other transactions, and it would be more difficult to distinguish the nature of the forward contract. However, it is clear that creating the forward contract in this fashion might be more useful to the firm.

[12] If the exercise price of the synthetic option could not be matched by the listed options, it could still be constructed using the rolling over of listed options by following the proper hedge ratio. For example, if the hedge ratio or delta of the listed option is .5 while the hedge ratio of the desired synthetic option is .75, then $.75/.5 = 1.5$ of the listed option would be held for each of the synthetic options to be constructed.

[13] This problem of path dependence has occasionally been overstated. While path dependence does lead to uncertainty, it need not be an overriding concern. In practice, any strategy, including the straight dynamic approach, will face uncertainty, because the market and security price movement will not fit the assumptions of any model precisely. The key issue is whether the risk imposed by this uncertainty, and the cost of employing the strategies, is large in proportion to the benefit derived from being able to form a return that comes closer to meeting the portfolio objectives. Furthermore, rolling over positions can enhance returns if the investor has expertise in execution.

[14] Applications can be found in Platt and Latainer (1983a, 1984b, 1985), Tilley and Jacob, and Tilley (1984a).

[15] In practice, it is unlikely that weekly adjustments will actually be necessary. Depending on market conditions, in particular the degree of price movement, as few as four adjustments a year may be sufficient.

[16] The relationship between market timing and option valuation was first pointed out by Merton (1981). As put-call parity suggests, this relationship can also be looked at through a put option strategy. The market timing service can be created with a put option by holding the equity and buying a put option with an exercise price equal to the bond return.

[17] A variation of this strategy can be used to form a variable beta portfolio, a portfolio with a high beta, and thus high leverage, in strong markets, and with a low beta, and thus little reaction to the market, when the market declines. The variable beta strategy is presented in Chapter 6 of Bookstaber and Clarke (1983).

[18] Strategy is presented in Tilley and Latainer (1985). A theoretical discussion of this concept is presented by Stulz

(1982), and by Stapleton and Subrahamanyam (1984).

[19] Further discussion of the problems addressed in this section is provided in Bookstaber and Clarke (1984).

[20] This bias will appear for the Sharpe measure (which measures performance as the difference between the portfolio return and the risk-free rate, divided by the standard deviation of portfolio returns), the Treynor index (which measures performance as the difference between the portfolio return and the risk-free rate, divided by the portfolio beta), and the Jensen measure (which measures performance by the "alpha" of the security market line regression, i.e. by the vertical distance between the portfolio return and the capital market line).

[21] For this reason, care must be taken in using the expected return as the sole criterion for selecting the best portfolio insurance strategy. The protective put option may be the least-cost strategy in that it provides the desired protection for the lowest drop in expected return *while preserving the features of the underlying security return distribution*. But it will not be the least-cost strategy if no constraints are placed on alteration of the security return structure above the point of protection. The same is true of other option strategies. Unless the return structure is specified over the entire range of possible outcomes, there will be some strategies that fulfill the stated objectives at an apparently low cost but do so only by making unfavorable tradeoffs in other regions of the return distribution.

[22] The potential conflict of the manager between meeting the sponsor's objectives and maximizing relative performance suggests that the sponsor of the investment program might be better suited to the performance structuring role. We have discussed above how futures can facilitate this.

Morgan Stanley's approaches to product design take these differences into account at the outset. For example, strategies in the insurance area include hedging single-premium deferred annuities and universal life policies. For savings and loans, these techniques have been applied to asset-liability management and cash management. Other applications range from protecting investments in foreign currencies from adverse currency price movements to hedging the credit risk of high-yield bond portfolios.

[23] For other patterns of return structuring, the strategy may initially lead to positive inflows rather than costs as, for example, does the writing of covered call options. But in this case the cost balancing the initial inflow will be a reduction in the potential return from the later price movements.

REFERENCES

1. Arditti, F., and John, K. "Spanning the State Space with Options." *Journal of Financial and Quantitative Analysis*, 15 (March 1980), pp. 1-9.

2. Arditti, F., and Levy, H. "Portfolio Efficiency Analysis in Three Moments: The Multiperiod Case." *Journal of Finance*, 30 (June 1975), pp. 797-809.

3. Black, F., and Scholes, M. "The Pricing of Options and Corporate Liabilities." *Journal of Political Economy*, 81 (May 1973), pp. 637-654.

4. Bookstaber, R. *Option Pricing and Strategies in Investing*. Reading, Mass.: Addison-Wesley, 1981.

5. Bookstaber, R., and Clarke, R. "Options can alter portfolio return distributions." *Journal of Portfolio Management*, 7 (Spring 1981a), pp. 63-70.

6. ——. "An Algorithm to Calculate the Return Distribution of Portfolios with Option Positions." *Management Science*, April 1981b.

7. ——. *Option Strategies for Institutional Investor Management*. Reading, Mass.: Addison-Wesley, 1983.

8. ——. "Option Portfolio Strategies: Measurement and Evaluation." *Journal of Business*, 57 (October 1984), pp. 469-492.

9. ——. "Problems in Evaluating the Performance of Portfolios with Options." *Financial Analysts Journal*, 41 (January/February, 1985), pp. 48-62.

10. Breeden, D., and Litzenberger, R. "Prices of State-Contingent Claims Implicit in Option Prices." *Journal of Business*, 52 (October 1978), pp. 621-651.

11. Brennan, M., and Solanki, R. "Optimal Portfolio Insurance." *Journal of Financial and Quantitative Analysis*, 16 (September 1981), pp. 279-300.

12. Cox, J., and Ross, S. "The Valuation of Options for Alternative Stochastic Processes." *Journal of Financial Economics*, 3 (March 1976), pp. 145-166.

13. Kraus, A., and Litzenberger, R. "Skewness Preference and the Valuation of Risky Assets." *Journal of Finance*, 31 (September 1976), pp. 1085-1100.

14. Leland, H. "Who Should Buy Portfolio Insurance?" *Journal of Finance*, 35 (May 1980), pp. 581-594.

15. Leibowitz, M., and Weinberger, A. "Contingent Immunization, Part I: Risk Control Procedures." *Financial Analysts Journal*, 38 (November/December 1982), pp. 17-31.

16. Merton, R. "Theory of Rational Option Pricing." *Bell Journal of Economics and Management Science*, 4 (Spring 1973), pp. 141-183.

17. ——. "Option Pricing when Underlying Stock Returns are Discontinuous." *Journal of Financial Economics*, 3 (March 1976), pp. 125-144.

18. ——. "On Market Timing and Investment Performance. I. An Equilibrium Theory of Value for Market Forecasts." *Journal of Business*, 54 (July 1981), pp. 363-406.

19. Merton, R., Scholes, M., and Gladstein, M. "The Returns and Risk of Alternative Call Option Portfolio Investment Strategies." *Journal of Business*, 51 (April 1978), pp. 183-242.

20. ——. "The Returns and Risks of Put-option Portfolio Investment Strategies." *Journal of Business*, 55 (January 1982), pp. 61-67.

21. Platt, R., and Latainer, G. "Risk-return Tradeoffs of Contingent Insurance Strategies for Active Bond Portfolios." *Financial Analysts Journal*, 40 (May/June 1984), pp. 34-39.

22. ——. *Replicating Option Strategies for Portfolio Risk Control*. New York: Morgan Stanley Fixed Income Research, 1983a.

23. ——. *Replicating Option Strategies — Part II: Applications of Portfolio Insurance*. New York: Morgan Stanley Fixed Income Research, 1983b.

24. ——. "The Use of Synthetic Option Strategies in Fixed Income Portfolios." In F. Fabozzi, editor, *Winning the Interest Rate Game*, Chicago: Probus Publishing, 1985.

25. Ross, S. "Options and Efficiency." *Quarterly Journal of Economics*, 90 (February 1976), pp. 75-89.

26. Rubinstein, M., and Leland, H. "Replicating Options with Positions in Stock and Cash." *Financial Analysts Journal*, 37 (July 1981), pp. 63-72.

27. Rubinstein, M., and Cox, J. *Option Markets*. Englewood Cliffs, N.J.: Prentice-Hall, forthcoming.

28. Stapleton, R. C., and Subrahamanyan, M. G. "The Valuation of Multivariate Contingent Claims in Discrete Time Models." *Journal of Finance*, 39 (March 1984), pp. 207-228.

29. Stulz, R. M. "Options on the Minimum or the Maximum of Two Risky Assets." *Journal of Financial Economics*, 10 (July 1982), pp. 161-185.

30. Tilley, J. and Jacob, D. *Asset/Liability Management for Insurance Companies*. New York: Morgan Stanley Fixed Income Research, 1983.

31. Tilley, J. *Hedging Interest Rate Risk for Interest Sensitive Products*. New York: Morgan Stanley Fixed Income Research, 1984a.

32. Tilley, J. and Latainer, G. "A Synthetic Framework for Asset Allocation." *Financial Analysts Journal*, forthcoming.

Real estate: The whole story

We allocate too little to it and pay too little heed to real estate diversification.

Paul M. Firstenberg, Stephen A. Ross, and Randall C. Zisler

Investors traditionally have thought of equity real estate as an inefficient market in which the key to success is in the skill with which an individual investment is selected and negotiated. The general approach seems to be to buy properties when they become available if they look like "good deals," with little regard for the equally important issue of how the acquisition fits with the other holdings in the portfolio and what effect, if any, it will have on the overall risk and return objectives of the portfolio. Only recently have some investors begun to think of the aggregate of their real estate investments as a *portfolio*, with its own overall risk and return characteristics, and to adopt explicit strategies for achieving portfolio goals.

This article takes the view that investors should examine equity real estate investments not only on their individual merits but also for their impact on the investor's overall real estate portfolio. In addition, investors need to assess how the real estate segment fits into their entire portfolio. In turn, this means:

- setting risk and return objectives for the equity real estate portfolio as a whole that are compatible with the goals for the investor's entire portfolio,
- devising a strategy for achieving these objectives, and
- evaluating the extent to which individual transactions conform to the strategy and are likely to further portfolio objectives.

These processes are, of course, familiar to anyone in the business of managing security portfolios. By contrast, there has been a nearly complete neglect of such theory and techniques in the management of real estate portfolios and in their integration into institutional portfolios. This, in turn, has deprived managers of the modern tools that they now employ when considering other financial decisions. Often, for example, the pension fund asset allocation process that results in a decision to "put 10% of the portfolio into real estate" seems governed at least as much by hunch as by any rational mechanism.

Again by way of contrast, probably there is not a single major institutional portfolio in the common stock area that does not make serious use of modern portfolio techniques to continually monitor overall portfolio risk and to assess portfolio performance. These techniques are often the central mechanism for determining management strategy and selecting managers.

While some funds rely much more heavily on quantitative techniques than others do, the implementation of these procedures clearly has moved well beyond the cosmetic and lip service stage. Furthermore, a good general rule is that the larger the portfolio, the greater the reliance on such techniques. This is no doubt a consequence of the realization that even a few good stock picks will have less of an influence on the performance of a $5 billion portfolio than over-

PAUL M. FIRSTENBERG is Executive Vice President of the Prudential Realty Group in Newark (NJ 07101). STEPHEN A. ROSS is Sterling Professor of Economics and Finance at the Yale School of Management in New Haven (CT 06520) and consultant to the Real Estate Research Group at Goldman Sachs & Co. RANDALL ZISLER is Vice President of Goldman Sachs & Co. and director of their Real Estate Research Group in New York (NY 10004). The authors are grateful to William N. Goetzmann of the Yale School of Management for his fine assistance.

all structuring decisions will. These decisions include how much to put into different categories of assets or stocks and the overall risk level of the portfolio.

Moreover, within an asset category, the selection of sectors in which to invest is likely to have more impact on results than the choice of individual investments. These types of decisions for real estate are likely to be as critical for performance as a few good individual property "investments" and individual property asset management will be.

Our intention is to show how pension funds and other large investors can use modern portfolio techniques both to construct real estate portfolios and to allocate funds to asset categories including real estate. Our concern, however, is not with a cookbook application of some handy formulas to the real estate market.

Because the real estate market is not an auction market offering divisible shares in every property, and information flows in the market are complex, these features place a premium on investment judgment. Managers who want to own some of IBM simply buy some shares. Managers who want to participate in the returns on, say, a $300 million office building must take a significant position in the property. One alternative is to purchase a share of a large commingled real estate fund, but that does not relieve the fund's managers from the problems of constructing their portfolio.

Our aim is not to eliminate the analysis of each individual property acquisition, but rather to supplement it with a thorough consideration of its contribution to overall portfolio performance. Modern portfolio analysis provides the tool for examining the risk and return characteristics of the overall portfolio and the contribution of the individual elements. The result of its application is a method for selecting properties whose inclusion in the portfolio is of overall benefit.

Before we consider this point in more detail, we examine how real estate performance results compare with those for stocks and bonds. In this analysis, the absence of the large and continuous data record available in the securitized markets presents some special problems.

TOTAL RETURN AND REAL ESTATE DATA

In all modern investment work, the focus of interest is on the total rate of return on assets, that is, the return inclusive of both income and capital gain or loss. The logic underlying this is the basic philosophy of "cash is cash." An investment with a total return of 10%, all from capital gains, is equivalent to one with a total return of 10%, all from income, be-cause the sale of 9% of the shares in the investment that has risen in value will realize for the holder the same cash as the all-income investment provides. This basic truth, though, does not deny the possibility that, for some holders, there may be an advantage to receiving the return in one form or another.[1]

A real estate fund might rationally have an income as well as a total return objective, yet the transaction cost of selling appreciated property to realize income is particularly severe for real estate. While we recognize that this is an important issue, space considerations do not permit us to deal with it explicitly. Fortunately, too, this is not a serious limitation to our analysis, because the income component of large real estate funds is relatively insensitive to the decision as to how to allocate the funds across different types of real estate.

To determine the total return on real estate or any other asset, we just add the income component and the capital gain or loss. The income component of an asset's return is relatively straightforward to determine, as it is just a cash flow, and good data generally are available for the computation.

The price appreciation component, however, is much more difficult to assess. If an asset is traded in a continuous auction market, like the common stock of a major company, price quotes in the market provide a good method for valuing the asset. Most real estate assets trade infrequently, however, and valuation is more problematic. For some of the commingled funds, appraisals are the only source of property valuations.

The appraisal process merits a paper of its own, but a few points are sufficient for our purposes. Appraisals usually are conducted annually and are based on one of two methods or a combination of the two. If comparable properties have recently been bought or sold, then the appraisal can use their prices as benchmarks for estimating the value of properties that have not been traded. Comparability is increasingly difficult to achieve as the number and complexity of leases increases. Alternatively, the property can be valued by the discounted cash flow (DCF) method of discounting the projected net cash flows at some discount rate determined by prevailing market conditions. Neither of these methods can be as accurate as an actual market price, but there is also no reason to think that they will be biased in the long run. Furthermore, even if appraisals are biased, the appreciation computed from appraisals will not be biased as long as the bias is constant over time.

Although appraisals are not necessarily biased, there is evidence of considerable sluggishness or inertia in appraised values. By any of the common measures of the volatility of returns, real estate returns from appraisals appear to vary far less over time than other asset return series. Standard deviation is a measure of the spread or volatility of investment returns, and we will use the standard deviation also as a measure of the riskiness of real estate returns.[2]

The data below reveal that the standard deviation of stock returns, for example, is over five times greater than that of real estate returns. The extent to which this difference is a consequence of real estate returns actually being far less volatile than stock returns or a consequence of the use of appraisal values is not really known. In the data that follow, we make a correction that raises the volatility of the real estate returns to a level that seems more reasonable to us.

The major sources of data on real estate returns come from commingled funds. We have made use of three series of aggregate real estate returns and a separate series of the returns on different subcategories of real estate. For comparison purposes, we also use returns on other assets such as stocks and bonds. The data and the sources appear in the Appendix.

Table 1 describes how real estate returns have compared with the returns on stocks and bonds and with inflation. As the Frank Russell (FRC) and Evaluation Associates (EAFPI) series are based on appraisals, they might move more sluggishly than a true

market value series — if one were available. The two adjusted series under the FRC heading report the result of alterations in the FRC data designed to recognize this weakness. The "cap-rate adjusted" series estimates the change in value from a DCF model, and the "appraisal adjusted" series adjusts the standard deviation of the series upward.[3]

Even when the standard deviation of real estate returns is adjusted upward, both the return and the standard deviation make real estate an attractive asset category in comparison with stocks and bonds. Its lower risk and its comparable return partially offset the lack of liquidity inherent in real estate investments.[4]

We turn now to the issues involved in managing an equity real estate portfolio and the implications of modern portfolio analysis for real estate.

REAL ESTATE PORTFOLIOS: THE BASIC PRINCIPLES

In an imperfect real estate market, the skill with which individual assets are acquired, managed, and disposed of will be a major determinant of total return. Portfolio management is not a substitute for, nor should it divert attention from, property-specific management. Nevertheless, the composition of the portfolio as a whole will impact both the level and the variability of returns.

The twin considerations of individual property-specific management and portfolio analysis require different human skills and make use of different information. This leads naturally to a two-tiered approach to management:

- A macro analysis that employs portfolio management concepts and focuses on the composition and investment characteristics of the portfolio as a whole, identifying major strategic investment options and their long-run implications. Each property that is a candidate for acquisition or disposition should be analyzed for its impact on overall portfolio objectives.

- A micro analysis that employs traditional real estate project analysis, and focuses on the selection of the individual properties that make up the portfolio, evaluating a property's specific risk–reward potential against the investor's performance targets.

We will not have much to say here about the micro analysis; it is the traditional focus of real estate analysis. We make suggestions for it, but we do not propose changing it. Our interest is in the macro analysis.

Macro analysis derives the characteristics of risk and return for the portfolio as a whole from different combinations of individual property types and

TABLE 1

Real Estate Series and Other Assets

Index	Annualized		Series Begins (*)
	Total Return (%)	Standard Deviation (%)	
Real Estate			
FRC	13.87	2.55	6/78
FRC (cap-rate est.)	13.04	11.28	6/78
FRC (appraisal adj.)	13.87	4.37	6/78
EAFPI	10.78	2.80	3/69
EREIT	22.26	19.71	3/74
Other Assets			
S&P 500	9.71	15.35	3/69
Small Stocks	14.51	23.90	3/69
Corporate Bonds	8.38	11.29	3/69
Government Bonds	7.91	11.50	3/69
T-Bills	7.51	0.82	3/69
Inflation	6.64	1.19	3/69
Risk Premium (spread over T-Bills)			
EAFPI	3.27	2.43	
FRC	4.36	1.29	
S&P 500	1.48	17.54	
Small Stocks	7.38	18.04	

* All series end in December 1985. For details and full titles of each series, see the Appendix.

geographic locations. It establishes the trade-off between the given level of return and the volatility of return that result from different mixes of assets. Selecting the particular risk–return trade-off that best meets an investor's requirements is the most crucial policy decision one can make and is one of our major concerns.

The macro policy is implemented only through the individual selection of properties at the micro level. A thorough analysis of a property should involve an analysis of its marginal contribution to overall portfolio return, volatility, and risk exposure. The difficulty in conducting such an analysis at the individual property level is what gives rise to the separation between the micro and macro analyses. In general, the macro goals are implemented at the micro level by choosing categories of properties to examine with the micro tools, rather than by examining each individual property's marginal effect on the portfolio.

We will employ some familiar principles from modern portfolio theory as guides in portfolio construction:

- To achieve higher-than-average levels of return, an investor must construct a portfolio involving greater-than-average risk. An investor whose risk tolerance is lower than that of the average investor in the market must expect relatively lower returns. Risk may be defined as the variability or dispersion from the mean of future returns or, simply put, the chance of achieving less-than-expected returns. The variability of returns usually is measured by the standard deviation.

- It is possible and useful to measure risk and return and to develop, in an approximate manner, a portfolio strategy that balances the trade-off between these two performance criteria. Because of the difficulty and costs of transacting in the real estate market, and because of the resulting lack of precise "marked-to-market" prices for real estate, it is unrealistic to attempt to fine-tune actual investment decisions in response to risk–return estimates. Even if an investor specifies a preference for a mean return of 15% with a standard deviation of 3%, to a 14% mean return with a standard deviation of 2.5%, translating that preference into a precise strategy is probably not feasible. Broader relationships between risk and return must guide real estate investment strategy.

- The total risk on any investment can be decomposed into a systematic and an unsystematic component. Unsystematic risk will largely disappear as an influence on the return of a well-diversified portfolio. To the extent that the return on an individual property is influenced by purely local events, it is

unsystematic and washes out in a large diversified portfolio.[5] A regional shopping center, for example, might find its sales adversely affected by a plant closing. A chain of shopping centers spread across the country, however, would find total revenues unaffected by such local influences. Its revenues would depend on the overall economic conditions that affect costs and consumer demand. An investor who owned many such centers would not be subjected to the ups and downs of individual industries and markets and would be affected only by the general economic conditions that influence all retail businesses simultaneously.

- The risk from changes in economic conditions throughout the country is systematic and will influence any portfolio, no matter how large and well-diversified, because it influences each of the parts. For example, a downturn in consumer demand and a rise in wages will probably adversely affect all business, which means that even a conglomerate would suffer a decline in profits. Systematic risk can be lowered only by lowering long-run average returns. A conglomerate might attempt to lower such risks by implementing a strategic decision to sell some businesses and invest the proceeds in cash securities. The resulting revenues will have less sensitivity to the business cycle but also will have a lower average return. An investor could do the same.

In the sections that follow we will illustrate how investors can apply these principles in portfolio construction by examining how different combinations of property types and economic regions affect the risk and return characteristics of a portfolio.

Investors can reduce the unsystematic and, therefore, the overall risk level of the portfolio without sacrificing return by diversifying real estate investments among property types that have non-covariant returns and across geographic areas or leaseholds that are not subject to the same macroeconomic variables. Diversification also protects the investor from overemphasizing a particular asset class or area of the country that then falls victim to unforeseen, or more often unforeseeable, negative developments.

Spreading assets geographically has been a commonly used rough proxy for selecting areas that are economically non-covariant. A more detailed analysis, however, is required to determine whether geographically separate areas are actually subject to the same macroeconomic variables. The economic base of a particular geographic area may be broad-based, with multiple and widely diversified sources of revenues, or its economy may be largely dependent on a single economic activity. The latter is obviously a riskier area in which to invest, but much of its risk is unsystematic.

As a consequence, a diversified portfolio of areas, each of which is influenced by a different industry-specific risk, can avoid such risk at no cost in returns. For instance, the economies of Houston, Denver, and New Orleans were all highly vulnerable to one variable — oil prices; San Jose, California, Austin, Texas, and Lexington, Massachusetts, are all vulnerable, to a lesser degree, to the fortunes of the high-tech industries. A portfolio made up of properties in these cities is diversified geographically, but subject to significant systematic risks. By contrast, a portfolio made up of properties in Lexington, New Orleans, and, say, New York and Reno would have less overall risk.

This line of reasoning explains the power of diversification across geographic areas whose economies are independent. Within a given city, the same economic forces that influence the business demand for industrial and office space also affect the demand of workers for residential space, the demand of customers for hotel room nights, and the demand of retailers who sell to the workers. Too often, casual real estate market research leads to a claim of urban or regional diversification without an adequate analysis of the inter-industry and inter-occupational linkages affecting returns. Diversifying across different areas lowers risk to the extent to which the economies of the areas are independent of each other. Ultimately, the goal of diversifying a real estate portfolio should be to diversify across leaseholds.

Intuition also suggests that international diversification would be a powerful tool for accomplishing this goal. The question of whether a portfolio with London and New York properties is more economically diverse than a portfolio of Boston and New York is really the question of whether the underlying economy of Boston will move more or less with that of New York than will London.

REGIONAL DIVERSIFICATION

Figure 1 illustrates the trade-off between risk and return that is available when we break real estate investment into different regions and examine various portfolio possibilities for diversifying holdings across the regions. The four regions are the East, the Midwest, the South, and the West.[7] Figure 1 displays all the possible combinations of return and risk available from the different combinations of holdings across these four regions.

The expected return is graphed on the horizontal scale in Figure 1, and the vertical scale gives the standard deviation. The data are all historical.

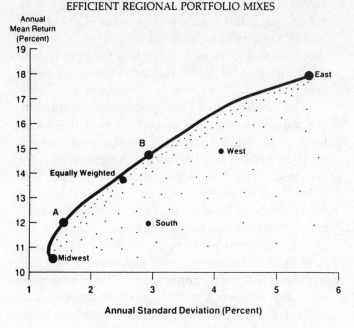

FIGURE 1

EFFICIENT REGIONAL PORTFOLIO MIXES

History is a guide to the future, but this is not to say that the next ten years will mimic the last ten. Rather, we are asking how different portfolios would have performed in the past. We contend that an intelligent look at past risk and return patterns is necessary for an understanding of the future. This, of course, is a weakness of all analysis, whether quantitative or not, but what else can we use to study the future if not the past?

By choosing different combinations of the four regions, all the points in the shaded part of Figure 1 are available. The labeled points describe the four pure regional portfolios. The East alone, for instance, shows a return of 17.9% and a standard deviation of 5.6%. The equally weighted portfolio in Figure 1 gives the return and the risk of a portfolio that puts one-quarter of its investment in each of the four regions.

Table 2 gives the background data underlying Figure 1. Here we have listed the return and standard deviation for each of the regions as well as the correlations in the returns across the four regions. Correlations are interpreted in the usual fashion. A positive correlation between two regions indicates that the returns tend to rise and fall together, and, as the table shows, all the regional correlations are positive. A zero correlation means that the returns tend to move independently of each other. All the correlations are low, and the correlation between the Midwest and the South is nearly zero. Combining asset categories that are only weakly correlated with each other greatly lowers overall portfolio risk. Figure 1 certainly reveals that this is the case for regional diversification.[8]

TABLE 2
Returns by Region, 1978-1985

Region	Annualized Mean Return (%)	Standard Deviation (%)
East	17.91	5.58
Midwest	10.49	1.44
South	11.96	2.92
West	14.83	4.11

Regional Correlation Matrix

Region	East	Midwest	South	West
East	1.00	0.16	0.25	0.32
Midwest	0.16	1.00	0.04	0.14
South	0.25	0.04	1.00	0.46
West	0.32	0.14	0.46	1.00

TABLE 3
Efficient Portfolio Mixes by Region (Proportions, %)

East	Midwest	South	West	Mean (%)	Portfolio Standard Deviation (%)
	99		1	10.50	1.43
0%	81	18%	1	10.80	1.31
5	74	17	5	11.30	1.36
9	66	15	9	11.80	1.49
14	59	13	13	12.30	1.67
19	52	12	18	12.80	1.89
23	45	10	22	13.30	2.14
28	38	8	26	13.80	2.41
32	31	7	30	14.30	2.70
37	23	5	35	14.80	2.99
41	16	3	39	15.30	3.30
46	9	2	43	15.80	3.60
51	2	0	47	16.30	3.91
64			36	16.80	4.28
80			20	17.30	4.80
96			4	17.80	5.43

Using Figure 1, we can show that investing the entire portfolio in any single region is unnecessarily risky. For three of the regions, there is a superior alternative that involves combining the regions. The only exception is the all-East portfolio. As it had the highest return in the period used to construct Figure 1 (see Table 2), putting the entire portfolio into the East would have been the best choice, but, of course, we have no basis for assuming that the next ten years would still put the East on top.

As for the other three choices, take, for example, the South. The South had a mean return of 11.96% and a standard deviation of 2.92%. Compare these results with those of Point A, directly above the South on the curve that bounds the possible combinations of return and risk. This point has the same standard deviation of 2.92% as that of the all-South portfolio, yet its return is nearly 15%, or 300 basis points, greater than that of the all-South portfolio. Similarly, Point B, just to the left of the South, is also superior to the all-South portfolio. It has the same return of 11.96% as the all-South portfolio, but its risk level is about 1.5%, or nearly half that of the all-South portfolio. The points on the curve of Figure 1 are called efficient portfolios, because they give the best possible returns for their levels of risk. The points between A and B are efficient portfolios that dominate the all-South portfolio.

Table 3 lists the efficient regional portfolios for each level of return and shows their risk level. These portfolios are the ones that give the returns and standard deviations on the curve in Figure 1. Table 3 provides a great deal of valuable information on the optimal regional diversification of a real estate portfolio.

As we move from low returns to high returns — and higher risk — we see that in the range from an 11.3% return with a 1.4% standard deviation to a 15.8% return with a 3.6% standard deviation, the efficient portfolios diversify to include all the regions. In other words, as we avoid the extremes of the highest returns and risks and the lowest returns and risks, a characteristic of the efficient portfolios is that they are fully diversified. Indeed, as Figure 1 shows, the equally weighted portfolio that puts exactly the same investment into each region is essentially an efficient portfolio with its return of 14% and its standard deviation of 2.3%.

This is as far as this quantitative analysis can take us. At this point judgment takes over. The quantitative analysis can weed out the inferior choices, but, in the end, it cannot make the final choice for the manager. The manager is left with the central question: What combination of risk and return should be chosen and, therefore, which efficient portfolio.?[9] Each investor will have particular requirements for establishing the trade-off between risk and return.

We offer here only some broad considerations. For a publicly-held fund, the basic issue is one of marketing; the combination of return and risk and, therefore, the regional diversification should be chosen according to an evaluation of the clients' demands. For a pension fund, the decision should be based on how the real estate portfolio is expected to contribute to the overall objectives of the fund. We will look at this matter more closely when we consider allocating funds across asset classes, including real estate. When regional diversification and property type diversification are combined, the resulting reduction in risk is considerable.

PROPERTY TYPE DIVERSIFICATION

Figure 2 illustrates the trade-off between risk and return that is available from forming portfolios of the five different property types, and Table 4 gives the data underlying Figure 2. The properties are classified into five major property types: apartments, hotels, office buildings, retail properties including shopping centers, and industrial properties such as warehouses. This classification corresponds both to the available data and to an a priori sensible breakdown into non-covariant business groupings. As we would expect, the efficient portfolios are diversified by property type, but here the results are different from those obtained when we consider regional diversification.

As Table 5 reveals, the efficient portfolios can have as few as two asset types in them. For returns above 16.3%, the efficient portfolios are dominated by hotels and office properties. For the low-risk alternatives, apartments, industrial properties, and retail dominate. At all levels of risk and return, though, some diversification is appropriate.

It is difficult to say to what extent these results predict future patterns and to what extent they are the consequence of the relatively short statistical history. There is reason to believe, though, that we should depend less on the property diversification results than on the regional analysis. For one thing, the numbers themselves are less reliable. The hotel category, for example, is based on a relatively small number of properties, and they are unduly concentrated in New York City. For another, it may well be

TABLE 4

Returns by Property Type, 1978-1985

	Annualized	
	Mean Return (%)	Standard Deviation (%)
Apartments	15.29	3.97
Hotels	18.25	12.08
Industrial	13.63	2.27
Office	15.38	4.72
Retail	11.56	2.19

	Property Type Correlation Matrix				
	Apartments	Hotels	Industrial	Office	Retail
Apartments	1.00	0.56	0.41	0.21	0.13
Hotels	0.56	1.00	0.17	0.11	−0.01
Industrial	0.41	0.17	1.00	0.65	0.59
Office	0.21	0.11	0.65	1.00	0.21
Retail	0.13	−0.01	0.59	0.21	1.00

TABLE 5

Efficient Portfolio Mixes by Property Type
(Proportions, %)

Apartments	Hotels	Industrial	Office	Retail	Mean (%)	Portfolio Standard Deviation (%)
4		4		92	11.80	2.10
9		20		71	12.30	1.97
13		36		51	12.80	1.94
18		50	1	31	13.30	2.01
23		61	3	13	13.80	2.18
30		61	9		14.30	2.43
41	2	34	24		14.80	2.81
53	3	7	38		15.30	3.29
38	16		46		15.80	4.03
15	33		53		16.30	5.23
	49		51		16.80	6.67
	67		33		17.30	8.40
	84		16		17.80	10.29
	98		2		18.20	11.88

that some of these returns reflect the economics of relatively tight leasing markets in the late 1970s and early 1980s. Furthermore, fundamental changes in the tax laws since 1986 probably will affect these property types differently.

For these reasons, we would advocate using Table 5 as a rough guide and tend to give greater weight to the middle region where all property types are represented. The final choice of a risk and return trade-off, as with regional diversification, rests with the manager and is governed by the same considerations as affect the regional choice.[10]

IMPLICATIONS FOR PORTFOLIO MANAGEMENT

We conclude from the foregoing analysis of the risk–return characteristics of portfolios constructed with different mixes of property types and geographic regions that:

FIGURE 2

EFFICIENT PROPERTY TYPE MIXES

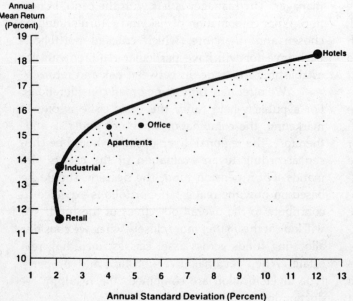

- There is a trade-off between the riskiness (as measured by standard deviation) of a real estate portfolio and the total expected return it generates. Consistent with experience with financial assets, the degree of risk an investor is willing to assume will be the single most important factor in determining return.
- Diversifying the composition of a portfolio among geographic locations and property types can increase the investor's return for a given level of risk. Diversification among holdings with non-covariant returns will reduce risk without sacrificing return. To construct such a portfolio, each investment category identified as offering diversification potential should be represented; the goal should be to have a substantial minimum threshold investment across property types and geographic regions (e.g., no property type or region should be below, say, 15% of the total portfolio).
- There are at least two alternative strategic approaches to diversifying a real estate portfolio. One approach calls for all investments to be made in strict accordance with diversification criteria, even though the assets allocated to different categories may exceed the minimums necessary to gain significant benefits. Under such a strict policy, an investor would not shift allocations because of perceived future changes in the payoffs from different allocations. The investor would modify the initial diversification slowly and generally only in response to some sort of significant long-term change in the marketplace. The assumption underlying this approach is that such modifications always create additional risk and that the investor lacks the forecasting ability to earn sufficient additional return to compensate for the risk.

The second approach allows for strategic deviations from the strict plan, provided that the threshold minimum allocations are met. Such an approach could reflect an investor's confidence in the ability to project changes in the risk–return differential of various geographic areas or property types. Or it could stem from pursuing a high risk–return strategy of, say, investing in development projects or in less than fully leased properties in currently out of favor markets in the hope of producing results outside of the efficient frontier of Figures 1 and 2. In such cases, the portfolio will reflect the strategic investment selections that deviate from a strict diversification policy, with the expectation that the added risk will be compensated for by additional return. One way to implement such a strategy is to divide the portfolio into a strictly diversified component (a core portfolio) and a higher risk/higher return portion (an opportunity portfolio), with the blend between the two reflecting an overall risk–return target.

In sum, an investor can target a real estate portfolio to lie at any point along the risk–return continuum; the crucial step is to articulate and explicitly adopt an investment strategy that fits this goal and that both the investor and the investment manager fully understand and agree upon. The strategies to be pursued in managing a real estate portfolio should be explicit, not unspoken.

- We need to learn a good deal more about the factors that, in fact, produce genuine diversification (i.e., non-covariant returns). Present categories of broad geographic regions or property types provide only crude guidelines for achieving efficient mixes. This lack of the proper economic classifications and the accompanying data are the most serious weaknesses of our analysis.

ASSET ALLOCATION: STOCKS, BONDS, AND REAL ESTATE

In principle, the same considerations that govern the construction of the all-real estate portfolio apply to the asset allocation decision. Table 1 gives the basic return and risk information, while Table 6 gives the correlations between real estate and other asset categories.

TABLE 6

Correlations Among Asset Classes*

	FRC	EAFPI	EREIT	S&P 500	Government Bonds	T-Bills	Inflation
FRC	1.00	0.71	−0.14	−0.26	−0.38	0.30	0.38
EAFPI	0.71	1.00	−0.20	−0.28	−0.10	0.54	0.48
EREIT	−0.14	−0.20	1.00	0.78	0.36	−0.23	0.03
S&P 500	−0.26	−0.28	0.78	1.00	0.49	−0.43	−0.15
Government Bonds	−0.38	−0.10	0.36	0.49	1.00	−0.09	−0.35
T-Bills	0.30	0.54	−0.23	−0.43	−0.09	1.00	0.41
Inflation	0.38	0.48	0.03	−0.15	−0.35	0.41	1.00

* For details and full titles of each series, see Appendix.

In constructing Table 6, we have treated real estate as a single category, even though different regions or property types will have different relations with other assets. Whenever we aggregate asset classes and consider their relationship with each other as classes, we always lose some of the fine detail. This is true of stocks as well as real estate. As these asset categories are managed as individual classes, however, the separation of management forces the separation of our analysis.[11]

From a portfolio perspective, the great attractive feature of real estate is its lack of correlation with other assets. Even if real estate risk is understated, the lack of correlation makes real estate a particularly attractive feature of a well-diversified portfolio.

Look first at the correlations among the three real estate indexes FRC, EAFPI, and EREIT. The two appraisal-based indexes, FRC and EAFPI, are highly correlated with each other, and both are negatively correlated with the stock market-traded REIT index, EREIT. This striking difference points up the difficulty with the real estate data. Indeed, both FRC and EAFPI are negatively correlated with the stock market as well, while EREIT with a 0.78 correlation with the S&P 500 actually looks like a stock index rather than the other two real estate indexes. (A closer look reveals that individual REITs can behave like the other real estate indexes; it all depends on the particular REIT.) Presumably, the truth lies somewhere between these two, and we can conclude that real estate returns, if not negatively correlated with those on stocks, are at least far from perfectly correlated with them.

One point with which all of the real estate indexes agree, however, is that real estate hedges against increases in inflation. All three indexes are positively correlated with changes in inflation. By contrast, the S&P 500 index has responded negatively to inflation.

Our argument for including real estate as a substantial portion of an overall investment portfolio is, thus, based on its significant diversification value in reducing risk, whatever the goal for returns.

Using the correlation data from Table 6 and the return data from Table 1, we created the efficient frontier of real estate, stocks, and bonds displayed in Figure 3 and tabulated in Table 7. We used the upward adjustment in the standard deviation of real estate in constructing Table 7 so as to avoid any possible underemphasis of its risk. The efficient portfolios in Table 7 display the same characteristics as the efficient portfolios of the real estate categories. In the middle ranges of return and risk, the portfolio is evenly diversified among the three categories, although real

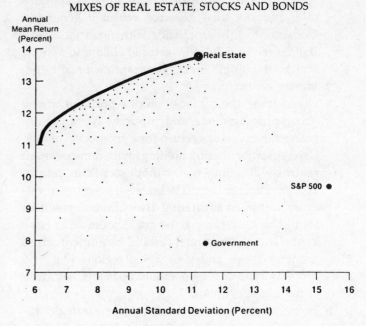

FIGURE 3

MIXES OF REAL ESTATE, STOCKS AND BONDS

TABLE 7

Efficient Portfolio Mixes of Real Estate, Stocks, and Bonds.
Real Estate Standard Deviation 'Cap-Adjusted' = 11.28%
(Proportions, %)

Real Estate (FRC Index)	Stocks (S&P 500)	Government Bonds	Mean (%)	Portfolio Standard Deviation (%)
49	11	40	11.00	6.16
52	12	36	11.20	6.20
55	13	32	11.40	6.29
58	14	28	11.60	6.44
61	15	24	11.80	6.65
65	16	19	12.00	6.91
68	17	15	12.20	7.22
71	18	11	12.40	7.56
74	19	7	12.60	7.94
77	20	3	12.80	8.35
80	20		13.00	8.79
85	15		13.20	9.30
90	10		13.40	9.89
95	5		13.60	10.56
100	0		13.80	11.28

estate has the major share. Insofar as the risk of real estate is still understated by the 11.3% standard deviation, these numbers will overstate real estate's role in an efficient asset allocation.

To examine this matter further, we raised real estate's standard deviation to be the same as that for the S&P 500, 15.4%. The resulting efficient portfolios are given in Table 8. Although the increase in the risk level of real estate lowers its contribution to the efficient portfolios and raises the proportion of bonds, the amount of the change is surprisingly small. For example, the efficient portfolio with a 12% mean return has a 61% holding in real estate when real estate

TABLE 8

Efficient Portfolio Mixes of Real Estate, Stocks, and Bonds.
Real Estate Standard Deviation = Stock Standard Deviation = 15.35%
(Proportions, %)

Real Estate (FRC Index)	Stocks (S&P 500)	Government Bonds	Mean (%)	Portfolio Standard Deviation (%)
38	13	49	10.40	7.05
41	15	44	10.60	7.09
44	17	39	10.80	7.19
47	18	35	11.00	7.37
50	20	30	11.20	7.61
53	21	26	11.40	7.91
56	23	21	11.60	8.26
58	25	17	11.80	8.66
61	26	12	12.00	9.10
64	28	8	12.20	9.57
67	30	3	12.40	10.80
71	29		12.60	10.61
76	24		12.80	11.22
80	20		13.00	11.92
85	15		13.20	12.70
90	10		13.40	13.54
95	5		13.60	14.42
100	0		13.80	15.35

is assumed to be as risky as stocks and a 65% holding when real estate is assumed to have a risk level below that of stocks but above its measured level. Of course, this result is dependent upon the limitations of the data and our model.

The important conclusion to draw from this analysis is that, even with an upward risk adjustment, real estate belongs in efficient portfolios at significantly higher levels than the 3.6% allocation for the top 200 public and private funds in 1986. Taking a pragmatic perspective, we feel that pension funds should seek initial real estate asset allocations of between 15 to 20%.

A second level of consideration in choosing among these possible asset allocations makes use of the additional data presented in Table 6, the correlations between asset returns and inflation and interest rates. Similar data can be collected for other major economic variables that influence asset returns, such as real productivity and investor confidence (see Chen, Roll, and Ross, 1986). We can see from Table 6 that real estate is positively correlated with inflation and, at least for the FRC and the EAFPI indexes, it is also positively correlated with interest rates. This is in marked contrast to stock returns, which are negatively correlated with the inflation variable and with interest rates.

This means that real estate returns have been a superior hedge against an increase in inflation or in interest rates, as compared with the experience of the stock market. As inflation or interest rates have risen, the stock market historically has tended to fall, and

real estate returns have tended to rise. Of course, this will depend on the source of the increase in inflation and interest rates. The Monday, October 19, 1987, crash in the stock market produced the opposite result, where sellers of stock ran to the bond market, pushing these prices up. Rather, we are primarily concerned here with a change in stock prices accompanied by a change in inflationary expectations. This differs from a once-and-for-all shift in prices, such as a jump in commodity prices because of formation of a cartel.

A corporate pension fund that is funded ultimately by the earnings of the company would find real estate a relatively attractive asset category if its earnings tend to be negatively related to inflation. For example, suppose that a manufacturing company believes that an increase in inflation brings about a more rapid rise in its wage and material costs than in the prices of its products. A fund with a tilt toward real estate would tend to offset this profit squeeze by rising when corporate earnings fell off.

This does not mean that companies whose earnings rise and fall with inflation should shun real estate. For example, a natural resource company with relatively fixed costs would find its earnings down in a period of low inflation. But the analysis of Tables 7 and 8 is still relevant, and the pension fund of such a company should still hold a significant proportion of its assets in real estate, simply to take advantage of the return and risk diversification characteristics. The proper conclusion to draw is that such a company should hold relatively less real estate than the manufacturing company.

In the end, the allocation decision among the three categories we have studied involves a judgment that is associated with the particular needs of the fund being considered. If, in addition to the considerations of risk and return on which we have focused, there is also a concern for liquidity, this will tend to push the fund toward marketed assets such as stocks and bonds and out of real estate.[12] There is no single answer that is best for all portfolios, only a range of desirable choices. Modern portfolio analysis limits this range to the manageable alternatives presented in Tables 7 and 8.

CONCLUSION

We have shown how modern portfolio analysis can be used both to optimally diversify a real estate portfolio and to allocate overall fund assets among real estate, stocks, and bonds. Real estate is an enormous percentage of world assets, and, as our final tables show, even with an upward risk adjustment, it may belong in efficient portfolios at significantly higher levels, such as 15 to 20%, compared to the 3.6% allocation in 1986 for the top 200 public and private pension funds.

REFERENCES

The two modern portfolio techniques used in the paper are the Capital Asset Pricing Model (CAPM) and the Arbitrage Pricing Theory (APT). Expositions of these approaches can be found in most textbooks on corporate finance. Two references are:

Brealey, Richard, and Stewart Myers. *Principles of Corporate Finance*, 2nd ed. New York: McGraw-Hill Book Company, 1984.

Copeland, Thomas, and J. Fred Weston. *Financial Theory and Corporate Policy*, 2nd ed. Reading, Mass.: Addison-Wesley Publishing Company, 1983.

The following article outlines the APT approach to strategic planning:

Roll, Richard, and Stephen A. Ross. "The Arbitrage Pricing Theory Approach to Strategic Portfolio Planning." *Financial Analysts Journal*, May/June 1984.

Other articles of interest include the following:

Chen, Nai fu, Richard Roll, and Stephen Ross. "Economic Forces and the Stock Market." *Journal of Business*, July 1986.

Hoag, J. "Toward Indices of Real Estate Value and Return." *Journal of Finance*, May 1980.

Miles, M., and T. McCue. "Commercial Real Estate Returns." *Journal of the American Real Estate and Urban Economics Associations*, Fall 1984.

Zerbst, R. H., and B. R. Cambon. "Historical Returns on Real Estate Investments." *Journal of Portfolio Management*, Spring 1984.

[1] Regulatory and accounting conventions may lead to a preference for income over capital gains. Tax issues also influence this preference. Furthermore, some funds may be precluded from realizing income through sales, and, even if they can sell appreciated assets to generate income, the transaction costs of doing so will detract from the return. On the other side, some investors actually may prefer capital gains to income (ignoring tax effects) to avoid being faced with the need to reinvest the cash.

[2] A rule of thumb is that two-thirds of the returns tend to fall within one standard deviation of the mean return and 95% of the returns fall within two standard deviations. The higher the standard deviation, the greater the range of the effective returns, and the greater the probability or likelihood of loss.

[3] The first correction uses a "cap-rate" proxy in place of appraisal returns. Net operating income is a commonly used yardstick for the valuation of real estate. By treating changes in the current income stream as indications of changes in the market value of the asset, we can estimate an appreciation return. Although this approach has a number of problems, at least it allows us to base the estimate of appreciation on known data. The result is an FRC series with an annual standard deviation of 11%.

We generated a series of appreciation returns on the change of an estimated value of the real estate index, where the value is given by the present value of a perpetual stream of income flows. The income flows are taken to be the current period income, and the discount rate can be modeled either as a spread over T-bills, or simply as a fixed rate.

$$Cr_t = \frac{(Ve_{t-1} - Ve_t)}{(Ve_{t-1})},$$

$$Ve_t = D_t/r_t,$$

where:

Cr = cap-rate return

Ve = cap-rate value

D = income per invested dollar

r = discount rate

Y = income return

I = appreciation index value

This simplifies to:

$$Cr_t = \left[\frac{I_t}{I_{t-1}} \cdot \frac{Y_t}{Y_{t-1}} \cdot \frac{r_{t-1}}{r_t}\right] - 1.$$

This method may have some validity, insofar as a similar procedure on the stock market produces estimates near the true value for volatility.

The appraisal-adjusted series is derived from an analysis of the appraisal process and estimates a volatility of returns based on the reported data. This method is an attempt to correct returns by removing any inertia or sluggishness inherent in the appraisal process. True rates of return should be uncorrelated with each other across time. Insofar as there is excessive correlation in the FRC returns, they will not accurately reveal the true return on real estate.

To model the appraisal process, we assumed that a property's appraised value is a mixture of the series of previous appraised values and the appraiser's estimate of the current market price the property would bring if sold. In other words, the appraiser incorporates past appraisals into the current appraisal.

The basis of this estimation is as follows. An estimated mean return can be expressed as the true mean, M_t, and some random error term, e_t:

$$M_t = R_t + e_t,$$

where the standard deviation of e_t is the true standard deviation of returns.

The appraiser can be thought of as combining the true mean return with a lagged return to make the following estimation:

$$E[R_t] = (1 - A)M_t + AR_{t-1}.$$

More generally, the process might use a whole year's worth of past returns in combination with the true mean to produce the current estimation:

$$E[R_t] = (1 - A)M_t + a_1R_{t-1} + a_2R_{t-2} + a_3R_{t-3} + a_4R_{t-4},$$

where

$$A = a_1 + a_2 + a_3 + a_4.$$

A linear regression based on this model yields the following information:

$$R_t = b_0 + b_1R_{t-1} + \ldots + b_4R_{t-4} + z_t,$$

where z_t is the residual error term.

Combining these two equations, we can solve for the true mean and standard deviation from the estimates of b_1, b_2, b_3, and b_4 as follows:

$$b_1 = a_1, b_2 = a_2, b_3 = a_3, \text{ and } b_4 = a_4,$$

and, therefore, the true mean:

$$M = b_0/(1 - A), b_0/(1 - A),$$

where

$$A = b_1 + b_2 + b_3 + b_4,$$

and the true standard deviation of returns is given by:

$$\sigma = \sigma(z_t)/(1 - A),$$

where $\sigma(z_t)$ is the standard deviation of the regression residual, z_t.

[4] We know very little about the effect of illiquidity on investment returns beyond the intuition that liquidity is certainly no worse than illiquidity. As we do not know much more than this, we will adopt the sensible policy of not saying much more.

[5] In practice, real estate managers spend most of their resources investigating local market conditions and negotiating terms of sale. Little if any attention is directed toward the role of a property in the overall portfolio. This is not as misdirected as it might seem. While diversification removes individual and unsystematic property risk, it does not help portfolio returns if misunderstanding the local markets results in overpaying for every property. Nevertheless, without understanding the marginal contribution that properties make to overall portfolio goals, the whole can be less than the sum of the parts.

[6] It is important that property returns be noncovariant, that is, that they not move together, or the risk will be systematic and the advantages of diversification will be lost. For example, a $100-million stock portfolio with 100 holdings of $1 million each will not be terribly well diversified if all of the stocks are utilities.

[7] Data are reported by the Frank Russell Company on a quarterly basis.

[8] We have used the appraisal based returns and have not adjusted the resulting standard deviations in Table 2 and Figure 1, but the possible low volatility of appraisal returns has no effect whatsoever on our analysis. If we were to increase all of the standard deviations by, for example, a factor of two, then this would double all of the numbers on the vertical scale of Figure 1, but all of the points would remain in the same position relative to each other. The analysis of Figure 1 would change only if the appraisals distort volatility by different amounts in the different regions. However, that seems unlikely (not to mention unknowable.)

[9] This is probably a good place to dispel another notion that sometimes surfaces in discussions of risk and return. Often a manager will say that "Risk is important, but over the long run, the risk will wash out and all that will matter is the expected return." This is a misunderstanding of risk and its relation to return and, in fact, both the return and the risk increase over time. The exact form this takes depends on various technical features, but generally over very long periods, the greater the standard deviation of a portfolio's returns, the more likely it is that the value of the portfolio will fall below a given level.

[10] It might have occurred to the reader that we should consider breaking real estate into twenty classifications according to both property type and region. For example, hotels in the West would be one of the twenty classes. This is possible, but we have chosen not to do so because of the small number of properties in some of these classes and the resulting lack of reliability of the figures.

[11] A subtle technical point arises from our focus on constructing efficient real estate portfolios. Because of the different interactions between individual stock categories and real estate, we are not assured that an efficient portfolio of stocks and real estate will make use of an efficient real estate portfolio. In practice, though, the difference will be small and the data are not accurate enough to discern the difference.

[12] Liquidity concerns, however, generally should not be a cause to forgo the diversification of benefits of real estate, because real estate constitutes a small percentage of most portfolios. Other assets can better serve as sources of ready liquidity.

APPENDIX

Data Series and Sources

Source	Data Description
Frank Russell Company (FRC Indexes)	A quarterly time series of equity real estate returns extending from 1978 to the present. The series is broken down by income and capital gains and also by region and property type. Currently, the data base has approximately 1000 properties owned by real estate funds with an average value of about $10 million per property.
Evaluation Associates (EAFPI)	A quarterly time series extending from 1969 to the present. It is an index constructed by an equal weighting of the returns on a number of largely all-equity real estate funds. The data base currently includes about thirty-three tax-exempt funds with a total asset value of about $25 billion.
Gs & Co. Equity REIT Returns (EREIT)	A monthly time series extending from 1974 to the present. It is an equally-weighted index constructed from thirty-three REITs holding more than 80% equity assets. In comparison with the FRC index, EREIT is more heavily concentrated in shopping centers and apartments and less in office properties.
Stock, Bond, and Inflation Data	Ibbotson and Associates provide a comprehensive monthly data base that begins in 1926.

THE SURBERS CONSIDER ASSET ALLOCATION

Carter and Hazel Surber are quite pleased with the help you provided to them in answering their four specific questions as part of financial and investment planning. During your discussion with the Surber family, Hazel inquires as to whether you believe their financial assets are properly invested or not. You explain to Hazel that her question really is one of "asset allocation."

In other words, Hazel Surber has inquired about the first-level of allocation of total investment funds into asset categories such as cash (or equivalents), bonds (or fixed income), or stocks (or equity). You point out that there may well be a fourth category -- perhaps labeled "other" -- that includes all other investments that do not fit easily into one of the other three groupings.

To help answer their further questions about asset allocation, you refer to the Surbers' recent balance sheet:

```
---------------------------------------------------
                  Assets:
    Home                              $121,800
    Retirement accounts                163,400
    Savings accounts                    10,600
    Investment portfolio               63,000
    Art and antiques                     6,700
    Automobiles (3)                     16,800
    Personal possessions                26,900
       Total                         $409,200


                Liabilities:
    Mortgage                          $77,400
    Credit card balances                2,700
       Total                          $80,100


               Family equity:
    Carter and Hazel Surber           $329,100
---------------------------------------------------
```

In further discussion with the Surbers, you learn that their retirement accounts are 60% invested in a bond mutual fund and 40% invested in a common stock fund. Their investment portfolio consists of approximately equal investments in seven blue-chip common stocks. Based on this additional information, you decide to try and be prepared to answer further questions for the Surber family such as the following:

(1) Based on the Surbers' balance sheet and the added
     information that is provided, what is their family's
     current asset allocation?

(2) Again, based on the Surbers' balance sheet, what is
     their family's current asset allocation, but without
     consideration of their investment in their home?
     Compare the answers to these first two questions.
     Which is the best starting point for their
     consideration of asset allocation?

(3) Hazel Surber reports that she recently read an article
     in the WALL STREET JOURNAL that revealed considerable
     differences in the recommended asset allocations of
     several large brokerage firms. She wonders how can
     they make an appropriate decision when the
     professionals themselves disagree so much?

(4) In turn, Carter Surber reports that he recently was
     given a copy of a September-October 1987 article in the
     FINANCIAL ANALYSTS JOURNAL (see Reading #15). Surber
     admits, though, that the article was difficult to
     understand because of the math. He wonders if any of
     the concepts from "modern portfolio theory" might be
     helpful to his family's decision on what to do about
     asset allocation?

(5) Based on your analysis of the above, what would you
     recommend in terms of asset allocation for the Surbers?
     In other words, what asset allocation do you believe
     would be most appropriate for the Surber family?

(6) To add perspective to the above questions, you also are
     asked to make recommendations on appropriate asset
     allocations for three additional scenarios:

     (a) A single professional, age 28

     (b) A married couple, ages 32 and 34, about to start a
          family

     (c) A retired couple, ages 62 and 63

FORMULA PLANNING IN VOLATILE MARKETS

As usual every month, there is a full agenda for the next scheduled meeting of the Investment Committee of the Peoples' National Bank. Brian Burford, recently appointed as president of Peoples' Bank, normally would not attend the meeting that is scheduled for Monday, August 22, 1988. But on this occasion, one item on the agenda catches his eye -- and he has informed Lawrence Ogilvie, senior vice president and chairman of trust services, of his intent to attend and possibly even to participate in the meeting. The item of interest to Mr. Burford is a scheduled discussion of his trust department's policy on asset allocation.

Peoples' National Bank is the fourth largest commercial bank in Seattle, Washington. The 1987 annual report of Peoples' shows net income of just over $8 million, on assets of $437 million, and which translates to a return on equity of just under 16%. And with a policy of careful attention to local business and families, Peoples' Bank has grown steadily in recent years to a position of being well respected among smaller and regional banks on the west coast. Peoples' president of almost two decades retired in 1987, and after an extensive national search, Brian Burford was hired as his successor.

After growing up in the Seattle area, and with an undergraduate degree in history and economics from the University of Washington, Burford took a position in corporate banking in New York City. After three years, he switched to another large New York City bank, and with greater responsibilities in corporate lending. Five years later he was named vice president and head of that bank's growing credit card business. During the next three summers, Burford attended the Pacific Coast Banking School in Seattle -- and that is where he became particularly interested in the trust side of banking. He decided to remain in the mainstream of corporate banking, however, and that paid off for him as he was selected to become Peoples' new president in the fall of 1987, and, coincidentally, just three weeks after Black Monday.

Since returning to Seattle, Mr. Burford has been mainly involved in trying to chart a course for Peoples' Bank for the next several years. He has assembled an excellent management team, and together they have developed a comprehensive strategic plan for most areas of the bank. The kernel of the plan is twofold: (a) to continue to stress personal service and quality in all activities, and (b) to try and carve out certain niches where Peoples' may be able to develop a comparative advantage.

But conspicuously absent from the strategic plan at this point is any serious attention to the trust activities of the bank. Like most financial institutions of its relative size, the trust side of the business has always been something of an enigma to Peoples' Bank. The trust and investment business is at best only marginally profitable -- and that is only when an appropriate credit is given for deposits generated. At the same time, Lawrence Ogilvie and certain other senior managers strongly believe that to do away with the trust and investment business would seriously jeopardize overall bank profitability. In sum, Ogilvie and his staff are devoted to doing as well as they can in a difficult part of the banking business. They also are eager to hear any constructive input from their new president.

The stock market crash of last October has not helped the situation. For apart from significant losses sustained in most of the accounts which they manage, there is a growing concern by many trust customers about the future prospects for the equity markets. And while many of those customers have urged Ogilvie to switch more of their funds into fixed income securities, other customers have expressed just the opposite viewpoint. Namely, those customers believe that long term prospects for the stock market are quite good, and thus they would prefer to have additional funds switched into the equity side. Yet a third group of customers admit that they have no idea what to expect -- other than that the Peoples' trust department hopefully will make correct investment decisions on their behalf.

Sensing a growing restlessness among their customers as well as among employees of the trust department, Lawrence Ogilvie has decided to devote a portion of the next meeting to reviewing the asset allocation policy. As part of the prepared agenda for the meeting, Ogilvie reviews the allocation guidelines set by his committee during the past four years. He also includes the quarterly yield on 90-day U.S. Treasury bills, and the quarter-end values of the Standard & Poor's 500-Composite Stock Market Index.

Quarter End	% Fixed Income	T-bills	% Equity	S&P 500
September 1984	20-30	9.9%	70-80	166.1
December 1984	30-40	9.5	60-70	164.5
March 1985	30-40	8.5	60-70	180.7
June 1985	40-50	8.0	50-60	191.7
September 1985	30-40	7.1	60-70	182.1
December 1985	20-30	7.2	70-80	211.3
March 1986	20-30	6.6	70-80	238.9
June 1986	30-40	6.2	60-70	250.8
September 1986	40-50	5.2	50-60	231.3
December 1986	40-50	5.5	50-60	242.2
March 1987	30-40	5.6	60-70	291.7
June 1987	30-40	5.7	60-70	304.0
September 1987	20-30	6.4	70-80	321.8
December 1987	40-50	5.8	50-60	247.1

| March 1988 | 40-50 | 5.7 | 50-60 | 258.9 |
| June 1988 | 40-50 | 6.5 | 50-60 | 273.5 |

Ogilvie appends a note to Burford's agenda and data indicating that the existing policy calls for each portfolio manager to keep each account under her/his control within the guidelines -- unless there is special approval from himself or another senior trust officer. As a practical matter, however, Ogilvie admits that a large number of accounts are viewed as "special cases," and thus the guidelines have not been honored.

Brian Burford suspects part of the problem is that Peoples' Bank never has had a coherent policy for asset allocation. Instead, Peoples' trust department has tended to change their asset allocation policy as the markets themselves have changed, and in very much of a short-term response mode. What Peoples' Bank needs is a longer-term consistent policy for managing their trust business. In sum, Burford is convinced that Peoples' Bank needs to tighten up on the management of their trust accounts.

In thinking about what he might be able to add to the meeting, Burford remembers a discussion of "formula planning" which was part of an investments course that was part of his work in the Pacific Coast Banking School several years ago. According to the notes which he saved from that course, a professor from Oregon State suggested that formula planning is a disciplined technique for asset allocation that seems to work especially well when markets fluctuate about achieved plateaus. And while the last few years have not been like that, several market commentators believe that the late 1980s and perhaps the early 1990s will see continuing volatile markets, but they may be markets for which formula planning could once again be useful.

Brian Burford decides to listen carefully during the first part of the meeting next Monday to see if there are any consensus views on what sort of asset allocation policy should be followed. If the discussion does not lead to that, the president is prepared to ask a number of penetrating questions. Among them are the following questions on formula planning:

(1) What are the pros and cons of formula planning during distinctly rising markets? During market downturns? During market cycles?

(2) Over the last four years, what would have been the achieved results of a fixed-ratio formula plan that allocates total trust assets (assume $100 million) to 60% stock market (e.g. S&P 500) and 40% fixed income (e.g. 90-day U.S. Treasury bills)? Assume 1% round-trip transaction costs for equity transactions.

(3) What would have been the achieved results of a variable-ratio formula plan that varies stock market allocations between 30% (when bearish) and 70% (when bullish)?

(4) In view of these results, what do you think about the feasibility of utilizing formula plans by the trust department at Peoples' National Bank?

254

PORTFOLIO MANAGEMENT USING MUTUAL FUNDS

James Hancock has been investing in the stock market for most of the six years since he received his baccalaureate degree from the University of Oregon. You met Hancock at an alumni party three years ago, you quickly became good friends, and now you regularly play racquetball with him on Saturday mornings. After you beat him once again last Saturday, he bought you a beer and shared some serious thoughts about his changing investment strategy.

Jim Hancock, age 29 and single, works for the Seattle advertising agency of Bachus and Whimple. Jim has done quite well in his professional position and is now responsible for several of his firm's smaller but growing accounts. His annual salary and bonus have grown by at least 20% on average, and by rather frugal living and a dedication to savings, your friend has accumulated an investment portfolio something in excess of $90,000. His only other asset of any magnitude, apart from the investment portfolio and a vintage foreign automobile, is a generous retirement account provided by Bachus and Whimple.

Hancock describes his investment strategy as the systematic purchase and holding of round lots of common stocks listed on the New York Stock Exchange. Of his current twelve holdings, eight were based on his own reading and research at the business school of the University of Washington, while the other four stocks were bought on the basis of tips from his broker and/or friends. Jim further shares that during the past six years, he has sold only two common shares -- both the result of recommendations from his broker.

In terms of achieved investment performance, Jim Hancock believes that he has done pretty well overall -- although in answer to your question, he has no idea what annual rate of return he has experienced from his common stock portfolio. But after another beer and further conversation, Jim admits that he has recently been somewhat more concerned about just how well he is doing. In particular, two of his purchases last year, again on the basis of broker and friend recommendations, have either not advanced or declined somewhat in what has been an otherwise upward stock market. With his increasing responsibilities at Bachus and Whimple, Hancock begins to wonder just how long he should continue to manage his investment portfolio by himself?

That same question occurred to him again last weekend when Jim had an opportunity to view an interesting video tape entitled, "Portfolio Management Using Mutual Funds." The speaker on the tape, a representative of a large mutual fund management company, argued convincingly that many investors may be more comfortable with, and, indeed, even fare better with, a strategy of investing in mutual funds -- rather than in individual common stocks. An important part of the suggested strategy is to carefully match the expressed goals of the investor with the objectives and investment philosophies of each alternative mutual fund.

The speaker went on to illustrate his firm's suggested mutual fund strategy for several different scenarios involving investors at different age levels, occupations, and economic situations. Perhaps not surprisingly, the mutual funds used in those illustrations were those offered by his firm. Hancock watched the tape a second time and took copious notes which he shares with you.

Hancock also reports to you that he has decided to switch his account to the local office of Merrill Lynch, Pierce, Fenner & Smith. He is impressed with his new broker who seems to have a somewhat more conservative perspective on the stock market. In addition, Hancock is impressed by the large group of mutual funds that is offered by Merrill Lynch. He gives you a copy of those mutual funds, together with their objectives and portfolio concepts (see Exhibit 1 below).

Jim Hancock asks if you will help him go through an exercise of thinking about how he should revise his portfolio from common stocks to mutual funds, and how that portfolio should be managed over time. You point out that the answer depends heavily on Jim's age, married status, and level of investment wealth. In particular, you agree to try and decide on appropriate mutual fund investments for each of six different scenarios, somewhat like what Jim viewed on the video presentation -- except that he wants to use the Merrill Lynch group of mutual funds.

Next Saturday, the two of you agree to compare your suggested portfolios for the following scenarios:

(1) Single professional, age 30, $90,000 investment wealth

(2) Two-career married couple, ages 35, $150,000

(3) Married couple, ages 45, two children, wife not working, $220,000

(4) Two-career married couple, ages 55, kids in college, $270,000

(5) Retired couple, ages 65, $450,000

(6) Bachus and Whimple pension plan, 15 covered employees, average age 47, $3.2 million

High need of tax exempt

Less need of tax exempt

256

Exhibit 1

MERRILL LYNCH MUTUAL FUNDS

A. Growth and Income

1. **Merrill Lynch International Holdings, Inc.**
   Objective: Highest total investment return consistent
   with prudent risk
   Portfolio concept: Investment in a world-wide portfolio
   of securities, primarily common stocks, to reduce
   volatility and enhance potential return

2. **Merrill Lynch Capital Fund, Inc.**
   Objective: Highest total investment return consistent
   with prudent risk
   Portfolio concept: Emphasizes stocks of financially strong
   companies exhibiting above-average profitability
   characteristics, selling at lower-than-average market
   valuations; corporate bonds and money market instruments,
   when appropriate

3. **Merrill Lynch Basic Value Fund, Inc.**
   Objective: Capital appreciation, then income
   Portfolio concept: Equities that appear undervalued,
   especially those selling at a discount from book value or
   at historically low price/earnings ratios

4. **Merrill Lynch Strategic Dividend Fund, Inc.**
   Objective: Long-term total return
   Portfolio Concept: Investment primarily in a diversified
   portfolio of common stocks which yield more than the
   Standard & Poor's 500 Composite Stock Price Index

5. **Merrill Lynch Global Convertible Fund, Inc.**
   Objective: High total return
   Portfolio Concept: Investment primarily in an
   internationally diversified portfolio of convertible
   debt securities, convertible preferred stocks and
   "synthetic" convertible securities

B. Growth

6. **Merrill Lynch Special Value Fund, Inc.**
   Objective: Long-term growth
   Portfolio Concept: Emphasizes securities of relatively
   small market capitalization companies, frequently with
   some unique product or service, that sell at very modest
   valuations at time of purchase

Age	30	35	45	55	65	Pension
A	30	25	20	15	10	
B	40	50	30	10	0	25
C	10	5	15	10	60	30
D	10	10	25	25	20	40
E	10	10	10	40	10	0
				10	10	5

257

7. Merrill Lynch Pacific Fund, Inc.
    Objective: Long-term growth
    Portfolio Concept: Securities of corporations located in
       the Far East and Western Pacific providing international
       diversification for United States investors

8. Merrill Lynch Phoenix Fund, Inc.*
    Objective: Long-term growth
    Portfolio Concept: A diversified portfolio of equity and
       fixed-income securities that are significantly under-
       valued, given current or future prospects

9. Merrill Lynch Fund for Tomorrow
    Objective: Long-term growth
    Portfolio Concept: Investment in a portfolio of good-
       quality securities, primarily common stocks, positioned
       to potentially benefit from demographic and cultural
       changes as they affect consumer markets

10. Merrill Lynch Natural Resources Trust
    Objective: Long-term growth and protection of capital
    Portfolio Concept: Investment in securities of domestic
       and foreign companies that possess substantial natural
       resource assets

11. Sci/Tech Holdings
    Objective: Long-term capital appreciation
    Portfolio Concept: Worldwide investment in securities of
       companies deriving income from sales of products or
       services in science or technology

12. Merrill Lynch EuroFund
    Objective: Capital appreciation
    Portfolio Concept: Investment primarily in equities of
       corporations located in Western European countries

C. Income

13. Merrill Lynch Corporate Bond Fund, Inc. -- Intermediate
    Term Portfolio
    Objective: High income through managed portfolios
       primarily of taxable corporate fixed income securities
    Portfolio Concept: Medium and high-quality corporate
       bonds of intermediate maturities to help limit wide
       fluctuations in share value while providing attractive
       income
----

*Merrill Lynch Phoenix Fund, Inc. is not related to Phoenix
   Life Insurance Company or any of its subsidiaries or
   affiliates, including the Phoenix Series Fund.

14. Merrill Lynch Corporate Bond Fund, Inc. -- High Quality Portfolio
    Objective: High income through managed portfolios primarily of taxable corporate fixed income securities
    Portfolio Concept: Long-term corporate bonds rated A or better, offering attractive income, subject to cyclical market fluctuations

15. Merrill Lynch Corporate Bond Fund, Inc. -- High Income Portfolio
    Objective: High income through managed portfolios primarily of taxable corporate fixed income securities
    Portfolio Concept: Lower-rated corporate bonds for current high return, subject to greater market fluctuations and risk

16. Merrill Lynch Federal Securities Trust
    Objective: High current return through a fully managed portfolio of U.S. Government and agency securities
    Portfolio Concept: Fully managed portfolio of U.S. Government and agency securities

D. Tax-Exempt Income

17. Merrill Lynch Municipal Bond Fund, Inc. -- Limited Maturity Portfolio
    Objective: Federally-tax-exempt income through investment in municipal securities
    Portfolio Concept: Relative stability of principal through short to intermediate-term municipals with somewhat lower tax-exempt income

18. Merrill Lynch Municipal Bond Fund, Inc. -- Insured Portfolio
    Objective: Federally-tax-exempt income through investment in municipal securities
    Portfolio Concept: High quality municipals, for which timely payment of interest and principal is insured by an independent insurer (Neither market value of the bonds nor share value of the portfolio is guaranteed.)

19. Merrill Lynch Municipal Bond Fund, Inc. -- High Yield Portfolio
    Objective: Federally-tax-exempt income through investment in municipal securities
    Portfolio Concept: Medium to lower grade long-term tax-exempt issues for current high return, subject to greater market fluctuations and risk

20. Merrill Lynch Municipal Income Fund
    Objective: As high a level of income exempt from Federal

259

income taxes as is consistent with the Fund's investment
policies and prudent investment management

Portfolio Concept: Municipal bonds with remaining
maturities of twelve years or less; under normal market
conditions, it is anticipated that the average maturity
of the Fund's portfolio will be between five and ten
years

21. Merrill Lynch New York Municipal Bond Fund
Objective: As high a level of income exempt from Federal,
New York State and New York City income taxes as is
consistent with prudent investment management

Portfolio Concept: Investment primarily in a diversified
portfolio of long-term investment grade obligations

22. Merrill Lynch California Municipal Bond Fund
Objective: As high a level of income exempt from Federal
and California State income taxes as is consistent with
prudent investment management

Portfolio Concept: Investment primarily in a diversified
portfolio of long-term investment grade obligations

E. Cash Reserves

23. Merrill Lynch Ready Assets Trust
Objective: Preservation of capital, liquidity, and current
income

Portfolio Concept: Short-term money market instruments,
including U.S. Treasuries and Government agency
securities, certificates of deposit and commercial paper

24. Merrill Lynch U.S.A. Government Reserves
Objective: Preservation of capital, current income and
liquidity

Portfolio Concept: Primarily short-term U.S. Government-
guaranteed securities providing money market yields
and liquidity

A Composite Portfolio Benchmark for Pension Plans

by Gary P. Brinson, Jeffrey J. Diermeier and Gary G. Schlarbaum

Successful management of a pension plan portfolio requires the focusing of investment attention on the asset configuration of the total portfolio. This focus is facilitated by a composite benchmark portfolio called the Multiple Markets Index (MMI). The MMI measures the composite performance of nine distinct asset classes representing the broad spectrum of primary wealth-generating investments available to the institutional investor. It is designed to offer an attractive return at risk levels acceptable to such investors.

Of the 80 asset classes and subclasses considered for inclusion in the MMI, nine were selected—domestic large capitalization equities, domestic small capitalization equities, international equities, venture capital, domestic bonds, international dollar bonds, nondollar bonds, real estate and cash equivalents. Portfolio optimization procedures were used to assign appropriate weights to these classes. The weights assigned were supported by the theoretical implications of New Equilibrium Theory, which suggest that institutional investors should overweight higher-risk asset classes such as domestic common stock and venture capital and underweight bonds, cash and international securities.

The MMI should outperform an equal-risk portfolio comprising only domestic stocks and bonds (the 60-40 mix typical of pension portfolios) by approximately 60 basis points a year. Furthermore, data over the 1960–84 period indicate that the MMI would have outperformed the SEI linked median balanced manager by approximately 3 per cent per year.

THE PORTFOLIO MANAGEMENT process of most pension plan assets has been splintered. In an age of specialization, balanced managers have become passé; specialty managers are in demand. Large plans with a single manager are uncommon, while plans with multiple managers are the norm. Individual vagaries within the pension plan are given more attention than the total, overall result. Investment talent is focused on the segments; the total asset configuration is a matter for administrative attention. The emphasis is precisely the opposite of that needed for successful overall results.

Consider the record. Figure A plots wealth indexes for the SEI median large pension plan, the investable capital market and the personal

consumption deflator over the 1969–84 period.[1] Their compound annual rates of growth, based on beginning and ending index values, are 7.1, 8.7 and 6.2 per cent, respectively. The rate of growth of the median large plan exceeded the rate of inflation, but lagged the rate of growth of the passively managed investable capital market portfolio. Moreover, the median large plan lagged the rate of growth of every class included in the investable capital market portfolio. Table I gives the geometric mean returns for the median large plan and each of the asset classes.

There is clearly room for improvement. But improved total fund performance requires placing greater emphasis on those decisions that have the greatest impact on total performance:

(1) the policy decision concerning the asset classes included for potential investment;

(2) the investment policy weights assigned to those investment classes, where asset allocation is approached under the extended corporate planning horizon;

1. Footnotes appear at end of article.

The authors are President, Managing Director and Vice President, respectively, of First Chicago Investment Advisors.

Figure A Median Large Plan Performance vs. Inflation and the
Capital Market (12/31/1969 = 100)

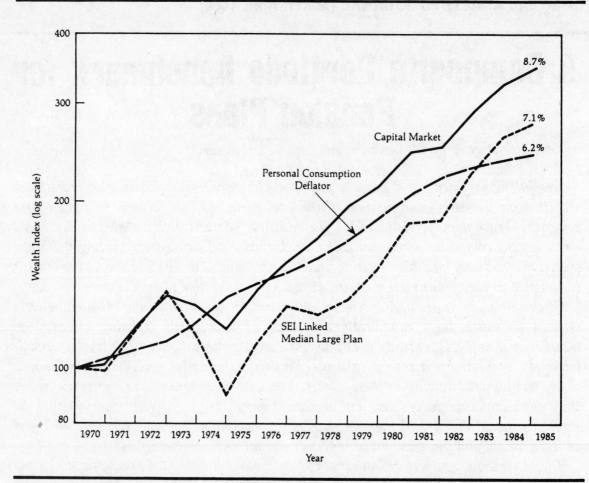

(3) the shorter-term strategic weighting of these asset classes, which may differ from the policy weights; and

(4) the selection of individual managers within or across those investment markets.

To ensure a plan's overall health, a substantial amount of investment resources and controls must be devoted to these key policy decisions.

Table I Asset Class Data Summary, 1970–1984

| | Annualized | |
| | Geometric | Standard |
Asset Class	Mean	Deviation
Domestic Equities	9.01%	19.02%
International Equities	9.54	19.85
Venture Capital	13.81	40.78
Domestic Bonds	8.74	8.13
International Dollar Bonds	9.57	7.10
Nondollar Bonds	8.60	9.86
Real Estate	10.81	3.28
Cash Equivalents	7.86	3.02
SEI Linked Median Large Plan	7.06	14.01

Source: First Chicago Investment Advisors.

The first two decisions, in particular, explain 90 to 95 per cent of the variation in total plan performance.[2]

This article describes a composite benchmark portfolio that facilitates a focus on the total portfolio with particular emphasis on the asset allocation decisions. The Multiple Markets Index (MMI) measures the composite performance of nine distinct asset classes representing the broad spectrum of primary wealth-generating investments available to the institutional investor.[3] As an integrated market index that is fair and representative of the institutional investment environment and that offers an attractive combination of expected return and risk exposure, the MMI provides the pension plan sponsor with an invaluable performance measurement tool.

Constructing the MMI

Construction of the MMI is based on the assumption that plan sponsors desire portfolios that are efficient in mean-variance terms.[4] With-

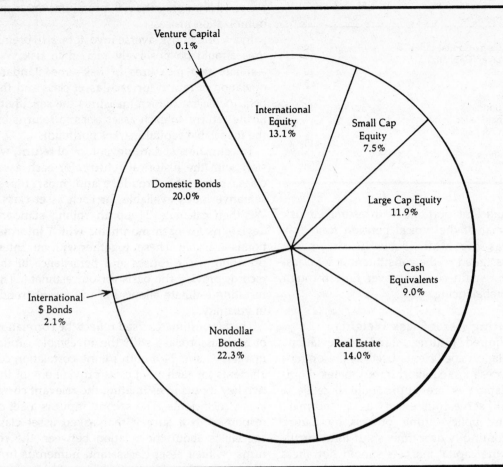

in this framework, construction proceeds by first selecting a set of asset classes for inclusion and then determining the appropriate weights to assign to these classes.

Asset Classes

We considered over 80 asset classes and subclasses for inclusion in the MMI. All asset classes that enhance the opportunity for meaningful diversification are at least potentially of interest. Moreover, it is desirable to participate in as broad a capital market as possible. Nevertheless, not all asset classes initially considered make sense for a pension plan portfolio.

Table II presents the criteria we used to reduce the list of potential asset classes to what we call the "investable capital market." In short, the investable capital market consists of primary wealth-generating assets where sufficient markets have developed and legal hurdles do not prohibit meaningful investment by tax-exempt investors. Figure B displays the nine asset classes, together with their market weights. The appendix describes the return series used to represent these classes.

Of course, the typical institutional investor will probably not hold these assets in the same proportions by which they are represented in the overall market. We thus used the portfolio optimization process to obtain an efficient (in mean-variance terms) set of asset class weights for the MMI.[5] The only constraints placed on the optimizations were that all weights had to be non-negative, and the maximum weight for venture capital had to be 5 per cent.[6] The mean-

Table II   Suitability Criteria

Analytical
    Adequate Control and Regulation
    Marketability and Liquidity
    Meaningful Impact
    Nonredundant
    Manageable Estimation Risk
Legal
Talent Availability

Table III Composition of the Multiple Markets Index

Asset Class	Weight
Equities	
Domestic Large Capitalization	30%
Domestic Small Capitalization	15
International	10
Venture Capital	5
Fixed Income	
Domestic Bonds	15
International Dollar Bonds	4
Nondollar Bonds	6
Real Estate	15
Cash Equivalents	0
	100%

variance efficient portfolio with estimated risk equal to that of the typical pension fund was selected as the MMI. Table III shows the weights assigned to the constituent asset classes. These remain constant over time through quarterly rebalancing.

Computing Asset Class Weights

The required returns, standard deviations and correlation coefficients used in the optimization process are equilibrium estimates. Equilibrium estimates are appropriate because a benchmark serves, in effect, as a "normal" policy. The policy-setting process by nature requires continuity over time; short-term fluctuations in the capital markets should not affect policy decisions.

We assess long-term equilibrium rates of return by separately estimating a risk-free real rate of return, an inflation premium and a risk premium, and adding them together.[7] We assume that the inflation premium and the real rate of return are the same for each asset class.

Only the risk premium varies across the asset classes, hence only the risk premiums enter the optimization process.

In a world of risk-averse investors, risk premiums should be positively related to risk. We estimate two measures of risk—the standard deviation of return for each asset class and the beta coefficient (which measures the sensitivity of the returns in each asset class to returns on the investable capital market portfolio).

To estimate standard deviations of return, we start with the historical returns for each asset class, using the broadest and most representative index available for each asset class.[8] We then calculate 24-month rolling standard deviations for each month for which information is available. These, together with our interpretation of the causes and persistence of the record, provide the basis for our estimate. The resulting estimate allows for any recent trends in volatility.

The beta estimates used reflect the correlation of each asset class with the investable capital market. Again, 24-month rolling correlation coefficients for each asset class provide one of the two key inputs in estimating the relevant correlation coefficients. The second input is a set of responses to a survey that asked asset class specialists about the relation between the returns on their asset classes and numerous fundamental and political variables.

We use two risk-return relations to obtain equilibrium risk premiums. At one extreme, we assume that capital markets are completely segmented. This approach assumes that investors in risky assets limit their focus to one asset class—i.e., investment decisions are made in

Table IV Equilibrium Asset Class Risk Premium Assessments

Asset Class	Segmented Markets Approach		Integrated Markets Approach	
	Std. Dev.	Risk Premium[a]	Beta	Risk Premium[b]
Equities				
Domestic Large Capitalization	16.50%	6.60%	1.31	4.74%
Domestic Small Capitalization	22.00	8.80	1.81	6.55
International[c]	17.80	7.12	0.46	1.94
Venture Capital	40.00	16.00	2.44	8.83
Fixed Income				
Domestic Bonds	8.50	3.40	0.59	2.14
International Dollar Bonds	8.00	3.20	0.56	2.03
Nondollar Bonds[c]	7.25	2.90	0.20	0.87
Real Estate	14.00	5.60	1.02	3.69
Cash Equivalents	1.50	0.60	0.00	0.00

a. Price of risk assumed to be 40 basis points per unit of risk.
b. Assumes risk premium to the investable capital market portfolio of 3.6 per cent.
c. Risk measured from the viewpoint of the local currency investor.

Table V Optimization Inputs

	Risk Premium	Less Passive Fee	Realizable Risk Premium*	Risk*
Domestic Large Capitalization Equities	5.80%	0.10%	5.70%	16.50%
Domestic Small Capitalization Equities	7.55	0.20	7.35	22.00
International Equities	6.35	0.25	6.10	20.50
Venture Capital	15.00	2.00	13.00	40.00
Domestic Bonds	2.30	0.10	2.20	8.50
International Dollar Bonds	2.25	0.10	2.15	8.00
Nondollar Bonds	2.70	0.15	2.55	12.00
Real Estate	4.80	0.80	4.00	14.00
Treasury Bills	0.00	0.00	0.00	1.50

* Optimization inputs.

isolation, as individual asset class specialists consider none of the alternative classes except cash equivalents. Standard deviations of return are the appropriate measure of risk in this case. We use a linear relation between standard deviation and risk premium to assess segmented risk premiums. Table IV gives these standard deviations and resulting risk premiums.

At the other extreme, we assume that capital markets are thoroughly integrated. This approach assumes that investors evaluate investment alternatives within a portfolio context, taking into account the diversification, or lack of perfect correlation, between markets. The relevant measure of risk in this setting is beta—a measure of the contribution of an asset or asset class to the risk of a diversified portfolio. Again, we use a linear relation to determine risk premiums. Table IV gives the betas and resulting risk premiums.

The final estimates of risk premium for each asset class, based on our best judgment, are constrained to lie between the estimates obtained using these two extreme views of risk—integrated and segmented.[9] The rank ordering of the risk premium estimates across the asset classes is the same for both approaches and is preserved in the final estimates.

The first column of Table V presents the equilibrium risk premium estimates. Each estimate is reduced by a passive management fee specific to each asset class in order to reflect the unavoidable costs of investing in the asset classes. The third and fourth columns of the table present the resulting realizable risk premium estimates and the estimated standard deviations that enter the optimization process. Table VI gives the relevant correlation coefficients.

Additional Support

An alternative approach to determining investment policy weights provides results consistent with our optimization results. This approach uses the New Equilibrium Theory (NET) of Ibbotson, Diermeier and Siegel to suggest appropriate shadings of market value weights.[10] NET is qualitative in nature, hence does not generate specific policy weights for each of the asset classes. It does suggest, however, which asset classes should be overweighted and which underweighted relative to market value weights.

NET explicitly recognizes that investors are heterogeneous, having different tax situations, institutional constraints and time horizons. NET assumes that investors regard each asset as a bundle of characteristics, some risk-oriented and some non-risk-oriented. Different investors react differently to different characteristics. Each investor translates each characteristic into a cost and requires compensation, in the form of expected return, for bearing this cost. Investors are thus interested in returns net of all costs, which are individually determined and include costs of all risks, taxes and lack of marketability.

The point of departure for the NET approach is the determination of market value weights.

Table VI Long-Term Asset Class Correlation Forecasts

	1	2	3	4	5	6	7	8	9
1. Domestic Large Capitalization Equities	1.00								
2. Domestic Small Capitalization Equities	0.85	1.00							
3. International Equities	0.55	0.55	1.00						
4. Venture Capital	0.40	0.45	0.55	1.00					
5. Domestic Bonds	0.45	0.40	0.30	0.15	1.00				
6. International Dollar Bonds	0.45	0.40	0.35	0.20	0.90	1.00			
7. Nondollar Bonds	0.15	0.25	0.70	0.40	0.40	0.40	1.00		
8. Real Estate	0.50	0.55	0.50	0.45	0.30	0.35	0.30	1.00	
9. Cash Equivalents	0.00	0.00	0.00	0.00	0.00	0.00	0.00	0.00	1.00

Table VII   Plan Sponsor Characteristics

Large Size
Long Horizon
U. S. Based Domicile
ERISA Governance
Tax-Exempt Status
Total Return Objective

The first step is to identify the relevant characteristics of plan sponsors. Table VII shows a sample list of these characteristics. Knowledge of individual plan characteristics comes into play at this juncture.

The second step is to identify the relevant characteristics of the available asset classes. The interplay of investor characteristics and asset characteristics determines how the policy weight of each asset class differs from its market weight. Our analysis suggests that pension fund portfolios should be overweighted in the higher-risk asset classes of domestic common stocks and venture capital. Conversely, bonds, cash and international securities should be underweighted. These qualitative conclusions support the quantitative conclusions of the optimization process.

Finally, we applied one additional check on the consistency of the set of estimates given in Tables V and VI. We set the long-term estimates of equilibrium return so that the market-weighted sum of the implied real returns was consistent with our forecast of real economic growth.[11] We forecast long-term world economic growth to be approximately 3 per cent per year, in real terms. This is consistent with the market-weighted sum of the asset classes' risk premiums, which is 3.6 per cent per year on a pretax basis. This macroconsistency is vital to realistic and proper estimation of long-term rates of return.

Representing the Institutional Arena

One of the requirements of any investment benchmark is that it be a fair and representative proxy for what investors could have achieved. By fair, we mean that the targeted audience should see the MMI as a viable alternative to their current total investment portfolio. By representative, we mean that the returns of the MMI should be relevant to the environment in which the pension sponsor operates.

The test of fairness is met in several ways. First, the MMI does not include any asset class in which the pension industry does not already invest sizable sums of capital. Second, the MMI uses passive, fixed policy weights, hence requires no unusual or creative skills in market timing. Third, the returns to the individual asset classes are passive and based on broadly defined markets. Fourth, ignoring transaction costs, the returns of the MMI can be readily duplicated in the real world by participation in any of the designated markets.[12]

The MMI meets the test of representativeness in two ways. First, as in the fairness test, the asset classes used are both available and used by the pension sponsor population. Second, the MMI is carefully calibrated to have the same degree of risk as the "typical" pension fund. As risk is believed to be the key characteristic systematically related to excess rates of return, forcing the risk of the MMI to equal that of the typical pension plan allows for meaningful performance measurement.

The calibration of the MMI's risk to match that of the typical pension plan is a two-step process. First, we estimate the risk of the typical plan. The average pension fund investment mix over the past 25 years has been approximately 60 per cent domestic equities and 40 per cent domestic bonds. Furthermore, an annually rebalanced "60-40 mix" and the median volatility fund of the SEI balanced funds universe had approximately the same standard deviation of return over the past decade.

Second, we target the forecast risk of the MMI to that of the 60-40 portfolio mix. Our long-term forecasts of standard deviations for domestic stocks and bonds and our forecast correlation coefficient imply an annual standard deviation of 12.5 per cent for the 60-40 mix. This serves as the target for the MMI standard deviation. The actual standard deviation—12.8 per cent—results from rounding to obtain even numbers for the final MMI weights.

Expected Return and Risk

The MMI should outperform an equal-risk portfolio comprising only domestic stocks and bonds (the 60-40 mix portfolio) by approximately 60 basis points a year, after deduction of passive fees. It should outperform the total pension plan account median by at least as much. This systematic gain of 60 basis points is highly significant: A 1 per cent increase in the actuarial investment assumptions for most plans would reduce overall plan costs by roughly 20 to 25 per cent.[13]

Figure C illustrates the attractiveness of the

Figure C   Attainable Efficient Frontiers

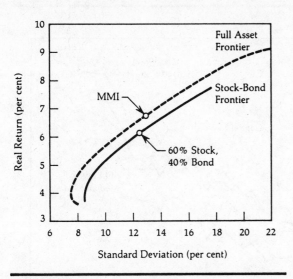

MMI relative to the traditional 60-40 mix. The figure shows two sets of efficient portfolios in risk-return space—the first set being in the set of mean-variance efficient portfolios that can be constructed using the nine asset classes included in the MMI and the second the set of mean-variance portfolios obtainable if investments are limited to domestic stocks and bonds. The expected real return of the MMI portfolio is approximately 60 basis points per year higher than that of the 60-40 mix.

Historical Performance

The historical performance of the MMI is also very impressive. Table VIII shows several measures of performance based on annual return data for the 1960–84 period. The MMI has the highest geometric mean return of any of the indexes examined. Notably, the geometric mean return of the MMI is approximately 3 per cent per year greater than that of the SEI linked median balanced manager.

The last column of the table shows the Sharpe ratio for the various indexes. This ratio is defined as the ratio of the excess return (mean return for the index less the mean return for Treasury bills) to the standard deviation of return for the index. It combines risk and return measures into one useful measure of performance for the investor interested in mean and variance. A comparison of the Sharpe ratios of the indexes indicates that the MMI has a much higher ratio than any of the other indexes.

The historical performance of the MMI based on quarterly data is just as impressive. Table IX shows relevant statistics for the 1970–84 period. Again, the MMI has the highest geometric mean return and the highest Sharpe ratio. Figure D compares the performance of the MMI with the various balanced indexes. Again, the superior performance of the MMI is evident.[14]

In sum, the MMI significantly outperformed the typical pension fund over the two time periods considered. In addition, it outperformed all the alternative performance benchmarks examined. We believe it will continue to do so in the future.

Implications

In 1973, William Sharpe wrote:

"For present [investment policy] purposes, we concentrate on bonds and stocks, assuming they are the only available media. Extensions to include other assets must await further research."[15]

MMI allows us to add to the traditional set of pension investments the asset classes of real estate, venture capital and international stocks and bonds. We have melded these diverse asset classes into a suitable benchmark for the typical pension plan total account.

Table VIII   Historical Mean Returns, Standard Deviations and Sharpe Ratios, 1960–1984 (annual data)

Index	Arithmetic Mean	Geometric Mean	Standard Deviation	Sharpe Ratio
MMI	10.36%	9.67%	12.40%	0.328
Inv. Cap. Market	7.60	7.37	7.03	0.186
60–40 Stock-Bond Mix	8.64	8.03	11.46	0.205
SEI Linked Median Balanced Manager*	7.36	6.81	10.82	0.099

* 1963–84.

Table IX   Historical Mean Returns, Standard Deviations and Sharpe Ratios, 1970–1984 (quarterly data)

Index	Arithmetic Mean	Geometric Mean	Standard Deviation	Sharpe Ratio
MMI	2.70%	2.49%	6.45%	0.122
Inv. Cap. Market	2.22	2.11	4.70	0.066
60–40 Stock-Bond Mix	2.46	2.24	6.76	0.081
SEI Linked Median Balanced Manager	2.06	1.85	6.49	0.023

Figure D   Multiple Markets Index and Three Balanced
Indexes (12/31/1969 = 100)

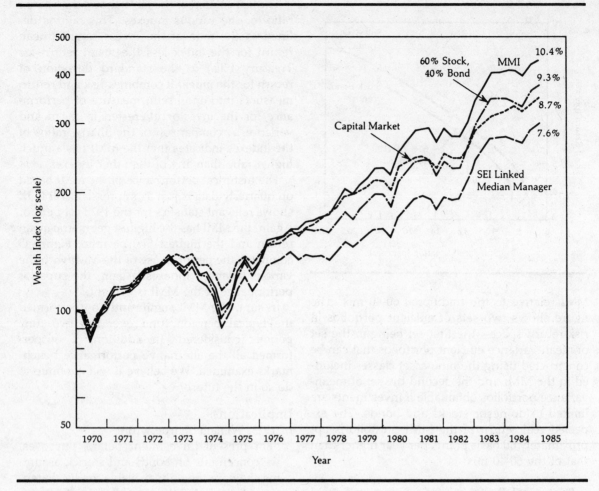

This index, updated quarterly, should redirect plan sponsor attention toward the total portfolio, and away from its important, but less critical, investment components. The result should be better bottom-line performance for the total account and reduced pension charges to the corporation.

The MMI will not, of course, be a suitable proxy for every pension plan. Each plan sponsor must determine the appropriate risk level for its plan. The method of benchmark construction underlying the MMI is, however, useful for most plan sponsors. It is a method that focuses attention on the most critical aspects of plan performance—management, measurement and control of the total portfolio—and away from the specialized asset segments that have too long dominated the thinking of pension plan sponsors. ■

Appendix

The following is a brief list of sources and method for data contained in the text.

Domestic Equities: For the purposes of constructing the MMI, large capitalization equities are defined as the total return to a portfolio containing the top 20 per cent (by number) of the firms on the New York Stock Exchange when ranked by capitalization. Since 1970, large capitalization equities have comprised about two-thirds of the total U. S. domestic equity market. Small capitalization equities are the residual of the total U. S. domestic equity market and the large capitalization equity portfolio returns. Weights for the two portfolios were calculated for each year end and held constant throughout the year. For 1971 to the present, the performance of the U. S. domestic equity market is proxied by the Wilshire 5000 Total Performance Index. For 1970, actual portfolios were constructed for both large and small capitalization, and their returns were calculated.

Non-U.S. Equities: Price performance, yield and total return for separate countries were taken from data available in the Capital International Perspective. For 1970 to the present, the non-U.S. index was created from Capital International Perspective by removing the effects of the U.S. market from the world index. Weights were updated quarterly, and allowed to drift within the quarter in accordance with changes in capital values. The yield series used is adjusted to reflect a 15 per cent withholding on most foreign dividends.

Venture Capital: Returns were generated by equally weighting the returns on publicly held venture companies as reported in the *Venture Capital Journal*. SBIC's were excluded.

Domestic Fixed Income: From 1973 to the present, the Lehman Brothers Kuhn Loeb Government/Corporate Bond Index was used. A proxy for the LBKL based on the Salomon Brothers High Grade Corporate Bond Index was used for 1970–72.

Dollar Bonds: The entire population of international dollar-denominated bonds was gathered and summarized on a bond-by-bond basis. Beginning in 1981, a weighted average of the Lehman Brothers Kuhn Loeb Yankee and Global Indexes was used.[16]

Nondollar Bonds: Returns for foreign cash, foreign crossborder bonds and foreign domestic bonds were taken from Ibbotson, Carr and Robinson. Beginning in 1981, returns for the nondollar bonds are based on a proxy of all nondollar bonds relative to the U.S. dollar provided by Salomon Brothers Inc.

U.S. Real Estate: Returns for 1970 through 1981 were based on equally weighted averages of equity real estate returns from commingled fund unit values made available by the Frank Russell Company.

Cash Equivalents: Cash returns used for MMI are 30-day Treasury bills rolled over at maturity.

Footnotes

1. The investable capital market is a value-weighted portfolio of all asset classes allowing meaningful investment by tax-exempt investors. It is discussed more fully later in the text.
2. See G.P. Brinson, G. Beebower and L.R. Hood, "The Determinants of Portfolio Performance," *Financial Analysts Journal*, forthcoming.
3. There are, of course, many different ways of dividing the universe of investable assets into asset classes. Our choice of nine classes is only one of these, but it is a natural and meaningful division. We have work in progress that, based on correlations of returns between possible asset classes, could lead to a slightly different set of classes. In addition, we intend to investigate the feasibility of using major factors affecting asset returns as the basis for asset classification.
4. This assumption is not universally accepted. Some have argued for a pension portfolio of all bonds. (See F. Black, "The Tax Consequences of Long-Run Pension Policy," *Financial Analysts Journal*, July/August 1980, pp. 21–28, and I. Tepper, "Taxation and Corporate Pension Policy," *Journal of Finance*, March 1981, pp. 1–14.) Their argument is based on tax arbitrage. It is an interesting argument. Nevertheless, the structure of pension plan portfolios indicates that the argument has not been accepted by plan sponsors.
5. The process of generating an efficient set was first advocated by H.M. Markowitz, "Portfolio Selection," *Journal of Finance*, March 1952, pp. 77–91 and Markowitz, *Portfolio Selection* (New York: John Wiley & Sons, 1959).
6. The weight assigned to venture capital was constrained to 5 per cent because of the relative size of the industry.
7. This basic framework is attributed to I. Fisher, *The Theory of Interest*, reprinted from the 1930 edition (New York: Augustus M. Kelley, 1965).
8. The MMI is rooted in a broadly based joint effort by First Chicago Investment Advisors and the firm of R.G. Ibbotson and Company in which historical returns and market values for over 80 different asset and subasset classes were gathered for the period 1960 to the present. See R.G. Ibbotson, R.C. Carr and A.W. Robinson, "International Equity and Bond Returns," *Financial Analysts Journal*, July/August 1982, pp. 61–83, and R.G. Ibbotson and L.B. Siegel, "The World Market Wealth Portfolio," *Journal of Portfolio Management*, Winter 1983, pp. 5–17.
9. Work in progress focuses on the question of which measure of risk is more appropriate for the purpose of assessing required returns. The question of whether the risk-return relation is in fact linear is also being considered.
10. See R.G. Ibbotson, J.J. Diermeier and L.B. Siegel, "The Demand for Capital Market Returns: A New Equilibrium Theory," *Financial Analysts Journal*, January/February 1984, pp. 22–33.

11. For a method and rationale for translating a long-term economic forecast into estimates of capital market return, see J.J. Diermeier, R.G. Ibbotson and L.B. Siegel, "The Supply of Capital Market Returns," *Financial Analysts Journal*, March/April 1984, pp. 74–80.

12. The transaction costs incurred in managing an MMI portfolio would be minimal. Once initial portfolio positions were taken and the costs of structuring paid for, relatively little rebalancing would be sufficient to replicate the performance of the MMI.

13. See D. McGill, "Fundamentals of Private Pensions" (Pension Research Council, 1979). A specialty manager with 10 per cent of a total portfolio would have to outperform his standard by 6 per cent per year to have the same impact on the total portfolio.

14. Although the risk-return characteristics of the MMI make it likely that it will provide superior performance over longer periods of time, it will not necessarily provide superior performance over shorter time intervals.

15. W.F. Sharpe, "Bonds vs. Stocks: Some Lessons from Capital Market Theory," *Financial Analysts Journal*, November/December 1973, pp. 74–80.

16. For a more complete description, see Ibbotson, Carr and Robinson, "International Equity," *op.cit.*

Integrated Asset Allocation

William F. Sharpe

Integrated asset allocation provides a framework for viewing the key elements of the important asset allocation decision. Its general perspective subsumes more traditional asset allocation procedures in current use, including strategic, tactical and insurance approaches.

Integrated asset allocation is concerned with the optimization of an investor's net worth. It thus deals with expected net worth (assets less liabilities) and standard deviation of future net worth, given the investor's willingness to take on added net worth risk in order to increase expected net worth.

The asset allocation procedure involves several major steps. The investor's current net worth is transformed, via a risk tolerance function, into the investor's risk tolerance. At the same time, current capital market conditions—prices, earnings, dividends—are transformed (via a heuristic or complex process) into expected returns, risks and correlations for various asset classes. Given these predictions and the investor's risk tolerance, an "optimizer" (ranging in complexity from a simple rule of thumb to a full-scale quadratic program) determines the most appropriate asset mix. The mix determines actual returns to the investor over the period. These returns feed back, via investor net worth and capital market conditions, into the next period's allocation procedure.

ASSET ALLOCATION ANALYSIS is hardly new. The first formal strategic allocation studies were performed well over a decade ago. Asset mixes have been managed using market timing models for several years. Portfolio insurance procedures have been used to allocate assets dynamically for at least three years.

This article provides an overview of a general approach to asset allocation—one that subsumes more traditional procedures as special cases. We begin with a description of the overall approach, termed *integrated asset allocation*. Next we discuss alternative objectives for asset allocation analyses. As many studies are limited to two asset classes, we treat such cases in some detail. Finally, we describe the three major

William Sharpe is President of Sharpe-Russell Research, Inc.

The author thanks Keith Ambachtsheer, Ernest Bianco, George Chow, Peter Dietz, Don Ezra, Mark Friebel, Kelly Haughton, Martin Leibowitz, Douglas Love, André Perold, Andrew Turner and Jan Twardowski for their comments and suggestions.

types of asset allocation analysis currently being performed—*strategic, tactical* and *insured*.

Integrated Asset Allocation

Figure A illustrates the major steps involved in asset allocation. The boxes on the left are concerned with the capital markets; those on the right are specific to an investor. The boxes in the middle bring together aspects of the capital markets and the investor's circumstances to determine the investor's asset mix and its performance. The process begins at the top and proceeds downward, then repeats.

Box I1 represents the current values of the investor's assets and liabilities and, by implication, net worth. An individual investor's net worth is his or her *wealth*; a pension fund's net worth is the plan *surplus*. Net worth will generally determine the investor's current tolerance for risk, shown in box I3. The relation between the investor's circumstances (box I1) and risk tolerance (box I3) can be portrayed by a *risk tolerance function*. It is shown in box I2.

Box C1 represents the current state of the capital markets. Included are such things as

Figure A   Integrated Asset Allocation

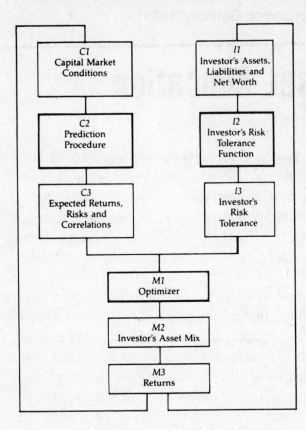

current and historical levels of stock and bond indexes, past and projected dividends and earnings. These data are the major inputs for predicting the expected returns and risks of various asset classes and the correlations of their returns (shown in box C3). Some procedure must be used to translate capital market conditions (box C1) into predictions about asset returns (box C3); it is represented by box C2.

Given an investor's risk tolerance (box I3) and predictions of assets' expected returns, risks and correlations (box C3), an optimizer can be employed to determine the most appropriate asset mix (box M2). Depending on such things as the number of assets, the optimizer (shown in box M1) may be a simple rule of thumb, a mathematical function or a full-scale quadratic program.

Box M3 represents actual returns to the investor. Given the investor's asset mix at the beginning of a period (box M2), the asset returns during the period (box M3) determine the value of the investor's assets at the beginning of the

next period. Given the nature of the investor's liabilities at the beginning of a period, changes in capital markets (including returns on fixed income obligations) and accrual of new obligations determine the investor's liabilities at the beginning of the next period. Returns in one period thus influence the investor's assets, liabilities and net worth at the beginning of the next period, as shown by the "feedback loop" from box M3 to box I1.

Returns during a period also constitute part of the overall capital market conditions at the beginning of the next period. This is shown by the feedback loop from box M3 to box C1. As these loops show, the process is a continuing one, with decisions from one period affecting those of the next.

From period to period, any (or all) of the items in boxes C1, C3, I1, I3, M2 and M3 may change. However, the items in boxes C2, I2 and M1 should remain fixed, because they represent the *decision rules* (procedures). Thus the investor's risk tolerance (box I3) may change, but the risk tolerance *function* (box I2) should not. Predictions of returns (box C3) may change, but not the *procedure* (box C2) for making such predictions. The optimal asset mix (box M2) may change, but not the *optimizer* (box M1) that determines it.

Many investors make some or all of the decisions shown in boxes I2, C2 and M1 "by hand" (and/or heuristically). In an increasing number of organizations, however, some or all of these procedures have been automated, with decision rules specified in advance, then followed routinely. Portfolio insurance procedures fall clearly into this category, as do certain process-driven tactical asset allocation methods.

To implement a fully *integrated asset allocation* procedure, one only (!) has to fill in (or leave out) the boxes. Traditional approaches do so, but in rather extreme ways.

Asset Allocation Objectives

To arrive at an optimal asset mix, an optimizer must have an explicit *objective function*. Typically, this involves the risk and expected value of some key attribute.

In integrated asset allocation analysis, the attribute is the investor's *net worth* at some future date. Optimization thus deals with expected future net worth and the standard deviation of future net worth.

272

Traditional analyses usually concentrate on the value of the investor's *assets* at some point in the future. Optimization thus deals with the expected return and standard deviation of return on current assets.

The nature of the objective function must also be reflected in the measure of risk tolerance, which indicates the investor's willingness to accept greater risk in order to obtain a greater expected reward. In traditional analysis, risk tolerance is typically concerned with the trade-off between expected return and standard deviation of return. In integrated asset allocation analysis, risk tolerance measures the investor's willingness to take on added net worth risk in order to increase expected net worth.

"Asset only" analyses can be considered special cases of integrated asset allocation in which liabilities equal zero (or are positive, but not subject to uncertainty).

Two-Asset Allocation

The remainder of this article will focus on cases in which only two assets are considered and liabilities equal zero. Many traditional asset allocation analyses conform to these restrictions, and we will discuss such approaches in this context. The appendix analyzes conditions for an optimal asset mix when multiple asset classes and liabilities are considered.

When only two assets are involved, the relation between the inputs and the optimal asset mix is particularly simple. Let the assets be S (e.g., stocks) and B (e.g., bonds or bills). As shown in the appendix, the optimal (dollar) amount to be invested in S can be computed as:

$$D_S = k_0 W + k_1 ART,$$

where k_0 and k_1 are parameters, W is the investor's current net worth, and ART is his or her *absolute risk tolerance*.

To determine the proportion of assets to be invested in stocks, divide both sides of the equation by W, giving:

$$\frac{D_S}{W} = k_0 + k_1 \frac{ART}{W}.$$

The latter ratio is termed the investor's *relative risk tolerance*. Representing this by RRT, and using the standard notation X_S to represent the relative amount invested in stocks gives:

$$X_S = k_0 + k_1 RRT.$$

If asset B is riskless, the value of k_0 becomes zero, giving:

$$D_S = k_1 ART$$

and

$$X_S = k_1 RRT.$$

The appendix shows that the values of k_0 and k_1 depend on the expected returns and risks of the assets and on the estimated correlation between their returns. Of particular importance is the fact that k_1 is proportional to the difference between the assets' expected returns:

$$k_1 = \frac{E_S - E_B}{k_2},$$

where k_2 depends (as does k_0) solely on the risks of the two assets and on the estimated correlation between their returns.

To avoid excess notation, no indication of time has been included in the equations. Each value is assumed to be relevant for the single period over which a decision is to be made. As will be seen, traditional approaches to asset allocation make different assumptions concerning the constancy of various aspects of these relationships over time.

Strategic Asset Allocation

Figure B portrays a typical strategic asset allocation analysis in terms comparable to those used for the more general integrated asset allocation.[1]

Strategic asset allocation studies are usually done episodically (e.g., once every three years). Relatively few asset mixes are considered (e.g., bond/stock combinations with 0, 10, 20, . . . , 100 per cent invested in stocks). An analysis (typically using Monte Carlo simulation) is performed to determine the likely range of outcomes associated with each mix. The outcome analyzed may be pension contributions over the next five years, or pension surplus five years hence.

When the analysis is complete, the investor is asked to examine the ranges of outcomes associated with each of the mixes, then choose the preferred one. This constitutes the "policy," "long-run" or "strategic" asset mix.

In the vast majority of strategic analyses, each

---

1. Footnotes appear at end of article.

273

Figure B   Strategic Asset Allocation

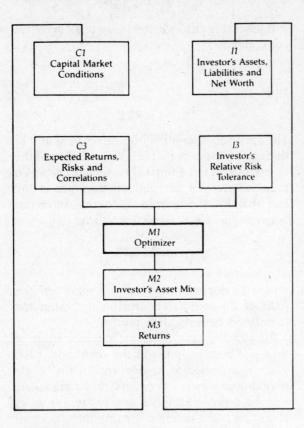

mix is expressed in terms of the percentage of total value invested in each asset class. Such an approach can be termed a *constant mix strategy*. It differs from a "buy-and-hold" strategy, because transactions required periodically to rebalance the mix after market moves change relative asset values. Although liabilities are usually included in the simulation results, no explicit attempt is made to alter the asset mix to take the nature of the liabilities into account.

Strategic studies almost always employ long-run capital market conditions. In particular, asset expected returns, risks and correlations remain constant throughout the simulation. Thus Figure B omits a connection between boxes C1 and C3. Changing capital market conditions from period to period do not influence predictions concerning asset returns.

If predictions are constant, the parameters k_0 and k_1 in our equations will remain the same from period to period. Letting the subscript t denote the time period, we can write the equa-

tion for the proportion to be invested in stocks over the period as:

$$X_t = k_0 + k_1 RRT_t.$$

For each set of simulations in a strategic study, the percentage asset mix is held constant. In the case of two assets, this implies that X_t remains the same from period to period. As the equation indicates, however, this can be optimal only if the investor's relative risk tolerance remains unchanged. Figure B portrays this condition by omitting a connection between boxes I1 and I3 and by using the term *relative risk tolerance* in box I3. Changing circumstances from period to period do not influence the investor's (relative) attitude toward risk.

Each of the possible strategies considered in a strategic study can be represented by a different level of relative risk tolerance. The lower the tolerance for risk, the more conservative the asset mix. The analysis is framed in terms of asset mix. By selecting one of the strategies analyzed, however, the investor provides information about his or her risk tolerance.

Tactical Asset Allocation

Tactical procedures are applied routinely, as part of continuing asset management. Their goal is to take advantage of inefficiencies in the relative prices of securities in different asset classes.

Until recently, tactical asset allocators switched funds between bonds and stocks.[2] Some tactical allocators now use bonds, stocks and cash equivalents. A few managers apply tactical approaches to multiple asset classes, including both domestic and international securities.[3]

Figure C portrays a typical tactical asset allocation analysis in terms comparable to those used earlier. Explicitly or implicitly, tactical procedures assume that the investor's relative risk tolerance is unaffected by changes in his or her circumstances. As in Figure B, this is portrayed in Figure C by the absence of a connection between boxes I1 and I3 and by the use of the term *relative* risk tolerance in box I3.

Tactical changes in asset mix are driven by changes in predictions concerning asset returns. In simpler systems, only predictions of expected returns on stocks and bonds change. In more complex systems, expected returns, risks and

Figure C   Tactical Asset Allocation

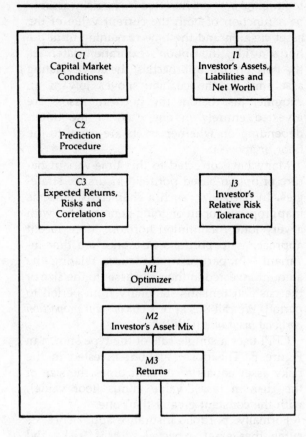

even correlations change.

In many systems, the percentage invested in stocks is related linearly to the spread between the expected returns of stocks and bonds. This can be seen to follow directly from the assumed conditions. Given constant estimates of risks and correlation, the parameters k_0 and k_2 in our equations remain the same from period to period. Assuming constant relative risk tolerance, and letting the subscript t denote time, we can write the equation for the proportion to be invested in stocks as:

$$X_{St} = k_0 + \frac{RRT}{k_2}(E_{St} - E_{Bt}).$$

In practice, tactical asset allocation systems are often "contrarian" in nature. Typically, the expected return on stocks is based on the relation between the current level of a stock market index and projections of dividends for its component stocks. Variations in projected dividends are usually smaller than the correspond-

ing variations in stock prices. Expected returns thus tend to fall when prices rise, leading to a decrease in stock holdings.

Changes in asset expected returns, risks and correlations take place in even the most efficient security markets. However, tactical asset allocation procedures typically operate on the assumption that markets overreact to information. In this sense, they base decisions on deviant beliefs, rather than on the consensus of investors.

Insured Asset Allocation

Portfolio insurance procedures are applied routinely, as part of continuing asset management. In principle, they aim to improve the "fit" between long-run results and an investor's objectives, without attempting to "time" the market. In practice, they are sometimes used for "closet" market timing. We focus here on portfolio insurance in principle.

Figure D   Insured Asset Allocation

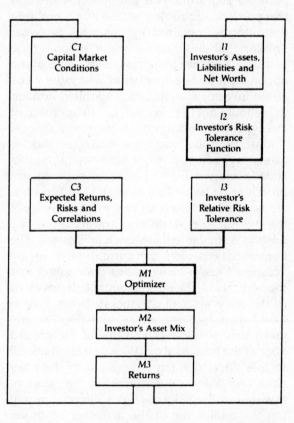

275

Figure E   Option-Based Portfolio Insurance

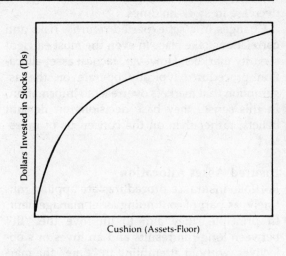

Figure D portrays an insured asset allocation procedure in the terms used earlier.

The earliest forms of portfolio insurance involved dynamic changes in asset allocation designed to replicate effects obtainable with certain option positions. For example, one might replicate the outcomes obtained by holding a portfolio plus a one-year put option written on that portfolio. Equivalently, one might replicate the outcomes obtained by holding a one-year Treasury bill plus a one-year call option on the portfolio. In either case, the striking price of the option represents a floor below which the value of the investor's assets at the specified horizon date should not fall.[4] We will call an approach of this type *option-based portfolio insurance*.

Most portfolio insurance strategies allocate assets between two major classes (e.g., stocks and Treasury bills). In essence, such an approach provides a rule that relates the appropriate asset mix to the excess of the current value of the investor's net worth over a desired *floor*. The relation is similar to that shown in Figure E. The horizontal axis plots the current value of the "cushion" (asset value minus floor value) and the vertical axis the dollar amount to be invested in the risky asset (e.g., stocks). In an option-based insurance procedure, the floor at any given time is the present value of the desired floor at the horizon date. When asset values fall to that floor, nothing is invested in the risky asset. As asset values increase, the amount invested in the risky asset can increase, reaching the total value of the assets as an upper limit.

Option-based portfolio insurance strategies require the amount invested in the risky asset to be a function of both the current value of the asset cushion and the time remaining until the horizon (i.e., the option's expiration date). As the horizon date approaches, the curve relating asset mix to the cushion moves toward an extreme; just before the horizon, assets are invested entirely in one class or the other, depending on whether assets are equal to the floor or above it.

Many have objected to this time-variant nature of option-based portfolio insurance strategies. In particular, such a characteristic seems inappropriate for an ongoing pension fund with a very long (or infinite) horizon. More recent approaches to portfolio insurance are time-invariant.[5] In particular, the curve relating the amount invested in the risky asset to the size of the cushion remains stationary from period to period. We call this approach *constant proportion portfolio insurance* (CPPI).[6]

CPPI uses a simple rule of the type shown in Figure F. The dollar amount invested in the risky asset equals a constant times the size of the cushion (asset value minus floor value), with the constant greater than one.

Formally, portfolio insurance approaches assume that asset expected returns, risks and correlations remain the same over the period during which the insurance is "in force" (although some *ad hoc* procedures have been de-

Figure F   Constant Proportion Portfolio Insurance

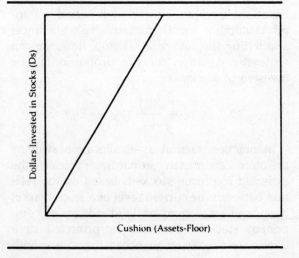

Figure G   A Linear Risk-Tolerance Function

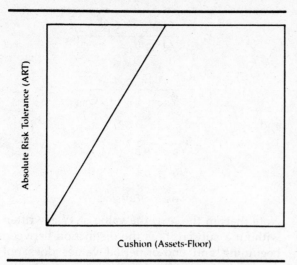

Absolute Risk Tolerance (ART) *(vertical axis)*

Cushion (Assets-Floor) *(horizontal axis)*

veloped to deal with unexpected changes in risk). Figure D portrays this assumption by omitting a connection between boxes C1 and C3.

While portfolio insurance strategies are normally *analyzed* in terms of a relation such as that shown in Figure F, they are *motivated* by a relation of the type shown in Figure G. As before, the horizontal axis plots the level of the asset cushion, but the vertical axis now indicates the investor's absolute risk tolerance. Risk tolerance is zero when assets reach the minimum value at which the floor can be assured. As asset value increases, so does the investor's risk tolerance.

The relation between the decision rule (e.g., Figure F) and the investor's underlying risk tolerance function (e.g., Figure G) is especially straightforward when one of the two assets is riskless. As shown earlier, in such a case:

$$D_S = k_1 ART.$$

Thus Figures F and G differ only by the "scaling factor" k_1, because:

$$ART = \frac{D_S}{k_1}.$$

Figure G plots the basis for constant proportion portfolio insurance: The investor's one-period absolute risk tolerance is assumed to be proportional to the size of the asset cushion. Merton has shown that such a policy is optimal if the investor's overall utility function displays linear absolute risk tolerance relative to wealth

at a specific horizon date or relative to consumption at many dates.[7]

Different portfolio insurance approaches imply different relations of the type shown in Figure G. Some are time-variant; some are not. Some give linear relationships; some do not. However, all can be viewed as implicit specifications of the investor's *risk tolerance function*.

Conclusions

Asset allocation is probably the most important task an investor undertakes.[8] The extensive effort that has been devoted to the development and application of procedures provides evidence that a number of practitioners recognize its importance. However, much of this work has been fragmented, and many of the models are subject to severe constraints. We hope the structure presented here can provide a more general framework for truly integrating the important aspects of this key investment activity. ∎

Appendix

Conditions for an Optimal Asset Mix

Assume that an investor's utility is related to net worth at the end of a relatively short decision period by the function:

$$U = f(W),$$

where W represents net worth at the end of the period.

Pratt defines *absolute risk aversion* as follows:[9]

$$ARA = -\frac{dU/dW}{d^2U/dW^2}.$$

The reciprocal is termed *absolute risk tolerance*:

$$ART = -\frac{d^2U/dW^2}{dU/dW}.$$

Because the time period is short, the range of possible values of W will be small. Over a small range of values of W, the investor's actual utility function can be adequately approximated by another function displaying constant absolute risk tolerance. Such a function can be written as:

$$U = 1 - e^{-cW},$$

with

$$ART = \frac{1}{c}.$$

Because the time period is short, changes in net

worth can typically be assumed to follow a normal distribution without excessive loss of precision.

Following Von Neumann and Morgenstern, assume that the investor's objective is to maximize expected utility of wealth.[10] As shown by Lintner, if returns are normally distributed and the investor has constant absolute risk tolerance, expected utility can be written as:[11]

$$EU = -e^{-c(E_w - c/2(V_w))}.$$

To make this as large as possible, one should maximize:

$$E_w - \frac{c}{2} V_w$$

or

$$E_w - \frac{1}{2ART} V_w,$$

where E_w and V_w are the expected value and variance of end-of-period wealth, respectively.

Assume that the investor's current wealth is W_0. Let R_i be asset i's *value-relative*—the ratio of end-of-period value to current value. Let D_i represent the current (dollar) value of asset or liability i. (As a liability is a "negative asset," it will have a negative value of D_i.) Clearly, end-of-period wealth will equal:

$$W = \sum_i D_i R_i.$$

Because the sum of the D_i values must equal W_0, optimality requires that an additional dollar invested in asset i must contribute as much to the objective function as an additional dollar invested in asset j. That is:

$$\frac{\partial E_w}{\partial D_i} - \frac{1}{2\,ART}\frac{\partial V_w}{\partial D_i} = K \text{ for all assets i.}$$

Substituting equations for the partial derivatives gives:

$$E_i - \frac{1}{ART}\sum_j D_j \sigma_i \sigma_j \rho_{ij} = K \text{ for all assets i,}$$

where

E_i = the expected value of R_i,
σ_i = the standard deviation of R_i and
ρ_{ij} = the correlation between R_i and R_j.

Note that, although the equations hold only for assets, the summation (over j) includes assets and liabilities.

In the case of two assets (S and B), this implies:

$$D_S = k_0 W_0 + k_1 ART,$$

where

$$k_0 = \frac{V_B - C_{BS}}{V_S + V_B - 2C_{BS}},$$

$$k_1 = \frac{E_S - E_B}{V_S + V_B - 2C_{BS}},$$

and

$$V_B = \sigma_B^2$$
$$V_S = \sigma_S^2$$
$$C_{BS} = \sigma_B \sigma_S \rho_{BS}.$$

Note that, in the text, the value of W is written without a subscript, as the distinction between beginning and end-of-period values does not need to be emphasized there.

Footnotes

1. See L. Kingsland, "Projecting the Financial Condition of a Pension Plan Using Simulation Analysis," *Journal of Finance*, May 1982.
2. See W. L. Fouse, "The Evolution of Asset Allocation Theory and Practice," in *Asset Allocation for Institutional Portfolios* (Charlottesville, VA: Institute of Chartered Financial Analysts, 1987).
3. See G. B. Brinson, "Implementing and Managing the Asset Allocation Process," in *Asset Allocation for Institutional Portfolios* (Charlottesville, VA: Institute of Chartered Financial Analysts, 1987).
4. See M. Rubinstein, "Alternative Paths to Portfolio Insurance," *Financial Analysts Journal*, July/August 1985.
5. F. Black and R. Jones, "Simplifying Portfolio Insurance," *Goldman, Sachs Research Report*, August 1986. For the foundation of this approach, see R. C. Merton, "Optimum Consumption and Portfolio Rules in a Continuous Time Model," *Journal of Economic Theory* 3 (1971).
6. Following A. F. Perold, "Constant Proportion Portfolio Insurance" (Harvard Business School, August 1986).
7. Merton, "Optimum Consumption," *op. cit.*
8. See G. P. Brinson, L. R. Hood and G. L. Beebower, "Determinants of Portfolio Performance," *Financial Analysts Journal*, July/August 1986.
9. See J. W. Pratt, "Risk Aversion in the Small and in the Large," *Econometrica*, January-April 1964.
10. J. Von Neumann and O. Morgenstern, *Theory of Games and Economic Behavior*, 3rd ed. (Princeton, NJ: Princeton University Press, 1953).
11. J. Lintner, "The Market Price of Risk, Size of Market and Investor's Risk Aversion," *Journal of Business*, April 1968.

THE MAJOR ASSET MIX PROBLEM OF THE INDIVIDUAL
INVESTOR

KEITH V. SMITH
UNIVERSITY OF CALIFORNIA, LOS ANGELES

INTRODUCTION

Many of the decisions made by individuals can be grouped into two distinct categories. There are those decisions which deal with current consumption and those in which current consumption is foregone in favor of
investment toward greater consumption at a future date. Rationale for
making consumption decisions has been well developed in the economic theory of consumer demand, while investment decisions have been treated in
the theory of portfolio selection. However, a closer look at portfolio
theory reveals a primary focus on allocation of investable wealth within
single categories of investment assets--notably, common stocks.[1] Little
work on allocation of investable wealth among asset categories such as
savings bonds, stocks, real estate, commodities and business ventures has
appeared in the literature. The purpose of this paper is to further ex-
plore an individual's decision problem of allocating wealth among several
asset categories. Perspective on multiasset portfolios is presented, and
the limitations of existing methods are discussed. As a preliminary step
toward improving the multiasset investment decision making of individuals,
a multiattribute model is suggested and illustrated.

MULTIASSET PORTFOLIOS

Every individual eventually must make portfolio decisions. During any
period in which regular disposable income is not completely spent on current consumption, the individual must decide what to do with the excess.
Even if only a small portion of disposable income is placed in a savings
account each month, the individual still has made a portfolio decision.
And even if all disposable income were spent, it may be that some part of

the individual's total wages automatically was allocated to social security or to a retirement program on his or her behalf.

Other individuals may find themselves with more extensive portfolio decision making. (Such decision making is, of course, identical for men and
women. For sake of convenience, married male heads of households are
used as examples throughout this paper.) Consider the case of an individual, who is 35 years old, well-educated and is married with two children. His family is protected by a life insurance policy and a portion
of his annual premiums is invested in the asset portfolio of his insurance company. Although the individual is employed as an accountant by a
manufacturing firm, he is beginning to plan for his retirement. His retirement income will come from the firm's pension fund, which is managed
by an investment advisory company. Equity in his home is increasing each
year. The security portfolio of the individual consists of 100 shares of
each of three blue-chip common stocks which he purchased several years ago
and is holding for long-term appreciation. Recently, he inherited a
large sum of money which was placed in a trust fund for the college education of his children. The trust fund is managed by the trust department of the city's largest commercial bank. Also, our individual makes
contributions annually to the small university he attended several years
ago. Such contributions are invested in the various securities that comprise the endowment fund of the university. Because of his recent promotion by his firm, he also finds that he has a few thousand dollars
that can be invested in the securities markets. He has little time for
analyzing particular stocks and bonds, so he has decided to purchase
shares of a mutual fund in order to gain the diversification of an entire
portfolio as well as the benefits of full-time management.

Although this is an exaggerated scenario, it does indicate the many con-
texts in which investment decisions are made, either by professional money
managers or by the individual. The former category includes the insurance
company portfolio, the company pension fund, the trust fund, the university endowment fund and the mutual fund. The individual has selected his
home, the blue-chip stocks, the particular insurance company, the commercial bank trust department and the particular mutual fund. But, more important for purposes of this paper, the individual decided on the amount
of life insurance coverage, he has some option on the amount of his retirement benefits, he determined what to do with his inheritance and he
chose to allocate his additional income to a mutual fund.

Table 1 traces the composition and growth of financial assets held by individuals over the past two decades. The assets are grouped into savings, fixed-income securities, other corporate securities, insurance and retirement benefits and other assets. The only asset category not included in Table 1 which probably is significant to most individuals is home real estate. While the overall compound growth of financial assets has been 7.8 percent over the two decades, investment companies (notably mutual funds) and private uninsured pension reserves have grown by almost 15 percent annually. The scope of multiasset portfolios also can be seen by examining the aggregate holdings of insurance portfolios, pension funds, trust funds, endowments, etc.

How do individuals make investment decisions about financial assets like those in Table 1? It is likely that practices range from habit or hunch, to copying the decisions of others, to enlisting the advice of friends, to using investment advisory services of one sort or another or to just doing it alone based on available information. An important observation in this regard is that decisions about financial assets cannot be avoided and that individuals somehow must decide how to allocate portions of their nonconsumed wealth to specific investment opportunities within various asset categories.

Despite the staggering importance of multiasset portfolio choice, both at the individual and the aggregate levels, little of a prescriptive nature has appeared in the literature of finance and investments. Textbook treatment tends to identify the goals of the individual and to describe the investment opportunities which are available, but only as a part of a broader-scale approach to investment analysis. Some writers have narrowed the focus to the investment problems of the individuals and family but have added little beyond a description of the environment in which the investment process takes place. Even within the academic literature, there is little help. The plethora of work on return-risk portfolio theory has been confined primarily to portfolios of common stocks. Apart from brief efforts to extend portfolio theory to the mixed-asset case, the problem facing an individual has not been addressed in a systematic manner.

Table 1

Financial Assets of Individuals in the United States, 1952-1972 (in billions of dollars)

Financial Asset	1952	1955	1958	1961	1964	1966	1968	1970	1972	Annual Increase, %
Demand deposits and currency	79.9	84.2	89.3	94.4	105.0	116.6	140.5	151.8	175.8	4.0
Savings accounts	80.0	106.3	142.1	181.8	259.5	306.8	371.7	422.3	568.6	10.3
U.S. savings bonds	49.1	50.2	47.7	46.4	49.0	50.2	51.5	51.4	57.1	0.8
Other U.S. Government securities	18.4	18.6	20.0	26.2	30.4	39.3	44.8	49.4	35.1	3.3
State and local government securities	11.4	19.2	24.0	32.0	34.6	40.0	37.0	45.6	46.0	7.2
Corporate bonds	6.3	7.1	10.2	11.3	11.8	15.1	23.8	41.2	54.8	11.4
Investment companies	3.9	7.8	13.2	22.9	29.1	34.8	52.7	47.6	59.8	14.7
Corporate stock	166.5	278.8	360.7	478.9	536.9	541.1	807.9	684.7	907.5	8.9
Life insurance reserves	54.5	63.5	72.3	82.1	94.2	103.5	112.9	122.9	136.2	4.7
Private insured pension reserves	7.7	11.3	15.6	20.3	25.3	29.4	35.0	41.2	51.6	10.0
Private uninsured pension reserves	9.6	18.3	29.2	46.3	63.9	75.8	101.4	110.8	152.3	14.8
Government pension reserves	21.2	26.6	34.0	43.5	55.2	65.5	77.2	92.6	112.8	8.7
Other financial assets	36.7	42.9	50.8	59.2	65.3	74.1	85.3	95.2	99.7	5.1
Total financial assets	545.3	734.9	909.3	1145.2	1360.1	1492.3	1941.7	1956.7	2451.3	7.8

Source: Federal Reserve System.

After observing the investment practices of individuals and the limited efforts appearing in the literature, it becomes clear that an approach is needed which captures the full spectrum of variables of concern to individuals in such a way as to provide useful guidelines for making multi-asset portfolio decisions. A central feature of such an approach is that it must somehow bring together two distinctly different types of information, as shown in the following schematic diagram.

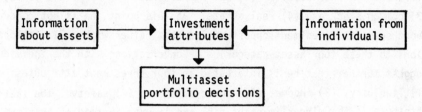

The first type of information describes alternative investment assets. Such information is common to all investors and is obtained from investment textbooks, from other publications or from individuals who are involved in various ways or who are familiar with the markets for stocks, bonds, real estate and other types of investment assets. The second type of information describes how individuals perceive or feel about such investment assets relative to their own unique circumstances—it is obtained from the individuals themselves.

As shown in the schematic, the two types of information are brought together via investment attributes, which can be defined as characteristics of investment assets about which individuals have feelings and can express preferences. While introductory treatment of consumer choice in economics begins with individuals having preferences for specific objects, such as refrigerators and television sets, many writers show that preferences (and, hence, choice decisions) are more logically based on certain attributes of those objects, such as design and reliability.[2] Popular examples of attributes within an investment context are income, appreciation and risk. Appreciation and income frequently are combined into the single attribute of return, and many decisions center on return and risk as two central attributes. Other examples of investment attributes are liquidity, taxability and manageability. Although some writers have built their analysis of portfolio management around the concept of investment attributes, such analyses typically are qualitative and offer little in the way of specific guidelines to the individual who must allocate investable wealth to various asset types.[3] We turn now to a suggested approach which uses investment attributes to develop quantitative answers to multiasset portfolio choice.

Suppose that a 35-year old individual (not necessarily the one described above) finds himself with wealth of $30,000 which he does not need for immediate consumption. He decides to allocate this wealth among four different types of assets: (1) savings account, (2) corporate bonds, (3) common stock and (4) real estate. At this point, he is not concerned about specific investment opportunities, but rather with dollar allocations to these four asset categories. Conversations with the individual suggest further that he is interested in four investment attributes: (1) liquidity, (2) income, (3) appreciation and (4) safety. The last attribute is the mirror image of risk and is used instead so that the four attributes are all desirable.

Further conversations with the individual are designed to elicit relative preferences for the four attributes which have been identified. One way to do this is to divide 100 percentage points among the attributes, with greater numbers being given to those attributes that are preferred by the individual. While the assignments can be made directly if the individual feels comfortable in doing so, an alternative method is to begin with equal assignments as follows:

Liquidity	Income	Appreciation	Safety
25 percent	25 percent	25 percent	25 percent

Changes then are made based on paired comparisons. For example, if the individual decides that he prefers appreciation twice as much as safety, it could be reflected in the revised assignments:

Liquidity	Income	Appreciation	Safety
20 percent	20 percent	40 percent	20 percent

After a series of such iterations, let us suppose that the individual arrives at the final assignment,

Its not that they prefer

Should be faced as need

Horizon should be an important ~~Attribute~~ ingredient

① Would I need this money in the near future

② Risk

284

Liquidity	Income	Appreciation	Safety
15 percent	0 percent	60 percent	25 percent

which implies greater preference for appreciation, less preference for safety and liquidity, respectively, and no preference for income (presumably because of his adequate salary).[4] Given such a set of preferences, what portfolio of assets chould be chosen?

To obtain an answer, it is necessary to examine the four asset types as to their suitability with respect to each attribute. We shall begin with liquidity and, again, it is convenient to use 100 percentage points to portray relative suitabilities. A possible set of assignments, again using paired comparisons and an iterative process, is as follows:

Liquidity, %	Asset
60	Savings account
20	Corporate bonds
20	Common stock
0	Real estate

100

This indicates that a savings account is quite liquid on a relative basis; that bonds and stocks are equally liquid, but less so than savings; and that real estate is relatively illiquid. Proceeding in a similar manner for each of the attributes might yield the following assignments:

Liquidity, %	Income, %	Appreciation, %	Safety, %	Asset
60	30	0	40	Savings account
20	50	10	30	Corporate bonds
20	10	40	20	Common stock
0	10	50	10	Real estate

100　*100*　*100*　*100*

These percentages reveal that a savings account is more suitable for liquidity and safety, corporate bonds are more suitable for income and real estate is better for appreciation. Note that each column totals 100 percent and is assumed to be independent not only of the assignments in other

Never buy single bonds

Liquidity:
being able to withdraw funds any time.

Horizon / Safety	1	3	5	10	20
All important	Money Market		Treasury Bonds or Money Mkts		
Relatively Unimport	Money Market	Bond Port			Portfolio of stocks
	Common Stock			Single companies or Portfolio	

columns but also of the preference information obtained from an individual. Suitability assignments are made after a careful study of the different asset types and, thus, are assumed to be the same for all individuals. Multiasset suitability measures usually are not provided by investment advisory services and thus, individuals as a practical matter may have to participate in making suitability assignments.

The final step is to weight the suitability measures for each asset with the preferences of the individual, attribute by attribute, in order to get an overall measure for that asset type. Each of the four attributes is desirable to an individual, hence, the weighted-suitability measure for each asset is an overall index of suitability to the individual based on his or her unique set of preferences. Calculations for the illustrations are as follows:

Weighted-Suitability Calculation					Asset
Liquid-ity, %	Income, %	Apprecia-tion, %	Safety, %	%	
(15) (60) +	(0) (30) +	(60) (0) +	(25) (40)	= 19.0	Savings account
(15) (20) +	(0) (50) +	(60) (10) +	(25) (30)	= 16.5	Corporate bonds
(15) (20) +	(0) (10) +	(60) (40) +	(25) (20)	= 32.0	Common stock
(15) (0) +	(0) (10) +	(60) (50) +	(25) (10)	= 32.5	Real estate

Results indicate that real estate and common stock offer greater weighted suitability for the individual than do corporate bonds or a savings account. This, of course, is consistent with the individual's concern for appreciation and the greater suitability of common stock and real estate for the appreciation attribute. Some readers may notice that the concept of weighted suitability suggested here somewhat resembles the Value Line system for evaluating common stocks.[5]

Because the weighted-suitability measures calculated above total 100 percent, they conveniently can be used as target percentages for the individual's $30,000 portfolio. In other words, the model suggests that the individual should place $5,700 in savings, invest $4,950 in corporate bonds, etc., as follows:

Asset	Weighted-Suitability, %	Suggested Investment, $
Savings account	19.0	5,700
Corporate bonds	16.5	4,950
Common stock	32.0	9,600
Real estate	32.5	9,750
Totals	100.0	30,000

Therefore, what we have is a quantitative solution to multiasset portfolio choice. The solution is obtained by bringing together, through a list of investment attributes, information about investment opportunities and information about individual preferences. Clearly, there are problems in trying to obtain the necessary percentages which are used in the weighted-suitability procedure. In particular, many individuals may not feel comfortable with a precise set of relative weights reflecting their preferences. Nevertheless, multiasset portfolio decisions have been made and will continue to be made. The suggested model is intended to be a more systematic approach to decision making, which usually is done almost entirely on an intuitive basis.

It also should be noted that the results of the model are intended to be helpful guidelines rather than absolute answers to the multiasset portfolio problem. For example, if the individual finds that the equity in his home is about $11,000, then the above results confirm this part of his portfolio. The result should not be interpreted literally as a signal that he must somehow reduce his real estate equity by $1,250. In other words, institutional factors and rigidities may well preclude perfect implementation of the results of the suggested approach. If, on the other hand, the individual does not own his home, the results suggest that he might well consider home ownership as a potential investment.

INTERTEMPORAL PORTFOLIO CHOICE

Another way of using the multiattribute model is in examining changes in suggested portfolio holdings over time. This is accomplished by allowing preferences of the individual for attributes to vary over time while keeping constant the suitability measures relating assets to attributes. Changing preferences by an individual reflect age and occupation, marital and family circumstances, overall wealth level and consumption patterns over time.

To illustrate, we extend the scenario of the individual described above to five distinct age levels. Suppose that at age 25, he is a graduate student, his family must exist on a limited income and safety is important for their limited investment wealth. At age 35, the individual has a good job; he and his family are becoming established in the community and appreciation is important as they plan for a future. At age 45, preferences are about the same, except that his children are entering college and he needs extra income. A decade later, at age 55, educational expenses are replaced by travel expenses as our individual and his wife begin to enjoy their success. Finally, at age 65, they are in retirement, and income and safety replace appreciation as the most important attributes.

Following the procedures described above, the qualitative description of this scenario conceivable might be transformed into the following array of percentage assignments:

Age	Liquidity, %	Income, %	Appreciation, %	Safety, %
25	30	10	0	60
35	15	0	60	25
45	10	10	70	10
55	10	20	50	20
65	0	60	0	40

The percentages reflecting the preferences of age level 35 are the same as before, while those for the other age levels, spanning a total period of 40 years, vary considerably.

When each row of such an array is combined with the suitability measures already defined, it is possible to develop a lifetime investment plan. For our illustration, the result is as shown. By looking down particular columns, one can see how the suggested holdings of a given investment type change over time. Savings is the largest holding for age levels 25 and 55. Common stock and real estate are the largest suggested holdings for age levels 35 and 45. For the retirement age, 65, corporate bonds become the largest suggested holding.

Age	Asset			
	Savings Account, %	Corporate Bonds, %	Common Stock, %	Real Estate, %
25	45.0	29.0	19.0	7.0
35	19.0	16.5	32.0	32.5
45	13.0	17.0	33.0	37.0
55	20.0	23.0	28.0	29.0
65	34.0	42.0	14.0	10.0
Average Holding	26.2	25.5	25.2	23.1

The average holdings of each asset type over the 40-year period are also presented. One notices that the average holdings over time are quite similar for the four investment assets of the example. On the other hand, there is considerable diversity at the different age levels. Although real estate is the largest suggested holding for three of the five age levels, it is the smallest average holding over the entire horizon because real estate is given very little importance in the suggested portfolio of age levels 25 and 65, the two extremes.

CONCLUSION

The problem of multiasset portfolio decisions has been identified and its importance stressed. A multiattribute model brings together two distinct types of information: (1) preferences of individuals and (2) suitability of investment assets. With attributes as the basis, these two types of information are combined to give the weighted suitability of each investment type, which also can be taken as the suggested portfolio holdings for the individual. Then, using a scenario of a typical individual at different age levels, the multiattribute model is illustrated and shown to be useful in intertemporal portfolio planning.

Several limitations of the multiattribute approach should be mentioned. First, procedures for obtaining the probability assignment have been discussed only briefly, with greater attention given to how they are combined. Much effort remains in learning how to obtain both quantitative attribute weights and quantitative suitability measures. Second, there is no sense of optimality in the model, except that the preference

289

assignments of the individual at each age level can be thought of as somehow reflecting the individual's highest level of preference. Third, no transaction costs have been included, and, thus, the intertemporal planning approach is simply a sequential application of a static model. As the number of age levels increases, transaction costs clearly would become more critical. Fourth, suitability measures for asset types have been held constant for all age levels and, more importantly, they are developed independently of each other and of the individual's wealth level.

Despite these limitations, the multiattribute approach to multiasset portfolio choice is felt to be a promising compromise between rigor and usability. It lacks the theoretical basis of standard portfolio theory, yet it addresses an important decision problem that has yet to receive adequate attention. Perhaps more importantly, it is offered as a first step in focusing on the several attribute dimensions which individuals do (and should) use in making investment decisions. Hopefully, the multiattribute model can be further developed to overcome some of the limitations which have been identified. At minimum, it should prove useful in providing broad guidelines for portfolio choice to those individuals who are willing to quantify their preferences.

MATHEMATICAL APPENDIX

The use of matrix algebra allows a succinct statement of the multiattribute model for multiasset portfolio choice. The scope of the problem is to use $1 \leq a \leq A$ attribute to determine the suggested holdings of $1 \leq i \leq I$ investment assets for each of $1 \leq g \leq G$ investor groups (or age levels). The indices a, i and g can assume only integral values and, in general, $A \neq I \neq G$.

Let $\bar{B} = [b_{ia}]$ represent an I x A matrix of suitability measures normalized such that $\sum_{i=1}^{I} b_{ia} = 1$. Also let $\bar{W} = [w_{ag}]$ represent an A x G matrix of individual preferences, normalized such that $\sum_{a=1}^{A} W_{ag} = 1$. If the suggested portfolio holdings are given by the matrix $\bar{X} = [X_{ig}]$, with $\sum_{i=1}^{I} X_{ig}$ ensuring total allocation of investable wealth, then the suggested portfolio holdings are calculated by the matrix multiplication $\bar{B} \bar{W} = \bar{X}$, where

$X_{ig} = \sum_{a=1}^{A} b_{ia}w_{ag}$. For illustration of the previous section, I = 4, A = 4,

G = 5 and the calculation would be:

$$
\begin{bmatrix}
.60 & .30 & .00 & .40 \\
.20 & .50 & .10 & .30 \\
.20 & .10 & .40 & .20 \\
.00 & .10 & .50 & .10
\end{bmatrix}
\begin{bmatrix}
.30 & .15 & .10 & .10 & .00 \\
.10 & .00 & .10 & .20 & .60 \\
.00 & .60 & .70 & .50 & .00 \\
.60 & .25 & .10 & .20 & .40
\end{bmatrix}
=
\begin{bmatrix}
.450 & .140 & .130 & .200 & .340 \\
.290 & .165 & \boxed{.170} & .230 & .420 \\
.190 & .370 & .330 & .280 & .140 \\
.010 & .325 & .370 & .290 & .103
\end{bmatrix}
$$

The encircled element of the $\bar{X}$ matrix is found by matrix multiplying the second row of $\bar{B}$ by the third column of $\bar{W}$ as follows:

$$(.20)(.10) + (.50)(.10) + (.10)(.70) + (.30)(.10) = .170$$

The same procedure of matrix multiplication is used for each element in $\bar{X}$.

FOOTNOTES

[1]Portfolio theory can be traced to the work of Harry Markowitz, *Portfolio Selection: Efficient Diversification of Investments* (New York: John Wiley and Sons, 1959). Many of the extensions to this work are discussed in Keith V. Smith, *Portfolio Management* (New York: Holt, Rinehart and Winston, 1971).

[2]For example, see Kevin J. Lancaster, "A New Approach to Consumer Theory," *Journal of Political Economy*, 74 (April 1966), pp. 132-157.

[3]An excellent qualitative discussion involving attributes is Harry Sauvain, *Investment Management*, 4th ed. (Englewood Cliffs, N.J.: Prentice-Hall, Inc., 1973).

[4]Procedures such as this and their implications are explained in Howard Raiffa, "Preferences for Multi-Attributed Derivations," RM-5868-DOT (The Rand Corporation, April 1969). See also James R. Miller, "Assessing Alternative Transportation Systems," RM-5865-DOT (The Rand Corporation, April 1969).

[5]The Value Line system is explained in Arnold Bernhard, *The Evaluation of Common Stocks* (New York: Simon and Schuster, 1959). For each of 1400 common stocks, Value Line provides ranking measures for four attributes (12-month market performance, 3-5 year appreciation potential, dividend yield and quality). The investor determines the relative weights for the four attributes, and a weighted index value is calculated for each common stock.

Bonds versus stocks: Another look

The look is at the market portfolio as well as at its components.

Meir Statman and Neal L. Ushman

Which is the better investment, stocks or bonds? William Sharpe examined this question in 1973 and concluded, based upon both theory and evidence, that the question is misstated: Neither stocks nor bonds are superior to the other. Rather, a portfolio combining both stocks and bonds is superior to portfolios containing only stocks or only bonds.

Sharpe's analysis is grounded in the Capital Asset Pricing Model (CAPM), and the combination of stocks and bonds that he used plays a special role in that model. Specifically, Sharpe used the "market" portfolio, combining stocks and bonds in proportion to their market values.

Any study where theory and evidence solidly reinforce each other is part of a small group, but Sharpe's study does not belong there. While the market portfolio was superior over Sharpe's entire thirty-four-year period 1938-1971, a portfolio containing only stocks was the best choice for the twenty-six-year postwar period 1946-1971. Sharpe argued that "all things considered, it seems more appropriate to attribute the somewhat negative results in the postwar period to unanticipated events than to reject the theory" (p. 79).

More than a dozen years have passed since Sharpe's paper was published. We now have better data and more of it. Sharpe's question is as relevant today as it was when he first presented it, so we ask the question once again. Is a portfolio combining stocks and bonds better than one consisting of only stocks or only bonds? We find that the market portfolio was no better than a portfolio of stocks alone for the sixty-year period from 1926 through 1985. A portfolio composed entirely of stocks was best over the forty-year postwar period 1946-1985, while a portfolio composed entirely of bonds was best over the earlier twenty years.

SHARPE'S REWARD/RISK RATIO

As we noted earlier, Sharpe's analysis is grounded in the CAPM. It compares the performance of stocks and bonds to the performance of the market portfolio, which is composed of stocks and bonds in proportion to their market value. We replicate Sharpe's analysis using the market portfolio. In addition, however, we also use a more general approach, grounded in Markowitz's normative framework for diversification, to compare the performance of stocks and bonds individually to the performance of the best portfolio that combines both in fixed proportions.

Figure 1 is an illustration of the risk and expected returns of stocks, bonds, and a portfolio that combines both. Risk and expected return are measured in terms of excess return, the return in excess of the riskless return. Point P, the origin, with zero expected excess return and zero risk, represents a riskless investment.

Stocks are typically higher in both risk and expected return than bonds. Points S and B, for stocks and bonds respectively, conform to this pattern. The curve connecting S and B represents risk and expected

MEIR STATMAN is Associate Professor of Finance at The Leavey School of Business and Administration at Santa Clara University in Santa Clara (CA95053). NEAL L. USHMAN is Assistant Professor of Accounting at the same institution. The authors wish to thank Peter Bernstein, Evan Schulman, and Laurence Siegel for helpful comments on an earlier draft. We retain full responsibility for all errors. Meir Statman acknowledges support of a Batterymarch Fellowship.

FIGURE 1

Risk and Excess Returns of Stocks, Bonds, and Combinations of Both

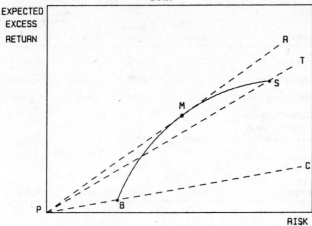

returns of portfolios that combine stocks and bonds in various proportions.

The relative performance of a portfolio is measured by the expected reward/risk ratio, which is the slope of the line connecting the origin and the point representing the expected return and risk of the portfolio. The expected reward/risk ratio of the stock portfolio is the slope of line PST, and the ratio of the bond portfolios is the slope of line PBC. Rational investors prefer high ratios to lower ones. Thus, the best portfolio is the one providing the highest expected reward/risk ratio. The best portfolio according to the CAPM is portfolio M, which combines stocks and bonds in proportion to their market values.

A COMPARISON WITH SHARPE'S RESULTS

Our returns data are from Ibbotson Associates' 1985 Yearbook, and the Stocks, Bonds, Bills and Inflation: Quarterly Service (Fourth Quarter 1985) update. The riskless rate of return is represented by the return on Treasury bills. Stock returns, including dividends, are represented by Standard & Poor's Composite Index. The index is market value-weighted and currently consists of 500 of the largest stocks in terms of stock market value in the United States. The index consisted of 90 of the largest stocks prior to 1957. Sharpe's study used the Dow Jones Average of 30 industrials to represent the stock market.

Returns on long-term corporate bonds for the years 1946-1985 are represented by Salomon Brothers High-Grade Long-Term Corporate Bond Index. Returns for the years 1926-1945 are represented by Standard & Poor's monthly High-Grade Corporate Composite yield data, assuming a 4% coupon and a twenty-year maturity. Long-term corporate bonds were represented by Keystone B-2 bond fund in Sharpe's study; Keystone has maintained a portfolio of about forty medium-grade corporate bonds.

Sharpe did not analyze long-term U.S. government bond returns, but we do evaluate them. Returns data are those obtained by Ibbotson Associates from the U.S. Government Bond File.

Sharpe estimated market values of domestic stocks, corporate bonds, and government bonds using data from the *NYSE Fact Book* and the *Federal Reserve Bulletin*. He used NYSE data to estimate the values of stocks and the total of corporate and government bonds. The value of government bonds, derived from the *Federal Reserve Bulletin*, was subtracted from the value of all NYSE bonds to arrive at an estimate of the value of corporate bonds. This estimation procedure presents problems, because the NYSE data pertain only to NYSE-traded securities, while Federal Reserve data pertain to all securities.

We use market values of United States stocks, corporate bonds, and government bonds as estimated by Ibbotson, Siegel, and Love (1985).[1] Unfortunately, year-by-year data are available only for the period from the end of 1959 through the end of 1984. We use the mean proportions of the market values of the three assets over the period 1959-1984 as estimates of the proportion that prevails in each year from 1925 through 1958.

The market value proportions of stocks, corporate bonds, and government bonds at the end of each year from 1959 through 1984 are presented in Figure 2. A market portfolio is formed at the begin-

FIGURE 2

Market Value Proportions of Stocks, Corporate Bonds, and Government Bonds at the End of Each Year 1959-1984

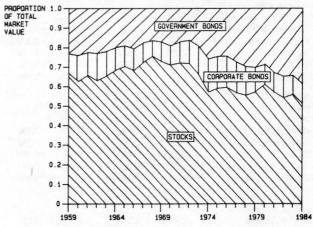

ning of each year based upon market values at the end of the preceding year.

Like Sharpe, we used a three-month holding period for calculating returns for the periods 1938-1971 and 1946-1971. We present his results side-by-

1. Footnote appears at the end of the article.

293

side with ours in Tables 1 and 2 to highlight differences in the two data bases.

Stocks have higher average excess returns and higher risk than corporate bonds in both data bases, but the numbers themselves differ. For example, the average excess return of long-term corporate bonds over the period 1938-1971 is 1.069% per quarter in Sharpe's data, but only 0.172% in our data. (The difference in returns may be due, at least in part, to the use of high-grade bonds in the Ibbotson and Associates data, while Sharpe used medium-grade bonds.) Equally important, the correlations between the excess returns of stocks and corporate bonds in our data are much lower than those in Sharpe's data: The coefficient of determination for the 1938-1971 data is 0.46 in Sharpe's data but only 0.03 in our data.

Reward/risk ratios for the entire 1938-1971 period and the postwar subperiod 1946-1971 reveal that the market portfolio, composed of stocks and corporate bonds, was inferior to a portfolio of only stocks in both periods. On the other hand, Sharpe found that the market portfolio was superior to a portfolio of only stocks over the period 1938-1971.

Sharpe included only corporate bonds in his analysis, excluding government bonds. The results in Table 2 show that the dominance of stocks in both

TABLE 1

Performance: Bonds and Stocks

| Measure | Period | | | |
| | 1938-1971 | | 1946-1971 | |
	Sharpe	Statman-Ushman	Sharpe	Statman-Ushman
Average quarterly excess returns (% per quarter)				
(1) Corporate bonds	1.069	0.172	0.330	−0.053
(2) Government bonds	N.A.	0.104	N.A.	−0.209
(3) Stocks	2.290	2.652	2.033	2.372
(4) Ratio: (1)/(3)	0.467	0.065	0.162	−0.022
(5) Ratio: (2)/(3)	N.A.	0.039	N.A.	−0.088
Standard deviation of quarterly excess returns (% per quarter)				
(6) Corporate bonds	4.069	2.496	2.703	2.750
(7) Government bonds	N.A.	2.701	N.A.	2.783
(8) Stocks	7.745	8.130	6.491	6.888
(9) Ratio: (6)/(8)	0.525	0.307	0.416	0.399
(10) Ratio: (7)/(8)	N.A.	0.332	N.A.	0.404
(11) R^2 of corporate bond and stock excess returns	0.46	0.03	0.37	0.05
(12) R^2 of government bond and stock excess returns	N.A.	0.01	N.A.	0.02
(13) Beta of corporate bond excess returns on stock excess returns	0.356	0.056	0.252	0.086
(14) Beta of government bond excess returns on stock excess returns	N.A.	0.028	N.A.	0.056

TABLE 2

Reward/Risk Ratios

| Portfolio | Period | | | |
| | 1938-1971 | | 1946-1971 | |
	Sharpe	Statman-Ushman	Sharpe	Statman-Ushman
Stocks	0.2957	0.3262	0.3132	0.3444
Corporate bonds	0.2627	0.0689	0.1221	Negative
Government bonds	N.A.	0.0384	N.A.	Negative
"Market" portfolio (Corporate bonds and stocks only)	0.3160	0.3245	0.2994	0.3331
"Market" portfolio (Corporate bonds, government bonds, and stocks)	N.A.	0.3195	N.A.	0.3058

the 1938-1971 and 1946-1971 periods becomes more pronounced when government bonds are added to the market portfolios.

We want to emphasize that neither Sharpe's analysis nor ours can be viewed as a proper test of the CAPM, for two important reasons. First, the estimates of market proportions and asset returns are not precise. Second, we know from Roll (1977) that a proper test requires inclusion of all assets. The market portfolio includes many asset categories in addition to the stocks and corporate bonds used by Sharpe. While the addition of government bonds brings the analysis closer to the "true" market portfolio, we know that even small deviations from the true market portfolio can have serious estimation consequences.

THE 1926-1985 PERIOD

On average, corporate bonds provided only 19% as much excess return as stocks over the sixty years from 1926 through 1985; government bonds provided even less. The variability of bond returns is also lower than that of stocks, but not proportionately.

The reward/risk ratio of stocks is almost double the ratio of corporate bonds and almost three times the ratio of government bonds. The market portfolio is no better than a portfolio consisting of only stocks, although a portfolio composed of 49% in stocks, 50% in corporate bonds, and 1% in government bonds is superior to the market portfolio and to any portfolio containing only one of these three assets.

CHANGES OVER TIME

The market portfolio performed as well as a portfolio of only stocks during the 1926-1985 period, but this result is sensitive to the period under study. We have divided the entire sixty-year period into the twenty-year prewar and war period 1926-1945, and the forty-year postwar period 1946-1985. Bonds were

TABLE 3

Portfolios over the 1926-1985 Period

	Mean quarterly excess return	Standard deviation of excess return	Reward/risk ratio
Stocks only	2.202	12.388	0.178
Corporate bonds only	0.410	3.981	0.103
Government bonds only	0.240	3.973	0.060
"Market" portfolio	1.480	8.334	0.178
Optimal portfolio with fixed proportions (0.49 in stocks 0.50 in corporate bonds 0.01 in government bonds)	1.286	6.958	0.185

Correlation of the excess return on stocks with the excess return on corporate bonds = 0.30

Correlation of the excess return on stocks with the excess return on government bonds = 0.19

Correlation of the excess return on corporate bonds with the excess return on government bonds = 0.92

dominant in the prewar and war period. A portfolio composed of 95% corporate bonds and 5% government bonds provided the highest reward/risk ratio. Stocks, on the other hand, were dominant in the postwar period. A portfolio consisting exclusively of stocks provided the highest reward/risk ratio.

Was the postwar period structurally different from the earlier period? The period under investigation is probably too short to establish such a conclusion, but it seems worth investigating further by

TABLE 4

Portfolios over the 1926-1945 Period

	Mean quarterly excess return	Standard deviation of excess return	Reward/risk ratio
Stocks only	2.938	18.681	0.157
Corporate bonds only	1.108	1.993	0.556
Government bonds only	0.922	2.330	0.396
"Market" portfolio	2.223	12.039	0.185
Optimal portfolio with fixed proportions (0.95 in corporate bonds 0.05 in government bonds)	1.099	1.974	0.557

Correlation of the excess return on stocks with the excess return on corporate bonds = 0.45

Correlation of the excess return on stocks with the excess return on government bonds = 0.11

Correlation of the excess return on corporate bonds with the excess return on government bonds = 0.68

TABLE 5

Portfolios over the 1946-1985 Period

	Mean quarterly excess return	Standard deviation of excess return	Reward/risk ratio
Stocks only	1.834	7.543	0.243
Corporate bonds only	0.060	4.653	0.013
Government bonds only	−0.102	4.548	Negative
"Market" portfolio	1.109	5.656	0.196
Optimal portfolio with fixed proportions (1.00 in stocks)	1.035	5.909	0.175

Correlation of the excess return on stocks with the excess return on corporate bonds = 0.40

Correlation of the excess return on stocks with the excess return on government bonds = 0.33

Correlation of the excess return on corporate bonds with the excess return on government bonds = 0.95

examining subperiods in both the postwar and the earlier years.

We analyzed subperiods of twenty-six years each. We chose the twenty-six-year period because it is identical in length to the postwar period, 1946-1971, used by Sharpe. We examined portfolios over the periods 1926-1951, 1927-1952, . . . , 1960-1985, and found that the market portfolio was best only for portfolios in the twenty-six-year periods ending in the years 1958 through 1965. A portfolio of corporate bonds was best over the periods ending in 1951 through 1957, and a portfolio of stocks was best over the periods ending in 1966 through 1985. The results of further analysis, using ten-year subperiods, are similar to the findings from the analysis of the twenty-six-year subperiods.

It is also important to note that correlations between stock and bond returns fluctuated greatly over time. The correlation between stock and corporate bond returns ranged from −0.08 in the twenty-six-year period 1939-1964, to 0.50 in the twenty-six-year period 1960-1985 (see Figure 4). Similarly, the correlation ranged from −0.24 in the ten-year period 1955-1964 to 0.70 in the ten-year period 1969-1978. These variations may be systematic, but the evidence suggests they are random; none of the correlation coefficients is different from the sixty-year correlation coefficient (0.30) in a statistically significant way.

NOMINAL AND REAL RETURNS

Sharpe's analysis, as well as our preceding analysis, uses nominal returns. Investors may be more interested in an analysis using inflation-ad-

295

FIGURE 3

Reward/Risk Ratios of Stocks, Corporate Bonds, Government Bonds, and the "Market" Portfolio for 26-year Periods Ending in 1951-1985

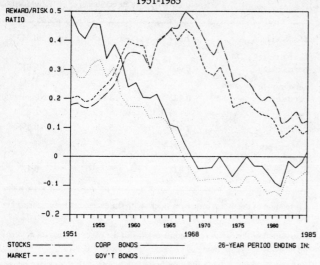

STOCKS ——— CORP BONDS —————— 26-YEAR PERIOD ENDING IN:
MARKET - - - - - GOV'T BONDS ....

FIGURE 4

Correlations Between Excess Returns of Stocks, Corporate Bonds, and Government Bonds for 26-year Periods Ending in 1951-1985

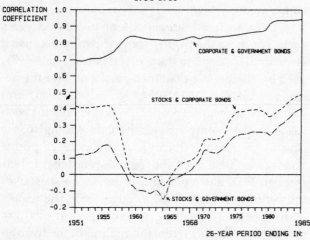

26-YEAR PERIOD ENDING IN:

justed real returns, because such returns provide a better picture of the changes in the purchasing power of the stocks and bonds in their portfolios. We wondered if optimal portfolio compositions with real returns are different from those with nominal returns.

To answer this question, we first converted all nominal quarterly returns into real returns, according to the following formula.

$$\text{Real return} = \frac{1 + \text{nominal return}}{1 + \text{change in the Consumer Price Index}} - 1$$

Next, we calculated the optimal portfolios for the entire period 1926-1985 and for the subperiods 1926-1945 and 1946-1985.

The results in Table 6 show that optimal portfolio combinations with real returns are virtually identical to the optimal combinations with nominal returns. For example, the optimal portfolio with fixed

TABLE 6

Portfolios with Nominal Returns and Real Returns over the 1926-1985 Period

	Average excess return		Standard deviation of excess return		Reward/risk ratio	
	Nominal	Real	Nominal	Real	Nominal	Real
Stocks only	2.202	2.200	12.388	12.394	0.178	0.177
Corporate bonds only	0.410	0.411	3.981	3.960	0.103	0.104
Government bonds only	0.240	0.242	3.973	3.952	0.060	0.061
"Market" portfolio	1.480	1.480	8.334	8.334	0.178	0.178
Optimal portfolio with fixed proportions*	1.286	1.268	6.958	6.858	0.185	0.185

* The proportions are 0.49 in stocks, 0.50 in corporate bonds, and 0.01 in government bonds using nominal returns. The corresponding proportions using real returns are 0.48, 0.51, and 0.01.

proportions for the 1926-1985 period is composed of 0.59 in stocks, 0.40 in corporate bonds, and 0.01 in government bonds when nominal returns are used. The corresponding numbers when real returns are used are 0.58, 0.41, and 0.01.

CONCLUSIONS

Are stocks or bonds the better investment? Sharpe concluded, based on data for the thirty-four-year period 1938-1971, that the market portfolio, combining stocks and corporate bonds in proportion to their market value, is superior to portfolios containing only stocks or only corporate bonds. Our analysis, based on data for the sixty-year period 1926-1985, suggests that results are sensitive to the choice of time period as well as to the composition of both the market portfolio and its components.

A portfolio of only stocks was best over the forty-year postwar period, according to our measurements, while a portfolio of only bonds was best over the twenty-year earlier period. Sharpe found that his market portfolio was superior over the period 1938-1971, but we found that a portfolio of only stocks was better than our market portfolio over the same period.

These results should be interpreted with caution. First, the CAPM, which is the basis of Sharpe's analysis, is defined on expected returns. Realized returns on stocks and bonds vary so much that even a sixty-year sample such as ours may not provide for a good estimate of expected returns. Indeed, there is evidence that realized returns are likely to differ significantly from expected returns. For example, Ibbotson and Sinquefield (1982, pp. 53-54) estimate that mean annual realized returns on bonds over the fifty-five-year period 1926 through 1981 were more than 1% lower than expected returns.

Second, we investigated only stocks and bonds, ignoring all other assets such as human capital, homes, and other real estate. It is quite possible that both stocks and bonds have a place when the market portfolio includes all other assets.

What should an investor conclude from this analysis? The sensitivity of results to changes in the time horizon leaves an investor with little direction. Should investors hold 49% of their assets in stocks, as the analysis over the 1926-1985 period seems to suggest? Or perhaps they should ignore the prewar period data and hold only stocks, as the analysis over the 1946-1985 period seems to suggest?

Investors are likely to feel uneasy about a recommendation to forgo diversification even if an analysis of returns and covariances over long periods of time indicates that such a policy is optimal. What is the source of the strong intuition favoring diversification? And how do investors construct their portfolios?

We suspect that the intuition that favors diversification is not rooted in a framework, such as Markowitz's, where a portfolio is viewed as a whole. Rather, evidence on portfolio construction suggests that investors do not view a portfolio as a whole: They view portfolios as loose collections of parts, or mental accounts, each designed to satisfy a particular need.

For example, investors may use bonds as a source of certain income and will classify those bonds into a "safe" or "income" mental account, while they use stocks with the hope of becoming rich and classify those stocks into an "adventurous" or "growth" mental account. The proportions of stocks and bonds in a portfolio may change as investors balance their need to climb into the upper class through investment in

stocks with their need to avoid falling into the lower class through investment in bonds. Different words but similar concepts would fit institutional investors. Covariances between stocks and bonds are not very important in the mental accounting framework, even though they are a crucial part of the Markowitz and the CAPM frameworks.

Conclusions will certainly become clearer as time passes and more data arrive. It is possible that future data will confirm the existing theory of portfolio construction. On the other hand, we might benefit from an exploration of alternative theories as we wait for new data.

---

[1] The government bonds category consists of bonds, notes, and agency bonds. Corporate bonds include both medium- and long-term bonds.

REFERENCES

Roger G. Ibbotson, Laurence B. Siegel, and Kathryn S. Love. *World Wealth: U.S. and Foreign Market Values and Returns.* R. G. Ibbotson Associates, Inc., Chicago, 1985.

Roger G. Ibbotson and Rex A. Sinquefield. *Stocks, Bonds, Bills and Inflation: The Past and the Future.* Charlottesville, Virginia: The Financial Analysts Research Foundation, 1982.

Ibbotson Associates, Inc. *Stocks, Bonds, Bills, and Inflation (1985 Yearbook).* Ibbotson Associates, Inc., Chicago, 1985, and *Stocks, Bonds, Bills and Inflation: Quarterly Service: Fourth Quarter 1985.*

Richard Roll. "A Critique of the Asset Pricing Theory's Tests; Part I: On Past and Potential Testability of the Theory." *Journal of Financial Economics* 4 (March 1977), pp. 129-176.

William F. Sharpe. "Bonds Versus Stocks: Some Lessons From Capital Market Theory." *Financial Analysts Journal* (November-December 1973), pp. 74-80.

Hersh Shefrin and Meir Statman. "A Mental Accounting-Based Portfolio Theory." Working Paper, Santa Clara University, November 1985.

RONALD HANSEN INVESTMENT COUNSEL

In January 1989, Ronald Hansen added another client to his growing investment advisory business. The new account is non-discretionary, but the client has asked for advice on a series of matters involving the family assets.

Ronald Hansen, age 49, was born in Los Angeles and educated in economics at the University of California, Berkeley. After receiving an MBA from New York University in 1963, he joined Lehman Brothers in their New York office as a security analyst. During seven years with Lehman, he gained experience both as a security analyst and as a portfolio manager.

In 1969, Mr. Hansen became a Certified Financial Analyst (CFA). The next year, he returned to San Diego as a principal in the investment advisory firm of Jackson, Lee, and Hansen. Clients of the firm included individuals, pension and profit-sharing trusts, and charitable foundations. Mr. Hansen became involved in all facets of investment counseling for assets under management totaling $300 million.

On his fortieth birthday in 1979, Mr. Hansen initiated and organized his own investment counsel firm, Ronald Hansen Investment Counsel (RHIC). As the sole principal, his business has grown steadily to its current position of having just under $60 million under management, consisting of about 50 clients with a total of 72 accounts. At year-end 1988, fee income to RHIC was just over $425,000. Of this, Mr. Hansen draws about $8,000 per month in salary and is also putting about $2,500 per month into a variety of retirement programs. Mr. Hansen, who is divorced, has an expressed goal of remaining independent, to enjoy his work, and to build toward a comfortable retirement. As part of that, he has decided not to add other principals -- but to continue with a small but loyal office staff, research obtained through the brokerage commissions he is able to direct, and two academic consultants: Professor Black who teaches behavioral science at an eastern college, and Professor White who teaches investments at a midwestern university.

The new client, Mr. Jason Walters, age 72(!), is married, with one son (grown and professionally successful), and still active as a corporate consultant. The Walters were introduced to Ronald Hansen through a mutual friend whose portfolio also is managed by RHIC.

The Walters have an impressive balance sheet. It includes a $1,300,000 pension fund (invested in second-trust deeds and high quality corporate bonds), an individual account of just over $1,500,000 (including $400,000 of municipal bonds, $900,000 of common stocks, and $200,000 in three high-quality mutual funds), $600,000 of non income-generating land, and a lovely home (without mortgage) recently appraised at $2 million. Without any appreciable debt, Walters' total assets and net worth position are approximately $5.4 million. The $900,000 stock portfolio consists of about nine issues, but with about 40% invested in the firm that he worked for almost fifteen years.

The new account for Ronald Hansen is the Walters' $1,500,000 individual account -- although they are admittedly seeking advice on their family's total assets. The expressed goal for the individual account -- according to Mr. Hansen -- is to "make it larger by taking on more risk." Apparently, Mrs. Walters (age 55) has strongly urged Jason to mortgage their home and invest in the extended stock market boom that has been predicted.

The first substantive meeting between client and advisor is scheduled in Mr. Hansen's office for 4:00 p.m. on Thursday, 21 February 1989. As always, Mr. Hansen is anxious to get off to a good start with any new client. In doing some homework for that meeting the prior weekend, he tried to anticipate possible questions from the Walters such as the following:

(1) Should we mortgage the home and invest in common stocks?
(2) How should our common stocks portfolio be revised?
(3) What about our pension fund account?
(4) What about our municipal bonds?
(5) What about the land?

After conversations with his two academic consultants, Mr. Hansen is wondering what to do, if anything, about potential questions such as the following:

(6) What if, as Professor Black suggests, Mr. and Mrs. Walters might disagree during the meeting? If so, what should Mr. Hansen do?
(7) What further financial and investment planning should the Walters do before investment from RHIC is really apropos?
(8) What if, as Professor White suggests, the Walters bring up the question of whether or not professional money managers are really able to outperform a passive investment strategy, such as an index fund?
(9) How does Mr. Hansen's responsibility change, if at all, if the Walters' account was to become discretionary?

TIMING AND PERFORMANCE FOR ALPHA BETA GAMMA

It was a crisp October morning as Britt Airlines flight #504 landed at the O'Hare Airport in Chicago. Professor John Copeland completed a review of his notes and headed for the airport shuttle that would take him to a nearby hotel -- and the site of the annual review of the Alpha Beta Gamma (ABG) investment portfolio.

John Copeland is a finance professor at Ohio State University. Since 1980 he has served on his fraternity's investments committee -- and he has been chairman of that committee since 1983. Agenda for the October 1988 meeting included the annual presentation by Firststar Investment Counsel, the professional investment manager that handles the $3.2 million portfolio of the Alpha Beta Gamma fraternity. The ABG portfolio exists to help individual chapters improve their fraternity houses, as well as to provide a working capital reserve for the national fraternity.

For several years prior to 1981, the ABG portfolio was managed by a large, well-regarded bank in New York City. Unfortunately, the relatively small size of their portfolio precluded any personal attention -- and the achieved performance was quite poor. As a result, a decision was made to change investment managers. In April 1981, the ABG investment committee heard presentations by four professional managers that had been recommended. During the ensuing discussion, it was clear that Firststar Investment Counsel (FIC) should be retained. The unanimous decision was a result of FIC's smaller size, their above-average performance record in recent years, and a very concise and competent presentation by Bradley Miller, executive vice president of FIC, and the one ultimately assigned to the Alpha Beta Gamma account.

Results were mixed during the next few years. On the one hand, and from an operational standpoint, the relationship of Alpha Beta Gamma with Firststar Investment Counsel was quite acceptable. Performance reports to the committee and fraternity headquarters were always prompt, annual presentations were well organized and executed, and the investment committee seemed to have confidence in the integrity and ability of FIC.

But on the other hand, achieved performance (see Exhibit 1 below) was inconsistent. ABG's portfolio outperformed the market averages during the early months and years, subsequent results were just the opposite, and as of the third quarter 1988 just ended, ABG's cumulative results were almost "dead even" with that of the Standard and Poor's Composite Stock Index (S&P 500).

Professor Copeland recently sent to each member of the investment committee a copy of INVESTMENT POLICY by Charles Ellis.

Brief in length, but insightful in content, Ellis is able to clearly demonstrate the important distinction between the responsibilities of the client (i.e. ABG) and those of the investments manager (i.e. FIC). Copeland was especially struck by the advice given in Chapters 10-11 (see Reading #23). Professor Copeland hopes that this advice will lead to an improved understanding of the relationship overall -- and especially to an improved oversight function by the ABG investments committee.

Professor Copeland also has concerns about both the performance and timing that has been achieved for the ABG portfolio. Although FIC has stayed even with the S&P 500, Copeland feels that on a "risk-adjusted" basis, FIC might have actually under-performed the overall market. He also wonders why FIC discontinued showing performance comparisons against the Dow Jones Industrial Average (DJIA) at the end of 1985. Possibly it was done because the DJIA is judged not to be a good benchmark. Conversely, it may have been done because the Alpha Beta Gamma portfolio had begun to trail the DJIA in a conspicuous manner.

The issue of timing looms even larger in the thoughts of John Copeland as the shuttle arrives at the airport hotel. From the beginning, the investments committee has established an equity/fixed income policy of 25-75%. In other words, FIC must keep the percentage of equity investments in that range at all times. In addition to the quarter-by-quarter returns of the portfolio and the market, Copeland has kept track of the equity/fixed income mix at the end of each quarter.

Professor Copeland hopes to chair a congenial and pleasant meeting. But he also feels responsibility to bring the issues of performance and timing into sharp focus. His personal calculations, done during the past few days, are not particularly encouraging. And thus he wonders what Bradley Miller will report? Will anyone else have looked at the numbers -- and perhaps thought about questions such as the following:

(1) What is the annualized rate of return on the ABG portfolio since Firststar Investment Counsel was given the account in mid-1981?

(2) What is the annualized rate of return achieved by the S&P 500 index during the same period?

(3) How would you compare the performance of the ABG portfolio against the S&P index during that period? Would your evaluation change if performance were measured on a risk-adjusted basis?

(4) How would you evaluate the investment timing of FIC with respect to the Alpha Beta Gamma portfolio?

Exhibit 1
QUARTERLY PERFORMANCE REPORT
ALPHA BETA GAMMA INVESTMENT PORTFOLIO

QUARTER	ABG	S&P 500	EQUITY
1981-3	-5.1%	-10.2%	18%
1981-4	5.8	7.1	28
1982-1	1.2	-7.4	29
1982-2	-1.1	-0.5	47
1982-3	15.3	11.4	57
1982-4	26.8	18.2	72
1983-1	12.6	10.1	77
1983-2	13.7	11.1	81
1983-3	-14.6	0.1	60
1983-4	-8.8	0.4	62
1984-1	-9.4	-2.4	32
1984-2	3.4	-2.6	58
1984-3	6.9	9.7	76
1984-4	-1.0	1.8	65
1985-1	11.1	9.1	72
1985-2	14.2	7.3	74
1985-3	-8.5	-4.1	62
1985-4	16.4	17.1	65
1986-1	16.3	14.1	71
1986-2	10.3	5.9	65
1986-3	-11.1	-7.0	43
1986-4	4.2	5.6	60
1987-1	21.1	21.3	67
1987-2	3.4	5.0	68
1987-3	5.0	6.6	73
1987-4	-15.6	-22.5	58
1988-1	4.3	5.7	63
1988-2	3.6	6.6	54
1988-3	1.6	0.4	62
1988-4			

ANALYSIS OF PENSION FUND PERFORMANCE

Although he is simply staying at home, Lawrence Duncan is really enjoying a week of vacation. Mr. Duncan has an interesting but demanding position as chief financial officer of Kellogg Instruments, a rapidly growing, high technology firm in the suburbs of San Francisco. His overall responsibilities include the coordination of treasury, accounting, and budgeting. He also is responsible for Fund K, the firm's defined-benefit pension plan.

A primary reason for his enjoyment is that his daughter Debbie is spending the summer at home. After completing her baccalaureate degree in economics at the University of Santa Clara, Debbie Duncan was accepted into the MBA program at U.C.L.A. She just completed her first year in that program, and is beginning a summer internship at a commercial bank in downtown San Francisco.

During her high school and college years, Debbie always thought that she wanted to follow in her dad's footsteps and pursue a career in corporate finance. But during her first year in graduate school, she really became interested in investments -- and now believes that she would prefer a career as a security analyst or portfolio manager. As a result of this interest, Debbie and Lawrence Duncan have had several interesting conversations about investments management, and, in particular, about how he oversees the professional management of Fund K.

During their latest conversation, Debbie showed her dad a copy of an academic paper by Professor Eugene Fama entitled "Components of Investment Performance" (see Reading #20). While the paper was published in 1972, it describes an interesting methodology for analyzing the performance of a managed portfolio. Debbie suggests to her father that he should try to apply some of those ideas to Fund K.

Lawrence Duncan quickly responds that the article has far too many equations for him -- but that he would welcome some help from Debbie in doing an analysis of the achieved performance of Fund K. They agree to look at performance over the past five years, since the current manager has had the responsibility for Fund K for that period.

The next evening, Mr. Duncan informs Debbie that the annual time-weighted return for Fund K over the five-year period was 30%, and that the associated standard deviation was 40%. During the same period, the Standard & Poor's 500 index achieved an annual return of 20%, and with a standard deviation of 20%.

Debbie explains that she also needs to know the "beta" for Fund K, and Mr. Duncan reports that it was estimated to be 1.2 over the five-year period. That number seems pretty high to both of the Duncans, and Debbie inquires as to just what risk level the employees of Kellogg Instruments would prefer to have their pension assets managed. Laurence thinks about that for a while, and concludes that he and his colleagues at Kellogg would probably be comfortable with a beta of 0.9.

Over the weekend, Debbie Duncan begins her assignment. She re-reads the Fama article and reviews her class notes from the graduate investments course that she had at U.C.L.A. during the spring quarter. In preparation for her next discussion with her father, Debbie focuses on several questions:

(1)   How well did Fund K perform relative to the market?

(2)   How well diversified was Fund K?

(3)   What was the implication of the risk level of Fund K being quite a bit higher than what the employees really wanted?

(4)   How well did the professional manager for Fund K do in selecting securities for the portfolio?

Charlie Colvin, treasurer and chief financial officer of the Mayfield Manufacturing Company, reluctantly cancels his participation in next Saturday's regular morning tennis foursome. The reason for this is that Charlie is saving the weekend to try and get prepared for a meeting the following Monday with Frank Riley, senior vice president of trust services at the Second National Bank of Allentown, Pennsylvania. The subject of the meeting is the bank's management of Mayfield's $5 million pension fund.

Mayfield is a manufacturer of air conditioning, heating, and refrigeration equipment. With manufacturing plants in three states, Mayfield's sales totaled $46 million in 1987. At year-end 1987, assets of $18 million were provided by $12 million debt and $6 million equity. One concern of Mayfield is that its debt-equity ratio of 2.0 is conspicuously higher than the industry average of 1.6.

Both sales and after-tax profits have grown steadily over the past decade, and especially so during the last five years. One of the main reasons for Mayfield's successful growth is a work force that is well-trained, experienced, and intensely loyal to the firm. An excellent profit-sharing program at Mayfield is supplemented by a generous defined-benefit retirement plan. Investment assets of the Mayfield pension fund are managed by the trust department at the Second National Bank. The pension fund portfolio currently consists of approximately $2 million in money market funds, plus $3 million in a well-diversified portfolio of investment grade common stocks.

In addition to his myriad of duties as chief financial officer, Charlie Colvin is responsible for overseeing the management of the company's pension fund. He meets quarterly with Frank Riley and other trust officers at bank headquarters to review investment policy, achieved pension fund performance, and future investment prospects. Mayfield's chief executive also attends on occasion, but clearly the responsibility belongs to Mr. Colvin.

Recently, Colvin met with an actuarial firm in Allentown to check the latter's report on Mayfield's pension plan liability. Based on conservative forecasts of manpower, retirement benefits, and portfolio returns, it is estimated that the present value of future retirement payments for Mayfield is approximately $3.8 million. And thus the retirement plan is currently overfunded by $1.2 million. Colvin is very anxious to maintain a healthy cushion (i.e. portfolio market value minus plan liability). For if the plan liability exceeds portfolio market value (i.e. the retirement plan is underfunded), then Mayfield's effective debt/equity ratio is even greater -- and it may become increasingly difficult for the firm to raise further external financing.

With the stock market crash of October 1987 still a vivid memory, and with a newly elected Republican president not yet in office, Charlie Colvin has growing concerns about the stock market's prospects for 1989 and beyond. He is comfortable that current stock market holdings of the portfolio (i.e. exposure) exceed the $1.2 million cushion in Mayfield's pension plan -- but that comfort level could certainly change if the stock market were to experience a significant correction, or even the more serious downturn that some analysts are predicting near the end of 1988.

Recently, Charlie skimmed an article (see Reading #18) that discusses the concept of portfolio insurance, and ways in which portfolio assets are revised to ensure that a pension plan does not become underfunded. He wonders if this would be a good time for Mayfield to implement portfolio insurance?

As an alternative for portfolio protection, Colvin remembers a comment made by Frank Riley at his last meeting with the Second National trust department. Namely, that it is possible to use stock index options to protect a pension fund portfolio against adverse market declines. Charlie thus wonders if perhaps this might be a good time for Mayfield to consider index options as an alternative for portfolio insurance.

Before leaving the office on Friday afternoon, Colvin gathers all relevant data on the Mayfield pension plan and portfolio. He asks his secretary to make him copies of the article on portfolio insurance, as well as to provide him with the latest market quotations on index options (see Exhibit 1).

With all this information, Charlie Colvin will use a good part of the weekend to prepare for the meeting with Riley on Monday. There are a number of issues and questions which he probably should consider in advance of that important meeting. Included are the following:

(1)   At present, Mayfield's pension fund has an exposure multiple of 2.5 ($3 million stock position <u>divided</u> by the plan's $1.2 million cushion). Suppose the firm agrees on a policy of maintaining that exposure multiple of 2.5, and with appropriate adjustments being made between common stocks and money market funds. What would be the necessary adjustment if the pension portfolio increased by 10% in value (assume that changes in portfolio value occur only with the common stocks)?

(2) What would be the necessary adjustment if, instead, the pension portfolio decreased by 10% in value?

(3) What would be the necessary adjustment if the pension portfolio subsequently decreased by another 15% in value?

(4) What should Colvin conclude about the impact of this type of portfolio insurance on portfolio holdings for the Mayfield pension fund?

(5) According to the current index option quotations, a January 280 put option on the S&P 500 Index could be purchased for (12)(500) = $6,000. What would be the dollar cost of providing complete (i.e. 100%) downside protection for the Mayfield pension portfolio using that particular put option? What is the annualized percentage cost of such protection?

(6) In view of that cost, it may be practical for Mayfield to provide only partial protection against adverse market movements. What, for example, would be the dollar and percentage costs of providing only 80% protection with the same January 265 put options?

(7) An alternative would be to utilize index put options with lower strike prices. Compare the cost of providing 80% protection in that manner. What should Mr. Colvin conclude?

(8) Based on these alternatives for portfolio insurance, what should Charlie Colvin recommend to Frank Riley and his colleagues at the bank? What other considerations should be brought into their discussion on Monday?

Exhibit 1

Chicago Board Index Option Trading
Tuesday, November 1, 1988

S&P 500 Index

Strike Price	Calls-Last Nov	Dec	Jan	Puts-Last Nov	Dec	Jan
235	...	...	...	...	9/16	...
240	...	40 1/4	...	...	3/4	...
245	...	...	...	...	15/16	...
250	...	...	...	...	1 5/16	4 1/4
255	...	...	...	1/2	1 3/4	...
260	19 3/4	...	28	3/4	...	...
265	15 3/4	17	22 1/2	1 1/4	3 1/8	6 3/4
270	...	...	...	2 1/8	4	8 1/8
275	6 3/4	10 1/4	16 3/4	3 1/8	6 1/8	...
280	3 5/8	6 3/4	13 7/8	4 7/8	...	12
285	1 11/16	...	...	8	10	...
290	11/16	2 11/16	...	...	...	...

The index: High 279.57; Low 278.01; Close 279.06. +0.09

310

Reverend Kevin White, senior pastor of First Community Church of Birmingham, Alabama, is in need of sound, albeit rather quick, investment advice. A distant relative, he sends a letter to you at the beginning of January 1989 in which he explains his relatively new position as a member of the Pension Fund Board of Advisors for the United Community Churches of America. Reverend White encloses two articles from the July-August 1986 issue of the FINANCIAL ANALYSTS JOURNAL (see Readings #19 and #21) that deal with South African divestiture -- the issue for which he seeks your advice.

Kevin White, age 52, has been the senior pastor at First Community for over seven years, during which the membership of that inner-city church has grown by over 30% to about 2,000 members. In so doing, Reverend White has established a wide following for his overall ministry, and especially his weekly sermons that are Biblical, conservative, but also quite practical. So much so that during the past three years, First Community has established an audio-tape ministry of White's sermons that now has circulation well beyond the city of Birmingham.

In the summer of 1987, Reverend White was elected to the Pension Fund Board that oversees the retirement assets for all Community churches in the United States, Canada, and Central America. Total retirement funds of that institution had a market value of $2.4 billion at the end of 1988, and with a cost basis of $2.1 billion. At that time, retirement funds were invested as follows: short term (i.e. money market) instruments 15%, high quality corporate and government bonds 30%, and blue-chip common stocks 55%. The investment portfolio has not been changed greatly in recent years, and, overall, its total market value has increased quite well.

The immediate issue has to do with the extent to which such a well-performing portfolio is invested in U.S. firms that do business in South Africa. Because of the considerable concern about the apartheid policies of the South African government, an increasing number of pastors and lay-leaders of the United Community Churches are greatly concerned about how the investment dollars of the institution's retirement assets are indeed invested. In sum, there is considerable feeling that the United Community Churches should sell all equity holdings of firms that do any business at all in South Africa. A recent study prepared by church headquarters staff indicated that almost 21% of the portfolio's common stocks would have to be sold if that feeling were to be implemented.

The Pension Fund Board meets twice a year to review investment performance and strategy -- as well as to discuss other matters pertaining to the pension assets of the United Community Churches. South African divestiture was not on the formal agenda of the August 1988 meeting in San Diego, but it was easily the most heated issue at that meeting. It is on the agenda for the February 1989 meeting in Orlando, and it is anticipated that the heated discussion will continue, and that certain members will put heavy pressure on the board to substantially alter the investment portfolio.

Although Reverend White did not speak up at the meeting in San Diego, he has rather strong feelings about the divestiture issue. Part of that is because his mother, age 76, has had to live extremely frugally the last fifteen years on the very modest retirement of her late husband, who like their son Kevin, was a minister in the United Community Churches. In particular, White feels that his mother and other pensioners who depend on the investment portfolio should not be put at a disadvantage just to satisfy certain board members' desire for social action. Moreover, White wonders about just what is "prudent" in this instance, and that is one reason why he enclosed the two articles on South African divestiture.

To further complicate the situation, Reverend White has been asked to lead the twenty-minute devotional time at the beginning the day on which divestiture is scheduled. That particular assignment has always been a focal point in setting the tone for the semi-annual meeting. As such, White is both honored and challenged -- for he has rather strong, albeit mixed, feelings about the scheduled agenda.

His letter to you asks that you review the two articles and give him your thoughts about the meeting in Orlando next month. In particular, he asks you for your advice on the following questions:

(1) Based on the two articles which were given to Reverend White, what seems to be the prevailing view about the relative merits of South African divestiture?

(2) Are there any factors unique to the goals and organizational structure of the Community Church that would seem to have a bearing on White's view toward divestiture?

(3) How important should the retirement status of White's mother be in his view toward divestiture?

(4) If you were Reverend White, what position would you take at the forthcoming meeting in Orlando?

(5) If you were Reverend White, what would you do about your devotional assignment?

312

William Winthrop is a leading and recognized citizen of Columbus, Ohio. After a very successful managerial career at Apex Chemicals, Mr. Winthrop, age 68, is now formally retired but quite busy in a number of civic and charitable activities. Among these activities, he is perhaps most proud of his participation since 1980 on the Board of Trustees of Central Columbus University (30 members). Winthrop was elected to the board while still active at Apex Chemicals, and thus his early years were more as a quiet participant. By now, however, he is the senior member of the Board, and thus is quite respected and often looked to for advice and leadership. Winthrop also serves as chairman of the Board's Investment Committee (6 members). He has enjoyed these roles, although recent developments have tended to complicate the situation.

Central Columbus University is a well-respected institution of higher education. It was founded in 1905 and currently has 25,000 students enrolled in schools of arts and sciences, business administration, law, and nursing and health. Total budget for fiscal year 1987 was $300 million, with tuition and fees (85%), private gifts and grants (13%), and endowment income (2%) as the major financial sources. While enrollments and private giving have been relatively stable during the past decade, endowment income has been somewhat erratic. In fact, the performance of the university's endowment funds, which currently total $76 million, has been a growing concern to Winthrop and his fellow trustees.

Part of the difficulty was that prior to fiscal 1984, Central Columbus University operated without any formal investment policies, objectives, or guidelines. One university administrator, as a part of his duties and supported by a single clerical personnel, operated the portfolio and maintained all necessary records. Another difficulty was that all funds were invested with three bank investment managers -- none of which had discretionary authority for the funds under their care. And there was a virtual lack of either criteria or comparable data for judging investment performance.

Several important changes were implemented at the beginning of fiscal year 1984. First, a formal statement of investment policy (see Exhibit 1) was approved by the investment committee and subsequently by the full board of trustees. Second, a master custodian trust (see Exhibit 2) was established with Columbus National Bank as the single conduit between all endowment funds and the institution's professional investment managers. Annual cost of the master custodian trust was $50,000 in directed commissions. Third, Superior Investments, Inc. was hired as a consultant to help select managers and subsequently monitor the investment performance of those professional managers. The fee to Superior Investments was also $50,000 in directed commissions. Fourth, relationships with the prior bank investment managers were terminated, and, after a careful search process, seven new managers were enlisted -- two responsible for fixed income funds, and five responsible for equity funds. Finally, Mr. Richard Roundtree, Vice President and Treasurer, retired after thirty years of loyal service to Central Columbus University.

Mr. Roundtree's successor, Mr. George Jacobson, came to his new position after several years as treasurer at a leading private university, in addition to considerable consulting experience in higher education. Jacobson very much agreed with the investment policy statement and the new master custodian arrangement, and he has spent a substantial part of his first two years implementing and coordinating these changes.

Indeed, George Jacobson has spent a good deal of time explaining these changes to William Winthrop, especially the procedures and advantages of the master custodian relationship. Although Winthrop serves as chairman of the Investment Committee, he relies heavily on Jacobson for establishing the agenda and providing appropriate materials for that bi-monthly meeting. At their last preparation meeting, Winthrop and Jacobson came up with the following list of issues and concerns that should be discussed at the next monthly meeting of the Investment Committee.

(1) To what extent should the trustees continue to be involved with investment matters, now that the new changes have been implemented? And to what extent should the Investment Committee involve the full Board in important decisions regarding the management of Central Columbus University's endowment funds?

(2) What information concerning the university's investment funds should be given to the Investment Committee and to the full group of trustees on a regular basis?

(3) Is the statement of investment policy still apropos for Central Columbus University?

(4) How are asset allocation decisions made within the new structure? How often should that decision be reviewed by the Investment Committee?

(5) What is the process whereby the investment managers are monitored and possibly changed by the Investment

Committee? Should the full Board be involved in that process at all?

(6) Does Superior Investments continue to serve a useful role?

(7) How good was the recent performance of the seven investment managers (see Exhibit 3)? In particular, has Delta Fund exhibited any improvement yet?

(8) What about the possibility of investing part of the endowment funds in real estate? International investments? Venture capital? How should such expanded strategies get decided?

(9) Is $100,000 in directed commissions a reasonable fee for consulting and master custodian services? Are these real costs?

(10) Central Columbus University would like to receive more annual income from the endowment funds. What are the best options for doing so?

In preparation for the next meeting of the university's Investment Committee, and subsequently its Board of Trustees, William Winthrop worries about the agenda, the issues, and what he -- as elder statesman among the thirty trustees -- can bring to those important meetings. What other advice would you give Winthrop on how to deal with each of the ten agenda items?

Exhibit 1
STATEMENT OF INVESTMENT POLICY, OBJECTIVES, AND GUIDELINES
CENTRAL COLUMBUS UNIVERSITY ENDOWMENT FUNDS

<u>Overall</u>

Central Columbus University, while recognizing that ultimate responsibility for satisfactory investment performance rests with the Central Columbus University Board of Trustees, believes this responsibility is best exercised by managing the investment management function, rather than being the investment manager. The Investment Committee believes it can best exercise its fiduciary responsibilities by:

1. Establishing investment philosophy and setting policy guidelines and objectives, which will be reviewed on at least an annual basis by the Investment Committee.

2. Selecting qualified independent investment managers.

3. Communicating closely with those responsible for investment results.

4. Monitoring investment results to assure that objectives are being met.

5. Taking appropriate actions if objectives are not being met.

<u>Philosophy</u>

The philosophic basis of this statement consists of the following statements:

1. The assets of the Endowment Fund are to be managed in accordance with the philosophy, objectives, and guidelines expressed herein. The investment managers are responsible for optimizing the return on the assets within these guidelines.

2. The endowment fund is a permanent fund. As such, the investment objectives require disciplined and consistent management philosophies that accommodate all those events which are relevant, reasonable, and probable. Extreme positions or variations in management style are not consistent with these objectives.

3. Careful endowment asset management should insure a total return (yield plus capital appreciation) necessary to preserve and enhance in real dollar terms the principal of the Fund while providing a dependable source of income from the Fund for current University purposes.

4. The purpose of equity investments is to provide current income, growth of income, and appreciation of principal.

5. The purpose of fixed income investments is to provide a predictable and dependable source of income and to reduce portfolio volatility.

6. The fixed income and equity portions of the investment portfolio shall be diversified in order to provide reasonable assurance that a single security (investment) or class of securities (investments) will not have a disproportionate or significant impact on the total portfolio.

7. Other than indicated herein, investments managers will have complete investment discretion for it is expected that the assets of the Fund will be invested with care, skill, prudence, and diligence.

General Investment Objectives and Guidelines

1. An average annual total real return of 4-6%, as measured over a three to five year market period, is the return objective.

2. The asset mix of the Endowment Fund will range within the following limits:

Fixed income securities	20-35%
Stocks (including convertibles)	65-80%

Equity Investments

1. Industry and company investments shall be based upon demonstrable analysis of prospects for above average return over a three to five year period. Emphasis should be placed on capital appreciation and growth of earnings.

2. Investment shall be made primarily in well-established, quality companies whose securities enjoy marketability adequate for this portfolio. Quality is not synonymous

with size or recognition. Further, it is recognized that equity investments in high quality, well established, and smaller companies (e.g. $100-500 million capitalization) could represent superior vehicles for preservation and enhancement of capital.

3.   For each manager, no more than 5% (at time of investment) of the net assets of the Fund shall be invested in securities of issues having a record of less than 3 years of operation.

4.   For each manager, concentration in any single industry and in any company shall not exceed 15% and 5% respectively of the market value of the Fund at the time of investment without prior approval of the Investment Committee's designee(s).

5.   Investments in equity (or debt issues) of smaller or small emerging companies may be made, but within the overall guidelines expressed herein. These investments (as distinguished from gifts) may not be made in letter stock, unregistered or privately placed securities without prior approval of the Investment Committee's designee(s).

Fixed Income Securities

1.   The bond portfolio structure as well as security selection are matters of investment management discretion, developed primarily in response to changing market relationships, interest rate forecasts, and liquidity requirements.

2.   The portfolio should be comprised of high quality issues consisting of Moody's A ratings and above or equivalent.

3.   Call protection should be emphasized to assure stable and current income.

Execution

1.   As a general guideline that applies to all assets managed, transactions should be entered into on the basis of best execution, which normally means best realized price. Commissions may be designated for the payment of investment services rendered to the University upon the approval of the Investment Committee's designee(s).

Investment Managers

1. The Investment Committee shall allocate funds to individual managers and from time to time may withdraw funds from or reallocate funds between managers.

2. Each manager's performance shall be compared regularly with the performance of equity and fixed income market indices, with mutual funds having similar objectives, with other funds managed by "peer group" managers, (e.g. similar types and objectives), and with other endowment funds.

3. Equity managers will be expected to achieve an average total rate of return over a three to five year period which exceeds the Standard and Poor's 500 rate of return by 1.5 - 2.0% compounded annually.

4. Fixed income managers will be expected to achieve an average total rate of return 1.0 - 1.5% compounded annually higher than the rate of return on the Salomon Brothers Index.

5. Custodial responsibility for all securities will be determined by the Investment Committee or its designee(s).

6. Investment managers are responsible for frequent and open communication with the University on all significant matters pertaining to the assets managed. Periodic objective evaluations of investment managers will be done.

7. The Investment Committee will meet as necessary with the investment managers. The frequency of these meetings will be determined by the performance evaluation results compared to predetermined objectives and manager characteristics.

Exhibit 2

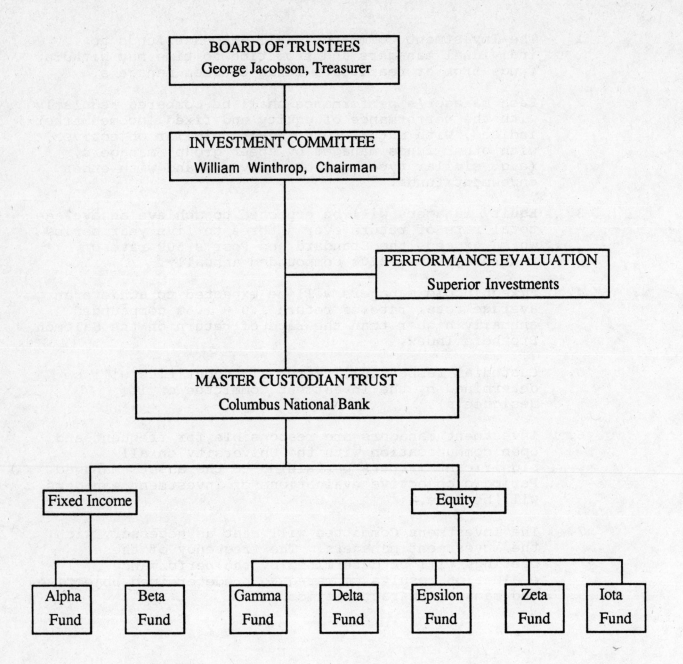

EXHIBIT 3

PERFORMANCE EVALUATION
FOR
CENTRAL COLUMBUS UNIVERSITY

INVESTMENT MANAGER	INVESTMENT POLICY	ASSETS MANAGED	PERCENT PORTFOLIO	PERCENT SECTOR	(%) QUARTERLY				(%) PERIODS ENDED JUN 86			(%) SINCE INCEPTION
					Sep 85	Dec 85	Mar 86	Jun 86	1/2 YR	3/4 YR	1 YR	
Fixed Income:												
Alpha Fund	Lower quality	9,199,952	12.11	44.16	1.9	6.7	8.0	1.1	9.2	16.5	18.8	14.0
Beta Fund	Higher quality	11,634,199	15.31	55.84	2.1	5.7	5.3	1.6	7.0	13.1	15.5	14.0
Subtotal		20,834,151	27.42	100.00	2.0	6.1	6.5	1.4	7.5	14.1	16.4	14.0
SLAE Index					2.0	7.7	8.4	1.8	10.3	19.8	21.2	15.9
Salomon Index					2.1	12.1	10.8	0.7	11.6	25.1	27.7	18.2
T-Bills					1.7	1.7	1.6	1.6	3.2	4.9	6.7	8.4
Equity:												
Gamma Fund	Value/income	18,169,579	23.91	32.95	-3.6	11.4	8.2	0.3	8.6	21.0	16.6	17.5
Delta Fund	Quality/growth	10,490,291	13.81	19.02	-7.7	15.7	16.1	2.6	19.2	37.8	27.3	16.6
Epsilon Fund	Aggressive Growth	7,363,919	9.69	13.35	-3.7	14.1	13.6	4.5	18.7	35.4	30.4	20.6
Zeta Fund	Growth/income	13,732,724	18.07	24.90	-0.6	12.4	15.2	6.8	23.0	38.2	37.4	23.1
Iota Fund	Smaller firms	5,387,172	7.09	9.77	-3.2	16.3	18.5	14.0	35.1	57.2	52.1	31.3
Subtotal		55,143,685	72.58	100.00	-3.8	13.4	13.0	4.3	17.8	33.6	28.6	19.8
S&P500 Index					-4.1	17.2	14.1	6.0	20.9	41.7	35.9	23.2
Total		75,977,836	100.00		-2.2	11.3	11.0	3.5	14.9	27.9	25.0	17.9
70% S&P/15% SLAE/15% Salomon					-2.3	15	12.7	4.6	17.9	35.6	32.5	21.5
Consumer Price Index					0.6	0.9	-0.4	0.4	0	0.9	1.5	3.1

Superior Investments, Inc.   Report as of June 1986

Simplifying portfolio insurance for corporate pension plans

A simplified method for protecting the surplus.

Fischer Black and Robert Jones

Changes in the value of pension assets relative to pension liabilities can affect reported earnings. Portfolio insurance can prevent the value of a pension plan's assets from falling below the present value of its liabilities. FAS 87, which requires companies that fail in this regard to post a balance sheet liability, has increased the importance of this objective.

To avoid a balance sheet liability, the pension plan needs a floor on the value of its assets equal to the present value of its obligations. To avoid a charge against earnings, the plan needs a floor to keep pension assets from falling too much relative to the present value of its obligations.

These floors will vary, because market interest rates vary. Market interest rates are what determine the present value of pension obligations. If interest rates go up, the present value of pension obligations (and the floor) will probably go down. If interest rates go down, the present value of pension obligations (and the floor) will probably go up. For a portfolio insurance strategy to work under these conditions, it needs a variable floor.

In our article, "Simplifying Portfolio Insurance," in the Fall 1987 issue of this Journal, we introduced a simple, flexible approach to portfolio insurance. Because you need to know only the current value of your portfolio and floor to determine your target asset mix, this approach easily accommodates a variable floor.

HOW FAS 87 AFFECTS A CORPORATE PENSION PLAN

FAS 87 increases the impact the pension plan has on corporate financial statements. The new rules require pension fund managers to report more complete information about the plan's status while reducing flexibility in measuring that status. Most important, by linking the pension plan to the balance sheet and income statement, FAS 87 encourages firms to maintain a surplus of pension assets over the present value of pension liabilities.

FAS 87 requires you to use market interest rates to compute the accumulated benefit obligation and the projected benefit obligation. The accumulated benefit obligation is the present value of earned benefits based on current and past compensation levels. The projected benefit obligation is the present value of earned benefits based on expected future compensation levels. In other words, the projected benefit obligation is the present value of the payments that you expect you will ultimately have to make for earned benefits. Both calculations take into account estimates of such future events as employee turnover and mortality. If benefits do not depend on future compensation levels, the accumulated benefit obligation equals the projected benefit obligation.

Under FAS 87, significant changes in pension plan status can affect reported earnings. In calculating earnings, you must amortize over ten to twenty years any unrecognized net change in the difference be-

FISCHER BLACK is a Partner and Director of the Quantitative Strategies Group at Goldman Sachs in New York (NY 10004). ROBERT JONES is in the Trading Group of the same organization.

tween the value of pension assets and the projected benefit obligation, provided the unrecognized change is more than 10% of the greater of the projected benefit obligation or the value of plan assets. You do not have to amortize changes until the year after they occur. You may also spread the effect of swings in asset values over a five-year period before calculating the change. Although FAS 87 may increase volatility in reported earnings, these smoothing techniques let you delay and reduce its effect.

For the balance sheet, you subtract the accumulated benefit obligation from the value of pension assets. Any deficit must be reported as a balance sheet liability.

To avoid a liability, the value of pension assets must stay above the accumulated benefit obligation. This makes the accumulated benefit obligation a floor for the value of the portfolio. To set such a floor, you must adopt an asset management strategy aimed at that goal.

HOW PORTFOLIO INSURANCE WORKS

Most portfolio insurance strategies have much in common. Usually, you start by choosing a floor for the value of the portfolio. The cushion is the difference between the value of the portfolio and the floor. As the cushion decreases (the portfolio approaches the floor), you sell risky assets to reduce your exposure. As the cushion increases, you buy risky assets to capture more of their appreciation.

Some forms of portfolio insurance use intricate mathematical models to determine what the asset mix should be in a given situation. But you don't need complex formulas for portfolio insurance. In "Simplifying Portfolio Insurance," we introduced a method that avoids complex math while offering the flexibility you need to accommodate a moving floor.

Professors Jay Light and André Perold of the Harvard Business School have produced an academic evaluation of the approach and conclude that it is optimal, in theory, for a broad class of investors. They have two papers forthcoming: "Constant Proportion Portfolio Insurance" is a general presentation of the approach, and "Conditional Allocation Policies for a Self-Insured Pension Fund" discusses some of its implications for pension plan management.

We assume the insured portfolio consists of two assets, an active asset and a reserve asset. Most pension funds hold several types of assets, and the concept works for a multi-asset portfolio; the two-asset case is just easier to understand.

The reserve asset has an acceptable minimum rate of return. Its value should move closely with the value of the floor. If it does not, then the floor might

rise above the portfolio's value or the portfolio might fall below the floor, even if you hold only the reserve asset.

Remember that the floor is your accumulated benefit obligation if you are trying to avoid a balance sheet liability. Your reserve asset should move closely with the accumulated benefit obligation.

A good choice for the reserve asset would be a package of securities that has the same sensitivity to interest rates that the accumulated benefit obligation has. Although the accumulated benefit obligation is affected by several factors that you cannot fully offset with exchange-traded assets, interest rate changes cause a large part of its variation.

A typical accumulated benefit obligation has about the same interest rate sensitivity that a long-term Treasury bond has. So let's say that your reserve asset is a long-term Treasury bond with the same sensitivity to interest rates that the accumulated benefit obligation has.

The active asset has a higher expected return than the reserve asset. The amount you have in the active asset is your exposure. Let's say that your active asset is the S&P 500.

Figure 1 compares the recent performance of certain long-term Treasury bonds against the S&P 500 and certain medium-term Treasury bonds. The long-term bond returns show how changes in interest rates might have affected a typical accumulated benefit obligation. The returns of the S&P 500 and medium-term bonds represent the performance of assets most widely held by pension plans to pay benefit obligations.

On average, from the beginning of 1982 until September 30, 1986, the long-term bond had a higher return than either of the other assets. This means that despite the substantial returns enjoyed by many pension portfolios in recent years, many accumulated benefit obligations have been rising even faster. If your portfolio was near its floor at the beginning of 1982, and you didn't use portfolio insurance with the long-term bond as your reserve asset, your portfolio could easily have gone below the floor, even though

FIGURE 1

Average Returns from 12/31/81 to 9/30/86 (annualized)

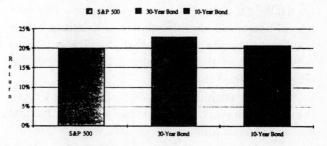

323

it might have done very well by historical standards. Figure 2 shows the performance for each year.

FIGURE 2

1-Year Returns

(1986 returns through 9/30 annualized)

One way to avoid posting a balance sheet liability is to invest an amount equal to the accumulated benefit obligation in long-term bonds. In this case, your exposure will equal the cushion. But this will leave just a small portion of the portfolio in stocks. Our method lets you increase your exposure to stocks without sacrificing the floor.

HOW OUR METHOD WORKS

KEY CONCEPTS
$e = mc$
e = exposure
c = cushion
m = multiple

Floor	Lowest value for the portfolio
Cushion	Portfolio value minus floor
Exposure	Amount in the active asset
Multiple	Exposure divided by cushion
Tolerance	Deviation from target exposure that triggers a trade
Limit	Maximum percentage of the portfolio in the active asset

You choose your initial exposure. Your multiple is your initial exposure divided by your initial cushion.

As the cushion changes, either because of changes in asset values or changes in the accumulated benefit obligation, you trade in order to bring exposure back to the multiple times the cushion. As the cushion approaches zero, allocation to bonds approaches 100%. Normally this will keep the cushion from falling to zero. The cushion will become negative only if assets fall sharply relative to liabilities before you have a chance to trade, or when the reserve asset falls relative to the accumulated benefit obligation when you are at the floor.

As the cushion rises, your exposure may reach the maximum you can have in stocks. During the time you are at your limit in stocks, you will not trade.

Choosing a high initial exposure when you have a small cushion will give you a large multiple. The higher the multiple, the more you will participate in a sustained stock market rally. But if stocks move up, then down, or down, then up, you will be moving quickly in and out of stocks, buying high and selling low. So the higher the multiple, the more you will lose in volatile markets.

Because it is impractical to trade continuously, you have to specify a tolerance for how far you will let the exposure drift from its target value before trading to restore the relation between exposure and cushion. When your tolerance is lower, exposure will be more closely related to the cushion, but your turnover and the frequency of your trades will be higher. More turnover means higher trading costs.

STRATEGY SIMULATIONS

Suppose you had started to use this strategy in 1975 with pension assets worth $100 million, an accumulated benefit obligation of $90 million, and an initial exposure to stocks of $60 million. That means your plan had an initial cushion between assets and liabilities of $10 million. Your multiple was a $60 million initial exposure divided by a $10 million initial cushion, or 6. When you traded, you did so to restore the 6-to-1 exposure-to-cushion ratio.

Assume the active asset was the S&P 500 and the reserve asset was a Treasury bond of between twenty-four and thirty years to maturity that moved precisely with the accumulated benefit obligation.

Suppose that you decided to trade when exposure was 10% more than your target exposure (the multiple times the cushion), or a corresponding amount less than the target exposure. If the floor did not change, that means you traded after roughly a 2% increase in the S&P 500 or a corresponding decrease. Assume that the full cost of your trades, including market impact or the effects of futures mispricing, was 0.5% of the value of your trades.

If you started using this strategy at the beginning of 1975, our simulations suggest that by the end of 1979, your floor would have grown from $90 million to $111.69 million. Your portfolio would have grown from $100 million to $192.46 million. So your cushion increased from $10 million to $80.77 million.

Most pension plans do not hold only long-term government bonds. They tend to hold mostly shorter-term bonds. So, for comparison, we simulated the performance of portfolios that kept constant percentages in the S&P 500 and in Treasury bonds of about ten years to maturity. We used the same trading cost assumption as for the insured portfolio simulations and tolerances tied to a 2% increase or a corresponding decrease in the S&P 500. So for a 60% S&P 500/ 40% ten-year bond portfolio, allocations were restored when there was a 0.8% surplus in exposure or a corresponding deficit.

If you started at the beginning of 1975 with a $100 million portfolio that had 60% in the S&P 500 and 40% in ten-year bonds, it would have been worth $166.24 million by the end of 1979. Your cushion would have risen from $10 million to $54.55 million. Table 1 shows detailed results for five-year

TABLE 1

Simulation Results for Five-Year Portfolio Insurance Strategies

Active Asset: S&P 500.   Reserve Asset: 30-Year Treasury bonds
Initial Portfolio = 100.   Initial Floor = 90.   Initial Cushion = 10
Initial Exposure = 60,   Multiple = 60/10 = 6

Tolerance: Rebalance when there is a 10% surplus exposure or a corresponding deficit
Trading Cost: 0.5% of amount traded

Years	Insured Portfolio's Final Value	Final Floor	Final Cushion	Final Exposure	Buys	Sells	Total Trading Cost	Constant Mix Strategies Using 10-Year Bonds 100% in S&P	60% in S&P	10% in S&P
1974-78	115.25	114.10	1.15	7.37	70	85	1.46	123.30	126.90	129.35
1975-79	192.46	111.69	80.77	192.46	3	0	0.38	198.73	166.24	131.57
1976-80	151.63	98.00	53.63	151.63	47	44	4.21	191.64	159.79	125.41
1977-81	121.53	83.03	38.50	121.53	37	33	2.59	146.86	128.76	107.25
1978-82	175.32	122.36	52.96	175.32	19	16	1.70	192.87	173.76	148.47
1979-83	211.08	123.22	87.86	211.08	8	5	0.77	222.08	192.89	157.48
1980-84	151.17	143.82	7.35	41.40	61	66	5.63	199.38	189.00	171.90
1981-85	198.16	197.59	0.57	3.18	86	109	2.24	198.71	207.83	215.19

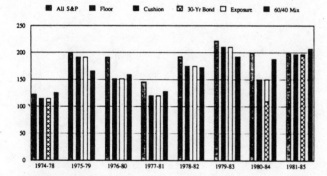

strategies initiated between 1974 and 1982. In each year, we assume that the portfolio starts at $100 million, the floor starts at $90 million, and exposure starts at $60 million. The first column lists the years of the simulation. The second column has the value of the insured portfolio at the end of the simulation, five years later. The third, fourth, and fifth columns show ending values of floor, cushion, and exposure, respectively. The sixth and seventh columns tell how many buys and sells were triggered over the simulation interval. The total cost of these trades is shown in the eighth column. And for comparison, the last columns show the results of three constant mix strategies: the first keeps the entire portfolio in stocks the whole time, the second starts with 60% (the initial exposure) in stocks and 40% in ten-year bonds, and the third starts with only 10% (the initial cushion) in stocks and 90% (the initial floor) in ten-year bonds.

Tables 2 and 3 show intermediate and ending portfolio and cushion values for simulations starting at the beginning of the years between 1974 and 1986,

TABLE 2

Insured Portfolio Performance

Active Asset: S&P 500.   Reserve Asset: 30-Year Treasury bonds
Initial Portfolio = 100.   Initial Floor = 90.   Initial Cushion = 10
Initial Exposure = 60,   Multiple = 60/10 = 6

Tolerance: Rebalance when there is a 10% surplus exposure or a corresponding deficit
Trading Cost: 0.5% of amount traded

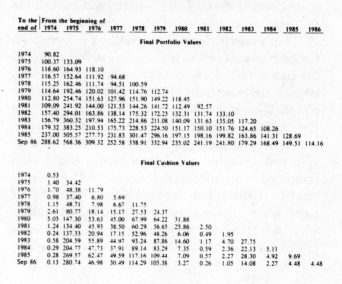

Final Portfolio Values

To the end of	1974	1975	1976	1977	1978	1979	1980	1981	1982	1983	1984	1985	1986
1974	90.82												
1975	100.37	133.09											
1976	118.60	164.93	118.10										
1977	116.57	152.64	111.92	94.68									
1978	115.25	162.46	111.74	94.51	100.59								
1979	114.64	192.46	120.02	101.42	114.76	112.74							
1980	112.80	254.74	151.63	127.96	151.90	149.22	118.45						
1981	109.09	241.92	144.00	121.53	144.26	141.72	112.49	92.57					
1982	157.40	294.01	163.86	138.14	175.32	172.23	132.31	131.74	133.10				
1983	156.79	360.32	197.94	165.22	214.86	211.08	140.09	131.63	135.05	117.20			
1984	179.32	383.25	210.53	175.73	228.53	224.50	151.17	150.10	151.76	124.65	108.26		
1985	237.00	505.57	277.73	231.83	301.47	296.16	197.15	198.16	199.82	163.86	141.31	128.69	
Sep 86	288.62	568.36	309.32	252.58	338.91	332.94	235.02	241.19	241.80	179.29	168.49	149.51	114.16

Final Cushion Values

To the end of	1974	1975	1976	1977	1978	1979	1980	1981	1982	1983	1984	1985	1986
1974	0.53												
1975	1.40	34.42											
1976	1.70	48.38	11.79										
1977	0.98	37.40	6.80	5.69									
1978	1.15	48.71	7.98	6.67	11.75								
1979	2.61	80.77	18.14	15.17	27.53	24.37							
1980	5.03	147.30	53.63	45.00	67.99	64.22	31.88						
1981	1.24	134.40	45.93	38.50	60.29	56.65	25.86	2.50					
1982	0.24	137.33	20.94	17.15	52.96	48.26	6.06	0.49	1.95				
1983	0.58	204.59	55.89	44.97	93.24	87.86	14.60	1.17	4.70	27.75			
1984	0.29	204.77	47.73	37.91	89.14	83.29	7.35	0.59	2.36	22.13	5.11		
1985	0.28	269.57	62.47	49.59	117.16	109.44	7.09	0.57	2.27	28.30	4.92	9.69	
Sep 86	0.13	280.74	46.98	30.49	114.29	105.38	3.27	0.26	1.05	14.08	2.27	4.48	4.48

TABLE 3

Constant Asset Mix Portfolio Performance

60% in S&P 500 and 40% in 10-Year Treasury bonds
Initial Portfolio Value = 100

Tolerance: Rebalance when there is a 0.8% surplus in exposure or a corresponding deficit
Trading Cost: 0.5% of amount traded

Final Portfolio Values

To the end of	1974	1975	1976	1977	1978	1979	1980	1981	1982	1983	1984	1985	1986
1974	85.53												
1975	106.13	124.08											
1976	129.15	150.99	121.69										
1977	122.98	143.78	115.88	95.24									
1978	126.90	148.36	119.57	98.27	103.18								
1979	142.19	166.24	133.98	110.11	115.61	112.05							
1980	169.58	198.26	159.79	131.32	137.88	133.64	119.26						
1981	166.28	194.40	156.67	128.76	135.20	131.03	116.94	98.05					
1982	213.71	249.86	201.37	165.49	173.76	168.42	150.30	126.02	128.53				
1983	244.77	286.17	230.63	189.54	199.02	192.89	172.14	144.33	147.20	114.53			
1984	268.74	314.19	353.22	208.10	218.50	211.78	189.00	161.62	125.75	109.79			
1985	352.46	412.07	332.10	272.93	286.57	277.75	247.88	207.83	211.96	164.92	143.99	131.16	
Sep 86	402.07	470.07	378.85	311.35	326.91	316.85	282.77	237.08	241.80	188.14	164.26	149.62	114.08

Final Cushion Values (When Floor Starts at 90)

To the end of	1974	1975	1976	1977	1978	1979	1980	1981	1982	1983	1984	1985	1986
1974	-4.76												
1975	7.16	25.41											
1976	12.25	34.44	15.38										
1977	7.39	28.54	10.76	6.25									
1978	12.80	34.61	15.81	10.43	14.34								
1979	30.16	54.55	32.10	23.86	28.38	23.68							
1980	61.81	90.82	61.79	48.36	53.97	48.64	32.69						
1981	58.43	86.88	58.60	45.74	51.23	45.96	30.31	7.98					
1982	56.55	93.18	58.45	44.50	51.39	44.45	24.05	-5.23	-2.62				
1983	88.56	130.44	88.58	69.29	77.40	69.68	46.65	13.87	16.85	25.08			
1984	89.71	135.71	190.42	70.28	79.11	70.57	45.18	8.95	12.22	23.23	6.64		
1985	115.74	176.07	116.84	90.69	102.26	91.03	57.82	10.24	14.41	29.36	7.60	12.16	
Sep 86	113.58	182.45	116.51	89.26	102.26	89.29	51.02	-3.85	1.05	22.93	-1.96	4.59	4.40

and ending on September 30, 1986. Table 2 shows the performance of the insured portfolio and Table 3 the performance of the 60%/40% constant mix portfolio.

Portfolio insurance helps most when the market goes straight up or straight down relative to the floor. Insured portfolios perform worst relative to constant mix portfolios in periods when the market and floor finish very close to where they started but had large fluctuations in between.

The period from the beginning of 1974 to the end of 1975 illustrates all three of these cases. In 1974, the S&P 500 lost 26.5%, while the floor rose only 0.3%.

In 1975, the S&P 500 gained 37.2%, and the floor rose 9.6%. If you had invested $100 in the S&P 500 at the beginning of 1974 and reinvested dividends, at the end of 1975 you would have made 40 cents.

Tables 2 and 3 show that the insured portfolio outperformed the 60%/40% constant mix portfolio in the separate one-year periods starting in 1974 and 1975 but underperformed the constant mix portfolio for the two-year period from the beginning of 1974 to the end of 1975. During 1974, the insured portfolio's cushion declined from $10 to $0.53 million while the 60%/40% constant mix portfolio finished below the floor with a cushion of −$4.76 million. If you started the strategy at the beginning of 1975, at the end of 1975 your cushion would have been $34.42 million compared to a static mix cushion of $25.41 million. If you had started the strategy in 1974, during 1975 your cushion would have grown from $0.53 to $1.40 million while the static mix portfolio's cushion would have grown from −$4.76 to $7.16 million.

The size of the cushion at the end of any period depends mostly on how the market does, how interest rates change, and how many times you trade. How many times you trade depends on the volatility of the market relative to the accumulated benefit obligation. If volatility is considerable, the cushion will decline even if the market level and interest rates are unchanged for the period.

When you adopt our strategy, there is no need to make any sudden adjustments to your asset mix. The choices of the floor and the initial exposure are independent of each other. You can increase your allocation to risky assets or keep the asset mix as it is.

Because our approach does not involve complex mathematical formulas, you can see what trades need to be made without using a computer. You can even adjust your multiple, your tolerance, or your floor to fit changes in your circumstances or changes in market conditions.

South African Divestment: Social Responsibility or Fiduciary Folly?

Richard M. Ennis and Roberta L. Parkhill

Although hundreds of U.S. corporations do business in South Africa, U.S. corporate investment there represents a small fraction of both U.S. corporate assets and the South African economy. It is thus not clear that South African divestment would have a material impact on South African policies or would benefit black South Africans.

The real issues for pension fund trustees are how divestment affects investment portfolios and the discharge of fiduciary duty. Statistical analysis confirms common sense: Divestment leads to the concentration of investment portfolios and introduces a risk of failing to earn the rate of return on an unconstrained portfolio. Divestment increases the cost of administering an investment program, too.

To pursue a policy of divestment with fiduciary funds is to ignore the "exclusive purpose" and diversification mandates of trust stewardship. Trustees may be held personally liable for additional costs and investment losses arising from divestment actions.

Although trustees make the decision to divest, investment managers are the ones who generally implement it. Inasmuch as divestment could hurt portfolio performance, it poses an ethical dilemma for investment professionals, who must choose whether to comply with or resist divestment directives.

THE BOARDS OF PUBLIC pension funds, endowed colleges and universities, foundations and other eleemosynary funds have faced or will soon probably have to face the question of divesting their portfolios of stocks of companies doing business in or with South Africa. All these funds have two things in common—an investment portfolio and political or social exposure. Corporate pension and profit-sharing funds, largely private and almost exclusively economic in their operation, are for now largely absent from the arena of the divestment controversy.

This article reviews the scope of U.S. investment in South Africa, the types of divestment activities under way in the U.S., and matters relating to the effectiveness of divestment as a means of bringing about reform in South Africa. A review of these issues may enable trustees to understand better the controversy in which they find themselves a party.

The article also addresses the issues of real importance to trustees and others involved with the management of institutional funds—namely, the effect divestment has on the risk and expected return of an investment portfolio and how divestment might impinge upon the discharge of fiduciary duty. We hope discussion of these issues can provide some policy guidelines for trustees and help clarify the ethical dilemma divestment poses for investment professionals.

Two Types of Divestment Activity

What is the mechanism by which divestment is intended to contribute to the solution of the South African problem? There are two closely related but distinct South African divestment strategies. One is *unqualified divestment*, which means the divestment of all companies doing business in South Africa. This strategy makes no attempt to distinguish between the employment practices of the various corporations oper-

Richard Ennis and Roberta Parkhill are associated with Ennis, Knupp & Gold, Inc., Chicago.

ating in South Africa. Unqualified divestment may be seen politically as an attempt to sanction Pretoria by pressuring all U.S. corporations to cease doing business in and with South Africa.

Qualified divestment is the sale of securities issued by those U.S. corporations not considered to be doing enough to promote fair and equal treatment of non-whites in South Africa. Qualified divestment is not so much aimed at sanctioning South Africa as at pressuring U.S. companies to adopt and abide by morally sound employment practices. Advocates of qualified divestment generally use the Sullivan Principles in selecting companies for divestment. (The appendix provides a summary of the Sullivan Principles.)

To understand the ramifications of either form of divestment, it helps to know the scope of U.S. investment in South Africa.

U.S. Investment in South Africa

The scope of U.S. investment in South Africa may be viewed as broad or narrow, depending on definitions employed. For divestment policy-making, the most useful definitions correspond to the types of divestment strategies that may be employed—namely, qualified or unqualified.

Unqualified U.S. Investment

As of December 31, 1984, approximately 620 U.S. firms had operations in South Africa. These tend to be among the largest companies headquartered in the United States, hence they represent a large proportion of the securities in which institutional funds generally invest. Of the companies included in the S&P 500 stock index, 166 do business in or with South Africa. Although they represent only one-third of the companies included in the index, they account for approximately 52 per cent of the index's market capitalization. Furthermore, U.S. companies doing business in South Africa issue approximately one-third of the corporate bonds rated "A" or better.

Companies with operations in South Africa represent not only a large proportion of the S&P 500, but also the bulk of several industry groups within the index. Table I identifies 10 industries in which 75 per cent or more of the companies have operations in South Africa.[1]

Although the number of U.S. companies with operations in South Africa is large, their South

1. Footnotes appear at end of article.

Table I Major U.S. Investments in South Africa by Industry (percentages based on market capitalization)

Industry	% of S&P 500 Industry Group With Operations in South Africa
Industrial Equipment	99%
Banks	97
Photographic Equipment	93
Chemicals	87
Drugs	87
Conglomerates	86
Tire and Rubber	85
Office Equipment	84
Motor Vehicles	81
International Oils	76

African operations are small. The Department of Commerce has estimated that direct U.S. investment in South Africa amounts to approximately $2.3 billion.[2] As Table II shows, the 10 companies with the largest investments have, on average, less than 1 per cent of their total assets invested in South Africa.[3]

Sullivan Signatories

We said that qualified divestment is an attempt to bring about change in South Africa *through* corporations that do business there and that the most common qualified divestment schemes involve use of the Sullivan Principles. The Sullivan Principles describe standards for desegregation of work facilities, equitable employment, compensation and promotion practices, and the initiation of training programs. Arthur D. Little, Inc. monitors compliance and assigns companies to the following categories:

I. Making Good Progress
II. Making Progress
III. Needs to Become More Active
IV. Endorsers With No Employees and No Equity
V. New Signatories

Table III summarizes how unqualified divestment and various qualified divestment schemes involving the Sullivan Principles would affect investors who consider the S&P 500 to be a proxy for their investment opportunity set. Unqualified divestment eliminates over half the S&P 500 stock universe. Various forms of qualified divestment eliminate from as much as 32 per cent of the S&P 500 (excluding all companies not signatory to the principles and not "making good progress") to as little as 13 per cent (excluding only non-signatory companies). The

Table II Ten Largest U.S. Corporate Investments In South Africa

Company	South African Assets (in millions)	Total Assets (in millions)	South African Assets as a % of Total
Mobil Oil Corp.	$ 400	$ 41,851	1.0%
Ford Motor Co.	230	27,449	0.8
Burroughs Corp.	150	4,504	3.3
General Motors Corp.	140	52,001	0.2
Newmont Mining Corp.	86	2,133	4.0
Xerox Corp.	42	15,406	0.3
Sperry Corp.	33	5,741	0.6
Phelps, Dodge Corp.	37	1,728	2.1
Norton Co.	26	1,060	2.5
Minnesota Mining & Manufacturing Co.	26	6,094	0.4
Total/Average	$1,170	$157,967	0.7%

wide range of results makes it all the more important for trustees contemplating divestment to think through their social motives.

Divestment Legislation Affecting Public Funds

The most comprehensive (restrictive) divestment legislation calls for divestment of investments in any banks making loans to the South African public and private sectors, as well as of investments in any companies doing business in or with South Africa. The appendix contains examples of unqualified divestment legislation.

The most common form of qualified divestment legislation identifies those companies that are signatories to the Sullivan Principles as being acceptable for investment. Other legislation requires Sullivan signatory companies to receive a specific performance rating in order to be considered an acceptable investment. The appendix provides several examples of specific legislation.

The majority of this legislation has been enacted since late 1984. Because these restrictions are so new, there have yet to be many legal challenges. The Attorney General of the State of Florida and the City Attorney of Dallas have issued opinions holding that divestment legislation would be contrary to trustees' fiduciary responsibility. Generally speaking, members and trustees of public retirement systems have not sought this legislation and have, in fact, in most instances strongly opposed it.

Effectiveness of Divestment as a Social Strategy

It is probably accurate to say that the majority of Americans feel a sense of moral outrage over the treatment of black South Africans by the white minority there, and the seeming intractability of Pretoria has done nothing to mollify its critics. The question remains, however, whether divestment can do anything to change Pretoria's policies.

Table III Effect of Alternative Divestment Schemes on Limiting Investment Opportunities Within the S&P 500 (dollars in billions)

	Number of Companies	Value at March 31, 1985	% of the S&P 500
S&P 500	500	$1,311	100%
Exclude all companies with South African operations (unqualified divestment)	166	684	52
Exclude all companies not "making good progress" (Categories II-V)	135	424	32
Exclude all companies that "need to become more active" (Category III)	68	180	14
Exclude non-signatory companies only	64	170	13

Many proponents of divestment seem to evince no doubt that it is obviously the right and efficacious thing to do—at least from a moral and strategic standpoint, if not from a fiduciary one. A number of reasonably well informed observers disagree, however; they question the efficacy of U.S. divestment as a social strategy, apart from any fiduciary considerations. They argue that divestment, *per se*, will neither alter much in South Africa nor benefit black South Africans.

If Divestment Succeeds

If divestment efforts succeeded in causing U.S. companies to abandon their South African operations, would the withdrawal contribute meaningfully to the end of apartheid? U.S. investment in South Africa represents only a small fraction of South African industry. As of 1983, U.S. companies operated only 3 per cent of South Africa's industrial plant.[4] Furthermore, it is entirely probable that the U.S. presence would merely be replaced by local interests or other foreign concerns. The ultimate success of divestment strategies might thus have little impact on the economy of South Africa; its repercussions for blacks in South Africa may actually be negative.

According to the *Ninth Report on the Signatory Companies to the Sullivan Principles*, U.S. companies employ more than 62,000 South African workers, of whom approximately two-thirds are black, colored or Asian.[5] Working conditions for blacks employed by U.S. firms are among the best in South Africa. These companies have a record of providing equal pay for equal work and virtually all have desegregated work facilities.[6] (Desegregated work facilities are illegal in South Africa, but the government does not enforce this law at the facilities of U.S. companies.)

U.S. companies have also spent substantial sums of money to improve working and living conditions of black employees. During the last six years, these companies have spent more than $80 million to provide housing, training and educational programs for employees and non-employees.[7] Were U.S. firms to cease operations in South Africa, these programs would presumably be discontinued, and some black workers would undoubtedly become unemployed. If non-U.S. companies were to take over U.S. operations, the record suggests that they would not likely be as fair to black workers.

How Do Black South Africans Feel About Divestment?

It is not clear how black South Africans feel about U.S. divestment. One survey by a leading South African poll analyst, Lawrence Schlemmer, addressed the specific question of U.S. divestment and found that a majority of black South Africans opposed U.S. divestment, and most said that American companies exert a constructive pressure for better jobs and working conditions. Another poll, published by *The Sunday Times of London* and conducted by Markinor, a Gallup-affiliated organization, indicates that three out of four blacks in South Africa now—and for the first time—favor "sanctions against the Pretoria Government."[8] There is no indication, however, that the poll dealt specifically with how blacks feel about U.S. divestment. The signals from black South Africans appear to be mixed at best.

These are some of the reservations concerning the wisdom of divestment as a social strategy. It is a controversial issue and the controversy is likely to continue. Fortunately for trustees, however, resolution of this controversy is not essential to their determining whether divestment is appropriate for their funds. The issues of real importance to trustees are (1) the effect of divestment on the cost of administration and on the risk and return of investment portfolios and (2) how divestment might affect the discharge of fiduciary duty.

Portfolio Implications of Divestment

Divestment has an impact on investment portfolios, both in terms of the cost of administration and the return that can be earned for a given level of risk. Some of the added costs and risk considerations are difficult to quantify, but they exist nonetheless.

Divestment Costs

Should a fund's trustees decide to divest South Africa-related issues, they must begin by restructuring the fund. This involves not only the sale of prohibited securities, but also the purchase of replacement securities. Such restructuring does not come without cost. Wells Fargo Investment Advisors has estimated that a $1 billion portfolio would incur a one-time cost of 1.5 per cent of assets, or $15 million, to effect unqualified divestment; qualified divestment would, of course, cost less.

Divestment also involves increased costs of

investment research, which may be passed on to funds in the form of higher management fees. As noted, the companies doing business in South Africa tend to be among the largest-capitalization companies in the United States. Eliminating these companies means that small-capitalization companies would constitute a greater proportion of permissible investments. Because there is considerably less research readily available on small-capitalization corporations, research activity may be expected to increase for divested portfolios.

Small-capitalization stocks are also less liquid than large-capitalization stocks. It is likely that the increased demand for fewer securities will result in higher trading costs and prices. This problem is magnified for large funds, which must buy large share positions in order to achieve proper diversification.[9]

In addition to increased investment costs, divestment programs also cost more to administer. Trustees must insure that portfolio managers are adhering to investment restrictions and must also be aware of changes in the status of restricted and non-restricted companies. Evaluating the performance of investment managers is complicated because the manager's investment universe is restricted; standard performance benchmarks such as the S&P 500 and the Shearson Lehman Government/Corporate Bond Index are no longer appropriate. It will generally be necessary to construct and monitor appropriate performance benchmarks.

Portfolio Risk Implications

Table I identified 10 S&P 500 industries in which 75 per cent or more of the companies (by market-capitalization weight) have operations in South Africa. Table IV gives a further indication of the reduction in the investment universe that results from divestment.[10] This table divides the S&P 500 by economic sector, market sector and company size. Regardless of how one views the stock market, divestment will severely restrict investment (diversification) opportunities. This means a South Africa-free portfolio will be *more concentrated*, hence prone to producing a rate of return that is different from that of an unconstrained portfolio.

Through the use of portfolio optimization techniques, it is possible to construct South Africa-free portfolios with statistical risk characteristics similar, but not identical, to those of the S&P 500.[11] What such analyses fail to portray effectively, however, are the consequences of the unusual occurrence.

For example, in mid-1982 a manager could have constructed a South Africa-free portfolio that, statistically, was not much riskier than the S&P 500. But such a portfolio would have ex-

Table IV   Proportion of South Africa-Related Issues by Various Market Segmentations

	S&P 500 Market Value (in billions)	South Africa-Related Issues Market Value (in billions)	% of S&P 500
Economic Sector			
Consumer Nondurable/ Services	$315	$131	42%
Consumer Durables	59	37	61
Technology	132	93	71
Energy	176	62	35
Basic Industry	230	103	45
Interest Rate Related	209	23	11
Market Sector			
Growth	$382	$229	60%
Growth/Cyclical	290	80	27
Cyclical	209	87	42
Defensive	225	53	23
Other	15	—	1
Company Size			
Large Capitalization	$510	$295	58%
Medium Capitalization	584	149	47
Small Capitalization	27	5	18

cluded approximately 70 per cent of the technology sector. During the 12-month period from June 30, 1982 to June 30, 1983, the technology sector was the best-performing sector in the index, earning a return greater than 90 per cent. The second best-performing sector, consumer cyclicals, earned approximately 80 per cent; nearly 60 per cent of the companies in this sector have operations in South Africa. These two sectors represent approximately one-third of the S&P 500 and contributed substantially to its favorable return in that 12-month period. The South Africa-free portfolio would have forgone a material fraction of these returns.

If divested portfolios achieve a lower rate of return than their unconstrained counterparts, or if they cost more to operate, the trustees of these funds may be held responsible for the loss incurred. Given the size of the sums involved, this is not an inconsequential consideration.

Legal Issues

Private-sector pension plans have been regulated by the Employee Retirement Income Security Act (ERISA) since 1974. It requires of trustees that (among other things) they administer funds solely in the interest of the beneficiaries and for the exclusive purpose of providing benefits to participants and their beneficiaries. This means trustees may not be guided by the interest of a third party. In 1981, the Supreme Court of the United States reaffirmed the "exclusive purpose" provision of ERISA.[12] In a case involving Amax Coal Company and the United Mine Workers (191 S.Ct. 2789), the Court said:

> "Under the principles of equity, a trustee bears an unwavering duty of complete loyalty to the beneficiary of the trust, to the exclusion of the interests of all other parties."

Although this interpretation of "solely in the interest of" and "exclusive purpose" arose from a case not involving a social investment issue, it makes it clear that trustees may not attempt to serve two masters with fiduciary funds, whether the second be the welfare of black South Africans, a cleaner environment or a safer world.

ERISA also requires that trustees diversify the assets of the plan so as to minimize the risk of large losses, "unless under the circumstances it is clearly prudent not to do so." The portfolio concentrations that tend to result from divest-

ment are contrary to the spirit of ERISA's diversification language. To concentrate a plan's assets in order to serve an excluded purpose would seem doubly imprudent.

Although public pension funds are not covered by ERISA, a number of state legislatures have adopted ERISA's "solely in the interest of," "exclusive purpose" and diversification language *verbatim* in legislation governing their public pension systems. More generally, under the common trust law from which ERISA's fiduciary standards evolved, public pension fund and most other trustees operate under the same standard of care. This concept was reinforced in New Hampshire, where the State Supreme Court ruled that the New Hampshire Retirement System is a trust fund rather than a state agency and, as such, its trustees are subject to ERISA-like standards.[13]

Personal Liability

In instances where legislation requires public university funds or public employee pension funds to divest securities of companies operating in South Africa, trustees may be obliged to divest. But where trustees act on their own accord, or on the basis of resolutions lacking the force of law, they may breach their fiduciary responsibility. This could have serious consequences for trustees; they may be held personally liable for losses sustained as a result of violation of fiduciary standards.

ERISA states:

> "Any person who is a fiduciary with respect to a plan who breaches any of the responsibilities, obligations, or duties imposed upon fiduciaries by this title shall be personally liable to make good to such plan any losses to the plan resulting from each such breach . . . and shall be subject to such other equitable or remedial relief as the courts may deem appropriate, including removal of such fiduciary."

The bite of personal liability could be felt by non-ERISA trustees as well. If there is any doubt concerning the standard of care applicable in a given circumstance, legal counsel should be consulted.

Adherence to the "solely in the interest of" and "exclusive purpose" tenets of prudence provides trustees with what the legal profession refers to as a "safe harbor." Some trustees, as a matter of conscience or for the perceived greater good of their institution, have elected to abandon the safe harbor. Others are likely to feel obliged to follow suit. A question then arises: For those who choose to divest, is there another safe harbor further down the shore?

Some trustees have minimized the extent of the exclusion of investment opportunities by eliminating only non-signatories to the Sullivan Principles. Others have attempted to optimize the diversification of remaining investments and thus to minimize the concentration effects of divestment. From the standpoint of minimizing the potentially adverse impact of divestment, these are constructive measures. But these acts are more akin to hugging the shore in times of stormy weather than they are to anchoring in a safe harbor—a subtle distinction perhaps, but one worth noting nonetheless.

An Option for Foundations

Inasmuch as foundations exist to give away money in socially beneficial ways, they have an option generally unavailable to others contemplating divestment. A foundation board with an earnest desire to bring about change in South Africa might estimate the economic cost of divestment—but not divest—and make a grant in that amount to further justice in South Africa, in a manner of the trustees' choosing. Not only are the trustees assured of not breaching their fiduciary responsibility (assuming the grant is in keeping with the foundation's charter), but it would seem that a well aimed grant could be at least as effective as divestment in furthering the interests of black South Africans.

A Postscript on Insurance

It is ironic that the divestment issue would come to a head at the same time that many boards are reevaluating their directors and officers (D&O) coverage. For reasons unrelated to divestment, premiums for D&O insurance have recently skyrocketed. In many instances, policies have been canceled outright as fewer and fewer insurance companies remain willing to write D&O coverage. As a result, some boards are doing without it. With the market for D&O coverage in disarray, it seems an especially inopportune time to take liberties with fiduciary standards. The concept of personal liability seems to take on greater meaning in the face of uncertain D&O protection.

An Ethical Issue for Investment Professionals

Although trustees make the divestment decision, they ordinarily direct their investment managers to execute it. Should the managers comply? Apart from the legal questions raised by divestment, we believe it raises an ethical question.

Is the business of investing fiduciary funds not also a profession? Intrinsic to a profession are its precepts, or doctrines. Divestment bruises one precept central to the investment profession by precluding a portfolio from owning a significant fraction of the universe of stocks; a portfolio that is constrained does not offer the same expected risk-adjusted return as one that is not. Must not the investment professional, therefore, make an ethical judgment before he invokes the paraphernalia of optimization, or whatever other means of compromise by which he identifies the portfolio of his second or third choice? Must he not ask himself, "Could this action have a materially adverse impact on the portfolio's rate of return?"

If the investment professional is concerned that, by yielding to a divestment directive, he may hurt portfolio performance to a meaningful degree, he should think twice about complying. Would it require a Thoreauvian constitution to resist? There is, of course, the possibility that the client would dismiss the manager for dragging his heels; that would be painful. On the other hand, there is the possibility that the investment manager's reluctance to be a party to divestment would have a mitigating influence on the client. In weighing the pros and cons of divestment, it would seem that prudent trustees would be reluctant to take an action that would cause their professional co-fiduciaries to go on strike.

Indeed, the investment manager should not overlook the possibility that *compliance* with a divestment directive could also jeopardize his job. A future generation of trustees—a group not favorably disposed to divestment—coming upon a divestment-damaged portfolio might fire the manager on the all-too-familiar, retrospective grounds, "The professionals should have known better."

Divestment literature has little to say concerning the ethical implications of divestment for the investment professional. Perhaps we are mistaken in thinking it an issue worthy of debate. Or perhaps the time is approaching when we will conclude that we have dawdled long enough among the politics, the investment technicalities and the legal ambiguities of South African divestment and must, as a profession, come to grips with the ethical dilemma it has created.

As a socioeconomic strategy, divestment is problematic at best. As an act of trusteeship it appears to be in conflict with basic precepts. For the investment manager, it clashes with professional doctrine and thus presents an ethical dilemma. All things considered, trustees would be wise not to mix social activism with the discharge of their fiduciary duty, and investment professionals should think twice before acceding to divestment directives. ■

Footnotes

1. From W.H. Wagner, A. Emkin and R.L. Dixon, "South African Divestment: The Investment Issues," *Financial Analysts Journal*, November/December 1984.
2. *Overseas Business Reports* (Washington, DC: U.S. Department of Commerce—International Trade Administration, November 1984).
3. *The Chicago Tribune*, July 14, 1985.
4. R. A. Schotland, "Divergent Investing of Pension Funds and University Endowments: Key Points About the Pragmatics and Two Current Case Studies," in *Divestment, Is it Legal, Is it Moral, Is it Productive?* (Washington, DC: National Legal Center for the Public Interest, February 1985), p. 45.
5. *Ninth Report on the Signatory Companies to the Sullivan Principles* (Cambridge, Mass.: Arthur D. Little, Inc., October 1985), p. 13.
6. Communications Task Group of Sullivan Signatory Companies, *Meeting the Mandate for Change* (New York: Industry Support Unit, 1984), p. 6.
7. Ibid, p. 20.
8. Editorial, *The New York Times*, August 1985.
9. Wagner et al., "South African Divestment," *op cit.*, p. 6.
10. From D.A. Love, "On South Africa," *Financial Analysts Journal*, May/June 1985.
11. Analyses of this problem indicate that one could construct a portfolio with a beta equal to that of the S&P 500 and an R-squared (the degree of diversification compared with that of the market) slightly lower. But even these analyses make it explicit that expected return per unit of risk is sacrificed.
12. J.G. Gillis, "Securities Law and Regulation," *Financial Analysts Journal*, January/February 1982.
13. T. Ring, "Court Supports New Hampshire System," *Pensions & Investment Age*, March 4, 1985.

Appendix

Sullivan Principles

Principle 1: Nonsegregation of the races in all eating, comfort, locker rooms and work facilities

Principle 2: Equal and fair employment practices for all employees

Principle 3: Equal pay for all employees doing equal or comparable work for the same period of time

Principle 4: Initiation and development of training programs that will prepare blacks, coloreds and Asians in substantial numbers for supervisory, administrative, clerical and technical jobs

Principle 5: Increasing the number of blacks, coloreds and Asians in management and supervisory positions

Principle 6: Improving the quality of employees' lives outside the work environment in such areas as housing, transportation, schooling, recreation and health facilities

The following performance rating categories were established by Dr. Leon H. Sullivan to assess the efforts of signatory companies in implementing the six principles. Signatory companies are evaluated annually by Arthur D. Little, Inc.

I. Making Good Progress
II. Making Progress
  A. Based on full report
  B. Based on abbreviated report
III. Needs to Become More Active
  A. Received low point score
  B. Did not pass basic requirements
IV. Endorsers With No Employees and No Equity
V. New Signatories

A Summary of Divestment Legislation

Unqualified Divestment

The states of Nebraska, New Jersey, New Mexico, Massachusetts and Michigan prohibit investments in any financial institution making loans to the South African public or private sectors and any companies with operations in South Africa, although Michigan's restriction applies only to public university funds.

The following cities have enacted the same

type of ordinance: Atlantic City, New Jersey; Berkeley, California; Boston, Massachusetts; Grand Rapids, Michigan; Newark, New Jersey; Philadelphia, Pennsylvania; Washington, D.C.; and Wilmington, Delaware. We note, however, that Berkeley, California specifically exempts pension and employee compensation funds from its ordinance.

Qualified Divestment

Davis, California, Rahway, New Jersey and the state of Maryland prohibit the deposit or investment of any public funds in a bank or financial institution with outstanding loans to the Republic of South Africa.

Charlottesville, Virginia prohibits the investment of city retirement funds in companies that do business in South Africa *if* they have not signed or are not adhering to the Sullivan Principles.

Connecticut legislation requires the state to divest of companies that have not signed the Sullivan Principles or that do not obtain a performance rating in the top two categories of the Sullivan Principle rating system.

Nebraska must divest state funds of the stock of any U.S.-based company doing business in South Africa that has not signed the Sullivan Principles and any signatory company that has not received a Category I performance rating by January 1, 1987. Nebraska is further restricted from making new investments in corporate bonds of companies doing business in South Africa and banks with loans outstanding to the South African public sector.

The New York City Employees Retirement System has a four-phase divestment program that could result in near-total divestment of the fund's South Africa-related holdings within five years. Phase I calls for divestment of securities of companies that support apartheid or are not signatories to the Sullivan Principles or do not employ a similar corporate policy. Phase II requires divestment of the securities of those companies that are Sullivan signatories but fail to file annual reports with Arthur D. Little, Inc., or another independent monitor. Phase III requires divestment of companies not receiving a Category I Sullivan rating. Phase IV calls for divestment of any remaining South Africa-related securities with the exception of those that receive a Category I Sullivan rating and are "of substantial assistance in efforts to eliminate apartheid."

COMPONENTS OF INVESTMENT PERFORMANCE*

EUGENE F. FAMA‡

I. INTRODUCTION

THIS PAPER SUGGESTS methods for evaluating investment performance. The topic is not new. Important work has been done by Sharpe [21, 22], Treynor [23], and Jensen [13, 14]. This past work has been concerned with measuring performance in two dimensions, return and risk. That is, how do the returns on the portfolios examined compare with the returns on other "naively selected" portfolios with similar levels of risk?

This paper suggests somewhat finer breakdowns of performance. For example, methods are presented for distinguishing the part of an observed return that is due to ability to pick the best securities of a given level of risk ("selectivity") from the part that is due to predictions of general market price movements ("timing"). The paper also suggests methods for measuring the effects of foregone diversification when an investment manager decides to concentrate his holdings in what he thinks are a few "winners."

Finally, most of the available work concentrates on single period evaluation schemes. Since almost all of the relevant theoretical material can be presented in this context, much of the analysis here is likewise concerned with the one-period case. Eventually, however, a multiperiod model that allows evaluations both on a period-by-period and on a cumulative basis is presented.

II. FOUNDATIONS

The basic notion underlying the methods of performance evaluation to be presented here is that the returns on managed portfolios can be judged relative to those of "naively selected" portfolios with similar levels of risk. For purposes of exposition, the definitions of a "naively selected" portfolio and of "risk" are obtained from the two-parameter market equilibrium model of Sharpe [20], Lintner [15, 16], Mossin [18] and Fama [10, 11]. But it is well to note that the two-parameter model just provides a convenient and somewhat familiar set of naively selected or "benchmark" portfolios against which

* Research on this paper was supported by a grant from the National Science Foundation.
‡ Graduate School of Business, University of Chicago.

the investment performance of managed portfolios can be evaluated. As indicated later, other risk-return models could be used to obtain benchmark portfolios consistent with the same general methods of performance evaluation.

In the simplest one-period version of the two-parameter model, the capital market is assumed to be perfect—that is, there are no transactions costs or taxes, and all available information is freely available to everybody—and investors are assumed to be risk averse expected utility maximizers who believe that return distributions for all portfolios are normal. Risk aversion and normally distributed portfolio returns imply that the expected utility maximizing portfolio for any given investor is mean-standard deviation efficient.[1] In addition, investors are assumed to have the same views about distributions of one-period returns on all portfolios (an assumption usually called "homogeneous expectations"), and there is assumed to be a riskless asset f, with both borrowing and lending available to all investors at a riskless rate of interest R_f.

It is then possible to show that in a market equilibrium all efficient portfolios are just combinations of the riskless asset f and one portfolio of risky assets m, where m, called the "market portfolio," contains every asset in the market, each weighted by the ratio of its total market value to the total market value of all assets. That is, if $\tilde{R}_m$, $E(\tilde{R}_m)$ and $\sigma(\tilde{R}_m)$ are the one-period return, expected return, and standard deviation of return for the market portfolio m, and if x is the proportion of investment funds put into the riskless asset f, then all efficient portfolios are formed according to[2]

$$\tilde{R}_x = xR_f + (1-x)\tilde{R}_m \qquad x \leqslant 1, \qquad (1)$$

so that

$$E(\tilde{R}_x) = xR_f + (1-x)E(\tilde{R}_m) \qquad (2)$$

$$\sigma(\tilde{R}_x) = (1-x)\sigma(\tilde{R}_m). \qquad (3)$$

Geometrically, the situation is somewhat as shown in Figure 1. The curve b m d represents the boundary of the set of portfolios that only include risky assets. But efficient portfolios are along the line from R_f through m. Points below m (that is, $x \geqslant 0$) involve lending some funds at the riskless rate R_f and putting the remainder in m, while points above m (that is, $x < 0$) involve borrowing at the riskless rate with both the borrowed funds and the initial investment funds put into m.

In this model the equilibrium relationship between expected return and risk for any security j is

$$E(\tilde{R}_j) = R_f + \left[\frac{E(\tilde{R}_m) - R_f}{\sigma(\tilde{R}_m)} \right] \frac{\text{cov}(\tilde{R}_j, \tilde{R}_m)}{\sigma(\tilde{R}_m)} \qquad (\textit{Ex ante} \text{ market line}). \quad (4)$$

Here cov $(\tilde{R}_j, \tilde{R}_m)$ is the covariance between the return on asset j and the return

1. By definition, a mean-standard deviation efficient portfolio must have the following property: No portfolio with the same or higher expected one-period return has lower standard deviation of return.

2. Tildes (~) are used throughout to denote random variables. When we refer to realized values of these variables, the tildes are dropped.

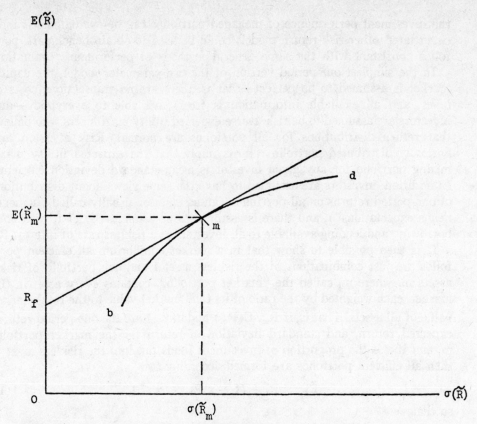

FIGURE 1
The Efficient Set with Riskless Borrowing and Lending

on the market portfolio m. In the two-parameter model $\sigma(\tilde{R}_m)$ is a measure of the total risk in the return on the market portfolio m. Since the only risky assets held by an investor are "shares" of m, it would seem that, from a portfolio viewpoint, the risk of an asset should be measured by its contribution to $\sigma(\tilde{R}_m)$. In fact this contribution is just $\text{cov}(\tilde{R}_j,\tilde{R}_m)/\sigma(\tilde{R}_m)$. Specifically, if x_{jm} is the proportion of asset j, $j = 1, \ldots, N$, in the market portfolio m

$$\sigma(\tilde{R}_m) = \sum_{j=1}^{N} x_{jm} \frac{\text{cov}(\tilde{R}_j, \tilde{R}_m)}{\sigma(\tilde{R}_m)}. \tag{5}$$

In this light (4) is a relationship between expected return and risk which says that the expected return on asset j is the riskless rate of interest R_f plus a risk premium that is $[E(\tilde{R}_m) - R_f]/\sigma(\tilde{R}_m)$, called the market price per unit of risk, times the risk of asset j, $\text{cov}(\tilde{R}_j,\tilde{R}_m)/\sigma(\tilde{R}_m)$.

Equation (4) provides the relationship between expected return and risk for portfolios as well as for individual assets. That is, if x_{jp} is the proportion of asset j in the portfolio p (so that $\sum_{j=1}^{N} x_{jp} = 1$), then multiplying both sides of (4) by x_{jp} and summing over j, we get

338

$$E(\tilde{R}_p) = R_f + \left[\frac{E(\tilde{R}_m) - R_f}{\sigma(\tilde{R}_m)} \right] \frac{\text{cov}(\tilde{R}_p, \tilde{R}_m)}{\sigma(\tilde{R}_m)} \qquad (6)$$

where, of course,

$$\tilde{R}_p = \sum_{j=1}^{N} x_{jp} \tilde{R}_j.$$

But (4) and (6) are expected return-risk relations derived under the assumption that investors all have free access to available information and all have the same views of distributions of returns on all portfolios. In short, the market setting envisaged is a rather extreme version of the "efficient markets" model in which prices at any time "fully reflect" available information. (See, for example [7].) But in the real world a portfolio manager may feel that he has access to special information or he may disagree with the evaluations of available information that are implicit in market prices. In this case the "homogeneous expectations" model underlying (4) provides "benchmarks" for judging the manager's ability to make better evaluations than the market.

The benchmark or naively selected portfolios are just the combinations of the riskless asset f and the market portfolio m obtained with different values of x in (1). Given the *ex post* or realized return R_m for the market portfolio, for the naively selected portfolios, *ex post* return is just

$$\tilde{R}_x = xR_f + (1-x)\tilde{R}_m, \qquad (7)$$

that is, (1) without the tildes. Moreover,[3]

$$\beta_x = \frac{\text{cov}(\tilde{R}_x, \tilde{R}_m)}{\sigma(\tilde{R}_m)} = \frac{\text{cov}([1-x]\tilde{R}_m, \tilde{R}_m)}{\sigma(\tilde{R}_m)} = (1-x)\sigma(\tilde{R}_m) = \sigma(\tilde{R}_x). \quad (8)$$

That is, for the benchmark portfolios risk and standard deviation of return are equal. And the result is quite intuitive: In the homogeneous expectations model these portfolios comprise the efficient set, and for efficient portfolios risk and return dispersion are equivalent.

For the naively selected portfolios, (7) and (8) imply the following relationship between risk β_x and *ex post* return R_x:

$$R_x = R_f + \left(\frac{R_m - R_f}{\sigma(\tilde{R}_m)} \right) \beta_x \qquad (\textit{ex post} \text{ market line}). \qquad (9)$$

That is, for the naively selected portfolios there is a linear relationship between risk and return that is of precisely the same form as (4) except that the expected returns that appear in (4) are replaced by realized returns in (9).

In the performance evaluation models to be presented, (9) provides the benchmarks against which the returns on "managed" portfolios are judged. These "benchmarks" are used in a sequence of successively more complex suggested performance evaluation settings. First we are concerned with one-period models in which a portfolio is chosen by an investor at the beginning of the

---

3. Henceforth the risk $\text{cov}(\tilde{R}_j, \tilde{R}_m)/\sigma(R_m)$ of an asset or portfolio j will be denoted as β_j.

period, its performance is evaluated at the end of the period, and there are no intermediate cash flows or portfolio decisions. Then we consider multiperiod evaluation models that also allow for fund flows and portfolio decisions between evaluation dates. We find, though, that almost all of the important theoretical concepts in performance evaluation can be treated in a one-period context.

III. The Benchmark Portfolios: Some Empirical Issues

Before introducing the evaluation models, however, it is well to discuss some of the empirical issues concerning the so-called "market lines" (4) and (9). Since this paper is primarily theoretical, and since empirical problems are best solved in the context of actual applications, the discussion of empirical issues will be brief.

First of all, to use (9) as a benchmark for evaluating *ex post* portfolio returns requires estimates of the risk, β_p, and dispersion, $\sigma(\tilde{R}_p)$, of the managed portfolios as well as an estimate of $\sigma(\tilde{R}_m)$, the dispersion of the return on the market portfolio. If performance evaluation is to be objective, it must be possible to obtain reliable estimates of these parameters from historical data. Fortunately, Blume's evidence [3, 4, 5] suggests that at least for portfolios of ten or more securities, β_p and $\sigma(\tilde{R}_p)$ seem to be fairly stationary over long periods of time (e.g., ten years), and likewise for $\sigma(\tilde{R}_m)$.

But other empirical evidence is less supportive. Thus throughout the analysis here normal return distributions are assumed, though the data of Fama [6], Blume [3], Roll [19] and others suggest that actual return distributions conform more closely to non-normal two-parameter stable distributions. It would conceptually be a simple matter to allow for such distributions in the evaluation models (cf. Fama [11]). But since the goal here is just to suggest some new approaches to performance evaluation, for simplicity attention will be restricted to the normal model.

Finally, the available empirical evidence (e.g., Friend and Blume [12], Miller and Scholes [17], and Black, Jensen and Scholes [2]) indicates that the average returns over time on securities and portfolios deviate systematically from the predictions of (4). Though the observed average return-risk relationships seem to be linear, the tradeoff of risk for return (the price of risk) is in general less than would be predicted from (4) or (9). In short, the evidence suggests that (4) and (9) do not provide the best benchmarks for the average return-risk tradeoffs available in the market from naively selected portfolios.

Even these results do little damage to the performance evaluation models. They indicate that other benchmark portfolios than those that lead to (9) might be more appropriate, but given such alternative "naively selected" portfolios, the analysis could proceed in exactly the manner to be suggested. For example, Black, Jensen and Scholes [2] compute the risks (β's) for each security on the New York Stock Exchange, rank these, and then form ten portfolios, the first comprising the .1N securities with the highest risks and the last comprising the .1N securities with the lowest risks, where N is the total number of securities. They find that over various subperiods from 1931-65 the average monthly returns among these portfolios are highly correlated, and when plotted against risk the average returns on these portfolios lie along a straight line with slope somewhat less than would be implied by the "price of risk" in (4) or (9). As benchmarks for performance evaluation models, their empirical risk-return lines seem to be natural alternatives to (9). And with these alternative benchmarks, performance evaluation could proceed precisely as suggested here. But again, for simplicity, we continue on with the more familiar benchmarks given by (9).

It would be misleading, however, to leave the impression that all important empirical problems relevant in the application of performance evaluation models have been solved. To a large extent the practical value of such models depends on the empirical validity of the model of market equilibrium—that is, the expected return-risk relationship—from which the benchmark or "naively selected" portfolios are derived. And though much interesting work is in progress, it would be rash to claim that all empirical issues concerning models of market equilibrium have been settled.

For example, an important (and unsolved) empirical issue in models of market equilibrium is the time interval or "market horizon period" over which the hypothetical expected return-risk relationship is presumed to hold. Does the model hold continuously (instant by instant), or is the market horizon period some discrete time interval? This is an important issue from the viewpoint of performance evaluation since if the market horizon period is discrete, evaluation periods should be chosen to coincide with horizon periods.

The evidence of Friend and Blume [12] and that of Black, Jensen, and Scholes [2] suggests that meaningful relationships between average returns and risk can be obtained from monthly data, while the evidence of Miller and Scholes [17] indicates that this is not true for annual periods. Within these broad bounds, however, the sensitivity of risk-return relations to the time interval chosen remains an open issue.

But unsolved empirical questions are hardly a cause for disheartenment. It is reasonable to expect that some of the empirical issues will be solved in the process of applying the theory. And in any case, application of a theory invariably involves some empirical approximations. The available evidence on performance evaluation, especially Jensen's [13, 14], suggests that the required approximations need not prevent even more complicated evaluation models from yielding useful results.

IV. Performance Evaluation in a One-Period Model When There Are No Intraperiod Fund Flows

Let $V_{a,t}$ and $V_{a,t+1}$ be the total market values at t and t + 1 of the actual (a = actual) portfolio chosen by an investment manager at t. With all portfolio activity occurring at t and t + 1, that is, assuming that there are no intraperiod fund flows, the one-period percentage return on the portfolio is

$$R_a = \frac{V_{a,t+1} - V_{a,t}}{V_{a,t}}.$$

341

One benchmark against which the return R_a on the chosen portfolio can be compared is provided by $R_x(\beta_a)$, which by definition is the return on the combination of the riskless asset f and the market portfolio m that has risk β_x equal to β_a, the risk of the chosen portfolio a. One measure of the performance of the chosen portfolio a is then

$$\text{Selectivity} = R_a - R_x(\beta_a). \qquad (10)$$

That is, *Selectivity* measures how well the chosen portfolio did relative to a naively selected portfolio with the same level of risk.

Selectivity, or some slight variant thereof, is the sole measure of performance in the work of Sharpe [21, 22], Treynor [23] and Jensen [13, 14]. But more detailed breakdowns of performance are possible. Thus consider

$$\overbrace{[R_a - R_f]}^{\substack{\text{Overall} \\ \text{Performance}}} = \overbrace{[R_a - R_x(\beta_a)]}^{\text{Selectivity}} + \overbrace{[R_x(\beta_a) - R_f]}^{\text{Risk}}. \qquad (11)$$

That is, the *Overall Performance* of the portfolio decision is the difference between the return on the chosen portfolio and the return on the riskless asset. The Overall Performance is in turn split into two parts, *Selectivity* (as above) and *Risk*. The latter measures the return from the decision to take on positive amounts of risk.[4] It will be determined by the level of risk chosen (the value of β_a) and, from (9), by the difference between the return on the market portfolio, R_m, and the return on the riskless asset, R_f.

These performance measures are illustrated in Figure 2. The curly bracket along the vertical axis shows *Overall Performance* which in this case is positive. The breakdown of performance given by (11) can be found along the vertical line from β_a. In this example, *Selectivity* is positive: A portfolio was chosen that produced a higher return than the corresponding "naively selected" portfolio along the market line with the same level of risk. *Risk* is also positive, as it is whenever a positive amount of risk is taken and the return on the market portfolio turns out to be higher than the riskless rate.

A. *Selectivity: A Closer Look*

If the portfolio chosen represents the investor's total assets, in the mean-variance model the risk of the portfolio to him is measured by $\sigma(\tilde{R}_a)$, the standard deviation of its return. And the risk of the portfolio to the investor, $\sigma(\tilde{R}_a)$, will be greater than what might now be called its "market risk," β_a, as long as the portfolio's return is less than perfectly correlated with the return on the market portfolio. To see this, note that the correlation coefficient k_{am} between R_a and R_m is

---

4. For greater descriptive accuracy, we should, of course, say "return from risk" or even "return from bearing risk," rather than just *Risk*. Likewise, "return from selectivity," would be more descriptive than *Selectivity*. But (hopefully) the shorter names save space without much loss of clarity.

$$k_{am} = \frac{\text{cov}(\tilde{R}_a, \tilde{R}_m)}{\sigma(\tilde{R}_a)\sigma(\tilde{R}_m)}.$$

It follows that

$$\beta_a = \frac{\text{cov}(\tilde{R}_a, \tilde{R}_m)}{\sigma(\tilde{R}_m)} = k_{am}\sigma(\tilde{R}_a)$$

so that $\beta_a \lessgtr \sigma(\tilde{R}_a)$ depending on whether $k_{am} \lessgtr 1$.[5]

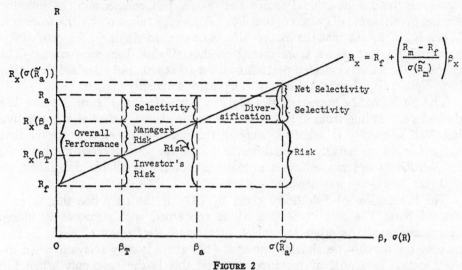

FIGURE 2

An Illustration of the Performance Measures of Equations (11), (12), and (13).

Intuitively, to some extent the portfolio decision may have involved putting more eggs into one or a few baskets than would be desirable to attain portfolio efficiency—that is, the manager places his bets on a few securities that he thinks are winners. In other words, to the extent that $\sigma(\tilde{R}_a) > \beta_a$, the portfolio manager decided to take on some portfolio dispersion that could have been diversified away because he thought he had some securities in which it would pay to concentrate resources. The results of such a decision can be evaluated in terms of the following breakdown of *Selectivity*:

$$\overbrace{[R_a - R_x(\beta_a)]}^{\text{Selectivity}} = \text{Net Selectivity} + \overbrace{\left|R_x(\sigma(\tilde{R}_a)) - R_x(\beta_a)\right|}^{\text{Diversification}}; \qquad (12a)$$

or

$$\text{Net Selectivity} = \overbrace{[R_a - R_x(\beta_a)]}^{\text{Selectivity}} - \overbrace{\left|R_x(\sigma(\tilde{R}_a)) - R_x(\beta_a)\right|}^{\text{Diversification}}. \qquad (12b)$$

By definition, $R_x(\sigma(\tilde{R}_a))$ is the return on the combination of the riskless asset f and the market portfolio m that has return dispersion equivalent to

5. In fact the naively selected portfolios are the only ones whose returns are literally perfectly correlated with those of the market portfolio (cf. equation (8)). But the theoretical work of Fama [9] and the empirical work of Black, Jensen and Scholes [2] suggests that the return on any well-diversified portfolio will be very highly correlated with R_m.

343

that of the actual portfolio chosen. Thus *Diversification* measures the extra portfolio return that the manager's winners have to produce in order to make concentration of resources in them worthwhile. If *Net Selectivity* is not positive, the manager has taken on diversifiable risk that his winners have not compensated for in terms of extra return.

Note that, as defined in (12), *Diversification* is always non-negative, so that *Net Selectivity* is equal to or less than *Selectivity*. When $R_m > R_t$, *Diversification* measures the additional return that would just compensate the investor for the diversifiable dispersion (that is, $\sigma(\tilde{R}_a) - \beta_a$) taken on by the manager. When $R_m < R_t$ (so that the market line is downward sloping), *Diversification* measures the lost return from taking on diversifiable dispersion rather than choosing the naively selected portfolio with market risk *and* standard deviation both equal to β_a, the market risk of the portfolio actually chosen.

The performance measures of (12) are illustrated in Figure 2 along the dashed vertical line from $\sigma(\tilde{R}_a)$. In the example shown, *Selectivity* is positive but *Net Selectivity* is negative. Though the manager chose a portfolio that outperformed the naively selected portfolio with the same level of market risk, his *Selectivity* was not sufficient to make up for the avoidable risk taken, so that *Net Selectivity* was negative.

The breakdown of *Selectivity* given by (12) is the only one that is considered here. The rest of Section IV is concerned with successively closer examinations of the other ingredient of *Overall Performance, Risk*. Before moving on, though, we should note that (12) itself is *only* relevant when diversification is a goal of the investor. And this is the case only when the portfolio being evaluated constitutes the investor's entire holdings, and the investor is risk averse. For example, an investor might allocate his funds to many managers, encouraging each only to try to pick winners, with the investor himself carrying out whatever diversification he desires on personal account. In this case *Selectivity* is the relevant measure of the managers' performance, and the breakdown of *Selectivity* of (12) is of no concern.

B. *Risk: A Closer Look*

If the investor has a target risk level β_T for his portfolio, the part of *Overall Performance* due to *Risk* can be allocated to the investor and to the portfolio manager as follows:

$$\overbrace{[R_x(\beta_a) - R_t]}^{\text{Risk}} = \overbrace{[R_x(\beta_a) - R_x(\beta_T)]}^{\text{Manager's Risk}} + \overbrace{[R_x(\beta_T) - R_t]}^{\text{Investor's Risk}} \tag{13}$$

$R_x(\beta_T)$ is the return on the naively selected portfolio with the target level of market risk. Thus *Manager's Risk* is that part of *Overall Performance* and of *Risk* that is due to the manager's decision to take on a level of risk β_a different from the investor's target level β_T, while *Investor's Risk* is that part of *Overall Performance* that results from the fact that the investor's target level of risk is positive. These performance measures are illustrated in Figure 2 along the dashed vertical line from β_T.

Manager's Risk might in part result from a timing decision. That is, in part at least the manager might have chosen a portfolio with a level of risk higher or lower than the target level because he felt risky portfolios in general would do abnormally well or abnormally poorly during the period under consideration. But if an estimate of $E(\tilde{R}_m)$ is available, a more precise measure of the results of such a timing decision can be obtained.[6] Specifically, making use of the *ex ante* market line of (4)[7] we can subdivide *Risk* as follows:

$$
\overbrace{[R_x(\beta_a) - R_f]}^{\text{Risk}} = \overbrace{\{\underbrace{[R_x(\beta_a) - E(\tilde{R}_x(\beta_a))]}_{\text{Total Timing}} - \underbrace{[R_x(\beta_T) - E(\tilde{R}_x(\beta_T))]}_{\text{Market Conditions}}\}}^{\text{Manager's Timing}}
$$
$$
+ \underbrace{[E(\tilde{R}_x(\beta_a)) - E(\tilde{R}_x(\beta_T))]}_{\text{Manager's Exp. Risk}} + \underbrace{[R_x(\beta_T) - R_f]}_{\text{Investor's Risk}}. \quad (14)
$$

The first three terms here sum to the *Manager's Risk* of (13). *Manager's Expected Risk* is the incremental expected return from the manager's decision to take on a nontarget level of risk. *Market Conditions* is the difference between the return on the naively selected portfolio with the target level of risk and the expected return of this portfolio. It answers the question: By how much did the market deviate from expectations at the target level of risk? *Total Timing* is the difference between the *ex post* return on the naively selected portfolio with risk β_a and the *ex ante* expected return. It is positive when $R_m > E(\tilde{R}_m)$ (and then more positive the larger the value of β_a), and it is negative when $R_m < E(\tilde{R}_m)$ (and then more negative the larger the value of β_a). The difference between *Total Timing* and *Market Conditions* is *Manager's Timing*: it measures the excess of *Total Timing* over timing performance that could have been generated by choosing the naively selected portfolio with the target level of risk. *Manager's Timing* is only positive when the sign of the difference between β_a and β_T is the same as the sign of the difference between R_m and $E(\tilde{R}_m)$, that is, when the chosen level of market risk is above

---

6. $E(\tilde{R}_m)$ might be estimated from past average returns on the market portfolio m. Alternatively, past data might be used to estimate the average difference between R_m and R_f. In any case, it should become clear that the expected values used must be naive or mechanical estimates (or at least somehow external to those being evaluated), otherwise the value of the timing measures is destroyed.

Admittedly, given the current status of empirical work on the behavior through time of average returns on risky assets, we can at most sepeculate about the best way to estimate $E(\tilde{R}_m)$. Hopefully empirical work now in progress will give more meaningful guidelines. And perhaps the development of theoretical methods of performance evaluation will itself stimulate better empirical work on estimation procedures. In any case, the discussion in the text should help to emphasize that one cannot obtain precise measures of returns from timing decisions without mechanical or naive estimates of equilibrium expected returns.

7. That is,

$$
E(\tilde{R}_x(\beta_a)) = R_f + \left[\frac{E(\tilde{R}_m) - R_f}{\sigma(\tilde{R}_m)}\right]\beta_a
$$

and similarly for $E(\tilde{R}_x(\beta_T))$.

(below) the target level and R_m is above (below) $E(\tilde{R}_m)$. It is thus somewhat more sensitive than *Total Timing* as a measure of the results of a timing decision.

A target level of risk will not always be relevant in evaluating a manager's performance. For example, an investor may allocate his funds to many managers, with the intention that each concentrates on selectivity and/or timing, with the investor using borrowing or lending on personal account to attain his desired level of market risk.

If a target level of risk is not relevant but the expected value or *ex ante* market line is still available, a breakdown of *Risk* similar to (14) can be obtained by treating the market portfolio (or the appropriate proxy)[8] as the target portfolio. That is,

$$\overbrace{[R_x(\beta_a) - R_f]}^{\text{Risk}} = \overbrace{\{[\underbrace{R_x(\beta_a) - E(\tilde{R}_x(\beta_a))]}_{\text{Total Timing}} - \underbrace{[R_m - E(\tilde{R}_m)]\}}_{\text{Market Conditions}}}^{\text{Manager's Timing}}$$

$$+ \underbrace{[E(\tilde{R}_x(\beta_a)) - E(\tilde{R}_m)]}_{\substack{\text{Expected Deviation} \\ \text{from Market}}} + \underbrace{[R_m - R_f]}_{\text{Market Risk}}. \quad (15)$$

The idea here is that even in the absence of a target level of risk, the measure of *Manager's Timing* must be standardized for the deviation of the market return from the expected market return, that is, for the "average" spread between the *ex post* and *ex ante* market lines.

Finally, the goal of this paper is mainly to suggest some ways in which available theoretical and empirical results on portfolio and asset pricing models can provide the basis of useful procedures for performance evaluation. But the various breakdowns of performance suggested above are hardly unique. Indeed any breakdown chosen should be tailored to the situation at hand. For example, if a target level of risk is relevant but the subdivision of Risk given by (14) is regarded as too complicated, then the approximate effects of the timing decision might still be separated out as follows:

$$\overbrace{[R_x(\beta_a) - R_f]}^{\text{Risk}} = \overbrace{[R_x(\beta_a) - E(\tilde{R}_x(\beta_a))]}^{\text{Total Timing}}$$

$$+ \overbrace{[E(\tilde{R}_x(\beta_a)) - E(\tilde{R}_x(\beta_T))]}^{\text{Manager's Expected Risk}} + \overbrace{[E(\tilde{R}_x(\beta_T)) - R_f]}^{\text{Investor's Expected Risk}}. \quad (16)$$

The one new term here is *Investor's Expected Risk*, which measures the expected contribution to *Overall Performance* of the investor's decision to have a positive target level of risk. Alternatively if a target level of risk is not

8. For example, if one were faced with portfolio evaluation in a multiperiod context, one might use the average of past levels of market risk chosen by the manager as a proxy for the target risk level when the latter is not explicitly available.

relevant for the situation at hand, but an expected value line is available, *Risk* can nevertheless be subdivided as follows,

$$\overbrace{[R_x(\beta_a) - R_f]}^{\text{Risk}} = \overbrace{[R_x(\beta_a) - E(\tilde{R}_x(\beta_a))]}^{\text{Total Timing}} + \overbrace{[E(\tilde{R}_x(\beta_a)) - R_f]}^{\text{Total Expected Risk}}. \quad (17)$$

And these few suggestions hardly exhaust the possibilities.

V. COMPONENTS OF PERFORMANCE: MULTIPERIOD MODELS WITH INTRAPERIOD FUND FLOWS

In the one-period evaluation model presented above, (i) the time at which performance is evaluated is assumed to correspond to the portfolio horizon date, that is, the time when portfolio funds are withdrawn for consumption; and (ii) there are assumed to be no portfolio transactions or inflows and outflows of funds between the initial investment and withdrawal dates, so that there is no reinvestment problem. If in a multiperiod context we are likewise willing to assume that: (i) though there are many of them, evaluation dates nevertheless correspond to the dates when some funds are withdrawn for consumption, and (ii) all reinvestment decisions and other portfolio transactions are also made at these same points in time, then generalization of the one-period model to the multiperiod case is straightforward.[9] Indeed the basic procedure could be period-by-period application of the performance measures presented in the one-period model. The major embellishments would not be in the nature of new theory, but rather would arise from the fact that multiperiod performance histories allow statistically more reliable estimates of the various one-period performance measures.

But this pure case is unlikely to be met in any real world application. Often performance evaluation would be carried out by someone with little or no knowledge of the dates when funds are needed for consumption by the owner of the portfolio, and often (e.g., in the case of a mutual fund or a pension fund) the portfolio is owned by many different investors with different consumption dates. As a result evaluation dates, withdrawal dates, and reinvestment dates do not usually coincide.

The rest of this paper is concerned with how the concepts of the one-period model must be adjusted to deal with such intraevaluation period (or more simply, intraperiod) fund flows. The procedure is to first present detailed definitions of variables of interest in models involving intraperiod fund flows, and then to talk about actual measures of performance. And it is well to keep in mind that though the analysis is carried out in a multiperiod context, the problems to be dealt with arise from intraperiod fund flows. With such fund flows, the same problems would arise in a one-period evaluation model.

A. *Definitions*

Suppose the investment performance of a portfolio is to be evaluated at discrete points in time, but that there can be cash flows between evaluation

9. For the development of the underlying models of consumer and market equilibrium for this case see [8].

dates. That is, there can be intraperiod inflows in the form of either cash receipts (dividends, interest) on existing portfolio holdings or net new contributions of capital by new or existing owners. And there can be intraperiod outflows in the form of dividend payments to the portfolio's owner(s) (e.g., a mutual fund declares dividends) or withdrawals of capital (e.g., by a mutual fund's shareholders).

In simplest terms, the major problem with intraperiod cash flows is obtaining a measure of the return on the beginning of period market value of a portfolio that abstracts from the effects of intraperiod new contributions and withdrawals on the end of period value of the portfolio. One approach is what might be called the mutual fund method. Specifically, when performance evaluation is first contemplated, the market value of the portfolio is subdivided into "shares." Subsequently, whenever there are contributions of new capital or withdrawals of capital from the portfolio, the current market value of a share is computed and the number of shares outstanding is adjusted to reflect the effects of the cash flow.[10]

Thus let evaluation dates correspond to integer values of t and define

$V'_{a,t}$ = actual market value of the portfolio at time t. It thus includes the effects of investment of new capital or reinvestment of any cash income received on securities held in the portfolio, and it is net of any dividends paid out to owners or other withdrawals of funds prior to t.

$V_{a,t}$ = market value the portfolio would have had at t if no dividends were paid out to owners since the previous evaluation date. In computing $V_{a,t}$ it is simply assumed that dividends paid to the portfolio's owners were instead reinvested in the entire portfolio. At the beginning of each evaluation period, however, $V_{a,t}$ is set equal to $V'_{a,t}$.

n_t = number of shares outstanding in the portfolio at t. As indicated above, this is adjusted when new capital comes into the portfolio and when capital is withdrawn, but it is unaffected by reinvestment of cash income received on securities held or by dividends paid to the portfolio's owners.

$p'_{a,t} = V'_{a,t}/n_t$ = actual market value at t of a share in the portfolio.

$p_{a,t} = V_{a,t}/n_t$ = value of a share at t under the assumption that dividends paid to owners of the portfolio were instead reinvested in the entire portfolio.

$R_{a,t} = (p_{a,t} - p'_{a,t-1})/p'_{a,t-1}$. Assuming t corresponds to an evaluation date, this is the one-period return on a share with reinvestment of all dividends paid on a share since the last evaluation date.

$R_{a,t}$ is an unambiguous measure of the return from $t-1$ to t on a dollar invested in the portfolio at $t-1$. This is not to say, however, that it is unaffected by intraperiod fund flows. Such fund flows are usually associated with redistributions of portfolio holdings across securities and these affect the

10. This is in fact the method of accounting used by open end mutual funds. It is also closely related to the "time-weighted rate of return" approach developed by Professor Lawrence Fisher. On this point see [1, Appendix I and p. 218].

return on a share. Moreover, $R_{a,t}$ as defined above is not the only unambiguous measure of the return from $t-1$ to t on funds invested in the portfolio at $t-1$. For example, one could define $R_{a,t} = (p'_{a,t} + d_t - p'_{a,t-1})/p'_{a,t-1}$, where d_t is the dividend per share paid during the evaluation period to the portfolio's owners. The more complicated definition, that is, with dividends assumed to be reinvested, is "purer" (especially for the purpose of inter-portfolio comparisons of performance) in the sense that funds invested at the beginning of a period remain invested for the entire period, but it is less pure in the sense that it assumes a reinvestment policy not actually followed in the portfolio.

The next step is to define prices per share for the benchmark or naively selected portfolios that also take account of intraperiod fund flows.

$p_{xt}(\beta_T) =$ price at t per share of the naively selected portfolio with the target risk level. To avoid double-counting of past performance, at the beginning of any evaluation period (for example, just after an evaluation takes place at $t-1$) this price is set equal to the price per share of the actual portfolio. Then this amount is invested in the naively selected portfolio with the target risk level, and the behavior of the market value of this portfolio during the evaluation period determines the end-of-period price per share, $p_{xt}(\beta_T)$. Any intraperiod cash income generated by the securities of this naively selected portfolio is assumed to be reinvested in this portfolio.

These conventions for the treatment of beginning-of-period values and intra-period cash income will be taken to apply in the definitions of all the benchmark portfolios. Thus

$p_t(R_f) =$ price at t per share of the naively selected portfolio obtained by investing all funds available at $t-1$ in the riskless asset.

The benchmarks provided by $p_{xt}(\beta_T)$ and $p_t(R_f)$ are unaffected by intra-period fund flows in the actual portfolio. This is not true of the following two benchmarks.

$p_{xt}(\beta_a) =$ price at t per share of the naively selected portfolio with market risk equal to that of the actual portfolio. At the beginning of any evaluation period and after any transaction in the actual portfolio during an evaluation period (that is, after any cash flow or exchange of shares in the actual port-folio) the market risk of the actual portfolio is measured, and the current price per share of this benchmark is shifted into the naively selected portfolio with that level of market risk. Thus the value of β_a could be shifting more or less contin-uously through time as a result of inflows and outflows of funds and decisions to shift the holdings in the portfolio.[11]

11. Indeed even if there are no transactions taking place, the value of β_a shifts continuously through time as a result of shifts in the relative market values of individual securities in the portfolio. Aside from adjusting the value of β_a at the beginning of each evaluation period, we have chosen to ignore the effects of such "non-discretionary" shifts here.

$p_{xt}(\sigma(\widetilde{R}_a)) =$ price at t per share of the naively selected portfolio with return dispersion equal to that of the actual portfolio. The definition of $p_{xt}(\sigma(\widetilde{R}_a))$ is obtained by substituting $\sigma(\widetilde{R}_a)$ for β_a in the definition of $p_{xt}(\beta_a)$ above.

Thus $p_{xt}(\beta_a)$ and $p_{xt}(\sigma(\widetilde{R}_a))$ take account of changes in β_a and $\sigma(\widetilde{R}_a)$ that result from intraperiod fund flows and portfolio shifts. Computationally, keeping tract of β_a and $\sigma(\widetilde{R}_a)$ in the way required for these benchmarks is not a difficult problem. At any point in time the market risk β_a of the chosen portfolio is just the weighted average of the market risks of the individual assets in the portfolio, where the weights are the proportions of total portfolio market value represented by each asset. Thus if one has estimates of the market risks of the assets from which portfolios are chosen, the value of β_a is updated by combining these with current measures of the weights of individual assets in the chosen portfolio. And a similar procedure can be followed with respect to updating values of $\sigma(\widetilde{R}_a)$.[12]

B. *Multiperiod Measures of Performance*

Given the beginning and end-of-period prices per share for these benchmark portfolios, their one-period returns are obtained in the usual way. Then the performance history of a portfolio can be built up (for example) through period-by-period application of the breakdowns given by (11)-(13). Alternatively, one can define performance measures in terms of profit per share rather than return. Thus, in line with (13) and using end of evaluation period prices, define

$$\overbrace{[p_{a,t} - p_t(R_f)]}^{\substack{\text{Overall} \\ \text{Performance}}} = \overbrace{[p_{a,t} - p_{xt}(\beta_a)]}^{\text{Selectivity}}$$
$$+ \overbrace{[p_{xt}(\beta_a) - p_{xt}(\beta_T)]}^{\text{Manager's Risk}} + \overbrace{[p_{xt}(\beta_T) - p_t(R_f)]}^{\text{Investor's Risk}}. \quad (18)$$

This type of breakdown can of course be computed both period-by-period and cumulatively. And from such multiperiod histories one can get more reliable measures of a portfolio manager's true abilities than can be obtained from a one-period analysis. For example, one can determine whether his *Selectivity* is systematically positive or simply randomly positive in some periods.

For some purposes one may wish to compare the multiperiod performance histories of different portfolios. For example, an investment company may be interested in the relative abilities of its different security analysts and portfolio managers. Or an investor who has allocated his funds to more than one manager may be interested in comparing their performances. On a period-by-period basis such performance comparisons can be carried out in terms of percentage returns. Alternatively, if the prices of shares in different portfolios

---

12. Keeping track of $\sigma(\widetilde{R}_a)$ is especially simple if one assumes that returns are generated by the so-called "market model." On this, and for additional computational suggestions, see Blume [3, 4, 5].

are set equal at the beginning of comparison periods, profit-based performance measures such as (18) could be computed both on a period-by-period basis and cumulatively.

One must not get the impression, however, that all the problems caused by intraperiod fund flows have been solved. Though the performance of a "share" during any given evaluation period (or across many periods) gives an unambiguous picture of the investment history of funds invested in a given portfolio at a given point in time, comparisons of the performances of shares in different portfolios are not completely unambiguous. This is due to the fact that even when things are done on a per share basis, intraperiod fund flows necessitate portfolio decisions that usually have some effect on the performance of a share. And when such fund flows occur at different times (and thus during different market conditions) in different portfolios, the observed performances of shares in the portfolios may differ, even if the portfolios are managed by the same person trying to follow the same policies in all of his portfolio decisions. But though such ambiguities seem unavoidable and to some extent unsolvable, their effects on performance comparisons should be minor except in cases where portfolios experience large cash flows (relative to their total market values) in short periods of time and/or when evaluation periods are long.

Finally, if an *ex ante* market line is available to compute expected values through time for the three benchmarks, $p_{xt}(\beta_T)$, $p_{xt}(\beta_a)$ and $p_{xt}(\sigma(\tilde{R}_a))$, then the one-period performance breakdowns of (14)-(17) can be carried out either in terms of returns or market values, and these can be used as the basis of even more detailed multiperiod performance histories.

But we terminate the discussion at this point. We do this not because of a lack of additional interesting problems, but because in the absence of actual applications, suggested solutions become increasingly speculative and thus of less likely usefulness.

VI. SUMMARY

Some rather detailed methods for evaluating portfolio performance have been suggested, and some of the more important problems that would arise in implementing these methods have also been discussed. In general terms, we have suggested that the return on a portfolio can be subdivided into two parts: the return from security selection (*Selectivity*) and the return from bearing risk (*Risk*). Various finer subdivisions of both *Selectivity* and *Risk* have also been presented.

To a large extent the suggested models can be viewed as attempts to combine concepts from modern theories of portfolio selection and capital market equilibrium with more traditional concepts of what constitutes good portfolio management.

For example, the return from *Selectivity* is defined as the difference between the return on the managed portfolio and the return on a naively selected portfolio with the same level of market risk. Both the measure of risk and the definition of a naively selected portfolio are obtained from modern capital market theory, but the goal of the performance measure itself is just to test how good the portfolio manager is at security analysis. That is, does he show

351

any ability to uncover information about individual securities that is not already implicit in their prices?

Likewise, traditional discussions of portfolio management distinguish between security analysis and market analysis, the latter being prediction of general market price movements rather than just prediction of the special factors in the returns on individual securities. The various timing measures suggested in this paper provide estimates of the returns obtained from such attempts to predict the market. And modern capital market theory again plays a critical role in defining these estimates.

REFERENCES

1. Bank Administration Institute. *Measuring the Investment Performance of Pension Funds.* Park Ridge, Illinois: B.A.I., 1968.
2. Fisher Black, Michael Jensen, and Myron Scholes. "The Capital Asset Pricing Model: Some Empirical Tests." To appear in *Studies in the Theory of Capital Markets,* edited by Michael Jensen and published by Praeger.
3. Marshall Blume. "The Assessment of Portfolio Performance," unpublished Ph.D. dissertation, University of Chicago, 1968.
4. —————. "Portfolio Theory: A Step Toward Its Practical Application." *Journal of Business* XLIII (April, 1970), 152-173.
5. —————. "On the Assessment of Risk," *Journal of Finance* XXVI (March, 1971), 1-10.
6. Eugene F. Fama. "The Behavior of Stock Market Prices," *Journal of Business* XXXVIII (January, 1965), 34-105.
7. —————. "Efficient Capital Markets: A Review of Theory and Empirical Work," *Journal of Finance* XXV (May, 1970), 383-417.
8. —————. "Multiperiod Consumption-Investment Decisions," *American Economic Review* XL (March, 1970), 163-174.
9. —————. "Portfolio Analysis in a Stable Paretian Market," *Management Science* XII (January, 1965), 404-419.
10. —————. "Risk, Return and Equilibrium: Some Clarifying Comments," *Journal of Finance* XXIII (March, 1968), 29-40.
11. —————. "Risk, Return, and Equilibrium," *Journal of Political Economy* LXXIX (January-February, 1971), 30-55.
12. Irwin Friend, and Marshall Blume. "Measurement of Portfolio Performance under Uncertainty," *American Economic Review* XL (September, 1970), 561-575.
13. Michael Jensen. "The Performance of Mutual Funds in the Period 1945-64," *Journal of Finance* XXIII (May, 1968), 389-416.
14. —————. "Risk, the Pricing of Capital Assets, and the Evaluation of Investment Portfolios," *Journal of Business* XLII (April, 1969), 167-247.
15. John Lintner. "Security Prices, Risk, and Maximal Gains from Diversification," *Journal of Finance* XX (December, 1965), 587-615.
16. —————. "The Valuation of Risk Assets and the Selection of Risky Investments in Stock Portfolios and Capital Budgets," *Review of Economics and Statistics* XLVII (February, 1965), 13-37.
17. Merton Miller, and Myron Scholes. "Rates of Return in Relation to Risk: A Reexamination of Some Recent Findings." To appear in *Studies in the Theory of Capital Markets,* edited by Michael Jensen, and published by Praeger.
18. Jan Mossin. "Equilibrium in a Capital Asset Market," *Econometrica* XXXIV (October, 1966), 768-783.
19. Richard Roll. *The Behavior of Interest Rates: Application of the Efficient Market Model to U.S. Treasury Bills.* New York: Basic Books, Inc., 1970.
20. William F. Sharpe. "Capital Assets Prices: A Theory of Market Equilibrium under Conditions of Risks," *Journal of Finance* XIX (September, 1964), 425-442.
21. —————. "Mutual Fund Performance," *Journal of Business* XXXIX (Special Supplement, January, 1966), 119-138.
22. —————. "Risk Aversion in the Stock Market," *Journal of Finance* XX (September, 1965), 416-422.
23. Jack L. Treynor. "How to Rate Management of Investment Funds," *Harvard Business Review* XLIII (January-February, 1965), 63 75.